THE LETTERS OF ELIZABETH RIGBY, LADY EASTLAKE

The Letters of Elizabeth Rigby, Lady Eastlake

Edited by Julie Sheldon

LIVERPOOL UNIVERSITY PRESS

First published 2009 by
Liverpool University Press
4 Cambridge Street
Liverpool
L69 7ZU

British Library Cataloguing-in-Publication data
A British Library CIP record is available

ISBN 978–1–84631–194–9

Typeset by Carnegie Book Production, Lancaster
Printed by the MPG Books Group, Bodmin and King's Lynn

Contents

Acknowledgements

I would like to thank the following libraries and archives for granting permission to publish letters: The Trustees of the National Library of Scotland; General Manuscripts, Wilson Library, the University of North Carolina at Chapel Hill; Camden Local Studies and Archives Centre; The British Library; The Master and Fellows of Trinity College Cambridge; Huntington Library; National Gallery Archive, London; National Portrait Gallery, London; Norwich Castle Museum and Art Gallery; Manuscripts and Special Collections Department, University of Nottingham; Nottinghamshire Archives and Southwell Diocesan Record Office; Pierpont Morgan Library; Powys County Archives Office; Royal Botanical Gardens Archives Kew; Bristol Record Office; the John Rylands University Library, The University of Manchester; the Archives of the Stirlings of Keir; Special Collections, UCL Library Services; The Mistresses and Fellows, Girton College, Cambridge; the Norfolk Record Office. I am grateful to Henry Ropner for his permission to publish the letters to Henry Sandbach and to Christopher Barker for his permission to include the letters to Hannah Brightwen here.

I have met with great generosity in all my transactions with librarians and archivists during the course of this research. I am indebted to Virginia Murray for her many kindnesses to me at Albemarle Street. I thank Alan Crookham at the National Gallery Archives for his prompt and patient attention. I also thank Rachel Beattie, Ruth Boreham, Elspeth Hector, Richard Knight, Sheila Mackenzie, Christine Nelson, Catherine Richards, Mary Robertson, and Norma Watt. I have been greatly assisted by the generous and unstinting attention of Christopher Barker whose family papers have been such an invaluable source of interesting and candid letters.

I owe a special debt of gratitude to Susanna Avery-Quash for generously sharing her research on Charles Eastlake for her forthcoming scholarly edition of his travel notebooks. I have profited greatly in my research from Joan Gibbons, Alex Kidson, Suzanne May, Edward Morris, Sara Stevenson, and Monica Thorpe. I thank Penny Marney and Sue Wellings for their kindness to me at Framingham Earl. I am indebted to my good friend Pam Meecham for her cheerful support and, with Neil Hall, for all their hospitality. Lynn Halliday is thanked for her help. Anthony Cond, Andrew Kirk and Helen Tookey at Liverpool University Press have been encouraging in the preparation of this edition and I thank them for their attention to detail. Rosemary Mitchell is thanked for her helpful comments. I thank Colin Fallows for all his encouragement and support throughout the duration of the work.

Finally I acknowledge the support of the Getty Research Center for making me the fortunate recipient of a Library Research Grant and the Paul Mellon Centre for British Art for a Research Support Grant.

Abbreviations

Standard reference works and bibliographical material relating to Elizabeth Rigby, Lady Eastlake's publications are abbreviated thus:

J&C — *Journals and Correspondence of Lady Eastlake*, 2 vols. (London: John Murray, 1895)

LSB — *Letters from the Shores of the Baltic*, 2 vols. (London: John Murray, 2nd edn, 1842)

BL — The British Library

BRO — Bristol Record Office

CLS — Camden Local Studies and Archives Centre

GC — Girton College, Cambridge

HL — Huntington Library

ML — Morgan Library and Museum, New York

NASDRO — Nottinghamshire Archives and Southwell Diocesan Record Office

NCM — Norwich Castle Museum and Art Gallery

NG — The National Gallery Archives London

NLS — National Library of Scotland

NOTT — Manuscripts and Special Collections Department, University of Nottingham

NRO — The Norfolk Record Office

PCA — Powys County Archives Office

RBGA — Royal Botanical Gardens Archives Kew

SRA — Strathclyde Regional Archives, Glasgow (The Archives of the Stirlings of Keir)

TCC — Dawson Turner Correspondence, Trinity College Cambridge

UNC — General Manuscripts, Wilson Library, the University of North Carolina at Chapel Hill

Introduction

On his deathbed in 1851, the painter J. M. W. Turner was reported to have said 'I saw Lady Eastlake'.[1] The object of Turner's hallucination was Elizabeth Eastlake, a 42-year-old reviewer, translator and essayist who had been married for nearly three years to the President of the Royal Academy, Sir Charles Eastlake. Just why the President's wife should appear to the most famous English artist as he drifted in and out of consciousness will never be known. Perhaps her statuesque physique left an impression upon the diminutive artist, or perhaps his mind was wandering back to dinner parties at which he had met the socially confident and opinionated lady with a reputation for being something of a bluestocking. Whatever the reason, by December 1851 Elizabeth had impinged upon the consciousness of most artists and writers in London society in one way or another – charming some and offending others – to become one of the most articulate and well connected women in the Victorian art world.

As the letters printed here demonstrate, Elizabeth Rigby, Lady Eastlake was happily situated in the Victorian literary and art worlds, linked by birth and friendship to an intellectual aristocracy of reputable artists, writers and influential figures. Although never a part of Bohemian or radical intellectual circles, she occupied a prominent position in conventional Victorian culture. Today her name is remembered, if at all, for one of three reasons. She wrote one of the first articles on photography, she reviewed *Jane Eyre* and *Modern Painters*, and she married Sir Charles Lock Eastlake. The article on photography and the marriage to Eastlake bring approbation. She continues to be credited in the history of photography for her acumen and foresight[2] and no account of Charles Eastlake fails to credit her part in his career. The reviews of *Jane Eyre* and *Modern Painters*, however, have cast her in a villainous bit part in the biographies of Charlotte Brontë and John Ruskin,[3] and Elizabeth's pert opinions have proven a rich source of quotations for scholars in need of soundbites representing the worst of Victorian opinion.[4]

However, Elizabeth Eastlake was responsible for much more than acerbic prose and a fortunate marriage and her reputation is in need of a thorough overhaul. The biography written by Marion Lochhead in 1961 is now rather outdated.[5] David Robertson provides more informative and erudite work on Elizabeth in his study of *Sir Charles Eastlake and the Victorian Art World* of 1978.[6] Beyond this there has been little scholarship on either of the Eastlakes; although, ironically, many scholars of the Victorian art world express their bewilderment about the collective amnesia that has condemned the Eastlakes to relative obscurity.[7] In *The Consort of Taste* (first published in 1950) John Steegman expressed surprise that Elizabeth Eastlake had yet to receive 'the recognition due to her', warning that 'the reader of this book will find [her] recurring so often that she becomes nearly as prominent as Ruskin'.[8] In 1957 Bernard Denvir remarked upon the fact that both of the Eastlakes had 'suffered an undue amount of neglect'.[9] In 1980 Francis Haskell recommended Elizabeth as 'one of the most articulate, representative, and influential figures of Victorian England'.[10] However, while all parties are keen to point out just how significant the name of Eastlake is in the cultural life of the nineteenth century, with the noble exception of an article by Adele Ernstrom there has been little contibuted. While Elizabeth's peers Anna Jameson, Emilia Dilke, Lucie Duff Gordon, Harriet Martineau and Maria Graham, Lady Callcott have had recent biographies,[11] she remains without any significant interpretation, contextualization or discussion of her life and work.

Elizabeth's now rather obscure status appears to me to stem from the perception that she was a woman writer without being a women's writer. By this I mean that she appears to have little to recommend her to historians in search of artists and writers validating a particular kind of female experience. Elizabeth has been regarded as a 'phallic speaker', earning herself a place with Margaret Oliphant, Mrs Humphry Ward and Queen Victoria among those since dubbed 'Eve's Renegades'.[12] Her apparently orthodox views were articulated with confidence and aplomb but seemingly out of alignment with the campaigns of the day. As her butler later put it, 'though not exactly a freethinker or a New Woman, [she] had opinions of her own, and a will of her own'.[13] In point of fact, although she did not contribute to important women's issues of the day, neither did she oppose them. As the correspondence printed here shows, she had little sympathy for any cases of special pleading. For instance, she supported the Society of Female Artists, and she also patronized a Society for the Employment of Women, yet she was dismissive of women's art education. Many letters testify to Elizabeth's other philanthropic interests, in particular her promotion of the fortunes of single women: recommending nurses to Florence Nightingale and governesses to ladies of her acquaintance, or intervening on behalf of the indigent relatives of artists. She was an enthusiastic supporter of several charities, lending her name to the causes that appealed for sponsors in the pages of *The Times*, and towards the end of her life she became an anti-vivisectionist.

The broadest biographical details of Elizabeth's life can be traced through the *Journals and Correspondence of Lady Eastlake*, compiled and edited by her nephew Charles Eastlake Smith in 1895.[14] Smith, as his aunt's literary executor, compiled two volumes from an uneven collection of sources (a journal, an unspecified number of notebooks and miscellaneous correspondence with friends and family), extracting passages for what he calls 'public interest'. The sources for the *Journals and Correspondence* are poorly distributed and only ten pages document the first thirty years of her life. Between 1840 and 1842 Smith quotes from what he calls 'Miss Rigby's notebooks', a series of disconnected thoughts and aphorisms without specific reference to events in her life. The title *Journals and Correspondence* is misleading, since Elizabeth did not begin her journal until she was 33 and finished it shortly before she became engaged six years later. Her journal keeping was, at best, uneven, and Elizabeth views the gaps in her journal as her 'besetting sin'.[15] Moreover, her journal entries are often oblique and contribute very little to our knowledge of her life. Following the suspension of the journal towards the end of 1848, Smith tells his aunt's story through letters to her mother and, following Mrs Rigby's death in 1872, to a handful of close friends, most frequently to Austen Henry Layard. Smith provides continuity statements between sources and fills in the broadest biographical detail. However, as a family member Smith tends to be silent on personal aspects of the Rigbys. There were many portions of his aunt's letters, printed here, that Smith would not have published, and there are a few instances of his bowdlerizing her letters that are uncovered here.

Elizabeth Rigby was the fifth of twelve children born to Dr Edward Rigby and Anne Palgrave. She was born at her father's medical practice in St Giles Street in Norwich on 17 November 1809. The Rigbys divided their time between Norwich and a model farm, a 300-acre country estate at Framingham Earl, six miles outside Norwich, where Dr Rigby perfected the latest techniques of animal husbandry and crop cultivation.[16] The term 'gentleman farmer' only partially describes Dr Edward Rigby (1747–1821). He was also a noted physician and obstetrician, an advocate of public health measures and, for a time, Mayor of Norwich.[17] Dr Rigby was a gregarious host, and his children were allowed to mingle freely with the many gentlemen-scholars and scientists who called at Framingham Earl Hall and St Giles Street. The picture that emerges from the very brief outline of her childhood in the *Journals and Correspondence of Lady Eastlake* is a bucolic one of the Rigby children 'climbing trees and haystacks, making fires in a dry ditch, and roasting potatoes'.[18]

Following the custom of the time, Elizabeth Rigby, along with her five sisters, was educated at home by a governess, while her brothers, Edward[19] and Roger, were sent to the local grammar school. The Rigby daughters, like countless other daughters of gentlemen, followed a prescribed programme of studies that included French, some German and Italian, piano lessons, conventional dance steps, needlework and drawing. Dr Rigby's death in 1821 substantially reduced the educational provision for the Rigby daughters. Mrs Rigby removed the family permanently to Framingham Earl and the 'men of note in literature, agriculture, natural history, science, and other branches of learning' ceased to call. In the move to Framingham Earl Mrs Rigby was pinning her family's fortunes to land, at a time when the future of the agrarian economy was uncertain. Economies were made to the girls' education: the French governess was retained but the tutors in Italian, arithmetic and geography were paid off. Elizabeth was retrospectively critical of her education, complaining in later life about its deficiencies.[20]

In 1827 the Rigby family moved to Heidelberg – in Smith's version of events, so that Elizabeth could convalesce from a severe attack of typhoid fever.[21] Just why the family should move to Heidelberg to aid Elizabeth's recovery when they already inhabited a model farm in the East Anglian countryside is a mystery. Smith only gives half a page to the two and half years that the Rigbys spent in Heidelberg and, as some of the letters reveal, Elizabeth preferred to draw a veil over the time abroad. The most likely explanation is that long-standing money worries caused the Rigbys to retrench. In a letter of 1824 to her sister Mary, wife of Dawson Turner, Mrs Rigby appeals for help in finding out about the 'economy' of living in Germany:

> Dear Mary
> I write to you, as to you I am indebted for all the information
> I have obtained on the subject of my expatriation, and beg you
> to accept my thanks for it; and to allow my further troubling
> you with further questions – would Mr. Turner write ... for the
> purpose of learning those further particulars, concerning education
> of females, economy of living etc – which it is needful I should
> know before I quit these peaceful abodes ... I am fully aware of
> the painful step I shall be obliged to take provided I left my house
> in the manner I have prepared; and that the increase of distance
> will serve only to extend the aggravation of my separation from
> home – but the inevitability of this necessary step loses of its
> horrors, when on looking at the other side of the picture, I see and
> feel poverty paralyses every effort I have to make. There I stand

between two evils, on examination, the former as more endurable, for a space, than the latter. I can encompass the former the better educating my children – with the latter they and their education must submit to every privation – and the term, three years, will I hope do much for them ...[22]

The choice of Heidelberg was probably on account of Edward Rigby, who was at the start of a promising career in medicine. He matriculated from Edinburgh University on the day of his twenty-first birthday in 1825 and went to Berlin University in 1826 and then to the lying-in hospital at Heidelberg to study midwifery. There is little to be gleaned from the two and half years that the Rigby family spent in Heidelberg, although three of the Rigby daughters – Anne, Maria Justina and Gertrude – became engaged to Balto-German barons. The unhappy fate of her three expatriated sisters in Estonia came to colour Elizabeth's view of Germans. In a letter to her cousin Hannah Brightwen she describes a visit to the city years later in 1873, remarking, 'Heidelberg is full of pathetic recollections. Sisters sacrificed to a dream'.[23] The 'sacrifice' of her sisters to apparently advantageous marriages that failed to live up to either material or marital expectations is hinted at in some of the letters. But her antipathy towards the Germans is a blatant and recurring theme in the letters, for example in those addressed to Layard.

The diminished Rigby family returned to Norwich in 1829. In the early 1830s Elizabeth made her first efforts at establishing a career for herself as a writer. Although I have been unable to find either piece, Smith informs us that she wrote a short story for *Frasers* in 1829[24] and a letter printed here confirms that she produced an article of unknown designation or description on Passavant early in the 1830s.[25] Throughout her youth, Elizabeth entertained ambitions to be an artist, claiming 'my pen has never been a favourite implement with me; the pencil is the child of my heart'.[26] She continued to draw regularly, leaving two thousand drawings to a niece on her death. Those that survive date mainly from the 1820s and 1830s and illustrate something of the young Elizabeth Rigby's world – a portfolio of unnamed portraits of friends and family in comfortable surroundings: women seated, women sewing, elderly women asleep in their chairs, sleeping children, men in profile and three-quarter views of elegantly dressed young women. In Norwich Elizabeth and her sisters were taught drawing by John Sell Cotman[27] and the artist E. T. Daniell also appears to have been co-opted into her art education.[28] According to Smith, Elizabeth was talented enough to warrant the short-term investment of a year in London from July 1832 to July 1833, in order to study under the tutelage of Henry Sass.[29] Although she was never to be a professional artist, the pencil remained the 'child of her heart' and she even published some engravings after her drawings in her various books.[30]

The obstacles to women's writing were arguably relatively fewer than those that prevented women from becoming professional artists in Victorian England. For instance, literary success was not predicated on entry to an academy. Elizabeth, in common with other women writers, began her literary life as a translator, electing to translate Passavant's *Tour of a German Artist in England with Notices of Private Galleries, and remarks on the state of Art*. In common with other women, she was employed on translating standard reference works into English.[31] Translating was an area of expertise in the family,[32] although it was still relatively unusual for women to be fluent in German.

In 1838 Elizabeth made her first journey to the Baltic to visit her two elder sisters Baroness Maria Justina de Rosen and Baroness Gertrude de Rosen. 'Justina', as her family called her, and Gertrude had married into one of the old established families of the 'Balto' overlords, members of the Teutonic aristocracy who had the governance of the Estonian peasantry under the Russian government. This extended visit was recorded in her first book, *Residence on the Shores of the Baltic* (hereafter referred to by its title in subsequent editions, *Letters from the Shores of the Baltic*). In distilling the narrative thrust of *Letters from the Shores of the Baltic* readers followed a vague topography as Elizabeth moved between various country estates in Estonia and the elite Toompea district of the capital, Reval (now Tallinn). In her bulletins home, she created vignettes of daily life in the Baltic, dwelling on what was distinctive in the habits of the Baltic German nobility and the native Estonian peasants. English readers were regaled with anecdotes about substandard living, quaint customs, strange meals, and the idiosyncrasies of the Lutheran faith. Readers would also learn about the petty tyranny of the Estonian nobility, and the iniquities of its government. The attribution of the experiences and views of the writer to a lady were important to the reception of the book. Lady travellers were acquiring a reputation for insight that their male counterparts lacked, and Elizabeth's authorial posture is an interesting blend of affinity for her Balto hosts and pity for the Estonian peasants.[33]

A Residence on the Shores of the Baltic was published by John Murray in 1841. Following the success of the book, she was invited to write for the *Quarterly*, an arrangement that was to last, on and off, for the rest of her life. It is not certain whether it was John Murray or John Gibson Lockhart, the editor of the *Quarterly*, who gave her the first commission to write a review. Both men seemed to have a flirtatious relationship with her; in particular Lockhart. Lockhart gave Elizabeth at least three soubriquets ('Lofty Lucy', 'Miss Esthonia' and 'Queen Bess') and some observers expected him to propose in 1844.[34] Harriet Martineau wrote to Jane Carlyle in 1844: 'For these two years nearly I have been hoping she wd marry [John] Lockhart. [John] Murray is far too good for her. She & Lockhart will match exactly; & the whole world will be saved from the peril of marrying either of them.'[35] A candid letter written to Margaret Outram in 1844 tells of her unchaperoned meetings with Lockhart in London while she was visiting the Murrays between February and April:

> I have many friends to see here, among them the redoubtable Mr. Lockhart, who is a kind friend to me. I shall see how he pleases me this time, for I have seen much of men and manners since I last saw him, but entre nous the impression he left on my mind was that there were few men who could win so much by their warmth, as he by his *coldness*. I know you won't approve this, but this is only an observation in the abstract. I am as safe from him as he from me. Our mutual situation however is odd and *piquant* – a man of such mental power and extraordinary personal beauty, and a young woman to be closeted together to talk of Quarterly Reviews, strikes me sometimes as thoroughly absurd, and is a new leaf in my many-leaved book of experience ...[36]

In October 1842 Elizabeth, her mother and her two sisters Jane and Matilda moved to Edinburgh. Mrs Rigby sold Framingham Earl, unable to maintain the rambling estate any longer. Again, it is not entirely certain why the Rigbys should have chosen to live in Edinburgh. Perhaps the city's reputation for intellectual society suited Elizabeth's literary aspirations, or perhaps it suited the family purse. Elizabeth arrived in Edinburgh equipped with letters of introduction from John Murray to the city's society, and the *Journals and Correspondence* show that she was swiftly admitted into the best drawing rooms, a distinction that was unprecedented: 'No one can more enjoy the kind of society with which we here mix, and which, except abroad, we had always been debarred from'.[37] From the Rigbys' rented house in St Bernard's Crescent, in the New Town of Edinburgh, Elizabeth made a concerted effort to assume a literary life and she published numerous articles and stories in this period. *The Jewess: A Tale from the Shores of the Baltic* appeared first as a slim John Murray publication in 1843, followed by 'The Wolves of Esthonia' for *Fraser's Magazine* in 1845 and a collection of *Livonian Tales* in 1846. She also began to write for the *Quarterly Review*, contributing on topics such as 'Books for Children', 'Evangelical Novels', 'The Lady of the Manor', and 'Biographies of German Ladies'. She complained mischievously about her allocation to John Murray III: 'I see that you and the Editor of the Q:R: persist in keeping me to the articles about "women on women"'.[38] Of her first article on children's books in

1842 Lockhart writes to her that he has 'read it with more pleasure than I can well express. It seems to me one of the most admirable specimens of review-writing I ever met with – full of sense and taste, equally instructive and interesting.'[39] And again in 1843 Lockhart praised her contributions: 'You seem to have it in your power to render the "Q.R." an instrument of great improvement among classes of readers that have hitherto probably given no attention to its contents. You are the only lady, I believe, that ever wrote in it except Mrs. Somerville, who once gave us a short scientific article; and I had long felt and regretted the want of that knowledge of women and their concerns which men can never attain, for the handling of numberless questions most interesting and most important to society'.[40] The judgements she expressed in her *Quarterly* reviews reveal her confidence in the quality of her opinions and the certainty that she is articulating the shared values of Tory society. Their tone occasionally caused offence. Harriet Martineau measured Elizabeth's articles as evidence of her distant cousin's character; citing her review of German women in the *Quarterly* she warned her friend Jane Carlyle:

> Learn her from her own works: but, my friend, *beware of her*. She is dangerous ... As for Eliz*th*'s talents ... her feelings will never rise above a superficial sentimentality, nor her wit above smartness: while her virtue will always consist of mere got up invective ag*st* whiggish religion and politics. Be sure, dear, not to trust her, not put yourself in her power in the least thing, till you are satisfied yourself of my being mistaken in all this. My very heart wails over these literary women who are not true to their womanhood – to responsibilities far far exceeding those they spend themselves on.[41]

The journal shows that Elizabeth generally took around two months to complete her articles and that she was in more or less constant employment. The journal fails to illuminate her emotional or intellectual life in Edinburgh, instead painting a sociable picture of Elizabeth as a benign flirt, escorted into dinner by a succession of Edinburgh men and taking an immodest delight in recording the comments of attentive dinner guests. There are several photographic images of Elizabeth from the mid-1840s by the Edinburgh partnership of Hill and Adamson that corroborate this bookish and yet vivacious sense of self, some showing her contemplative and others showing her posing in her best apparel, in the manner of contemporary fashion plates.[42] Elizabeth was often described by her contemporaries as a 'handsome' woman, code perhaps for her striking but not conventionally beautiful features. Her unusual height (she was almost six feet tall), combined with her rather Roman nose, made her 'imperial looking', in the words of her nephew. From the very few images we have of Elizabeth in later life we can see that she retained her fondness for styling her hair in two braids, fixed with pins, around her ears. The photographer David Octavius Hill certainly found her attractive, recalling years later that his 'old sweetheart Elizabeth Rigby' was 'the tallest, cleverest & best girl of these parts'.[43]

It is not known exactly when Elizabeth first met the painter, former Keeper of the National Gallery and Secretary to the Fine Arts Commission, Charles Lock Eastlake. Eastlake was a frequent guest at the Murrays' and it can be deduced from a letter of 5 May 1843 that the two had first met shortly before, thereafter sporadically renewing their acquaintance at various dinner tables. John Murray observed enough to think that Eastlake was 'a little in love' with Elizabeth as early as 1845.[44] The feeling may have been mutual since Eastlake is mentioned gratuitously in some of her *Quarterly* reviews and flatteringly in her journal.[45] Charles Eastlake and Elizabeth Rigby became engaged in January 1849. We can only speculate, albeit with some confidence, that theirs would have been an utterly punctilious and protracted courtship. Eastlake's personality does not present itself very clearly in the letters but his contemporaries remarked variously on his circumspect behaviour, courtier-like bearing and methodical habits. His reputation as a painter was founded on rigorously academic views of the Roman campagna and history paintings. However, he was painting less frequently and increasingly acting as an administrator, in which role he was equally thorough and workmanlike. At the age of 56, Eastlake was qualified to present himself to Elizabeth Rigby. He was an established Royal Academician, public servant, writer and, more reliably, a land-owning gentleman, capable of supporting a family within the socially acceptable limits of his class.[46] Following his engagement he wrote to Elizabeth's uncle, Dawson Turner, 'You who know the worth and excellence of Miss Elizabeth Rigby can well estimate the prospect of rational happiness which is before me'.[47] His hopes of 'rational happiness' are entirely in character and not without foundation. Miss Rigby was a measured risk.

Eastlake brought his new bride back to his home at 7 Fitzroy Square, a solid Georgian house on the east side of the square, in an area of eighteenth-century property development that had become unfashionable and often bypassed by Victorians who headed west to Mayfair and Belgravia. Inside number 7 the Eastlakes lived on the light and airy first floor, which was divided into a front drawing room with its large windows facing the square and what Elizabeth called the back drawing room. The rooms were large enough to accommodate music parties and they frequently entertained the Royal Academicians. The Eastlakes quickly became a social fixture of the London season, although the first appearances of a tall, striking-looking bluestocking on the arm of a shorter, slightly built, confirmed bachelor aroused some short-lived comment and there are some irresistibly comic sketches of the couple among the recollections of various Victorians.[48] Soon after their marriage Eastlake became President of the Royal Academy and, as was customary, he was knighted in recognition of his services. The Eastlakes' new position and responsibilities put the pair at the heart of the London season, which was unofficially opened by the Private View at the Royal Academy in May each year. They presided as gregarious and companionable hosts of what Elizabeth described as 'the most exclusive meeting of rank and fashion, intermingled with artists and their wives'.[49] The London season was over at the start of the grouse shooting season, when the Eastlakes usually left town to start their continental tour of Europe. Many letters printed here testify to Elizabeth's feelings of 'dissipation' each summer, as she managed both her 'At Homes' and a busy schedule of evening parties. Her circle of friends extended in this period to literary and artistic residents of London, and included Euphemia ('Effie') Ruskin. As the letters document, Elizabeth was Effie's close friend and confidante during the period leading up to the annulment of her marriage to John Ruskin. The letters demonstrate how Elizabeth used her position to campaign for Effie among her large circle of acquaintances, in particular marshalling the ladies to prevent her friend from becoming a social outcast.

Fixed to the outside of number 7 Fitzroy Square since 1985 is a blue plaque which records that Charles Eastlake lived there for 22 years (1843–65), not mentioning that Elizabeth lived there for 44 years. This is a particularly contemporary oversight and not, perhaps, one which would have been made in the 1850s and 1860s. The married life of the Eastlakes is one of many distinguished Victorian partnerships that contravene the early feminist indictments of 'separate spheres'.[50] To be sure, Eastlake was a public man and Elizabeth would have had dominion over the private sphere of home, but her career as a writer between 1849 and 1865 was as productive as that she had had before her marriage: she wrote nine reviews, translated three volumes of Waagen and completed Anna Jameson's *History of Our Lord*. It could be observed that Elizabeth diverted her interests to those of her husband and that she concentrated her efforts on more art-historical material, as she acquired a reputation as an authority on art, although she regarded her knowledge of the history of art as 'small'.[51] Nonetheless, she was at the outer edges of the scholarship that contributed to the formation of the discipline we call the history of art. Knowledge about art history was generally in the orbit of literary people or of gentlemen artists; and despite her demurrals, Elizabeth's credentials in the history of art, and particularly in connoisseurship, were exceptional. She had a sound practical knowledge of art, albeit one whose technical expertise was limited to drawing and watercolour; and an extensive knowledge of European art collections.

As the letters printed here show, her main art-historical concern was with connoisseurship. Elizabeth's life straddled important changes in what constituted knowledge about art, based upon the systematic and scientific study of art and of attribution. Her connection to European connoisseurship was made through Charles Eastlake but maintained beyond his death through her friendship with Austen Henry Layard. Charles Eastlake became the first Director of the National Gallery in 1855. The few commentators on the history of the National Gallery have treated Elizabeth very kindly, unanimously arguing that Eastlake's successful tenure as Director was very much the result of a partnership with his wife. John Steegman writes: '"Eastlake" really means "them", a perfect and wonderfully fruitful partnership' or 'rather a joint personality'.[52] Holmes and Baker in an early history of the National Gallery give Elizabeth all the credit for Eastlake's successful transition from Keeper to Director, crediting the difference between the Eastlake who had resigned as Keeper in 1847 and the Eastlake who took on the Directorship in 1855 entirely to his wife: 'The single external cause to which we can assign a share in this development was Eastlake's marriage. Lady Eastlake was one of the most remarkable women of her time ... every autumn, from 1855 onwards, this talented lady accompanied her husband on his travels in search of pictures for the Gallery, and the extraordinary improvement in the quality of Eastlake's purchases can hardly fail to have been assisted by her companionship'.[53] Winslow Ames credits the couple with the fortunate purchases at the National Gallery: 'he and his wife, with their remarkable *expertise*, mobility, and knowledge of private sources, worked as one to build up what was already an important gallery'.[54] Denys Sutton describes Elizabeth as making a 'major contribution to Eastlake's assured position in the London art world'.[55]

In some ways the idea of a partnership presented by Steegman, Holmes and Baker and Sutton is overstated. What the letters seem to show is that the practicalities of their partnership were clearly devolved along private and professional lines. There are many letters (not reproduced here) written by Elizabeth on behalf of Sir Charles – sending replies to dinner invitations, allocating tickets, writing letters of introduction for private art collections and, more significantly, acting on his behalf when absent from town. Sir Charles authorized Elizabeth to open his mail in 1861 when he was on the Continent alone.[56] The real question of partnership, however, is that of her influence over his professional activities. Was her influence merely one of providing secretarial support or can it be traced in the actions of Sir Charles as the Director of the National Gallery? In a letter of 6 April 1861 she appears to be more than her husband's companionable helpmeet, suggesting to Layard that she will accompany Eastlake on his inspection of Piero della Francesca's *Baptism* and remarking that 'what influence I have will probably be execcuted in favour of trying to obtain it'. The extent of her putative influence over Eastlake's purchases for the National Gallery is still a matter of conjecture. However, it seems that she gave her unequivocal support to her husband in his professional activities. Adele Ernstrom has written on the working and married lives of the Eastlakes and has argued cogently in favour of 'their professional as well as personal solidarity'.[57] And perhaps 'solidarity' is the operative word. There are several letters in which Elizabeth takes up the cudgels in defence of her husband. For example, in one letter to Layard she pulls him up for an article in *The Times* questioning the progress of the decoration of the Houses of Parliament, overseen by Sir Charles' Fine Art Commission;[58] and in a set of letters to John Blackwood she beleaguers the publisher into printing a retraction of a remark in his magazine about Sir Charles' alleged policy of glazing pictures.[59]

Elizabeth did not make her first tour of the Continent with Eastlake until 1852, and she accompanied Eastlake on all or part of his travels except in 1853 and 1856. Eastlake went to Europe for five weeks each year to view and purchase paintings for the National Gallery collection. In their packed itinerary, Elizabeth often accompanied her husband to view the disassembled panel paintings and detached frescoes in dealers' shops or in private collections. To what extent her presence influenced Eastlake in his judgements about the eligibility of purchases for the National Gallery is unclear. For example, was she consulted over the purchase of works for Eastlake's own collection? The letters are inconclusive in this respect. Eastlake had formed a decent collection of old master drawings and some paintings – including a Rembrandt – before his marriage. However, the salaries that came with his new posts gave him a discretionary income to spend on art; and he was in an excellent position for picking up bargains.[60] The overwhelming majority of works purchased by the Eastlakes were quattrocento paintings of the virgin and child, including work by Botticelli, Bellini, Mantegna and Ghirlandaio. The quality of the Eastlake collection is summarized by Robertson when he observes that 'of the Eastlakes' 67 old pictures and drawings, 26 are now in the National Gallery, and a dozen more are in other galleries open to the public'.[61]

The Eastlakes made their last journey abroad together in August 1865. Almost as soon as they had crossed the Alps Eastlake became ill, suffering from familiar respiratory problems, and the pair remained at Milan, waiting for his health to improve sufficiently to return home. Eastlake attempted to carry out his business with Elizabeth acting as his secretary, writing most of his correspondence and coordinating his visitors. A few weeks into this regime it became clear that any plans to return to England would have to be postponed and that they would have to winter in Italy. By the end of

October the weather in Milan was too cold and wet for Eastlake's health and the pair headed to Pisa, hoping for a better climate and believing that they would be well placed to return home via Leghorn and thus avoiding the Alps. They lingered at Pisa for six weeks. The letters written by Elizabeth give successively encouraging and discouraging reports, as Eastlake alternately rallied and then relapsed. Eastlake made out his last will and testament on 22 December, and died two days later on Christmas Eve.

Elizabeth returned to England in January 1866 to live out what she called 'the altered remainder of my life'.[62] As she assumed the prescribed pattern of mourning followed by Victorian widows,[63] Elizabeth channelled her grief into a number of literary outlets, including a slim volume entitled *Fellowship: Letters Addressed to my Sister Mourners*, a perceptive pathology of grief that charts the stages of bereavement before consigning all suffering to the inscrutable will of the Almighty. The letters written in the late 1860s show her efforts to keep Sir Charles' flame burning, through his literary legacy and the future of the National Gallery. Her proprietorial interest in the National Gallery is thoroughly documented in the letters to the new Director William Boxall and to one of the trustees, Austen Henry Layard. The letters generally concern the disposal of Eastlake's art collection and library, although many also comment upon Gallery business. Elizabeth probably had little direct influence on the affairs of the National Gallery but she was certainly indulged by Boxall and Layard, both of whom courteously or diplomatically allowed her to imagine her importance. For example, in one letter to her cousin she confesses 'I grudge that the "talent" – i.e. the knowledge of art lies so useless with me. I had such an exceptional education in connoisseurship at my beloved One's side – & there is scarcely a creature with whom I can share it. I feel that I shd have been his best successor in the direction of the Nat: Gallery … Without vanity I know I shd have been the right person, tho' the world wd be astonished at such an idea'.[64] Following Boxall's resignation the letters are mainly critical of the new Director, Frederick Burton, and of his purchases for the nation, and some of her letters try to promote the career of her nephew Charles Locke Eastlake as he followed his uncle into the post of Keeper at the National Gallery.

Elsewhere her mandarinism wielded a traditionalist influence in the opinion-forming press. She continued to write for the *Quarterly* and, following a temporary rift with the Murrays, for the *Edinburgh*. Her topics were generally related to art and, when viewed in combination with the correspondence here, her articles help form a picture of the spirited and outspoken Lady Eastlake, who used her position to contribute to the cultural controversies of the period, illuminating the part that a confident and well-connected woman could play in debates about art scholarship.

Long after Eastlake's death, many prospective sellers of art works continued to approach her for verification of an artist's name, and she was regularly invited to comment upon paintings for descriptive notices and periodical reviews. As her nephew recalled, 'She was considered one of the best connoisseurs of Old Masters, and well known people came to her daily to talk pictures and art, and to get her advice thereon'.[65] Her correspondence with connoisseurs and historians including Austen Henry Layard, Rawdon Brown and William Boxall shows not only how much positive agency she wielded in their respective careers but also the extent to which she promoted the interests of friends in her writing.

Elizabeth ventured abroad periodically but she passed most of her time in London, punctuated by visits to family and friends, and she spent most summers out of town, frequently with her closest friend Harriet Grote in Surrey. Mrs Grote destroyed all her correspondence before her death and we are deprived of the letters that might have animated their friendship. Conversely, the correspondence with her great friend Austen Henry Layard is intact and the letters here reveal the scope of their shared interests, while some of the playful banter that passed between the pair gives colour to their relationship. The letters to Layard disclose the partisanship of the pair in the debates about connoisseurship at the end of the nineteenth century, showing the convivial relationships among their friends – Gustav Waagen, Giovanni Morelli, Jean Paul Richter and Bernard Berenson – as well as their common enmity towards J. A. Crowe, G. B. Cavalcaselle and Wilhelm von Bode.

By the 1880s the grand dame at number 7 was an oddity to the younger visitors to Fitzroy Square. Elizabeth had inherited the family condition she called rheumatism, and she became increasingly less mobile. She was still able to make house calls until 1883 but after that became more or less housebound, until she obtained a new carriage that could accommodate her wheelchair. Thereafter she still called at friends' doors and they obliged her disability by coming down to her in the street. At home she was virtually confined to her rooms on the first floor, receiving guests in her front drawing room and in her final years sleeping in the room at the rear. She was attended by five servants, and a succession of young friends and nieces. Visitors to her home usually found Elizabeth next to the fireplace, working at a writing desk on top of a great round table covered with manuscripts and periodicals, surrounded by unfashionable furniture covered in faded chintz.[66] She arranged what remained of the Eastlake collection across her two drawing rooms: two Veronese paintings over the chimneypiece, on the opposite wall various quattrocento paintings of the virgin and child intermingled with Sir Charles' views of the Roman campagna. She had too many paintings for the walls and kept some on easels, and others propped on chairs. The publisher Charles Kegan Paul recalled Elizabeth as 'a complete survival of a lady of the last generation. I never saw her wither sitting on a sofa or in an easy chair, but she sat up at a table with a little slanting writing-desk before her, surrounded with the stiffest of furniture, although priceless works of art hung upon the walls.'[67]

Bessie Rayner Belloc paints a graphic image of the elderly Elizabeth, loyally inhabiting Fitzroy Square despite its decline as the surrounding roads were filling with fish and chip shops and rag and bone men:

> During the last years of her long life she spent her days sitting between the window and the fire-place, at the convenient edge of a comfortable round table of the old-fashioned sort, littered over with new books and periodicals; and though she moved with difficulty, and had renounced her ceremonious habit of accompanying her visitors to the door of the room, she always apologised with stately politeness, and, except in that one particular, wholly declined to admit the infirmities of age. This room at number 7 Fitzroy Square, where the President had dwelt with persistent dignity, ignoring the western march of London, was inhabited to the last by 'Dame Elizabeth Eastlake'. It was large and handsome, with very high old windows, and the walls were covered with a profusion of fine pictures, many of them of great value; and intermingled were works by Sir Charles Eastlake, which although weaker in conception, did not jar at all with those of the Italian masters; and this was exactly what his widow intended to express by the arrangement. It was a delightful room, with a refreshing absence of any attempt at decoration, and exactly suited its imposing mistress.[68]

This view of the dowager Lady Eastlake is corroborated by a number of her visitors. G. E. Flower remembered, 'it was an intellectual treat to sit with her in her old house in Fitzroy-Square, surrounded by her splendid pictures and other works of art, enjoying her refined and elevated conversation, piously resigned to bodily sufferings, but bright in mind and warm in heart to the last'.[69]

The last two articles that Elizabeth published were, fittingly enough, reminiscences. 'Reminiscences of St. Petersburg Society' and 'Reminiscences of Edinburgh Society Nearly Fifty Years Ago' were published in *Longman's Magazine* in 1892 and 1893 respectively. In the new year of 1891 she began destroying her papers in order to save her executors trouble.[70] By the summer of 1893 it was evident to her friends and family that Elizabeth was dying. She remained conscious throughout her illness but suffered from breathlessness and restless nights and she ceased her correspondence in September. She added a codicil to her will on 30 August 1893, revoking some legacies and reducing others.

Elizabeth Eastlake died on 2 October 1893 and was buried beside her husband and their stillborn daughter at Kensal Green Cemetery four days later. She left £27,945 13s 4d to be divided up between a considerable number of family members and friends, giving proportionate sums to old friends, faithful servants, cousins and numerous nephews and nieces.

The death of Lady Eastlake generated a handful of perfunctory obituary notices but, by and large, collective amnesia had relegated her to the status of a widow of a distantly remembered public servant. However, following the publication of *The Journals and Correspondence of Lady Eastlake* on 4 December 1895 there was a belated press interest in her contribution to Victorian literature. The first crop of reviews were generally enthusiastic and adjectives such as 'charming' or 'delightful' are recurrent.[71] The *Daily Chronicle* called it 'one of the books of the season' and stated that it 'deserves, and cannot fail to secure, a permanent place in the libraries of all who have learned to understand that lively and just observation of men and manners, places and pageants, is seldom so valuable as when the observer is a shrewd, amiable and witty woman'.[72] However, the publication of the *Journals and Correspondence* also revealed Lady Eastlake's identity as the *Quarterly* reviewer of *Jane Eyre* and aroused more press interest.[73] The *Daily News* admitted that while 'happy in her intellectual gifts and inclinations, she was not less happy in her opportunities'.[74] Augustine Birrell in the *Speaker* hotly contested her reputation as a 'woman of letters': 'Accident threw open to her the "pulpit" of the Quarterly Review, and from that pulpit she preached many a sermon, inflicted many a wound, promulgated much mischievous nonsense without a tremor or a misgiving'.[75] James Payn writing in the *Illustrated London News* also queried Lady Eastlake's credentials: 'her style was admirable, and her opinions would have been valuable if only she had been right ... The past loomed before her eyes, like a hill in mist, while the present was a mole-hill'.[76] *The Times* appeared to sum up her contribution with acumen: 'The truth is that the note of Lady Eastlake's character was a robust commonsense which brought with it all its usual accompaniments of intolerance for sentiment and the tendency to hate what she could not sympathise with. Such a type of mind does not excite the highest kind of admiration, but in a woman who, through long life, makes such strenuous use of her endowments and opportunities, who does so much in the world, and who writes so much and so well, it arouses an admiration that is, after all, very real and very warm'.[77]

A final interesting footnote to these early considerations of Lady

Eastlake is the attempt by her butler, Stephen Springall, to contribute his own memoir. Stephen Hatcher Springall entered Fitzroy Square around 1870 and left service some time before 1891. Springall alerted 'the Eastlake Family' to his intentions shortly after the death of his former employer:

> It probably is known to you that I have written considerably about her and hers in the shape of 'Reminiscences of Lady Eastlake' and 'Facts and Fiction of Painters' Diction'. I have taken good editorial opinion concerning them, find they are up to the popular mark, and am advised as to where to plant them. Before making this venture I wish to bring the matter before the 'Eastlake Family'. I have been associated with the old House at Fitzroy Square for over a quarter of a century and consequently my writings exhibit much intimate and personal knowledge connected with persons and things about it of present and bygone days. This put together in an entertaining manner would doubtless please the popular mind, and bring me some remuneration for my trouble. It would also undoubtedly cause much displeasure and disapproval in the 'Eastlake Family' for while I have found much in my old mistress to laud and honour somethings [sic] there are I am forced to adversely criticize. This would hardly be relished by many members of the Family, but as I have taken the greatest pains to be strictly truthful and accurate I am not disposed to tone them down or to make any alteration whatever. But I am disposed to give the 'Eastlake Family' the first chance of possessing my 'Fitzroy Writings' should they care to do so.[78]

Charles Eastlake Smith put the matter in the hands of a solicitor and Springall capitulated; but in 1908 he published a novel entitled *That Indomitable Old Lady: A Romance of Fitzroy Square*. In Springall's thinly disguised but bizarre version of her life (told twice; once in prose and again in verse) 'Lady Lisbeth Simpson' is the titled daughter of the Earl of Haroldover. The Haroldover family consists of one daughter who marries a Norwegian, Herr Bjorsen; two brothers, the younger of whom ('Burly Jack') is a shady character who is murdered in Australia; and Lady Lisbeth Simpson, a 'stately and Brobdignagian' [sic] painter living in Fitzroy Square with her housekeeper, Mrs Sanderson. Boating at Regent's Park one day Lady Lisbeth falls into the water and is rescued by a young man, whom she never quite forgets. Her early career as an artist is enabled over a twenty-year period by her friends, Professor Vargon and Sir William Roxhall (evidently Waagen and Boxall), the latter an ageing painter who dies and leaves Lady Lisbeth all his possesions. On the proceeds, she and Mrs Sanderson make a tour of Germany and Italy, meeting a Welsh sculptor in Rome, John Gibson. Gibson gives her a letter of introduction to his friend the sculptor Henry Lockyer, whom she recognizes as the young man who had saved her years earlier following her dunking in Regent's Park. They subsequently marry and Lockyer becomes curator of an unnamed museum. Following Lockyer's death his widow becomes an active hospital visitor. The narrative is embellished with petty details about life in Fitzroy Square, particularly about Mrs Sanderson's management of the household. Springall's attempt to blackmail the 'Eastlake family' suggests that he may have had an unsavoury view of events, but at worst this appears to be the view of his employer as bellicose and the suggestion that her brother Roger was involved in some scandal in Australia. Springall settles his scores by making his former employer a little comical and putting her in demeaning situations (particularly her mud bath in Regent's Park).

Recently, Elizabeth Eastlake has been brought to life in two semi-fictional works. In Gregory Murphy's play based upon the annulment of John Ruskin and Effie Gray's marriage, *The Countess*, Lady Eastlake is a strident and sharp-tongued bluestocking friend of Effie. Her presence on stage, in a couple of key scenes, has her volleying barbed comments with Ruskin's parents.[79] In James Wilson's book *The Dark Clue* Lady Eastlake is cast as a bookish, untidy and rather slippery London hostess who may be a possible conspirator in a plot to discredit J. M. W. Turner's will.[80] The *Letters of Elizabeth Rigby, Lady Eastlake* presented here offer a clearer picture of Elizabeth's character. Her chief personality traits are remarkably consistent – strident, punctilious, proper, stern, judgemental, loyal. She liked Mendelssohn, fresh flowers, early Italian art, good food, and handsome men. She disliked Germans, 'fast' women, racy novels, and Gladstone. Her opinions remain fairly fixed and steadfast. There are, to be sure, some shifts in the authorial voice, from the confident young woman of the 1830s and 1840s, playfully communicating with John Murray, to the elderly Lady Eastlake, sometimes brittle and full of dowager importance, but capable of humour and great loyalty.

A Note on the Letters

Portions of some of the letters to A. H. Layard appearing in this volume were originally published by Charles Eastlake Smith in the *Journals and Correspondence of Lady Eastlake*. However, they were heavily edited and Smith tended to collapse letters together and occasionally to bowdlerize the text. Smith also loses his aunt's conversational style, her liberal emphases and her customary salutations; and he is silent on any aspect that he regards as outside the 'public interest'. A very small number of letters by Elizabeth Rigby, Lady Eastlake have been published outside the *Journals and Correspondence*, in the main appearing in the collected correspondence of other Victorians.[81]

The most significant source for the *Letters of Elizabeth Rigby, Lady Eastlake* is within the John Murray Archive, now in the National Library of Scotland, containing letters dating from 1841 to shortly before Elizabeth's death. The Archive includes letters addressed to three generations of John Murrays, as well as some addressed to Murray family members and some to successive editors of the *Quarterly Review*. There are gaps in the collection and only a very small number dating from the 1850s appear to have survived. In addition, the Archive includes a seemingly intact run of letters from Elizabeth to her friend and confidant Sir Austen Henry Layard and all of Layard's letters to Elizabeth.[82] Their correspondence is frequently lengthy and all the more interesting since Layard lived the itinerant life of an ambassador before settling in Venice and the two often corresponded at a distance. Consequently Elizabeth's letters to Layard include her reports on domestic matters and her opinions on political and world events.

Other important manuscript sources are dispersed among various libraries and public record offices. The Bowerswell Papers at the Morgan Library & Museum in New York include the correspondence of Euphemia ('Effie') Ruskin, later Millais. There are several lengthy letters from Elizabeth to Effie Ruskin and to her mother written during the annulment proceedings of the Ruskin marriage in 1854, and although portions of some have been previously published, they are included here in their entirety. The letters among the Dawson Turner papers at Trinity College Library, Cambridge are highly significant because they are among the earliest surviving letters, dating from 1834 to 1836, and provide a fascinating account of Elizabeth's earliest work.[83] The National Gallery holds letters written after Charles Eastlake's death – in the main to her husband's successor as Director, William Boxall. The University of North Carolina has more of Boxall's letters, which, in combination with the National Gallery Archive, offer a unique picture of Elizabeth's life immediately following Eastlake's death. Other smaller collections of letters supplement the larger archives, often providing continuity between letters or demonstrating the sheer range of Elizabeth's concerns and interests.

This volume represents about two-thirds of the correspondence I have read. On balance the process of tracing and transcribing letters occasions more disappointments than fulfilments. Lady Eastlake was an inveterate letter writer (she called herself 'an incorrigible scribbler'), although the letters that have survived and are represented here can only be a small part of her overall correspondence. In addition to her own letters she would have been the recipient of many letters, the majority of which she appears to have destroyed in 1891.[84] The letters in this volume span 63 years and they are printed in chronological order.[85] The broadest biographical details of Elizabeth's life, from 1830 to 1893, will be evident from the letters published here; I have annotated them with biographical details when relevant to the content of the letters. There is a general continuity to the letters, although there are gaps in the correspondence; for example, there are only two surviving letters to John Murray between 1848 and 1857, a regrettable gap that deprives us of correspondence about two of her most infamous *Quarterly* publications, the review of *Jane Eyre* and the review of Ruskin's *Modern Painters*.

I have made every effort to transcribe faithfully the letters, adopting the policy of not deleting passages even where the text is repetitive or purely solicitous. The rare instances of my inability to decipher the text are marked with '[*illegible*]'. Most of Elizabeth's letters can be read with ease, once the idiosyncrasies of her handwriting have been established, although proper names and foreign words can give trouble. All spellings, wordings and punctuation have been retained and *sic* is used sparingly, so that I have not added it to Victorian spellings such as 'accomodation', 'favor' or 'surprize'. Because of Elizabeth's tendency to drag her pen between words, leaving many connected by a thread of ink, it is sometimes not easy to tell whether words are connected or not: 'to day' and 'to morrow' occasionally appear unconnected and so I have transcribed them accordingly. The most difficult letters to transcribe have been those that are cross-written – that is, written vertically over horizontally written lines to save paper and postage costs. Particularly difficult are the cross-written letters on onion-skin paper addressed overseas (most often in the case of the correspondence with Layard), where the ink from the reverse side is visible and the process of determining which set of marks belongs to which side of the paper can be an arduous one.

Elizabeth tends to use em-dashes very liberally and sometimes I have had to judge between a full stop and an em-dash where the intention is not obvious. The other notable feature of her letters is her underlining of certain words or phrases for emphasis. In her early letters this conceit is rare but by the 1850s she is using the underline frequently. This gives a certain animation to the letters and some indication of how she might have modulated her speech, as does her use of exclamation marks. We know very little about how she sounded in conversation but a report by Beatrix Potter in 1886 describes her conversational emphases when she talked about Gladstone: "'I don't think I've ever met him at dinner when he had not his cuffs all frayed; that's Mrs. Gladstone. Oh yes, no doubt she's a terrible slut" (said Lady Eastlake with emphasis). "I believe Hawarden is a very dirty place, no punctuality, the meals any way. Mr. Gladstone would not mind it if she hadn't her stockings on!" Lady Eastlake talks rather slowly and at times mumbles a little. I should think she soon gets tired. Her voice is rather deep'.[86] The artist Catherine Maud Nichols recalled that her voice was 'measured and distinct'.[87] Elizabeth's underline is not only used for emphasis; foreign names (particularly artists' names) are underlined, as often are dates. I have retained her spelling of foreign names. Where Elizabeth used superscript letters in abbreviations, I have lowered them. I employ the customary square brackets for editorial insertions, but I have endeavoured to minimize these. Any hyphens occurring in line breaks have been removed. All brackets rendered () are Elizabeth's.

There are inevitably some stylistic changes to the format of Elizabeth's letters over the 63 years represented here. For example, in early letters the address and date appear at the bottom of the letter. This is changed between 1846 and 1847 to the top of the letter. Similarly, in August 1867 she starts to invert the day and the month in her dating of letters. In the 1860s she begins to write 'FitzRoy' instead of 'Fitzroy'. I have preserved her formatting of the date and address, on the basis that these details may be of some significance to someone, somewhere at some time.

Finally, annotations are provided with a view to contextualizing Elizabeth's correspondence and providing information that will contribute to a picture of the events or matters described or discussed. The first intention of the annotations is to identify, where possible, named (and sometimes unnamed) individuals, to give brief biographical details or to make suggestions for further reading. The annotations also give citations for bibliographical references and to works of art where possible. Significant events are verified where relevant, particularly in reference to the reports in *The Times*.

Notes to Introduction

1. There are two sources for this story. In the *Journals and Correspondence of Lady Eastlake* Smith reports that 'he [Turner] suddenly looked steadily and said he saw "Lady Eastlake"' (J&C1, p. 273). The second source is Millais' *Life and Letters*, which states that Turner took rooms at an inn in Cheyne Walk under an assumed name: 'at last, one day he became seriously ill, and it was only by his constantly calling out for Lady Eastlake … and on her being sent for, that his identity became known'; J. G. Millais, *The Life and Letters of Sir John Everett Millais*, 2 vols. (London: Methuen & Co., 1899), vol. 1, p. 158. This version is corroborated, in spirit at least, by Jack Lindsay, *J. M. W. Turner: A Critical Biography* (London: Cory, Adams & Mackay, 1966). It is unlikely that Elizabeth visited Turner on his deathbed; she thought that the circumstances of his life were 'sordid in the extreme' and that the terms of his will were 'stupid' (J&C1, p. 273). They had met at John Murray's in 1844, and in May 1846 she visited Turner's studio, where she saw a painting

'with all the elements in an uproar, of which [she] incautiously said: The "End of the World," Mr. Turner? "No, ma'am; Hannibal Crossing the Alps"' (J&C1, p. 188).

2. See my entry for 'Lady Eastlake' in the *Routledge Encyclopaedia of Nineteenth Century Photography* (New York: Routledge, 2007).

3. See Elizabeth Gaskell, *The Life of Charlotte Brontë* (London: Penguin, 1997 [1857]), pp. 281–82; Tim Hilton, *John Ruskin: The Early Years* (New Haven and London: Yale University Press, 1985), p. 242.

4. There are innumerable instances of Elizabeth's review of *Jane Eyre* being quoted in Brontë studies. Kathryn Hughes uses Elizabeth's phrase 'a tabooed woman' as a chapter title in her book *The Victorian Governess* (London and Rio Grande: The Hambledon Press, 1993).

5. Marion Lochhead, *Elizabeth Rigby, Lady Eastlake* (London: John Murray, 1961). Lochhead's work retells the narrative established in the *Journals & Correspondence*, adding some supplementary description of Elizabeth's published writings and drawing upon the writer's knowledge of material from the John Murray Archive.

6. David Robertson, *Sir Charles Eastlake and the Victorian Art World* (Princeton, NJ: Princeton University Press, 1978).

7. Dictionaries of Victorian literature usually give Elizabeth Eastlake a perfunctory credit; see e.g. Sally Mitchell (ed.), *Victorian Britain: An Encyclopedia* (New York: Garland, 1988); John Sutherland, *The Longman Companion to Victorian Fiction* (London: Longman, 1988).

8. John Steegman, *Victorian Taste: A Study of the Arts and Architecture, 1830–1870* (London: Century in Association with the National Trust, 1970 [1950]), p. 7. In fact, consulting the index of this book, the two are virtually equal for print inches. Steegman published sporadically on the Eastlakes over his career, including 'The Eastlakes and Lord Lindsay', *The Listener*, 14 July 1949, pp. 61–62, and 'Sir Charles Eastlake: 1793–1865', *The Architectural Review*, vol. 138 (November 1965), p. 364.

9. Bernard Denvir, 'The Eastlakes', *Quarterly Review*, vol. 295 (January 1957), pp. 85–97 (p. 85).

10. Francis Haskell, *Rediscoveries in Art* (Oxford: Phaidon, 1980), p. 19.

11. Namely: Katherine Frank, *Lucie Duff Gordon: A Passage to Egypt* (Harmondsworth: Penguin, 1994); Shelagh Hunter, *Harriet Martineau: The Poetics of Moralism* (London: Scolar Press, 1995); Judith Johnson, *Anna Jameson: Victorian, Feminist, Woman of Letters* (London: Scolar Press, 1997); Kali Israel, *Names and Stories: Emilia Dilke and Victorian Culture* (London: Oxford University Press, 1999); and Susanne Knecht, *Flora Tristan und Maria Graham Lady Callcott. Die zweite Entdeckung Lateinamerikas (Gebundene Ausgabe)* (Hamburg: Europäische VA, 2004). Vernon Lee has had two recent biographies: Vineta Colby, *Vernon Lee: A Literary Biography* (Charlottesville and London: University of Virginia Press, 2003) and Christa Zorn, *Vernon Lee: Aesthetics, History and the Victorian Female Intellectual* (Athens, OH: Ohio University Press, 2003).

12. Valerie Sanders, *Eve's Renegades: Victorian Anti-Feminist Women Novelists* (London: Routledge, 1996).

13. Stephen Springall, *That Indomitable Old Lady: A Romance of Fitzroy Square* (London: Henry J. Drane Ltd, 1908), p. 21.

14. Charles Eastlake Smith was the second child of her youngest sister Matilda and James Smith, a brother of Marion Murray; hence a mutual nephew of both Elizabeth and John Murray. See Obituary, *The Times*, Friday, 2 February 1917, p. 9, col. E.

15. J&C1, p. 57.

16. These are described by Dr Rigby in his book *Framingham, its Agriculture, &c., including the economy of a small farm* (Norwich, 1820).

17. For details of his agricultural innovations see A. M. W. Stirling, *Coke of Norfolk and his Friends*, 2 vols. (London: John Lane – The Bodley Head, 1912), vol. 1, pp. 291–300.

18. J&C1, p. 5.

19. See letter, 10 November 1830, n. 3.

20. See letters, 5 September 1843.

21. J&C1, p. 6. In the first half of the nineteenth century the terms 'typhoid' and 'typhus' were used interchangeably, although strictly referring to pathologically different diseases. It was most probably typhoid fever, since the disease was most commonly caught in the summer from bacteria in food and drink and is marked by intestinal inflammation.

22. TCC, July–December 1824 (92).

23. See letter, 23 July 1873.

24. Smith states that her first work was 'My Aunt in a Saltmine'. It is not in *Frasers* and despite intermittent efforts over the years to locate this short story, the piece eludes me.

25. See letter, 25 November 1834.

26. J&C1, p. 10.

27. Letter from Cotman to Dawson Turner, 30 October 1841, Norfolk Record Office: '...Yesterday we carried Madam Du Wall [Wahl] & her two Children to Framingham, where we saw Miss E. Rigby's very, very fine Portraits of Russian Nobility &c – they really are exceedingly beautiful, & they appear to be her strong points of excellence. Mrs R. I was glad to find looking well & in fine health. The family, saving Dr R – & Roger – & the two Russian Ladies, were all at home. They were all once my pupils – & expressed their pleasure at seeing their old Master. – Madam Du Wall is a delightful creature but a less observer than I own myself to be – must see with pain that a Canker lurks in the beautiful Rose that still damasks her lovely cheek! ...'. I am very grateful to Norma Watt for this information.

28. See letter, 15 March 1891.

29. Henry Sass (1788–1844) ran a drawing academy on Bloomsbury Street to prepare entrants for the Royal Academy. Frustratingly, details about Sass's academy are scant and there is no evidence to connect Elizabeth to his

school. However, Sass did take female students. See Caroline Davidson, *The World of Mary Ellen Best* (London: Chatto & Windus, 1985).

30. Engravings after her drawings were published in *Letters from the Shores of the Baltic, The Jewess* and most notably in her jointly authored work on *The History of Our Lord*. She also illustrated two volumes of *Recueil de meubles et d'ornement intérieurs, composés et dessinés dans les differents styles depuis l'epoque Louis XIII, jusqu'a nos jours par E. Eastlake*, 2 vols. (Brussels: C. Muquardt; London: Williams & Norgate; The Hague: Martinus Nijhoff, 1866–69).

31. Many standard reference works of art history were translated by women in this period: Mrs Merrifield translated Cennino Cennini's *Treatise on Painting* in 1844, Mrs Jonathan Foster translated Vasari from 1850, and Mrs Margaret Heaton translated the first English edition of Kugler's *Handbook* in 1842.

32. Her father Dr Rigby translated from the French Jacob Frédéric Lullin de Châteauvieux, *Italy, its Agriculture, etc. from the French of ... Chateauvieux being letters written by him in Italy, in 1812 and 1813. Translated by E. Rigby* (Norwich, R. Hunter, 1819) and wrote a medical book in German, *Versuch über die mutterblut flüsse*. Her brother Edward Rigby translated Carl Naegele's 'Lehrbuch der Geburtschülfe für Hebammen' in 1836.

33. Around 200 Baltic-German families had the governance of 800,000 Estonian peasants.

34. In fact Lockhart proposed instead to Letitia Mildmay and was refused. See Marion Lochhead, *John Gibson Lockhart* (London: John Murray, 1954), p. 256.

35. Kenneth Fielding and Ian Campbell, 'New Letters of Harriet Martineau to Jane Carlyle', *Women's Writing*, 9.3 (2002), pp. 379–93 (p. 389).

36. Mary F. Outram, *Margaret Outram 1778–1863, Mother of the Bayard of India* (London: John Murray, 1932), pp. 324–25.

37. J&C1, p. 45.

38. See letter, April 12 1845.

39. J&C1, p. 29.

40. J&C1, p. 51.

41. Fielding and Campbell, 'New Letters of Harriet Martineau to Jane Carlyle', p. 389.

42. Colin Ford and Roy Strong (*An Early Victorian Album: The Hill and Adamson Collection* [London: Jonathan Cape, 1974]) have compared her poses to those found in fashion plates for *Heath's Book of Beauty*, pp. 74–75 and pp. 61–62.

43. Letter from D. O. Hill to his sister-in-law, Jane Macdonald, July 1853, NLS, Acc 11782. I am very grateful to Sara Stevenson for bringing this letter to my attention.

44. George Paston, *At John Murray's: Records of a Literary Circle 1843–92* (London: John Murray, 1932), p. 193.

45. His name appears in her review of 'Modern German Painting' (*Quarterly Review*, vol. 77, 1846, p. 330) and he is even flattered in her 'Art of Dress'

(*Quarterly Review*, vol. 79, 1847, pp. 391–92). In her journal she calls him the 'Raphael of England' (J&C1, p. 118).

46. Eastlake inherited (in 1845) St Mary's Hill, a small country seat at Plympton. See Elizabeth Eastlake, *Contributions to the Literature of the Fine Arts by Sir C. L. Eastlake: with a memoir by Lady Eastlake* (London: John Murray, 1869), p. 181.

47. 27 March 1849. TCC, January–June 1847 (77).

48. Bessie Rayner Belloc remembered: 'In middle life she was an unusually tall, fine-looking woman, and her distinguished husband … looked extremely small and frail by her side'. See Bessie Rayner Belloc, *A Passing World* (London: Ward & Downey, 1897), p. 11. Beatrix Potter reported the gossip that Lady Eastlake 'used to be able to lift up her husband under her arm'; *The Journals of Beatrix Potter from 1881–97*, transcribed from her code writing by L. Linder (London: Warne, 1966), p. 55. Isobel Violet Hunt reported that he was known as 'Little Eastlake', while she was known as 'Lago Maggiore'; Isobel Violet Hunt, *The Wife of Rossetti: Her Life and Death* (London: John Lane, 1932), p. 107.

49. J&C1, p. 227.

50. For the 'separate spheres' thesis see Joan Landes, *Women and the Public Sphere in the Age of the French Revolution* (Ithaca, NY: Cornell University Press, 1988), Joan N. Burstyn, *Victorian Education and the Ideal of Womanhood* (London: Croom Helm, 1980), Martha Vincinus, *Suffer and Be Still: Women in the Victorian Age* (Bloomington: Indiana University Press, 1972), and Martha Vincinus (ed.), *A Widening Sphere: Changing Roles of Victorian Women* (Bloomington: Indiana University Press, 1977).

51. See letter to John Murray, 14 March 1868.

52. Steegman, 'Sir Charles Eastlake', p. 364.

53. Sir Charles Holmes and C. H. Collins Baker, *The Making of the National Gallery, 1824–1924* (London: The National Gallery, 1924), pp. 32–33.

54. Winslow Ames, *Prince Albert and Victorian Taste* (London: Chapman & Hall, 1967), p. 126.

55. Denys Sutton, 'Aspects of British Collecting Part IV', *Apollo*, 123 (1985), pp. 84–129 (p. 92).

56. See letter to R. N. Wornum, NG02/4/2/57/2.

57. Adele M. Ernstrom, '"Equally Lenders and Borrowers in Turn': The Working and Married Lives of the Eastlakes', *Art History*, 15.4 (December 1992), pp. 470–85 (p. 482).

58. See letters to Layard, 31 December 1859 and 21 January 1860.

59. See letters to Blackwood, 3, 10, 20 December 1853.

60. So much so that there was some suggestion that Eastlake had dishonestly acquired his collection, a suggestion that Elizabeth was anxious to dispel by disposing of the works he had collected privately during his time as Director of the National Gallery. See letters to Boxall, 1867.

61. Robertson, *Sir Charles Eastlake*, p. 275.

62. See letter to Boxall, 10 May 1866.

63. See John Morley, *Death, Heaven and the Victorians* (London: Studio Vista, 1971), pp. 63–79.

64. See letter to Hannah Brightwen, 14 October 1875.

65. Charles Eastlake Smith, letter to John Murray, 18 May 1895, NLS Acc 12604/2104.

66. For example, see Potter, *The Journals of Beatrix Potter*, p. 167.

67. Charles Kegan Paul, *Memories* (London: Routledge & Kegan Paul, 1899), p. 345. Because Paul's account is not a diary, there is no date for his recollections, except that they appear in a chapter dated from 1874.

68. Belloc, *A Passing World*, pp. 11–12.

69. *The Times*, 13 October 1893, p. 5, col. f.

70. See letter to Layard, 1 January 1891.

71. *Morning Post*, Thursday 5 December 1895; *Glasgow Herald*, Wednesday 4 December 1895; *Manchester Guardian*, 4 December 1894; *London Quarterly Review*, April 1896, p. 98.

72. *Daily Chronicle*, Wednesday 4 December 1895.

73. In point of fact Elizabeth had been known as the author of the review since 1873. I have documented reactions to the publication of Lady Eastlake's name in full in '"In her Own Metier": The *Quarterly* Review of Jane Eyre', *Women's History Review*, forthcoming 2009.

74. *Daily News*, Wednesday 4 December 1895.

75. *Speaker*, 'A Literary Causerie: Lady Eastlake by A.B.', Saturday 14 December 1895, pp. 647–48.

76. *Illustrated London News*, Saturday 14 December 1895, p. 722.

77. *The Times*, Wednesday 4 December 1895, p. 7, col. A.

78. Copy of a letter from Springall to W. S. Carver, 15 November 1893, NLS uncatalogued.

79. Gregory Murphy, *Countess* (New York: Dramatist's Play Service, 2000). The character of Lady Eastlake also featured in a previous play in the West End, *The Bride of Denmark Hill* by Lawrence Williams and Nell O'Day, which played at the Royal Court Theatre in 1952.

80. James Wilson, *The Dark Clue* (New York: Atlantic Monthly Press, 2001).

81. For example in Mary Charlotte Mair Senior, *Letters and Recollections of Julius and Mary Mohl* (London: Kegan Paul & Co., 1887); W. N. Bruce (ed.), *A. Henry Layard, Autobiography and Letters*, 2 vols. (London: John Murray, 1903); Outram, *Margaret Outram 1778–1863*; Cornelia Carr (ed.), *Harriet Hosmer, Letters and Memories* (London: John Lane – The Bodley Head, 1913).

82. The letters came to the Murray family through a marital connection: Enid Layard's niece Alicia du Cane married Henry Hallam Murray in 1885.

83. Dawson Turner was an inveterate collector and there are 82 volumes of his correspondence bequeathed by his daughter Eleanor Jacobson to the University. Regrettably, some of Elizabeth's letters seem to have been removed, almost certainly by her cousin. For this information I am grateful to Diana Chardin.

84. J&C1, p. 6. Those that survived her bonfire passed to her nephew and

executor Charles Eastlake Smith on her death. Following Smith's death his widow Lizzie began to dispose of those parts of the collection that had historic or resale value.

85. There are a small number of undated letters, which I have placed according to the most likely date of composition.

86. Potter, *The Journals of Beatrix Potter*, pp. 168–69.

87. C. M. Nichols 'Personal Reminiscences of Lady Eastlake'. This newspaper cutting is in the Norwich Scrapbooks of Edward A. Tillett in the Millennium Heritage Library, Norwich. I have been unable to find its original source, presumably a local newspaper.

Letter to Francis Turner Palgrave[1]   *Private Collection*

Framingham Earl
Nov 10th 1830
My dear Mr Palgrave

I am quite sorry that I was not sooner able to send you some of my drawings and to acknowledge your kind letter. I was not however quite prepared with copies, which I could lay before you with satisfaction, these four I now send you are finished (according to Mr Cotman's opinion)[2] enough for the engraver and may serve as an example of what others will be. I have no idea in what form a publisher would bring them forth, but of course as my only object is to dispose of my drawings that will be of little consequence to me; should they be published in the form of an annual or any thing of that kind I should be equally happy to furnish short descriptions and anecdotes to each print. In case you should be able to arrange this affair for me, Mr Cotman strongly advises that the Impressions should be sent to me while in progress, for me to correct, this seems very presumptuous task for me to undertake but he assures me it will be of great benefit to the print as well as improvement to myself. I am very anxious as to the success of these drawings and I am sure you and Elizabeth will understand my feelings. I would have sent my original sketches but I was advised not to run the risk.

Edward[3] is now in London and I doubt not will soon do himself the pleasure of seeing you, he was so much improved in health that Mamma parted from him with comparatively little anxiety, pray tell Elizabeth that I was a day in Yarmouth last week and saw my aunt who was looking very well, though terribly reduced in number of family, Ellen being the only one with her.

Mamma desires kind love to yourself and Elizabeth, thank her also in my name for the few kind lines she addressed to me, and believe me my dear Sir, sincerely your
Eliz Rigby

1. Sir Francis Palgrave (1788–1861), antiquarian and historian, was married to her cousin Elizabeth Turner.

2. John Sell Cotman (1782–1842), landscape artist associated with the Norwich School, and employed as a drawing tutor to the Rigby daughters. See Derek and Timothy Clifford, *John Crome* (Greenwich, CT: New York Graphic Society Ltd, 1968), who suggested that Elizabeth was 'Cotman's favourite pupil'. A letter from Cotman to Francis Palgrave dated 16 October 1830 gives his opinion of Elizabeth's sketches thus: 'They are the best Amateur Sketches ... I ever saw – highly picturesque, well chosen, and splendidly drawn. A sufficient number may be selected from them to form a valuable work – but they want finish and effect' (Private Collection). For this information I am very grateful to Norma Watt, Assistant Keeper (Fine Art) at the Norwich Castle Museum and Art Gallery.

3. Dr Edward Rigby Jr (1804–60), Elizabeth's elder brother. Like his father, Dr Rigby became an eminent obstetrician, holding many posts in London hospitals and at the University of London. He wrote the *System of Midwifery* (1851) and *On the Constitutional Origin of Female Diseases* (1857). Rigby's significant contribution to midwifery was to bring his knowledge of German advances in obstetrics to London. See Walter Radcliffe, *Milestones in Midwifery* (Bristol: John Wright & Sons Ltd, 1967), and Peter M. Dunn, 'Dr. Edward Rigby Junior of London and his System of Midwifery', *Archives of Disease in Childhood: Fetal and Neo-Natal Edition*, 84.3 (May 2001), pp. 216–17.

Letter to Dawson Turner[1]   *TCC July–December 1834 (147)*

Framingham Earl
25 November 1834
My dear Uncle

I thank you much for your letter and questions with regard to Passavant[2] – his having communicated with you on the subject, and the additional inducements, and probabilities of success, which are now held out, make me answer without hesitation, that I shall gladly continue the translation, and trust with diligence to make rapid progress, which under present circumstances I feel necessary.[3]

From the length of time which has elapsed since my first essay upon him,[4] my mind had become sanguine as to the eventual success of the undertaking; I had therefore applied to Mrs. Austin[5] for her opinion. I have, however, as yet received no answer. Nor do I now require one. I have been much employed on other things lately, but I shall set to work on him immediately: and now I must ask you whether I may not send you a few sheets at a time as fast as I translate, as I feel aware how much correction I shall require. Also may I trouble you to send me back the first sheets which you took with you to London.

I feel there is much more to be said about this and I shall want to hear further about Passavant's proposed additions and amendations but in the mean while I had better not be losing time.

We should be sincerely glad to hear better accounts of your dear Mary and trust such are not far distant. Mamma and all here desire their loves to all your party, and with my own particular one to dear Ellen,[6] I am dear Uncle

Your affectionate niece

Elizth Rigby

Framingham Earl[7]

Nov 25th 1834

1. Dawson Turner (1775–1858), Yarmouth banker, antiquarian, amateur botanist and Elizabeth's uncle, who superintended the translation of Passavant. See Nigel Goodman (ed.), *Dawson Turner, A Norfolk Antiquary and his Remarkable Family* (Phillimore, 2007).

2. Johann David Passavant (1787–1861), art historian, curator and artist, based in Frankfurt. His *Kunstreise durch England und Belgien* was first published in 1833.

3. This and subsequent letters addressed to Dawson Turner relate to Elizabeth's translation of J. D. Passavant's *Tour of a German Artist in England with Notices of Private Galleries, and Remarks upon the State of Art*, 2 vols. (London: Saunders & Otley, 1836). For an account of the translation see Neil Macgregor, 'Passavant and Lady Eastlake: Art History, Friendship and Romance', in Hildegard Bauereisen and Martin Sonnabend (eds.), *Correspondances: Festschrift für Margret Stuffmann zum 24 Nov. 1996* (Mainz: H. Schmidt, 1996), pp. 166–74. Macgregor praises Elizabeth's sensitive translation of Passavant: 'she has a fluency in rendering him which is never forced or literal, and a happy knack of catching his occasionally purple prose' (p. 168).

4. This corroborates Smith's claim that she did publish some translation of Passavant in 1830. J&C1, p. 6.

5. Sarah Austin (née Taylor) (1793–1867), Elizabeth's cousin and translator of numerous German texts, significantly including Pückler-Muskau's *Tour of a German Prince in England*. See Lotte and Joseph Hamburger, *Troubled Lives: John and Sarah Austin* (Toronto: University of Toronto Press, 1985) and *Contemplating Adultery: The Secret Life of a Victorian Woman* (New York: Fawcett Columbine, 1991).

6. Eleanor Turner (1811–95), daughter of Dawson Turner and Elizabeth's cousin.

7. Framingham Earl, just outside Norwich, was the home of the Rigby family,

where they had a large estate and model farm. For an account of the farm see Dr Edward Rigby, *Framingham, its Agriculture, & c., including the economy of a small farm* (Norwich, 1820).

Letter to Dawson Turner   *TCC Dawson Turner & Palgrave Private Etchings and Autographs Vol. II (39)*

Framingham Earl
26 December 1834
My dear Uncle

I enclose you Mrs. Austin's letter which I received a few days ago. You will see what she says about the review of Passavant in the approaching Foreign Quarterly; this does not damp my courage, if you do not feel there is <u>real</u> cause for doubting of ultimate success.[1]

I am rather troubled by occasional inaccuracies which seem to occur in his statements, but I conclude that with proper references and your good help these can be corrected in the translation. You have also mentioned corrections and improvements on his part which would probably meet their objections.[2]

Will you be inclined to send up what we have already translated to a publisher for further opinion? If so, as soon as you can return the book to me I will send you a portion I have been translating from the private collections, and these two pieces would give a fair sample of the work. Although this is a <u>business</u> letter, dear Uncle, I must introduce a few of those good wishes which this season brings more especially to mind; may the approaching year bring fresh health and strength to the dear invalids of your family, and comfort to your's and my aunt's hearts. We thought particularly of you all yesterday, and of our Christmas party under your roof last year. We had Mrs. and John Simpson[3] with us yesterday, which at once gave us the pleasure of their company, and eased my poor aunt of some of her numbers on a trying occasion. We have not heard of our boy Roger[4] since the first announcement of his safe voyage, but now we can afford to wait for further news. Be so good as to tell us particulars of dear Mary's state, we have heard indirectly but not satisfactorily of her progress. Also tell my aunt that Miss Emily Morse who called here today made many enquiries after her and the different members of your family.

With our united loves, believe me my dear Uncle,
Your very affectionate niece
Elizth Rigby

I had a little lithographic drawing sent me the other day from Heidelberg, copies from a light profile I had taken of Professor Naegele[5] when there: the circumstance is gratifying to me, tho' the drawing is such as I would now be glad to replace with another.

1. Sara Austin's enclosed letter dated 18 December 1834 recommends that Elizabeth persevere in her approaches to publishers since she has ascertained that the book is regarded as 'rather dull'. It was not unusual for translators to pitch publishers with proposals since, as Susanne Stark has noted, translators also had to have 'the entrepreneurial talent to decide which foreign books would be appropriate for translation and would go down well on the English book market'. See Susanne Stark, *'Behind Inverted Commas': Translation and Anglo-German Cultural Relations in the Nineteenth Century* (Clevedon: Multilingual Matters Ltd, 1999), p. 45.

2. There a a great number of translator's footnotes in the volumes, pointing out the changes since the original publication. In the Translator's Preface she writes, 'In all important changes the necessary notes have been added. By means of correspondence, also, the translator has obtained the advantage of the author's own corrections and emendations, which will account for some seeming discrepancies between this and the original version' (p. xx).

3. Elizabeth's aunt Katherine and uncle John Simpson, parents of John Palgrave Simpson, the playwright and popular dramatist.

4. Roger Rigby (1814–76), Elizabeth's younger brother. Three accounts of his travels were published under the pseudonym 'Benjamin Bunting' for *Bentley's Miscellany*: 'Ten Days in Quarantine' (February 1843), 'Shooting in Brazil' (May 1843) and 'Burning of a Roca' (June 1843). See Bentley Papers, BL Add 46650 ff289 and 293.

5. Franz Carl Naegele (1778–1851), Professor of Medicine at Gröningen. Elizabeth's brother Dr Edward Rigby translated Naegele's essay 'On the Mechanism of Labour' in 1829.

Letter to Dawson Turner   *TCC January–June 1835 (104)*

Framingham Earl
2 May 1835
My dear Uncle

I must have seemed very remiss in the acknowledgement of your kind letter to me of many weeks back, but in the mean time, my patience has been not a little tried with Mr. Bentley's delays. In consequence of your letter I wrote to Mr. Simpson, he being I considered, more fitted for the execution of such a commission than my brother Edward. He had been with Bentley, and received so many promises of the MS being read, and an answer returned within a few days, none of which have been fulfilled, that I feel reluctant to press the matter further upon him. Might I beg you, dear Uncle, to use your influence; I send a few lines to Bentley, requesting him to come to a speedy decision, one way or other.[1]

I sent William a host of arguments in favour of the undertaking and I quite believe he employed all his powers of persuasion, but I understand from others Bentley is notorious for his procrastinating habits, and gives endless trouble thereby.

Should he refuse the work, I am anxious to prepare parts of it, for articles in some periodical publication, and this month is all the time I can dispose of, as I fully expect to start for Heidelberg the beginning of next month. It is not unlikely that I may visit Frankfort, where I should make a point of seeing Mr. Passavant. At all events I shall be happy to be the bearer of any parcel from you to him.

We hear frequently from Roger, who writes very agreeably and we watch the tone of his letters with much interest, as this period of his life will greatly determine his future lot. He is becoming quite reconciled to the country, and likes his situation, superiors and companions. James Powys[2] is reported of, in the highest terms, for his abilities and industry.

I have read the accounts of Mr. Buchanan's exportations[3] with much pleasure, and return you the second volume with many thanks.

With my best love to my aunt and cousins, believe me my dear Uncle to remain
Your obliged and affectionate niece
Elizth Rigby
Framingham Earl
May 2nd 1835

1. Richard Bentley & Son was a publisher and bookseller based in London.

2. James Murrell Coventry Powys (b. 1810), a cousin of the Rigbys and eldest of triplets born to Elizabeth and Rev. Thomas Powys.

3. Most likely a work by Francis Buchanan (afterwards Francis Hamilton), a zoologist and botanist who published several accounts of his travels, including *A Journey from Madras through the Countries of Mysore, Canara and Malabar* in 1807 and *An Account of the Kingdom of Nepal* in 1819.

Letter to Dawson Turner   *TCC (uncatalogued item)*

Framingham Earl
9 June 1835
My dear Uncle

I received your kind note to-day and I am much pleased with the prospect which Saunders & Ottley hold out to me.[1] I am truly obliged for the exertions which you and Mr. Thurgen have made for this purpose. I know Mr. T. very well, and he has been very interested in the fate of Passavant, but I don't at all know how he came to make so unceremonious an attack upon you. My sisters have just written that Mr. Simpson has left the M.S. with them not having heard anything from Wm I conclude he could not extract it out of Mr. Bentley's hands. I expect to be in London myself this week, or at all events the beginning of next; and I will forward the translation, as far as it goes, to Saunders & Ottley: and perhaps dear Uncle you will be so kind as to write what you think proper to Saunders & O. and direct it for me to my aunt Powys'[2] under cover to Sir Eardley Wilmot,[3] M.P. 44 Parlliament [sic] St. (should you have no other means of sending it free) and I will enclose it with the M.S. to the publishers. Also if you would wish to send any letter by me to M. Passavant it would reach me by that means. I <u>may</u> start for Rotterdam on Sunday morning next but I am not sure owing to my expected escort being still undecided. But I fear I must restrict you to this time. I expect to return to England at the end of August, and if nothing mars the present prospect shall be able to continue translating with the greatest ease during my absence. Whatever may be the ultimate result of this association, do not my dear uncle let the thought of your having been the means of my undertaking this work annoy you for one instant. I have enjoyed the occupation and the practise [sic] it has afforded me in writing, has been of great service to me in some other little short pieces, which I have been trying my head and hand upon. Should I never see a 6d for it, I would not regret what I have done. <u>You</u> are the only one who have suffered, and will have to suffer (for I doubt not that I shall be very glad of your kind assistance) unprofitable trouble. You say nothing of your dear Mary's health; but we trust in this instance that "no news is indeed good news".

With Mamma's and my best love to my aunt, yourself and all believe me dear Uncle
Your obliged and affectionate niece
Elizth Rigby

1. Saunders and Otley were publishers in London.

2. Elizabeth Powys, née Palgrave (1772–1842), sister of Elizabeth's mother, married the Rev. Thomas Powys. See C. J. Palmer and Stephen Tucker (eds.), *Palgrave Family Memorials* (privately printed, 1878).

3. Sir John Eardley Wilmot (1783–1847), MP had married Elizabeth Parry (1789–1818), sister of Admiral Parry and hence a relation of the Rigby family.

Letter to Dawson Turner   *TCC July–December 1835 (71)*

Framingham Earl
24 September 1835
My dear Uncle

Last Saturday evening brought me to my old quiet home again, after rather a boisterous journey, and after spending 3 months in every respect as happily as I expected; which is saying very much.[1] The old complaint of "Time Flies" I never found more applicable than to these same, short, bright summer months, which have passed over me like a dream, but a dream which has left me not empty-handed, nor I trust quite empty-headed either. I must first tell you that I have not seen Passavant,[2] who is still in Italy, which he will not leave before November. I managed, however, to reach him by letter, and heard from him very fully before I left. I believe, however, dear Uncle, that I am still beginning at the middle of my story, and that I should first acquaint you, that the day previous to my leaving England, I agreed with Saunders & Ottley for the publication of Passavant. They did not require to have the manuscript left with them, as they were perfectly satisfied with the report they had heard of the work – they undertake everything, allowing me the half of the profits. Whether this will be much or little I know not, but I am not sanguine. I accordingly continued the translation assiduously abroad, and carried it as far as I was there able. I was very sorry not to be able to see Passavant. He seems to be much industriously collecting material for his life of Raphael, and I am not without a private design upon this work, should it prove translatable, and should this my first attempt succeed.[3] The kind contents of your letter were communicated to me from home, and I almost hoped from what you said of your plans to have been able to welcome you in Germany. Passavant's absence, however, would have frustrated one of your expectations. On my return through London I called on Saunders

& Ottley, [sic] who will require sufficient of the manuscript, as will form one volume (my wish to make 2 octavo <u>Post vol's</u> of it) in about 3 weeks from this time.[4] And I am now occupied in working the whole MSS, as far as I am able. May I venture my dear Uncle now to draw upon your patience, and ask your assistance on many points which I do not understand. Passavant has sent me further corrections, and also referred me to a letter which he wrote to you from Rome, which perhaps you will be so good as to allow me to see. I enclose a few words which I do not understand, will subjoin a short explanation to them – also can you give me any account of the statues in Langley, and of the curiosities in Narford Hall.[5] An history also of the forum collection at Houghton.[6] If you could refer me to works where I could obtain a general idea of the picture galleries and <u>show houses</u> in Norfolk I would be very much obliged. Saunders & O. seemed to think that it would require an extension of the work to complete the 2 vols: and therefore I have been endeavouring to collect a few materials, and for this purpose I thus trouble you. I saw Mr. Woodburn[7] when in London who kindly overlooked the description of his own rooms in Passavant, where we found several little inaccuracies which make me rather anxious for the fate of the rest. You have probably heard of Professor Raumer who is now travelling through Great Britain upon a commission from the King of Prussia for the purpose of obtaining a complete survey of the state of art. I fear his work will quite eclipse Passavant, but at all events we have the start.[8]

The news of your dear Ellen's engagement, greeted me immediately on my arrival. I can congratulate Mr. Jacobson[9] very safely. Pray assure her of my affection and sincere good wishes. I know how new this subject must be at your's and my dear aunt's heart and I can only hope that you will have the blessing of seeing her as happy in this connection as she deserves. I shall venture to trouble you again when I come to doubtful parts – but I send off their questions in the mean time, as I am anxious to get all to rights.

With mamma's and all our loves to aunt and your dear party I remain my dear Uncle
Your obliged and affectionate niece
Elizth Rigby

1. She had been on a three-month visit (June to September) to Heidelberg.

2. She finally met Passavant in 1848 at Frankfurt.

3. Passavant's biography of Raphael, *Rafael von Urbon und sein Vater Giovanni Santi*, 2 vols. (Leipzig, 1839).

4. Standard book size of 8 ½ x 11 inches made from standard size sheets of paper folded three times to make eight leaves. Each leaf is usually printed on each side, making 16 pages in total. Books were customarily sold with the pages folded and had to be cut by hand. See letter, 6 March 1845.

5. Narford Hall in Norfolk, the seat of the Fountaine family, had a collection of paintings, coins and bronzes.

6. See reference to Houghton in LSB1, p. 67.

7. Samuel Woodburn (1786–1853), collector and picture dealer.

8. Friedrich Ludwig Georg von Raumer (1781–1873) published *England in 1835: Letters Written to Friends in Germany* (Philadelphia: Carey, Lea and Blanchard, 1836) and *Contributions to Modern History, from the British Museum and the State Paper Office* (London: Charles Knight & Co., 1836–37).

9. Eleanor Turner married William Jacobson (1803–84) who was, from 1865, the Bishop of Chester.

Letter to Dawson Turner   *TCC July–December 1835 (96)*

Framingham Earl
20 October 1835
My dear Uncle

Many thanks for your answers and speedy return of my manuscript. I must now trouble you again. Passavant's letter rather frightens me, as he seems to look forward to a mass of information being added by the translator, which I am by no means in a state to give. In some instances, I have procured matter for notes, but these are few in number. I should be truly obliged if you would look through the work, and send me the cases of attention since its publication, which have come to your knowledge – and also the two catalogues of Mr. Aders' sale[1] which you mention, and from which I conclude sufficient information may be extricated. I also write to Mr. Woodburn today, enquiring more particularly into the number and nature of the drawings in his possession. Some have been already disposed of, of which he has informed me.

I think I mentioned to you that Passavant had sent me a drawing of himself, by himself. I send it you. It is an ordinary concern as you will see. I proposed it, and I showed it, to Saunders & Ottley, who seemed little inclined to add any frontispiece to the work, and said in case they decided on taking it they could get it slightly executed themselves. I showed it to some of his relations in Germany, and to Mr. Woodburn,

who all condemned it as a likeness. Under these circumstances would
you advise me to offer myself as etcher or lithographer of it (I think I
could manage either) to Mssrs. S. & O.? I thank you much for the offer
of Hannah's services but if done at all, and out of the publisher's hands
I think I should like to attempt it myself. Passavant's letter is a valuable
help. I will return it to you if possible by this parcel. I must also ask
you for the sketch of the preface which I sent you, and the likeness of
Passavant back as soon as is convenient – i.e. when you like. Will you
tell me what's the meaning of "der Schäfer des Apulejus p.58 Claude
No 3.

I have delayed this parcel till the return of my messenger from
Norwich, and find that not one of the works you mention are at the
Public Library – will you, Uncle, be so good as to supply me with them
as far as you can. I have procured a catalogue of Nat: Gal: by Ottley,
but it is as early as 1827. Is there another later, and if you have it will
you enclose it to me? Also if you have catalogues of any of the other
collections in the work,[2] they would be of the greatest service to me,
as he makes many significant mistakes which are sillier to leave, than
great ones. I want very much to see the outline [?] galleries of Mr.
Hope, Stafford, Grosvenor etc. and I cannot procure them in Norwich.
If you would trust yours to me, I can only say that I would take great
care of them and return them in a day. Give [sic] me dear Uncle I have
taken most unscrupulous advantage of your kind offers of assistance and
have told you openly all I want and wish for, otherwise how should
you know it. With regard to your proposal of adjoining an account of
the Norfolk collections, it certainly would give the work a great local
interest, and make myself of rather more importance, but do you think
that can be accomplished without visiting all the places in question
myself, and delaying the work still further, which I am only to anxious
now to wind up. There is a word in Passavant's letter I can't make out
S.III Z 24 – "und eine andere in der Brera" &c.[3] What is this? I shall
adopt your advice about putting Passavant's additions as notes, except
when they are intended to be inserted in the text.

I have troubled you long enough, and think I have mentioned all I
intended. My aunt Simpson is staying with us, and is better than she
has been. She and mamma and all join in love to you and your dear
party and assuring you again of my sense of your unremitting kindness,
believe me dear uncle
Your affectionate niece
Elizth Rigby
Framingham Earl
Oct 20th 1835

1. Charles Aders' collection of early Netherlandish and German paintings was on display at Suffolk Street Gallery in 1832. See Michael Kennedy Joseph, *Charles Aders, A Biographical Note, together with some unpublished letters addressed to him and others, and now in the Grey Collection, Auckland City Library*, Auckland University College, Bulletin no. 43 (1953).

2. Dawson Turner had an prodigious collection of exhibition and gallery catalogues. When his library was sold in 1859 Lots 2272–2322 were catalogues and some individual lots contained 70 items. See Trevor Fawcett, *The Rise of English Provincial Art: Artists, Patrons and Institutions outside London* (Oxford: Clarendon Press, 1974), p. 108 n. 225.

3. 'And another in the Brera', i.e. the gallery in Milan.

Letter to Dawson Turner   *TCC July–December 1835 (129)*

Framingham Earl
13 November 1835
My dear Uncle

I have delayed acknowledging your delightful loan of books, which, as you will believe, have been of the greatest service to me, and also dear Mary's kind letter, which I will hope to answer in kind, more worthily another time. I have many questions to trouble you with. I have a letter from Saunders & Otley to-day in answer to a packet of MS I sent them almost a fortnight back; wherein they say, that before commencing printing they must know the quantity of my MS in the whole "Their impression being that the whole was expected to make 2 vols: of about 300 pages each – each page containing 22 lines of 8 words".

On calculation, I find that with such wide printing and my additional notes, I am likely far to exceed the stipulated number of pages. This, however, may be obviated by their printing the descriptions of pictures in a smaller text; as Passavant himself has done. At all events, this seems to preclude my making any additional description of the local collections in Norfolk, which under your kind means of information and by visiting the chief places myself, I had rather wished to do. What say you Uncle?

Passavant has offered me the plates for £12 ... 6 including those two beauties in his account of the Netherlands. This, I submitted to Messrs S.&O. who think the terms reasonable, and that it is better they should have them. I have ordered them from Frankfort. They further ask whether it will be necessary to send the proofs for correction to <u>me</u>, or whether that can be dispensed with. I think decidedly <u>not</u>, and should like to know your opinion. I have some intention of going up to London to Edward, for a few weeks, in order to facilitate the correction and obtain other points; your advice as to the advantage incurred by this or not would decide me. Also in that case, can you give me my introductions or directions which would in general promote the work. If not imposing too much trouble on you or dear Mary, I should very much like to know your opinion as soon as convenient, as my answer to Mssrs S.& O. would be accordingly. I will further request you, if in your power, to lend me your catalogue of Mr. Aders' sale, which you mentioned as having prices and names of purchases amended, not finding it in the parcel of books, I wrote to Mssrs Foster and Sons the auctioneers of that sale for their details. I have waited long for deliverance in vain, I am getting rather impatient to conclude this part. From Mr. Woodburn I have obtained particulars of the Laurence col: and a few other things but they know nothing of Mr. Aders'. With regard to Passavant's account of Oxford; I find on commencing to translate it, that a large part beginning with Magdalen College p.100, is <u>verbatim</u> from Slatter's "Oxford Guide" – which I have here.[1] Would you not advise me to leave this out, and give my reasons in a note, as Mrs. Austin sometimes does in her "German Prince". Also will you be so good as to look through the latter part of Oxford, and tell me whether you think it possible for translation. I add a few questions in a list.

Was Mary Queen of Scots confined in Chatsworth 13 years? P.185
What are Schienen? 156 12 from bottom
Do you term Pracht Werke – "works of splendour"?
How do you express modellirt? 186 2 from top
Also "Miniaturen" upon old MS p.200 10 from bottom. That occurs often – surely our word miniature won't do.
In his account of Cambridge there is an architectural sentence I cannot understand p.202 2 lines from the bottom, beginning "Die Capitale breiten sich and ending with "entstehen".[2]

I am ashamed of the trouble I give, but I must trust to your kindness, and at all events won't add to it by annexing a list of excuses. We have heard from dear Anne lately, as suffering in body, but very cheerful in spirit. We are anxiously awaiting the news of her confinement.[3] From Roger we continue to have the most comfortable letters. I delivered dear Ellen's message to my aunt Simpson, and trust she has long received the result.

With kindest love from all here to all around your care dear Uncle, your affectionate niece
Elizth Rigby

1. The translator's note explains the omission on the grounds that these details 'although interesting to a foreigner, are so familiar to the English reader, as to authorize the translator in omitting this part' (footnote, p. 334).

2. Many of these specific translations are elided in the publication which makes a precis of Passavant.

3. Anne de Wahl (1804–69), Elizabeth's sister, married to Carl George de Wahl of Wattel, Estonia. She was expecting her last child, Thomas Alexis de Wahl, later a Captain in the Royal Navy (1835–67). In 1837 Anne divorced her husband and returned to England to run a succession of girls' schools in Norwich and London. She also wrote *Practical Hints on the Moral, Mental and Physical Training of Girls at School* (London: John W. Parker, 1847).

Copy of Letter to Dawson Turner   *TCC January–June 1836*
(112)

Framingham Earl
16 April 1836
My dear Uncle

I conclude by this time, you may have seen Mr. Passavant in his English dress. A copy was sent to me a week back, the day before publication, but having been absent from home, I have not been able to address you on the subject. To tell you all the anxiety and trouble it has caused me, through printer's delays and wilful mistakes, would only take up your time, and exhaust my own temper, which is already sufficiently sore. The greatest pinch of all, however, has been the sight of this frontispiece of vol: 1st which, I think you will agree, is sufficient to appal any one from reading the author who wears such a countenance.[1] In my own justification, I send you the accompanying impression which is also by no means a just representation of the state of the plate when I sent it to Mr. Saunders; it having in the course of several impressions been corrected of what you see here to be the prominent blemishes and otherwise improved by myself. On sending the best impression to Mr. Saunders, which considering my little, or rather no, practice in etching, was really not bad, I offered to have the proofs in case he should approve the specimen sent, taken off under my own eye in Norwich, which could have been done at the same expense. He perfectly approved of the etching, but declined my offer, and the vile impression which now disfigures the work is the result. I was much distressed on seeing it, and immediately wrote to Mr. Saunders, requesting to know whether all the impressions were bad alike; and in that case begging the frontispiece might be at all events subtracted from the work, before its further circulation. Mr. S. has not answered me; and being a poor helpless woman, I turn to you, dear Uncle, for advice in this matter, and should you feel with me the necessity for its not appearing in the work, would beg you to write to Mr. S. and use you authority in obtaining its extraction. Your advice and opinion, any how, will be of much comfort to me; as this frontispiece has given me more pain than I would like to suffer in such a cause.

On 2nd thought I send you my own copy; so that, in case the work has not reached you, no time may be lost.

We have very good accounts from Russia. Anne very sanguine with regard to spending the summer here; and may we not be disappointed![2] From Roger we have most interesting letters: he is happy and contented, and from other corroboratory accounts in good esteem with his superiors. In case my dear Aunt Turner has not heard from Aunt Simpson, I will also add a report of her, mamma having received a long and most cheerful letter, showing that she is much enjoying change of scene, and is improved in health. Mamma would write to acknowledge Aunt's kind present of gingerbread, but is now so completely prostrate with a regular <u>bone</u> cold, that she must defer writing,

Trusting to your kindness to excuse the trouble I give you; and looking forward to your advice in this annoying little matter – I am with our united loves to dear Aunt and cousins
My dear Uncle, your affectionate niece
Elizth Rigby

1. The engraving of Passavant at the front of volume 1 is a very crude rendering.

2. Anne de Wahl in fact separated from her husband in 1836 and they divorced in July 1837.

Letter to Dawson Turner   *TCC January–June 1836 (175)*

Framingham Earl
21 June 1836
My dear Uncle

You have bestowed a most undeserved kind letter upon me, and were I not aware of your opinions on such a subject, gain acknowledgements for a present I have never made you, would have caused me to reproach myself for a want of proper attentions towards one who has made me so much his debtor. It was, however, that very acquaintance with your sentiments which withheld me from the gratification of sending you a copy of my translation, for indeed dear Uncle, I am innocent of the matter. I suspect it must be Mr. Saunders affection which prompted the act, and as I expect to spend the last few days of this month in London I will ascertain all about it. I am much annoyed by the mistakes you mention and by many others which I know myself, and this forms a prominent one among the many reasons for my desiring a 2nd edition – of which however I am not very sanguine. I have sent a copy to M. Passavant and begged for the earliest sight of his work on Raphael, which I have no doubt will prove very valuable.

We can fully sympathise with your feelings in the approaching separation from Ellen; few fathers have such a daughter to part with. The sight of her happiness can be literally the only palliation for such a loss, and as far as human foresight can go you will not be disappointed. Pray tell her that we add our warm good wishes to the many which are offered up for her.

We are much enjoying the company of our dear Anne, and would fair make up for all she and we have foregone during the long period of separation. Our minds are much occupied with a subject on which we are eager to consult with you. M de Wahl's tastes have always been wedded to England, I need not say what Anne's are, and if some specific employment could be procured which would both give scope to his literary talents and afford a small addition to his income he would willingly exchange his Russian residence for one nearer us. He and Anne, however, will doubtless have the opportunity of talking over this matter with you face to face and at all events will be thankful for your advice.

Your intention of noting the margins of Passavant is indeed the most valuable service you can render me. With regard to the preface you will find, on reference, that I have alluded to the advantage of Mr. Passavant's communications.

Should you see the Foreign Quarterly of this month (not Cochrane's) will you favour me by looking at the article subtitled "Göthe, Wieland, Herder" &c a contribution from my humble hand which they have paid me the compliment of accepting.[1] The incognito is you will agree the only warrant for my presumption, and having thrown it up to you I shall look for indulgence in your inspection. I am anxious for many reasons to persevere in such attempts, the chief of which is the hope of improving in information and style.

M de Wahl is in London but Anne and all of us unite in best loves to yourself, my dear aunt and cousins and believe me my dear uncle
Your affectionate and obliged niece
Elizth Rigby

1. 'Letters to John Henry Merck, from Goethe, Herder, Wieland &c', *Foreign Quarterly Review*, vol. 17 (July 1836), pp. 391–417.

Letter to J. Barwell[1]   *NRO BOL 5/51, 742X6*

My dear Sir

Since I had the pleasure of meetg you at the Palace, I have quite made up my mind that I shall not want that <u>hand</u> wh: you were kind enough to promise me. What I shd be most thankful for, is some antique female head; & havg understood, that through yr mediation, I mt obtain the loan of one at a time from the draw.g Academy in Norwich, I venture frankly to ask you if such be the case; & if peradventure not, to recommend in all humility that such privilege be granted to select individuals of my unfortunate sex in future. May I trouble you, in case my position meet with a denial, to let me have a line to that effect at Cheverton's Livery Stables – All Saint's Green; & provided you are silent I shall venture to call for a head on Saturday abt 3 o'clock as I pass through Norwich homewards.

With kind regards to Mrs. Barwell, & many apologies to yrself for givg you so much trouble.

I beg to remain
Yr's sincerely
Eliz: Rigby

Hethersett. Novr. 30th 1837.

1. John Barwell (1798–1876), Norwich-based artist and secretary of the Norwich Society of Artists.

Letter to John Murray II[1]   *NLS Ms.42174*

Framingham Earl
Decr 31st 1840
My dear Sir

I fear you will have thought me extremely dilatory in remitting to you this specimen of M:S:S: from Reval & its neighbourhoods. But I wished them to be accompanied by the enclosed etchings, which have been subjected to great delays by the printer, who, after all, has done his part of the work very badly – havg bitten them in, especially the building much too severely. Also my part in them is by no means done to my satisfaction, but I enclose them with all their defects, trusting that your eye will see rather what my etching will be with a little further practise than what it now is.[2]

In the event of these letters being to Mr. Murray's satisfaction I shd wish to know what you wd desire regarding the illustrations of the work – whether etchings instead of woodcuts. I prefer the former in themselves, & whether the size I have transmitted be suitable, or upon a smaller scale.

I will trouble you to address me "at Wm Burt's Square Bracondale, near Norwich" where I shall remain for a week from this time, & with the compliments of the season I beg to remain my dear Sir – yr's obliged
Eliz: Rigby

1. John Murray II (1778–1843), publisher and founder of the *Quarterly Review*.

2. This and subsequent letters refer to the publication of *A Residence on the Shores of the Baltic; Described in a Series of Letters*, 2 vols. (London: John Murray, 1841). Second and subsequent editions were titled *Letters from the Shores of the Baltic*. Since the second edition (1842) became the standard edition, I have used it for references. What follows is a selection of the numerous letters relating to the preparations for this publication in order to give the overall sense of Elizabeth's chief concerns, rather than a week-by-week bulletin of its progress.

Letter to John Murray   *NLS Ms.42174*

My dear Sir

I have to apologise for detaining the proof, finding that the heads of the letters which I forwarded to you have not been inserted. I have written the head in the accompanying proof & will do so with all in future. Letter 3rd therefore is the only one which I will request you to see inserted.

I detained this parcel in order to enclose a few specimens of etchings, of which I shall be glad to hear of your opinion. Not being able to rely on the Printers for careful biting in I have undertaken that part myself. But these are seen to disadvantage, having rolled off on any scraps of paper, & not having undergone, from want of proper instruments, the corrections & amendments they are capable of.[1]

But I shall be glad of your opinion – your matter of fact opinion as concerns the public, otherwise your own feeling for art might give them an interest which others will not feel.

I beg to remain my dr Sir
Your's truly
Eliz: Rigby
Framingham Earl
May 11. 1841.

1. Elizabeth's etchings after her drawings made in Estonia illustrated the various
   editions of *Letters from the Shores of the Baltic*. Etchings were printed onto
   separate plates and pasted into the book, often by the purchasers.

Letter to John Murray   *NLS Ms.42174*

Framingham Earl
May 21 1841
My dear Sir
From the delay in your usual packet, I am in danger of believing that
the specimen of my etchings must have disgusted you. However, knowg
your better judgement & probable press of occupation I beg you will not
take this for any suggestion of impatience. In order, at the same time to
avoid all delay on my part, I shd much like to know, when ever your
time permits you & as nearly as you can tell me, <u>when</u> you desire the
work shd appear. I am engaged, in etching, & have a few more which I
flatter myself are better than those you have seen.
I beg to remain
Your's faithfully
Eliz: Rigby
I think of being in town as soon as my labours finish.

Letter to John Murray   *NLS Ms.42174*

My dear Sir
I feel but little disposed to quarrel with a slight additional task which
has procured me the honour of yr kind communication of the 10th.
The favourable remarks on my M.S. with which you have favoured
me, cannot be otherwise than deeply gratifying to me, altho' my poor
judgement cannot be induced to concur with that of Mr. Lockhart in
the matter of approbation.[1]
But at all events the good opinion of such a critic has made me very
happy – especially by proving that the confidence & liberality with

which you accepted a work of which you had seen so small a portion may not have been misplaced. For I can say with entire truth that the only part of my work which affords me any pride is the circumstance of its being published by Mr. Murray.

It is rather strange that Mr. Lockhart's life of W: Scott was the only work of importance I perused during the progress of my writing, & I was often made aware of its useful influence. Certain it is that I concluded the work with a profound veneration for Sir Walter, & a lively desire to become acquainted with his Biographer.

I feel deeply indebted for your kind wish to see me at your residence, & only regret that I have no immediate prospect of visiting London.

Begging to repeat my thanks for your flattering letter I have the honour to remain, my dear Sir
your's obliged
Eliz: Rigby
Framingham Earl
Augst 13. 1841.

1. John Gibson Lockhart (1794–1854), Scottish writer and biographer of Walter Scott. Lockhart was editor of the *Quarterly Review* between 1825 and 1854. Lockhart's approbation is recorded: 'I have been reading the manuscript with great admiration for the most part. I wish the lady would score out a few fine words, but beyond these trifles she is unassailable. I have no doubt she is the cleverest female writer now in England, the most original in thought and expression too; and she seems *good* beside, which after all has its charms even for old sinners like you and me' (J&C1, p. 9).

Letter to John Murray   *NLS Ms.42174*

My dear Sir
According to desire I have forwarded the last proofs to Messrs Clowes & Son, & with the exception of a few corrections they are now ready for press.[1]

I take this opportunity of sending you a selection from some of the hitherto best printed of my etchings, which I beg you to submit to Mr. Murray, & also to inform him that I can have them printed here in the best manner for ten shillings a hundred on India paper, or for eight shillings on plain paper. Will you also add that my vanity leads me to prefer the India paper, & that I hope he will be so good as to indulge it. I will superintend the printing & ensure their being executed with all care & neatness. The expenses of copper-preparing &c will be included in about half a crown each.

I suspect my printer will have finished his work before your's on with the 2nd Not: But do not interpret this as impatience, for my time is of little importance.

I beg to remain

My dear Sir

your's faithfully

Eliz: Rigby

Framingham Earl

Augst 21. 1841.

May I request you to return these etchings when you next forward proofs – & also to tell me how many hundred will be required of each.

1. Clowes & Son was a printing company founded in London in 1803. By the 1840s it was one of the largest printing firms in the world.

Letter to John Murray   *NLS Ms.42174*

My dear Sir

The printer having applied to me for title page & preface, I must for the former refer him to yourself, not being exactly aware of the title by which it has been advertised. Only I shd prefer "by a lady" to be omitted.[1] As to the preface is it permissable to dispense with one altogether? For I have nothing either common or uncommon to say – or may a short dedication be substituted? That I will do as you like, or whatever is usual. Not havg recd your answer about printing the etchings I am inclined to think you must have been absent from town, or that you have conceived a higher opinion of my patience than I may find it convenient to support. In order to undeceive you I fear I must proceed to printing before I am favoured with your feats. Respecting Preface &c, however, I will await your wish.

I beg to remain my dear Sir

yr's faithfully

Eliz: Rigby

Framingham Earl

Septr 17. 1841.

1. The phrase 'by a Lady' was retained in all editions. The first edition sold 1,000 copies, a further 1,000 were issued in the second and the book was reprinted in 1844 in the Home & Colonial series. In all, 4,750 copies were printed.

Letter to John Murray   NLS Ms.42174

My dear Sir

I am much obliged to you for the candour with which you have explained to me your wishes regarding the etchings, & also I am so entirely persuaded of your superior judgement, & of the impossibility of your proposing anything prejudicial to the interests of the work that I beg whatever I may urge here may be considered as subservient to that conviction. My only objection to "a separate publication" is that the etchings are not fit to stand alone, being much too slight – in short not good enough. At the same time as I feel that the proposition you have made may in part arise from a feeling of delicacy towards myself, I am anxious to assure you that no measures you might think expedient to adopt towards the etchings would offend me. If the increase of price for the work, which you justly deprecate, can be avoided by a restriction of number of etchings I shall be quite satisfied to see three or four at most, including Frontispiece, of the <u>best</u>, introduced into each volume. I remember with something like contrition being very tenacious for the introduction of many etchings, although assured by yourself that they were not necessary, but this willingness, I beg you to believe, arose less from a vanity of my pencil than from a mistrust of my pen. Even if you shd think better to dispense with them altogether I shd not feel hurt; my chief motive, after that of a supposed advantage to the work, being to fulfil my engagement to yourself. And at present an expense of only a few pounds has been incurred. However, this I leave to your better determination, though I must repeat that I shd be unwilling to see them standing in a separate publication, the more so as my portfolio contains so many subjects so far superior in size, interest, & finish to those I have been able to include in these small etchings.

I have been this moment favoured with your second letter, & in return for your kind expressions can only hope that you have not many writers so <u>troublesome</u> as myself. I was happy to hear that I may dispense with a preface. If I include a short Dedication it shall be forwarded quickly.[1] With regard to the title I should be better pleased simply thus, "A Residence on the Shores of the Baltic – described in a series of Letters". But I am greatly ashamed to proposed alterations to one who knows so much better than myself, & requesting your indulgence, beg to remain my dear Sir yr's obliged & truly

Eliz: Rigby

Framingham Earl

Septr 19 1841

I shall feel myself much honoured of a notice in the Quarterly.

1. The work is dedicated 'to her whose presence enhanced every pleasure, whose affection shared every trial ...'. Although addressed in the singular, the dedication is probably to her two sisters Maria Justina de Rosen and Gertrude de Rosen, both living in Estonia.

Letter to John Murray   NLS Ms.42174

Framingham Earl
Septr 30. 1841.
My dear Sir

The insertion of one extra letter into my usual address caused your last parcel to make a longer circuite than was necessary. Our residence is simply "Framingham Earl nr Norwich", & though not totally destitute of all modern attractions does not possess antiquarian ones in the same degree as Framlingham in Suffolk can boast. This accounts for my not receiving your obliging note, with the Quarterly Review, till two days later than your intention. Nevertheless, I owe you apologies for not sooner acknowledging both. With regards to your note I shall be happy to profit of your kind injunction to take off some few copies of the other etchings for myself. The two Frontispieces are now in hand, & you shall shortly receive a supply. Pray receive my thanks also for the Quarterly. The general circumstance of a notice therein is in itself an honour, & further, the manner in which I am treated is so undeservedly flattering, that I cannot but think your press exercises an improving influence no less over the matter than the form of a M:S: Such being the case you may be sure that I shall not be unwilling to trouble you again.

And now the only objection I can raise to this service, if I may be permitted to criticize such a critic, is that I would rather he had left my "elder sister" "the expatriated Baroness" alone – whom he has introduced to the public more distinctly than I have done. However, it was perhaps needful to assign some respectable motive to my wanderings, which otherwise hardly assimilate with the appended name of "Spinster" (is this a right application of the unfortunate word?) The truth is, I have not only one but two most dear expatriated sisters in Estonia – the recollections and associations with whom have supplied a kind of under current in my letters, visible perhaps to none but myself, but which constitutes their only real charm in my eyes.[1]

I beg to apologise for trespassing on your time thus frivolously, & beg
to remain my dear Sir

Yr's obliged & truly

Eliz: Rigby

1. Richard Monckton Milnes (1809–85), afterwards Lord Houghton, reviewed
   the work in the *Quarterly Review*, vol. 68 (1841), pp. 444–69.

Letter to John Murray   *NLS Ms.42174*

My dear Sir

Your previous parcel reached my hands half an hour back, & thus
having only had time to inhale the rich odours of the feast you have
prepared for me, & this with a running accompaniment of
exclamations of delight, I sit down to thank you. But indeed I am at
a loss how to thank you for your kindness is so entirely unmerited,
and perhaps the only way in which I can at all show my sense of
it is by fully acknowledging the same. I had looked at the notices
of the "Spanish Ballads" with longing eyes,[1] & you have so entirely
anticipated my wishes that I must repeat my conviction of there being
some 'magic' in Albemarle St.[2] I can but admire your son's energy in
giving the world such a beautiful present. I beg also to thank you for
the letters from yr traveling friend wh: I reserve for the first leisure
moment, after the Ballads. With regard to Mr. Lockhart's letter, for
which I am also greatly your debtor, I shall be glad to consider his
proposal thought not under the pleasing delusion of being able to
realise what he points at. But as you & also Mr. Lockhart, having a
few fine words, appear to be no more strict towards my manner of
writing than I am myself, I am not entirely without a criterion. At
the same time were I to attend only to my own suggestions they wd
tell me I might aspire to illustrating his Ballads, but certainly not to
appearing in his Quarterly. Though I have not yet thanked you for
the inscription in the Blank Leaf of the Ballads yet I assure you this
does not stand least in my estimation & I can only with all respect
echo the kind expressions.

I beg to remain my dear Sir

Your's obliged & truly

Eliz: Rigby

Framingham Earl

Octr 8. 1841.

I have omitted to say that if you wd kindly allow me the loan of either the German works on Russia you mention & also of the For: Quarterly I shd be much obliged.

1. John Gibson Lockhart, *Ancient Spanish Ballads* (London: John Murray, 1841).

2. 50 Albemarle Street was both the home of John Murray and his family and the location of his publishing business.

Letter to John Murray   *NLS Ms.42174*

My dear Sir

I find I cannot be so good as my word in sending your <u>fair</u> impressions of the other etchings, for I now find, as probably you are already aware, that a plate of this kind does not print well until after a number have been rolled off. You will see that I have sent you many more than six, not with any intention of <u>beguiling</u> you with more, but because you are yourself, & have around you those, much better able to judge which subjects will be most attractive to the public, than I can. I shall be thankful for any suggestions which an artist may give. At the same time I daresay they will see, as I now do, that the inefficiency is mainly owing to their being too feebly <u>bitten in</u>, & this arose from my not having either courage or experience at the beginning. The more effective are those latest done. There is some mode of rebiting etchings but this I shd think hazardous. If you and your friends will select the subjects you prefer, & if these include some of the ineffective ones, I shall, with your leave, (or perhaps without it) etch the same over again. The expense of the coppers are so trifling as to be no object, & I can execute more than one etching a day with ease. Nevertheless, if, upon second thoughts, you shd again decide not to introduce more, pray have no scruple in telling me so. In the narrow circle of friends who are aware of my having written these "Letters" I find that the absence of the etchings is regretted, but this is of no importance. Therefore recommending them to your mercy, I beg to remain my dear Sir, yr's truly & obliged
Eliz: Rigby
Framingham Earl
Octr 15. 1841.

Letter to John Murray   *NLS Ms.42174*

My dear Sir

Allow me to thank you for your kind sympathy in our late affliction. The death of my sister in law is indeed a severe blow to both families.[1] You are kind and liberal that I feel quite delicate in availing myself of it, & yet you will hardly believe this assertion when I request you to allow me to have eight copies of the letters <u>embossed</u> for I will have all the etchings inserted here for my own family. If I were to thank you as much on paper as I do in my head I fear you would have rather too much of the subject. But, whatever the merits of the work, I shall owe its favourable reception only to the most indulgent of publishers & reviewers. I have been mustering my ideas for an article on Russia, & find I have some light troops in service from my last campaign. But whether their paces will assimilate with the majestic movements of the Quarterly is matter of great apprehension to me. I am no politician, and have only looked on Russia in a somewhat philosophic light. However "faint heart & c".[2]

Captn Sterling's translation will I think suit me. I am reading Miss Richardson with much attention.[3] I think an English public will hardly appreciate her Definitions so much as a foreign one. With your leave I shall keep the work longer, but return you her letter, having taken a short transcript. I am quite satisfied with your decision respecting the etching, & well pleased with your extract.

I heard from a friend (Sir E Wilmot) the other day who is very happy at my debût in the Quarterly. He advocates my giving my name (to which I remain however equally averse) and adds "I think it wd procure you some good Editor for your own Edition of <u>yourself</u>". Now high as I have rated your services to me I never looked upon them in this light. You must have thought me <u>very</u> ungrateful.

Nevertheless I am with truth my dear Sir yours obliged and truly

Eliz: Rigby

Framingham Earl

Octr. 22. 1841.

1. Dr Edward Rigby's wife, Susan Taylor.

2. A reference to the article she is preparing, 'Jesse, Kohl, and Sterling on Russia', *Quarterly Review*, vol. 69 (March 1842), pp. 380–418.

3. *Russia under Nicholas the First, translated from a Supplement to the Conversations Lexicon*, by Captain Anthony C. Sterling (London, 1841).

Letter to John Murray II   *NLS Ms.42174*

Framingham Earl
Octr. 28. 1841.
My dear Sir

I am your debtor for two letters recd yesterday & to-day. In the last especially not only for your very kind deviation in my favour, both in amount and time of payment, but for the expressions with which you have accompanied the act. Indeed I should be unjust towards myself if I did seek to assure you that your gratuitous kindness has awakened in me feelings of the warmest and most respectful gratitude. And as I can only rely far better on my heart than on my abilities I may add that so far you will not be disappointed.

Though yr liberality in presentg twelve copies is a rule to all your authors, yet I am not the less thanked for its extension to me. I shall also be happy to embrace the offer of sending the etchings to you with directions for placing them, & very proud to send six copies for your daughter & yourself as you request. I shall also probably trouble you with the three copies of the Letters to exchange with a repetition of my thanks. Knowing so well the need of indulgence myself I felt some compunctions in having influenced yr judgement with regard to Miss Richardson's work, & though I hazarded what I was hardly competent to say respecting the taste of the public, yet upon further & entire perusal I cd urge much in favour of its good tendancy & intrinsic merit. I had hoped that its English garb wd have annulled what I was inclined to criticize but from yr own judgement expressed in yr last letter this appears not to be the case.

I enclose you the Receipt with my signature & beg you to believe me my dear Sir
Your's truly & obliged
Eliz: Rigby

Letter to John Murray   *NLS Ms.42174*

Framingham Earl
Novr 13. 1841.
My dear Sir

I am truly concerned & amazed to find by the contents of your note recd this morning that I have been instrumental in delaying the sale of the work. And, altho' far from wishing to exonerate myself, I must add that I have had much trouble with the printer, who, it now appears promised more than he could perform either in execution or dispatch & has much harassed me with his impunctuality. At the same time we have been visited with much domestic affliction – my mother having lost, since the short period of my inlaw's death, a nephew, a dear grandchild, & a young friend to whom we were much attached, & the temporary relaxation in the spurring system which I had been obliged to keep up with the printer, which these calamities induced, has been taken advantage of by him. This must also be my excuse for not acknowledging your nephew's communication – a parcel of etchings was sent off on the 7th inst, enclosing Miss Richardson, & another on the 12th, & I will take care by intimidation of some kind that next week makes up the whole number.

I am almost afraid of asking your forgiveness (for I feel myself the responsible person) knowing how inconvenient this interruption must have been to you. The delay in my forwarding you sets of all the other etchings has been occasioned by my discovering a person who understands all the secrets of rebiting them, & in a few days I hope to send them to you in a state worthier of yr regards than before. Trusting that my first tardiness may prove my last, I beg to remain my dear Sir, yr's truly & obliged
Eliz: Rigby
I hope quickly to forward to you a contribution of the nature desired my Mr. Lockhart.

Letter to John Murray   *NLS Ms.42174*

My dear Sir
The thought of my book paining you for want of its absent frontispiece, or rather the sense of your just resentment at my breach of faith, has troubled me much, & even disturbed my slumbers, though this I fear will do the cause no good. Therefore having prefaced my visit with a very severe warning by letter, I began the week yesterday by an admonition to the printer in a style which I had never before deemed myself a proficient. I found he had been so silly as to run one etching almost 400 a head of the other! However I recd the firm promise that a parcel of 200 of one sort shd leave Norwich last night, & overlooked some of them myself, tho' I cd not stay late enough to examine all. This, with the knowledge that you recd a parcel on the same day that

I received yr letter hs eased my mind, & in the course of the week you will be supplied with the whole number.

In a letter from one of my dear Estonian Baronesses recd to-day she tells me that the Dorpat Gazette mentions "<u>der Verühmte</u> [sic Berühmte] <u>Buchhändler Murray</u>" as having published Lockhart's Spanish Ballads in a form of decoration which has never been surpassed. By this time she has read a more minute description in a letter from me. My sister also gives me a deeply interesting account from a correspondent in Livonia of an insurrection in that Province. The peasants abjuring the Lutheran faith for the Greek, & refusing all subordination to their Lords. But perhaps you have other advices of this. Unfortunately she begs that no publicity may be given to her information.[1]

I see the "letters" on many tables. The Quarterly has so spoilt me with its indulgence that I am hardly fit to endure any rude dissection. Nor, perhaps you will kindly add, need I fear it.
I beg to remain my dear Sir, your's truly and obliged
Eliz: Rigby
Framingham Earl. Novr 16. 1841.

> 1. In the article she elaborates: 'the late disturbances in Livonia, where the oppressed were freedmen, and their oppressors enlightened German barons? All public accounts of the real nature of this insurrection were carefully suppressed or qualified by the Russian government, but we know through private sources that no abuses of the feudal power were ever more crying than those which urged the free Livonian peasant to violence' ('Jesse, Kohl, and Sterling on Russia', *Quarterly Review*, vol. 69 (1842), p. 391).

Letter to John Murray   *NLS Ms.42174*

My dear Sir

I conclude that it is to yourself that I am indebted for a sight of the three various forms of review upon my work, & therefore I return to my pleasant theme of thanks for your kindness, & hope I may never give you occasion to change the subject.

Like most people, probably, in a similar situation, I find myself swallowing all the good things they say of me with considerable relish, and imputing their criticisms to any misconceptions of style or judgements save to my own; for which arrogance I deserve the severest of all animadversions in my eyes, viz: a reproof from <u>yourself</u>. Nevertheless, I believe I shall never be so blind as to mistake what the book owes to you for any merit of its own.

I forward you hereby a packet of frontispieces, making up, according
to my printer, the full thousands of each. But if you have found
occasion to throw out any I beg you to let me know, & they shall
be instantly made up. I also enclose you two woodcocks from our
plantations,[1] with many apologies for the insignificance of the offering,
& I hope these samples of Art & Nature may travel safely together. The
poor birds ended their mortal career only this morning. I am waiting
for a parcel from Norwich wh: I expect will bring me sets of the other
etchings.

I have been disappointed by my etchings, but cannot this time rail at
the deceitfulness of view in general, for the engineer who undertook has
been very ill. I fear I cannot now promise them before next Monday,
though very impatient to claim yr kind allowance of copies.

Begging also to thank you for the little note of forgiveness I remain
my dear Sir
Yr's obliged & truly
Eliz: Rigby
Framingham Earl
Novr 23. 1841.

1. Framingham Earl was a large estate with extensive plantations where Dr
   Rigby perfected his techniques of animal husbandry and agriculture. The
   model estate is described in Dr Edward Rigby's *Framingham, its Agriculture,
   & c., including the economy of a small farm* (Norwich, R. Hunter, 1820).

Letter to John Murray   *NLS Ms.42174*

Framingham Earl
Nov 25. 1841.
My dear Sir
I am at length able to forward you these sets of etchings. The small
size, with nine of each, are intended for those copies which you have
kindly offered to bind up for me, & are accompanied by directions
respecting their position. The others, on larger paper, are for yourself,
since you have done me the honour of desiring them. I think you
will agree with me that the etchings are actually improved, & much
better taken off. I shall be glad to receive any criticism you may hear
upon them. I also forward you a paper which I submit to your's &
Mr. Lockhart's mercy. I have written it with the fear of Mr. L: greatly
before my eyes, though I fear it will hardly be found to have served the
purpose of inspection. At all events you will not think worse of it than

I do. But I am rather tired of the subject, & neither my information nor my powers are equal to the task, such as it <u>ought</u> to be done. Indeed I should not have undertaken it save at Mr. Lockhart's most honourable behest. But I need not add that I should be ill pleased if his acceptance of it were to be influenced by that consideration.

If Mr. Lockhart had not drawn so awful a balance in favour of the <u>pen</u>, I should venture to beg one of the sets of etchings might be forwarded to him.[1]

I will be obliged to you to forward a copy of "The Letters" with <u>all the etchings</u> to my brother, 23 New Street, Spring Gardens. Also may I request you to send the enclosed to Sir E: Wilmot to its direction. The other copies of Letters I must trouble you to send to me at yr convenience.

I beg to remain my dear Sir

yr's obliged & truly

Eliz: Rigby

You will find the paper somewhat, or rather, very dull at first, but I think it improves.

1. A letter from Lockhart to Murray weighing up her literary versus her artistic merits: 'pen against pencil; 1,000*l*. to an orange, say I' (J&C1, p. 11).

Letter to John Murray   *NLS Ms.42174*

My dear Sir

Very many thanks for your charming parcel recd to day. I think also the etchings improved the book. I shall now forward a copy to each of my sisters in Russia, who can enter more into the intention of the work than any body else.

I find the Monthly treats me most handsomely. Thank you much for it, & also for the sight of the German works which I shall look through.

I hereby send you a corrected copy to the passage I alluded to in my yesterday's letter. I have given a different terming, which, if you like it as well, had better be substituted, also there is a passage about Lady Hamilton which I never liked & to which I have appended an alteration. Otherwise there is nothing of importance. Do you wish for the Frontispieces as in the 1st edition, or will you drop them entirely?

I beg to give in my congratulations, however late, upon the occasion of your birthday. I think all your authors ought to club together to spare a portion off each of their lives to prolong the life of one infinitely more valuable – you should have a very large donation from

your's very truly
Eliz: Rigby
Framingham Earl
Decr. 9. 1841.
I have ordered the etchings to be made up immediately

Letter to John Murray   NLS Ms.42174

My dear Sir
  I return you the proof but <u>not</u> Mr. Lockhart's letter. I was truly glad
the article has found space in his sight, but I rather fear I was indebted
more to his <u>humanity</u> than his judgements. I have endeavoured to lop
away a few parts tho' I fear not enough and have also substituted others,
but will you tell him that their adaption depends of course only on his
approval. Though I greatly admire the little volume on which my paper
turns yet I would make my range of information fit but clumsily upon
it & felt I could not do justice to myself, far less to the society in which
it was to appear. I find that by a fortunate mistake instead of "Kohl's
Southern Russia" you have sent me "Kohl's Petersburg". I have only
had time to glance at it but find it so graphic, interestg & even witty
(that rare ingredient in a German head) that I almost lament I had it not
sooner. Nevertheless, what I have written would not have applied to it. I
will translate a few of the most striking passages & forward them to you
to give you an idea of its interest. Will you apologise for my retaining
of the proof for so long, but I could not complete it by return of post.
I remain my dear Sir
Your's very truly
Eliz: Rigby
Framingham Earl
Decr. 12 1841

Letter to John Murray   NLS Ms.42174

Framingham Earl
Decr. 16. 1841.
My dear Sir
  I have submitted the matter to the printer, and he makes his estimate
of expense, one with another, at <u>eight shillings per hundred</u>. India paper

of course, will this be suitable? He wishes to know by what time you wd require to have 400 of each plate ready. A proof shall be sent you, lettered & numbered in the way you describe, except that I have taken the liberty of directing the letters to be smaller, as some of the plates do not allow room for similar letters as the Frontispieces. And now I must assure you, that however agreeable it is to me that the work shd appear with more etchings, yet I hope that you have thought more of your own interest than of my pleasure. But will you wish for them all? With the frontispieces they amount to 23, which is a large number. Therefore I beg you to <u>weed</u> without mercy, & let me know exactly the subjects you prefer.

You are very good to interest yourself about my other drawings, you shall receive them by an early opportunity.

Have you in your possession any work with arabesques – architectural backgrounds- old carvings – cupids &c. If you cd remember such a work without thought, put yr hand upon it without trouble, & spare it without inconvenience, I wd venture to ask you to lend it to me. I am long upon a drawing in which I want more reference than I can command here.

I enclose the bill from the other printer – you will see that he has charged for 1200 of the small size. If you feel the least hesitation about his having printed or sent you this number, pray cut off the 200 surplus, & I will settle the matter.

The printer I have recently employed & whose estimate I hereby forward, is himself a fine etcher, & your son who I hope is returned to you well, may remember when in Norwich, seeing some etchings of the antiquities of Norwich by him.

I beg to remain my dear Sir
Yr's very truly
Eliz: Rigby

Letter to John Murray   *NLS Ms.42174*

Decr 23 1841
My dear Sir

The <u>Ritterschaft</u> of the Province of Estonia having been informed that you have recently published a work, in which themselves & their territory, with descriptions of their manners & customs, form the principal subjects, they come to the resolution at the last <u>Landtag</u> of passing you a public vote of thanks. It is true that, owing 1stly to an ignorance of the English Language, 2ndly to a national objection to

much reading, & 3rdly to not having seen the work at all, they are by
no means certain what it is all about. Nevertheless, from the high repute
in which your name stands, & which has penetrated far beyond the
shores of the Baltic, they feel assured that you would publish nothing
which did not equally redound to your credit & to their own; they also,
it would seem, entertain a far greater confidence in the publisher that
in the writer of the volumes in question. In consideraiton, therefore,
of your services in bringing them thus honourably before the notice of
the world, a discussion respecting the best mode of renumerating the
same, took place among the assembled members of the Ritterhaus – a
discussion which, owing to the great importance of the subject itself,
& partly also to the paucity of other subjects, occupied them actively
during the greater portion of the session. At first it was proposed, as a
mark of their esteem, to register you among the matriculated nobility
of the province, whereby you & your heirs for ever would have enjoyed
the right of voting in the Senate upon all matters not so important
as to come under the cognissance of the Russian Government – the
privilege of considering yourselves subjects of the Emperor of all the
Russias – & other advantages. But the Senate, thinking that it would
be ungenerous to require from an Englishman such proofs of unsullied
descent as thirty-two quarterings on the family shield, &c., especially
as you could not be considered actually accountable for being born
of 'la nation bourgeoise' – to say nothing of the further necessary
qualifications, such as the possession of landed property not measuring
less than fifty square miles in extent, & a residence in the province of
not less than six months in duration (without which conditions no one
may sit upon the Ritterbank) – finally resolved to reject this proposition.
It was then suggested by some of the members that the Senate could not
better testify their gratitude than by electing you, after the precedents
of Catherine II., Paul, Alexander, & other of your great predecessors in
history, a member of the far-renowned corps of Schwarzen Häupter: but
this was also abandoned on the considerate plea of the possibility of your
finding the uniform, which consists in heavy pieces of armour, rather
inconvenient to adopt. Again, the expediency of voting you a more
sterling testimony in the shape of a sum of money (to be paid when
the work should have reached the tenth edition) was warmly discussed:
but, as a sagacious member remarked that sending money to England
would be like sending 'owls to Athens,' or, in our phraseology, 'coals to
Newcastle,' this proposition was dismissed as well.

  Finally, as all plans, whether directed to the gratificaiton of your
ambition for family honours, thirst for fame, or love of lucre, seemed
equally impracticable, it was unanimously resolved in full Senate to

adopt a mode which should, at all events, recommend itself to your palate. Now, as the woods of Estonia are famed for the resort of a bird – almost as unique as the Phoenix of antiquity – called in Russian Kuritza Indiskaya, in Estonian Kalkuni–issa, & in Latin Gallina Icenorum, &, as such, greatly in request, both for the delicacy of its flavour & the substantiality of its dimensions, it was determined to increase you Christmas board with a specimen of this rara avis. I need hardly add that the bird reached England in a frozen state; but so exactly had the Senate calculated the time, allowing always for the difference of style, that its dissolution, I am happy to inform you, took place only yesterday.

I can now only beg your indulgence for the very unworthy & imperfect way in which I have interpreted the wishes of this noble body, & fear that their language has lost much of its dignity in my hands. Nevertheless, I will venture to add my most sincere wishes to theirs for a merry Christmas & many to come Mr. Murray & his family, & beg to remain his obliged & truly
Eliz: Rigby
The writer of this very impertinent letter feels so many scruples of conscience in thus trifling with one for whom she entertains to profound a respect, that, were in not for the sanction of her mother, she would not venture upon sending it. At all events she solicits early pardon.

Letter to John Murray   *NLS Ms.42174*

My dear Sir
You must take my plain self in plain prose. At present all the flatteries you forward me have brought me no further on the road to inspiration than to make me very conceited which I fear is the wrong end to begin at. But for this you are excusable.

I fear you will think this etching business never-ending – but on examining them all I find that in some plates there is not enough room for any lettering while other subjects, such as 'The Man at the Wheel" speak for themselves.[1] The difficulty could be removed by my writing the name in a vacant corner, as the plate I now enclose you – if this mode does not shock your eye for regularity & ideas of business too much. At all events will you let me have a line by return of post as the printer can begin to work on Monday. The only consolation I can allow you for all this annoyance is permission to scold me as much as you like, & the reflection that this is the last time I shall trouble you – – – this year.

With regard to the Quarterly for which I thank you much, & for
Captain Jesse's work, does Mr. Lockhart wish that I should remodel
my present paper & combine it with a review of Captn Jesse? If so I
shd suggest admitting Kohl's Petersburg, which is admirable in parts, &
very tempting for extracts. Will you kindly ask these questions & let me
know the answer. I fancy a more interesting article cd thus be made, but
I <u>sigh</u> at the prospect of going over old work.

I cannot repress my sympathy for the death of Mr. Chas Scott. The
fate of his father's family must be endeared to every heart.

I am happy to see that your hand has recovered its use & with every
wish for the happiness of the ensuing year I beg to remain my dr Sir
Your's truly
Eliz: Rigby
Framingham Earl
Decr 31st 1841.
I hope my drawings are safe in your hands – there are two readings to
this phrase but I hope you will take only what I mean.

   1. The second edition, *Letters from the Shores of the Baltic*, was illustrated with
      twenty etchings after Elizabeth's own drawings.

Letter to John Murray   *NLS Ms.42174*

My Dear Sir
   I am as much annoyed as yourself by the tardiness of the printers. I
have just heard from him, in answer to our expostulation, saying that he
will put on more hands this week and hasten the completion as much
as possible. I have had reason to place much more confidence on him
with regard to execution, than upon the former printer but they seem
much alike in despatch. In case you wish to apply to him yourself I will
subjoin his address.

   I authorised Mr. Reeve[1] to submit to you a short tale[2] which I
have written lately, and which I wd have submitted to you in the first
instance had I thought it worthy of your attention. Perhaps you will tell
me, either directly or through him, whether is is worth anything, and
what can be done with it.

   I remain my dear Sir, yours truly
Eliz: Rigby
Framingham Earl
Febry 1. [poss. 7.] 1842.

Printer's address
Mr. Ninham
Chapel Field
Norwich

1. Henry Reeve (1813–95), Elizabeth's cousin. Reeve was a regular contributor to the *British and Foreign Quarterly Review*. He joined the staff of the *Times* in 1840 and in 1855 became editor of the *Edinburgh Review*.

2. This short tale called *The Jewess* was published in 1843.

Letter to John Murray   *NLS Ms.42174*

Framingham Earl
Febry 27. 1842.
My Dear Sir

I forward you hereby my paper about Russia, in its altered form. Will you plead any excuse with Mr. Lockhart for my not having recopied some of the printed portion, which will therefore meet his eye in rather a shabby condition. The paper is necessarily much increased in length with the insertion of one work, & the appendage of another, but he will, I hope, not hesitate to curtail where he thinks proper. Mr. Lockhart will observe that I am not altogether pleased with Captain Jesse, but I hope he will not consider that I have transgressed the injunction of doing as I would be done by. I don't know whether my translations of M: Kohl do justice to his work – or whether a stranger to Petersburg will feel the liveliness of his pictures as I do. Upon this, & upon the article in general, you will kindly let me know your opinion & Mr. Lockhart's decree.

Though of little moment I wd rather my name shd not be mentioned as the writer.

I beg to remain my dear Sir
Your's truly
Eliz: Rigby

Letter to John Murray   *NLS Ms.42174*

London April 20. 1842
My dear Mr. Murray[1]
   Pray present my compliments to your daughters, & tell them that I
am delighted to see that they keep you in such order. The only thing
I had to complain of this morning was that you did not present me to
them, & I was too stupid or awkward to ask you to do so.
   You are very kind to think of me in the friendly way you propose –
it will give me true pleasure to accompany your family to the Hanover
Sqre rooms to-morrow evening & I will be ready at 7 o'clock. I also
hope that my pleasure will not be purchased by the disappointment of
any of your party. The sight of D: Wilkie's pictures[2] I must reluctantly
forego, as I am obliged to leave London early to-morrow mg & shall
probably not return till between four & five.
   As some equivalent to the scoldings you have received I must beg
you to accept my sincere thanks & believe me with compliments from
Mamma (not the good lady you saw this morning)
Your's truly
Eliz: Rigby
24 Sackville Street
Tuesday Evg

   1. John Murray and Elizabeth had met for the first time in person earlier that
      day, so all letters are now addressed to Mr Murray as opposed to 'dear
      Sir'.

   2. David Wilkie (1785–1841), Scottish painter whose work was on show at a
      Memorial Exhibition at the British Institution.

Letter to John Murray   *NLS Ms.42174*

Framingham Earl
June 24. 1842
My dear Mr. Murray
   As it is our duty to return good for evil – I am going to do you
the questionable good of writing you a long letter, in return for your
negative evil of not having written at all.
   Since receiving your daughter Hester's last kind letter, in which I am
sorry to say she speaks very disrespectfully of you, I have been looking

every day for Mr. Lane's[1] beautiful version of my Jewess[2] – & fearing that when she does appear, she will engross me too much too much [sic] of my attention. I begin this before post time in order to give my undivided heart (if you have no objection – nor Mrs. Murray) to you. From this beginning I fear you will think that home life has by no means corrected the thorough spoiling I had in Albemarle St. – not that I can impugn, my dear mother, also is a proverbial disciplinarian, & as absolute at home as somebody else I dare not name. Only to be sure she does not begin reading Ld. Byron to us at one o'clock in the morning!

And this reminds me how much pleasure I am now enjoying from your beautiful present.[3] When I was <u>young</u> Ld B: was my beau idéal of men and poets – but then cares came over me, and my beau idéal only made bad worse and Moore's Life put the finishing blow to my enthusiasm.[4]

Now, however, that I have seen more of life – have been in the company of the Emperor of Russia, Mr. Murray (& the Bishop of Norwich) & thus strengthened my mind without extinguishing my fancy, I return to him with a double zest, and enjoy him the more because I pity him the less.

I am agreeably surprised also with the number of works, and quantity of contemporary history and biography which this very perfect edition presents. I go picking about for Sir W: Scott's notes, who, if he was not my "first love", is what all lovers whether literary or literal, will acknowledge to be much better – viz my <u>last</u>. I think it gives some definition of the respective characters of Byron and Scott to say that each could have equally engrossed a woman's heart – but the former it would have been the greatest misfortune in the world to have loved – the latter the greatest privilege.

I am not surprised to hear that Kohl is being translated – I hear from my sisters that it is strictly forbidden to enter Russia – and any quotations from it in foreign papers cut out at the Censor's Office.

All Russia is also talking about the <u>Silver Wedding</u> or anniversary of the 25th year of the Emperor and Empress's <u>happy</u> marriage – for the celebration of which so much money is required that they feared the Emperor, and Cancrin, [sic][5] his minister of Finance would split upon it. On occasion of this Silver Wedding an amnesty is to be proclaimed releasing all criminals, <u>except</u> those confined for <u>debts</u> to the <u>Crown</u>. Thus it is with the present government no act of enfranchisement but what covertly increases their own power, no act of humanity by which they are to lose any money. There never was a meaner government nor a more extravagent Court. Its absolute power is its least blemish.

I know you will be kindly interested in what nearly interests us – & therefore, tho' not formally settled, I cannot help telling you that I fear our estate is sold. And this has spread a gloom over our party. But it is a very necessary step, and we have been long prepared for it by seeing & feeling that it pulled us down without our being able to keep that up. We have therefore long had the mortification of seeing our favourite trees gradually disappear, our miles of walks neglected, our ponds fill with weeds and empty of water, & all the signs of decay which by both showing the present state and recalling the past, cut two ways at once. But I must not talk about it, for tho' I dwell upon all the disadvantages of stopping, I cannot reconcile myself to leaving. We have not formed any plans for the future yet.[6]

And now my dear Mr. Murray I think it high time I should release you having given you as much of my [*illegible*] nature as I think you can manage at once. Your daughter is so undutiful as to call you "lazy" but how should you have so much leisure as other people when your duty to your family compels you to lie in bed till ten of the morning! Whereas we careless young people can take our own pleasure and be up at six.

I think however that you will consider yourself bound to favour me with a letter now and then when you reflect that, but for you I might have gone on corresponding with your son to this day!

Post is in and brought neither Jewess nor last proofs to revise – but I am in no hurry if you are not. Pray tell your daughter Hester that I will have the pleasure of writing to her in a few days and thank her much for her letter. That Mrs. Murray is regaining her strength I am truly thankful to hear. My kindest wishes and regards attend her and all your party.

Most truly your's
Eliz: Rigby
I hope Mr. Lockhart is better.

1. Richard Lane (1800–72), sculptor and engraver, who engraved Elizabeth's drawing of the Jewess for the frontispice of her book.

2. *The Jewess: A Tale from the Shores of the Baltic* (London: John Murray, 1843) was published as 'by the author of "Letters from the Baltic"'. *The Jewess* tells the story of an Anglo-Estonian baroness's fight to save a young Jewish wife from penal servitude in Siberia. The idea for *The Jewess* originates from an incident described in the first volume of *Letters from the Shores of the Baltic*, where Maria Justina (presumably) and Elizabeth had encountered a Jewish peasant whose beauty attracted their attention (LSB1, pp. 277–83). See Joseph Garver, 'Lady Eastlake's "Livonian" Fiction', *Studia Neophilogica*, 51.1 (1979), pp. 17–29. For an account of the general treatment of the

subject see Nadia Valman, *The Jewess in Nineteenth Century British Literary Culture* (Cambridge Studies in Nineteenth-century Literature and Culture; Cambridge: Cambridge University Press, 2007).

3. Murray made Elizabeth a gift of an edition of Byron's works.

4. The reference is to Thomas Moore's *Life of Byron*, first published by John Murray in 1835.

5. E. F. Kankrin (1774–1844), Minister of Finances to Tzar Nicholas I.

6. Framingham Earl was sold in 1842.

Letter to John Murray   *NLS Ms.42174*

Framingham Earl
July 8. 1842.
My dear Mr. Murray

   I have just received your parcel, & beg to thank you much for the Quarterly, which will be a great treat to me. With regard to the work on female education, Mrs. Sherwood's,[1] which Mr. Lockhart pays me the compliment of offering me, I cannot yet look at it properly, but will soon, & ascertain how far I have any right or power to judge it.[2] I know & remember your kind sentiments, & know also that it is only in efforts above our powers that we can test the latter properly. I am for the present, however, surrounded with juvenile books, & except in the trifling item of grandchildn feel quite ready to act grandmamma. I shd like to see those American books – if you have them actually – & I will send you word how they may be conveyed to me by a friend who is in London.

   With regard to the detention of the Jewess from the public, I feel only sorry for the cause, & shall be truly happy when the depression upon your business & your spirits is equally relieved. Also as I feel the infirmities of age fast creeping upon me the Jewess may have the distinction of being a posthumous work! I wish I cd promise you a little companion to her by next season. I am going to the land of inspiration. I need hardly say that we shall accept yr offer of letters of introduction to Edinburgh with gratitude, hitherto we have scarcely known a name there.

   Mr. Lane has written to me respecting the stone, & knowing the great delicacy of such drawings I concur with him in thinking it had better not run the risk of the transport hither. It is very possible that our emigration may include a visit to London, or that Mamma may require

one of my sisters or myself to precede her to yr beautiful Northern
Capital. I must take a hasty leave of you, & begging the kindest regards
to yourself & all your family I remain, dear Mr Murray
Your's very truly
Eliz Rigby
I forwarded a parcel a few days ago to Miss H: Murray, containing
Valerius, & Mr. Eastlake's Passavant. If I had known his address I shd
have written to this latter! not Passavant.[3] There is a little children's
book of the Hist: of England which has gone through twelve editions,
published by yourself, is it written by Lady Calcott?[4]

1. Mary Martha Sherwood (1775–1851), writer of children's literature and one
   of the subjects of Elizabeth's review.

2. 'Books for Children', *Quarterly Review*, vol. 71 (December 1842), pp. 54–83.
   Lockhart writes to her that he has 'read it with more pleasure than I can
   well express. It seems to me one of the most admirable specimens of review-
   writing I ever met with – full of sense and taste, equally instructive and
   interesting' (J&C1, p. 29).

3. This is the first mention of Eastlake.

4. *Little Arthur's History of England* by Maria Graham, Lady Callcott (1786–1844)
   was first published in 1835.

Letter to John Murray   *NLS Ms.42174*

Framingham Earl
July 26. 1842.
My dear Mr. Murray
    I have to thank yourself & your daughter for most kind letters telling
me of your removal & residence for the summer upon which I sincerely
congratulate the whole party. My second letter to your daughter Hester
will have explained to you my approaching movements northward & the
hopes I had ventured to entertain of being assisted in my enquiries by
Miss Murray. This morning I have received a letter from her, worthy of
her very sweet self, in which she assures me of kind help from herself
& her friends, & obviates all necessity of my asking for any other
introduction. She conveys to me also a truly friendly message from Mrs.
Henderson proposing that I shd pay her a visit, that in this instance
neither my time nor my position will permit me to accept her kindness.
    We start as proposed from Yarmouth next Sunday, & I fear also that
our final move will be by the same route, i.e. not include London.

Otherwise you may be assured that I should be too happy to give
myself the pleasure of seeing yourself & your dear family again, before
I remove so much further from them, & I am truly gratified with the
kind expression of <u>your</u> wish. We are as you suppose, much engaged
with arrangements – resulting from our change in residence, & which
include also visits from friends & relatives who are anxious to come "for
the last time" & long confabulations, & much advice & debate on legal
matters, &, last not least, feelings which cannot always be <u>exorcised</u> on
this account. I have not been able to devote myself entirely to that <u>word</u>
which you were "content with obtruding". Nevertheless I am tolerably
forward with a paper, which I look forward to completing immediately
on my return, & submitting to the approbation of the Editor in due
time for insertion if found eligible.

   I must beg your Hester's indulgence for not answering her charming
letter, & your's for the hasty epistle & with very kindest regards to Mrs.
Murray & all I remain
Your's very truly
Eliz: Rigby
I think it is a great privilege to see your Christina again so soon & it
not possible that she may return with me?

Letter to John Murray   *NLS Ms.42174*

9 St Bernard's Crescent[1]
Novr 16. 1842.
My dear Mr. Murray
   I am indebted for kind letters to yourself & both your daughters, &
I am glad to address you again in Albemarle Street where I can think
of you all with more distinctness. At the same time I trust that your
absence from home has been the source of pleasure & health to all your
party & that to Mrs Murray Brighton has retrieved what Tunbridge
Wells failed in. We are meanwhile beginning to take root here, & are
helping ourselves, instead of being always chargeable upon those friends
which you & your family have procured us. We venture on voyages
of discovery & actually discovered the most charming basket-maker
& promising milliner both on the same day! Within doors we feel
domesticated, & it is only on returning from a walk that we wonder
how that strange looking Crescent can ever be our home. I am glad
to say that Mamma is in good health & spirits to which I think the
attentions of our kind new friends have not a little contributed. Of the

Drysdale's[2] we see much, as their frequent pleasant evening parties are at present our chief sources of relaxation. They gather people together & entertain them in so agreeable a manner as to impress us with a most favourable idea of Edinburgh society. We met the other night George Combe the phrenologist, but I liked the man as little as I liked the writer.[3] He is returned from Germany with the conviction that man & wife ought to separate as soon as they disagree! It may be supposed therefore that he has another Mrs. Combe in his eye. The present one has a fine Kemble countenance. She has done us the favour to call & knows some of our Norfolk acquaintants. Mr Laing[4] the Norway traveller was the requisition of another evening, & we compare notes about Northern natives with, I think, mutual interest. I am happy to say that Mrs Smith is somewhat better, & kindly insisted on our all joining her tea circle last Saturday, it being the first meeting between herself & my family. The two elder Miss Smiths are looking very sweetly. I am truly grieved that the eldest should have so severe a trial, & also not a little that all outward sympathy in the subject should be interdicted. As for Mr. David Smith,[5] I must roun to Christina for a key to his character.

Edinburgh is now filling, & Princes' Street looks less like Picadilly deserted. Nonetheless George St, Gt King St. & others are still almost entirely abandoned to hands of school boys who play lengthways & crossways without the slightest fear of interruption. Altogether Edinburgh is a wonderful mart for children if you know of anybody wanting a few. Mr. Reeve is now in London, & his wife with her little Scotch lassie follow as soon as able. We have been much concerned at the death of Mr. Daniel in Lycia.[6] He was first playfellow & then friend of us all. I think your son knew him. Pray tell your daughter Hester that as soon as I can report any progress in the portraits I will write. Meanwhile she has given me an occupation which I shall much enjoy. I shall be glad to know that her cold is better & that both she & dear Mrs. Murray are home to you safe & sound. We are endeavouring to understand & make ourselves understood in return, but Mamma & her butcher can't come to right terms at all; our ladservant also who by no means does discredit to the Norfolk accent is very indignant because the Scotch housemaid says he can't speak English. That, dear Mr. Murray, excuse this selfish letter, & believe me with love, if I may, to your & your's, your's most truly

Eliz: Rigby

i. St Bernard's Crescent in Edinburgh's New Town was home to Mrs Rigby and three of her daughters – Jane, Elizabeth and Matilda.

2. 'Drysdales' were evidently Sir William Drysdale (1781–1847), treasurer of Edinburgh and advocate of sanitary reform, his wife Lady Elizbath Drysdale (1781–1882), noted for her interest in literary and scientific thought, and his sons George and Charles, birth control activists.

3. George Combe (1788–1858), the leading British advocate of phrenology. See C. Gibbon, *The Life of George Combe: Author of 'The Constitution of Man'*, 2 vols. (1878). ·

4. Samuel Laing (1780–1868), travel writer on Scandinavian countries.

5. David Smith was the eldest of the thirteen children of the banker Alexander Smith. His sister Marion married John Murray and his brother James married Matilda Rigby.

6. Rev. E. T. Daniell (1804–42), Norwich artist and printmaker. Daniell had accompanied an expedition to Lycia; see T. A. B. Spratt and Edward Forbes, *Travels in Lycia, Milyas and the Cibyrates, in company with the late Rev. ET Daniell*, 2 vols. (London, 1847). See also letter, 15 March 1891.

Letter to John Murray   *NLS Ms.42174*

9 St Bernard's Crescent
Novr 23. 1842.
My dear Mr. Murray

As I no longer have any birds from our own woods to offer you, I have directed three grouse to take their passage by the steam boats today for Albemarle St. They travel in a box with some fellow grouse from Lady Drysdale, but mine I beg to say are for <u>you</u>. I trust that they will be in good order for the 27th for which occasion I beg to offer my warm good wishes, hoping that for many years to come I may be permitted the same pleasure. I look back to the past year with peculiar gratification as having procured me the friendship of yourself & your excellent family — a circumstance which has materially increased my happiness & also directly & indirectly much contributed to the pleasure & comfort of those I love around me. & without any of those fine words which Mr. Lockhart thinks <u>de trop</u> in my writing I will simply add that I heartily hope this regard may ever continue.[1]

I find from Christina's kind letter that we may look forward to the acquaintance of Lady McNeill, & also of Mrs. Murray's relatives — both of which will give us much pleasure.

This is a beautiful morning for Miss Smith's first sitting and I trust her likeness may be as successful as one just finished of my younger sister.[2] Mamma joins her good wishes to mine for your birthday & I remain dear Mr. Murray

Your's very truly Eliz: Rigby

   1. A reference to Lockhart's comment to John Murray: 'I wish the lady would score out a few fine words, but beyond these trifles she is unassailable.' See letter to John Murray, 13 August 1841, n. 1.

   2. Two of Elizabeth's drawings of unnamed women from the Smith family are now in the possession of John Murray.

Letter to John Murray   *NLS Ms.42174*

9 St Bernard's Crescent
Novr 29. 1842.
My dear Mr. Murray

   Perhaps you have heard already, & I am sure with the deepest concern, of the blow that has fallen up Mr. Reeve, & the Richardson family.[1] The joy & pride of their hearts was taken from them last Monday, & surely a sweeter angel never visited nor quitted this earth. It is dreadful to think of the grief that now reigns in this late so happy family, as to the poor husband I can conceive no human sorrow greater than his. He has high religious principle but nature must have way. They had entertained hope in an increasing degree beyond last Friday, & the change must have been sudden. I have not heard particulars, & indeed we are quite cut down with our own personal sorrow & the sense of their's. I hope & yet dread to hear – & will let you know for I am aware of the deep interest you & yours take in my lamented cousin & friend. We have also just seen tidings of a most distressing fire at the rectory of my nephew,[2] to which we removed on leaving dear Framingham. He & the man servants were absent & his sister, her young daughter, & the female servants were saved by the sagacity of a little dog who awoke the former. She is a most delicate young woman, & her exertions to save the parishioners & control & direct the frightened servants & the reaction of those have greatly prejudiced her health. But the house was insured, tho' many a treasure is lost that no money cd regain.

   I trust you & your dear party are under God's blessing all well, & that Mrs. Murray is nicely regaining her accustomed strength. I have

completed my portraits, but – not quite satisfied with Miss Smith.
Marion is very sweet upon paper & indeed she is so in nature. We are
more & more pleased with this truly worthy & refined family. Mrs S:
paid us her first visit today. The Drysdales are well & untiring in
kindness. Mrs Hasting [sic] Sand's called, but I am sorry we were not at
home. We hope soon to return it. In haste dear Mr. Murray but always
with sincere regard your's most truly
Eliz: Rigby

   1. Mrs Reeve (née Hope Richardson) died eleven months after her marriage
      to Henry Reeve. Elizabeth's drawing of Hope Reeve was later engraved by
      Richard James Lane, 1 June 1860 (1842). A coloured lithographic copy is in
      the National Portrait Gallery, NPGD22342.

   2. Edward Rigby Postle (1799–1878), Rector of Hevingham. His sister Mary
      Ann Beevor had long-term mental health problems. See Anne Carter, *The
      Beevor Story* (Norwich: privately printed, 1993).

Letter to John Murray   *NLS Ms.42174*

9 St Bernard's Crescent
Decr 29. 1842.
My dear Mr. Murray

Your account of dear Mrs. Murray's gradual improvement has given
me, & indeed all my family, the most sincere pleasure. Within an hour
the cheering tidings were communicated to our now mutual friends,
with whom the first question for the last ten days has been "any news
of Mrs. Murray"? We shall now be content to wait a while in the hope
that her recovery is gradually progressing & meanwhile we shall think
of you on Sunday.

I am truly glad to see the Jewess finds favour. I founded some hopes
upon the testimony of a cousin, who tells me he has read it three times,
& cried every time! I recd the "Bible in Spain" on Tuesday evening
& thank you truly for your kind thought of me. Evening engagements
& morning sitters have not allowed me to do it justice yet, but in the
first few pages I am reminded of my old German master, who used to
assure us we cd never expect to speak German unless we would open
our mouths. I have heard it much praised by Mr. Kinnead, who is now
on his way to London, where he hopes to see you & your family, for
which I much envy him. Indeed I have a great longing to Albemarle
Street-ward, & wish I may be so happy as to indulge in the Spring.

Nonetheless Edinburgh is gaining greatly upon our affections. Our acquaintances increase very much, but our aboriginal ones remain the favourites. Of the Smiths we see very much, & with increasing pleasure, but I do not speak in way of comparison for dear Lady Drysdale is unique in my estimation in the act of diffusing happiness. Yesterday morning was chiefly occupied in taking lunch with Miss Stewart in company of Mrs Henderson & Miss Miller. We greatly enjoyed the drive & Miss Stewart's society. That truly we find Edinburgh all that we can wish, excepting that its hospitalities take you from occupations not nearly so tempting.

Mr. Lockhart's letter contained some kind suggestions regarding future attempts upon the Q:R: also a cheque for £26,,5, which I beg to acknowledge with many thanks. He did not send any "sexagenerian love".[1]

Be kind enough to tell Christina with my love that what we think a very successful likeness of Anne Smith has been finished this morning, & soon as the drawing can be put in travelling order they shall be forwarded to Albemarle St. I conclude if I meet with no private means I may enquire when Messrs Oliver & Boyd[2] are next sending a despatch to you.

I am sorry to say that our mother is not quite well. We attribute it to this too mild season & trust that a day or two may remove it. She wishes very much to spend the evening with Mr & Mrs Ramsay (of St. John's Church) but I fear she won't be able for it, as the Scotch say.[3]

Now dear Mr. Murray, I must apologise for this very irreverent note, & wishing that 1843 may be rich in blessings & happiness to you all, I remain with much affection your's most truly
Eliz: Rigby

1. In 'Biographies of German Ladies' (*Quarterly Review*, vol. 73 (December 1843), pp. 142–87 (p.166)) she refers to the sexagenarian Goethe's relationship with Bettina von Arnim.

2. Oliver & Boyd, Edinburgh-based publisher and bookseller.

3. Dean Edward Bannerman Ramsay (1793–1872), founder of the Scottish Episcopalian Church Society and Dean of the Diocese of Edinburgh. He was Priest in the Church of St John's, where the Rigbys, as Anglicans, worshipped and where Elizabeth later married.

Letter to John Murray   *NLS Ms.42174*

9 St. Bernards Crescent
Janry 12 1842 [sic; 1843]
My dear Mr. Murray

It is long since I heard from any of your party, but as the last news of Mrs. Murray conveyed to me by Miss Miller was very cheering I persuade myself that she is making that progress, however slow, which all who know her so fervently desire. Your dear daughters are I know truly "better engaged" than in note writing and as for <u>you</u> I am perfectly aware that Lady Sale[1] has taken that position in your affections which, with her military knowledge, she will not fail securely to fortify. I shall have to get in again by <u>strategem</u> if at all. I need not say however that I have much more occasion to think of you all, than you of me, for every day, in the increasing enjoyment I find in the Edinburgh society. I was reminded to whose kind mediation I owe it. We are gradually making our way into that improving & rational kind which we most desire, for which we are in the second place, indebted to the Drysdale's, Smith's and good Mrs. Henderson. This latter and her niece have shown us much valuable kindness. We are particularly pleased with the family of Mr. Swinton whom they introduced to us, and at whose house, my younger sister and myself met a most delightful and distinguished party – Lord Jeffries and Sir John and Lady McNeill[2] were of the number, none of whom had met before. I looked down at Ld Jeffries and up to Sir John with equal curiosity through with different interest. Sir John is very magnificent – a splendid man – but as the Lord showed me most attention he carried the day. His knowledge of the dear Mrs Reeve was a subject which made me forget the individual who was speaking through the fire and acuteness of his glance did not fail to remind me. Lady McNeill is so natural and kind in manner that it is impossible to fell any constraint with her. I had the honour of dining at her table yesterday, and was placed next a Count Hamilton – a Swede – with whom I had many Estonian and Russian acquaintances in common. Sir John, at the first glance, is like Mr. Lockhart, but the impression is not long maintained, nor to the advantage of the former, who though perhaps more regularly handsome has a common face. There is a beautiful picture of him, worthy of Van Dyke both in treatment and subject, by Mr. Phillips – the other day I saw a painting of the Mr. Lockhart by a Mr. Landerr – which has so studiously kept the care and omitted the expression of his face that it might not to go down to posterity [sic]. A few days back I ws seated at a table near the Dean of

Faculty who so much amused me that I could hardly laugh within the bounds of decorum. It was too much to look at him and hear him both. He is an enthusiastic friend of Mr. Lockhart's of whom <u>he looks</u> almost 20 years the senior. Tonight we dine at the Smith's when the honour of Professor Wilson's acquaintance awaits us.[3]

Marion Smith has just been in, & shown me a kind message in a letter from Hester, and also corroborated Mrs. Murray's gradual improvement. I am expecting the drawings back in packing order to night, & then through Lady Drysdale expect to find a speedy opportunity of conveying them to Albemarle Street free. At this time our engagements and particularly mine are rather numerous – but after this week I intend to resist temptation for a short time as I must have more time. I was much struck with quotations from Lieut Eyre's book, & much delighted with Mr. Borrow's forcible frankness. It is a highly romantic work. But I will tell you more about it.

I have a great desire, if within your obtaining, to have two German works – "Charlotte Stieglitz" and "Goethe's Briefwechsel mit einem Kinde".[4] These, with others I possess, would, I am inclined to think, give me materials for a very interesting paper relating to the lives, education, and correspondence of German women. The Advocate's Library, through Mr. David Smith's kindness, keeps us amply supplied with English books. I will tell Christina that we are become acquainted with Mr. Ramsay and his lady, but we are startled to find through him the poverty-stricken state of the Scotch Episcopal church.

I am afraid I have been writing you a very rambling letter, but I have had a succession of callers who were not satisfied with hearing that <u>Mrs.</u> Rigby was out. We are not yet certain of continuing in our present nice house – we have made our Landlady's acquaintance, and are awaiting her decision. Now, dear Mr. Murray, banish Lady Sale a moment from your thoughts & think of me as your's most truly
Eliz: Rigby

1. Lady Florentina Sale, wife of Sir Robert Sale, at his side during the defence of Jalalabad and whose *Journal of the Disasters in Afghanistan 1841–2* was published by Murray in 1843.

2. 'Lord Jeffries' appears to be Francis, Lord Jeffrey (1773–1850), Scottish judge, writer and co-founder of the *Edinburgh Review*. Sir John McNeill (1795–1883), Ambassador to the Court of Persia and Privy Councillor.

3. Professor John Wilson (1785–1854), Scottish writer, frequently under the pseudonym of 'Christopher North'.

4. Bettina von Arnim, *Goethe's Correspondence with a Child*, 3 vols. (London: Longman, 1837–39).

Letter to Hester Murray   *NLS Ms.42174*

9 St Bernard's Crescent
Friday Eveng Febry 10. 1843.
My dear Hester[1]

You must kindly forgive me for addressing you thus unceremoniously, but I find it difficult to insert the formal "Miss" when I feel so much regard, & to one of whom I speak & hear spoken, without this little monosyllable among the many here to whom you & your family are dear. I will not let any of our few quiet evenings slip by without thanking you for your kind letter. Altogether, a letter from Albemarle St, is the most acceptable harvest the heavy post can bring me in. Your account of dear Mrs. Murray is cheering, & I willingly give myself to the hopes you entertain knowing that all that medical skill & tender nursing can do, will be done for her. I am sorry Mr. Murray is not quite the thing, but if he finds my letter too entertaining to answer, I daresay I can oblige him with a few <u>dull</u> ones. I wish indeed I were at hand to give whatever of help & pleasure it cd be in my power to give to either of your parents, & hope truly for many reasons that the spring may find me once more a happy guest beneath your roof. I have just finished packing, with the assistance of my constant help-mate Matilda, the long delayed drawings, which proceed to-morrow to London under convoy I believe of one of Lady Drysdale's nephews. I trust there is no doubt of their reaching you soon & safely & I shall be very happy if I have succeeded in recalling to your's & dear Christina's minds the faces of your two valuable friends. We are become so fond of them both, that I felt a greater twinge in parting with their likeness than I had anticipated. I trust I may see them again in Albemarle St. I know I can't tire you in speaking of your friends here, & therefore I shall begin upon them first. High as they all stand in my estimation, dear Lady Drysdale stands highest of all. I never met with so warm hearted & unselfish a woman. The more I see of her the more I love her, & cannot live without the sunshine of her face for above three days. My family are so wilful as to think this is all for <u>Sir William</u>, but I beg to know my own mind best. They are now a very small party, having only Anne with them, & she leaves for Liverpool next week, so that I shall decidedly feel it my duty to devote myself much to the lovely parents. I began a drawing of Anne this morning which promises well – her face is one which will look very well on paper. As for the Doune Terrace party,[2] we meet somehow & somewhere, almost daily. Mamma is very much smitten with David & we all begin to share <u>Christina's sentiments</u>, though we have not yet expressed them so candidly. I think the picture of this united & well-doing family is one of the most charming possible. Mrs. Kinnear is also a great addition, & her husband, who spends part of every week here. And now if I launch into the wide mile of mere acquaintances I shall hardly know where to begin or where to stop, for indeed they extend so rapidly, that the task of returning calls is no slight one. Our two most interesting dinners have been this week at Lord Jeffrey's & Lord Murray's. At the former I had Professor Napier[3] for a companion, who was infinitely deafer & not near so interesting as his brother Editor. Lord Jeffrey, however, was in most gay spirits, but is mistaken in thinking that a succession of French words, not always too well pronounced, is a needful set-off to his beautiful English.[4] Mrs Jeffrey's simplicity & good nature also pleased me much, & knowing many of my friends & relatives we had many subjects in common. At Lord Murray's we <u>all</u> made our debût last night. We have not yet traced our connection but it is very evident from their quartering our <u>Cross</u> in their arms, she was a Miss Rigby. After dinner there was a musical party, at which Lady M: is herself a great performer, & I was so happy as to enjoy Sir John McNeill's conversation during the whole of Beethoven's <u>Septuor</u>, which was a very great treat, only that he took snuff to all seven movements. I am afraid I don't feel very charitable towards Lady McNeill, in spite of the snuff. He is rather too handsome to go about loose in society, especially when he talks philosophy & quotes Burns in a soft whisper. I was also at a very agreeable dinner at Lady Sinclair's, where Sir Norman Lockhart fell to my share, or I to his. I asked him whether he belonged to Mr. Lockhart's family, he replied "No" – "But he does to mine". I hear this latter gentleman much spoken of with the greatest affection & enthusiasm by a few of his intimate friends, but rather the severe by the rest of the world who seem piqued that he cares so little for them.

Miss Cath: Sinclair pleases me much – I am sorry she has written that poem.[5] The family & company were so gigantic at this house, that I felt uncomfortably <u>small</u>. Among the <u>young</u> people we feel most attracted to the Miss Swintons of Inverleith Place,[6] & to Lord Medwyn's daughters.[7] We are also much interested in a blind Mr. Anderson & his wife & sister in law, who were <u>Petersburg</u> English. It is strange that we here meet <u>three</u> blind gentlemen in society – Mr. Anderson, Mr. Walpole & Colonel Abercrombie. I never remember meeting <u>one</u> elsewhere. We meet Mr. Yorke occasionally, who is <u>very</u> agreeable, indeed the Episcopal clergyman shine both actually & comparatively. I don't think I have told you of Professor Wilson's acquaintance.[8] Speaking of <u>McNaughten</u>, he said that if he was sure to have a verdict of <u>insane</u>

brought in, there were <u>nine</u> men in Edinburgh whom he should be delighted to shoot.

The clock striking reminds me to break off for the night. I am glad to hear the Jewess is in favour. I am as interested as you to know <u>what</u> children's books are fit to read now a days, & shall hope to see the question answered in some future number. Pray thank Mr. Murray for the German books. And now begging you to excuse a very egotistical letter, & with my kindest love to your father, mother, & sisters, believe me dear Hester your's affectionately

    Eliz: Rigby

We shall be thankful to hear of Mrs Murray soon again, be the lines ever so few.

Tell Christina that we have had some interviews with the mysterious Mrs. MacKinnon who turns out to be a young & pretty woman, & that we have hired her house <u>furnished</u> as now for another year from next April.

1. Hester Murray, daughter of John Murray II and close friend of Elizabeth's.

2. The Smith family lived at Number 3, Doune Terrace.

3. Macvey Napier (1776–1847), Professor of Law at the University of Edinburgh and editor of the *Edinburgh Review.*

4. Jeffrey lost his Scottish accent and spoke with what his contemporaries described as a high-pitched English accent. See G. W. T. Omond, *The Lord Advocates of Scotland from the Close of the Fifteenth Century to the Passing of the Reform Bill*, 2 vols. (1883), vol. 2, p. 301.

5. Catherine Sinclair (1800–64), poet, novelist and writer of children's books, romances, travel guides and social guides such as *Modern Accomplishments* (1836) and *Modern Flirtations* (1841).

6. The Swintons of Inverleith Place were the family of John Swinton. His daughter Henrietta was a lifelong friend of Elizabeth's and her son later married Matilda Rigby's daughter Anne. The larger Swinton family included the family of John Campbell Swinton of Kimmerghame. His children included the jurist Archibald Campbell Swinton, the painter James Rannie Swinton (see letter, 5 May 1843, n. 2), and his daughters Catherine and Elizabeth, who were also artists.

7. Daughters of John Hay Forbes, Lord Medwyn (1776–1854), Scottish judge.

8. See letter, 12 January 1843, n. 3.

Letter to John Murray III   *NLS Ms.42174*

9 St. Bernard's Crescent
May 5 1843
My dear Sir[1]

The bearer of this, Mr. Swinton,[2] is a gentleman whom I beg to introduce to your acquaintance. You are probably aware of the high standing of this old Scotch family here. They were among the earliest of our acquaintances here, & we owe them much hospitality & kindness. This Mr. Swinton has chosen the profession of an artist from pure love & has had great opportunities of improvement in Italy & Spain. From some of the finest pictures in the latter country he has made splendid sketches which I hope you will have the pleasure of seeing. His crayons portraits are also most beautiful in my eyes.

If you would kindly procure him an introduction to Mr. Eastlake, Mr. Swinton would consider it a great advantage & I a great favour. I would have given him a letter to that gentleman myself, but feared he might wonder at this liberty from one, whom he has by this time probably forgotten.[3]

Had it not been for the state of Mrs. Murray's health I should have ventured to give Mr. Swinton an introduction to your father & family – as it is I can only trust that the skill & care with which Mrs. Murray is surrounded may be the means, under the divine blessing, of restoring her to that health & strength of which she made so good a use. With my best wishes & love to her & your sisters

I beg to remain
Your's very truly
Eliz: Rigby
May 5 1843
9 St. Bernard's Crescent

1. This and subsequent letters are addressed to John Murray III (1808–92). See Samuel Smiles, *A Publisher and his Friends: Memoirs and Correspondence of the late John Murray* … (London: John Murray, 1891).

2. James Rannie Swinton (1816–88), Scottish portrait painter who later had a successful career in London.

3. Eastlake was a frequent guest of the Murrays but first met Elizabeth perhaps in 1843, given her own account of their meeting at dinner in 1846 where she records, 'Eastlake took me in to dinner, and was most refined and amiable; quite the stamp of gentleman in the utter absence of all anxiety to show it; remembered, too, what we had talked about three years ago

– laughed at my asking him whether he was a grouse-shooter' (J&C1, p. 187).

Letter to John Murray　　*NLS Ms.42174*

9 St. Bernard's Crescent
Septr 5. 1843
My dear Mr. Murray

It is with very mournful feelings that I find myself addressing another Mr. Murray,[1] though at the same time I feel that I can pay no more grateful homage to your dear father's memory than by expressing my entire regard & respect for his son. May that son ever reap the benefit of his own & his father's good sense. I must beg you to accept my thanks for your kind expressions, & I trust long to enjoy that friendship with your family which I consider the best fruits of my connection with Mr. Murray as a publisher. That you all consider Mrs. Murray decidedly better is indeed welcome news. I truly hope that Albemarle Street is destined long to be the scene of the best kind of happiness to herself & her family.

Your wishes & those of Mr. Lockhart that I should continue to be a contributor to the Quarterly are in every way gratifying and flattering to me. But I hope by this time that you quite understand that in many matters which writers for the Quarterly are supposed to have at their finger's ends I am perfectly ignorant & shall probably always remain so. In addition also to a very deficient education, I do not lead, nor wish to lead, that life which should keep me au courant du jour. But such thoughts as a woman of the most private station & habits may have, & those plainly spoken, will ever be at your service, & you & Mr. Lockhart are only too good to be pleased with them. I will do my best to mend the sheets you have sent me, but this catalogue is a very troublesome matter & one in which I want help which now I cannot command. Thank you for the coming books – I will endeavour to ascertain whether there are more which it might benefit me to see. Could you also obtain for me the address of Mrs. Austin – or is there any person of your own acquaintance who could give me a little information respecting those extraordinary Berlin ladies – Rahel, Bettina & Charlotte Stieglitz – further than what appears in their most extraordinary biographies & letters?[2] I know that their private histories are matters of public conversation in ... [second page missing]

1. John Murray II died on 27 June 1843.

2. 'Biographies of German Ladies' reviews Rahel, *Ein Buch des Andenkens für ihre Freunde*, 3 vols. (Berlin, 1834); Goethe's *Briefwechsel* (second edition, Berlin, 1837); and Charlotte Stieglitz, *Ein Denkmal* (Berlin, 1835). Henry Crabb Robinson remembered that the article 'gave offence' at the time. See Edith J. Morley (ed.), *Henry Crabb Robinson on Books and their Writers*, 3 vols. (London: J. M. Dent & Sons Ltd, 1938) p. 367.

Letter to John Murray   *NLS Ms.42174*

Edinr
Saturday Octr 7 1843
My dear Mr. Murray

I have been much interested of late in an instrument called the Calotype, of which probably you, (knowing everything,) know something, but the better results of which, having chiefly been exercised and improved here, you may perhaps not be acquainted with.[1] Therefore I venture to send you a few specimens, being assured that you will appreciate their truth and beauty, though few do. It appears to me that this is the only line of photographic drawing which can at all assist an artist – it was absurd to think that any would supersede him. I send you various specimens of the subjects to which it has been turned here, but fear I can only beg you, as you have so kindly done me with your Lexicon, to keep them till I ask for them back. I have enclosed three of myself, not the best impressions, which you and your sisters will doubtless recognise. I <u>admire</u> myself very much, but cannot get the world to agree with me. The downcast eyes were a necessary consequence of the most brilliant sun which prevented their being raised the least higher. With old faces it is most successful – producing the most exquisite Rembrandt effect, but I have none of that kind to send you. If these are new to you I shall be glad to hear your opinion, but if well known do not let me trouble you.[2]

Mr. D: O: Hill the landscape artist here has undertaken the picturesque part of the Calotype.

I wish also to day to tell you about Lady Drysdale – She is seriously ill, but the worst symptoms are an utter despondence and conviction that she shall not live, to a degree which frustrates all medical help. Wm Alison, I am happy to say, is called in now and goes to Queensferry daily. He says her state of mind is more against her than the actual fear. She has only Miss D: & Mary with the two lads about her, and the

two first although so tenderly affectionate have had no experience of illness or nursing. Therefore Mamma thinks of going over to-morrow to offer what her knowledge and experience may see fit. Mrs. Crowe may possibly go, being equally anxious. I will give your sisters tidings after their return. Begging you to excuse this hastily written note.
Remain your's truly
Eliz: Rigby

1. A calotype was a photograph printed on paper from a negative. Unlike the daguerreotype, the calotype yielded multiple copies.

2. David Octavius Hill (1802–70) and Robert Adamson (1821–48) were Edinburgh-based photographers. Elizabeth Rigby sat for around 17 portraits between 1843 and 1847. Thumbnails of each are reproduced in Sara Stevenson, *David Octavius Hill and Robert Adamson: Catalogue of their Calotypes taken between 1843 and 1847 in the Collection of the Scottish National Portrait Gallery* (Edinburgh: National Galleries of Scotland, 1981). See Julie Sheldon, 'Elizabeth Rigby and the Calotypes of Hill and Adamson: Correspondence from the John Murray Archive, 1843–1880', *Studies in Photography* (2007), pp. 42–48, where all Elizabeth's letters regarding the calotype are printed in full. See also Julie Sheldon, 'Elizabeth Rigby, Lady Eastlake', in *Encylopaedia of Nineteenth Century Photography* (New York: Routledge, 2007), pp. 1195–96; and L. Wolk, 'Calotype Portraits of Elizabeth Rigby by David Octavius Hill and Robert Adamson', *History of Photography*, 7 (July/September 1983), pp. 167–81.

Letter to John Murray   *NLS Ms.42174*

Edinr
April 20 1844
Dear Mr. Murray

I am exceedingly obliged to both Mr Portland & Captn Beaufort for their respective shares in the kind offer which your letter communicated. I shd have no hesitation in accepting it but my sister now accompanies me (of which my Thursday's letter to Christina appraised you) & though most unwilling to appear to encroach upon such liberality, yet unless it cd be extended to her also I must decline it. May I request you therefore ascertain whether a companion wd be permitted me, the which, had not my sister decided on becoming it, wd have been a servant, assuring Captn Beaufort that under any circumstances I shall consider myself much his debtor for the kind readiness he has showed to assist me.

In this uncertainty, however, I shall have every thing in readiness so as to be able to start on the 1st May, & should leave Edinr this day week by steamer & be in London on the Monday.[1] I shall add a few words to Christina to announce an arrangement which, without lodging us in Albemarle St, will trouble Mrs. Murray quite sufficiently. Of course I am <u>exceedingly</u> anxious to know whether the Captain be <u>married</u> but till the chief question be ascertained I will forebear troubling you about that.[2] Your answer therefore will decide us as to what to do, & meanwhile let me thank you for the trouble you have taken in communicating this matter to me. Indeed I should be proud to enter Russia under Her Majesty's flag. All Calotype questions shall be answered with a <u>Navy List</u> exactitude! The prices I am assured are written very <u>small</u> on a corner of the card back so you must look <u>very close</u>. I believe I can say that the paper is of no peculiar make.
Believe me dear Mr Murray your's very truly
Eliz: Rigby
Pray present my best compliments to Mr. Portland

1. Steam packet ships between Leith and London took 60 hours. The rail link was not completed until 1846.

2. It was customary for unmarried women to travel with a chaperone, usually an older married or widowed woman or a married man.

Letter to John Murray[1]   NLS Ms.42174

Wardes[2] July 14/26 1844
My dear Mr. Murray
    I received your kind letter yesterday & am glad that a letter in hand to Hester enables me immediately to acknowledge it. I am only too glad to have such letters as I receive from Albemarle St. to pay for. Also for yr satisfaction I must inform you that the foreign postage is here lisscensed [sic], probably as a slight compensation for the enormous tax imposed on all subjects leaving the country wh: is one among too many sources of his I.M.'s great unpopularity. We have much entertained some of the natives here by extracts from the English papers concerning the Emperor wh: have been quoted in our letter from home. I learn from a General Aide de Camp who received him that his Majesty returned in the worst possible humour, owing it is concluded to the future of those plans for wh: this visit was undertaken. The Grand Duchess Alexandra is in a state wh: forfeits all hope. Nevertheless she is expected to reach

her confinement though no to survive it. The Imperial daughters have
been brought up in a manner wh: must entail early death, or, like their
mother premature old age.

You will hear from Hester that we have been in some delightful
society lately. I learnt from Prince Volkonsky[3] a circumstance wh:
interested me deeply, namely that he knew a Russian who had been in
some way witness to the murder of Col: Stothard & Captn Conolly.[4]
The Prince promised me to obtain precise information on his return to
Petersburg where he now is. I find Custine's[5] work most tremendously
forbidden here, also a long list of books the various nature of which
wd in chief give a characteristic picture of Russian precautions.
Nevertheless all <u>defense</u> is evaded, & all save Custine be openly on
tables in St Petersburg. I certainly have had no inconvenience to
suffer from [*illegible*], unless a great stimulation of a very burdensome
popularity among a set of good people whom the love of royalty only
attracted to me, be so called. Here also I pay much more for what
I did <u>not</u> say than for what I <u>did</u>. I can least hope for forgiveness
for having asserted that the Estonian homes smell of <u>onions</u>! & that
the Estonian ladies were given to <u>drinking</u>! I am glad the article on
Childn's Books gives satisfaction. Wd you kindly pay over the money
you mention for wh: accept my thanks, to Sir Wm Forbes Bank (now
called I think the Union Bank) in Edinr to my account, deducting
always the £5 for which I owe my debtor. I trust the No. of the Q:
R: may reach me, but as it is often the <u>forbidden</u> list I fear it may
not. I will therefore beg you to send one for a gentleman here, who
wishes regularly to take the Quarterly, in the following way. Addressed
to "Christopher Grammann & Sohn – "Lubeck" – within that cover
to "Herr Eggers Buchhandler Reval". & within that to Count de la
Gardie, Hapsal,[6] also you may enclose the smallest & cheapest edition
of Scott's Life, & direct Eyre's book. I am responsible for the amount
wh: is easily settled as [*illegible*] delay the [*illegible*] in question, is my
chargé d'affaires for some money placed here of which we receive
the annual interest. This is giving you much trouble but this is a side
door for the admittance of English books wh: we have already found
to answer. We are much tried with the worst summer wh: has been
encountered for years – cold & rainy – so that everything is put back,
& the hearts of the wholesale farmers are very low. Also some late
crown regulations are depriving Estonia of much [*illegible*] of profit.
Our frequent journeys & interruptions do not give much time for
regular occupation & now our short month will find us thinking of
our departure. We intend coming home by Stockholm at all events, but
whether we shall see more of Sweden circumstances must determine. I

am promised letters of introduction & hope to see a little with Swedish life. Most of all do I hope that it may please God to bring us safe through our various autumnal voyages home again. You shall hear fully of our plans beforehand. I have only space to say how I rejoice in the good account of yr dear mother & to remain with love around you yr's very truly

Eliz: Rigby

1. This letter is particularly difficult to transcribe, being written in tiny close handwriting on onion-skin paper.

2. Probably Alt- or Neu-Wartz in Estonia.

3. Perhaps Prince Pyotr Mikhailovich Volkonsky (1776–1852).

4. Captain Arthur Conolly was captured on a mission to rescue Lieutenant Colonel Charles Stoddart in Bukhara. The two were executed in 1842 on the charge of spying. See Joseph Wolff's *Narrative of a Mission to Bokhara, in the years 1843–1845, to Ascertain the Fate of Colonel Stoddart and Captain Conolly* (London: J. W. Parker, 1845).

5. Astolphe-Louis-Léonor, Marquis de Custine wrote *Empire of the Czar: A Journey Through Eternal Russia* (1839).

6. Now Haapsalu in Estonia.

Letter to John Murray   *NLS Ms.42174*

9 St Bernard's Crescent
Novr 18. 1844
My Dear Mr. Murray

Mr Lockhart has sent me a suggestion respecting some future article upon Lady Travellers, to wh: I have agreed with pleasure, & in wh: he tells me you concur. He also tells me to ask you for books, as if I had no modesty at all, wh: I assure you I have. Will you therefore think a little which English works are necessary for such a project & most of them I may be able to procure from libraries here. But the foreigners I must request you to procure. At present I think of none but the Gräfein Hahn Hahn.[1] Her "Jenseits der Berge", Reise Versuch in Schweden u Norwegen" & the recent work on Egypt. But there must be others of importance & I will set seriously to enquire through some foreign correspondents.

I look forward with impatience to more leisure, at present the kindness of our friends is so hot that I have <u>none</u>, unless I give myself airs which I myself shd condemn much more than the incessant interruption.

I owe Hester two kind notes. Will you tell her that she and your cousin shall hear fully as soon as some canvass arrives which you understand nothing about. Mr. Gruner's plates reached us on Saturday to our great satisfaction, & now we are expecting the letter press.

I heard from Russia the other day that Ct de la Gardie had recd his importation of English books, & also that the June Quarterly you sent of first had reached my sisters. They were greatly delighted. Their long absence from English scenes and topics prevents them from relishing many of the light modern books, & Gertrude writes me that she turned from "Ten thousand a year" to bury herself in the Quarterly.

I can give no great change in the accounts of Mrs Smith. Upon comparing week with week & telling us little minutia about the hours of keeping up & amount of nourishment taken, her daughters & ourselves came to the conclusion that improvement was going on though very slowly. Hester's account of your mother greatly disappointed me the other day. I hear a rather better one from a letter to the Smith's this mg. My mother is a terrible absentee but seems to be getting used to it. She is now staying with her venerable step-daughter of nearly four score years. Meanwhile Matilda and myself are not left to spend many days together wh: I should rather prefer.

With our kindest love to your family I remain
Your's very truly
Eliz: Rigby

    1. Ida Gräfin von Hahn Hahn (1805–80), authoress and travel writer, whose *Orientalische Briefe* was reviewed in 'Lady Travellers'.

Letter to John Murray   *NLS Ms.42174*

9 St Bernard's Crescent
Janry 11 1845
My dear Mr. Murray

The accompanying M:S: is not at all what you might expect – not at all in your way, & I owe you an apology for troubling you to run your eye over it. They are two little nondescripts, done at times lately which have been too much interrupted to attempt anything more serious. But before sending them to take their chance in some magazine I have thought it better to submit them to your inspection, in case, wh: I don't in the least anticipate, you should care to have a volume of such – since there are plenty more where those came from. The one is merely put together of anecdotes of wolves which I heard abroad –[1] the other was suggested by a dreadful scene which occurred on Loch Lomond, but it harps too much on one string. You need not be in the least embarrassed in telling me they are great trumpery, & that you are ashamed at my not employing my time better.

Many thanks for the Quarterly. I have been not much pleased but much amused with Mr. McKee's Harem and Woman's rights. I fancy I recognise Mr. Milman in every line, especially in that wise supposition that even if the English law did allow of polygamy, English women wd have nothing to fear. This is one of his own true awkward bits – not less monstrous an idea than false in conslusion. Pretty Mrs. Milman herself would have no great chance of a monopoly if that were the case.[2] Eothen also speaks for itself, so you <u>need not tell me</u>.[3]

I can give you in the main no better account of our dear Mrs. Smith. The last two days have been easier but on Monday, when I last saw her, I thought her much altered. Dr. Davison was called in & has disheartened them all much, but he is known always to take the worst view of all cases. It is a comfort to think that the hopes of your patient are so much better founded. We expect Mamma at the end of the month fully, & then I hope for my usual leisure wh: in her absence is much taken up by necessary matters in her place. Wishing you joy of the new year & much comfort in it I remain
your's very truly
Eliz: Rigby

1. One of the 'nondescripts' is 'The Wolves of Esthonia', later published in *Frasers* and republished, titled simply 'The Wolves', in *Livonian Tales*. Again the story has its origin in *A Residence on the Shores of the Baltic*, where Elizabeth describes being stalked by 'a great brute of a wolf' on a journey to a neighbouring house (LSB1, pp. 161–63).

2. Wife of Henry Hart Milman (1791–1868), historian, writer. Milman was not the author of the review; it was Alexander Kinglake.

3. 'Eothen' is Alexander Kinglake, reviewed in the *Quarterly Review* by Bartholomew Elliott Warburton (*Quarterly Review*, vol. 75 (December 1844), pp. 54–76. Confusingly, Kinglake reviewed 'Milnes on the Hareem – The Rights of Women' in the same issue (pp. 95–125).

Letter to John Murray   *NLS Ms.42174*

9 St. Bernard's Crescent
March 29. 1845
My dear Mr. Murray

I sent off a parcel to you this morng through Mr. Blackwood's intervention. It contains some books for my sisters in Russia which I shall be much obliged to you to forward with the forthcoming Quarterly's for them and for Count de la Gardie. May I also trouble you to add to these your Colonial Edition of Borrow's Bible in Spain & of Mangle's & Irby's Travels.[1] Also wd you procure me a copy of the old school book <u>Mangnall</u> & enclose it too. Wd you also kindly let me know what I owe in your debt for books ordered for Russia, as my sisters leave me <u>no peace</u> till I tell them.

I find the Quarterly comes out on Monday – as my Lady Tourists proved too long for this number I have been letting them stand over a little, & have taken that opportunity of being poorly from which, however, I am quite recovered. I am told by a foreign correspondent that I ought to see the <u>Beilage</u> to the <u>Allgemeine Zeitung</u> for the last months of January & February, as it contains some excellent remarks on Madame Hahn Hahn and others – is it to be had in London? & cd you procure it me – as I shall soon have this subject off my hands I am anxious to know what I can treat next. The little that was said of "the Rights of Woman" in the last Q:R: was too good to permit of being followed up.[2] I fancy something might be said of the light Puseyite books – the Tales of the Village by Paget Rudolph, the Voyager by Sewell &c unless you think it is a subject the Quarterly had best let alone. But perhaps with your constant opportunities something has occurred to you that would be in my small way.

I was dining at Ld Robertson's last night – he has suffered terribly on his daughter's account, & his family & medical man are thankful that his is compelled to think about his poetry now. He will be in London in about a week as you probably know. I was also at a charming party at the McNeill's <u>after</u> the dinner, both host & hostess very charming. There was a pyramid of immensely tall even of which Sir Henry Bethune[3] was the top & Sir John the base. I shall have to come to London to feel myself acceptable height again, & for many other good reasons. A Miss Sinclair lords it terribly over me at a singing class which I have joined – the leader of which, a German of great talent & most exquisite voice I shall recommend to your good offices when he come later to London – at present his English, however, is not favorable to the shape of his pupils mouths! when singing.

I am expecting full accounts of the dinner in Albemarle Street yesterday.

The dear Doune Terrace party are really charmingly well, & receive our frequent visits with much cheerfulness. They are expecting two of Miss Kinnear's children today with them which will be better for them than other kind of guests.

Next week is a terribly gay one including the Waverly Ball for wh: I am booked. I rather wish the gaeities over – and so you must my letter so with much love to yr family

Believe me your's very truly

Eliz: Rigby

1. Charles Irby and James Mangles, *Travels in Egypt and Nubia, Syria & Asia Minor during the Years 1817 & 1818* (London: T. White & Co., 1823).

2. See previous letter, n. 3.

3. Sir Henry Bethune (1787–1851), army officer and commissary-general in Scotland. At six feet eight inches tall, his exceptional height made Elizabeth's remarkable height (she was five feet eleven inches tall) less conspicuous.

Letter to John Murray   *NLS Ms.42174*

April 12 1845

My dear Mr. Murray

I am indebted to you for your communications. I have immediately corrected & sent off the proof, <u>not</u> curtailing my part. I was rather in a rage with the Editor of Fraser for his having given the other tale such a title – he might be sure that if I had wished it to be known I shd not have taken such pains to keep away all allusion to Estonia – & now he has published it in the title.[1] I was rather puzzled for a title to this, and now fear I have sent rather a sentimental one viz: the Mourner & the Comforter, but it does not matter. Thank you for send.g me my debt, & also for mak.g it so little a one – by all means an embargo upon the money from Fraser. Thank you much also for the Q:R: I will send you some impertinent remarks upon it before long. I fancy I have discovered the means for seeing the Allgemeine Zeitung here, through Mr Dürrner the German musician, on whom I have been rather sweet this morn.g for that purpose.[2]

I hope soon to send off the Lady Travellers – but I have no idea how they will please. I have been putting in the "Letters from Madras" Lady, which though rather flippant is the liveliest picture of everday life in India. I have met with much English good sense besides – but I may be mistaken so tell me whether I am right in weaving her in, and praising her wh: I have done. Also can you tell me a little about her, and may I mention her name?[3] That's to day, if you will tell it me. I see that you and the Editor of the Q:R: persist in keepg me to the articles about "women on women" – so I suppose I must think abt. it again. But what business has Mr. Lockhart to put such fair words in his letter – 'what's mysogynical?

My rally are killing me with kindness here, or rather my time. Engagements accumulate this time of the year, and another Spring I must accept none at all – there's no drawing a line.

I am glad to find that Hester and Maria have left town, and that you have the prospect of getting your mother soon into the country. I hear of you all through my good friend and correspondant Miss Swinton – who describes you as all that's delightful and attentive – so I rejoice that you are improving. If you go one week I may perhaps take you to Paris next Spring, for this summer I think of being quite quiet – not even London, which is a great piece of self denial.

Our dear Smiths are charmingly well. David quite himself again. I believe I have nothing else to trouble you about – except that I have learnt the Hullachan and the Polka, which doubtless you will be glad to hear. Dear Christina is now alone with you and Mrs. Murray – I hope she is well. With my love to her believe me
Your's very truly
Eliz: Rigby
9 St Bernard's Crescent
April 12 1845
Can you insinuate in some way to the Editor of Frasers that I think his surmises very impertinent & that you know them to be wrong.

1. 'The Wolves of Esthonia', *Fraser's Magazine*, 31 (April 1844), pp. 392–400.

2. Mr Dürrner was a music teacher. 'The Siren Music has been the tempter: we have had such first-rate musicians at our beck, that, with my strong love for music, I have indulged myself far to much. Mr Dürrner is the ringleader, and his not speaking English has thrown him the more into our company' (J&C1, p. 167).

3. Julia Maitland was the anonymous 'Lady' author of *Letters from Madras* (London: John Murray, 1843).

Letter to John Murray   NLS Ms.42174

9 St Bernard's Crescent
May 8. 1845
My dear Mr. Murray

It is very long since I have had the pleasure of writing to any of your family, by which I am greatly the loser as I long very much to hear of you all. Also my friend Miss Swinton is no longer in the way to give me various little notices of your family's kindness, & your behaviour, which is a great loss.

I recd the draft from Fraser under your address. I think Mr. Nickisson[1] very impudent for boring me in my own person. In a day or so Mr. Lockhart will receive my Lady Travellers,[2] which has been rather lying about for mature reflection. I shall be anxious to know what he & you think of it. I am quite as little satisfied as usual. I have been getting acquainted with the last Quarterly greatly to my enjoyment Lord Malmesbury & Miss Berry I fancy I recognise both, & as far the capital "French Lake" it has such a dash of Eothen Impudence in it, with other better qualities, that I have rather a theory that it is by the same hand.[3]

We have been much annoyed this morng, as I hear many other people have been, by a very impertinent man belonging to Mr. Longman, who takes up his post in the Cartoon Exhibition now going on here. We went there today between two & three & found him lecturing & compelling people only to look at the Cartoons in the order & in the manner he chose. Of course we paid no attention to his harangue, though it very much interrupted us, & made our observations to one another upon the Cartoons in the tones usual in such cases when he gave us very impertinently to understand that we could keep our remarks to ourselves for that they interrupted his. We had no gentleman with us, & there was no one of any note or standing in the room to annihilate him but I have seen Mr. Blackwood & other gentlemen since, who recommended my making it known to you, so that you might apprise Mr. Longman if you think proper, of the discredit he does to their establishment. On another occasion he was found intoxicated – & always the greatest bore & annoyance. I think it is the same man who accosted you to put your name down when I visited the Cartoons with you in London – only grown infinitely more intolerable.

We have taken a deep & melancholy interest in this dreadful calamity at Yarmouth, & have had private accounts corroborating the worst that the papers say. The number of Norwich boys at school in Yarmouth gave rise at first to the most terrible anxiety.[4]

I was greatly obliged to you for all your information about "the letters from Madras" which has been of great service to me! What is to be done next?

Mr. Hamilton Grey[5] [sic] was here a short while back. He gave me to understand that Mrs. Grey did not proceed quite to your satisfaction. Also he informed me that any letters to her seem infinitely more interesting than her's to him, of which I don't quite see the connection. Edinburgh is becoming delightfully empty, & I have been luxuriating in a little leisure, as far as a dreadful fit of Menie will allow me. But next week I am to be carried off into the country for two visits – above of which if find two of the most splendid voices I believe England can furnish a Mrs. Gartshore,[6] & a Miss Monro whom not to know argues yourself unknown.

I am sorry Mr. Nickisson's mode of proceeding prevented you from defraying my debt to you, but I hope you will take the next opportunity.

Hoping to hear soon a good account of all your dear party & promising an immense chapter to my Christina before long. I remain dear Mr. Murray

Your's very truly

Eliz: Rigby

1. G. W. N. Nickisson, editor of *Fraser's Magazine*, 1842–47. *Fraser's* published the 'Wolves of Esthonia', 31 (April 1844), pp. 392–400.

2. 'Lady Travellers', *Quarterly Review*, vol. 76 (June 1845), pp. 98–136.

3. A. W. Kinglake, 'The "French Lake" [the Mediterranean]', *Quarterly Review*, vol. 75 (March 1845), pp. 532–69.

4. A crowded suspension bridge at Yarmouth collapsed, killing over 100 people, many of them children.

5. Rev. John Hamilton Gray. See letter, 14 July 1846, n. 1.

6. Mary Murray Gartshore (d. 1851), singer and composer.

Letter to John Murray   *NLS Ms.42174*

9 St Bernard's Crescent

May 24 1845

My dear Mr. Murray

I am very glad you like my article – I have sent it back to you, & have found but little to alter, which I suppose is a sign of great

barrenness of ideas. Mr. Lockhart promised me some marginal
suggestions, but I find none. He wished me to abate a little the quizzing
of Mrs D: Damer, but on fresh reading I can but think there is as much
<u>pour</u> as <u>contre</u> her.[1] At the same time I bow to his judgement & if he
really wishes for alterations can commit them upon the remaining proof.
Once little objection he has dexterously obviated himself.

We are all most thankful for the improved account of your mother
– though Christina's account of this morning is not very favourable. It is
indeed a great trial of patience & submission to you all – of which the
patient herself sets so beautiful & example.

We are all charmingly well. The country however, or something else,
did not suit me, & mamma scolded me for my disimproved looks, <u>but
they are recovering – I am told</u>. Of course I don't know myself.

We are enjoying charming musical evenings with a violin-artiste,
& three voices of whom we see more now that Edinburgh is so
nicely empty. The beautiful violin & tenor voice, in one, I intend
recommending to your good offices when it proceeds to London.

We hear better accounts of Sir John McNeill – will you let Mr.
Lockhart know this – his chief malady is sudden & most violent
palpitations, but it is ascertained that his lungs are perfectly safe. They
are now in the country somewhere close by. With much love to your
family believe me
Your's very truly
Eliz: Rigby

   1. Mrs Dawson Damer's *Diary of a Tour in Greece, Turkey, Egypt and the Holy
      Land*, 2 vols. (London, 1841) is reviewed in 'Lady Travellers'.

Letter to John Murray   *NLS Ms.42174*

Edinr
July 19. 1845
My dear Mr. Murray

I have continued to think over your suggestion, & am come to the
conclusion that I shall best be able to judge when I am once abroad, &
can make inquiries & form my own ideas. Thus far I go at all events
first to Cologne & Düsseldorf & you shall hear futher. I wish you to
give me your advice upon another little matter. There is to be a most
wonderful musical festival at Wurzburg consisting of <u>two thousand</u>
male voices! With accomodations preparing for 5.000 auditors. If my

nation can do such a thing well it will be the Germans – above seventy Vereins[1] are coming together for the purpose, & Schneider of Berlin I believe is the conductor. We hear much of it from our German musical friend here who wants us very much to combine this with our Rhine business, & can procure us all attention & accomodation there. Now as this is considerably out of our way, lying (vide Handbook) 28 hours by diligence from Frankfort, I should like to know whether I could do anything with it beyond the mere pleasure of hearing the monster. Is it sufficiently novel or interesting for me to give a description of it in the Times? Or in a Periodical? If I could have an object besides my own satisfaction I would much like to do it. It takes place for the 3rd to the 6th of August, so that we have no time to lose in making up our minds. Otherwise we think of starting about the 6th from this. Will you give me kindly your opinion.

Also will you tell Mr. Grüner that I am exceedingly interested in Count Racynsky's German Art,[2] & that it has greatly increased my desire to become acquainted both with the art & artists of the Düsseldorf school. If he can kindly give me letters to any of them by him not to mention me in any way as an authoress – neither my humility nor my vanity like the title – the latter assures me I can do very well without it. I must not write more except to hope that Hampstead is doing all the good you can desire.
In haste your's very truly
Eliz: Rigby

1. Organisations or societies.

2. Count Atanazy Raczynski, *Dictionnaire d'artistes pour servir à l'Histoire de l'art moderne en Allemagne* ... (Berlin, 1842).

Letter to John Murray   *NLS Ms.42174*

9 St Bernard's Crescent
July 23. 1845
My dear Mr. Murray
    I must thank you for your kind letter, altho' only in a few hurried words. Since I last wrote we have been obliged to give up the idea of Wurzburg as we cannot manage to get there in time – as it begins on the 3rd of next month, & we cannot contrive to leave Hull for Antwerp before next Saturday week the 2nd. But the Germans are determined we shall not be disappointed, & have fixed a grand musical festival at

Bonn in honour of Beethoven, on the 10th till the 12th, with trips
to Nonnenwerth & a great deal of German sentiment gratis. This we
shall in all probability attend, as we have friends in Bonn. Our plan is
therefore to go straight from Antwerp to Cologne & move up & down
between Bonn, Cologne & Dusseldorf as may suit us. There I hope
to digest at leisure & with every opportunity of enquiry your general
proportions, thanking you much for them, & for your financial offers,
but of this there will be no need, tho' I am equally indebted to you
for the kind thought. We start therefore probably on Wednesday or
Thursday of next week for Hull. My <u>elder</u> sister is my companion –
Matilda & I are not considered sufficient to make each other <u>respectable</u>!

Pray give my best thanks to Mr. Jordan for the much trouble he has
given himself. I am sure his letters will work wonders, & Sohn, I see,
is one of the corner stones of the Dusseldorf school.[1] Should I go to
Coblentz I shall not fail to trouble him (Mr. Jordan) with a visit. His
handsome face made far too vivid an impression to be forgotten.

I shall find time to write your sisters in <u>proper</u> letter before I
start – now I am horridly taken up, for my two sisters are staying in
Forfarshire, & we have a Norfolk friend with us whom I am obliged to
lionize about.

With the promise therefore of atoning for this shabby note.
I remain dear Mr. Murray
Yours very truly
Eliz: Rigby

1. Carl Ferdinand Sohn (1805–67), painter of the Düsseldorf School.

Letter to John Murray   *NLS Ms.42174*

Cologne
August 22 1845
My dear Mr. Murray

I have been intendg all along to write to you or one of your sisters as
soon as I shd have enough to say; & now I have so much <u>too much</u>, & so
may be limited a time for that, that I am almost afraid to begin. We
fancied we had given ourselves more leisure than travellers ever did
before, but what with unexpected sources of interest, or our superior
powers of research, we have managed not to have a moment to spare, &
the letters which filial piety demanded of us have, I am sorry to say, been
very few & far between. As I don't feel any filial piety to you this must

stand as my excuse. But our trip has been most successful in point of enjoyment, & can already look back upon it with great self gratification. The Antwerp Epoch was very exquisite. We revelled in churches & pictures, & Nuns & Jesuits & lace. I am sorry you don't require any further ideas about Rubens, for I have some very luminous ones. The modern Netherlandish painters, however, I conclude, are new to you – at least they were to me. We saw two of the first artists & their ateliers, more of the former than of the latter, for they had but little to show. But the men seem gentlemen, & originals – one of them rather fascinating – so I presented him with a Calotype as a souvenir. We liked Antwerp so much that we gave all the time there before heading on for the Bonn Epoch. This was a great change of subject, & increase of excitement. On the rail to Cologne on the 9th we picked up Henry Reeve, & his friend Mr. Shorty. Also Mr. Ford & his son were part of the time in the same carriage with us. I concluded he cd not possibly remember me, so I quite forgot him. But after a few reconnoiterings he claimed an acquaintance, & was very urbane. He was obliged to sleep at Cologne but got on to Bonn early the next day. We were recd there with waving banners & every demonstration of joy, & of course (just as at Stockholm) while other people were thankful for miserable little waves they had engaged five weeks beforehand & obtained the best accommodation in the town at five minutes notice. Henry Reeve with some other English gentlemen & a Sir J: & Lady Wilson & family were close to us & we formed a band of twelve English – 6 ladies & 6 gentlemen wh: did no discredit to our native soil. There were plenty of our countrymen there besides, but I can't say they were nearing such favourable specimens. Doubtless you have heard enough of the musical department through the papers, & will think me very old, so I will only say that the solo singers were ordinary, the choruses excellent, & the orchestra beyond all praise – it was magic! Not an infirm musician in it. I can't attempt to describe the wonderful effect, the touching grandness of the mass, the untouching animation of the military symphony. The pastoral mass of the Choral Symphony Beethoven was never done such justice to before. Mendelssohn & Litzt [sic] were made much of, but on this occasion the orchestra led them. On the Monday our loyal English all repaired to Brühl to await her Majesty.[1] We had to wait some time & grew very hungry & cold, but all thoughts of food & easement vanished the moment the scream of the engine was heard, in a few minutes the crowd was as lively as a German crowd can be. The regiment of lanterns soon clustered round the Palace, till at a distance it seemed to stand as a pedestal of fire, and then the mighty serenade of 8 bands comprising 400 drums struck up in tones never to be forgotten. It was the most immense music you can imagine – as if the

Cyclops were playing. We left her Majesty bowing got back in prudent
time to Bonn, having about 10.000 people to disperse as they cd, which
ended in some terrible scenes. The next day her Majesty appeared at
Bonn, at uncovering of the statue, & the following the royal party
entered the immense concert room through the very middle of us; but
tho' they enchanted everybody with their grace & condescension they
completely spoilt the last concert. The musicians wanted all to be asked
to perform & the audience none of them cared to hear, & when the
Queen left, half the orchestra took offence, & most of the audience
followed her out, so that what began so spendidly concluded most
ignobly. A worse finale followed this in the shape of a great <u>Fest Essen</u> in
the principal hotel where the quarrel & tumult was so great that ladies
fainted, & waiters fled, at least so we heard, for that time we were
implicitly obeying the directions of the Handbook & finding our way,
Henry & ourselves, to the loving valley of the Ahr. We all wanted repose
of mind, after the whirl & great enjoyment of Bonn, & thought a
temporary seclusion from the world wd be the best thing. Our expedition
answered completely we slept at Ahrweiler, & proceeded through
magnificent scenery to Altenahr, where we rumbled about some hours, &
then returned & went to Brohl, where we gave a day to the the
Brohlthal, mounting up to the Laacher See, & examining the monastery
& cathedral to our hearts content. Everything was delightful, except the
weather which tried us sorely tho' it cd not spoil our pleasure. Henry left
Bonn a <u>heavy gouty</u> old gentleman, but returned a light footed, light
hearted fascinating young man! We were delightful under all
circumstances! We moved on from Bonn to Dusseldorf for Henry's
convenience, who wished to share in our acquaintance with the
Dusseldorf School. We outstaid him, however, there as he was obliged to
return to Aix. I am almost afraid to speak of the Dusseldorf artists – I
was so <u>disappointed</u> in them! There never was such a mistake as that
School altogether, not tolerable in any department, & I saw all. Don't let
Mr. Gruner[2] know this or at least not in this degree. I wished to know
<u>what</u> it was, & am equally obliged to him for giving me the means, & I
am not a little interested in accounting for the causes of their most
erroneous ideas of art. The artists were very polite & kind, but either
they are very simple or very self-satisfied. We visited Heltorf, where the
frescoes are now finished, & tho' more tolerable than most we had seen
before yet the best were very second rate.[3] The only exception has been
the artist now employed at the new church on the Apollinaris Berg[4] –
altogether a most pleasing & beautiful object of examination. & Herr
Dager [sic] to whom Mr. Gruner gave me a letter is truly an artist, & a
very interesting, handsome, & gentlemanly creature besides. He & a Herr

Atenbach, [sic]⁵ also working there, seem to me the very painters of the
school who deserve the name. But perhaps I say too much against it.
Their aim & idea is always high & <u>unvulgar</u>, but their dreadful
colouring, & <u>laboured wax work</u> finish an intolerable. It is a pleasing
picture to me how harmonizing they all live together, but though this is
highly creditable to their Christian motives, it seems to be anything but
favourable to their artistic progress. They seem to me to see too little of
other schools, past or present & therefore to be little aware of the
deficiencies of their own. We arrived here on Wednesday, & have been
very busy since with various collections; & then the Cathedral! This is
alone enough, & I am eager to collect as much relating to its proceedings
& prospects as time will permit. We have promised namely to join Henry
at Aix on Monday at latest, & then after seeing an exhibition of the
moderns there to go on to Brussels where the chief exposure is to be.
The Netherlanders, however, beat the Germans in execution, tho' they
do not equal them in <u>intention</u>. And now I come to a principal object of
this long letter – namely to tell you our plans of return wh:, I am sorry
to say, do not promise to bring us round by London. I have thought very
much about it, & can find nothing but selfish pleasure in the matter for
us, & nothing but inconvenience for you, or your family, supposing, as I
feel I may suppose, that you wd wish to see me in Albemarle St. I have
therefore resolved to return by Antwerp & Hull, as the directest route, &
to relinquish the pleasure of seeing you all again till the Spring, when, if
I dare look forward so far, I threaten you with a complete visitation. I
have not mentioned you excellent mother, but I do indeed trust that your
next report will assure me that you are enjoying more comfort for the
present, & hope for the future. It wd be <u>very</u> good of you, or my dear
Christina or Hester to write to me to Brussels, post restante, where I
expect at all events to remain till Friday mg. I believe this will not be
hurrying you very much, & it wd give me the greatest pleasure, as I <u>long</u>
for intelligence. I have sacrificed all chance of beauty sleep for to night –
tho' this is a sad hurried scrawl. I give your Christina & Hester the right
for a full share of it, however. & with much love to them, & best wishes
for you all I remain dear Mr Murray your's very truly
Eliz: Rigby
You see I have no thought of continuing my wanderings for reasons wh:
I have not time to enter into. Also I shall soon have terrible heimwerk.
If you have not time to write to Brussels let me hear Post Restante
Antwerp.

   1. The Beethoven Festival in Bonn was attended by the Queen; see *The Times*,
      Saturday, 16 August 1845, p. 5; cols. A and C; and Monday, 18 August 1845,
      p. 5, col. A.

2. Professor Ludwig Gruner (1801–82), engraver (who undertook many copies on behalf of the Arundel Society) and designer. He was Prince Albert's personal art adviser from 1841, and from 1858 was Keeper of the Royal Print Room.

3. Heinrich Mucke's frescoes depicting *Scenes from the Life of Barbarossa* (1829–1838) at Schloss Heltorf near Dusseldorf.

4. The church of St Apollinaris in Remagen on the Rhine was built between 1839 and 1853.

5. A reference to two painters from the Düsseldorf Academy, Ernst Deger and Franz Ittenbach.

Letter to John Murray   *NLS Ms.42174*

9 St. Bernards Crescent
January 3 1846
Dear Mr. Murray

I am much your debt in every way – both for your kind letter and beautiful present. The first I received in East Lothian where were were staying immediately after the Christmas. It was an odd time of the year for the sea side, for the house is quite appropriately called <u>Seacliff</u> – but its position close to Tantallon and opposite the Bass makes it beautiful at any season. We went there, two of us, with the whole Doune Terrace party and therefore were sure of ample sources of enjoyment, to which several other guests contributed. David was in most uproarious spirits, laughing from morning till night. His sisters were also as bright and well as possible. We had very nearly enacted the scene of the Antiquary over again, being caught by the tide with a perpendicular cliff above us, but, like them, you see we escaped to tell the tale.[1]

Indoors our chief amusement was billiards, and very plentiful <u>eating</u>, for which the sea air rendered us particularly disposed. And then in our rooms at night we had such laughing – for one of the gentlemen – a Free Churchman – was so amicable as to make himself ridiculous. The others were all stupid and sensible!

As we drove up to our own door Oliver & Boyd's man came up with their parcel and your kind present had my immediate attention, and has been since the admiration of all friends. You have done so well in giving us a plenty of Raphaels – and those two grand things of Fra Bartolomeo. Overbeck also appears to advantage, especially his Christ before Pilate.[2] The borders are very beautiful. I don't quite like the fair designs by Horsley and Warren – but that's more the fault of our church than of them – as it is, Horsley has made his sinister cause as near a Roman Catholic priest as he could.[3] I have also to thank you much for the Quarterly. The Scotch Episcopal Church engrosses me immediately. It is not <u>gracefully</u> written, but is temperate and much to the point. I am glad to have more knowledge on the subject than I have hitherto possessed tho' my <u>faith</u> did not want it. I am rather discouraged, however, about the church matters, and shall want some stout lecturing from Hester when I come, but now that I have alluded to that I must thank you for the kind way in which you have promised me a welcome. You shall have no lack of <u>snubbing</u> when that does come to pass!

I have had a long kind letter from Mr. Drummond's lady wife inviting me to Albury Park[4] – this whole acquaintance is rather a mysterious affair to me.

Now with every good wish for your good health, happiness and <u>behaviour</u> believe me dear Mr. Murray your's very truly

Eliz Rigby

1. Walter Scott's *The Antiquary* describes scenes in north-east Scotland.

2. Johann Friedrich Overbeck (1789–1869), German painter and member of the Nazarenes.

3. Reference to the designs and illustrations to *The Book of Common Prayer, Illuminated and Illustrated* (London: John Murray 1845).

4. Albury Park, home of Henry Drummond (1786–1860), the banker and Irvingite. He purchased Albury Park in 1819 and engaged Pugin to convert the house to the Gothic style. Elizabeth describes how he asked to meet her at the end of 1845 without his wife and mother in the room, which she found shocking: 'he did not care a straw for me, but he wanted something new' (J&C1, p. 173).

Letter to John Murray   *NLS Ms.42174*

My dear Mr. Murray

You must not be alarmed at the packet of the M:S: which goes by the same post as this – I have no designs upon you, but simply like that you should see all the trumpery I may indite before any one else.

This in unEstonian tale which I began, thinking it was to be very short, but it went on spinning till it has reached the volume you see. Now, unless you have any time for it, it will find a place in Blackwood's Magazine or perhaps in a series of tales which Mr. Blackwood gave

me a hint he should be glad I would contribute to – though not
commenced yet.

It is a rather sad picture of the misrule in that part of the world, of
which I know too much, and therefore I have exchanged Estonia for
Livonia wh: would save me from reproach, and answers the purpose just
as well for all comprehensions.

I fear you will find it dreadfully simple.

We have enjoyed hearing of you all from dear Anne Smith who
seemed very unwilling to go out to Hastings. I have been a very bad
correspondent but I really have been much occupied though you may
think to very little purpose.

Have you got those numbers of the Dom Blatt from Germany? I shall
be setting to work upon Cologne now immediately.[1]

In haste yours ever truly

Eliz: Rigby

9 St. Bernard's Crescent

Febry 28. 1846.

1. 'Cathedral of Cologne', *Quarterly Review*, vol. 78 (September 1846),
   pp. 425–63.

Letter to John Murray   *NLS Ms.42174*

My dear Mr. Murray

Thank you much for your kind letter. I lose no time in assuring you
that I feel flattered at you proposing to include my tale in your Colonial
Lib: & that I am satissfied with the terms you mention. I alluded to the
alternative of Blackwood in order to set you more critically at liberty.
But I need not say that I wd rather have no literary transactions – trivial
as mine may be – with any but yourself. I have no tale either ready
or in prospect that would suit with that you have in hand, as Estonian
matter I think is pretty well exhausted now. Therefore if you will accept
of "The Wolves" to complete the volume – the matter is settled. I shall
be ready to alter any words you point out, especially that polite term
"jawed"! though when Estonians do get into a rage they make you
think of nothing else. As to connecting Anno's pleading scene more
into dialogue I must think about that. I am very inept at making my
personnages talk – & also I fear it would entail much repetition. I'll see
whether my rough copy be in a state for me to judge by.[1]

You speak of care as well as business which I am sorry to hear.

That our dear Christina should not be well I much regret, but your silence makes us hope it is nothing serious. I am indulging myself in some rheumatic pains in my head, which make me sit reading books on symbolism &c over the fire. But I am better today and intend to be quite well for a Bachelors' Ball to-morrow!
In haste your's truly
Eliz: Rigby
How soon do you propose printing?
March 23 1846
 I give you leave to announce it as by the "Author of Letters from the Baltic" being convinced that not doing so might be an inconvenience to you and no screen to me.

> 1. *Livonian Tales* is a collection of previously published tales, 'The Wolves of Esthonia' from *Fraser's Magazine* and *The Jewess: A Tale from the Shores of the Baltic*, with the additional and previously unpublished tale, 'The Disponent'. See Joseph Garver, 'Lady Eastlake's "Livonian" Fiction', *Studia Neophilogica*, 51.1 (1979), pp. 17–29.

Letter to John Murray   *NLS Ms.42174*

April 13 1846
Dear Mr. Murray
 A few words with this one sheet which is all I have had time to correct today. I am sorry yr printer misled you – that is for your sake. But if you have no objection to filling up the volume with the Jewess I can have none. Are you well sure that you like it thus. In that case I shall still expect to appear on May day.
 I like "Livonian Tales" myself better than any other title, & was going to propose it. I shall alter therefore the Wolves in Esthonia to Livonia. Especially as the insertion of Esthonia at all was a gratuitous impertinence on Mr. Nickisson's part.
 I have recd two parts of the DomBlatt.[1] I wanted to have had from last July, but I daresay I can do without it. I am eager to finish Cologne before I come to London, & have beside plenty of other occupation.
 Thanks to dear Christina for her note. I think it high time Anne Smith shd come home!
Your's ever truly
Eliz: Rigby

> 1. *Kölner Domblatt*, the magazine of Cologne Cathedral.

Letter to John Murray   NLS Ms.42174

9 St Bernard's Crescent
July 14 1846
My dear Mr. Murray

I think it is high time for me to trouble you with a letter now. This
being a favour which your modesty, I know, will not have expected
before. I must thank you first for your parcel and letters to Bolsover,
and for the Quarterly and other books which I have found awaiting me
here – where I am very glad to find myself after the dissipations of the
world, and especially the shocking Roman Catholic company I have
been keeping of late. I hope however I shall not corrupt you – if you
are afraid I should – you had better stop reading at once and take refuge
in the Times. You heard something of my life in Derbyshire from my
letters to Xtina, if you were permitted to share in them. The Grays did
as much as they could to amuse me, and much more than I liked, for I
longed for a little rustication after the excitement of your society! And
Bolsover is so very grand that I could have found endless employment
within and without. The few drawings I did accomplish after a fashion
will surprise you I think. The fine tower in which the Grays reside is
older than the ruins which surround it. These were built to receive Chas
1st and Hentte and correspond as much in general character as they
do in time with the most modern parts of Heidelburg Castle. Indeed
Heidelburg was always in my mind. These beautiful ruins contain the
longest gallery in England – 22 ft long.[1]

They took me to Chatsworth, Hardwick, Matlock, and other sights of
less note – especially Balborough House a beautiful Elizabethan mansion
belonging to the ancient family of Rodes. Chatsworth I criticised to
Xtina. Hardwick I admired excessively, and Matlock, after Scotch glens,
I thought but little of. We revisited this from the Lea Hurst – the home
of the Mr. Nightingale – whose wife is sister to Mrs. Nicholson, and
whose little plain, but nice and accomplished daughter, was one of the
party to the Queen's Summer House – if your intellect can reach so
far back.[2] I liked the party particularly, and they liked me for bullying
Mr. Gray, which it seems not many have the courage to do. But this
is all he requires to make him very agreeable – otherwise he would
lord it over you rather too much. Of Mrs. Gray I see more and more
to like, as a truly kind and amicable woman who is eager to fulful all
her duties, and does not slight the humblest neighbour but her literary
powers are beyond me! We had another literary lady too for a few days,
whom I met with interest and quitted with something very like the the

reverse – this was Mrs Clive. She reminded me much in manners and opinions of Mrs. Crowe only for worse.[3] The husband of such a woman is rather a riddle to me. But Mr. Clive was not there. She has been writing a pamphlet called "Saint Oldooman" in derision of the Puseyite tendencies, which I think very vulgar and rather profane.[4] Mrs. Gray was somewhat puzzled with her guest. Of Lady Sitwell I saw more at Lea Hurst and imbibed quite an affection for the old lady who has made two husbands very happy, and brought up two families of step children with great care and tenderness. I never thought to ask about Mrs. Borrow!

On taking the train at Chesterfield after leaving Bolsover Castle I found myself to my surprise in the same carriage with Miss Anderson and her brother. I was somewhat divided between their gaiety on the one hand and the misery of a young Pole on the other, who is one of the first fruits of this last insurrection – too young to hear much blame, tho' he suffers all the penalty. He was so rejoiced to find anyone who could speak German that he poured out his sorrows to me, and tho' I have but little interest for Poles in general the poor lad's distress was very moving. Would you look with the Court Guide and see whether you can find the address – town or country of a "Sir Reynolds F: Alleyne, Bt" and send it to me. My time was thus beguiled till I reached the station for Durham towards which my thoughts had been setting for some time. I found our good friend composed in mind and well in health, tho' it was evident how much suffering she had undergone. The matters stand as they did. Her strange husband has taken no step, except forwarding her a trifling supply of money. Her affectionate and submissive letter has remained unnoticed. He has broken with those friends who have expostulates & those that remain feel it better for her sake to wait with patience the turn that his diseased mind will take. She thinks very badly of the future herself. She does not doubt being recalled eventually, but fears that her influence wh: has hitherto kept him steady to the eye of the world will be utterly broken by this. Meanwhile his is doing such strange things here that the public were openly speaking of his oddness but I doubt whether it is odder now than it has been during his whole married life only she was too good a wife to let it be observed in a questionable light. My company was a great comfort to her and as I did everything as she did I lived a shockingly Romish life. We spent the greater part of one day in looking over a convent of Theresian nuns at Mt Carmel near Darlington. This order is but recently removed there and as soon as the house is finished intend to enforce the rule of St Theresa strictly and be enclosed. They being I understand the only sisterhood behind a grate in England. We were recd by Abbess Sist Prioness, & a

very pretty young nun who looked radiant with health and spirits. Their
costume is of Spanish peasant origin, and made of materials which it is
difficult to procure in England – picturesque and becoming in headdress,
but dreadfully clumsy & hot for the person. Their vocation is <u>prayer</u> and
their charities are only optional, tho' I hear they are great. They abstain
from all meat tho' their diet otherwise is delicate and plentiful. They
showed us their chapel, vestments, rooms &c and then we returned to the
parlour where we found a good plain dinner awaiting us and two priests
took top & bottom of the table and entertained us most courteously.
For your comfort I was <u>outrageously Protestant</u> on this occasion, which
occasioned some amusement to the good fathers, who agreed I was "an
<u>honest</u> heretic".

The weather was bad at Durham and that I saw little beyond that
stupendous Cathedral, for which Mrs Jones was an excellent Cicerone
– I had never before seen so grand a <u>Norman</u> interior. I think after all
it is more to my taste than the Gothic, though not so <u>symbolical</u>!! Do
you know about the beautiful Chapter House wh: has been recently
disinterred from a load of stucco & plaster & reveals endless riches of
Norman arches beneath?

I left our good friend with much regret but Romanism still kept its
hold, for my companion in the rail to Newcastle was Dr. Riddell the
Bp (R:C:) of Newcastle who made the most of the opportunity. After
such a trial I think my Protestantism is undoubted, much as I do hate
Luther. At Newcastle I was joined by my Norfolk companion, & with
her had a glorious day for crossing the Cheviots. Found all charmingly
well at home, & was declared greatly improved by my <u>London life</u>. Of
course I have seen Miss Swinton & many other friends & yesterday
brought Anne & Euphemia Smith to Edinr who gave us good accounts
of your dear sisters – especially of Hester. I long very much to see them
& am going to write a regular epistle to them. This reminds me of the
inordinate length of this, which is a sad breach of propriety. I intended
it to have been a mere bit of fash for the benefit of the Handbook,
but fear it is not even good enough for that! I shall expect however in
return an account of Mrs. Butt's last party at wh: I hear you were to
assist. I have kept Mr. Torrie's secret most faithfully, & have recd the
intelligence with all due surprise from everybody here.[5] I hope you will
keep <u>your</u> secrets better – but I doubt it.

Now, dear Mr. Murray, with many apologies for all impertinence
past, present, & future believe me
Yours obliged & truly
Eliz: Rigby
I am glad to hear that Mr. Torrie will require you as soon as the 22nd

at least this the Edinr talk. I am told that you were at Durham the same time as myself, but do not believe it.

1. Bolsover Castle was owned by the Dukes of Portland and rented to Reverend John Hamilton Gray, vicar of Bolsover. Mrs Hamilton Gray (née Elizabeth Caroline Johnstone), author of *A History of the Roman Emperors* and *A Tour to the Sepulchres of Etruria*, was the twin sister of Mrs King Harman and also sister of Lady Frederick Beauclerk, all lifelong friends of Elizabeth.

2. A copy after Elizabeth's drawing of Florence Nightingale, dating from this visit, is now in the National Portrait Gallery, London.

3. Catherine Ann Stevens Crowe (1790–1872), writer on the supernatural, in particular spiritualism and the occult.

4. Caroline Clive's anonymous publication *Saint Oldooman; a myth of the nineteenth century, contained in a letter from the Bishop of Verulanum to the Lord Drayton (a satire on J. H. Newman's 'Lives of the English Saints')* (London: Simpkin, Marshall & Co., 1845).

5. Thomas Jameson Torrie, geologist and friend of John Murray, who accompanied him on visits to Europe.

Letter to Lockhart   *NLS Ms.42174*

Dear Mr. Lockhart

I send you my performance – not at all proud of it, for I fear you will pronounce it very dull & dry.[1] I don't approve of ladies' meddling with history – although this is but local – I have put it together from a variety of odds and ends scattered through the <u>Domblätter</u> & elsewhere. You will see I have left a gap in one part, but I am expecting an answer from an acquaintance at Cologne which will fill it up & to add a few particulars which can be inserted in the proof. You have always been kind, but I shan't be surprised at a little <u>abuse</u> this time. I hear from Prof: Milman that he missed giving you a dinner on your way through.[2] I almost hope you went without or had a very bad one, since you did not give St. Bernards Crescent the chance of supplying it.

We are going to spend the evening at Craigbrook and expect Sir F. Palgrave[3] to breakfast tomorrow. This is the latest Edinr <u>news</u>. Will you direct your answer to Post Office Aberdarcer Fife

Your's very truly

Eliz: Rigby

9 St. Bernard's Crescent

Septr. 12. 1846.

I hope you won't object to that history of the Three Kings it is a very pretty little book.

1. 'Cathedral of Cologne' appeared in the *Quarterly Review*, vol. 78 (September 1846), pp. 425–63.

2. Henry Hart Milman (1791–1868), historian, ecclestiastic, Professor of Poetry at Oxford and from 1849 Dean of St Paul's Cathedral.

3. Sir Francis Palgrave (1788–1861), see letter to Palgrave, 10 November 1830.

Letter to John Murray   *NLS Ms.42174*

My dear Mr. Murray

Our correspondence has not got into its usual train of alternate respect and impertinence in which it ran of old so smoothly to <u>me</u> at least – nor is the hasty note a fit prelude, since it is only to give you trouble. I really am thinking of a <u>light</u> chapter on <u>costume</u> – having had a coaxing letter from Mr. Lockhart.[1] But what I want is what I fear there is no getting here – viz: old <u>fashions</u>, either frontispieces of Lady's Jacket Books, or old <u>Belle Assemblee's</u> to show me what they were in the reign of the George's. If you could help me to a sight of any old <u>store</u> of this description it would help some floating ideas now in my mind.

Meanwhile I have been translating some <u>verses</u> for Mr. Dürrner which is very undignified work in which I assure him I always improve the original, & he <u>believes</u> me! Our dear Smith's we expect tonight, but were not by five o'clock. Now I believe there are no other defaulting.

I wd not answer dear Hester in a hurry, or she shd have heard today – you see I don't mind how I treat <u>you</u>.

Your's very truly

Eliz: Rigby

Nov 10 1846

I have had one of the Iona green stones polished and Matilda says it looks like boiled cabbage.

1. Quoting Murray, Lockhart wrote encouraging her article for the *Quarterly Review* on 'Dress' of 1846: 'if you write on Dress as well as you dress yourself, you must produce a *chef-de' oeuvre*' (J&C1, p. 204). 'Planche's *History of Costume*', *Quarterly Review*, vol. 79 (March 1847), pp. 372–99 was later republished in Murray's 'Reading for the Rail' series as *Music and the Art of Dress: Two Essays Reprinted from the Quarterly Review* (London: John Murray, 1851).

Letter to John Murray   NLS Ms.42174

9 St. Bernards Crescent
Febry 6. 1847.
My dear Mr. Murray

It is so long since either of us wrote that it is impossible to say which did it last – at all events it was your undoubted duty to begin – I have a great deal of patience with people in your situation, but Matilda has not & before proceeding any further she desires me to say there are some mistakes in your letter which she begs you to recant.

I fear I have let many tokens of Albemarle Street kindness arrive without acknowledgement. "The Three Reformations" I consider one of the only notices of the subject worth reading.[1] I am delighted with it, & as I received at the same time a copy from Mrs. Jones I am now lending out both for the edification both of Presbyterians & Puseyites. The Book of Manufactures does not quite answer my purpose, & I shd like if you please to see one of a more domestic & household (which I am aware is the same thing!) scale, before making up my packet for Estonia.

Regarding the Song for the Highlanders there has been a slip between the cup & your lip. The M.S. was all ready revised, corrected, done up, & directed, when Peterson & Rag, our singing class shop, induced Miss Agnes Swinton to change her mind & give it to them, & it will be out on Monday. But you may have as many copies as you like for your private use. The lady begs me to make every apology for the trouble you have taken to enquire – but indeed it was my fault in not letting you know before. The singing class is flourishing. Our basses & tenors have considerably increased, but as if a very miscellaneous description & calculated not to divert the attention of the ladies. Dürrner gets very savage sometimes & blunders out much wrong grammar in his anxiety to correct our wrong notes – "was been" being a new mode of declension which often occurs. My altos who are recruited with two more & Miss Margaret Sinclair sides alternately with sopranos & altos, without either party being aware of the fact! We are to have a musical even.g on Tuesday at which I wish you could assist. I write to your cousin Mr. R: Cooke begging his good offices to procure me some more overtures, & am still hoping they will arrive this even.g.[2]

This morng I was at Inverleith Place & saw the Smith drawings. They have cost Mr. J.S. an unprecedented deal of trouble, & he has succeeded in making decided likenesses but nothing more. Neither Anne nor Menie have their peculiar sentiment – but don't tell David this – as his opinion is still to form & they hope he will be pleased. They are very like, & that's the chief thing.

We have been rather dissipated lately, & as my elder sister has been poorly with influenza Matilda has been doing double duty. We were at Lord Jeffrey's the other night. I met Mr. H: Gray, who had as many rings on as usual. I am sadly out of news of your dear sisters but fear they have too much to do & think of – so I shall soon write again. I am upon the whole relieved at Ch: Lockharts enfranchisement – I had heard much <u>pity</u> expressed at her taking such a boor.[3] I conclude you hear occasionally from Doune Terrace – I saw Miss <u>Menie</u> S: today, who desired her "best compliments" to you. After this I can only add that I am your's very truly

Eliz: Rigby

1. Walter Farquhar Hook, *The Three Reformations: Lutheran, Roman, Anglican* (London, 1847).

2. Robert F. Cooke (1816–91), cousin of John Murray III and a partner in the publishing business.

3. Charlotte Lockhart (1828–58), Lockhart's daughter, married the barrister James Robert Hope in 1847.

Letter to John Murray   *NLS Ms.42174*

Edinr June 21. 1847
Dear Mr Murray

I don't know whether you have even found out that I have not written to you for some time – at all events you can so well <u>afford</u> just now to bear a little neglect of that kind from me that I have no scruple in having committed it. Once more however before the final (not fatal) knot is tied must I write to congratulate you on the happiness it promises to you. I look forward to the 6th of July as a day I have long wished and hoped for, believed in and predicted (you <u>yourself</u> having always been my <u>informant</u>) and which I feel will, under God's blessing, bring to two very dear friends of mine the best happiness this world can give. You will receive a treasure such as falls to few men's share, and we can trust you with it.[1]

I think it rather hard you did not request me to be your <u>best man</u>, but at all events I shall be there to see how you behave.

I have just begun a drawing of Menie, but at present am very dissatisfied – in a day or two – as soon as one promises fair – the Calotypes are to be undertaken. Mr. Hill's coadjutor has been very

ill hitherto, or your wishes should have been complied with before.[2] I
have been having two agreeable country visits in opposite directions
and with my two different sisters. The one in Forfarshire, and the other
in Haddingtonshire. In the first I made acquaintance with Glammis
Castle which has left an indelible picture on my mind and also a little
one on my book, which I hope will give you some kind of idea of its
singular beauty. Our Haddingtonshire visit gave us Tantallon and the
Brass from the windows (Seacliff). We were the guests of Mrs. Geo:
Sligo and the first she has received since her widowhood so that we had
no amusement got up for us, I am happy to say, for I infinitely enjoyed
the quiet. The mother Mrs. Outram was staying there too, and that was
quite amusing enough.

I am infinitely obliged to you for the periodical supply of the Colonial.
The War of Liberation, and the Story of Waterloo are particularly fit to
go together and are both singularly interesting.[3] The latter somehow got
into my hands yesterday and would not get out again, tho' I had sundry
hints given me of the profaneness of my lecture. I am obliged to you also
for M: Feti's Autain de la Musique, which I find quoted by others and
spoken of highly. Could you get me this Life of Sebastian Bach by Forkel
in German – if it can be found in London.[4]

Now dear Mr. Murray I'll let you alone again for a time, and won't
take it amiss if you find no time to answer this till you do it in person
– and then you will have other fish to fry! Your's very truly
Eliz: Rigby
Mrs Butt complains she can never catch you. I have particularly
informed her what an agreeable better half you are about to present to
your London friends.

1. John Murray married Marion Smith on 6 July 1847. In an unpublished
   account of her life Menie Murray refers to a 'Painful discussion about the
   Wedding Ceremony. Hester [Murray's sister] at the instigation of clerical
   relations and encouraged by E.R. made a great point of a Service in Church
   according to the C of E rite, in addition to the Scottish Service. Greatly
   upset'. 'Account of the Life of Marion Murray', NLS Ms.43082, p. 14.

2. David Octavius Hill's partner in the photography business, Robert Adamson,
   was gravely ill. A letter from Marion Smith to John Murray (2 Ainslie Place,
   22 June 1847) records: 'I have been calotyping all day, seven different posi-
   tions have been taken of myself and I do not know how many of Elizth
   Rigby. I think all successful, but it has occupied the whole day & quite
   worn me out, altho' Mr. Hill was very interesting & Elizth charming!' (NLS
   Ms.43076).

3. John Murray's popular *Colonial and Home Library* series was issued in monthly
   parts at 2s. 6d.

4. Johann Nicolaus Forkel, *Life of J. S. Bach, with a critical view of his composi-
tions … translated from the German [by Stephenson]* (London: T. Boosey & Co.,
1820).

Letter to John Murray   *NLS Ms.42174*

My dear Mr Murray

Tho' I am perfectly aware that your state of <u>sanity</u> is questionable
at this time, and that probably, if it depended on you alone, this
letter would stand better chance of being understood or even read,
yet knowing the excellent <u>keeper</u> you are provided with I have some
hopes of its being made comprehensible to your mind – under these
circumstances you are welcome to continue this state of aberration as
long as you please as I am perfectly satisfied with your proxy. I have
heard of your's & Menies's progress with the greatest interest, and I
quite approve of you having commenced her episcopal and architectural
education with the <u>glories</u> of York and Canterbury. By this time you
have introduced her to beauties of a kindred style in Belgium, and I
almost envy you the pleasure which her admiration must have given
you. I don't mean her admiration <u>of you</u>, but ask Menie if you get
puzzled! We travellers <u>at Home</u> have been leading a very quiet reputable
life can since two good people left us endeavouring to make up for
lost time. This seems especially the case with some of the party both
in Ainslie Place & here and if they go on at the present rate I shd say
that object will be soon effected.[1] I leave Matilda however to report
matters in a regular official song and can only say that this gentleman
wins upon <u>my</u> regard whatever he may do upon her's. She & I are to
start this day week for Ardinconnal[2] where a large body of Smiths have
encamped, and I am sure we shall engage ourselves exceedingly. After
that I don't quite know what we are to do & would rather not look
forward, for there is an event to take place between this and <u>November</u>
which weighs very heavily on my mind. I like people to be engaged in
a <u>general</u> kind of way, but I do hate the selfishness of their insisting on
being married. If this be <u>beyond</u> you, just consult the lady again.

This heat has been excessive here – the thermometer at 80. I liked it
very well in one respect for it served as an excuse to neglect whatever
I did not care to do, but now St Swithin has <u>set in</u> with great severity
and I must call upon various people who are so tiresome as not to leave
town. When I shall ever find time to do anything <u>rational</u> appears more
and more problematical. Meanwhile I subjoin a little list of musical

works which Mr. Dürrner greatly recommends, & which you may find convenient to procure upon the spot, but do not give yourself trouble. Menie will be glad to hear that the report I received of my good friend Count de la Gardie's death is <u>untrue</u>.[3] Germans can't live without gossip and if materials fail they <u>invent</u> them. In this way the news of his death had been circulated while in fact he was much improved, and is to commence his proposed journey to the continent in August. I am so rejoiced – Mr. Hill seems to be much obliged for your communication & I picked out a number of Menie and myself, adding a <u>lovely</u> one of <u>Matty</u>, which your sisters conveyed to London. Tell Menie that we are all in great dugian [sic] with Mrs Outram for not informing her that James was coming,[4] before we knew it ourselves, and I have had some rather <u>emphatic</u> letters on the subject. This is partly also because she wished the whole party to go to Seacliff, and we chose to be preengaged to Ardinconnal. I don't think she will be appeased without <u>one victim</u> at least, & so I have some thoughts of laying the whole blame on <u>Menie</u> as it can do her no harm – so far off.

   Now I think I have written as much as is <u>good</u> for you, and indeed if I go on I shall forget altogether that I am writing to <u>you</u> and go on rambling to somebody else. So with very much love to Menie, and as much for yourself as she cares to spare – just the <u>dregs</u> – I remain dear Mr. Murray
Yours very truly
Eliz Rigby
Edinr July 16 1847
Many remembrances to Gilbert & Mrs G:[5]

   1. Ainslie Place was the Smith family home. The implications of romance relate to James Smith (recently returned from abroad) and Matilda Rigby.

   2. Perhaps Ardenconnel near Rhu, on the shores of the Gare Loch.

   3. Count de la Gardie was a family friend resident in Reval (now Tallinn) in Estonia. Elizabeth often acted as an intermediary between John Murray and the Count, ordering the books that were regularly sent to Reval.

   4. James Smith, who later became engaged to Matilda Rigby, was a merchant in Ceylon, and Mrs Outram (perhaps through her son, General James Outram) evidently had early news that he was travelling back to Britain. A letter (17 February 1847) from Menie Smith to John Murray elaborates on Elizabeth's dudgeon: 'Elizth especially has taken up the idea that James is trifling with Matilda's feelings – what can I longer say? The Rigbys are making preparations for his immediate appearance amongst us, and next mails will bring the tidings that he is not coming. When you were with us I observed a cooling in Mrs Rigby's manner to us, and I really <u>dread</u> the consequences

of the arrival of the next mails'. And in her next letter, 'all I can do is to treat my dear Matilda with the greatest affection & confidence & try and conciliate the rest of the family, but I do dread Elizth and her mother' (27 February 1847) (both NLS Ms.43076).

5. Probably Gilbert Smith, Menie Smith's brother, and his wife.

Letter to John Murray   *NLS Ms.42174*

Edinr Octr 1. 1847
My dear Mr. Murray
   I have been treating you very ill. In your present state of felicity you may not have found it out but I assure you I have. For I should long ago have acknowledged your very interesting and most kind letter from Basle. I shall like very much to talk about Milan Cathedral, and the nice theory of Monte Bosa, and many other things. Meanwhile I hope that dear Menie gave you a hearty welcome from me on your return to your paternal home. I will add my innigste congratulations on your first instalment at home with the sweet object of your affection, & hope that you may long be blessed in the society of each other. You have lost some very good & dear wives in the persons of your sisters, but though no longer living in the same house I know you will perpetually meet there. And I shall think it a very happy day whenever I have the double pleasure of seeing all my kind friends there. But that is a distant prospect. The more immediate one is that of seeing Menie & you among us here. Now that the occasion is so near I cd wish it were over, & all the sad followings after. For some time I have been very busy & now we are very glad to be so as without incessant employment I shd be lower that I ought to be. I know you agree with me that there is no family in the world to whom we can give a sister, or from whom we can take something nearer still, with greater happiness and confidence. Therefore I endeavour to silence all thoughts of my own selfish loss, and to keep the real good of my dear sister perpetually in sight. We are all very well and have been engaging in the visits of some Simpson and Hooker cousins,[1] which were only too short. My friend Miss Swinton is looking most blooming. It is almost amusing to observe how very similar are the occupations of respective families, for Miss Agnes S: day is also approaching, and indeed Matilda and she have had a pull for the same which would not do, since some of us are to be at each.[2]
   To make up for this very dull letter I enclose you the extract of a letter from a friend, whom Menie will remember under the name of

Mrs. Grant,[3] & with whom you may remember I once spent a day in a lunatic asylum. She is now the wife of the Cavaliere Buonarotti – an elderly gentleman – heir of Michel Angelo's house, treasures & name, of whom all the world knows at Florence, & for whom, being of Italian parents & a Catholic, our friend was well fitted. She has just written us an account of his present life, including some discoveries that I am sure will much interest you & Menie. If you thought them fitted for the Athenaeum I wd send the extracts there.

I have been much engrossed with Rachel, whom I saw two successive nights, & could have seen ten.[4] Nothing but that unprecedented deed of honor at Paris could have disturbed her image from my mind. But that upset every thing. Since then we have heard Jenny Lind & are in the very select minority who think her a deserving hardworking person, with many tricks, but no really great singer. As Mrs. Gartshore says, "an industrious Bulfinch but not a Nightingale." She in truth disappointed even the slender expectations I had formed.[5]

Now my dear Mr. Murray I must have done. You must be very busy. I shall be glad when I can be so – I mean in the Q:R: sense.
With warm love to my & yr dear Menie
Ever your's most truly
Eliz: Rigby
Wd not you like to have the Michel Angelo letters to publish!!

1. Joseph Dalton Hooker (1817–1911), Elizabeth's cousin, botanist and Director of Royal Botanic Gardens Kew between 1865 and 1885. See Leonard Huxley, *Life and Letters of Joseph Dalton Hooker, based upon materials collected and arranged by Lady Hooker*, 2 vols. (London: John Murray, 1918); and Ray Desmond, *Sir Joseph Dalton Hooker: Traveller and Plant Collector* (London: Antique Collectors' Club, 1999).

2. Matilda married James Smith on 11 October 1847.

3. Rosina Grant-Vendramin (1814–56), the Anglo-Italian wife of Count Cosimo Buonarroti (1790–1858) and instrumental in establishing the Casa Buonarroti in Florence.

4. Mademoiselle Rachel was Elisabeth Rachel Félix (1821–56), the French classical tragedienne who toured Europe.

5. The famous singer Jenny Lind (1820–87). On 25 September 1848 Marion Murray wrote to John Murray, 'On Saturday Anne & I dined at the Rigbys, and met there Mrs Jones, as one does. She, Elizabeth had been to Jenny Lind's concert, so our conversation turned altogether on music, abuse of the popular "Jenny" which Annie and I very soon tired of, not being able to enter into the very minute criticism that she was subjected to, poor thing. I was rather provoked to find our dear friend E.R. giving way to the weak-

ness of finding so much fault with one so highly gifted as Mrs Lind, & Mrs
Jones is an affected woman, & echos all that E. says, to be sure I never heard
the great Jenny, but I feel I am too ignorant not to be enchanted with her'
(NLS Ms.43076).

Letter to John Murray   *NLS Ms.42174*

Edinr Septr 21. 1848
My dear Mr. Murray
   I am glad to take advantage of an opportunity to write to you,
though it is one which will only give you trouble.[1]
   You were kind enough to interest yourself in Re[1] Matilda's harp, &
in case you should have time to call at Erard's I send you the necessary
M.S stating the whole complaint. My sister Jane has drawn it out from
Matilda's letters, I think very clearly, & you will find the different items
marked 1.2.3.4. in the paper and in the file. The object is to give Erard
a thorough blowing up so that he may feel himself "the most blowed up
man alive" & 2ndly that the bill may be materially reduced. I leave both
in your hands with great confidence. We were very sorry not to have a
peep of you on your passage through Edinr especially as we might have
dropped in upon you on the Thursday evening had we not been too
modest. But as long as you were kind enough to leave dear Menie among
us I forgive you. We meet often and remark with pleasure that she is
stranger. To day I have had a seat in the little phaeton as they were kind
enough to fetch me up from a call at Leith. I wish I could say my dear
mother's rheumatic suffering were milder, but she is so disabled with this
severe summer that I doubly dread the winter. We now expect my dear
and much tried sister by the next steamer from Petersburg. This will be
a trying time to all, and I own I do not at present see light through the
cloud, but I remember the motto "Faites bien − rien que pourra"[2]
   I am sorry that your dear sisters have have anxiety on Maria's
account, but I make not doubt your kind arrangements for them at
Brighton will restore all parties.
   I have received the several German handbooks. Arendt's life is very
interesting as far as his boyhood goes, with a picture of the life on the
shores of Pomerania intimately related, & as you know to the Provinces
of the Baltic. But as he grows up he becomes like most gentlemen,
much less fascinating. Nortiz & Munster I am gradually mastering.
Now dear Mr Murray believe me your's always truly
Eliz: Rigby

1. Latin, 'in the matter of'.

2. A reference to her sister Maria Justina (1808–89), evidently separated from her Estonian husband and en route to England. Unlike her elder sister Anne de Wahl, Maria Justina never divorced. Maria Justina appears to be the model for the Anglo-Estonian baroness in the *Jewess*, where Elizabeth removes her husband altogether from the narrative ('we must confess that it better suits our purpose to extract him from the scene', p. 176), leading her distant cousin Harriet Martineau to believe that Elizabeth had been malicious in her treatment of her Estonian in-laws: 'You see Eliz*th*'s malice in the abominable treatment of her brother-in-law, Justina's husband, in "the Jewess," where she makes insinuations wh he has no power of meeting'; Kenneth Fielding and Ian Campbell, 'New Letters of Harriet Martineau to Jane Carlyle', *Women's Writing*, 9.3 (2002), pp. 379–93 (p. 389).

Letter to John Murray   *NLS Ms.42174*

Edinr Octr 6. 1848.

My dear Mr. Murray

Many thanks for your kind letter and enclosure. You always treat me so handsomely that I can each time only reiterate my acknowledgements. I am glad "Music" meets with your approval.[1] I have lately been making up a paper on Edinburgh Old Town – chiefly the High Street, which I have sent to Fraser, when it comes out, which I conclude will be next month,[2] I shall remind you to look through it, for it sometimes strikes me that a pretty book might be made of Edinburgh and its environs – and one which would not offend a Scotch public.

I wrote to Marion yesterday informing her that my dear sister had arrived having absconded in an English schooner without a passport, as they might have waited three months longer for one. Not least what it will be duly made out, and then nobody will know that she no longer needs it. She and her two nice girls are well and recovering quickly from the fatigues of their journey. We have a full home, for Aunt and John Simpson are still with us. I am <u>so</u> thankful. Walter Lockhart is better. Let's hope for improvement in the other things afterwards.

Believe me dear Mr. Murray

Yr's very truly

Eliz: Rigby

1. 'Music', *Quarterly Review*, vol. 83 (September 1848), pp. 481–515.

2. 'Views of Edinburgh' appeared in *Fraser's Magazine*, vol. 38 (November 1848), pp. 481–94.

Letter to John Murray   *NLS Ms.42174*

My dear Mr. Murray

Can you kindly give me a little information as to the <u>Dames Houses</u> at Eton, & whether they be things which there is any natural hope of obtaining, if we were to take the steps. & also something about what those steps should be, or wd you refer me to somebody who can answer these questions. You may guess their object is for my sister – & if such an occupation for her be impossible to obtain with an average share of interest we shall dismiss it from our heads, & not trouble our friends to make further enquiries.[1]

I had a kind letter from Mr. Lockhart about Vanity Fair &c. I shall set about this directly. If there be anything about governesses published which I ought to see I know you will send it to me.[2]

In haste dear Mr. Murray

Yr's most truly

Eliz: Rigby

Oh: o/c[?] another very important thing. I have promised to look out for a young French girl of good character to be under nurse to Mrs Clive's two childn. That to wash & dress & work for them & <u>talk</u> to them (under a responsible servant) at £20 a year. Now this is so good an offer that among the number of refugees in London it surely can't be difficult to meet with a girl too happy to accept it. Will you mention it to any French friend.

Edinr. Octr. 9. 1848.

> 1. Maria Justina was to support herself and her daughters by running a Dame's House in Eton.
>
> 2. 'Vanity Fair and Jane Eyre', Quarterly Review, vol. 84 (December 1848), pp. 153–85. All correspondence relating to this infamous review of Jane Eyre and Vanity Fair is frustratingly absent from the correspondence with John Murray. See my article "'In her Own *métier*": The *Quarterly* review of *Jane Eyre*', in *Women's History Review*, forthcoming 2009.

Letter to Marion Murray   *NLS Ms.42174*

Edinr Janry 24 1849

My dearest Menie

How happy I am to rejoice with those that rejoice. Dear Annie's welcome news from Glasgow yesterday relieved our hearts of a very

heavy load and turned our fears into thanksgiving. I trust now you
may all await this next mail with well grounded hopes of seeing
your dear mother's handwriting. I trust indeed it will please our
gracious God to spare your tender hearts any further trials of this
kind, though I know that did He appoint them strength would be
given to bear His will.

I have obtained from Mr. E: a very ready assent to my informing
Mr. Murray and you of this matter. So you must <u>consider</u> yourselves
<u>now</u> put in possession of it. He indeed seems pleased that I should
desire it. He returns from Devonshire on Saturday. I suspect John
will beat him up on Sunday! He owns himself very ignorant of all
forms in such matters not having committed such follies, I suppose,
<u>often</u> before – as a proof of which he thinks that all the world might
know it without any harm, which idea will have to be put out of
him. He talks of coming for two days next month, and has some
<u>wild</u> ideas connected with that visit which will have to be <u>nipped</u>.
You will think me very composed through all this, but I must <u>nip</u>
that idea too – for in reality I am sometimes, <u>very</u> disturbed <u>very</u>
<u>often</u>! The slightness of our acquaintance still comes over me <u>most</u>
harrassingly, and sometimes I see nothing but the leaving all I hold
most dear, and dear <u>Edinburgh</u> into the bargain, for a stranger I
hardly know the look of yet! – for I have quite forgotten what <u>he</u>
<u>is like</u>![1]

I am not going to trifle with him, my dearest, nor to be
unreasonable, but I must be allowed to feel a little <u>variable</u> though I
may not act so. He is <u>improving</u> in the writing department, but terrifies
me with the piece of <u>perfection</u> he expects. Altogether there never was
an old bachelor committed such a willful bit of imprudence before. May
he live long to repent it!

I hope you see <u>my</u> dear John occasionally, but he has been very ill
with influenza – all for want of that little article of clothing.

Goodbye my dearest Menie – I long for your handwriting again.
Yr own <u>incomfortable</u> and <u>yet happy</u>
Eliz: R.
We have just received the tidings of my cousin Gurney Turner's death
in India. A great shock to my aunt and his family. Quite a young man
– left a widow & child.[2]

<ol>
<li>Elizabeth became engaged to Charles Eastlake in January 1849. They married on 9 April at St John's Church in Edinburgh.</li>
<li>Gurney Turner, son of Dawson Turner, died at Calcutta, 28 November 1848.</li>
</ol>

Letter to John Gibson Lockhart   *NLS Ms.929, no. 76*

Dear Mr Lockhart[1]

You will think that demur of mine about Miss Martineau[2] very
deceitful when I tell you that it was only a preface to a "notice to quit".

I have engaged myself to serve another master, &, I can only hope
that he will be as indulgent to me in all respects as I have every found
you in one.

I hope you will not think I have risked my happiness more than all
women must risk it, but rather less so, when I tell you that it is Mr.
Eastlake to whom the trust is given.

I don't say that I wish to cut the Q:R: – far from it – but I hope he
will employ me too much to leave me any spare time for independent
doings. & that at all events I shall retain what I have valued most in my
connection with the Q:R: which is your kind friendship.[3]

I have been much grieved at your dear sister's death. I was in some
measure prepared that it must be & that it was to be desired for her.
I had written her a long letter about three weeks before, to which I
received an affectionate answer through a third person.

Believe me dear Mr. Lockhart with much regard
Your's very truly
Eliz: Rigby
Edinburgh January 29 1849

1. John Gibson Lockhart; see letter, 13 August 1841, n. 1.

2. Harriet Martineau (1802–76), writer on social and economic issues of the
   day. She was a distant cousin to Elizabeth. In a letter to Jane Carlyle in May
   1844, Harriet Martineau wrote: 'I must answer you about Eliz*th* Rigby ...
   No cousin of mine, thank you ... The women of that family are (& esp*cy*
   Eliz*th* & her mother) most unprincipled; – ie, untruthful, scheming (but with
   too much rashness not to fail in the end) & malicious beyond the malice of
   scheming women. They took a vast fit of piety about 5 years since, all in a
   day. I suppose it has somehow come into combination with their London
   and Edinburgh objects. Just when most pious, they quarrelled with a bitterly
   slandered Dr. Rigby'; Kenneth Fielding and Ian Campbell, 'New Letters of
   Harriet Martineau to Jane Carlyle', *Women's Writing*, 9.3 (2002), pp. 379–93
   (p. 388).

3. In fact Elizabeth continued to contribute to the *Quarterly Review*. During
   the years of her marriage she wrote eight articles, all related to art.

Letter to John Gibson Lockhart   *NLS Ms.929, no. 78*

Edinburgh April 6. 1849
Dear Mr. Lockhart
    I had intended writing to you, at all events, today, for I was
unwilling to quit my old name without once more assuring you how
grateful I feel for all the kindness I have received from you under that
familiar appellation. I hope the new one may fare as well in that respect.
    I cannot tell you how much pleasure you give me, & I am sure Mr.
Eastlake also, by your very kind gift. You could have bestowed nothing
on me more valuable & acceptable. I only quarrel with its <u>munificence</u>,
which is far too great.[1] There is no gift I have rec.d on this occasion
which has given & will always give me so much real gratification. You
must only add to its value, if you have not done so already, by writing
your name & anything else you will in the first volume of the novels, &
also in that of the Life. If you have dispatched them already to Fitzroy
Square without this indispensable <u>enhancement</u> I shall bring the two
volumes one day myself to you, & <u>compel</u> you to fulfil my request.
    It is not a light or an easy thing to leave a happy house & a dear
mother, especially when the delusions of <u>youth</u> are past, but I believe
that I shall be happy, & feel that if I am so, Mamma will be so too.
    I remain dear Mr. Lockhart with much regard
Yours most truly & obliged
Eliz: Rigby

    1. Presumably a gift of the complete works of Walter Scott.

Letter to Mrs Acton Tindal   *CLS M10990*

7 Fitzroy Square
July 14. 1851
My dear Mrs Tindal[1]
    I have too long delayed not only returning as I now do your
most interesting M.S. but also writing to you which I was longing
& intending to do before I received them. I have read & reread, &
lingered over particular passages with that <u>sad</u> pleasure which the tone of
your writing always excites in me − & which proceeds from something
deeper than mere gratified <u>taste</u>. I have been in the country with my
husband for a few days − at quiet rural village inns. I took your packet

with me for solitary enjoyment, as my London life just now gives too little opportunity for such, but I had left your letter behind. "The Infanticide" made the deepest impression on me – witness many a tear – & now that I reread yr letter I find that it is also one of your favourites. You have such a rapid grasp in sketching events – on, on, you go – knowing so perfectly what to touch & what to omit. And yet though the Infanticide moved me so deeply I can hardly say there is one among these pieces that does not. "The Picture" is a beautiful summing up of a life. The Hymn to the Martyrs of Truth & Science is to my view exceedingly fine & tho' I mention our sweet departed one's name last it is only because that piece lies deepest of all in my heart. I can hardly judge how it may strike one who did not know her, but I am very sure that you conjure her up irresistibly to those who do. I would like when you come to town to ask you to let me send that piece to Lady Howard Douglas – the gentle unselfish mourner, who adored the wondrous being she yet has found grace & power to resign unmurmuringly into her Maker's Hands.[2] Thank you very much for trusting me with these precious papers. But I have much to thank you for, dear Mrs Tindal, sweet gifts have you sent me, when not only they, but the kind interest & sympathy which prompted them most welcome.

Ah! your sweet line "If ye love can ye wish them back again" was ever in my thoughts – a comfort to me. I hope I have given my sweet lifeless babe unmurmeringly to Him, a sinless soul, a bright link between the regions of light & this soiled earth, on which I may hold in my upward passage. I hope I am content, but you need not to be told of those yearnings which sometimes will interrupt the perfect sacrifice of the will & affections.[3] I am thankful to say I am well again & I have our house full of dear guests – a sister & niece from Russia – one long separated from her native land, & now returned to speak of scenes of girlhood 20 years ago, more than of anything that happened in the wide interim[4] – also my dear mother is here & another – or rather two other sisters coming & going. I rejoice to here that you are coming, but will not keep yr M.S. so long, that is to the 18th lest you shd want it before leavg home. I shall venture to bespeak a little of your's & Mr. Tindal's company during your stay in London, & in the hope of soon meeting.

Believe me dear Mrs Tindal
Your's very truly
Eliz: Eastlake

1. Henrietta Euphemia Acton Tindal (née Harrison) (1817–79), poet and
    novelist. She was the wife of Acton Tindal (1811–80), Lord of the Manor
    at Aylesbury and a close friend of Austen Henry Layard who was elected
    MP for Aylesbury in 1852. Mrs Tindal was a contributor to *Ainsworth's*

Magazine, for which she wrote on Old Masters, Dutch and Flemish painters and Albrecht Dürer in 1848. She published two volumes of poems, *Lines and Leaves* in 1850 and *Rhymes and Legends*, published posthumously in 1879. She sometimes wrote under the pseudonym 'Diana Butler', the name under which she published her novel, *The Heirs of Blackridge Manor* (1856).

2. Mother of Mrs Murray Gartshore. Mrs Acton Tindal published a poem, 'The Eve of All Souls, in memory of Mrs. Murray Gartshore', in the *New Monthly Magazine*, vol. 96 (1852), pp. 456–57.

3. Elizabeth gave birth to a stillborn daughter on 4 June.

4. Gertrude de Rosen, visiting from Estonia, was present at the birth.

Letter to John Murray   *NLS Ms.42175*

7 Fitzroy Square
March 8 1852
My dear Mr. Murray[1]
Many thanks for your liberal cheque – I return you the receipt signed by us both. I have nearly completed all I have in hand of Waagen,[2] but have no idea how much more there is to do – nor how much there will be to undo. This morning I spent at the British Museum following the course of priest as he describes them – which is a very interesting journey.[3]

I hear from one of my cousins that Mr. Dawson Turner's pictures will be sold at Christie's in the beginning of May, which will be a <u>pinch</u> to me, and how much more to all of them.[4]
Believe me dear Mr. Murray Your's most truly
Eliz Eastlake

1. Enclosed with receipt: 'London Mar 8 1852. Received of John Murray Esq the sum of fifty guineas for the entire copyright of two articles in the Quarterly Review nos 158 and 166 – respectively and entitled "Music" and "The Art of Dress" and I hereby promise a further assignment if required. C.L. Eastlake Eliz Eastlake'. The payment was to both Eastlakes because a married woman's earnings belonged to her husband.

2. Gustav Waagen (1794–1868), art historian and Director of the Gemäldegalerie in Berlin.

3. Elizabeth had undertaken to translate Gustav Waagen's *Treasures of Art in Great Britain, being an account of the chief collections of paintings, drawings, sculptures, illuminated mss etc*, 3 vols. (London: John Murray, 1854–57) and *Galleries and Cabinets of Art in Great Britain* (London: John Murray, 1857). See Frank

Herrmann, 'Dr. Waagen's Works of Art and Artists in England', *Connoisseur*, 161 (March 1966), pp. 173–77.

4. Dawson Turner had remarried following his wife's death in 1850 and was subsequently estranged from many members of his family. He moved from Yarmouth to London, selling much of his art collection and library.

Letter to John Murray   *NLS Ms.42175*

Dresden Hotel de Saxe
Septr 4 1852
My dear Mr. Murray

I have proposed writing to you for the last day or two, as I consider that our journey has now nearly reached its meridian, at least in point of time. You & dear Menie may profitably have had some report of us from that common recipient of all our news – my dear mother – as far at least as the assurance that the complete change of scene & occupation has in great measure fulfilled my hopes in its beneficial affect on Sir Chas' health, & I have had & have the great satisfaction of seeing him enjoying himself thoroughly & that in his own line. Our tour hitherto has been one succession of fine pictures, & we are reminded at every fresh halt how richly it answers to a city to possess a gallery. These are the shrines nowadays which bring the stranger from afar.

I am happy to say that all hitherto has prospered remarkably well with us – thanks to fine weather & "Murray".[1] We were very nearly run down by her Majesty on crossing, & very nearly lost Tucker in a confusion of railways between Lille & Bruges but escaped both dangers very happily & now this latter individual has become so accomplished a traveller that I will trust him anywhere for finding us & everything else.[2]

Our picture raptures began at once at Bruges with the great van Eyck picture, & we did not know how to part from that oyster aged, flabby cheeked old burgher who kneels before the Virgin with an expression of intense devotion which would beautify any face.[3] The Memlings also came in for their share of admiration, especially those exquisite specimens at St. John's Hospital, & nothing we have since seen has lessened them in our admiration. The simple portrait of v. Eyck's wife also enchanted us, tho' it throws a doubt on the fact of the picture in our Nat. Gallery being v. Eyck & his wife which rested chiefly on the supposed fact of the identity of the lady there with the lady in Bruges, who would have been greatly affronted at the comparison.

Ghent is a barren desert as respects pictures, but Antwerp was a feast, & Rubens I think now fully shares Sir Chas' affections with Titian & Palma Vecchio. He was fortunate in finding the great Ruben's Descent & Elevation already cleaned & not yet put up, but standing on a level with the eye in the great so called workshop of the Cathedral. They have been admirably cleaned, which has consisted chiefly in stripping off overpaintings & allowing the original work to emerge so that Rubens was seen in his glory. Antwerp is more delightful than ever & we heard good accounts of its improving prosperity, & we came in for part of the <u>Kermess</u> there (which I will trouble you to explain in Handbook)[4] there was more than the usual allowance of processions, bands of music, <u>Harmonic</u>, & other popular jollifications. Cologne which we took in one leap did not look to advantage after Antwerp – that is as regards the people – the hotels &c, but its glorious churches were reflected in the same glorious Rhine as ever – the Cathedral promising a far grander mass than when I saw it last. The interior is most exquisite now & we did full justice to the splendid old painted windows & also to the odious new ones. Nothing can be worse also than the painting of the choir – I don't mean with the colours which are becoming rather subdued now, but the general coating of heavy yellow which they have given to the walls & piers of the chair, & which is put the more to shame by the contrast with the piers of the nave which are as yet of the unpolluted stone than which nothing can be grander in tint. From Cologne to Berlin we took another leap, which proved so fatiguing that we have vowed in future always to divide our journeys when possible. We left Cologne at 10 at night, & reached Berlin at 3 the next afternoon "a regular grind" as Eton boys say, with nothing to beguide the way except an occasional chapter of abuse of my old antipathies the Germans, for which roadside accomodation gave plenty of occasion & which greatly refreshed me. At Berlin good old Waagen soon welcomed us & next morning was in full glory introducing us to the treasures of the museum. And well may he be vain of them, for never were more instructive and interesting pictures more exquisitely arranged and taken care of. Sir Chas instantly declared that he should be a fixture in that gallery for days to come, and Dresden and Vienna and all distant attractions faded from our thoughts and we felt that we could willingly devote our whole time to the Berlin Museum. We carried this to such an extreme that Waagen had the greatest difficulty in inducing us to see anything else and every morning we went half an hour earlier, bribing the good natured officials to open the doors earlier till at last 8 o'clock found us there. Sir Chas made the most complete examination of the most interesting pictures wheeling about a high ladder from room to room, and making hasty notes which he has great trouble in deciphering, but which will in due time contibute to swell the 2nd vol: of the Materials of Oil Paintings.[5] And indeed but for the gallery Berlin would not have detained us a day and that would have been chiefly devoted to doing homage to Rauch's magnificent monument to Fred: the Great.[6] Kaulbach's work we admired for what they were worth, which is immense grasp of mind and power of drawing, but Cornelius is the most thorough imposition that ever German wisdom worshipped.[7] Charlottenburg we voted a hoax. Their garten &c will only do for people who can get nothing better. In Dresden our ecstasies have been quite reversed – the city and all around & about it enchants us, & the gallery disappoints us. It is worth coming from Berlin here to prove how much the best pictures depend on good lighting, arrangement, and care to please. With the exception of the divine St Cecilia I find that the gallery has left me very cold. Its other chef d'oeuvres be in the late Italian school, for which the interesting, earnest early Italian school at Berlin have quite spoilt me – and even those are so badly seen and no chair to be had that I get out of humour with them. The Titians are poor, and the Tribute Money is a very disappointing picture. Sir Chas has found most gratifications among the grand Paul Veronese, whom he thinks the king of the gallery, but he too is much disappointed with the general effect. But a fine picture gallery is building, over which Schultz the Director kindly took us, and which promises to be beautiful and well adapted to purpose.[8] The plan of the screens and side lights is also adapted here, and we hope will be so in our future Nat: Gallery. After the first day or two I left Sir Chas to bury himself in the gallery alone and with Tucker's escort explored the picturesque beauties of the city, which are inummerable. Backgrounds and foregrounds are all charming, the hills and view so fresh and blue and the house architecture so sparkling and varied. The two bridges group beautifully together and wherever I wanted a view there was sure to be some pretty eminence ready at hand, with wide steps up to it and low benches exactly where wanted.[9] Tucker reciprocated all my feelings of admiration, or if his were over before mine he would philosophically sit patiently and study Murray. I am sure you have no more devoted admirer than he, and he knows you by heart from the tables of money change, to rules of conduct. He has brought the same good sense and good [paper torn] abroad with him which distinguishes him in Fitzroy Sqre and is invaluable as a traveling servant. The want of language is no impediment – he picks up information in the most surprising way, and has an instinct for smelling a cheat. The luggage he sticks to as a standard bearer to his flag, and the moment we alight from a train he

bustles up intuitively to the right official, and says with a good natured
smile no one could resist "I say – the luggage!" however the luggage
is sure to be all round him in course of time. He visits the galleries
with us, & knows at all events as much as most visitors – judging from
the sapient remarks I overhear – his opinion being summed up in one
unfailing trenchant remark "These here pictures must be worth a deal
of money"! Wherever we go he is on the look out for news of England,
& while I sit sketching he entertains me with "a dreadful burglary
committed in the North from fellows in masks" or "the Queen has
come in for a grand liggacy" & all that. He is very select in his choice
of acquaintances, & has no taste for foreign couriers, let them talk
English ever so well, & knows precisely in 12 hours what's the character
of an hotel by the manners of the waiter. Certainly I would not change
him for any courier in the world, & am daily thankful that we brought
him. We have all the comfort of an excellent English servant & none of
the penalties, for he is contented & happy with everything.

 Septr 12. This letter has halted till it finds us just leaving Vienna,
& now I am sorry to say must finish it off in a hurry, as packing time
is approaching. We left sweet Dresden with that vow of returning to
it which softens the pang of departure, travelled with very agreeable
English companions to Prague – crammed as fine a general conception
of that glorious city into three hours as was possible & were off.
The next day at 5 o'clock for Vienna where we have spent five most
interesting days. The Belvedere gallery has cast even Berlin into the
shade, & Sir Chas has reveled in his dear Venetian school, spending
the day there from early morning till late afternoon. The Lichtenstein
& Esterhazy Gallery we have also visited but otherwise excepting the
Ambras Museum which Tucker & I went over – & drives to Schönburn
&c we have done none of the sights, & make up our minds that our
time & our strength not more than enough to devote to our line.[10]
I must rejoice in seeing Sir Chas so interested & to hear of things &
places which must be left to "another year". Our time is fast running
out now, but still we have resolved to accomplish Venice, & shall
probably after a week there return as straight as we can by Munich &
Frankfort, so we start to-morrow for Gratz, & now I feel will being
some of our really severe travelling. We find you of inestimable comfort
& hear your praises as we come along, which do my heart good. I fear
you are too complete for us to bring you home any notes, but I have
made some hotel memoranda, & one or two corrections in the art way.
I shall bring home a few sketches which indulgent friends will take
interest in, tho' some of them very hurried.

 So now dear Mr. Murray God bless you & your's. Dear Menie

knows that this egotistical letter is for her as well as you. I trust she is well, & the dear childn, & Annie, to whom give my best love when you write. I have good news from my dear people at Eton, who are very kind in writing also from my kind Cath: Swinton.[11] The first week in October will see us home, & me very soon enquiring for news in Albemarle St.

Always dear Mr. Murray your's most truly

Eliz Eastlake

Kindest love to your sisters.

1. A reference to Murray's *Handbooks for Travellers*, a series of guidebooks begun in 1836, and in particular to Murray's *Hand-book for Travellers on the Continent: being a guide through Holland, Belguim, and Northern Germany, and Along the Rhine, from Holland to Switzerland*. The 1852 handbook was the eighth edition. Murray encouraged his friends to report back with comments and changes to the material contained in the Handbooks.

2. Nicholas Tucker (c. 1821–95), Eastlake's manservant. Tucker accompanied the Eastlakes on a number of their travels abroad and following Sir Charles's death he continued as Lady Eastlake's butler, before leaving service in 1869. He remained a great favourite of Elizabeth's and she left him a legacy of £250 in her will.

3. *The Madonna with Canon van der Paele* (1436), now in the Groeninge Museum, Bruges, but then in the Academy of Painting.

4. Kermess is a Flemish fair.

5. Charles Lock Eastlake, *Materials for a History of Oil Painting*, 2 vols. (London: Longman, Brown, Green & Longman, 1847).

6. Christian Daniel Rauch (1777–1857), German sculptor of the colossal bronze equestrian statue of Frederick the Great in Unter den Linden.

7. Wilhelm von Kaulbach (1804–74), German painter who worked with Peter von Cornelius (1783–1867) on the frescoes in the Glyptothek in Munich.

8. The Gemäldegalerie Alte Meister (Old Masters Picture Gallery) was built by Gottfried Sempter between 1847 and 1855 as a wing of the Zwinger Palace.

9. A view of Dresden is reproduced in J&CI, facing p. 286.

10. The collections of the Prince of Liechtenstein in the garden palace at Rossau, Vienna; Esterházy Gallery in Vienna; Ambras Castle is outside Innsbruck.

11. Eton was home to Maria Justina de Rosen and Mrs Rigby.

Letter to G. F. Watts   *Heinz Archive and Library,*
National Portrait Gallery, London, Letters to G. F. Watts Album 11, p. 66

Wimbledon
August 1 1853
Dear Mr. Watts[1]
I am not allowed to leave good John Murray's hospitable roof in time
for the proposed sitting tomorrow. If I hear nothing to the contrary
in Fitzroy Square from you I will be at Charles St. at 1/4 past 12 on
Wednesday.
In haste yrs truly
Eliz Eastlake

1. George Frederick Watts (1817–1904), English painter commissioned by John
   Murray to make portraits of the chief writers for his publishing house. This
   letter is docketed 'Lady Eastlake 1 charcoal drawing', although the present
   whereabouts of the drawing are unknown. The drawing is mentioned by
   Elizabeth in a letter from 1853, now lost but appearing in George Paston,
   At John Murray's: Records of a Literary Circle 1843–92 (London: John Murray,
   1932), pp. 118–19: 'I must tell you that Watt's drawing, for which I have given
   two very long sittings, is *most magnificent*. I can't conceive anything finer.
   It's like an animated marble. As to the likeness, I can't believe in it – the
   beauty is too much even for my vanity – but you will have a chef d'oeuvre
   of art, which is a comfort. He has every reason to be proud of his work,
   and might make his three thousand a year as well as Richmond'. See also
   letter, 9 October 1884.

Letter to John Blackwood   *NLS Ms.4101, no. 304*

7 Fitzroy Square
Decr 3 1853
<u>Private</u>
Dear Mr Blackwood[1]
   Sir Charles & myself derive much pleasure from the perusal of the
Magazine with which you do me the honour to supply me that I the
more regret to have to call your attention to an erroneous passage which
occurs in a paper on the National Gallery in the number just received.
Without any observation on the spirit & extent of knowledge displayed
in that paper I wd wish simply to ask you on what authority Sir Chas'
name is connected with a passage – page 650 column 1st – where he is

stated to have spoken ambiguously about glazing, & also to have said "he would not hesitate to clean a picture, & "to strip off the whole of its glazings". As a sole answer to this statement I can only assure you of Sir Chas entire denial of such words, or of such a sense in any words; which, independent of his assurance, those in any way acquainted with his practice as a painter will readily believe. The Report of the Committee containing the evidence is not yet published, & as I should be unwilling to think that you wd quote from the accounts given in the Morning Post, I am the more anxious to know the authority for the statement you have published in Sir Chas' name.[2]

I have written on my own responsibility relying on your long known kindness to give your full attention to my request. For while, like all individuals in any way before the public, Sir Chas is too much exposed to mere party attacks in the newspapers not to be indifferent to them, I know too well the estimation in which he holds your Magazine not to hasten to protest against what I hope will prove to be as great an injustice to yourself as it is to him.

Believe me dear Mr Blackwood

Your's truly

Eliz Eastlake

1. John Blackwood (1818–79), publisher and editor of *Blackwood's Edinburgh Magazine*.

2. *Blackwood's Edinburgh Magazine* ran an article on the National Gallery (vol. 74 (December 1853), pp. 643–62) accusing the gallery of picture cleaning and misquoting Eastlake. An article on the Report of Commission in the next volume (vol. 75 (February 1854), pp. 167–84) corrects the offending statement, admitting Eastlake's general aversion to cleaning pictures. Both articles were written by John Eagles, the art critic, artist and poet.

Letter to John Blackwood   *NLS Ms.4101, no. 306*

7 Fitzroy Square

Decr 10 1853

Dear Mr Blackwood

I shd be very sorry to be insensible to the kindness with which you have entered into this matter – & still more so that you shd think me so. Still I cannot agree with you as to the unimportance of the passage attributed to Sir Charles. On the contrary such worlds from his mouth are downright treason to art, & such as he cannot be otherwise than most impatient to be cleared from. I must therefore ask you to have the kindness, which believe me I shall highly estimate, to insert a plain contradiction of that passage as follows "Sir Chas Eastlake says that he would not hesitate to clean a picture & to strip off the whole of its glazings" in any form customary when a mistake is made, but of course as public as the mistatement has been. Even as regards his not hesitating to clean a picture the statement is untrue, since any one troubling themselves to look at the Minutes of the Nat: Gallery wd see that he strenuously opposed the cleaning the pictures at all.

As regards your correspondent I can have but little faith in the sincerity of his apology, when I find that he voluntarily quoted against Sir Chas & I doubt not against the other eminent parties he has amused himself with attacking from accounts notoriously supplied by Mr. Morris Moore to the Morning Post, & that also with the Report of the Commission in his possession. So much for the impartiality of his intentions – while his ignorance of the mearning of the word glazing wd leave a doubt of his ability to treat such as subject at all.

You must not for one moment think that I shd ever protest against any difference of opinion between your Magazine and Sir Chas, but I only trust that another time you will examine whence the evidence against, & in him against the Academy, proceeds.

I have not shown Sir Chas our correspondence, nor shall I till I can show him also the contradiction of the statement which annoys him. Believe me dear Mr. Blackwood

Your's obliged

Eliz Eastlake

Letter to Blackwood   *NLS Ms.4101, no. 308*

7 Fitzroy Square

Decr 20 1853

Dear Mr. Blackwood

I was in Devonshire when your letter of the 14th arrived, or I wd sooner have acknowledged the favor of it. I have since shown it to Sir Charles & spoken openly of the subject to him. He desires me to say that he wd rather you shd <u>not</u> insert the contradiction in question in yr next number, but prefers to rely on your setting the matter right & making the amende[1] you propose in the future article you allude to. I may also add for myself that a contradiction "on Sir Charles' authority" wd be no compensation in my eyes – for, having the means of entirely convincing yourselves from the real Evidence how utterly unfounded was the assertion your writer has put into Sir C's mouth I conceive that the contradiction, no less than the statement, should be on your own authority. Sir Chas further remarks that he believes himself well acquainted with the writer of the article in question & is therefore the more grieved that he shd have taken his materials from such a source, as he surely wd never expect Sir C. to have time or inclination to contradict the unwarranted statements made in the newspapers, however, he may regret those in such a periodical as your's. Sir Chas feels that he cd set this gentleman right on points regarding the Academy where he has been greatly misled – not that he means this as any expression of a wish to do so, but simply to show his regret that, in an article intended to lead the public mind, more care has not been taken to enquire into the nature of the evidence he has depended on, & so to obtain real fact. For though Mr. Morris Moore's name is unknown to you, you may be quite sure that it is well known to the writer of the article. But the Report of the Evidence is now out, & in Sir Chas evidence regarding glazing it wd be difficult to find sentiments more directly opposed than those which he really did utter & those which you have published under his name. Perhaps you wd let the gentleman in question see this letter.

I am glad to turn from this uncomfortable subject & to congratulate you on your marriage which I have reason to trust has taken place. I do trust it will be the date of much happiness to yourself & the lady, to whom I beg my compliments. Believe me dear Mr Blackwood your's very truly
Eliz Eastlake

    1. Reparation or recantation.

Letter to John Blackwood   NLS Ms.4105, no. 27

7 Fitzroy Square
Febry 2. 1854
Dear Mr Blackwood

I should be very ungrateful if I were not immediately to acknowledge the reparation you have made Sir Chas in your present paper on the National Gallery. I assure you that he as well as myself think it full & sufficient, & are very ready to forget that it was ever needed.

I am glad to have it in my power to congratulate you on your marriage, & I trust that you & your bride have been enjoying this fine

weather somewhere. With Sir Chas' complts & mine believe me dear
Mr Blackwood
Your's obliged & truly
Eliz Eastlake

Letter to Euphemia Ruskin[1]   *ML MA 1338 T.33*

7 Fitzroy Sqre
April 13. 1854
My dearest Effie

My heart is exceedingly occupied with you & I find it difficult to
be patient <u>for</u> you – so that I can the more keenly enter into your
exceeding state of suffering. The sooner that it is over, I am convinced,
the better. You need never scruple to disturb me at any time. My heavy
work is now quite over.

My dear mother leaves me on Tuesday & I intend going with her
till Thursday, but if you or your parents were likely to wish to see me
in that time, I would stay at home. I am thankful your mother comes
as well, for you will need her softer comfort & she need [sic] to give it
too. I have read you little paper with painful interest, & that <u>finale</u> with
as much disgust as yourself & perhaps more surprise.

I have often thought whether Dean Milman[2] could be of service to
you but feared his infirmities & the natural selfishness with which men
old enough to be trusted shrink from the trouble of it, but Mrs. Milman
is a true friend to you. You must trust your father on earth, & pray that
our Father in Heaven will lead him in the best way for you. I have not
seen Mr. Brown since he cd not dine with us yesterday. I am sure of his
kindness but I think he would sacrifice too much to mercenary interests
– especially that <u>openness</u> which you ought to <u>court</u>, when this comes
on.[3] I know your mother feels as I do in this which is a great comfort
to me.

God bless you my dearest child & lead you through this thorny way.
Yr truly affte
Eliz Eastlake

1. Euphemia Ruskin (1828–97), née Gray and known affectionately as 'Effie',
wife of John Ruskin and later of John Everett Millais. This and subsequent
letters refer to the annulment of Effie's marriage to Ruskin. The two women
had met for the first time in June 1850. Effie boasted to their mutual friend,
Rawdon Brown, that Elizabeth 'is one of my beauties and so charming in
every way, so good and so womanlike, so clever and not in the least of a

blue'. Elizabeth's proprietorial interest in Effie (in the letters she addresses her as 'my darling child') leads Mary Lutyens to surmise that Effie probably 'appealed to her frustrated maternal feeling' (*Millais and the Ruskins* (London: John Murray, 1967), p. 32). Lutyens reports (pp. 31–32) that Effie first confided the reason for her unhappy marriage to Elizabeth over lunch on 2 March 1854; reasoning that, as the daughter and sister of two eminent obstetricians, she might know something about the procedures for annulment on the grounds of non-consummation. It seems equally, if not more, likely that Elizabeth was one of the few women of Effie's acquaintance who knew anything about divorce, having one divorced sister and another separated from her husband.

2. Henry Hart Milman (1791–1868), poet, historian and Dean of St Paul's. According to Mary Lutyens, the Milmans' dislike of Ruskin stemmed from his speaking ill of St Paul's Cathedral (*Millais and the Ruskins*, p. 134n.).

3. Rawdon Brown; see letter, 25 May 1854.

Letter to Euphemia Ruskin   *ML MA 1338 T.36*

7 Fitzroy Sqre
April 18. 1854
My darling child
    You have been my waking & sleeping thought since I last saw you, & the thought that I shd not see your sweet face again & that no love, not even that of your admirable parents, could take this cup from you, has drawn many a bitter tear from me. But it does comfort me, as I know it comforts your dear mother, that you have been kept in purity & honour, & that no shadow of sin rests on your young brow. Your letter this morng comforts me, tho' it wrings my heart. It will be a pleasure to me to assist yr servants if I can. At this moment I know that dear Mrs. Murray's maid has given her warning, & if I hear that your Jane wd be likely to fulfil her wishes, which are quite domestic & humble, I will write to <u>Crawley</u> & tell him to send her to Albemarle St.
    I could hardly part from your mother yesterday. I felt that she was part of you. I cannot tell you the comforts I feel in <u>knowing</u> your upright excellent parents. I am convinced now from my own observations that you cannot be in wiser hands. The legal tidings she brought me were very welcome. God is surely working out some course for you in His love & wisdom, which will enable you hereafter to look back on this troubled time & acknowledge that all did really work together for good to those who love Him.

I saw Lady Davy late yesterday. She was very anxious to see me on this matter & though with many digressions she showed me that the whole intent of her heart was to serve you to the utmost of her power by securing the immediate adherence of a few influential friends – Lady Westminster, her niece Lady Octavia &c. I only begged her not to let anyone think they were admitted to this knowledge for the sake of gossip, but for the sacred privilege of assisting a much injured long suffering fellow creature. Also not to speak of it until you should really be gone.[1]

You will have seen whom I mentioned to your mother as deserving to serve you. If you have not time to write, which you cannot have, I will engage to mention it to Boxall[2] (who has often warmly espoused yr cause to me, little knowing how <u>crying</u> it was) to the Milman's, & to Lockhart,[3] also to the dear Murrays & to gentle Mrs. Gruner.[4] I return on Thursday early & my first duty shall be to see Mrs Murray – or him – if she be not strong enough.

I will write to you fully at Bowerswell, & tell you all I know – your friends will gather together by a strong sympathy & by the need of mutual comfort. I told my dear husband before I saw your parents – I felt that the time has come, & his manly indignation has only added strength to my own feelings. You may be sure of his voice.

Now dearest, the little keepsake you have sent me is far too good, but I accept it with true love & affection & I shall ever treasure it for your sake.

I shall leave a little hamper to be sent to Bury Street tomorrow for your use on your voyage.

I have told Mamma & my sister & their woman's sympathy is a great comfort to me. Mamma's feelings are a standard to me of what all sound plain woman's minds <u>must</u> feel. She is full also of tender personal emotion for you.

Farewell my darling Effie. Let not your heart be troubled. Throw all your sorrows on the Cross.

Your true loving
Eliz. Eastlake

1. Lady Jane Davy (1780–1855), widow of Sir Humphry Davy; Lady Westminster was Elizabeth Mary Leveson-Gower, wife of Richard Grosvenor, 2nd Marquess of Westminster.

2. William Boxall's correspondence with John Ruskin seems to have ended abruptly in 1854. See M. J. H. Liversidge, 'John Ruskin and William Boxall: Unpublished Correspondence', *Apollo*, vol. 85 (January 1967), pp. 39–44.

3. Lockhart wrote to his daughter on 18 April, 'I am not surprised, but sorry, to

hear whispers of a separation between _____ _____ [*blank in original*]
and her virtuoso, whose neglects have at last exhausted her patience; but I
shall have particulars whenever I meet the Eastlakes, and till then *mum*'. See
Andrew Lang, *The Life and Letters of John Gibson Lockhart*, 2 vols. (London:
John C. Nimmo, 1897), vol. 2, p. 388. In 1846 Lockhart's daughter Charlotte
had been the object of Ruskin's amorous interest.

4. Wife of Ludwig Gruner; she lived at 12 Fitzroy Square.

Letter to Mrs Gray   *ML MA 1338 T.37*

7 Fitzroy Sqre
April 18. 1854
My dear Mrs. Gray[1]
   I feel it a pain to say my last words to <u>you</u>. All I can say is that my
acquaintance with you & Mr. Gray is in the highest degree <u>comforting</u>
to me & I am sure it will not cease here, for I shall ever think of you
with the deepest interest. My dear young friend is in wise & tender
hands & I trust with God's blessings she will recover peace of mind &
some degree of strength before she is required to take a further part
in this sad affair.[2] I send my messenger for such last tidings as you can
send me. I trust nothing may impede the carrying out of those plans
which you told me of yesterday. I shall go to Eton easier in mind if I
can believe that tomorrow really will close this first painful act in this
tragedy.
   Sir Chas will probably see Mr. Murray in my absence & make him
acquainted with the subject (unless anything form your note today
should lead me to delay the communication) for his shop is the great
rendez-vous of reports & rumours & I wd like them to find him
prepared with the <u>truth</u> & by her wish.[3] Tomorrow a little hamper for
dear Effie's use will reach you – so that she can make you, or you her, a
little good port wine negus on your voyage without having recourse to
the ordinary wine of the vessel, & after, I shall be most thankful when
I can see her handwriting dating from her father's haven of rest. I will
write to her & tell her all I hear.
   Now dear Mrs. Gray give my kind regards to Mr. Gray, & may God
watch with especial love over your dear charge & over all that you hold
dear.
   Your's very truly
   Eliz Eastlake

1. Sophia Gray (1804–94), Effie's mother. Elizabeth was one of the few people to know that Mr and Mrs Gray had been secretly in London to assist Effie in her preparations to leave Ruskin.

2. Effie left for Perth on 25 April, Ruskin believing she was simply paying a visit her parents.

3. The Eastlakes devolved their management of the story so that Sir Charles informed their male acquaintances and Elizabeth campaigned on Effie's behalf in the drawing rooms of her large circle of acquaintances. Mary Lutyens entitles her chapter on this episode 'Lady Eastlake Rampant'.

Letter to Euphemia Ruskin   *ML MA 1338 UV.05*

7 Fitzroy Sqre.
April 27. 1854
My Darling Effie,
   I have been longing to write to you & longing to tell you how some of your friends have rec.d this intelligence – recd in some cases first from me. Much as you were loved & respected you were never so much so as now – not by me only but by all whom this sad tale has reached & who know not only what you have suffered, but how you have borne it. Your dear mother will tell you how late & long I was with her on Monday eveng (so <u>long</u> ago it seems now!). We both felt that the worst was indeed past, & that we could dwell now more exclusively on the comfort of your coming liberation & unsullied name.[1] But still Tuesday morning woke me early to thoughts of what was actually going on & imagination was too busy with you to submit to my <u>quiet</u>. I was almost as restless as you have so long been. My dear husband was a great relief & comfort to me – & is – he calls you ''a heroine of the best kind'' & occasionally he gratifies me by sentiments of a somewhat opposite kind regardg one who I wish could be struck out from your memory as utterly as he will be & already is out of the respect of all good people.
   On Tuesday eveng I saw dear Mrs Murray. She begged me to come upstairs – & only her gentle sister was with her. I asked the sister whether Menie cd bear to hear what wd <u>terribly</u> interest her – & she assured me there was no fear for her health now.[2] And then by that time your sorrows were so forcibly before me that I could not conceal my emotion & the story was out in its sad outline before I well knew what I said. Never shall I forget the tender womanly <u>anguish</u> with which dear Mrs. Murray caught at it – hiding her face on the sofa to conceal her sobs – all sympathy & pity – too much even for <u>indignation</u>

to be uttered. And amidst all, the sorrow for the <u>loss</u> of you. "Oh!
that I could have seen her sweet face once more". "& she has been
so often at this door to ask for me". Ah, dear child – those are true,
sweet friends who will ever give you the hand of comfort. I was cross
examined & questioned – & in short all was told, & she begged to tell
her husband in her own way, & doubtless did so that eveng. Still, as I
had not recd the agreed note from your Father I was glad to rest from
any mention of it on the Fast day when <u>you</u> divided my prayers much
more than half with our fleets & armies. I got yr father's note (they
had forgotten to put it with the post & I sent for it) by about 3 o'clock,
& after writing a long letter to my friend the Swinton who I think
can do you good in Edinr I went across to dear Mrs. Gruner. I then
began to feel the <u>relief</u> of <u>knowing</u> you as safe as you are pure, but still
it was a sad task to acquaint her for here again I found the pure true
<u>woman</u> – all overpowered with the sense of what a sister had suffered.
I feared the gentle creature wd have fainted – she could not conceive
the <u>reality</u> of such a tale – & then came, as with dear Menie Murray,
the fond looking back to when she had seen you last, & all that <u>love</u>
which rushes to the heart when a dear & interesting object has suffered
wrong. Your heart may take all this as a <u>balm</u>. I found Lady Lewis
had called in my absence, & so I wrote notes to her & Mrs. Milman
saying I would call early this afternoon, & I wrote a letter to dear Mr.
Lockhart – telling him that you had included him amongst those whom
you wished shd not learn this sad event by common rumour. I referred
him for particulars to John Murray. The <u>original</u> cause I am sure he
has long known. For I find now that many gentlemen never doubted
<u>that</u>, & so my only object was to tell him what you had done under the
circumstances & how you had been wickedly placed in dangers "which
one less pure, sound & pious wd hardly have escaped from". Then this
morng my darling I drove to Mr. Boxall & perhaps no interview has
<u>touched</u> me more than that. He had heard <u>nothing</u>, but expected he
knew not what, for you had referred him to me on that Sunday eveng,
when he said you interested him more than ever, & the good man was
not ashamed to weep before me – anxious, like a true knight to fight
your battles if fight shd be required – but <u>sure</u> that all must think as he
& others whom he mentioned. Then on to good Lady Lewis – kind &
plain & right, with all the women in her age – <u>greedy</u> for information
– thinkg of nothing else. She asked me if I thought she shd tell Louisa
Mackenzie but I left her to judge, saying that I cd not tell how far she
deserved the privilege of serving you.[3] I don't <u>think</u> she does, but I was
unwilling to say a word against her. Old Sir Frankland too came in
– full of few but manly words of <u>respect</u>.[4] Anxious to express them to

you himself, which I am sure he will do – also she was anxious to write quickly. Then to Fords (I must be quick) & from them I heard how it was being taken,[5] but one voice & that against "the blackguard" – they disputed a little as to the term – but both agreed as to the meaning, & I cannot tell you how much pleased I was with her. Her full oyster eyes, & pale lips were full of deep emotion & as I said something about the comfort her sympathy gave me she clambered up of me & kissed me. Next to the Deanery – Mrs. M: expecting me. Her whole heart full of tenderness – & anxiety. She is indeed one of the sweet women of this earth – unworldly, true & good. The Dean too was longing to hear her reports of my visit. Now I must hastily have done. Mr. Lockhart has been here – & full of you – he knew much, but far from all – expressed himself in curt grumbling, significant phrases, called names, & piped out something like "beast" – said there "never was or could be a word said against Effie", "a good sweet innocent pretty girl from Perth", & parting, told me to tell you that he was "much afflicted for her & felt the very sincerest interest".

   Now my darling I must end quickly – remember me to your dear Father & Mother, & let me hear that you are resting, mind & body, for my heart has many fears for you.

   Ever yr truly affte
   Eliz Eastlake

1. On 25 April Effie had parted from Ruskin at King's Cross railway station, he believing she was to visit her parents in Scotland, whilst he went abroad with his own parents. In fact he was served with a legal notification later the same day.

2. The Murrays' son Henry Hallam had been born on 1 April.

3. Louisa Mackenzie, later Lady Ashburton (1827–1903). See Virginia Surtees, *The Ludovisi Goddess: The Life of Louisa Lady Ashburton* (Salisbury: Michael Russell, 1984).

4. Sir Thomas Frankland Lewis (1780–1855), former politician and chair of the Poor Law Commission.

5. Richard Ford (1796–1858), Hispanist, connoisseur and writer. See Ian Robertson, *Richard Ford 1796–1858, Hispanophile, Connoisseur and Critic* (Norwich: Michael Russell (Publishing) Ltd, 2004).

Letter to Mrs Gray   *ML MA 1338 UV.06*

7 Fitzroy Sqre
April 29. 1854
My Dear Mrs. Gray

I was most thankful for your letter, for I had been much longing
for tidings of my dear <u>child</u> who is ever in my thoughts. Especially
had I longed to know how her last hour in company with that J.R.
had passed, & your account tallies much with my anticipations. I am
convinced that you have only <u>forestalled</u> him in the act of separation
& that if Mr. Gray had not acted with such excellent promptitude &
prudence now, he might have had a far more difficult task to perform
a year hence. Thus I feel more & more comforted that the decision is
already <u>over</u>.

I continue to hear the same buzz of pity for her & indignation at him
& I continue to tell the tale whenever & wherever I think the <u>truth</u> can
do good. Yesterday was the Private View at the Roy: Academy (she was
with me last year there!) & the story was circulating busily through the
rooms. I took Lady Davy & heard from her again what she had said to
me on Tuesday (when she called) tho' I omitted to tell dear Effie in my
letter, that she should be ready & willing to go into court if required to
speak for her. Also Lord Landsdowne had expressed the same willingness
to her, & he did it again yesterday to Mr. Ford – adding, as many have
done, that they shd be proud to take her by the hand & invite her when
she returned next year. I had not been long there when I saw Millais,
so I went to him with a cordial heart, & after a few commonplaces, we
found ourselves suddenly in the <u>subject</u> – my cheek white, his <u>crimson</u>.
I asked him if he had heard anything from the other side, & he told me
that he had a note from J.R. on the <u>Wednesday</u>, merely saying in usual
terms that he should delay a sitting till next week. Millais said that he
did not know how he shd bear to see him – truly I think it useless his
finishing a picture which <u>nobody</u> will <u>look</u> at.[1] He had known nothing
of the <u>truth</u> & asked me with painful blushes if I had. Our conversation
was very short from the numbers of acquaintances that beset me, & from
my knowledge of matters it was constrained, but I think he felt that I
have a great respect for him. In the course of the afternoon I introduced
him to the Ford's & to Sir Robt & Lady Inglis. Good David Roberts
was in great concern, & telling me of a little conversation with Effie
about a fortnight ago at the Bicknell's. I told him that I shd be glad to
hear anything he could gather regarding how the R. party had taken the
matter, i.e., without breaking any confidence.[2]

I conclude that Mr. Gray will hear through the lawyers or in some way from J.R.

I conclude also by this time dear Effie has had many a kind & consoling letter. Tell her that I have written to Mrs Boyle, whose heart was too pure & true not to have <u>reversed</u> her predicilections as soon as she know J.R. & her – also to Countess Salis, & today I have written a note to Lady Charlemont & asked to see her at any time that suits her for Sir Charles thinks that the Court is ignorant of the matter & that it is as well that our good Queen shd know the <u>truth</u>.

As to good Madame Bunsen[3] they have been out of town, but I enclose Effie a little note which shows her ignorance at present of the rumour, & which also will interest her from its goodness & sense. She will kindly return it to me.

Sir Chas has written or told it to his friends, & finds but one voice. Good Mr. Twopeny[4] owns to me that he suspected the parties when I enquired, & says there can be no two opinions on the lady's sufferings & merits.

I hope by this time that Mr Gray & your little Sophia are home safe with you. Tell my Effie that at some future time I shall like to have a description of the little ones I don't know, & whether yr 2nd little fairy is as pretty as she promised to be.

I must end in haste. To day is a great Academy Dinner for Sir Chas to conduct & I shall be nervous until it is over.[5]

Your's dear Mrs. Gray with much love – always afftly

Eliz Eastlake

Your letter was <u>so</u> interesting.

1. John Everett Millais (1829–96), painter and founder member of the Pre-Raphaelite Brotherhood, *Portrait of Ruskin at Glenfinlas* (1853), private collection.

2. Sir Robert Inglis (1786–1855), Tory politician and from 1850 the Professor of Antiquity at the Royal Academy; David Roberts (1796–1864), Scottish artist noted for his views of Egypt and the Holy Land.

3. Frances Bunsen (née Waddington) (1791–1876), artist and wife of Baron Christian Bunsen, Prussian ambassador to England 1841–54. See A. J. C. Hare, *Life and Letters of Frances Baroness Bunsen* (London: Routledge, 1880).

4. William Twopeny (1797–1873), lawyer, antiquarian and amateur artist.

5. The President of the Royal Academy gave an address to the academicians at an annual dinner.

Letter to Euphemia Ruskin   *ML MA 1338 UV.13*

7 Fitzroy Square
May 3. 1854
My darling child
   The sight of your handwriting is always dear to me, but now it
no longer inspires those feelings of anxiety, which however great,
were the greatest privilege to bear for you. I know you now safe
where you are, & I hear you honoured on all sides here, so that I
am indeed comforted & relieved of my burden. I have today a 2nd
letter to thank you for − but shd have written to you at all events &
wished to do so sooner, only that our house becomes fuller instead
of emptier & the <u>season</u> has burst upon us like a hurricane. Your
first letter was indescribably consoling, although sad, but you are
in all true to yourself, as I have ever found you, & I felt sure that
no weak <u>complaints</u> wd ever come from you. Your <u>strength</u> comes
from the only source & that is meant to be perfected in <u>weakness</u>. I
don't wonder that your harrassed mind & unstrung nerves can <u>apply</u>
to nothing yet. Only resist, & treat yourself like a dear sick child,
for whom kind nature provides restoration more than any medical
treatment. It is a calm to my heart to think of you in the garden
− with your little ones about you − & tenderly cherished by your
kind parents & brother. I shared your anxiety too on the delay of the
Dundee packet & am quite relieved at the arrival of the dear Papa
& of my little Sophy with her curls all dank & heavy. And now I
have seen good Madame Bunsen. I went there yesterday about 12
o'clock − with Mrs. Gruner (talked of nothing but you on the way)
& found both him & her. He was very interesting − owning with
tears that the <u>transition</u> was painful, because the thing had been done
so unhandsomely. But both were thankful for the retirement. The
very step has alienated him for ever from the <u>sneak</u> of a king, for, as
Bunsen said "<u>resignation</u> in Prussia is considered next to <u>rebellion</u>", as
the king considers them his abject servants to <u>think</u> of as he likes, so I
congratulated him on havg sounded the first note of true liberty in this
respect.[1] Then he went off to his last call on Lord Clarendon & I was
left alone with the kind lady. I asked her at once if she suspected my
errand − no − if she had heard anything − no. The truth is they have
denied themselves to everyone since his resignation − but I mentioned
your name only, & she guessed sorrow & distress, tho' of what kind
she knew not, except that it was not of <u>your</u> bringing. So the sad tale
was told, & no one has been more tenderly & deeply interested − no

one more appreciated you – more done you more justice, or expected more from you. She says that she has had some previous experience in such terrible exceptions to humanity & that she has invariably found them hard hearted & malignant. That it is one sign of the case. Dean Milman too who has met Sir Chas just now at the Levee says that the cold frigid imagination of his writings – uncheered by a single social or affectionate feeling – is all indicative of the same thing.

Well my darling child, Mdme Bunsen & I lingered together exchanging thoughts & anecdotes of you, & before I left her she put down your address. Mrs. Hardwicke too – our Academician's wife – you don't know her I think, but she is one of my favourites, came soon after I returned home – full of womanly tender interest in you, her husband & son chafing against him. Yesterday we dined at a Mr Geddes & met Ld Napier & the Longmans – all quietly telling his neighbour how high you stand & how low J.R. Another sad story divides yours with the public. Ld Ribblesdale, who married Col: Mure's young daughter last year, has left her for some wretched previous acquaintance. At all events, left her, & it is feared it can never be patched up, so that she is left a giddy thoughtless girl of 19, singularly unfitted from what I hear from my maid Ruth – who lived with them – to take care of herself.[2]

Now dearest for the tidings I have picked up of the R's. Wd you believe that father & son were boldly at the Water Colour Exhibition on Saturday in the middle of the day! Good Roberts fell in with them, & with his honesty said "I could not blink the matter" so he went to them & said he cd not pretend to be ignorant of what all the world was speaking of, & which had given him a sorer heartache than he had known for some time, & asked them if it were true. The young man treated it lightly & said that Mrs. Ruskin was gone to Scotland, & hummed & ha'ed. But the old man interposed that his son had been completely entrapped into marriage! that he had been attached to a French Countess & was an easy prey! but that they had overlooked that, & your father's absence of wealth &c &c & as the place was not the best in the world for discussing such a matter, he took his precious son by the arm & said "come along John, we shall have to pay for it but never mind, we have you to ourselves now". These words were exactly what Roberts heard & repeated to me. He repeated them to Sir Chas afterwds. Your father will understand no better perhaps than we do to the allusion to paying. I wd fain hope it means something more than the costs. I am convinced the son never meant to return, & that you are right in foreseeing his ending in Rome (if he be not there already) only that it is too good a place even for him. Mr Browne[3] brought me your letter to him on Sunday, & was very amusing, declaring that he will end as Pope Joan! & that he is now taking "the theraphic line" – looking down with thovereign contempt on the thins of this world & ethpecially on hith own".[4]

Well darling I must hurry on. Your two servants came here on Monday. Sir Jus: Ramsay was calling (Sir Chas told him) & I met them down in the kitchen for warmth & comfort. I saw them later & my tears started at the sight of them. What two nice girls! The cook not the least prepossessing. Old Mrs. R. & the old man too had been very harsh & rude to them & would fair have turned them out on Saturday, but they had protested against having till today, when your Jane comes to town & is to let Tucker know where she is. I have been disappointed of one place for her, but hope soon to hear of another. J.R. had not returned to the house till Monday except on Sunday for a moment.

Tomorrow I expect good Lady Charlemont who has sent me word that nothg but her duty prevented her coming sooner. Kind Lady Lewis called again yesterday afternoon when I was gone to the Bunsens – they also invited us to dinner but we unfortunately engaged. Lord Landsdowne the same with the same result. He told Sir Chas at the Academy Dinner his feelings on the subject & added kind things of me. All you tell me is interesting. I have a letter from Mrs. Boyle & enclose it. Also one from Louisa Mackenzie which I enclose too. You need not be supposed to have seen it. I have answered her kindly, but I have lost my confidence in her. Return both when you have done. Dear Mrs. Boyle is mistaken in her fears that people would speak against you. Give my kind love to papa & mamma & accept heartfull from yr ever affte

Eliz Eastlake

1. Baron von Bunsen, the Prussian Minister, was recalled from London in 1854 for supporting western forces in the Crimean War.

2. In 1853 Emma Mure (1833–1911) married Thomas Lister, Lord Ribblesdale on her twentieth birthday. Ribblesdale seems to have been an inveterate gambler but there is no suggestion that this was more than a temporary separation since they later had five children.

3. Elizabeth is not consistent in her spelling of Rawdon Brown's name.

4. She is making fun of Brown's lisp (see letter, 17 May 1854).

Letter to Euphemia Ruskin   *ML MA 1338 UV.21*

7 Fitzroy Sqre
May 9. 1854
My darling child

It is a long time since I have written & meanwhile I have a kind packet from your mother, & one yesterday from yourself. I have been longing to write daily, but have still our Eastlake guests with us & 4 sons of Mrs. E: backwards & forwards, which, with the average run of London interruptions just now, leaves me few moments in a day to spend quietly. But, I know you wd <u>fancy</u> all this even if I did not tell it, & will have made all allowance. You continue, my darling Effie, the object most engrossing my thoughts, & it will be long before I can dismiss you from my anxiety – never from my heart. Lady Charlemont called on me last Thursday – Mr Ford had already given her the outline of the sad tale, which I was glad of, for the good lady with all her kind heart seems to have a very confined <u>head</u>, & perhaps from her misfortunes has formed such a very low estimate of the male sex that she heaped upon J.R. every possible & impossible wickedness of motive & aim that has characterised the <u>roué</u> parts in the novels of the last half century – none of them being <u>his</u> particular wickedness, which was too new for her apparently to comprehend. She was all kindness & interest about you, & begged me to express as much to you. I asked her if the Queen were to hear the story at all whether she cd take care that H: M. heard it <u>rightly</u>, but she seemed to have too great a fear of the little woman even for that, & told me frankly that she cd not, but that <u>Bunsen</u> could best. All I care about is that the Q: shd hear it correctly if at all.[1] Lady Lewis – kind, worthy lady, was also early one morng early with me – from the wish to hear & speak of you. Out of evil comes all kind of indirect good, for this sad matter has brought me closer to her & to other excellent people. & you, the great sufferer, will I feel sure trace God's hand in countless ways bringing you comfort from the <u>deep</u>. Then Louisa Mackenzie has been here, & pleaded warmly that though appearances had been much against her & only time could prove to you that she was "true" to you, yet that she <u>was</u> so, & wished me to tell you so. She was very <u>earnest</u> in manner & her eyes overflowed with tears. On her saying to me at first "do you really think him so utterly devoid of feeling" I said "I think you need no further proof than the letter in the Times this morng" (it was on Friday she called). "What man of the slightest heart, having even a bad wife, could have written such a disgusting farrago not ten days after". I conclude you & yr people

have seen that letter – on Hunt's odious picture – it has condemned
him with many – even without knowing anything further. Mr Browne
dined here yesterday & was anxious to make out whether they were
really gone, wh: he said he should try to do from Smith & Elder. Also
I promised him the perusal of those copied letters you kindly have sent
me, & which are the most extraordinary things I ever read. The "loves
of my son" are horrid & monstrous to think of. Sir Chas hopes they are
not gone as J.R. has 2 or 3 books of his – single volumes out of sets
– but those will be easy to reclaim in some way. On Friday eveng we
met Millais at Sydney Cooper's & he interested me much by his upright
simplicity. He owned to me that he had remonstrated with J.R. on
exposing you so much in the Highlands, but that he laughed & said that
he (J.R.) was so much obliged to M: for teaching you to draw! Also
Henry Butler Johnstone came to me about it – a rattle – but a kind
manly heart – assuring me that he had heard but one voice & that he
longed to serve J.R. after the fashion of Mr. Oliveira, only much worse.
Mr. Boxall also gives the same tale.

I did not hear from your servants the account of the Ruskin surprise.
I was rather too scrupulous of asking & regretted afterwards that I had
not been bolder. I trust the bad old man's fury fell at first partially on
his son. Thank your mother for the kind letters & for the capital address
by Prof: Blackie, which is a masterpiece in its way. Tell me if I shd
return it. I am glad you have satisfied yourselves that we need not load
the jewels upon his guilty head. I was ready enough – but refrained
from mentioning the surmise till I heard further.

I enclose you a letter I recd from Miss Mary Boyle, to whom sweet
Ella had sent my letter about you. I rejoice to send you what I know
will be kind.

I have been much interrupted, my darling, in writing this, but when
our guests are gone which will be at the end of the week (if one of
them be well enough) I shall be much freer & shall like to tell you
more about our daily life. Now God bless you & your's – always your
affte

Eliz Eastlake

1. Lady Charlemont was Lady of the Bedchamber to Queen Victoria from 1837
   to 1854. There is some suggestion here that Elizabeth was hoping that Lady
   Charlemont would give the Queen a partisan account of the annulment.

Letter to Euphemia Ruskin   *ML MA 1338 UV.24*

7 Fitzroy Sqre
May 10. 1854
My darling Effie

I write you a few words again today having ascertained pretty
certainly that the R's must be gone. I met Millais last night at Lady
Inglis' who told me he had a note from J.R. saying that he was on the
point of starting though he did not say for where, & also saying that he
should probably be back before Millais left London. All this is little but
it is perhaps more than you have heard elsewhere.

You were still the theme last night of many an anxious enquiry from
many who knew half or less. Mrs. Wedgewood came to me. I asked her
what she had heard. She said "that Mrs. Ruskin ought never to have
borne that name, & that Mr. Ruskin is a villain". I said it was right in
the main outline & then answered many a kind & anxious question.
Also Mrs. Adolphus was full of kind womanly sympathy & Mrs.
Cardwell, who does not know you but who is a person I much regard
– a tender, gentle loving wife herself, appealed to me to clear up what
she could not understand, & the[n] great drops fell from her kind eyes,
& she said she shd ever think of you with the deepest interest – adding
"how we are blest".

Then in the afternoon I had been to Ella's concert – the first I have
attended since you, dear suffering child, were at my side. I can't tell you
how much I missed you. There was a pretty young bride near me with
massive wavy hair, & I twisted your life so well known to me round
her's of which I knew nothing, till I was sorry to think I shd not see
her again. She did not look happy, which increased the association. After
the concert I called on Ctss de Salis & found her & Hadie, & they drew
most affectionately round me to ask & hear of you. And no one have I
heard do you more justice than the old Ctss. She was charming in my
eyes. She said she always thought what the real fact must be. Hadie also
came out in her real fine colours. The Ctss said she should write to you
now she had seen me.[1]

I won't venture to begin another sheet. The E's are still with us, our
one remaining niece very faint & delicate. She has had a life of strange
suffering from an unkind Father, & after his death the debility he had
caused has told. The elder sister died last Octr & tho' I trust time may
recover this poor child – only 23 – yet I can't help being anxious. We
are feeding & petting her up & I wish I cd have the charge of her for 6
months.

God bless you, yr loving
  Eliz Eastlake

  1. Henrietta de Salis (1824–63), daughter of Count Jerome de Salis.

Letter to Euphemia Ruskin   *ML MA 1338 UV.28*

7 Fitzroy Sqre
May 17. 1854
My darling Effie
   It is such a pleasure to my heart to write to you, that you must never
think that I do so oftener than is quite convenient to me. I have at
the same time the most entire conviction that when I don't write you
are making far more kind excuses for me than I deserve. I have Mrs.
Murray's "most tender love to her" with the request that I wd tell you
how weak she still (I much regret to say) is, & that her hand shakes so
much that she is not fit to write, as she is longing to do, to you. This
I have in a letter from Miss Smith – from Wimbledon, where they
are now removed. Also old Lady Morley begs to be recalled to your
recollection & to express her sympathy & best wishes. You wd have
laughed, malgre vous,[1] had you seen the faces & heard the noises she
made at an imaginary J.R. before her, on my telling her the story which
I thought it quite right to put in her clever emphatic hands.
   Your letters & your kind mother's are most interesting to me, my
dearest child, & I can see you in the Kinnaird Woods – recalling you
wandering little party, & also your wandering <u>thoughts</u>. It is a marvel
how any people in the 19th century can conduct themselves in a trying
& peculiar position like this, as those old people are doing. Nothing can
be more <u>indecent</u> & <u>vulgar</u> than their affected glee at such a catastrophe
so disgraceful to their wretched son – "that Pre-Raphaelite fellow" as
I hear him called. Mr Brown lisps out the most burning indignation
at the folly as well as wickedness, & when there is any allusion to the
uncertainty of their being driven to make pecuniary amends he says
"<u>we'll</u> <u>see</u>" with an air as if he intended to see them himself. He seems
to find some consolation in occasionally coming here, & the other day
I took him to Mr. Monro's gallery, & then on to join Sir Chas in the
Bot: Gardens. Also the Messrs Cheney called the other day & found me
just in from a drive & staid some time. I liked the quizzical expression
of Mr Ed Cheney – Sir Charles & I have been very dissipated of late, &
so we have been making holiday together – he has a card of admission

"Sir CLE & friend" to the French Exhibition & I have one "Lady E & friend" so we take <u>each other</u> in. However, I must own I have varied my campaign oftener than he – to day we are going to the Water Colour, & in the eveng to the Queen's ball which, if as interesting as usual, I shall describe to you. To me it is always interesting to watch her fresh, unstudied ways.

I am now preparing a couple of <u>At Homes</u>, which I always dread beforehand & enjoy at the time. I have had a celebrated flutist from Germany recommended to my tender mercies, & I must do my best to bring him forward one of the evenings.

I was deeply interested by your first legal communication, & I thank you much for sending it. I find, from all who understand the matter, that this "contempt" does make his bad case even worse, & I hope he'll continue the same false course, tho' it is a <u>true</u> one in him. I shd be glad if Lady Trevelyan were to come in my way.[2] Mamma always calls Sir Walter "a Hamydryad" [sic][3] which may have confused Lady T's notions of conjugal duty. Louisa Mackenzie I have not seen again, but I find Hadie, whom I met last night, thinks very disparagingly of her, & is not inclined to trust her. Hadie is looking full blown & honest, & is all the quiety she can in the short time she is to be in London.

Our Eastlake guests left us last Saturday, & I hope the invalid, who interests me deeply, had really made a step towards recovery. She wants the cook more than the doctor, & my cook rejoiced in cheating her with various nourishing things.

God bless you & keep & comfort you, my Effie, my little dear friend. My heart is indescribably relieved about you, & a break in the Kinnaird Woods for the present is a paradise to my feelings in comparison to that dreadful position at Herne Hill. I trust to hear that piano & other things are sent to you. Give my love to your mother & <u>to your father</u>!

Your true loving
Eliz Eastlake

1. In spite of yourself.

2. Pauline Trevelyan (1816–66), writer, artist and patron of the Pre-Raphaelite artists. See John Batchelor, *Lady Trevelyan and the Pre-Raphaelite Brotherhood* (London: Chatto & Windus, 2006).

3. Sir Walter Calverley Trevelyan (1797–1879). A hamadryad is either a wood nymph or a venomous cobra, but it seems plausible that Mrs Rigby's phrase is a Malapropism for 'hermaphrodite'.

Letter to Rawdon Brown[1]   *NOTT PWM226*

7 Fitzroy Sqre
May 25 1854
Dear Mr. Brown

I am very sorry that you could not join us yesterday, but shall reserve
a ticket for you for the next show – for yesterday's was a sight worthy
being carried off even to Venice in your mind's eye.

I know that you are aware of our little friend's probable arrival
with her father this week. She recommended secrecy to me, & even
without her request I see sufficient reason for it in the nonsense I
hear if as talked, about her having to go publicly before the House of
Lords – Ladies thanking God that they are not like her – & c. – all of
which will be best refuted by its not being known even to her friends
when her evidence is taken. I am going today to 28 Bury Street to
ascertain whether they really come there, as intended, if they cd have
the lodgings. I was not to write again to Perth. I only wish she could
be in this house, but that cannot be. Dr. Waagen is now here. I enclose
you At Homes – & shall be delighted to see you even "in a crowd" but
hope for At Homes in a more rational shape beforehand.
Your's very truly
Eliz Eastlake

> 1. Rawdon Brown (1803–83), antiquarian and historian normally resident in
> Venice. He was a friend of the Ruskins. See Ralph A. Griffiths and John
> E. Law (eds.), *Rawdon Brown and the Anglo-Venetian Relationship* (Stroud:
> Nonsuch, 2005).

Letter to Mrs Gray   *ML MA 1338 UV.38*

7 Fitzroy Sqre
May 31. 1854
My dear Mrs. Gray

As I have your dear people today before they started I fancy I can
give you later intelligence of them than you can have otherwise. Dearest
Effie was looking much better than when I saw her first on Sunday.
Then her wasted looks went to my heart, but both times that I have
seen her since she has decidedly been better. I can't <u>tell</u> you how much I
rejoice that matters are thus far & from what both Papa & she state the
lawyers give them leave to consider the matter as good as <u>settled</u>. Much

had she to go through yesterday, dear child, & I longed for you to have been by her side. But God has always raised up kind & considerate friends for her, however trying the position.

At a party at Landsdowne House last night I saw Lord Glenelg[1] for the first time since all this, & it was also his first appearance for many weeks. I instantly resolved to address him on this subject, & discover his real sentiments, but there was no need for any movement on my part, for he eagerly came to me for tidings & begged to call & hear further. Nothing could exceed the kindness of his manner of speaking of her. So that has relieved me, for his shyness & long absence has weighed on my mind.

I saw also good Lady James & had a little talk with her on this engrossing subject. She told me that she had remarked from the first that J.R. had always spoken to them disparagingly of our dear one, & she "always loyally of him"!

Effie's coming has been kept perfectly secret, but now I shall be glad to retort when I hear foolish & malicious people talking about her giving "public evidence before the House of Lords", "scandal", "exposure" &c which a few have got hold of – & just assure them that all her evidence is already given, & nobody has known the how, where, or when.

Now dear Mrs. Gray I trust the travellers will have a good voyage back to you. I was delighted to hear of you & your childn.

Your's afftly

Eliz Eastlake

1. Lord Glenelg was Charles Grant, Baron Glenelg (1778–1866), Scottish politician who held numerous political offices, first as a Tory and later as a Whig. Evidently Elizabeth thought he might be useful to Effie's cause.

Letter to Euphemia Ruskin   *ML MA 1338 UV.43*

7 Fitzroy Sqre
June 3. 1854
My dearest Effie

Though time runs short as usual I must send you a few lines to say how perpetually you have been & are in my thoughts. The high wind has distressed me much, for I fear you are little able to stand sea sickness & the knocking about of such a voyage. Most thankful shall I be to hear that you have not been much tried for you strength, & not deluged in reaching Dundee, where I like to fancy you arrived today.

I have not seen many of our mutual friends – but Lady Inglis I caught hold of after the breakfast yesterday morng & most sweet & kind

she was about you – begged me to give her "love to you" which I think
I may send her, for I'm sure I feel it for her" with much sympathy, &
many thanks to you for remembering her at all in your time of trouble.
I told her that near the time one wd be most certain to remember one
so good as herself. Then last night we were at the Bunsen's, when I told
Mdme B: of your havg been in town, & of your being now free from
any further demand on your participation in the matter. She was, like
herself, all earnest kindness. We paid our visit to them at the Ernest
Bunsen's where the whole family is now staying – they leave soon.
Lady James called the day before yesterday, but I was not at home. Lord
Glenelg has not yet called.

Our engagements are very numerous just now & we have not been
allowed a quiet night this week. Dr. Waagen's presence contributes to
this a little, for he is so fresh & cheerful that he can enjoy everything.
Also we see exhibitions &c with him & in half an hour we are going to
the Private View of the British Institution – <u>Old</u> Masters – which is a
great feast. I shd like to have my Effie on my arm, but I know it is <u>well</u>
with her wherever she is, with Everlasting arms about her. My faith is
very strong for you, for you indeed have learned how to <u>wait</u> upon the
Lord. My kind love to Papa & Mamma.

Yr ever affte
Eliz Eastlake

Letter to Euphemia Ruskin   *ML MA 1338 UV.50*

7 Fitzroy Sqre
June 10. 1854
My darling Effie

I indite a few hurried lines before starting for the opening of
the Crystal Palace. Your most kind letter reporting your safe arrival
reached me on Monday mg just before starting to spend the day at
Eton, & made me happier for the blustering weather had given me
much anxiety. I do hope the extreme sickness has relieved you of much
superabundant bile.

Well, my dearest I can give you direct tidings of J.R. Sir Chas had
written to the old R: about his books ignoring the fact of their being
away too, & this morning he recd a short letter from J.R. himself dated
June 6th Geneva, in which he apologises for not having returned the
books on the score of being too hurried. "I was in much confusion,
owing to the unexpected necessity of removing all my things from my

former house to my father's in the last week before leaving Engld (I went abroad in order to give my father & mother a happy tour, & his time of departure could not be delayed) so I was a little hurried". All this speaks for itself. I leave you the easy task of pulling the sophistry to pieces. There was time enough to write that letter about Hunt's picture, which has condemned him in the eyes of the mere world more than anything. He adds that he will return the books "the moment I return – some time in August".

I send you also a letter from dear Mrs. Murray recd last night & one from Mrs. Boyle recd this morng.[1] The other morng at Christie's Mr. Bentinck came to me to ask for you, which he did very kindly & I promised to let you know of his sympathy & regard. Lady James has called on me & I on her, but we have not met, so I have writen her a few lines reporting about you, as she had been to Lady Davy's who had promised to get me to let her know all I know. Lady D: I saw on Wednesday. She was very energetic & agreed with me in regretting that the privacy which is so acceptable for you, shd also be the means of screening him. She still entertains a vision of going into court for you which I love her for, tho' it can't be realised. Ld Landsdowne also had repeated all his kind wishes & willingnesses to Mrs. Ford. Ld Glenelg has not been here but I like him too much to doubt him. Lady Lewis & other kind friends I shall see on Wednesday – my great awful party – if not tomorrow.

Now my dearest child, in haste yr true loving
Eliz Eastlake

1. Eleanor Vere Boyle (née Gordon) (1825–1916), a noted writer and illustrator of children's books, better known by her artist's signature, E.V.B. She was a lifelong friend of Elizabeth, writing the reminiscence at that appears at the end of *Journals and Letters of Lady Eastlake*.

Letter to Euphemia Ruskin   *ML MA 1338 UV.53*

7 Fitzroy Sqre
June 14. 1854
My Darling Effie
   I just send you a few lines to enclose this kind little note from Lady Inglis, which I have answered to the best of my power, telling her where you are & how much you value the sympathy of the good. I was with the kind Lewis' last night, & they both contrived in a crowded room to tell me that you had written cheerfully to them. Also dear Mrs. Milman,

whom I had not seen for some time, put her kind face closer to mine to hear & speak of you. Lady James I met later at the Milnes.

My great party comes off tonight & I confess to a little nervousness beforehand, tho' I warm to it when the flood is fairly set in. Mrs Gruner laughs at me. We are now very dissipated, & only surpassed by Dr. Waagen who is in request for breakfast, lunch, dinner & evening, & is as happy & jovial as possible. The Crystal Palace opening was very fine.[1] And tho' falling short of the first opening where like it it has other grand features of its own. The music was sublime, & the Hallelujah Chorus given with a perfection which must stand alone till the 1600 musicians are gathered together there again. Also the vast ampitheatre of orchestra one sloping mass of beings, which towered behind the throne, was a stupendously fine sight. Her Majesty was badly dressed in blue [b]varége, flounced, but did her part beautifully as usual, recd her various handbook presenters with the most gracious smiles, but looked polite ice upon one Phillips – a trader in criticism – to whom some of the slanders upon the Prince have been traced.

There is a dejeuner given at the C.P. on Saturday next to which we are invited &, I expect, shall go.

Now my darling child I must bid you good bye. Tell your dear Mother that there is a treat for her in Blackwood – an article upon J.R. which I drank slowly, enjoying every drop. Mr. Brockenden came here in delight about it, & prides himself on having always detested the fellow, before knowg what grounds there were for it.

I know I shall hear from you in a day or two. I only trust you are well.

Yr ever affte

Eliz Eastlake

1. The Crystal Palace was opened at Sydenham on 10 June by Queen Victoria in the presence of 40,000 spectators. The orchestra under the baton of Mr Costa played the Hallelujah Chorus. The Handbooks referred to were copies of guidebooks given to various departments of the Palace.

Letter to Euphemia Ruskin   *ML MA 1338 UV.56*

7 Fitzroy Sqre

June 25. 1854

My darling Effie

The sight of my handwriting cannot give you more pleasure than that of your's does to me. You are perpetually in my thoughts & even

if I were disposed to forget you I would not be allowed so many are
the friends known & unknown to you who enquire for you. Mamma
does not like to be many days without hearing of you. My sister in law
Mrs. Eastlake from Paris, acknowledging a letter from me says "you do
not mention Mrs. R." I was grieved to hear of the little suffering finger
which I fear was rather the sign of an enfeebled system, but truly my
heart is so relieved by the knowledge of the loving hands you are now
in that I have none of that pain of helpless sympathy which formerly
oppressed me.

Well my dearest child, I hope by this time that you have heard from
Ld Glenelg who came to see me by appointment last Thurdsay at 3
o'clock, & begged for all particulars of your last days before leaving
Herne Hill, & indeed for all I cd tell him. As the world has informed
him of the principal points in your history I was spared all that, &
found plenty to say in reminiscences which are deeply graven in my
heart & which I saw were more interesting to him to hear. He wanted
to hear all about you parents' proceedings, & what <u>they</u> were like, so
you may guess I held forth enthusiastically on dear Papa & Mamma,
& <u>how</u> you went & much about your health. He told me of the sad
alteration he had remarked in you, & that he quite believed you would
not have lived had you remained as you were. Inexplicable as is the
unwillingness he showed to take a personal part in assisting you, yet
as soon as he could he had evidently consulted a lawyer as to the
state of the law in your case. He asked who had been good & kind
to you, whether Fords & Lady Davy had been, & I told him of Ld
Landsdowne's readiness to stand by you – hoping that the old gentleman
wd take that a little to himself. But nothing could be <u>kinder</u> than
manner, attention to every word, & occasional ejaculation regarding
your many excellences. Somebody had told him, as I also heard, that an
amicable arrangement had been entered into on condition that nothing
should be said of J.R.'s temper(!) He merely mentioned it knowing that
it must be untrue. I have also heard that J.R. <u>intended</u> to have written
a statement of the truth, but that upon 2nd thoughts he felt it would
injure you so much, that he had made up his mind to refrain! Very
convenient forbearance. Ld G. came at 3 & I was to go out at 4 to see
the Munro's Turner drawings with Dr. Waagen, so, as he was walking,
I asked him whether he wd like to see them too & he came with us
& enjoyed them much. Once or twice while driving he asked me aside
"is so & so true to our friend?" I gave him your address & he said he
should write so I hope he will.

At the Fords' the other night I met Mrs Strutt – a nice unaffected
person – who drew her chair to mine to ask about you, was full of true

womanly respect & sympathy & begged her kindest regards to you. Also
we were at the Cheneys the other day.[1] Dr. W. I, & Lady de Tabley, &
Ed Cheney, whom I am rather in love with for his honest kind face &
manner, asked me quietly about you. Then last Sunday the Bp of Edinr,
Mr. Lockhart, & Mr. Hay (from Rome) were here to dinner, & when
Miss Farqhuar & I had left the room (Mr. L: havg started the subject
by asking me after you) the gentlemen continued the conversation &
the Bp – not knowing the real history – was duly informed – then all
agreed as to their long detestation of the writings & those were handled
accordingly, & then Mr. Hay said "it is very well to agree with the
writings – but what do you intend to do with the man. Surely when
women are banished from society for their faults, you will never admit
such a villain as that" & then Sir Chas & all said that they shd never
receive him & Mr. L: gnarled out his indignation at his having dared to
write to Sir Chas at all, which I do think the greatest assurance.

You will be enjoying this summer weather at St. Andrews. It is very
oppressive for London & for hot dinners & evenings. Dr. Waagen's
company brings more dissipation upon us & as it really seems to suit my
dear husband I make no complaint, we enjoy much of it exceedingly.
Last night after dining at the Davenport Bromley's[2] we went to Mrs
Seymour's (H. Danby's mother) whom I fancy must be a nice woman.
The pictures were attractive & the new conservatory decorated by
Gruner very pretty. Tomorrow is a concert at Landsdowne House, next
day a dinner at Murchison's, Wednesday at Ld Overstone's, Thursday we
dine with my dear Murray's at Wimbledon, Friday I do think is nothing
& with this next week much ends, for I hear of many leaving town.

Yesterday I spent the day with my dearest Mother, who is rather less
of a sufferer since the warm weather came. We discussed our little plans
together, as the only way to get her to a little warm seabathing is for
me to go with her, which is a mutual happiness. We think of Folkstone
this year. But all that requires much forethought as to comforts
indispensable for her. Sisters & nieces were all well, & Eton quite gay.

Last Tuesday I enjoyed an exceedingly beautiful Ella & with Mrs.
Gruner. I fear that we shall lose them from our neighbourhood soon,
as they find they can have a cheaper home & one more convenient for
his work. & the dear little woman is very sorry to leave F. Sqre & us, &
indeed I shall lose very much for she is one I value most truly. There is
not a more interesting person in the London guest world, little as she is
known. We do not meet often but it has been always a mutual comfort
to know that we are so near.

Now my own little Effie I must leave off & join Sir Chas to drive &
enquire for our friend Brockedon who is very ill. I don't think I have

thanked yr Mother for her interesting letter received just as mine was
off to the post. I am grateful for all she tells me. My kind love to that
handsome young couple who pretend to be your father & mother!

Ever yr most affte

Eliz Eastlake

1. Edward Cheney (1803–84), art collector and friend of Rawdon Brown.
He lived with his two brothers between the family home in Shropshire
and Audley Square in London. Lady de Tabley was Catherina Barbara de
Salis Soglio (1814–69), sister of Henrietta de Salis and the wife of George
Leicester, Baron De Tabley (1811–87).

2. Rev. Walter Davenport Bromley (1787–1863), collector of Italian Renaissance
art. See Denys Sutton, 'From Ottley to Eastlake', *Apollo*, cxxiii (1985), p. 88.

Letter to Euphemia Ruskin   *ML MA 1338 UV.64*

7 Fitzroy Sqre

July 8. 1854

My darling Effie

I shd have written to you at all events today for I have been long
wanting to talk to my dear child – & now I have your letter enclosing
Lady Sorel's for Ld Glenelg which I have sent him already with a few
lines saying "our little Friend was shy of sending you direct, because I
fancy she imagines what I am sure is not true". Thus I wd fair give him
a chance of doing himself justice, for though he must be judged by his
deeds yet I am sure in my heart that they are not the proper exponents
of his real feelings. But this comes of people allowing mere temperament
to be indulged on every occasion until it becomes quite the master.

Well dear, your long dear letter of the 29th gave me the greatest
pleasure as showing me how much stronger you really are, & so my
anxieties about you are gradually diminished, & I place the future with
more & more <u>practical</u> confidence in the Hands of Him whom you have
always trusted. I think of your parents with the greatest <u>comfort</u> & I can
see you & the dear, bright tender mother side by side, & shd like to be
between you! But here I am still in a round of engagements, & though
my evengs are much more frequently at home than before yet morning
& afternoon engagements have taken the place of dinners & At Homes,
& I fancy break more into my time.

Dr. Waagen's presence brings a good deal more to do, & it is hard
work acting wife to two gentlemen! Also there is much temptation, for

all picture galleries fly open at his approach & I am too happy to be
his companion. I can't remember all our dissipations but some of them
will interest you. Last Thursday week we dined at Wimbledon, & found
Fords & Hughes &c & it was a most pleasant dinner the more so as
Sir Chas was with us. But dear Mrs Murray had not been well & was
looking <u>beautifully</u> delicate, also the children had the chicken pox &
Master John, the little Hercules, was laid low. She & I managed a quiet
half hour to talk of the dear one in whom our hearts have much tender
interest. She was much touched with your letter, which she kindly let
me see, & she said it had gone deeply into her good husband's little-
displayed heart. I hear since that childn are better.

Our next party that I can remember (but I always write the accounts
of everyday to my dear Mother) was an afternoon one at the Fords'. The
little beehive swarming with <u>drones</u> – upstairs & downstairs – looking
at the pretty things, & eating strawberries & drinking champagne. The
little Meta standing looking out of the drawing room window as if she
did not belong to the gay scene, but I went to her & made her talk
of the 2 cats, & 3 dogs, & 6 birds in the house, & of her aversion to
the parrot which disturbs her at her lessons. A very pretty drawing has
been made of her by a Miss Holton – à la Richmond – but she really
is far from pretty.[1] Lady Davy was there looking extremely fragile,
& laughing in a way which shows that the enemy is close at hand. I
hope to see her today. I wish I cd get to her oftener, for no one is
more sensible to kind interest. She often speaks of your writing to her
weekly when she was at Northampton. And she always speaks of &
enquires for you, so as ever to satisfy <u>me</u>. Then Waagen & I were at
breakfast at Danby Seymour's last Tuesday – only a few besides – Lord
Elcho, Dav: Bromley's &c, Stirling of Keir.[2] I like the little bright eyed
man whom Waagen says looks "so glucklich wie ein Maus in einem
Mehltopf"[3] – tho' he is always attacking the Academy in Parliament
at night & then making up to Sir Chas & me the next day – quite
forgetting what he is about. And I like his sweet looking mother &
sister & <u>fancy</u> them happy good people. The house is full of beautiful
things which he is always increasing. Then in the afternoon was another
<u>breakfast</u> at the Cockerell's at Hampstead – always a pretty scene there,
but this year prettier than ever. Such a number of sweet young faces
– girls in all the pride of beauty, dancing going on the grass & old
bachelors looking on in ecstacies! Mr. Ford required sharp looking after,
for having been forbidden <u>ink</u> & <u>wine</u> he has taken to studying the
fair sea, & was continually running about "who <u>is</u> the blue bonnet?"
"who <u>is</u> the pink dress?" till Mrs. Ford & I agreed it was as well he
should be enlightened no further. Then we had a charming lunch at

the Overstones – strawberries & ice fruit, & pictures afterwards, some
of them first rate. Miss Lloyd I look at with great interest. Her aunt
tells me good thing of her – & that her father is bringing her up very
wisely. She is nicer looking than 8 millions require to be & I cd not
see a young man paying her the commonest attention without a sort of
mistrust for her.[4] Then we went in to Mr. Vernon Harcourts[5] close by,
for more pictures, & finished at Mr. Barker's in Picadilly who has those
true Pre-Raphaelites which captivate me more than my other masters.[6]
Then Mrs. Gruner & I have been to St. James' Theatre together to see
my cousin Mr Palgrave Simpson[7] & his troop act. It was for the benefit
of some poor lady – & it was exceedingly well done. Yesterday, but not
least, I drove to the Crystal Palace with the Clerks & Barlows – taking
one of the girls in my brougham. & certainly I do not hesitate to say
that that is the most enchanting place that ever has been devised by
man – high & low enjoying alike – all innocently if not improvingly
– pleasures which seem to have no limit, which is the painful part of
all others, & an air which gives you vigour faster than you can spend it.
For after 4 hours of perpetual excitement & fatigue I came away fresh &
fit for a small dinner party at home. There are pleasures for all, but to
me the Italian Court was like going to Italy. I saw much sculpture from
Genoa & Pavia & Florence as gave me the same sensations of intellectual
delight as a first rate picture gallery. It really is the finest thing in the
world that Palace – already perfumed with thousands of bright flower
beds, & every month & year will increase its beauties. The Clerks are
excellent people. The two girls far more interesting than the world
supposes, & Sir Geo: sharing my affections with a certain Mr. Gray!

From Hadie I had a sweet kind note the other day, announcing
her departure for Ems[8] & sending me the manners etc. of the Greeks
translated by Lady de T: & herself. Thankyou for her kind line about
me. I like Lady de T: much & fancy there is much more in her than her
rather weak manner lets appear.

Now my darling child I must have done but it is easier to continue
a letter than to begin one sometimes. I wish I cd give a good account
of Sir Chas but he is not well, & that always shows itself in depression
& incapacity to take interest in anything – at least he is up & down
& ought to seek a change of air, but I fear will not. I at all events do
not leave London until August, & nothing is settled about that. I am
perfectly well all but a hoarseness wh: I suspect will not leave me here.
Now dear Love God bless you. We have heard not a murmur about that
wretched trio!

Yr true loving
Eliz Eastlake

1. Meta Ford, daughter of Richard Ford.

2. Rev. Walter Davenport Bromley (1787–1863), collector of Italian Renaissance art; Henry Danby Seymour (1820–77), MP and writer; Lord Elcho (Francis Wemyss Charteris) was a frequent antagonist of Eastlake's in National Gallery debates in Parliament. See letter to William Stirling, 21 July 1859.

3. German expression, 'happy as a mouse in a flour jar'.

4. Miss Lloyd is evidently the hieress of large estates in Carnarvonshire.

5. Two contenders: Sir William George Granville Venables Vernon Harcourt (1827–1904), statesman and Chancellor of the Exchequer under Gladstone (1886, 1892–95), or William Vernon Harcourt (1789–1871), General Secretary to the first meeting of the British Association.

6. Alexander Barker had a fine collection of Italian art. See Waagen's *Treasures of Art in Great Britain* (London: John Murray, 1854), vol. 2, pp. 125–29.

7. John Palgrave Simpson (1807–87), Elizabeth's cousin, the playwright and author.

8. Ems, a German spa town.

Letter to Rawdon Brown   *NOTT PWM227*

7 Fitzroy Sqre
July 12. 1854
My Dear Mr. Browne [sic]

   You will think me a pretty correspondent to have been thus long in acknowledging your kind letter from Venice – & much as I regretted to be reduced to this form of communication I was truly glad to know that you were safely arrived in your adopted city. You need not fear that Sir Chas shd ever think you neglectful, tho' when he neglects to give you his commissions he deserves that you shd be so. He tells me I shall have them all ready to insert by the time I come to the end of this letter. As regards the Mantovani book he bids me assure you that he is inciting the Trustees of the B: Museum to it purchase & that some one will probably be in Venice this autumn to inspect it. In that case he wishes to know whether the fortunate druggist[1] will be in the way, or if absent from Venice, able to be summoned. I wish I cd assure you that this "someone" would be no other than himself but I am still in the dark as to our possible doings, & were I to tell you that I do hope that a trip to Venice will come to pass I shd fear to mislead you. I shall have to carry the question by assault at last I fear – but meanwhile am trying

negotiations. He very much requires for his health to have some change
of air, & if I can but frighten him a little I feel sure that he wd disdain
any lesser flights than Venice & Florence. Our friend Waagen, still
staying with us, most earnestly seconds all my wishes this way. I am sure
if you knew him as well as we do you would swell the number of the
Dr's devoted friends – for he is a man of most remarkable requirements
& with a sense, kindness, & humour that none would appreciate more
than yourself. We saw a little of your friend Hartzen before he left
London & I was much pleased with the modest little savant.[2] He &
Waagen have been pronouncing judgement on the Wallerstein collection,
& they have turned up a few prizes.[3] Waagen being glad to find that his
opinion coincides with that formed & written by Hartzen 8 years ago.

I have been very sorry for your friends the Cheney's in the sad loss of
their nephew, which they feel, I understand, with more than common
acuteness. Nevertheless they allowed me to take Dr. W: there one
afternoon with Lady De Tabley to see their "Treasures" & I was quite
enchanted with the Venetian portraits &c., & with them one gem of a
Titian. Sir Charles has been since & is equally delighted. They were so
kind to us & I fell very much in love with Mr. Edward C: This evening
I have an invitation for ourselves & Dr. W: to drive in Audley Sqre on
the 21st, & I hope Sir Chas will be tractable & not refuse. But, as you
may guess, he begins to think that the season has lasted long enough.
It is however declining now & dejeuners are coming into vogue, with
those who have pictures to show. Our friend Ford set the example one
afternoon with strawberries & ice – since then Lord Overstone has
thrown open his door of bright daylight & shown us many a fine Dutch
picture, & a grand oil sketch by Titian. Also a Mr. Phipps who has
some good things & on Friday is a similar party at Grosvenor House. I
live in the world of pictures just now, to my great delight, & have twice
been feasting on those belonging to Mr. Baring, a far finer collection
than Munro's which I should have liked to shown you.

I do not doubt that you hear from our little friend, but still you
will be glad to hear what little I can tell. The world is stating her
approaching marriage to Millais with the most utter positiveness &
untruth, & the report will be contradicted by time. These Philobiblions,[4]
a society who profess to talk of old books, but really meet only to
gossip, have set this report freshly about. I quarrel with any untruth
about the dear little lady, & especially that they can fancy that she
could think of such a thing yet. She deserves better of the world. At the
same time I can say, as far as I hear, that the feeling for her is steadily
increasing, & that against him the same. I hear no abuse, but down
right condemnation. John Murray, who was cautious at first, is openly

against him now. Lord Glenelg has been to me to hear about her, by
his own wish of course, & proved to me in divers ways that he had
been much more actively interested than he has given <u>her</u> to suppose.
Indeed he has been so cautious towards her, that she & her parents think
him not a false friend, but none at all. He amused me by hoping that
<u>you</u> were among her steady adherents. He told me that both by letters
when about, & now in person he has heard only <u>one</u> opinion expressed.
He told me that he is sure she wd not have lived much longer had she
remained at her post of suffering. She is now at St. Andrews as you may
know — a bathing place in Fife — & is considerably better — indeed, she
assures me, quite well. I hear frequently from her & all she says inspires
me with the utmost respect for her good sense, & admirable conduct
under circumstances which wd try most women. I fear no reaction for
her, but foresee that the further she is removed by time & habits from
her former life the more terrible & hateful will it appear to her. Of
him we have heard nothing since he had the audacity to write to Sir
Chas. He had borrowed some of Sir Chas' books & absconded without
returning them. After a time, as the fear of loosing them increased,
Sir Chas wrote to the <u>old man</u> requesting they might be returned, &
thus showing that he ignored the existence of the young one. But John
Ruskin understands no such hints, & in due time there came a letter
from Geneva — written in the most <u>empressé</u> way — regretting that he
had not had one <u>moment</u> of time before leaving Engld (time enough to
write in the Times about art & religion) — promising to return them as
soon as he came back — begging "kind regards to Lady E:" &c &c as if
quite sure of a welcome whenever he might please to present himself.
He there said that he shd be home in August & I since hear reports that
he will be back the first week in August — also that he has too much
<u>compassion</u> for her to publish her conduct to the world, as he intended
to do! This wd be a true Ruskin evasion.

My lightness of heart which had been much restored by little Effie's
present safety & comfort, has been much depressed of late by the sad
tidings of Ctss Rossi's death — of the cholera, at Mexico. I had known
her in Petersburg, & again here most intimately, & all her toils &
fatigues which she went through <u>heroically</u>, looking always to the bright
goal of a final private life with her childn. Two of them are at a convent
school at Roehampton, & it has been my pleasing duty to visit them
from time to time & report their growth & looks to the poor mother.
They have not yet been informed of their loss, tho' England is singing
with it, but I fear tomorrow I shall have to assist in putting this heavy
trial on them. They are a girl of 18 & a child of 8, each equally wanting
maternal care. It is a most sad dispensation. Her husband was with her,

& has been a kind one, as foreign counts go, but his family disdained the woman who alone has worked to rescue the Rossi race from poverty, & her son – a contemptible fool, secretary to some Sardinian Embassy – affected to be ashamed of his mother, & to be hipped at the name of <u>Sonntag</u>. Thus she is probably taken from the evil to come, but I am one of a numerous class of friends who deeply regret her.[5]

Now dear Mr. Browne, this letter has become unconscionably long – when you find time to write tell me about your book & whether I can do anything for you or it, & believe me
Your's very truly
Eliz Eastlake
Sir Chas did not pick Hartzen's brains about the price of the book. The following are the books or numbers he wishes for if they come in your way.
Memorie spellante a Tiziano – dal P. Luigi Pungileone, nel Giornale arcadico dio mesi d'agosto e di settembre 1831.
Aglietti, elogico storico dei Bellini – alti dell'academia Veneta 1812.
Lettera di Aless: Paravia al Conte Napione stampata in Venezia nel 1826. Ove si sende conti di tutto sio che pertione al guardo del Pietro Martine di Tiziano.

1. Brown's draft copy of his reply (dated 11 July 1854) also mentions the 'druggist', clearly the seller of the book. (See manuscript NOTT PWM228.)

2. Georg Ernst Harzen (1790–1863), a Hamburg art dealer and collector.

3. The Öttingen Wallerstein collection of early Italian, German and Flemish pictures was acquired by Prince Albert in the 1850s. See Lionel Cust, 'The Royal Collectors, Art 1, H.R.H. Prince Albert as an Art Collector', *The Burlington Magazine for Connoisseurs*, vol. 5, no. 13 (1904), pp. 7–11.

4. Philobiblon Society established by Monckton Milnes in 1853.

5. Henrietta Sontag, Countess Rossi (1806–54) was a German coloratura soprano who performed with great success in many cities across Europe and North America. Elizabeth first met her in Reval in the late 1830s (LSB2, pp. 170–73). Countess Rossi died of cholera on a tour of Mexico and, as an old friend, Elizabeth had been charged with breaking the news to her children. See *Life of Henriette Sontag, Countess de Rossi with Interesting Sketches by Scudo, Hector Berlioz, Louis Boerne, Adolphe Adam, Marie Aycard, Julie de Maguéritte, Prince Puckler-Muskau, and Theophile Gautier* (New York: Stringer & Townsend, 1852).

Letter to Euphemia Ruskin   *ML MA 1338 W.01*

7 Fitzroy Sqre
Aug 10 1854
My darling Effie

I have not willingly abstained so long from writing to you – but in preparing to leave home my time has been more disturbed. Tomorrow morng I expect my dear mother & my sister Jane, & in the afternoon we go on to a little cottage at Dulwich which we have taken together for 3 weeks or so. The Crystal Palace is directly before us & occasionally we shall spend a day there – especially if my dear mother can bear the motion of an easy wheel chair. Then I also hope Sir Chas. will will [sic] find he can't remain away & make me quite happy by joining us. You know he is always anxious to promote my havg change of air, though he is sceptical as to its effect upon himself. In several exploring drives which I made at Sydenham & Dulwich before I could find any suitable accomodation I have passed close to the scene of your former troubled & harrassed life & even to be in that neighbourhood gives me pain. But all that is <u>over,</u> & another life lies before you, my dear child – & one that cannot but sparkle brightly to your view – for your heart, however mistrustful it may have become, is now really engaged. I knew that it was so, I can only honour you for having held it in tight subjection at a time & during trials when a little sophistry might have argued you into believing that you were not bound to do so. All I hope & believe is that out of your past sufferings that good may have sprung, that all <u>delusions</u> may be powerless upon you, & that you may view your future with <u>safer</u> eyes. But don't think more of it than you can help. Be sure that you do more than enough for him in letting him look forward to the privilege of making you really happy – & let neither his happiness nor misery disturb that rest of body & peace of thought which you so much need. Think only of <u>yourself,</u> it won't be <u>selfishness.</u> I shd have better liked to have shipwrecked him – with canvas, colours & brushes on a desert island for two years & then rescued him. I like him very much – but I shd not want him yet awhile. I wanted my Effie to be <u>untroubled</u> till she was fit for this life's work again, knowing all the time that the two dear people were safe enough to come together at last. But all is overruled – & now my only refuge is in hoping that you will disturb yourself about his waving locks as little as you can, & give him just the scantiest <u>parish</u> allowance to keep him from starving.

Aug 11: So far I wrote last night & now I have the dear touching left-handed letter which goes to my heart. It will be long before you are thoroughly to be <u>trusted</u> in health – for all those poisoned thumbs & fingers are symptoms of nature's low funds, & no wonder indeed Everett must be content with very few lines now. You are too kind my Effie with your donation of preserves. They shall be greatly honored & Sir Charles shall cut his "rolly-polly pudding" & think of you – he happens to be particularly fond of that viand.[1]

Your last letter before this so full of sweet openness to me touched me indescribably. I have felt from the beginning that all things must work together for good to one who loved God & your history only strengthens my faith. Everett will feel that his once wretched & now happy love was a part in God's great & wise designs. Tell your dear mother that I agreed in every syllable of her letter to me but she knows like myself that it is well we have not the settling & choosing of our lots or the lots of those we love. Our part is to recognise the blessings given us, & not be anxious to cut & carve our lives exactly according to our own ideas. She was a brave woman indeed about her teeth, but I see she is paying the penalty. I trust she will be soon well & restored to <u>pristine beauty</u>. She is one of the brightest beings I ever met with.

I hope I may write in time to prevent your shaving your head – tell Mr. Brown I strictly forbid it. The cap & short hair wd be very pretty but the hair wd never come so well again. I have known this from experience. Nourish your hair well & keep your dear fair head cool – night & day.

Our old Waagen left us on Wednesday but probably returns after a turn in the <u>Shires</u> of three weeks. He spends a week first with yr old friend Danby Seymour – whom he calls from his bright eyes "die Maus im Mehltopf". We had Mrs Huskisson & her two annual guests – Lady Davy, Boxall &c on Tuesday to dinner. Calling also on Lady D: a day or two before I found Lady Westminster who did not know your history & listened to it with the deepest interest. Also I heard at the Carrick Moores that Lady Chantrey had showed them a letter from a gentleman with whom she had some argument regarding you – she being all wrong – but that he had discovered the <u>truth</u> & wrote to her to say that he could not sleep until he had told Lady C: how differently he now thought.

Now my dearest, I trust the <u>24</u> have had a merry dinner. Kind love to Papa & Mamma. My address is "Dulwich Common".

Yr ever affte

Eliz Eastlake

1. Food.

Letter to Euphemia Gray   *ML MA 1338 W.04*

Dulwich Common
Aug 14 1854
My darling Effie

Though I left Fitzroy Sqre on Friday yet I have heard from the faithful Tucker of the arrival "of Miss Gray's box" (for all my servants are anxious to send the old name to Coventry) & of the very large supply of good things it contains. Tomorrow I drive to Fitzroy Sqre & shall, after having inspected Sir Chas, inspect my storeroom treasures. I am only ashamed that you & your dear mother should bestow so much on us. I already do fancy myself one of the <u>family</u>, but I must not let you make me a burden to it. However, I shall eat your preserves during winter months with both real & imaginary gusto.

We are here comfortably settled – & my dear Mother's quarters are especially nice, convenient & airy which is the one thing needful. She effected her move hither very tolerably – especially the latter part of it & she has had no excessive suffering since she has been here, which she thinks quite a blessing. It is a very great delight to be together & Mamma is so utterly unselfish that her whole thought & aim is to avoid her suffering being a pain to others. But still, dear Effie, you can believe that they are a suffering to me, tho' one I do not grudge.

I have been grieving for sad events lately. Mrs. Proctor's widowed sister a Madame de Very, married on 26th of last month to Count Revel Swedish plenipotentiary, a very excellent anglicised man – after long attachment & engagement; & he dead with the cholera on the 30th. How the poor creature bears the shock of it is impossible to imagine – except in that strength which is in proportion to her excessive need. And then the death of Ld Jocelyn by cholera on Saturday, at Ld Palmerston's home, taken abt at noon & dead 12 hours after. These are indeed things to make us remember what we are. You are a loved –- [*letter torn*] but your heart I know is, for the present, more with those who weep than with those who make merry, & always will be so.

Mamma's & my sister's express love to you. They shall be glad to hear that the little thumb is better, but don't you write, my sweet darling, till you are able.

Yr always affte
Eliz Eastlake

Letter to Euphemia Gray   *ML MA 1338 W.13*

7 Fitzroy Sqre
Janry 1 1855
My Darling Effie

I have not indulged myself with a letter to you for an immense time during which time I have had one of your always comforting letters (for they always have both heart & heart satisfied & happy) & have thought & spoken of you often & often. And now I can't see the beginning of another year without thanking God with you for the especial mercies of the past, & for the so conspicious [?] working together of good of all things to one who truly loves Him. When I recall the trouble of hearts which you were in – & which I had the privilege of sharing with you – in which nothing broke the darkness of the present & future except the one polar star of trust & dependance on God, & then turn to complete deliverance which He has granted to you I can only lift up my heart in praise – & feel that your life had added fresh motives to my faith. And doubtless your history has done that for many – such is the blessed force of one right example. And now, darling, I share with you the hopes of happiness which this year holds out; tho' also a shyness of looking forward to any form of happiness except that which you now enjoy under your dear parents' roof.

My parties were delayed two days & came off on the 21st, the 23rd & the 27th on each of which occasions the dinners were 17 strong. My ladies on the first occasions were sweet Mrs. Boyle & my sister Miss Rigby. Mrs. Boyle is looking perfectly beautiful just now, being much stouter which greatly becomes her. Hadie & she struck up a friendship on the strength of "the dear Effie" – the first words that were spoken as I introduced the one to the other. Hadie looked to great advantage, & showed all her artless, lively honesty – quite captivating Sir Chas. She remained the night but had to leave directly after breakfast for her little nephew's christening. A certain young Apollo came in the evening, & Hadie frankly & innocently said "I won't be introduced to Millais because I can't talk on the only subject I most want to talk on". But the scruple did not last, for in 5 minutes afterwards they fell together without introduction, & were very inseparable for the rest of the eveng – he not knowing who she was. He told me afterwards that he thought her handsome & interesting.[1] The next dinner we had Mrs. Jameson, Miss John Carrick-Moore, dear Mr. & Mrs. Murray, & Miss Hosmer.[2] & on the 3rd & last our laity consisted of the Emerson Tennents, Mr. Tremenheere, Mr. Foster, Editor of Our Examiner, Miss Carrick Moore

& the little <u>Infanta</u>, whom I always find a most kind & well bred little girl.[3] People came in the evening each time & thus made the parties rather late which I must own tried me much. Then Christmas Day brought a few old friends & young nephews. And now I have finished for a while with a dinner party of my <u>own</u> last Saturday – Sir Chas being obliged to dine at the Academy – consisting of my old kind friends Mr. Murray's sisters, the Gruners, & cousins of our's & nephews of Sir Chas' – all so familiar & dear that our dearest mother joined us at the table. And now I must go back & tell you that she & my sister came to us on the 21st & will remain I trust until the end of this new month. Mamma shows her real improvement in being able to join us at every meal, when alone, & in such far happier accounts of her nights rest. For this we cannot be too thankful, especially at a time when our hearts are <u>excited</u> with the expectation of receiving my dear sister Matilda with the excellent husband (Mrs. Murray's brother) & 4 little ones <u>in a few days</u>. They started from Bombay on the 28th Novr, & we have heard of their safe arrival at Alexandria & now, with God's gracious blessing, we look for "the Euxine" to arrive at Southampton on the 4th, 5th or 6th. With their <u>not</u> favourable winds it may be the latest day. We send our invaluable Tucker to Southampton the 4th & he will telegraph me the time of their arrival, & the <u>train</u> by which we may expect them, & you will imagine the trembling emotion with which the beloved party will be welcomed. My sister has been away 7 years, & brings us there 4 new little ones – tender babes of 6 & 4 years, of 22 months & of 4 months. Sir Chas had kindly begged the whole party to come at once here, but they prefer a lodging until they are a little to rights. & as I must have sent away my dear mother & Jane to make room for them, I am reconciled to having them within the distance of a few streets at first. I have engaged roomy comfortable lodgings – & have been preparing many a little comfort to welcome the weary ones.[4]

Janry 2nd 1855

Now darling since beginning this I have recd your kind box full of good things through the medium of Mr. Halliday, who kindly sent it up here yesterday afternoon, & Tucker immediately expressed his opinion that it was from "Miss Gray". You are far <u>too</u> good my Effie, & so are dear father & mother to send these Scotch hospitalities so far to me. And the <u>thought</u> gives a further sweetneess to all. Our <u>Matty</u> will partake in your present, & the childn will experience for the first time that their father's Scotland is the land of <u>cakes</u>.

Last night we dined at the Murrays – our usual unusual dinner there which includes all their relatives, & even one of our's for they always have our favourite cousin Mr. Simpson. And then Mr. Murray steals

round to each, & has a nice kind present to each – beautiful books
or bonbon boxes – & the little childn in return get toys without end.
Dear Mrs Murray is looking so sweet, with her lovely hair, & sweet
expression. And Mrs Gruner who only returned about 10 days ago from
France has quite recovered health, & <u>hair</u>, & is looking her prettiest.
One of her first gentle questions was for <u>you</u>. And so you see I am
surrounded with rich blessings in store & expectation, & if any fail, I
can only the more prize the many that are left. Dear Sir Chas is upon
the whole well. Of mutual friends I have seen kind Lady Lewis, as you
know, who is full of interest & Mrs. Ford, who was alone in London
with her mother – but Ford is home now – & then kind Lady Davy,
who had had a bad cold, & could not come out to any parties. I have
succeeded in getting her a most worthy, cheerful & intelligent maid for
herself, & believe that I have done both parties a real service. This maid
has been accustomed to age & infirmity, & I am sure to more selfishness
than she will have from our eccentric old friend. This morning the
bargain was struck, & the maid came back & told me that Lady Davy
has told all her faults, & all that she would have to put up with, & was
very hopeful that she shd suit her. It will be a comfort to me, & I know
to you also, that she is in kind & sensible hands.

   Well darling, & now last but not least, for a few words on that other
<u>E</u> who interests me more & more. He has been in several times, & has
now quite worn off his shyness with me, & does himself <u>justice</u> for I see
into his refined intelligent nature, & into the sound religious principles
which animate him. On the last two occasions mamma & Jane have
been in the room so he has not been able to talk on the one dear
subject, & this has perhaps given me the opportunity of judging of him
with more impartiality. Immediately after my last hurried note to you
I drove to Hanover Terrace & saw that picture which he had finished.
I thought I could not have borne to look at it, & yet felt that I shd be
wrong to let the sight of it escape me. It was a very foggy day, & I
could only see that it was a <u>marvel</u> of art, & beg to bring Sir Chas the
next day. So we both went, & a better light showed us beauties which
I had not discovered before & enabled Sir Chas to pronounce it "a first
rate work of art". He was <u>enchanted</u> with it, & enthusiastically like
myself. & both of us forgot & <u>could</u> forget the <u>subject</u>, while we hung
spell-bound over the art. I could not have believed that any portrait of
him cod have given me any pleasure, but in truth the personality of the
portrait sitting vanished before the skill of the painter. Sir Chas said over
& over again that it was "one of the remarkable pictures in the world"
– & we could liken it to nothing but Van Eyck, for with all the minutia
of finish a greater breadth of grander feeling pervades the whole. As

we came away Sir Chas remarked to me that Millais stood in a most beautiful & interesting position – whether to the eye of painter or moralist, fairly started in a career of great distinction – his toil over, his pleasure to come, with unsullied reputation, finely constituted mind, & splendid person. And darling I listened & assented with a glowing heart, taking a tenfold pleasure in the praise unknown to Sir Chas – or not quite unknown for I am sure he understands in a quiet way why I take such interest in the fine young painter.

I have the parental feeling for you so strongly, that all this from a man so well able to judge, & never profuse in expressions was balm to me as I know it will be to your dear mother.

And now God bless you and yours my darling one – in this and all seasons – my next few lines shall tell you of our Matilda's arrival – my heart and even my stomach are in a whirl with thinking of it.

Ever your loving
Eliz Eastlake

1. Miss Rigby is Jane; Mrs Boyle was Eleanor Vere Boyle; see letter, 10 June 1854, n. 1.

2. Anna Jameson (1794–1860), Irish art historian and writer. See Adele Holcomb, 'Anna Jameson: The First Professional English Art Historian', *Art History*, 6 (1983), pp. 171–87; Mrs Steuart Erskine (ed.), *Anna Jameson: Letters and Friendships* (London: T. Fisher Unwin Ltd, 1915); Clara Thomas, *Love and Work Enough: The Life of Anna Jameson* (London: Macdonald, 1967); and Judith Johnston, *Anna Jameson: Victorian, Feminist, Woman of Letters* (London: Scholar Press, 1997). Miss John Carrick-Moore is one of the two daughters of James Carrick-Moore, surgeon and biographer; John and Menie Murray; and Harriet Hosmer (1830–1908), American sculptor.

3. Sir James Emerson Tennent MP (1804–69), traveller, writer and politician; Hugh Seymour Tremenheere (1804–93), author and barrister; Emilia Gayangos, daughter of Pascual de Gayangos from Madrid, is the little infanta (she later married Don Juan Facundo Riaño; see letter, 16 August 1876). This dinner party on 27 December is recorded by Richard Redgrave in his diary of 31 December 1854: 'When assembled in the drawing-room after coffee, Sir Charles proposed to us to play at the "new game" of "Post," and seated us in a circle, ladies and men together. We each took the name of some town, and Rome, Florence, Constantinople, and London … Our President, with his precise white tie, volunteered to be blindfolded, and blindfolded he was, and then the game began. Lady Eastlake called out the names of two towns, such as London to Sebastopol, and these had immediately to change places without going out of the ring, while the blindfolded member of the party was, if possible, to catch one or other in transit. The fun soon grew fast and furious … There was Barry dodging Stanfield, stout and burly both, and contrasting with the spare and compact President, who was on the watch

for them.' Frances Margaret Redgrave, *Richard Redgrave: A Memoir Compiled from his Diary* (London: Cassell & Co., 1891), pp. 114–15.

4. Matilda and James Smith were returning from Ceylon.

Letter to Mrs Gray   *ML MA 1338 W.27*

7 Fitzroy Sqre
July 4 1855
My Dear Mrs. Gray

You may be sure that my thoughts were seldom away from you yesterday, & that I took part in spirit in all that went on. You must be glad this too interesting event is over, tho' it is hard for you to part again with her even under the most promising auspices. Many a prayer was offered up for the pair by those who know that they were yesterday to be united, and I cannot but feel that if anyone may look for a Blessing in her now new state it is our much loved Effie.

It was so kind of you to write & give me many interesting particulars. Your & Mr. Gray's opinion upon <u>him</u> is of great weight with me. I had truly formed a very favourable estimate of him, & inclined as I was to be anxious rather than sanguine I still could see no sign of a <u>rock</u> in the path. I don't doubt that she will have those trials for which we women are all the better, but she will also I trust & believe enjoy more happiness than falls to the common lot, for she will be proud of his great gifts as well as secure in his right principles. Indeed he may well have thought the paradise of Bowerswell "a dream" for no man ever had <u>less</u> reason to believe in the accomplishments of his inclinations. It is seldom too that parents can draw such comparison between a daughter's first & second marriage. You will be sure to have made many, which I shall be truly interested to hear some day. Now I know that you are going with your numerous little ones to the seaside, & therefore I shall hardly look for a letter yet. The occasion was stripped of its mournfulness by the prospect of all being together again, when you & they respectively return. It is the most fortunate thing in the world to have them next door.

I hope that you will send the marriage to the Times not only that those who wish her well may know that it is over, but that the bad set who will have it that she has been <u>long</u> married may be discomfited. If you wd send me precise names – for I fancy dear Effie has another Christian name – I wd forward the announcement to Printing House Sqre with pleasure.

I wd not allude to that <u>other</u> creature but to tell you a story which will amuse you & Mr. Gray. It is this – that he wrote to Mr. Roberts the painter saying that he thought him a most amiable man &c but very <u>dangerous</u> to <u>art</u>, & that therefore he intended to attack every picture he painted, but that he hoped it would make no difference to their friendship! – Robert's answer was 'My dear Ruskin, I am very obliged by your letter. I beg to say that every time I meet you I intend to pull your nose, but I hope it will make no difference in our friendship &c &c". I think this is very likely to be true, at all events the world <u>believes</u> it.

Now dear Mrs. Gray I shall soon send a note to Effie to her old address, as she tells me it will be forwarded, & I shall hope to hear from you at your leisure. With kindest regards and congratulations to Mr Gray

I am ever yr's truly
Eliz Eastlake

Letter to Rawdon Brown   *NOTT PWM230*

7 Fitzroy Sqre
Novr 23 1855
My Dear Mr. Brown
I recd your kind letter yesterday and was very glad to be informed by yourself of your welfare, & here am I troubling you again with a letter still sooner than I purposed because I am <u>ordered</u> to do so. Sir Charles, who ignores all his bad behaviour to you when he wants to ask a favour, has received tidings of Schielin's having paid old Schiavoni his money for the 2 pictures – one for John Murray & the other for self last purchased, & of their being already in Zen's hands,[1] but contrary to his usual order in such matters, it does not appear that he has given Zen in any way instructions how to forward them to England. He wants you therefore (in his <u>cool</u> way!) to take the trouble of telling Zen that they are to be consigned to the case of McCracken[2] as before & to be expedited by as early an opportunity as possible. I believe he intends telling your beloved Mr. Mündler (to whom, however, you have been most kind) to have the proper insurance effected upon them.[3] This is all my message, accompanied by kind regards & so forth. You don't suppose that I read Sir Chas your opinion of Mr. Mündler's new acquaintance Della Rovere! He wd not have a moment's peace, & as meanwhile he has effected a most important purchase for the Nat: Gallery through the help – or rather instrumentality of this same individual – & feels himself greatly

obliged, the dear gentleman would not know what to do or think. This last transaction is a profound secret, and therefore of course I tell it you! The truth is that a magnificent Paul Veronese originally from the Church of S. Silvestro in Venice destined for Paris has been adroitly turned in the direction of London – was stretched & seen in our front drawing room for the first time – was on et approuvé, [sic][4] & wooed, married & a' in the course of a few hours. It is a grand thing, in excellent state, & has been obtained for a comparatively low price, & so far there is no mistake. Sir Chas considers this a great stroke of statesmanship on the part of Mr. Mündler, who attributes all the merit of it to his rogue friend. However, you must not know anything about the affair until informed by one of the good gentlemen themselves. Mr. Mündler may make what mistakes he pleases about his friendship, as long as he makes none about pictures!

And now I cannot help firmly believing that John Murray meant far more by what he said to me on the subject of yr present labours than he could have done on former occasions, for he seemed to wish to have it, & that for so cautious a man is going far. But time will prove – meanwhile go on & prosper – I rejoice at every additional sheet you add to the lump – & also meanwhile do not hesitate to send me by any favourable opportunity your worthy Chaplain's work – scored & rough as it may be, & I shall have true pleasure in going through it, & if I can't decipher I will let you know. I shall therefore expect a packet unless I hear to the contrary.

I heard of Mrs. Norton yesterday in Paris as rather taken with a handsome young man. This is so unlike the dear lady that of course it can't be true, but still I thought you wd like to know! Lady Lewis I saw the day before yesterday. She was very kind & we talked of you. Of dear Effie I hear that she was very serious at Keir – who can wonder! Now dear Mr. Brown goodbye again for the present. Yrs very truly
Eliz Eastlake

1. Natale Schiavoni (1777–1858), painter and seller of Italian paintings. Zen may be either Antonio Zen, a dealer and packer, or Catterino Zen, an agent.

2. Otto Mündler (1811–70), German art historian and dealer, appointed by Eastlake as travelling agent for the National Gallery on 2 July 1855. Mündler scouted for prospective sales of paintings on the Continent, keeping a travel diary for the Trustees that meticulously recorded potential acquisitions. Eastlake regarded the post as a great success; however, there was sustained criticism of Mündler in the press, and his post was abolished by the House of Commons in 1858, although he continued to work on an occasional basis for Eastlake and his successor, William Boxall. See Jaynie Anderson, 'Introduction to the Travel Diary of Otto Mündler', *The Walpole Society*, vol. 51 (1985), pp. 7–59.

3. Messrs 'J&R McCracken General & Foreign Agents, by appointment, to the Royal Academy, and Agents Generally for the reception and Shipment of Works of Art, Baggage, &c. From and to all parts of the world'.

4. I.e. *lu et approuvé*, 'read and approved'.

Letter to John Scandrett Harford[1]   BRO 28048/C/68/3

7 Fitzroy Sqre
Janry 2 1856
Dear Mr. Harford

You are most kind to have remembered us on New Year's Day, and I beg you to accept both Sir Chas' thanks and mine. The game arrived last night in excellent condition, and we shall make it the occasion for toasting you and Mrs. Harford with all the good wishes of the season.

Our travels last autumn took us to Florence – a first visit on my part, and I need not tell you the impression it produced on me. Comparatively little as a fortnight enabled me to get acquainted with its glorious treasures. I am full of them, and for life. Owing to an interruption one day Sir Chas visited S: Croce without me, but he tells me that your interposition has not availed and that it is a carpet manufactory still! We know the Cav: Buonarroti well – and good and worthy he is – but I am convinced from what we ourselves experienced that neither he nor any of the Tuscan government will even lift a hand to save a work of art, at least nothing older than Michael Angelo. We saw precious things perished and perishing, which the government won't save themselves anad yet won't allow others to rescue. With our tastes now stimulated for the great old Florentines it is doubly hard that it should be so difficult to rescue them.

Sir Chas' health took great good from the change of air and scene, and I truly hope that I may keep him well until we go again!

With our best compliments to Mrs. Harford believe me
Yours truly
Eliz Eastlake

1. John Scandrett Harford (1785–1866), banker, landowner, Quaker and abolitionist. Harford was the author of the *Life of Michelangelo* in 1857 and he had also financed an ambitious chromolithograph after the ceiling of the Sistine Chapel in 1852–53, published by Colnaghi in 1854 with a dedication to Charles Eastlake.

Letter to Rawdon Brown   *NOTT PWM232*

7 Fitzroy Sqre
April 25 1856
My Dear Mr. Brown

It is only within the last few days that I have obtained Mr. Murray's verdict, & I am sorry to say that it approaches nearer to your prognostics than to mine. He has not a soul for Busino and declines marshalling him into the world, tho' he dwells on the interest of many portions and thinks the translation most appropriately done.[1] So then I shall write to Mr. Cheney today (wd that you had said <u>Edward</u> instead of Henry! for I am faithful) & leave the book in Audley Sqre where I don't know yet whether they are arrived. I do hope that Smith & Elder will be more alive to what I feel the attraction of the book. I retain my opinion on it, & have repeated it to Murray.

We are getting rather giddy now – the season already getting up its steam though not yet with high pressure. I delay my personal hospitalities until after the Academy dinner & opening of the Exhibition which rather occupies Sir Chas. Then I have to give a few great dinners, & <u>aged</u> as I am, & hardened too, I assure you I can't anticipate 17 people at a time coming like some inexorable Fate upon us without a nervous shudder! I don't mind giving all these before <u>you</u> come, as, tho' not nervous like me, you have the good sense to despise them philosophically.

My prettiest party lately was at Marochetti's (the sculptor's) rooms – his great granary-like studios opened – with flaring gas, as in a butcher's shop, above, & a rope carpet beneath, & all the beauty and aristocracy of England circulating among his charming works of art.[2]

Sir Chas has not been so well as I cd wish. I hardly suppose that you saw that attack upon the Nat: Gallery in the House of Commons – but if you did you must not suppose that he cared for it. Indeed the defence was worth ten of the attack, which was both so violent & so shallow that it has turned the abuse upon itself – & now all the neutral papers are become our hearty partisans. In short the attack was very unEnglish and is therefore repudiated. Then my dear Sposo never cares for real bothers, it is only imaginary ones that assault & hurt his soul.

Millais has been here – as happy as in the honeymoon, & happier, intending to stay for the opening of the Exhibition but, finding he cd not live without the sweet Effie, he is gone back again. He has done much & well – has made great improvement in certain things, but has still to throw off much of the poisonous Ruskin-teaching, for the principal object of a painter – the true imitation of flesh – he is as deficient in as ever, while all the imitation of wood, & velvet & in which he is much improved only makes his flesh appear the more behind-hand. On this account I don't think his pictures will be the fashion this year, but that does not matter. They are most profitably sold – & it is better for him, morally, now to go on in the race at a safer pace. He is becoming more catholic in his tastes for pictures, & has evidently already learnt much good sense from his good angel. As to the Denmark Hill "party" as Millais calls him the Edinr & Quarterly have both opened simultaneously upon him and admirably to the point – the one having taken up his contradictions, the Q: his general ignorance of the principles of art.[3] He won't care, but I trust the public will be more convinced that he is a false teacher.

Now dear Mr. Brown goodbye – I hope your next letter will tell me that you are coming. Your's most truly
Eliz Eastlake

1. Brown had translated the diary of Orazio Busino, chaplain to the Venetian Ambassador in London in the early seventeenth century.

2. Carlo Marochetti (1805–67), Italian sculptor mostly of public monuments. His large studio and foundry was on Fulham Road, close to his home in Onslow Square.

3. She is disingenuously referring to her own attack, 'Modern Painters [by Ruskin]' in the *Quarterly Review*, vol. 98 (March 1856), pp. 384–433.

Letter to Rawdon Brown   *NOTT PWM233*

7 Fitzroy Sqre
Novr 16 1856
My Dear Mr. Brown

I have been intending to write to you ever since I had the pleasure of welcoming Sir Chas safe back again, and now, as I shall be year older tomorrow (when Sir Chas and I most properly celebrate the same birthday) I will not carry forward such a debt to the new page, but let the present year have the pleasure of discharging it. From all I hear, I gather that Sir Chas & you lived on the most amicable terms during his short stay in Venice. He indulges often in the warmest retrospect of your kindness, & as long as your tamarinds lasted he drank your health nightly in delightful probations, of which I was allowed an occasional spoonfull, & when the contents were done it was difficult to separate him from the pot! Tucker too had a tale to tell me about some beer, accompanied with great eulogies of the giver. It is true that Sir Chas insinuates that you liked him all the better for coming without me! But I disdain to listen to such a perversion of the truth. He was quite disappointed not to be able to clear up a question regardg a certain Christopher Urswick (he told me Eastwick at first till I corrected him from your book, & Richd the 3rd).[1] He went to the British Museum and looked over the Cardinals but found no such name. Had there been any catalogue of Bishops he would have searched it too, but none exist. You must tell me if he or I can pursue some better scent for you. Since then he has resumed his usual indefatigable life, & has brought so much health & strength back from Italy that I rejoice to see in him that "cheerful heart" which in the Proverbs of today say "is better than medicine" & which is all he usually wants. You may guess it was a very happy meeting between Baucis & Philomon when he returned one Friday night the 24th October.[2]

Meanwhile I had been solacing myself for his absence as I best could among kind friends in Scotland where I soon recovered my usually admirably behaved health. The visit to Perth was truly interesting. At the first sight I caught of her I saw how much she was improved in health & also in beauty.[3] She is not the little dainty pretty girl now, but, tho' equally slight & young looking, she has a far higher look. Distress of mind & body are both gone, & much sound happiness is in the bright full cheek, but also there is a something which tells of suffering overcome, which, however pathetic, adds much to her beauty. I need not tell you how warmly I was welcomed, & how soon a little gentleman was held up before me, the image of the Papa, who stared most assiduously at the stranger. It was very bad weather the two only days down there, but I almost enjoyed the excuse of sitting tête a tête with dear Effie and talking of so much that was deeply interesting. I trust her for her character of good Millais, & all I saw confirmed it. He is of a nice, upright nature, full of social as well as other talents & adores her. He was looking a very handsome fellow in a kilt & strode about fishing & shooting in a way that would not have paralysed the other party. I don't mean to say that our dear little friend has a literal bed of roses, for Millais is a painter, as well as a man, but his faults are such as she is particularly fitted to cope with, & she is a great God send to him. Her father & all about him, family, home and grounds, are all quite delightful, & it is quite true what Millais had told me before that Effie's first marriage was no advancement to her in point of luxury & comfort. Indeed Denmark Hill is not near so handsome a place as Mr. Gray's Bowerswell, near Perth. Effie even told me that she has now far greater

liberty in money matters than before, & I was glad to hear that Millais'
earnings are well invested & already amount to a very nice provision
for the future. They don't think of coming to London till next April,
& then probably not to live here, for fear that she is still quite unequal.
Also, stronger as she is, she is little fitted for anything but a very quiet
life, tho' no one can be more actively useful in that quiet sphere than
herself. You may believe that we talked of a certain gentleman in Venice
con amore!

And then I had a very enjoyable 2 days at the "brother in law's". If
you have not seen Keir you have not seen one of the most beautiful
places in the world. It is a Paradise of magnificent scenery and exquisite
rest combined. I did not think I could have liked the owner of such
a place so well. Or that one could forget that he was it, in his other
more personal attraction. He was charming, and many a little thing bore
witness to the sense & unaffected goodness of his character. The world
& you say that he is engaged to be married, but, to my dull eyes, there
were no signs of such a state, as usually precedes a marriage ceremony
– though I heartily wish it may be true, if the lady be good enough for
so interesting a man. I hear that the lady has been staying there since,
and is there still I believe – in her absence the few honours he does
not do himself were done by a lady cousin. I can pay Mr. Stirling[4] no
higher compliment than to say that splendid and enjoyable as is Keir, I
believe he would be quite as happy, and quite as delightful without it.

Now dear Mr. Brown, I must bring this year to an end. The world
is not come to town, at least not to my knowledge. Sir Chas & I are
enjoying a tolerably quiet life. Tucker left your little packet in Audley
Sqre and wd do (in spite of your difference about a tallow candle!).
Mr. Mündler had no sooner returned to Paris than he fell in with the
Duke Melzi, & face to face concluded the purchase of the exquisite
Perugino formerly in the Casa Melzi at Milan. With full powers he
immediately turned upon his steps & recrossed the Alps, intending to
carry the picture off at once. But tho' it is in his hands, that is not easy,
as some forms have to be gone through at Vienna. Poor Mr. Mündler
is therefore kept waiting at Milan, while Sir Chas has done his best
by help from the Foreign Office, & also by private application to Sir
Hamilton Seymour whose sister is one of my most intimate friends. So
altogether we hope to spur the laziness of the Austrian Chancellerie,
which Sir H: S: says is hard enough always, & worse in the absence of
Count Buol.[5] The picture, however, is such a prize, that when we do
get hold of it we shall forget all previous bothers. The other day I saw
Mrs. Norton – just starting for Italy, but not intending to go by Venice.[6]
She spoke of herself as the humble adorer of a certain impervious

individual at Venice who, by her description, lords it over her with all
the consciousness of unbounded power, & I roared with laughter most
indecorously as I contemplated the Rawdon-pecked gentle lady.

The other day I had a most kind note from Henry Cheney in answer
to a regret on may part for his note to some charity. Lady Somers and
other friends I have not seen, and Layard, who is a favourite of mine, I
must not talk to you about.

Sir Chas is pretty well, and I try and make him bravely indifferent to
the nonsense – malicious and ignorant – which goes, and will infallibly
go the round of the papers at the acquisition of every new picture in the
N: Gallery. A glorious Mantegna form the Casa Sommaglia at Milan is
just arrived, but not yet up.

I am back from Murray's who accepted your Crispin's bill with a
smile and a promise to "see about it". Also he will be much much [sic]
more for you than that with pleasure.

Sir Chas desires to be most kindly remembered – no more travelling
about <u>alone</u> for him again!
Ever yours most truly
Eliz Eastlake

1. Christopher Urswick, priest who appears in Shakespeare's *Richard III*.

2. Baucis and Philemon were an old married couple in Ovid's *Metamorphoses*.

3. She means Effie Millais.

4. William Stirling Maxwell; see letter, 21 July 1859.

5. Foreign Minister of Austria.

6. Caroline Norton would marry William Stirling Maxwell in 1877.

Letter to John Murray   *NLS Ms.42175*

7 Fitzroy Sqre
February 2 1858
Dear Mr Murray

I return your Cavalcaselle's[1] letter to which Sir Chas assents & begs
me to return it you quickly so that there may be no hindrance to your
replying to it!! I have conceived a very low opinion of Vasari from my
study of M.Angelo's life by him which seems to be a mass of folly &
mistatements – but Sir Chas assures me that this life is his very worst. I
know but too little at present of his other biographies.

What a day this has been for our young princess! Tucker met her in the city – open carriages, very tearful eye – an immense multitude despite the weather. Poor Helen has been better off in a railway carriage.

Your's dear Mr. Murray very truly

Eliz Eastlake

1. Giovanni Battista Cavalcaselle (1819–97), Italian painter and collaborator with Joseph Archer Crowe on a number of art historical texts. Cavalcaselle was exiled in 1848 for his revolutionary activities and moved to England, where apparently his name was mooted as the National Gallery's Travelling Agent in 1855 (J. A. Crowe, *Reminiscences of Thirty-Five Years of My Life* (London: John Murray, 1895), pp. 236–37) but rejected on the grounds that he was exiled from the very country he would need to travel in. In 1857 Eastlake, John Murray, Layard and Tom Taylor formed a support group to finance Cavalcaselle in a proposed new edition of Vasari, which never materialised.

Letter to John Murray   *NLS Ms.42175*

7 Fitzroy Sqre

June 7 1858

My dear Mr. Murray

I fear I may not find you at home by the time I make my way to Albemarle Street. I therefore scribble this note with Sir Chas' message – viz: that he <u>greatly approves</u> of Cavalcaselle's sendings, that he has received the accompanying letter from him this morning & has already replied to it, telling him that he must adhere more to the plan advised, & make one Life at a time <u>perfect</u>. This will meet your wishes I do not doubt.

I have met, & shaken hands with <u>Coningham</u>! His very handsome face dissipated the last feelings of malice which his wife had not removed![1]

No letter from Senhals today – I am owing Annie an answer to her kind note, which I will soon send. I trust all are well at Wimbledon. Sir Chas "no matters".[2]

Your's dear Mr. Murray always truly

Eliz Eastlake

1. William Coningham (1815–79), art collector and politician, and critic of Eastlake's management of the National Gallery. See letter, 21 July 1859.

2. John Murray built a handsome home at Wimbledon reportedly on the profits from his *Handbooks for Travellers*. The house was called Newstead, in honour of Lord Byron, but it was also mischievously known as 'Handbook Hall'.

Letter to John Murray   *NLS Ms.42175*

7 Fitzroy Sqre
July 21 1858
Dear Mr. Murray

I find, to my regret, that Sir Chas is really too much engaged, preparing for a special meeting of Trustees on Friday – up in arms at Ld Elcho's falsities – to allow himself to agree to your very kind proposal.[1] So it must be "as you were". We shall expect you and Layard at 2½ and I shall rejoice to have your company for the drive out.
Your's ever truly
Eliz Eastlake

> 1. Lord Elcho had told a Committee of the House of Commons that the expenses of the National Gallery would be improved by removing the Royal Academy from the premises. He was also perceived to be instrumental in the removal of Mündler from his post as travelling agent for the Gallery.

Letter to Mrs Austen[1]   *NLS Ms.42167*

Florence
Septr 26. 1858
Dearest Mrs Austen

I resolved when I last parted from you in F. Sqre that if time permitted I shd myself trouble you with tidings of our condition & doings instead of leaving you to pick up information from good Mr. Murray. Indeed there is no one whose ever sympathising kindness entitles her to more grateful recollection than you may well claim from me, & it is a real pleasure to have the leisure to tell you so. I have too plenty of leisure & rest just now for you will be surprised to hear that I am alone now in Florence. Sir Chas having left me just a fortnight ago for a round of remote places which he kindly judged would be too rough work for me. In some places he is following Layard's steps of the summer before last, and has (at Gubbio) met with great kindness from two of L's friends there – Counts Reni and Bonfatti, but he is searching the country still more thoroughly and writes me word that much as he writes for my companionship in scenes of beauty and before pictures, he is too glad to know that I am quietly laid up here. He himself knocked up at first with the heat, fatigue and most intolerably bad accomodations, but he assures me he has become more seasoned, and is stronger than

when he started. He has our invaluable manservant with him and also
a Signor Cavalcaselle of whom Layard knows, so that he is not without
care & kind companions. Still I shall be thankful to welcome him back.

And now I can assure you that I am quite well & have gained
strength & health, & not found the heat of our early start so oppressive
as I feared. It is only during the last fortnight that we have had Italian
heat, & with all the comforts of an excellent hotel & cool galleries
in which I daily live. I have rather enjoyed the heat, or rather the
exquisite weather – one day of sapphire skies, & golden sunsets after
the other. At first I dreaded the unusual solitude of my life, & did feel
it rather overwhelmingly (being spoilt with such a companion as I am
accustomed to) but human nature may be relied on for compassion
on a forlorn lady, & from the visitors in the hotel, & chiefly from
Americans, I have recd a succession of kind attentions, that the Yankee
dialect begins to sound musical in my ears! I have had many things to
see for Sir Chas in his absence & it is very delightful to have time also
to mature one's impressions of certain masters. I have many new loves
among the painters, & fortunately in the art world it is not necessary to
be off with the old before you are on with the new. I have all Vasari
too with me, & pore over him of evengs – & am compelled not only
to read but to talk such Italian as I can muster, to the great amusement
of my Italian friends who laugh quite as much & as innocently at my
mistakes in their own tongue as the English do. Our journey thus far
was very agreeable. We peeped successively into Holland, Germany
& France on our way. The first always delightful in my eyes, though
I prefer it at the season when there are no gnats! Germany always
detestable at any season! We made our way to Hanover & Brunswick
to see Galleries there – & at Brunswick were rewarded. Then at Cassel,
a very pretty town, we found a public gallery which no Handbook
has enough extolled, & where Rembrandt is seen in unprecedented
perfection both in number & quality. Paris we were at on the 15th
August – which is the greatest day now in the public calendar, which
means that it calls forth a greater display of colored lamps than any
other day in the year. Seeing the preparations for the solemn tomfoolery
I made up my mind that French and English were & ever would be as
distinct in their nature as ever they had been.

We crossed the Mt Cenis – just seeing where the tunnel which is
to perforate the Alps finds its opening on the Savoy side. It will be 12
miles long – at £40 a yard – & will be almost as wonderful, & I trust
more successful at once than our Grande Atlantic Telegraph, the very
disasters of which only develop that energy & science of which we may
be truly proud.

Turin was new to me, & I was delighted with the gay royal city, with
its mountains marshalled around it. Thence we passed to Milan, where
the first night we were roused by the guns for the birth of the heir to
the throne of Austria. But the Italians never heard them! nor knew that
an Archduke was born unto them! nor even that Milan was to be right
loyally illuminated! Venice was our next resting place, & the old Queen
of the Sea was fascinating like a real Circe – so much so that Sir Chas
made no end of plans about hiring a Casa & coming to it every summer,
saying "why shd one not have a country house at Venice, as well as at
Hampstead."² But I think Florence has superceded the old Enchantress
already. At Turin I shd tell you we made the acquisition of a glorious
portrait by Moretto of Brescia – as fine in his way as Titian, which I am
sure you, & all worthy judges will admire. Other things are simmering &
will perhaps be ready to carry off by another year – all of which are very
interesting & will give the public new names & wider ideas.

From Venice we came on to Ferrara – the very type of desolation,
where the old Palaces are more dilapidated & the modern Italians more
indolent than I have yet seen. Nor does the past shed any favorable
prestige over the grass grown streets & tattered population – for there
stands the gloomiest & strangest of fortresses (the residence of the old
Dukes) in the heart of the city to show their power, & within a mile
is the unfinished dilapidation of the Schifa Noia to show their idleness.
The two together speak volumes for the sort of sway excercised by
the Dukes of Ferrara. Whether Tasso's dungeon be true or not, does
not matter, there is enough to prove the tyranny without that. But to
leave mouldering walls & turn to the ever beautiful country – truly it
is worth enduring some heat to see Italy still with her summer garb.
Our drive from Ferrara to Bologna was a perpetual succession of all
that the richest soil & most beneficent air could display. The grapes in
such gorgeous abundance, the country festooned for miles – & every
single festoon a picture. Then the peaches coloured the trees like apples
in Herefordshire, the figs stood out in great knobs black and green, &
every flower that is sweetest perfumed the gale in full bloom – for they
seem never to be in bud!

And now dearest Mrs Austen I must close this selfish & incoherent
letter – hoping that it might find you in better health, & with no
anxiety about dear Mr Austen, to whom pray give my love. Shd Layard
be with you tell him that I have no end of things for the Arundel.³ I
fear he will be coming to Florence just as we are leav.g it. I fear tho'
that I must not expect Sir Chas for 8 or 10 days more! Then we proceed
to Rome – beyond that our plans are uncertain, but I suspect that
having prolonged his stay in these parts longer than he intended our

project of <u>Spain</u> will have to be abandoned, which I do not regret. You will be kindly glad to hear that I have excellent tidings from my dear Mother, who has been in Norfolk among old friends!

Now dearest Mrs. Austen accept my tender love & thanks for all your most valued friendship & believe me your's truly affectionate
Eliz Eastlake
Forgive my sending an unfranked letter. I have no one to trust with the commission.

1. Sara Austen (c. 1796–1888), wife of the lawyer Benjamin Austen, and Layard's aunt.

2. The Eastlakes toyed with the idea of taking a home in Venice. See Otto Mündler, 'Charles Lock Eastlake', *Zeitschrift für Bildenden Kunst*, vol. 4 (1869), pp. 99ff.

3. Arundel Society; see letter to Layard, Christmas Day 1870, n. 4.

Letter to A. H. Layard   *NLS Ms.42168*

Genoa
Octr 20 1858
My dear Mr. Layard

I had intended writing to you by Sir Chas' wish, before we left Rome, & leaving the letter there to find its way to you somehow on your arrival – but our stay there was so short & so over engaged that I am only able to fulfil my intention hurriedly here.

Much of my time in Rome was spent in the melancholy Campana house, thoroughly investigating the enormous collection of pictures. Here are the series of 14 grand heads of philosophers & poets which once decorated the Library at Urbino, some of which are copied by Raphael in his well known sketch book. Sir Chas when he saw these heads 2 years ago in the C. House gave them from conjectural evidence of his own the name of <u>Melozzo Forli</u> – which name was immediately adopted, & is now inserted in the Campana Catalogue. I was astonished at their grandeur of treatment & in many respects, sickness of colour, & we both became convinced that the two ruined pictures I showed you in the Casa Conti at Florence are by the same hand.[1]

Now Sir Chas wishes you very much to examine these same noble heads (tho' not all of equal attraction) & then to do as we did & visit all the other specimens of Melozzi in Rome, as follows – in a chapel of the SS. Apostoli at Rome (mentioned by Vasari in his life of Benozzo

Gozzoli) Melozzo executed a fresco of the ascension. This is destroyed, but fragments of it are preserved in the <u>Sacristy</u> of St. Peter's, & to be seen for the asking. These consist of half figures of angels & one male head. I thought them the grandest & most beautiful things in the world. At all events, making allowance for the difference of subject & of vehicle, I think you will agree with us (judging by the drapery &c) that they are by the same hand as the Campana heads. Then there is the figure of the ascending Saviour surrounded by angels, rescued from the same fresco, now on the stairs of the Quirinal, & also <u>magnificent</u> – like Mantegna, without his peculiarity, which you perhaps know already. & lastly, there is the picture in the Vatican Gallery – the last great Room I think – of the Pope appointing the Kneeling Platina as his librarian. All these together serve to raise Melozzo to one of the highest places in the temple of art, and also to establish the wide difference between him & the painter who signs himself <u>Marcus di Melotus</u>, in which the 1st editors of Vasari are all wrong, also there is no doubt is his scholar Marco Palmezzano.

So please do all this, when in Rome, for our pleasure & your own. Sir Chas has made a selection of the Campana pictures – including 9 of these heads, but it is uncertain whether he will be able to induce the Government to sell separately the comparatively small number of pictures to be found eligible. At Rome he concluded the purchase of a fine Marco Palmezzano (signed Marcus de Melotüs), & also of an unfinished Palma Vecchio female portrait – all this entre nous.

When there also you should see the Dosso Dossi presented by Gen: Moore to the N: Gallery, now standing at Freeborn's & say that you have Sir Chas' wish that you should do so, for he requested Freeborn not to show the picture too freely. It is very fine.

We have had a smooth quick passage from Civita Vecchia to Genoa, which we reached on the 18th & are now as Tucker expresses himself "creeping back again" – intending to be in London by the 30th if possible. When you return we must hear all about your impressions of Melozzo &c &c.

I send this through the hands of Macbean – a most obliging gentleman – who will be good enough to find you up.

Do look well also at the S. Botticelli Moses & the Burning Bush, & the daughters of Jethro in the Sistine Chapel. You should take an opera glass – it is a magnificent composition.

Sir Chas kind regards & mine
Your's very truly
Eliz Eastlake
Sir Chas advises Freeborn instead of Macbean

1. The Campana Collection belonged to the Marchese Giovanni Pietro Campana, a Roman banker who formed an extraordinary collection of antiquities and art works from the medieval and Renaissance periods. See Helen and Albert Borowitz, *Pawnshops and Palaces: The Fall and Rise of the Campana Art Museum* (Washington: Smithsonian Institute Press, 1991).

Letter to Mrs Gray   *ML MA 1338 ZE.04*

7 Fitzroy Sqre
Novr 30 1858
My dear Mrs Gray

The sight of you handwriting yesterday gave me a lively sensation of pleasure which was increased when I read the contents of the letter. I am <u>thankful</u> that the dreaded time is over, & quite delighted to welcome a little Effie into the world with all the promise of the dear mother's beauty. I congratulate dear Effie most cordially, & wish that every babe came into this weary world under such happy auspices. I am sure that her Everett is delighted with his new gift.

I am sure that you have so much to do, attendg to childn, grandchildn, as well as to husband & son in law — & most of all to the dear patient, that I shall thankfully consider no news as good news, & only look for a few lines when your hands are comparatively empty.

Tell Effie that I have seen a little of dear Hadie. She is so happy in her engagement that I must not criticise it. Also I know that Col: C: is truly noble & liberal in all his sentiments & actions towards her, but he is not very attractive looking, & indeed I thought on first sight more of his plainness that of his years. However, she will make his remaining years very happy & will find her happiness in that.[1]

Lady Ashburton's good fortune surprised me, for Ld A: is, as far as I understand, a very worthy man. I <u>hope</u> that she will study his happiness — but I hear him generally pitied for havg chosen as ungenially in the second as he did in the first instance. The later Lady A: patronized <u>J.R.</u> so in that respect also there will be no change for the better![2]

With kind love to yourself & Effie, Sir Chas' best congratulations, believe me dear Mrs Gray yr's ever truly

Eliz Eastlake

1. Henrietta de Salis married Colonel Thomas Chaloner Bisse-Challoner of Portnall Park, Virginia Water in Surrey.

2. Née Louisa Mackenzie; see letter, 27 April 1854.

Letter to A. H. Layard   *NLS Ms.42168*

7 Fitzroy Sqre
March 26. 1859
Dear Mr. Layard
   Before seeing you this eveng I must tell you how much interested, satisfied and gratified I am by the perusal of your paper.[1] The opinions and suggestions on general questions I have not call to differ from, but rather the reverse. The opinion on one particular person I am very grateful for – for it is as kind as it is just. You have said for good Mündler all that a non-partisan could be expected to say – and your strictures on Italian governments in their pretended zeal for the preservation of their pictures delights my worst feelings.
   I must find a little fault, or you will think I have not been myself. Don't you say more than you mean when you speak (p:5) of works being torn from their sanctuaries to gratify private Vanity. We know that these sanctuaries have been the graves of too many, and but for the private vanity then would have been much fewer at this day in the Florence galleries.
   Also I must raise a voice for our poor chairs at the Nat: Gal: At all events more tired people can sit there than in any other foreign gallery I know. Where there are 2 chairs to a room & those fastened to the floor!
   I am sorry I can't manage to see any more mistakes. Sir Chas will probably ignore the paper to you – but tho' he has not looked at it, you may be quite satisfied that he approves it.
In haste yr's very truly
Eliz Eastlake

   1. A. H. Layard, 'National Gallery', *Quarterly Review*, vol. 105 (April 1859), pp. 341–81.

Letter to John Scandrett Harford   *BRO 28048/C/33*

7 Fitzroy Square
March 31 1859
My dear Mr. Harford
   You are indeed increasingly kind to me. I have only delayed acknowledging your kind note and beautiful volume till I should have done a little more justice to the latter. I have now read your dissertation on Grecian Tragedy, with great interest, and with equal information

to myself, never before having had a clear idea of its derivation, local habituation, and mechanism. Your translation of Agememnon I reserve for another quiet evening, and meanwhile have feasted my eyes on your illustrations – always feeling <u>thankful</u> to find myself able to appreciate, (and to enthusiasm) the lofty charm of Greek forms. For they are a kind of revelation in art, which I find is "foolishness" with some.

I have been doing nothing original this winter, dear Mr. Harford, and am rather longing to get rid of a translation I have in hand. A second edition of Kugler's German and Flemish Schools, which good Dr. Waagen has undertaken.[1]

Sir Chas is at the R: Academy this evening, where he will have the pleasure of announcing or welcoming your most kind present of your 2nd edition of your M:Angelo.

Meanwhile, under his auspices, the B: Museum have purchased, a few letters, drawings and models, by M:Angelo which were the private property of the present degenerate possessor of the family honours. We inspected them at Settignano last October.[2]

Today I have seen the <u>sorrowing</u> Miss Alexander, and heard much of the particulars of Miss Joanna's death. She suffered from a malady which prevented the stomach from receiving nourishment – but she did not suffer much.

With my kind regards to Mrs. Harford and yourself, believe me dear Mr. Harford your's always and obliged and truly
Eliz Eastlake

1. Franz Kugler, *Handbook of Painting. The German, Flemish, and Dutch Schools. Based on the Handbook of Kugler. Enlarged and for the most part re-written by Dr Waagen*, 2 vols. (London: John Murray, 1860).

2. See Dora Thornton and Jeremy Warren, 'The British Museum's Michelangelo Acquisitions and the Casa Buonarroti', *Journal of the History of Collections*, 10.1 (1998), pp. 9–29.

Letter to Mrs Austen   *NLS Ms.42167*

7 Fitzroy Sqre
May 30. 1859
Dearest Mrs. Austen

Time is short, & I fear not to be able to come at the door when you are at home. I write therefore to say that it is decided for me to go over to my beloved sister in Estonia. Her state is now so utterly hopeless,

letters are so <u>few</u> & <u>scanty</u>, the call of Nature to her so loud, that as
no one of our family can stir <u>now</u> but myself, & as her life cannot
be prolonged many weeks, my dearest husband with sweet kindness
<u>promotes</u> my going. This has given great consolation already to my
venerable mother & all my family. I start on Saturday – unless required
to go earlier.[1]

This is a <u>solemn</u> mission. I can only go in the strength given me
from on High, & I trust with that grace to be able to fortify the
fainting spirit, & assist her to commit her beloved child^n undoubtingly
to God.

She is now being very wrongly treated, having removed into the
country, to an ignorant practitioner. I trust that an authoratative letter
from Dr. Rigby here will have arrested this system before I reach her.[2]
I go furnished with all that Dr. Ferguson can instruct me in – & with
certain opiates which he strongly recommends.

Now dearest Friend, give my [sic] your prayers. But I dare not ask
you to come & see me, lest I should make you break down with my
emotion. I ought to be back in 5 weeks. May they bring you no fresh
anxiety for your dear charge. I shall think of you <u>very often</u>. Yr obliged
& affectionate

Eliz Eastlake

1. Elizabeth travelled to Estonia to visit her sister, Gertrude de Rosen, who
   died in August 1859.

2. Dr Edward Rigby, the brother of Elizabeth and Gertrude.

Letter to William Stirling Maxwell   *SRA T-SK 29.9/38–39*

7 Fitzroy Sqre
July 21. 1859
Dear Mr. Stirling[1]

As Sir Chas is <u>much</u> engaged with business I venture, in my own
name, & at the risk of troubling you with a superfluous letter, to call
your attention to the two notices by Mr Coningham directed against Sir
Charles in the Times of today.[2]

I take for granted that you, in common with other unprejudiced
observers, are not inclined to admit that the present management of
the Nat: Gallery is "detrimental to the public service", but are rather
persuaded of the reverse.

I am only anxious that Mr. Coningham shd not, as on a former occasion, reap any success by default of advocates for the just cause – a cause so just as perhaps not to be supposed to be in danger & therefore too confidently left to its own merits. The question of the withdrawal of the supplies for travelling expenses, which, in lieu of the Travelling Agent, now include miscellaneous agents in all parts of Italy, & various incidental expenses, affects also the very existence of the present contribution of the Gallery.

Sir Chas has called Mr. Baring's especial attention to the subject, & qualified him, in his character of Trustee, to meet such falseness of logic as well as fact as may be brought forward, but you will forgive me if the desire to obtain a faithful ally – not precisely in the French sense of the term – has induced me thus to intrude on you. One sign of favour will be that you do not trouble yourself to answer this.

Believe me your's very truly

Eliz Eastlake

If anything should be said for Mr. Mündler it wd be both just & kind.

1. William Stirling Maxwell (1818–78), Scottish writer, politician, and connoisseur of Spanish art.

2. Coningham criticised the management of the National Gallery in the House of Commons as 'unsatisfactory' and 'detrimental to public service'. See *The Times*, 21 July 1959, p. 6, col. E. Francis Haskell describes him as a 'spiteful and vindictive critic' in 'William Coningham and his Collection of Old Masters', *The Burlington Magazine*, vol. 133, no. 1063 (October 1991), pp. 676–81 (p. 676).

Letter to John Murray   *NLS Ms.42175*

7 Fitzroy Square

Aug: 4 1859

My dear Mr. Murray

May I request you to order a fresh set of proofs to be sent me of the new Edition of Kugler's German, Flemish Handbook, up to page 74. I want to send Waagen a complete series of proofs, as far as they go, which is as p:264, & I have no duplicate of the first two sheets. He is very unhappy about the book's not being under his name.

I am now carefully going through my young lady's work during my absence, which costs me plenty of trouble to revise. I should be so much obliged to you if you could give me an idea of what she is entitled to from me, for just 90 pages of MS I propose sending her £20 but would rather have some standard to calculate by.

Sir Chas is returned from Cheltenham, satisfied upon the whole with what he has hitherto obtained. But Ld Hertford is bidding – by proxy – and a Cima on which we had set our heart for the N.G. after giving up to an absurd price was obliged to be ceded to one who will always bid the longest! All this <u>entre nous</u>.

I saw Mrs. de Rosen off yesterday mg and am thankful she is en route. I have long letters from the childn this morng but a sad chapter! Tho' the parting from her eldest married daughter, had, thanks to her self-command, been accomplished without evil effect to the dear sufferer.[1]

We shall enjoy your company tomorrow – ½ past 7 – but Layard is otherwise engaged.

Your's always truly

Eliz Eastlake

All quiet at Liverpool up to yesterday.[2]

1. Maria Justina de Rosen was perhaps en route to Estonia.

2. Matilda and James Smith lived at 18 Falkner Square in Liverpool.

Letter to A. H. Layard   *NLS Ms.42168*

7 Fitzroy Sqre

Aug: 13 1859

Dear Mr. Layard

You are very good, with your hands always more than full, to remember your friends in Fitzroy Sqre, altho' we are sorry to be taken leave of by you in this fashion. We wished very much to have seen you, & your absence from town has spared your answerg more than one dinner invitation. Our day of starting is not yet fixed but I have little doubt of being summoned to be ready for the middle of next week. Our program is promising, beginning with Paris, then Hanover, where there are fine Ruysdaels in the otherwise awful accumulation called the Söder Collection. Then Berlin and friend Waagen, who will be sure to ask about you. Dresden, Leipsic, Vienna – all with <u>covers</u> of some kind of game. And so to Venice and along Northern Italy to Genoa, where about the 20th we propose taking steamer for Marseilles en route to <u>Alicante</u>.

Of the Madrago Collection at Madrid we hear great things, tho' from not very great authority. At all events the head of the family is dead, and the collection to be sold piecemeal. This is our <u>excuse</u> for Madrid, but you may guess the real curiosity and interest is for the Gallery, which is more or less shrouded in mystery as to state of pictures.

Sir Chas has now terminated our visits to Cheltenham, having been there again since making you the proposal to join him. He has obtained, with one exception, the pictures he desired – viz: the great Moretto altarpiece, the Guilio Romano, Girolamo da Treviso, (fine signed picture) an <u>enchanting</u> head of an ugly grand man by Filippino Lippi called Masaccio, and a little Terburg of great beauty. The one exception was the Cima you remember at Manchester on which Lord Hertford had fixed his inevitable eye.[1]

I am sure what you say of our good friend's M.S. must be right. And I fear now I shall know nothing of her till our return – end of October.

I wish you could join us at Madrid! Pray accept our warm good wishes and hoping we may meet again in health and comfort. Believe me your's very truly

Eliz Eastlake

Sir Chas is very disquieted with Pinti's proceedgs towards you. He has reason to think that he is gone to Florence on some Gabalgna [?] – Salvator – Rosa mission for Ld Ward – whence he will soon return. Don't pronouce extreme judgement yet.[2]

1. Lord Northwick's sale of art works was held at Thirlstaine House, Cheltenham, between 26 July and 16 August 1859. See Oliver Bradbury and Nicholas Penny, 'The Picture Collecting of Lord Northwick: Part I', *Burlington Magazine*, vol. 144 (2002), pp. 485–96; and 'The Picture Collecting of Lord Northwick: Part II', *Burlington Magazine*, vol. 144 (2002), pp. 606–17.

2. Raffaele Pinti (1826–81), restorer and picture dealer employed by the National Gallery; William Ward, Baron Ward (1817–85), created Earl of Dudley in 1860.

Letter to William Stirling Maxwell *SRA T-SK 29.9/38–39*

7 Fitzroy Sqre
Aug: 13. 1859
Dear Mr. Stirling

Sir Charles' niece Mrs James Muirhead, & her husband are planning a little excursion about the Forth, the chief attraction of which will be beautiful Keir. They have begged me in case they should not be in your neighbourhood on a public day to take the quite unjustifiable liberty of requesting a <u>private</u> View for them. I can only say that I do so with due shame. I trust, however, that there may be no occasion to trouble you with this petition, or at least with the fulfilment of it.

I am glad to express to you my acknowledgements for the very kind as well as wise words you said about the Nat: Gallery. I find on talking with a few well known members that the sense of not being connoisseurs in matters of taste keeps them paralysed on such occasions. I have tried to convince them that knowledge of art is not really the available weapon, but rather those qualities which a shrewd & honest lawyer wd bring to the question. If there be small chance of Mr Coningham's becoming more modest I wd fain hope that other members, with one good exception, may become less so!

We are just starting for Italy, & propose seeing the Madrid Gallery before we return. The Life of Velasquez is my companion.

With many pleasant thoughts of Keir, which no Italy can obscure, believe me dear Mr Stirling
Your's very truly
Eliz Eastlake

Letter to Mrs Acton Tindal   *CLS M10989*

7 Fitzroy Sqre
Aug: 16. 1859
Dearest Mrs. Tindal

We are off on Thursday. Though travelling is stript of its attractions to me this year, yet I long to be off now for Sir Chas' sake.

I had heard from Layard how excellent he thought your Bucks – only "too conscientious" & I am very glad that you have determined to recast it, for the Q.R. after next. I shall see John Murray today to bid him goodbye and havg mentioned the subject to him already, & found him most desirous that it shd succeed, I shall not scruple to express my hopes to him today. Elwin[1] is a queer little man – immense learning & immense good in him, but not the big human sympathy and instinct which my beloved Lockhart had.

Alas! my letters from Russia are sadder and sadder. I long to hear that it is over – but for the childn who cling to her life, even when all that can make it tolerable is gone.

I shall hear on my route & expect that the arrow will reach me midway in Italy or Spain.[2]

I shall think often of you dear Mrs Tindal. I am so glad to know you, just when I was beginning to doubt whether this world contained any new person that an old careworn heart could rejoice in.

God bless you & yr home & husband & childn.

You ever affte friend
Eliz Eastlake

1. Whitwell Elwin (1816–1900), clergyman and writer. He was Lockhart's successor as editor of the *Quarterly Review* between 1853 and 1860, when he was succeeded by William Macpherson.

2. Gertrude de Rosen died on 14 August according to C. J. Palmer and Stephen Tucker (eds.), *Palgrave Family Memorials* (privately printed, 1878), but Elizabeth received the news in Vienna on 3 September according to J&C2, pp. 115–16.

Letter to John Blackwood   *NLS Ms.4138, no. 120*

7 Fitzroy Sqre
Decr 27. 1859
Dear Mr Blackwood
I will not longer delay telling you how much Sir Charles & I are pleased with the article of "the National Gallery, its Purpose & Management" in your present No. I was once before so bold as to criticise an article bearing on art, & therefore I am doubly bound now to trouble you with an expression of very contrary feeling. Your writer leaves nothing to be desired in what he says of the Management; it is just, generous & not partisanlike, the evident judgement of one who cares only for fairness & truth, & not for any party. His sentiments on art too are peculiarly interesting to us, as the feelings, not of a would be Connoisseur blundering about technicalities difficult to the most initiated, but of the true layman who leaves subtleties alone, & launches into the broad philosophy & poetry of pictures which speak to the general mind. I am inclined to nail this article on the turning point in a very vexed subject, & hope that people will not excuse themselves in future for not answering the attacks on the Nat: Gallery, as M.P.s have done, by the plea that they are no connoisseurs – Connoisseurship has less to do with these matters than common sense.
We enjoy your <u>Magn</u> as we ought to, & feel every month very grateful to you for your great liberality.
Pray accept & give to Mrs Blackwood my best wishes of the Season & believe me dear Mr Blackwood
Your's truly obliged
Eliz Eastlake

Letter to A. H. Layard   *NLS Ms.42168*

7 Fitzroy Sqre
Decr 31 1859
My dear Mr. Layard

I find that Sir Charles has read your letter in the Times of this
morng with much regret, owing to the allusion to the works now
going on in the Houses of Parliament. He feels unwilling to enter
into any agreement on the question of respective merits, & equally to
close it, as he would do to most, by that empty phrase that you have
a right to your opinion. But setting aside the merits or demerits of the
Experimental frescoes in the Upper Waiting Hall,[1] where Watts is far
outdone in all the conditions of fresco by Herbert, Sir Chas simply
asks whether you have seen Dyce's frescoes in the Queen's Robing
Room, Herbert's now in progress, or Maclise's cartoon for his Battle of
Waterloo?[2]

If not, on what is your opinion founded? & what is there to choose
between the "discouragement" to these painters from the sweeping
condemnation of a man of known taste who has never seen their
greatest efforts, or to Mr. Watts from his ignorant censure of one who
has seen his?

But Sir Chas especially condemns the system which cannot exalt one
painter except at the expense of justice to others. His conviction is that
there are works now going on in the Houses of Parliament unsurpassable
in merit by any man living. Yet you know that this conviction has not
interfered with his doing justice to Watt's great work. No one, he is
sure, is more ready to admit the necessity for upholding this principle of
catholic justice to all merit in art than your own most impetuous, willful
& generous self! & this is why he feels the more sore at the sweeping
expressions not more unjust to others than to a certain Mr. Layard.

I know well, dear Mr. Layard, how kindly & truly you estimate Sir
Chas' character, (& while I live shall never forget how generously you
have expressed that opinion) therefore you will not think him actuated
by a thought of retaliation in telling you that should any dinner be
given in honour of Watts he cannot now be present at it. Once you
make Watt's merits the mere watchery for a party condemnatory of
other painters of equal merit, & not more crotchets, Sir Chas can have
nothing to do with any of its demonstrations.

Now let me add a word for myself, which is the hope that you will
make a point of examining the works in Westminster for yourself, &
then come and fight it out with your old friend.

I am sorry to write you a scolding letter exactly for the first day of the new year. But for all that beg you to believe that none more than ourselves wish that it may bring you much happiness.

Believe me dear Mr. Layard

Your's always truly

Eliz Eastlake

1. Eastlake was Secretary of the Fine Arts Commission that oversaw the decoration of the Houses of Parliament. See T. R. S. Boase, 'The Decoration of the New Palace of Westminster, 1841–1863', *Journal of the Warburg & Courtauld Institutes*, vol. 17 (1954), pp. 319–58. The Upper Waiting Hall was decorated with frescoes after literary subjects, including Herbert's *King Lear* and Watts's scene from the *Faerie Queen, Spenser: The Red Cross Knight overcoming the Dragon*. William Dyce was responsible for the frescoes depicting Arthurian legends in the Queen's Robing Room, but the work was behind schedule and still unfinished. Watts's frescoes in the Upper Waiting Hall had begun to deteriorate and the Fine Art Commission sent several reports to the House of Commons in the 1860s on the matter. Maclise's work on the Battle of Waterloo for the Royal Gallery was detained by problems in the technique of fresco painting, which the Eastlakes attempted to rectify on a visit to Berlin, where Maclise joined them to seek advice from German experts.

2. Layard's letter appeared in *The Times* on Saturday 31 December 1859, p. 10, col. C. The letter is an encomium of Watts's work at the New Hall in Lincoln's Inn, but he does describe his fears that the decoration of the Houses of Parliament was 'proceeded on a false system, and that an opportunity not likely to occur again, was being thrown away'.

Letter to A. H. Layard   *NLS Ms.42169*

7 Fitzroy Sqre

Janry 21. 1860

Dear Mr. Layard

If disengaged on Wednesday next the 25th will you kindly dine with us at 1/4 to 7. You would meet a few R.A.s among them Maclise, and I would be glad if we could persuade him to show you his cartoon. Also you will find friends Murray here.

I did not answer your kind letter from Aldermaston for I feared the last word would be too long delayed where each party thought themselves in the right! But though you showed <u>fight</u>, I know there is no real difference of opinion between Sir Charles and you on such matters. I am much more likely to be the obstinate adversary!

Believe me always dear Mr. Layard
Your's truly
Eliz Eastlake
I am going today if possible for another view of the new Nineveh
room below the B:M. Those bas reliefs inspire me with more and more
admiration everytime I study them.[1]

1. Layard had been the lead archaeologist on an expedition to the site of the
   ancient ruins of Mesopotamia, described in *Nineveh and its Remains* (1849).
   See Giles Waterfield, *Layard of Nineveh* (London: John Murray, 1963).

Letter to John Murray   *NLS Ms.42176*

7 Fitzroy Sqre
March 21 1860
Dear Mr. Murray
    Sir Chas. & I returned from Paris last night, after a very rough
crossing, which to our surprise reduced us to the level of all the other
passengers! But he is none the worse for that. I hope, much the better
for the change of air & weather.
    I found your note, dated the 17th wh: I have read with others this
mg. I merely submitted the question to you, & was prepared that you
might take the view you have done & which you have quite the right to
take. But I, as a sister, have no such right, & should this disaster occur
again & with more serious consequences it would be small consolation
to think that a feeling of delicacy had withheld my urging a strict
investigation on this occasion & my the <u>more</u> urging it because I have
<u>no</u> suspicion of anything beyond an accident. Nor am I acting for myself
only, for I have my mother's extreme & natural anxiety to consider. No
one also who knows me can doubt my entire affection & respect for
James but I can the more afford to see his very few failings & know
that when much harrassed in mind, as his is now, it is difficult for him
to give his thoughts to other things. But tho' feeling most tenderly for
him, I have no right to be more tender of such a failing than of my
sister's life.[1]
    However, I am sorry to have troubled you with the subject & will do
so no further except to beg that all blame may be imputed to me, & not
any to Matty, who far from ever complaining, will bear so much fatigue
& suffering as to make me dread that, like my late sister, she may find
that she has one day overtaxed nature.
    I left London but too sadly certain that a few hours would close our

dear Mrs. Jameson's life. Her death is a very great grief as well as loss to us – for she was ever kind to me.[2]

Believe me dear Mr. Murray with <u>no</u> thought that you in any way are wanting in kind sympathy for Matty's late sufferings with love to Menie.

Your's ever truly

Eliz Eastlake

1. James Smith's failing business ventures caused the Rigbys and Murrays periodic consternation. See letter, 28 March 1865.

2. Anna Jameson died on 17 March 1860.

Letter to John Murray   *NLS Ms.42176*

7 Fitzroy Square

July 13. 1860

Dear Mr. Murray

You are always the most generous of employers. Pray accept my best thanks for your liberal payment of 100 guineas – of which I return you the receipt signed. I also feel obliged to you for your kindness to Waagen. I do trust the merit of the book will gain it a standard place. I owe it much information.

I heard from him today. He thinks your estimate of the cost of printing the wood cuts very moderate – as well he may – and was in treaty with his German publisher.

Your information about the change of ministery in the Q.Review takes me by surprise, as wondering that Mr. Elwin can prefer any literary occupation to his most interesting editorship. I have no doubt of your excellent judgement on the choice of Mr. Macpherson, tho' I had not heard of him. May he prove to have Elwin's many good qualifications and those few which he had not, and maybe be a worthy successor to the dear old friend whose like we shall never see![1]

I fear my hands are filled with other work for some time, not unprofitable for the general mental cultivation. The subject is of the highest interest, but requires such garnered materials as Mrs. Jameson alone possessed.

I have employed my week at Windsor with old and young – you will be delighted with the little quartet of girls.

Ever dear Mr. Murray your's obliged and affectionately

Eliz Eastlake

Poor Mr. Wornum's great affliction will probably render our continental trip later this year.[2]

1. William M. Macpherson was editor of the *Quarterly Review* from 1860 to 1867; the 'dear old friend' is John Gibson Lockhart.

2. Ralph Nicholas Wornum (1812–77), Keeper at the National Gallery, whose wife Elizabeth had recently died.

Letter to A. H. Layard   *NLS Ms.42169*

Milan – Septr 24. 1860
Dear Mr. Layard
 I have not forgotten my promise to let you know in Venice by the 25th whether Sir Chas would go to Ferrara. I think I can say positively now that he will. He starts the day after tomorrow, via Lodi & Cremona, for a trip of which Ferrara will be the extreme point. He will be accompanied by an Italian acquaintance who can be useful to him – Signor Orlandi from Turin[1] – & by the indispensable Tucker, but he leaves <u>me</u> here, & so I am making myself a little unhappy, altho' I am sure it is the wisest plan.
 I expect he will be away about a week. Should you come here during the time you will find me in the Hotel de la Ville.
 We altered our proposed course upon leaving Innspruck, & turned off to the Pusterthal, & the Ampezzo Pass, taking Pieve di Cadore on the way, & regaining the civilised world at Conegliano. All that & more you have I hope prosperarily done, ere this. Sir Chas hopes that you will have something to tell him about Udine which he leaves till another time on his way per rail to or from Trieste. We were 2 days in Venice – half a day in Padua & Verona, & hurried on here in order to get Sir Chas into more comfortable quarters, as he has caught cold & was far from well. Today he is alright, & has gone to see his beautiful Fra Angelico[2] at Molteni's, which <u>enchants</u> me.[3]
 While at Venice look in the Belle Arti for a small Pietro della Francesca in one of those small rooms leading out of the narrow corridor. It is ruined by still grand – a St. Jerome & another Saint, & the tree exactly like that in the Baptism at Mr. Uzzielli's.
 Also if you have not seen them look for 2 small Fillipino Lippis (called <u>Crespi</u>!) in the Seminario della Salute.
 I have nothing further to say except that Sir Chas is just in & repeats his hope to hear much about the Fruili from you.

His kind regards to you & mine always your's truly
Eliz Eastlake

1. Paolo Orlandi, Turin artist and (occasional) agent for Eastlake in Italy.

2. Fra Angelico, *Christ Glorified in the Court of Heaven* NG663 was purchased for £3,500.

3. Giuseppe Molteni (1799–1867), Italian painter, restorer and Director of the Brera in Milan from 1861. Molteni's studio restored Old Master paintings for clients such as Eastlake, while the works were awaiting export licences. See Cecil Gould, 'Eastlake and Molteni: The Ethics of Restoration', *Burlington Magazine*, 116 (1974), pp. 530–34; and Jaynie Anderson, 'The First Cleaning Controversy at the National Gallery, 1846–1853', in *Appearance, Opinion, Change: Evaluating the Look of Paintings*, with a preface by Stephen Hackney (London: Institute for Conservation, 1990), pp. 3–7.

Letter to Mrs Austen   NLS Ms.42167

Bologna – Octr 8 1860
Dearest Mrs. Austen

I have thought of you & dear Mr Austen continually, & have longed for more spare time to tell you how much I hope that your anxieties have been graciously mitigated. I do indeed long to hear of you, but have at present had no letters from those friends who cd give us tidings of you. Meanwhile I am thankful to say that we have done well. Sir Chas a little troubled with a cold caught from going from hot Piazzas into cold churches, but enjoying himself thoroughly & in excellent spirits. I know that Layard wrote to you – I think from Dresden – saying that we had fallen in with each other. We met again in Munich where we left him – or <u>them</u> – & I have since heard of them through the Ball's, whom we met 2 days ago, as having appeared at Mrs Ball's fathers house, near Bassano (he a Marchese Parolini) where good little Mrs Ball confessed that <u>Mr B</u>: was rather unwelcome.[1] But of this more when we meet, as I trust, dear Mrs Austen we may ere long. I will only add that Layard seemed rather dissipated & like a man truly in a false position. Mrs Drummond & her daughters had come to Munich before we left – so he had plenty on his hands!

We preceeded Layard in our movements in some measure – taking the route into Italy through the Pusterthal, & the Ampezzo Pass – the first one of the loveliest valleys, the last one of the most tremendous of gorges. This brought us down into Titian's country which Sir

Chas had not visited for many years – & so to Conegliano – another
birthplace of a great painter, a beautiful place where the rail brought us
into Venice. There we were caught at by the starving hotel keepers, as
drown.g men catch at a straw, & make much of. Venice was desolate &
beautiful – gondoliers talking loud on forbidden subjects when in the
middle of the Grand Canal! & the police revell.g in the new modes of
arrogance & extortion. We were glad to leave Austria behind us & to
breathe the air of liberty, & in this air we have continued to breathe
to our great comfort for we have no intentions of going beyond the
present extensive domains of the "King of Italy" in which one moves
about as freely as in our own England. The change is something
surprising – like a natural & good thing after a state of coercion &
restraint. From Milan we have taken a trip which we are just about
to conclude, tak.g us through Lodi, Cremona, over the greatly swollen
Po to Piacenza, to Modena, Bologna, Ferrara, Faenza, Ravenna &
now here we are in Bologna again & hope to be at Milan at the best
of all hotels by tomorrow eveng – the railway now embracing all the
intervening space – taking us round by Alessandria. Thus we have been
in the centre of the present festivities occasioned by the fall of Ancona,
& the King's progress hither through the principal cities. Everywhere
signs of enthusiasm, "Eviva Vittorio Emanuele – nostro legittimo Re"
on every house in some form or another. Piacenza is becoming a
very strong fortress, & swarms with 25,000 soldiers – the Bersagleri
with their flattering cock's feather, real fighting cocks they look, their
sailor-like dress, & astonishing rapidity of pace, the most conspicuous
objects. The telegram of the fall of Ancona reached Piacenza the day
we arrived, & in the eveng the old city burst into illuminations, which
harmonized well with the tramp of thousands of feet, the hum of
excited voices & the clang of trumpets. I went into the Piazza – with
our faithful Tucker – the statues of the old Great Gonzagas gleaming
strangely beneath the brilliant light – a scene I shall not forget. We
have had an Italian gentleman with us on this trip – a Piedmontese.
& our conversation has turned for once quite as much on politics as
on art. The more we hear & see, the more we are astonished at the
prudence & discretion & patience with which these changes have been
brought about, again I must say like a natural event, like a mighty
animal saved from torpor, & casting off its slough at the appointed
time, making one wonder how it could have laid inactive so long.
There is no doubt that the most important changes are contemplated
in the church – but "adagio adagio" – amounting to a Reformation
in our sense of the word, a protest against the folly & wickedness that
has long ruled. It is a sublime time, spoken of by Italians with more

than party feeling or enthusiasm, but with the acknowledgement that nothing but the Divine Hand could have brought it about.

Now a little about Ravenna which was new to me & nearly so to Sir Chas. It is <u>externally</u> the most disappointing place; one may drive through the city from morning till night without the suspicion of its containing any object of the slightest interest – a wretched, modern, filfthy, Italian fifth rate town without a tower conspicuous in the distance or any details worth seeing near. One must enter there low, common looking whitewashed buildings to find oneself suddenly transported from the 19th to the 5th & 6th centuries, to ancient Christian sarcophagi, sculptured with the simplest styles of early Christianity & to grand figures in gleaming mosaics stalking in solemn progression along the walls, or looking down from domes & apses – perfect as if executed yesterday. I mean such of them as still exist, for the hand of ignorance & violence has stripped much away that otherwise might have defied time itself. The art of these monuments is beautiful, the various engraving I know give no idea of its beauty. A Baptism in a deserted Baptistry gave me a more solemn impression of the reality of the scene, although a river God sits by with the Jordan streaming from his urn, than any representation by more recent hands. But nothing short of objects of such interest wd ever take me to Ravenna, which seems the very type of that Papal education, which has rendered its unfortunate subjects the most barbarous, ferocious & filthy of the Italian race. One other thing was fine – the ancient pine forest which stretches 20 miles in length & depth between Ravenna & the sea. I drove into its confines – about 3 miles off – & fed my eyes on its solemn grandeur, on the storm beaten groups of slow-grown trees in the foreground, & on the modulating line which stretched as far as an eye could reach & lost itself in the horizon.

Now, dearest Mrs. Austen, I should be truly thankful for a line to Paris – Hotel du Louvre – about the 25th of this month, merely, if you can, to say how you both are. If I do not hear I shall only conclude that your time is too much wanted by your dear invalid, & shall soon be at your door on our return at the end of the month.

I have not mentioned to you a wonderful meeting with one of my Russian nieces – of which I have much to say. But no more now. You will be indulgent to this selfish epistle & ever believe me in the true regard of your affectionate
Eliz Eastlake
Many kind things from Sir Chas

1. John Ball (1818–90), Irish politician, naturalist and author of the *Alpine Guide*, and his wife Eliza, daughter of the Italian naturalist Count Alberto Parolini. The Balls wintered every year at their estates in Bassano.

Letter to A. H. Layard   *NLS Ms.42169*

Paris – Octr 23. 1860
Dear Mr. Layard
I add a few words to Sir Chas' letter – were it only to thank you for your kind letter to Milan, which I found on my return from our inland trip. You have discovered that I accompanied Sir Chas after all which was quite necessary for my comfort, & I flatter myself for his too, as his cold & cough – now quite gone – dispirited him. We enjoyed ourselves much, especially at Ferrara which I thought brushed up, & where the Costabile Gallery is always delightful guessing & fishing. Would that we could bring anything up! I hope we shall succeed in time. It is nice to find that you recommend to Sir Chas exactly what he most covets, & for which he has bid. I hope you have not set your heart on the little Costas in the Costabile, because it happens that I have![1] Ravenna is a horrid place – wretchedly modernized, but the mosaics are bright as if done yesterday, & some of them beautiful in art – wonderful & sublime things indeed, & the pine Forest in keeping with them.
I heard from good Murray yesterday. Robert Cooke home from Italy, & the new Editor's Quarterly successfully out.[2] Murray resting at St. Leonard's. He tells me to my great thankfulness that your uncle has rallied materially. All good be with his nephew – pictures & everything else to his heart's content, only that member is rather a whimsical one. But it is always true to his friends. We caught a hasty sight of the Drummonds in Milan. The weather is beautiful, & Paris superb.
Your's always truly
Eliz Eastlake

1. The collection of Marchese Gian Battista Costabili in Ferrara was the source of a number of Eastlake's purchases, including Pisanello's *Virgin and Child with Saints George and Anthony Abbot*, and works by Bono da Ferrara and Cosimo Tura.

2. I.e. W. M. Macpherson's first *Quarterly Review*.

Letter to A. H. Layard   *NLS Ms.42169*

7 Fitzroy Sqre
Decr 11 1860
Dear Mr. Layard

I will be early on in the field of congratulation, for, by the time the
Times is read to-morrow, no end of kind notes will be pouring in upon
you.[1] Our good Tucker has shared in our deep interest for you, & his
return from Southwark this afternoon with the final result made us very
happy. Sir Chas rushed up to me hurrahing & conducting in a most
juvenile manner! We are very glad, & wish you everything in your fresh
public career that true friends may wish. It is a great victory, & won by
your own personal influence. I am sure the manner in which you have
fought must win some & convert others.

And now I hope you will have a goodnight.

We are not so selfish as to think of ourselves, but your readmission
into Parliament is a very great comfort to me for Sir Chas' sake. I hope
your good uncle is well enough to enjoy your victory.

Now God bless you
Your's very truly
Eliz Eastlake

1. Layard had been elected MP for Southwark.

Letter to John Murray   *NLS Ms.42176*

7 Fitzroy Sqre
Decr. 19. 1860
Dear Mr. Murray

I enclose a list of the articles in the Q.R. & their numbers – also the
number of Sir Chas article on Raphael which I would like bound in the
same volume.[1] But, by his stipulation, it is to be placed last. I am not
sure whether the materials will not be enough for two volumes. I will
call & see the sheets, please, before they are sewed up.

This is a discouraging day for Wimbledon to come to London! I trust
all are well. My messenger brings a haunch we have just received, &
which Sir Chas begs you to consume. We are too small a family for that
purpose.

I do not forget the New Year's day kind invitation, & I beg to bespeak all your party some day soon after – we think that Friday the 4th at 7 o'clock might suit, but I shall doubtless obtain some oral information before then.

I am kept in great heaviness of mind with the state of the sufferer in Berkeley Square.[2] Of course all cheerful Christmas & New Year engagements must depend on that, tho' the Drs. Still speak of <u>time</u>.

Your's always, dear Mr. Murray

Eliz Eastlake

1. Charles Lock Eastlake, 'Passavant's Life of Raphael', *Quarterly Review*, vol. 66 (June 1840), pp. 1–48.

2. Her brother Dr Edward Rigby, who lived at 35 Berkeley Square, died on 27 December.

Letter to John Murray   *NLS Ms.42176*

7 Fitzroy Sqre

Janry 4 1861

My dear Mr Murray

I am better than my word, for I leave the M.S. with you this afternoon, hoping that it may thus give you time on Monday mg. It has been an <u>arduous</u> job in the time allowed & I am very tired. But I have done my best & perhaps as it has been done <u>con amore</u>, it may answer your purpose. You will like the latter part, after the review of the Speeches, the best. I have introduced a few little things from Sir Chas Lyell's letter, though I have not alluded to his own work. I see that Blackwood has put a mourning line round a paper on the same subject – which I have not read. Will you think it necessary to do the same?[1]

I return you Hansard, & another public Library Book. Robert Cooke shall have back his own contributions all safe.

I shall submit gladly to any suggestions or alterations both material & immaterial for the hurry has not allowed me much judgement as to style. Also there may be some things which you know better.

Always yrs truly dear Mr. Murray

Eliz Eastlake

1. 'Late Prince Consort', *Quarterly Review*, vol. 111 (January 1861), pp. 176–200.

Letter to A. H. Layard   NLS Ms.42169

7 Fitzroy Sqre
April 6. 1861
Dear Mr. Layard

Sir Chas is anxious that you shd kindly inspect the Uzielli P. della Francesca on view at Christies on Monday – with a view to giving him your opinion as to the policy of endeavouring to secure it for the N: G: He is irresolute – considering its injured condition – & the silence of Vasari, & the criticism of Passavant. He will also examine it afresh on Monday but has not empowered me to say whether fore or afternoon. I shall probably accompany him, & what influence I have will probably be executed in favour of trying to obtain it.[1]

Sir Chas tells me also to ask you for the address of Sgr Marini Franceschi at Florence.

I will try & let you know what time Sir Chas is likely to be at Christie's on Monday so as to give him the chance of the same hour suiting you.

I rejoice to hear of your uncle's improvement.
Your's always truly
Eliz Eastlake

   1. Eastlake purchased the Piero della Francesca *Baptism* at the Uzielli sale on 13 April. The painting had been secured by J. C. Robinson for Uzielli (see letter, 29 June 1874).

Letter to A. H. Layard   NLS Ms.42169

7 Fitzroy Sqre
April 16. 1861
My dear Mr. Layard

Sir Chas is very eager that I shd report to you the great pleasure yr article in the present No of the Q.R. has given him.[1] Our copy only came to hand yesterday afternoon, & once opened, Sir Chas did not cease to pour over it – only coming up stairs occasionally to tell me how much he was enjoyg it. I took my turn in the eveng & can quite sympathise in his opinion. I could not lay it down either, but sat over it to the great sacrifice of 'beauty sleep'. It is a most able summary & never flags in its interest & is capital in style. Your feelings for <u>Nature</u> too – if you won't be insulted by the compliment – are most

delightfully expressed. In short we are so fascinated with the article
that the <u>snubs</u> to the translator at the beginning are quite forgotten
– tho' I suspect the word 'motive' will be kept in use till you provide
a better. I think our good old friends will be much pleased to have
given the text, &, in a certain sense the matter, to such an article – if
he is cosmopolite enough not to feel insulted at the charming way in
which you <u>pitch into</u> German vulgarity, & lowness of feeling which
rejoices <u>my</u> heart. I am writing to Dr. Waagen today & shall mention
the article. I believe he starts for Petersburg – to catalogue Hermitage
Gallery &c – in May. We also propose a short excursion abroad in the
first week of May & hope before then to see you. At all events Sir
Chas will be at the Academy Dinner.

I hope you have seen the effect of the new Room at the N. Gallery.[2]
I was there yesterday. Sir Chas thanks much for your kind answer to his
letter.

Always your's truly
Eliz Eastlake

1. A. H. Layard, 'German, Flemish and Dutch Art', *Quarterly Review*, vol. 109
   (April 1861), pp. 463–96.

2. For a discussion of the redecoration of the National Gallery see Charlotte
   Klonk, 'Mounting Vision: Charles Eastlake and the National Gallery of
   London', *Art Bulletin*, 85.2 (June 2000), pp. 331–47.

Letter to Mr Lumley   *NASDRO SSSR 226/24/120b*

7 Fitzroy Square
May 28 1861
Dear Mr. Lumley[1]
    Your kind letter of the 18th May reached me yesterday & gave
Sir Chas & me much pleasure. It found me just about to trouble you
with another parcel for one of my dear nieces, & therefore I write to
you a few hasty lines to thank you beforehand & to tell you a little
about ourselves. Our London season has been agreeably interrupted
by a short tour in France, Belgium, & Holland. There would be
little to tell you of places you know well, but that we met with
mutual friends & talked much of you. We hoped somehow to see the
Buchanans – and chance brought us a very agreeable meeting.[2] For
after resting unconsciously under the same roof at Antwerp we met
at the Station next morng & joined company in rail and steamer as

far as Rotterdam. There they branched off for the Hague, & we for
Utrecht & Amsterdam. They were both well, but rather depressed at
the change they have so unjustly suffered, in which I am sure you have
sympathised. They neither of them knew the Hague, & I tried to cheer
them by describg it to be, as I think it, one of the brightest & prettiest
& cleanest places in the world. But Lady B: has too Scotch an eye I
fear ever to relish the flat beauties of Holland, and she was dreadg to
find their house with a green door. I hope the kind, dear people will
have nothing worse than that! Ld Napier knows the home well as it
was &, I believe, still his [sic]. We saw a few interestg things in private
hands in Utrecht and Amsterdam. The Dutch are so close that they
are not eager to buy any stray pictures of their own School which may
come into the market. We have a large unfinished work by Rembrandt
"The Lord of the Vineyard". There is a small & excellent picture of
the same subject in the Hermitage. Sir Chas is rather wishing to know
its date, if there be one on it.

I am so glad of all you can tell me of Constance Manderstjerna.[3]
She is too lovely & young to have bestowed herself on one with such
painful personal disparity, though I quite believe that that is his worst
fault. She too had written me much of her pleasant talk with you, &
of yr kindness, & the Napiers. I am sure good. Dr. Waagen is enjoying
himself much. We have bespoken him for next summer. I do not
wonder at his admiration for the sentiment of your Velasquez. In the
light in which I am studying Art now I feel its peculiar pathos more &
more. I have already a small photograph from the large one, but in both
the relative light and dark is sacrificed, & the angel's figure has lost all
detail of drapery. Sir Andrew B:, pretending to no knowledge, said truly
that the picture had made an impression on him which never allows
him to forget it.

Sir Chas took cold abroad, where it was colder than here, but is quite
well now, rather overwhelmed with business, with Christie's rooms
perpetually full of pictures of some sort. I am now going to look at a
few there, & give him my ideas!

Give my love to Waagen, and something more still to either or both
of my nieces if you happen to meet. And with Sir Chas kindest regards
to you believe me dear Mr. Lumley
Your's very truly
Eliz Eastlake

1. Sir John Savile (1818–98), formerly John Savile Lumley and later first Baron
   Savile of Rufford, was ambassador to Italy and had also held other appoint-
   ments in the diplomatic service.

2. Sir Andrew Buchanan (1807–82) of Craigend Castle was a diplomat who was posted to many European cities, notably appointed ambassador at the Hague in 1861, Berlin in 1862, St Petersburg in 1864, and Vienna in 1871. Lady Buchanan was his second wife Georgiana.

3. Elizabeth's niece Constance Manderstjerna (daughter of Gertrude de Rosen) was married to General Manderstjerna, aide de camp to the Russian Tzar.

Letter to A. H. Layard   *NLS Ms.42169*

7 Fitzroy Sqre
July 27. 1861
Dear Mr. Layard
     I intended to write to you this morng to say how delighted we are with the article on Cavour[1] – which I read aloud to Sir Chas last night – and now there is another reason, which if true, makes it impossible for old friends to hold their peace. Sir Chas does not often bring the Times into breakfast with so happy a face as he did this morning. We both wish you heartily well, & go so far as to mingle some invocation of a blessing upon yr prospects, which you will think very profane![2]
     And now Sir Chas bids me tell you that he had already written a letter to Lord Russell on his retirement from office – for once asking a favour, viz: something in Foreign Office or elsewhere for his nephew – a well educated young man. He wishes you now to know that he has made this application in case by any chance you shd be referred to.
     I saw yr aunt yesterday and was grieved at her nervous prostration. But she will regain her bearing if she have rest.
     You will enough to do now [sic].
     Pray take all the care of yourself you can. I thought you looking far from well in addition to being so naughty the other evening.
Your's always truly
Eliz Eastlake

1. A. H. Layard, 'Cavour', *Quarterly Review*, vol. 110 (July 1861), pp. 208–47.

2. Layard had been appointed Under-Secretary for Foreign Affairs. See *The Times*, 27 July 27, p. 9, col. F.

Letter to Mrs Austen   *NLS Ms.42167*

7 Fitzroy Sqre
Septr. 20 1861
Dearest Mrs. Austen

I have been longing to write to you and have thought of you often daily. Your kindness in seeing me, & all your sweet confidence in me remains <u>graven</u> in my heart. The more I have thought of what you told me, the more I am convinced of the judgement & kindness & compliance with <u>his</u> wishes in all you have done. Your own mind will have derived peace from this conviction too.

I have seen Layard two or three times since – having spent a Sunday with him at the Acton Tindals. His spirits were not as usual, which I was glad to see. I have since met him at our good Murrays & brought him back to London in my little brougham.

I could not tell you when I last saw you that I had been astonished by a letter signed "Margeritta Higford Burr" [*name deleted*] inviting me in the most pressing terms to spend any time with them at Aldermaston, [*Aldermaston deleted*] during Sir Chas' absence that I could spare. I really could hardly believe my eyes! I felt as if I could have left such a document without <u>any</u> answer – however that would not do, so I merely declined the honor in civil and cold terms, & there it ends.[1]

Last Sunday I was with my dear Mother, who is still staying at Godalming.[2] She is wonderfully well, & both vivâ voce & by writing begs that I will remember her with deep sympathy to you. From my dear Sir Charles I have quite a charming <u>flood</u> of letters lately. He should now be in Naples, whence I hope for a letter everyday. He is doing some <u>business</u> for the Nation, & is also picking up little things for <u>me</u>.

On leaving you, dearest Mrs Austen, I thought that your old friend Sir Fenwick would be glad to hear more of you than Layard would have time to write, so I wrote him a letter the subject of which will excuse the intrusion.

Now dear Friend I need not say how I long to hear of your health & general state. You have gone through such exhaustion of mind & body that Nature may well make her <u>protest</u> in some respects. When you have been able to give her rest I quite look for the restoration of your strength and with it of your hearing. God is merciful & knows what your need has been.

Believe me dear Friend your truly attached
Eliz Eastlake

1. Margaretta Higford Burr (?–1892), English artist. Mrs Burr had accompanied Layard on some of his annual trips to Italy in the 1850s. She made water-colour copies after frescoes whilst Layard traced the figures or groups of figures on behalf of the Arundel Society. See letter, 7 February 1892.

2. Anne de Wahl was living in the High Street, Godalming according to the 1861 Census, presumably running another girls' school. Roger Rigby was also living in the same house, with his profession listed as 'Secretary and Mining Company'.

Letter to Mrs Acton Tindal   *CLS M10995*

7 Fitzroy Square
Feby 20. 1862
My dear Mrs. Tindal

Have I not been ungrateful? I am sure you are too good to think me so. I have felt all yr kind thoughts of me – the outpouring for those 'Giants of childlike faith' <u>eased</u> my heart, while it renewed my tears. Ah! what are <u>Essayists & Reviewers</u> to such! To what wd such as they hold fast in such dire extremity! Not in vain have those humble Christians died, not only to save their descendants from such a fate by wise enactments for their preservation, but surely also to fortify many a heart in the <u>simplicity</u> of the Gospel. The World by <u>Wisdom</u> will never know God, as it never did of old.[1] Those thoughts come to me the more in combination because two days ago at the B: Museum the <u>little Goodwin</u> came into the same department. We recognised each other, & we talked of the only good thing we can have in common – a certain dear Lady – & of these very verses. He seemed to me to be brewing some <u>mischief</u> among the MSS.

Then for the <u>flowers</u>, hearty thanks. They are still beautiful. But I fear you have stripped yourself in this niggardly season to give me such profusion. We have friends dining here to day. Milmans & <u>Browning</u> among them, & the flowers are smiling still.[2]

I have been very much engaged dear Mrs Tindal with work & play, which I never find answer together. London has no end of dinner parties just now, & after joining & giving a few Sir Chas & I are goint to be <u>wise</u> enough to <u>retire</u> for a short time. His health is very uncertain & often asthmatic distress prevents all engagement in the eveng. I want <u>quiet</u> evengs for my task & we both look forward to so fatiguing a season with the month of May as will require us to come to it fresh. So I am standg firm against all temptations & feel quite relieved in the prospect of some quiet weeks. My task advances & your vol: of Tillemont is frequently consulted.[3] From what that contains about our Lord, I suspect the remaining volumes wd be less profitable for me, however that I shall settle one day at the B: Museum.

I tell <u>you</u> what I have told none but my own that I had an extra job at Christmas & New Year time in getting ready at very short notice an article on our beloved Pce Consort in the Q.R. You have probably seen this No. I have been generally <u>taxed</u> with it, but I tell no one, so that you are to believe that I am not tell.g you what anyone else knows from me. It was a grateful task to my heart.[4]

Occasionally I see Mrs Dawkins – our unforgettable Mary's only remaining sister. She & her three girls are still in the Old Home in Green Street, but only for a short time. Old Sir Howard Douglas did not die rich, & there are 4 still to divide that little. Her eldest girl is very interestg & has the 'trick' of the dear aunt in her face which I look at greedily. Mrs Dawkins has given me a Photograph of dear Mrs Gartshore which I was ten years ago with <u>craving</u>, & which has passed through the hands of the dear mother & sister since. So it is doubly precious. You shall see it whenever we meet, tho' to those who loved her I almost dread the first sight of it, so true is it.

Now dear friend I trust the beautiful boys are all well. I have got a few <u>crests</u> & <u>shields</u> cut off letters if they ever wish for them. I have written the name usually behind for their edification.

Now God bless you dear Mrs Tindal

Ever yr truly affte

Eliz Eastlake

1. 204 men and boys died on 16 January when a mineshaft collapsed under falling equipment at Hartley Colliery in Northumberland.

2. Henry Hart Milman (1791–1868), Dean of St Paul's, historian and writer on ecclesiastical subjects, and his wife Mary; and Robert Browning (1812–89), poet and playwright.

3. Louis-Sébastien Le Nain de Tillemont, seventeenth-century ecclesiastical historian. Elizabeth was working on *The History of Our Lord*.

4. 'Late Prince Consort', *Quarterly Review*, vol. 111 (January 1862), pp.176–200. Henrietta Acton Tindal also wrote a poem, 'To the Most Illustrious Mourner in the New Year', in 1862 which was printed in *Rhymes and Legends with a Prefatory Memoir* (London: Richard Bentley & Son, 1879).

Letter to John Murray   *NLS Ms.42176*

7 Fitzroy Sqre
March 9 1862
Dear Mr. Murray

I am truly sorry I can't beg you to let me try my hand on the few pages you want about the artistic view of Turner.[1] But I feel I must <u>stick</u> to my present task. You know probably as much of Hart's literary prowess as we do. He can give a very good lecture, & he can give one very much the reverse! There is a gentleman who writes in Blackwood – & who attracted our notice by his review of Harford's Michel Angelo. "Mr. S. Beasington Atkinson Rosehill Cotham Park Bristol" also by a paper in Blackwood on the Nat: Gallery. He has <u>ability</u>. The only question is whether he knows what an <u>artist</u> wd say & think of Turner. He was Ruskin-bitten at one time, & wd have to be cautioned on that point, should you to him the favor to ask him. I think Layard knows him – he is a remarkable little man, with a very grand head.

I wish we could give you better suggestions. I leave off as I began, regretting that I must not do it myself. Won't I devote myself to the Q.R: when this clay/day is off my neck!

Your's dear Mr. Murray very truly
Eliz Eastlake

1. James Hamilton has attributed the review of Thornbury's *Life of Turner* to Elizabeth. See *Turner: A Life* (London: Sceptre, 1997), p. 336. James Craigie Robertson actually reviewed the book for the *Quarterly Review* (vol. 111 (April 1862), pp. 450–82). Elizabeth's only involvement seems to have been to make some suggestions to Thornbury in advance of the second edition. A letter from James Thornbury to Elizabeth on 2 February 1862 apologises that '[a] prolonged tour in Syria has prevented my writing sooner to thank you for your kind corrections of my story "marred in the telling". Any further anecdotes or facts you could give would much enrich my 2nd edition'. NLS Ms.42179.

Letter to Mrs Acton Tindal   *CLS M10993*

7 Fitzroy Sqre
April 9. 1862
My dear Mrs. Tindal

Your gorgeous flower garden came yesterday afternoon – too late to be acknowledged by post, indeed "a <u>famous</u> box" bringing Spring bodily into our London rooms. How can I thank you dear kind friend, who spoil me with your constancy of kind thought. I go from one glass & one plate to another, <u>kissing</u> them, & sniffing at them, & hanging over them. They welcome me in return every time I enter the room with a fragrance of past days, & of scenes to which I have become a stranger. Sir Chas paid loving homage to them too. Now he is just off to Osbourne on this Memorial business. His interviews with her Majesty have been more interestg than I can say. She <u>first</u> will never be forgotten. She never shone so brightly in the unaffected reality of her nature. No conventional long face or proprieties, but such genuine tears as don't refuse to be followed by gentle smiles, dwelling on the one subject & acknowledg.g extraordinary <u>comfort</u> in the midst of all sorrow. I am rejoiced that that [sic] she has seen the lines on Hartley Colliery – why not those also on herself?[1]

Dear Mrs Tindal I am lookg forward with eager pleasure to your Mr Tindal's company. At present our <u>distant</u> friends have not defined the time of their com.g, which keeps us a little uncertain about our arrangements. I think we shall be disengaged early in the time & hope in a few days to write & propose a definite period & if that wont suit you, another.

And now my thanks for a previous box of flowers – glorious darlings – left by Mr Tindal.

Ever yr affte

Eliz Eastlake

1. See letter, 20 February 1962.

Letter to Mrs Acton Tindal   *CLS M10996*

7 Fitzroy Sqre
Janry 7. 1863
My dear Mrs. Tindal

I am ashamed that you should have anticipated me in greetings. I wished very much on our return to tell you about our doings, but the anxiety to make the most of my always very curtailed leisure – in getting on with my heavy task – has made me neglect every correspondent whom I thought wd not <u>hate</u> me for it. But you have been <u>perpetually</u> thought of – & were so in our long wanderings – for your & Mr. Tindal's visit to us left reminiscences which will survive the evanescent dissipation of that time. It only comes across me painfully sometimes that I shd have burdened you with the troubles that hung so heavy on me just then. But yr friendship I know has looked on that in a different light.

We had a very charming time – the greatest enjoyment & the greatest rest at Florence, where we had your friend Fuller quite returned to his sculptor habits, & with the bust of his Lady love in his innermost studio.[1] We fell in with old friends travelling, & made new acquaintances, but happily Mr. and Mrs. Layard were always behind us.

At Paris I met young Annie Rigby, with her most kind friend & chaperon Miss Courtenay on their way to Cannes where for her health they are pass.g the winter.

I found my dearest mother wonderfully well, & I counted over no end of blessings this New Year in the health of all my survivg sisters. Like you I do all I can to cater for dear mamma's readg & for her sweet tooth too. She got more goodies and sweeties than any school girl this last Christmas.

How I congratulate on your vein of wealth! No fear of its failing. Isn't it delightful to make money? Mamma takes 'one a week' so when I next go to Windsor I shall pounce upon "The Strange Story of Kitty Hancombe" – far different are my cogitations.[2] Just now I am taken up with "The Last Judgement"! & I assure you as I have pored over the engravings from Fra Angelico's right hand scenes of bliss & sweet meetings, the tears have trickled down my cheeks.

My book cures have been cleaned & altered during our absence & I have for the present mislaid yr dear old "Lines & Leaves".[3] I want a quotation for the Last Judgement from them. Will you spoil me by send. g me yr copy per book post, to be returned in two days.

I can well believe that your verses were welcome to our august mourners on that anniversary. I have read them to Sir Chas & he responds deeply to them – as he does to all that comes from a pious heart in acknowledgement of our blessed Lord. Much do I look upon those wounds now in my researches into Early Christian art, which is always reverentially devout. You have a happy calm mind dearest Mrs. Tindal. I often feel mine too excitable.

Just now my little leisure is 'croached upon by our Exhibition to open next week – for benefit of Lancashire. All yesterday as long as daylight lasted I was there hanging pictures surrounded with idle people who hindered the busy ones. Layard got me into this scrape by recommending me as a useful hand. He dined here last night in great force & Sir Chas & I meet him at the N. Gallery at 2 today to see a new picture. He talks to me much of Mary Drummond still, who has been secretly engaged for the last 3 years to be married to a brother of Sir J.R. Shuttleworth – not a good thing I fear & is very anxious about her. He always says she is the most amiable & unselfish girl he has ever known.

Where is dear old <u>Mary</u> gone? that you talk of a new maid. <u>I</u> have a new one too – good Smith hav.g been spirited away for no fault of hers or mine. I am long in tak.g to a used one, but I think I have a very nice one, who manages <u>coiffures</u> too.

I would like to see the <u>delightful</u> boys – <u>Mr. Tindal</u> too. I don't know if <u>my</u> liking <u>him</u> would make you jealous, if so you have every reason to be so!

I had a dear funny letter from our little friend Hattie Hosmer not long ago – also one lately from good Gibson,[4] who has much of Pce of Wales & Pss Royal at Rome. Boxall our friend is spend.g the winter at Gibraltar with the Codringtons.[5] I want to write to him but hanve not managed it. My dear mother resisted leav.g her own home this year so I wait for warmer weather. Mrs Whm Leslie is a sweet little unspoiled creature really – you wd like her on better acquaintance. Now God bless you dear Mrs Tindal. Ever yrs affte

Eliz E.

1. Charles Francis Fuller (1830–75), British sculptor resident in Florence.

2. Mrs Tindal's first volume of poems, *Lines and Leaves*, was published in 1850.

3. Mrs Tindal's article 'The Strange Story of Kitty Hancomb' was first published in 1862 under her pseudonym Diana Butler.

4. John Gibson (1790–1866), sculptor and friend of the Eastlakes. Following his death, soon after Eastlake's, Elizabeth undertook to edit his life. See letters to John Murray, 9 January 1868ff.

5. Admiral Sir William John Codrington was Governor of Gibraltar, 1859–65.

Letter to A. H. Layard   *NLS Ms.42169*

7 Fitzroy Square
April 19. 1863
Dear Mr. Layard

I am always very sensible of your compliments to my good nature, however disguised they may be. I shall be very happy to use my very small influence with the Council of the R. Academy in favour of your friends, but it would be as well if I were to know who they are! But if there is any indiscretion in asking that question you shall have two blank tickets – if they can be had – sent to you.

I was quite longing to have your pleasure at the Andrea del Sarto &c.[1] And am also glad that you see beauty in the odd, idyllic Cosimo Roselli – the dear Procris and Satyr – for which I am always a champion with Sir Charles.[2] You would hear from Wornum of the purchase of the chef d'oeuvre of <u>Lanino</u>. I have not seen it yet.[3]

Sir Chas wants you much to see a picture from Hampton Court – a portrait of Bandinelli called Correggio[4] – which is now under Pinti's hands. He wants you to see what it is covered with before Pinti finally extracts it from its <u>pall</u>, so that you may better judge what Pinti does.[5] The name of Lorenzo Lotto has been laid clear in the corner. Pinti lives at 22 Howland Street – close here – & you wd have to make an appointment with him when you next visit the N. Gallery.

I am sure I wish they wd make you <u>Premier</u>, as there are several little jobs I want done! Sir Chas & I are both coughing and sneezing & very compassionate to each other.

Your's very truly
Eliz Eastlake

1. Eastlake had purchased Andrea del Sarto's *Portrait of a Young Man* NG690 for the National Gallery.

2. The work is now known as Piero di Cosimo, *A Satyr mourning over a Nymph* NG698. Cosimo Roselli was the teacher of Piero di Cosimo.

3. Bernardino Lanino, *The Madonna and Child with Saint Mary Magdalene, Saint Gregory, Saint Joseph (?) and Saint Paul* NG700 was purchased in 1863.

4. Now called Lorenzo Lotto, *Portrait of Andrea Odoni*, in the Royal Collection.

5. Raffaele Pinti (1826–81), restorer and picture dealer employed by the National Gallery.

Letter to John Murray   *NLS Ms.42176*

7 Fitzroy Sqre
Janry 18 1864
Dear Mr. Murray

I want to ask you a question before we have the pleasure of seeing you tomorrow – which you can answer verbally, or in any way <u>at yr leisure</u>.

I may however be committg a very great breach in etiquette in supposg the Q.R. wd notice my work published by Longman in which case I beg that you will <u>snub</u> me without mercy.

I am, as you know, now printing my book & it has struck me that I could furnish what might be interestg as an article on early Christian art (connected with present High Church perpetrations) if your editor wd put a <u>top</u> and a <u>tail</u> to it, so as to connect it with my book. I have no ambition to be blundered about it in the <u>Edinr Review</u> which will probably be my lot. & I could supply Mr. Macpherson with the sheets before the work appears, so as to give time. At the same time I am quite aware that any benefit accruing to the work from a notice in the Q.R. wd all go to Longman! So you can be quite frank with me.[1]

Strange to say at this <u>moment</u> arrives a note from your Editor himself kindly invitg me to do something with Mendelsohn [sic] & Weber. In my turn must now take a little time to think. And tho' as this letter is thus far written, I <u>send</u> it you, yet I quite anticipate the nature of your answer.

Eliz Eastlake

How much I have enjoyed the Sleswig Holstein article! & for the first time understood the question. <u>He</u> is a <u>capital</u> writer.[2]

1. *The Wellesley Index to Victorial Periodicals* credits the article 'Christian Art', ostensibly reviewing her work on the *History of Our Lord*, jointly to Elizabeth and Harriet Grote in the *Quarterly Review*, vol. 116 (July 1864), pp. 143–76.

2. Robert Cecil, 'The Danish Duchies', *Quarterly Review*, vol. 115 (January 1864), pp. 236–87.

Letter to Rawdon Brown   *NOTT PWM234*

7 Fitzroy Square
Janry 28 1864
Dear Mr. Brown

Your large letter arrived here on the 26th & was very nearly being answered by return of post. For Sir Chas & I were delighted with the contents, & with your great kindness in sending me such an addition to our repertory of the great Venetian. At first Sir Chas could not believe that the Photograph, however fine, could be from the fresco itself. But our magnifying glasses soon convinced him how veritably it is from the original. Certainly Titian, with all his power, never appeared to me so refined. The child is unspeakably beautiful, with its wide, downcast eyes. And its natural gesture of authority, the true infantine form so

wonderfully preserved through its solemnity of expression. The Saint
is magnificent. There is a reverential enquiry in the grand head which
is on the verge of adoration. The background is full of space and air. I
assure you you have given us great pleasure, and I am exceedingly proud
of my progression.

I wish you had said a little more of <u>yourself</u>, but as a punishment for
not doing so I shall set you the example! <u>You</u> know what it is to <u>work</u>
& therefore can sympathise with me in being so far through a long &
anxious job as to be in the Printer's hands. I means the job I undertook
by Longman's entreaty in completing – which means writing 5 parts
out of 6 – Mrs Jameson's History of Our Lord in Art.[1] I could not do it
superficially so, with <u>Mr. Rawdon Brown's</u> <u>help</u>, who sent me the gates
of S. Zeno besides a book upon that church, & also a number of little
vols: on St. Marks'. I have made it as <u>solid</u> as I could. You will find
some of the ancient mosaics of the Creation, in the vestibule cupolas
of St. Marks' engraved in my pages, which will reach you as soon as
they possibly can after the book is finally <u>born</u>.[2] Longman talks of end
of Febry – but he may tell that to the <u>Marines</u> rather than to me, if
Spottiswoode does not make more haste with the printing. I am proud
of having a great many new subjects, hitherto unengraved in any form.
Also I have a beautiful etching from Memling's Trinity in the Grimani
Breviary. Mdme Göethe had had that finely drawn for Mrs. J: & I
found it in her portfolio. Meanwhile Longman has put a fortune into an
illustrated New Testament – & will make one too out of it, for wonders
suit the million, & the idea of woodcuts being made to look like steel
engravings is fascinatg the world. I prefer things to look like <u>themselves</u>,
& I so have no wish for one of his 10 gn: copies. Also with all his
outlay he has not introduced a single new work of art to the work, &
only taken those which have been engraved over & over again, & much
<u>better</u>. You are not to think that good Murray & I have <u>coolled</u>. My
<u>liaison</u> with Longman is <u>temporary</u>!

Talking of <u>liaisons</u> there has been an immense scandal about our
friend Layard & the lady he <u>escorts</u> in Italy, & I believe has also
fascinated somewhat a friend of mine in <u>Venice</u>. However that may be
I wish Layard out of the nets, for she keeps him from what I know he
wishes, viz: to marry. He is so very fine a fellow that I don't like any
one shd be able to throw a stone at him.

Now I only have time to tell you that Sir Chas is but tolerably – that
little Effie Millais is better – near having recovered from her 6th baby,
& that Millais is an R.A.

Hoping that you are well believe me always your's truly
Eliz Eastlake

1. *The History of Our Lord as Exemplified in Works of Art, Commenced by the late Mrs. Jameson, continued and completed by Lady Eastlake*, 2 vols. (London: Longman, 1864). Elizabeth distinguishes between their work by adding the initials A.J. to any passages penned by Mrs Jameson. Ainslie Robinson has written very fully on the 'duet of female voices' in the *History of Our Lord*. See Ainslie Robinson, 'The History of Our Lord as Exemplified in Works of Art: Anna Jameson's coup de grâce', *Women's Writing*, 10.1 (2003), pp. 187–200. However, Kimberly VanEsveld Adams sees less concord and argues that Elizabeth 'imposed on Jameson's materials a chronological organization that reflected the Protestant understanding of providential history'. Distinguishing between the approaches of the two women Adams characterises Eastlake's as sectarian rather than aesthetic, whereas Jameson 'provided aesthetic rather than primarily theological criteria for her judgements'. See Kimberly VanEsveld Adams, *Our Lady of Victorian Feminism: The Madonna in the Work of Anna Jameson, Margaret Fuller, and George Eliot* (Athens, OH: Ohio University Press, 2001), p. 61.

2. *The Lady's Own Paper* of 9 March 1867 says that 'of the two volumes, consisting of some eight hundred and sixty pages, Lady Eastlake prepared over seven hundred, besides the three hundred illustrations with which the work is adorned'.

Letter to A. H. Layard   NLS Ms.42169

Hotel du Louvre Paris
Octr 28. 1864
Dear Mr. Layard

It is hard to trouble you to become a <u>Postman</u> for me, but I can think of no sooner way of getting the enclosed to Lady Buchanan as you are sure to know where Sir Andrew is. Many thanks in advance.

We are here resting a little after our rather fatiguing journey from Cannes. Sir Chas very well and much better. We think of being home by Tuesday or Wednesday next. Letters from Orlandi announce Molteni's enthusiastic admiration both of the Girolamo dai Libri, and of the Giolfino's.[1] But he has not succeeded for the present with the Portugalli Cavazzuola.[2] The <u>Sasso Ferrato</u> is secured, for 475 Nap: – a slight abatement of price, and it is shipped by this time.[3]

We found some interesting things at Marseilles. A 'Van der Meer' (of Delft). Sir Charles offered for, but unsuccessfully for the present.[4] One of our last days was at Arles, and Montmagein and Alis Camps we saw well. Weather – pouring rain – prevented Pont du Gard. Montpellier

Gallery is first rate in Dutch pictures. Avignon, how fine in landscape!
Sir Chas kind regards
Ever your's truly
Eliz Eastlake

1. Fifteenth- and sixteenth-century painters in Verona. There are several painters – Bartolommeo, Nicola, Niccolo and Giuliano – called Giolfino.

2. Cavazzuola was Paolo Morando, a painting offered by Lodovico Portalupi.

3. Sassoferrato, *The Virgin and Child Embracing*, NG740.

4. Eastlake's hope of securing the 'perfect' Vermeer for the National Gallery led to a degree of vacillation and consequently he did not purchase any of the paintings that were available in 1864. See David Robertson, *Sir Charles Eastlake and the Victorian Art World* (Princeton, NJ: Princeton University Press, 1978), pp. 224–25.

Letter to John Murray   *NLS Ms.42176*

7 FitzRoy Sqre
Novr 26 1864
Dear Mr Murray
   Many thanks for the packet of books. I am sure they will furnish much information. I have also been ransackg Sir Chas' library with good effect.
   I want to give you a little hint, with regard to a possible contributor to Q.R. I have reason to think that Ld Strangford wd respond to an invitation to contribute.[1] I need not dwell on his extraordinary ability, profound knowledge of all Eastern subjects, & also his tolerable experience in the line of reviewg. This <u>hint</u> is sufficient – but I must add that the idea must apparently come from the Q.R. editor or yourself. Ld S. is not to know that you have had any hint.
   What work is this by <u>Van Bury</u>? Or some such name. You will know & I fancy Lord S. is much interested with it.
   I send this to you – feeling that I may be the first to give you intelligence of a mutual old friends' death which had shocked us <u>unspeakably.</u> David Roberts is no more! He was seized with apoplexy in walkg Saturday afternoon in Berners Street, instantly conveyed to the hospital, & instantly surrounded with the best medical help. He was brought home & died last night at 7 o'clock. His son-in-law Bicknell came to Sir Chas. this morning.[2]
   I am quite <u>stunned</u> with it. He wrote us a note <u>yesterday</u> on

Munro's death which had greatly affected him. Alas! Alas! this life is too uncertain for anything but kindness to those we know & love.

Your's ever dear Mr Murray

Eliz Eastlake

1. Percy Smythe, Lord Strangford (1826–69), writer and former attaché at Constantinople. His only contribution was 'Travels in Central Asia', *Quarterly Review*, vol. 117 (April 1865), pp. 476–519.

2. David Roberts died on 24 November 1864.

Letter to W. E. Gladstone   *BL Gladstone Papers vol. CCCXIX 44,404 f.120*

7 Fitzroy Square

19 November 1864

Dear Mr. Gladstone

I was ill able to answer your questions last evening regarding the comparative merits of fresco and oil. I have since consulted my oracle and venture to give you the true answer in a few words.

The objection to oil painting as a substitute for fresco consists in the glossy nature of its surface, which requires certain conditions of light and can never, under any conditions, be visible and legible to the eye as a whole. Fresco, on the contrary, from the deadness of its surface, receives the light equally and favourably at any angle.

Sir Charles tells me that earnest attempts have been made, in the New Palace at Westminster, to discover some mode of correcting this shining surface in oil – with a view to substituting it for fresco – but without success.

You are aware perhaps that the expedient of executing the fresco on a slab of slate afterward fixed to the wall was adopted in the smaller subjects in the corridors.

I mentioned Pettenkofer's invention for restoring varnish. The results are given in an interesting paper 'Picture Regeneration' in the Fine Art Quarterly No.5 October 1864 and the process is given at p.176 of the same volume. I venture to mention this in case Mrs. Gladstone or yourself should care for more precise information on a subject likely to be talked of. I need hardly beg you not to trouble yourself to acknowledge this instructive letter in any form.

Believe me dear Mr. Gladstone your's truly

Eliz Eastlake

Letter to Dawson Turner   *The John Rylands University Library,*
The University of Manchester MS.597

7 Fitzroy Square
March 4 1865
My dear Dawson[1]

Sir Chas has willingly indicated such information as his library can give regarding John Downman[2] who was <u>A.R.A</u>. (associate). That fact shows that he attained a certain eminence. He is mentioned in Nagler's 'Kunstler Lexicon' – though without encomium.[3] Sandby's 'History of the Royal Academy' does him more <u>justice</u>.[4] I say justice because I have long known and much admired a small picture by him on copper of my two half sisters (Mrs. Postle and Mrs. Beevor) taken as children.[5] Mamma gave it to Edward Postle – whose death we are now mourning.[6] It is a very beautiful thing. It appears that he also painted for the Shakespeare Gallery and executed other fancy subjects, in which, according to both historians, he did not shine. Sir Chas believes that the R. Academy possesses some of his drawings – portraits of eminent painters. I would ascertain that fact, if important to your friend. Sandby says that he left a large collection of his work to his only daughter and that he was a man of 'very inferior abilities'.

I had not heard of the Cambridge Scheme in particular for the Examination of Girls. About 2 years ago I refused to put my name to one which I think emanated from University College. In all agitations for the employment of women I suspect the chief thing is overlooked – viz: their own <u>unreadiness</u>. It is the case disgracefully in art, where French women beat our own country, women follow, and for very good reasons. For they are in earnest and <u>work</u>. Whereas our girls hang upon Schools of Design and think everything can be <u>taught</u>. I investigated the wood drawing and cutting capacity of London women thoroughly when engaged on 'the History of Our Lord' and found only one professional cutter, and <u>no</u> draughtswoman. The Female Artists' Exhibition is worse than ever this year.

It pains me to hear that your beautiful Effie should have been suffering – give my kind love to her and to little Godson.[7]
Believe me dear Dawson
Your affectionate cousin
Eliz Eastlake
I return Sir Chas' card.

1. Dawson William Turner (1815–85), son of Dawson Turner and Elizabeth's

cousin, historian, philanthropist and writer on education and hygiene, and headmaster of schools including the Royal Institution School in Liverpool.

2. John Downman (c. 1750–1824), portrait painter famous for Georgian chalk drawings and oval portraits. His portrait of Elizabeth's two half-sisters (see n. 5 below) is now in the Fitzwilliam Museum, Cambridge.

3. G. K. Nagler, *Neue Allgemeines Künstler Lexicon* (Munich: E. A. Fleischmann, 1835–52).

4. William Sandby, *History of the Royal Academy of Arts* (London: Longmans, Green, 1862).

5. Elizabeth's father Dr Rigby had two daughters by his first wife. The elder, Sarah, married Jehosophat Postle in 1792. Their son was the Rev. Edward Postle. The younger, Mary, married James Beevor and had a son, Rev. Edward Rigby Beevor (1798–1878). See Anne Carter, *The Beevor Story* (Norwich: privately printed, 1993).

6. Rev. Edward Postle died at Yelverton Rectory on 26 January 1865.

7. Turner's son Dawson Fyers Duckworth Turner (1857–1928) was Elizabeth's godson; Effie Turner (1856–1929), his daughter.

Letter to John Murray   *NLS Ms.42176*

7 FitzRoy Sqre
March 28 1865
Dear Mr. Murray

I did not thank you for the valuable & kind present of the 'New Testament Illustrated' made more valuable by your handwriting in it. Your benefits to me & mine are not to be numbered. You have been the good star of my life – & when I think of what you have done, & the claims now made upon you further to do so, my eyes in the language of the Psalmist 'gush out with tears'.

We are busy preparg for our journey & have to attend H. M's Reception this afternoon. But the thought of the sufferers at Sydenham never leaves me & indeed Sir Chas share them as if they were his flesh & blood as well as mine.[1] He is for the present painfully placed with a chancery suit going on with rogues of nephews, who have treated him much as Wm Brougham has done Lord B: – ensnared him into having responsibilities.[2] But the worst will soon be decided & over & I am sure of his liberal contribution.

We both feel that if the house can be saved – by the exertions of the brothers & yourself – tho' aware of the heavy sacrifice that implies – we will among us undertake to provide the necessary income for the family. We propose naming that my mother & Jane should hire a part of the Sydenham home, throwing a considerable portion of mamma's income – at least £300 a year – into Matty's hands. I have been long preparing myself for this crisis & have at least £100 a year ready. Sir Chas will do much. This & other small helps & the let of the house ready furnished for 3 summer months, will produce a modique[3] sum – but a sure one. Should my dear mother's life fail Matty would be provided for in another way.

I put these views before you immediately – as being entirely practicable, & as enabling you & the brothers to see their way, in a small degree. The education of the boys is another thing, but even for that I do not despair of our contributing means.

Only let everything be looked up open-eyed & with no false scruples & reliances.

It is a great trial to leave just now & I would not increase your trouble by asking you to write to us. At the same time should you wish for an address it is simply 'Hotel du Londre, Paris'

Ever dear Mr Murray

Yours truly

Eliz Eastlake

1. James Smith's business was about to be declared bankrupt. See *The Times*, 25 March 1865, p. 12, col. D.

2. Eastlake v. Eastlake Chancery Suit, *The Times*, 18 March 1865, p. 13 col. D.

3. French, 'modest'.

Letter to A. H. Layard   *NLS Ms.42169*

Hotel de la Ville, Milan

Septr 10 1865

My dear Mr. Layard

I had your kind letter of the 6th yesterday. It was a great pleasure to Sir Chas to hear your affectionate interest for him, tho' we never doubt it. Sir Chas perhaps resisted the onset of such an illness better than a stronger man would have done, but the progress to recovery is slow. Still, I have every reason to think it sure. Friends in Engld

have been afraid of Italian Drs. but have had no reason to wish for
any English Dr. I ever knew I cannot imagine greater skill & care and
kindness than has been shown to my dear patient. He is still in bed
but today we take a step in diet, for in addition to the "minestra con
vermicelli"[1] he is to have a potato. I do not despair now that we may
still have time & strength to do a little business before returning. I
have seen the Girolamo dai Libri and the Giolfino pictures at Molteni's.
They are delightful. But my 2 visits have been but short, and I have
seen nothing else – tho' I ask to see your pictures next time. But the
poor Moltenis are in great sorrow, their eldest daughter – mother of a
family – is insane and in strict confinement. Good Mdme Molteni is
very depressed.

I do think we shall return to England for the winter. The Dr
thinking the lungs no tenderer than before. They were not the source
of the illness.

Sir Chas tells me that he wants me to write to Wornum, so I make
no doubt your complaint of non ventilation will be one of my subjects,
tho' without quoting you. I am so glad your dear Aunt is tolerably well.
Sir Chas love to you.

Your's ever truly

Eliz Eastlake

  1. Minestrone soup.

Letter to R. N. Wornum   NG5/161/12

Hotel de la Ville, Milan

Septr 10. 1865

Dear Mr. Wornum

I take up the pen to you by Sir Chas' wish. I conclude you have
heard of the serious illness which befell him nearly three weeks ago,
from which he is gradually recovering – and hopes in another week or
so to be able to resume his usual occupations.

Meanwhile he has recd intelligence of the possible sale of a very
important picture. This is communicated to him in strict secrecy,
which he also enjoins to you. It is the Perugino in the Villa Albani at
Rome. He would wish you to look at all your Roman guides & see
what they say of it, & whether something of its history can be traced.
He would also wish to see what is said of it in Bunsen's 'Beschreibung
der Stadt Rom'. You will find the work in Sir Chas Library in upper

shelf of the compartment opposite fire place. Our servant will let you
in. Also in lower shelf of same compartment you will find an early
edition of Vasi.[1]

He wishes to know whether Passavant or other writers speak of it.

The works which especially describe the Villa Albani confine them
he imagines, to the Sculpture.

As regards operations in the N. Gallery Sir Chas commends to yr
attention great care in the sponging the great Seb: del Piombo previous
to varnishing it. He depends upon you not to allow any operation of a
picture cleaning description.

Through a correspondent the other day I heard incidentally that the
atmosphere in the N. Gallery was unfit for men or pictures – the word
"offensive" was used. Sir Chas allows me to mention this to you.

I hear that you have had a few days of great heat. We have had
nothing else – today it is most oppressive, tho' splendidly fine.

I do trust that Sir Chas will soon be able to leave his bed. I have
every reason to be satisfied with the Italian Dr – even though they
found it necessary to take blood from the patient. The chief malady was
violent inflammation of the lungs.

Give my compts to Mrs. Wornum, who with all yr family, is I trust
well. Sir Chas will be glad of an answer addressed here.
Believe me your's truly
Eliz Eastlake

1. Giuseppe Vasi, *Delle Magnificenze di Roma Antica e Moderna*, 1747–61.

Letter to R. N. Wornum   *NG5/161/13*

Hotel de la Ville, Milan
30 Septr 1865
Dear Mr. Wornum

The faint hope that we must leave this place next week is now given
up. Sir Chas is not strong enough to move anywhere. Dr. Eastlake
therefore leaves tomorrow evening without us. Sir Chas is consigned by
him to the charge of an English medical man just arrived to settle here
– a Mr. Walker. How long we may still be detained it is impossible
to say. The present obstinate malady is entirely induced by the terrible
treatment of these ignorant Italian Drs. But as soon as he can move we
shall lose no time.

He bids me tell you that he regrets having requested you to write to

Genoa, and hopes this may be in time to prevent your doing so. At all
events he begs that you will answer him concerning the Pay Office here.

I had no idea that Sir Charles had such a strong constitution. What
he has gone through would have killed stronger men.

Believe me dear Mr. Wornum

Your's very truly

Eliz Eastlake

Letter to A. H. Layard   *NLS Ms.42169*

Hotel de la Ville, Milan

Octr 13. 1865

My dear Mr. Layard

I write at once to assure you that Sir Chas is going on as well as I
can expect. The speed is slow but steady. Today and yesterday he has
had a short drive in an open carriage and we try to keep him a little
longer out of bed every day. There is now no malady but weakness.

Both your letters have come to hand and Sir Chas has listened with
much interest to both. Form what he hears and knows of Ferrari there is
little chance of inducing him at present to sell the Carotto separately or
at a reasonable price. This affair will wait a little.

He hopes that the Cima business may be more promptly decided.
Supposing that the question of proprietorship be satisfactorily settled Sir
Chas would like you to see Count Morolin and sound him about the
price.

As regards your new treasure Sir Chas is much interested in your
description. The fact of its being on canvas is quite compatible with
the hand of Gentile Bellini. Sir Chas thinks that it would be wiser to
entrust to Pinti, and to have it repaired under your own eye. Pinti is
equally capable of managing either tempera or oil and the practice he
has had of late ought to have improved him.

I have seen your pictures at Molteni's. I am delighted with the
quattrocento portrait. I give it another name – viz: Marco Zoppo. There
are things in it which recall the picture of St. Dominic in N.Gallery.
Your Moroni head I do not envy you – you know my partiality for
handsome men! The little girl is very sympathetic.

Our plans are still unformed, except that all thought of wintering on
this side of the Alps is stoutly resisted by the dear patient. When strong
enough to go anywhere he intends going home. If this be safe for him I
shall be but too glad.

If you see kind Rawdon Brown tell him that I have his book and letter and will write very soon.

Please don't prejudice him against me!

Ever dear Mr. Layard

Your's very truly

Eliz Eastlake

Letter to A. H. Layard   NLS Ms.42169

Hotel de la Ville, Milan

Novr 8. 1865

Dear Mr. Layard

Many thanks for yr kind letter. Sir Chas thinks that yr impressions of the Signorelli are 'promising'. I have my doubts!

We now go to Pisa earlier than we anticipated. Our Dr is anxious to get Sir Chas off to Pisa – anywhere indeed out of this city where it has rained almost uninterruptedly for 9 days. We propose starting on Saturday next, & proceeding by easy stages, via Bologna, where we remain Sunday. I think that my dear patient will stand the journey well, tho' of course I am a little nervous. But good Tucker's assistance is the greatest comfort.

If Mr. & Mrs Ball are still in Florence, & if they can recommend their lodgings there, I should be greatly obliged by your asking Mr. Ball to let me know the address. We hope to be in Pisa by Tuesday next, & a note poste restante wd be fetched immediately & most gratefully received. We are not likely to want more room than they did.

Your account of Millais' growing feelings for the great old men interests me much. In a letter to Mrs. Millais I was very near saying that I anticipated his admiration of the Mantegna in the tribune. He is quite right about Maclise & Bronzino, in a certain sense. Both draw equally finely. That little chapel in the Palazzo Vecchio by Bronzino, Millais should see.

Sir Chas can't say be whom the picture belonging to Ct Mieni may possibly be. As to Ct Cottrell's so called Giorgione Sir Chas believes it to be a Romanino.[1]

We are longing to be out of this rapacious hotel, which has no heart, & an insatiable pocket which has traded on our distress. Pray get Murray to put a bad mark against it – just 12 weeks experience has taught us the truth.[2]

Sir Chas was carried up to Molteni's yesterday. He admires the
Pedrini very much, & the Belgioso picture looks magnificently.
Ever dear Mr. Layard your's truly
Eliz Eastlake
Tucker begs me to send you his 'duty'. You will never have it from a
better man.

> 1. Henry Cottrell was made a Count for his services as Chamberlain by the
>   Grand Duke of Lucca.
>
> 2. That is, to get Murray not to recommend the hotel in future editions of his
>   *Handbooks for Travellers in Italy.*

Letter to A. H. Layard   *NLS Ms.42169*

Peverada's Hotel, Pisa[1]
Novr 15 1865
My dear Mr. Layard

Just a hurried line to say that we are safe & to acknowledge yr most
kind letter. The journey here was easy as far as Bologna, but a night at
Pistoia was a great mistake & gave my dear patient much distress. It is
a place without accommodation but two Osterias – & Murray should
warn travellers off. Her also we are not well lodged, but I trust only
for a day or two. I have been seeing many apartments this morning &
am in love with one which is all cleanliness & quiet & sun, but off the
Lung Arno, which I prefer.

Now we have via Mr. Arthur Russell who gave us your kind
message & the very pleasant hope of seeing you on Monday next. That
will do Sir Chas much good, & I will back you to any extent about
my beloved Sandro Botticelli.[2] Also it will be a great pleasure seeing
Mr Millais & having the here on Sunday. I shall try & see some things
with them.

Tucker is gone to Leghorn to get wine from McBean, who I am glad
to find is a wine merchant as well as Consul.[3] The weather is lovely &
Sir Chas is basking in the sun on the balcony.

I have the kindest note from Mrs. Ball enclosing 2 letters of
introduction. My best love & thanks to her. I will write in a day or two
to her. We shall be glad perhaps to visit your pension at Florence when
Sir Chas can do a little business there.

Should we have left this odious hotel by the time you come we shall
leave careful address to our apartment – nothing is far off here.

Ever dear Mr. Layard
Your's very truly
Eliz Eastlake

   1. The Hotel Peverada was on the north side of the Lung'arno.

   2. Elizabeth's enthusiasm for Botticelli and for quattrocento artists in general located her amongst some of the earliest admirers of the so-called Italian 'primitives'. See D. Weinberg, 'Ruskin, Pater and the Rediscovery of Botticelli', *Burlington Magazine*, 129 [1006] (1987), pp. 25–27; and Francis Haskell, *Rediscoveries in Art* (Oxford: Phaidon, 1980).

   3. Messrs W. McBean & Co., correspondents of Messrs McCracken at Leghorn.

Letter to A. H. Layard   *NLS Ms.42169*

Casa Bacchioni
7 Via del Risorgimento, Pisa
Novr 22. 1865
My dear Mr. Layard

   Sir Chas begs me to write to you on some picture business in Rome, which he omitted to mention to you. I must premise it by saying that it is a <u>great secret</u>. The pictures in the Albani <u>Villa</u> (& statues) are for sale, tho' at present the fact is kept quite quiet. There is but one picture which Sir Charles would desire to acquire for the Nat: Gallery – which is a fine Perugino, in three compartments. No other picture of the master there. He would wish you, if you have time, to examine the picture. For this purpose you must apply to Minghetti the Dealer, in the Via Brabrino, telling him that Sir Chas has communicated to fact of proposed possible sale in <u>that expedience</u> to you & that he greatly desires that you shd see the collection. Minghetti is so very earnest for secrecy that you will have to make the most of Sir Chas' injunction to that effect. There is nothing else Sir Chas wd consider suitable for the Gallery. He reminds me to tell you that the lower part of the picture is injured. <u>In due time</u> he will be very glad to hear your opinion. He <u>hopes</u> that you may return to <u>Pisa</u> – so do I truly – tho' your words did not give me much hope. Should you do so I shall trouble you with a very small parcel for our friend Mrs. Acton Tindal – little things bought for the twins in Genoa, when I little thought how long our return could be delayed. – also a very small parcel for Fitzroy Square.

You will be kindly anxious to hear how Sir Chas is – much the same as when you saw him, only that last night was entirely sleepless. The Dr is intelligent & has stopped the quinine which after a time greatly disorders the digestion. That is now the uppermost ailment. I trust a few days care may relieve it. But we are comfortable in our little rooms & the quiet is very acceptable. Just now there is Sirocco & rain.

You will see Mrs. Millais. My kind love to her & assurance that, however suffering still, the dear patient is better than when I saw her last Sunday evening.

Sir Chas adds that there are some interesting pictures from Urbino (a portion of those philosophers & the characters whom young Raphael copied in his sketch book) in the Barberini Palace – Private apartments not generally shown. If you have not seen them he thinks they would much interest you. Half the number are in the Campana collection & more. But the Barberini half contains the portrait of Duke Federigo engraved in Dennistoun.[1] The fragments by Melozzo da Forli in the Sacristy of St. Peter & the great work in the Quirinal you of course know. They wd delight Millais.

Ever dear Mr Layards
Yr's very truly
Eliz Eastlake

> 1. James Dennistoun, *Memoirs of the Dukes of Urbino, illustrating the arms, arts & literature of Italy, 1440–1630*, 3 vols. (London: Longman, Brown, Green & Longmans, 1851).

Letter to R. N. Wornum   *NG5/161/19*

No 7 Via del Risorgimento
Pisa
Novr 27. 1865
Dear Mr. Wornum

I write by Sir Chas' wish to inform you that Sir Chas has approved of a suggestion from Zeno, the packet at Venice, to send the Carpaccio by land. The season is very treacherous now, and the Adriatic especially tempestuous. But the frame will go by sea, and will not need to be insured. The picture will be insured for £3.500 all the same.

Sir Chas remarks that you have not given him the amount in English money of the 85.000 francs. He concludes that in such transactions the value of money is taken at part and that therefore it will be right to consider £3.400 the equivalent for 85.000 francs. He concludes that in such transactions the value of money is taken as par, & that therefore it will be right to consider £3.400 the equivalent for 85.000 fcs.

He begs me to inform you that he has taken measures through Sigr Gualandi at Bologna[1] to purchase a picture, belonging to Count Mazza at Ferrar, pronounced by Cavalcaselle to be by Giovanni Santi. It is to be had for the comparatively small sum − £120 − & wd probably rise much in price if Cavalcaselle's opinion were generally known. Also the Count will not give more than a few days liberty for decision. Sir Chas has therefore empowered Mr. Gualandi to purchase it as for himself, & will nominally purchase it of him. But he has not himself seen the picture. Therefore till the Trustees have seen & approved of it he wishes the bargain to be suspended for the N. Gallery − as shd it turn out satisfactory he will purchase it himself.

He has recd a kind letter form Mr Wm Russell & begs you will express his thanks.

I am grieved to add that Sir Chas is again very ill. Causes more deeply seated than any change of air are responsible for this sad change. I summoned Dr. Wilson yesterday from Florence, & trust that the advice he gave will prove a great benefit.[2] But I cannot but own that my anxiety is great. A private home we now occupy and a good cook gives us many more comforts for my dear patient than we could have in an hotel. But he suffers greatly − chiefly from impeded respiration.

I grieve to send you this account & hope that a day or two − especially as his appetite has improved − may lighten my anxiety. Believe me dear Mr. Wornum
Yrs truly
Eliz Eastlake
In addition to £120 for the picture Sir Chas has directed 50 napoleons (£40) to be paid to Sigr Gualandi & Sigr _____ [*blank in original*].

1. Michelangelo Gualandi (1795–1865), art historian and picture dealer in Bologna.

2. Dr Wilson had a long established practice in Florence, 'and is consequently well acquainted with its climate and effects on disease; an important consideration in the selection of a physician in every part of Italy'. *Murray's Handbook for Travellers in Central Italy* (London: John Murray, 1864), p. 85.

Letter to A. H. Layard   NLS Ms.42169

7. Via del Risorgimento, Pisa
Decr 7 1865
My dear Mr. Layard

I received yr letter from Rome only last Thursday (the 5th) – too late to send you a few lines to Leghorn, where you were to be on the previous night. You will I trust have met Mr Millais and heard that improvement had commenced. I now write to you direct to London to confirm & continue the happy report, & to tell you that my dear patient was pronounced yesterday 'out of danger'. His rallying powers surprise the Drs. He has thrown off successively symptoms each sufficiently formidable in itself. Now his state is that of extreme weakness, but he has begun to take solid food, & has been lifted onto an arm chair for half an hour just now. Whilst there I read from your kind letter & respecting the request to have your picture Gentile Bellini cleaned & restored by Pinti in the lower story of the N: Gallery Sir Chas <u>nodded</u> assent. So pray tell Pinti – or rather Wornum – that you have permission.

I am recovering strength too & have seen the outside of this home more than once – driving with the kind people here to that grand pine forest between this & the sea, & feeding my eyes on scenery of a most solemn & monumental kind. Now my <u>horizon</u> enlarges again & I indulge the sweet hope of bringing my Sir Chas back to kind friends – among whom there is no one he values more than yourself. Meanwhile as soon as he can think, & allow me to write for hime, rely on my doing all I can to induce him to lay a retaining hand on those Preci Sandros.

This in great haste, having had many letters to write. I hope it may arrive as soon as you. I had written to you, as Millais would tell you, wondering why I did not hear.
Ever yr's truly
Eliz Eastlake

Letter to R. N. Wornum   *NG5/161/21*

No 7 Via del Risorgimento
Pisa
Decr 13. 1865
Dear Mr. Wornum

I have by degrees, with Sir Chas' instructions, been putting together what he has desired for his part of the Report of the National Gallery for the year endg Decr 31st 1865. The greater part of it is what you could have done as well, or better, being little more than a copy of the form of the last printed Report, & put together under his own eye.

Now, there are a few things to which he invites yr attention for insertion or correction on yr part.

1. Shd the number of Trustees be this year, he begs you to add the name or names to the list given in my page 1.
2. Should the picture by Gio: Santi not be approved by the Trustees he requests you to expunge the two notices of it in leaf 2 & the last page, also to alter the <u>balance</u> on sheet of accounts.
3. The notice of the bequest of the Derby Day to be added by you.
4. Details relating to the Gallery & Establishment to be added by you, includg the few words on the cleaning of the Seb: del Piombo which you will find over leaf 3.
5. To add the dates of birth & death of painter where I have omitted them.
6. The measure of the Carpaccio.
7. In case the Gio: Santi be approved (if it arrive in time for this Report) to add whether painted in oil or tempera, & the precise measure.

About Sir Chas' health I can say little. It is difficult to speak of progress in one who continues so very weak & has still so many grave symptoms. But his wish for food has improved & that is our sweet anchor. Lately the cough & flow of expectorations had increased, & the Dr ventured to put a small blister on the chest which has relieved him.[1] Day by day he holds his ground but when shall I get him on to a higher level?

Meanwhile the weather is <u>frosty</u> bright & very dry – with a north wind. We have had nothing of the mild depressing damp for which <u>it is said</u> Pisa is famous.

I hope that my arrangement of the Report will be clear to you. You will understand that he wishes the arrangement to be kept according to previous Reports.

Believe me dear Mr Wornum

Your's very truly

                 Eliz Eastlake

Sir Chas begs that this report, when made up by you, may be neatly copied before sent into the Treasury with (signed) before his name.

1. Most English visitors regarded the Italian physicians as a last resort. The *Illustrated London News*, in its report of Eastlake's death, lays the blame at the 'obstinate bigotry with which the Italian physician clings to a practice abandoned by more enlightened men'. *Illustrated London News*, January 1866, pp. 6–7 (p. 6).

Letter to R. N. Wornum   *NG5/161/24*

No. 7 Via del Risorgimento

Pisa

Decr 17. 1865

Dear Mr. Wornum

In the last letter it was omitted to tell you that Mr. Layard has requested leave of Sir Chas to have Pinti attend to a picture he has purchased in Italy, in the lower rooms of the Nat: Gallery.

Sir Chas has no objection & hopes that the Trustees will have none. He wd wish to oblige Mr Layard who (I say this in confidence) is likely to bequeath the picture to the Gallery. But he thinks that Pinti's work over it shd not go on in the room where pictures from the Nat: Gallery are restored, but in the Turner room.

I have much the same account to give of my dear patient. He fluctuates so much that I find it difficult to depend on any temporary improvement. The weather is <u>really</u> cold now here. I trust a return of mild weather may benefit him.[1]

Believe me yrs very truly

Eliz Eastlake

1. Eastlake died on 24 December 1865. *The Times* (2 January 1866, p. 8, col. E) carried a report of the funeral: 'Sir Charles Eastlake was buried at noon yesterday in the English cemetery at Florence. The body was brought from Pisa in the morning. His death was not known here until Tuesday, and then only to comparatively few persons. The attendance at the cemetery was consequently smaller than it would otherwise have been. Lady Eastlake brought her husband's body from Pisa, and attended his funeral. She was accompanied by Mrs Romilly and the Misses Horner. The British Minister at Florence was present, also Mr. Webster, R.A., and several English and Italian artists, Power, the American sculptor, and a number of English visitors and residents in this capital.'

Letter to William Boxall[1]   *UNC Elizabeth Eastlake Letters* #11,617

Florence, 6. Lung Arno Nuovo
2 Janry 1866
My dear Mr. Boxall

I am thus far on my sad journey. I had yr few lines of immediate & affte sympathy – so painful, yet for his beloved sake so sweet. I need not speak of my sorrow – you knew him, you knew <u>us</u>, as we lived & loved. God's will be done. Earthly parting <u>must</u> be, but there remains the sure & certain Hope. Be assured that my poor heart is <u>staid</u> & that my health does not suffer.

Now I must speak to you on business. I received the Academy telegram dated <u>29</u>th Decr. On Saturday evening the 30th I received Mr. Knight's[2] letter expressg the condolence of the Council and offer to meet my wishes "in every way most acceptable" on Sunday mg the 31st (This letter is a <u>private</u> one to you – not meant as an official answer). You wd receive from Mr. Elliot our British minister here a telegram sayg that I accepted the offer of the R. Academy. You received from <u>me</u> a telegram on Sunday (a few hours perhaps after) begging the Academy to wait till I shd send again. You can enter with my feelings – a little reflection had showed me that I ought to hesitate before <u>disturbing</u> that recent grave – that my Beloved One wd not wish for pompous honor – that he <u>had</u> <u>often</u> told me that he desired no pomp at his internment. In short a few hours (after the first natural impulse of joy that I could through the Academy's offer have my Beloved One in his own land) a few hours had shown me that it wd be my duty to decline that offer.

I felt that <u>you</u> wd agree with me <u>not</u> to disturb that grave, that all those whose opinion I shd value would agree with me. Had I received the slightest intimation from the R. Academy <u>in time</u> how gladly would I have obeyed it – but the laws of this country require almost immediate sepulture. I had obtained the delay of one day in addition, on a particular favor. I was strongly urged to place him here. I was (as I now believe) unintentionally <u>deceived</u> as to the enormous expense of attempting to convey the precious remains myself. In short our good Tucker – second only in grief to myself – & I were <u>compelled</u> to a prompt decision – & we followed him to the grave. Thus matters stood yesterday when I arrived & even till after I had visited that fresh raised mound!

But a few hours have changed all! The rumour reached me that the <u>cemetery</u> was not guaranteed – that city alterations wd disturb it. I went

straight to the minister Mr. Elliot & it was with something like joy that
I heard him confirm this idea.[3] He told me that he had been making
particular enquiries of the Italian Govt & cd get no guarantee – that it
was believed that interments wd soon cease in that cemetery & that only
a few year's quiet after that wd be allowed as the extension of the city
wd require that ground. He told me that in my place he wd not leave
him there – he gave me leave to quote him on his 'strong opinion'. You
may guess how this changed my views, became my duty. I need not
say more to you. I do now most gratefully accept the Academy offer. I
cannot now say to what extent. St. Paul's is repugnant to me, because
his modest spirit wd have forbidden it – his desire was to lie in the
Kensall Green Cemetery – with our babe – who lies there – next him,
& me finally at his side. But on this point of place I reserve my answer
till my return. It will be my duty to consult his nephews first. Also it
will depend on the Academy whether to permit this less ostentatious
way of doing him honor.

Meanwhile our Tucker is laboring with pious affection to smoothe the
way for removg his beloved Master – if possible for accompanying him
directly & immediately by land – for wh: many formalities are needed
to be gone through.

Perhaps I may not be in possession of positive information before I
close this – perhaps I may require to remain here a day or so longer on
this account. At all events I write formally to Mr. Knight today with
my acknowledgements but postponing the complete answer to their most
consoling offer till my return. Meanwhile you can tell him what you
please as to the particular reasons which have finally guided me. You
can also do the same – if you will kindly to Dr. Eastlake, and tell him
to acquaint our good Anderson in Fitzroy Sqre. You shall immediately
hear of my return.[4]
God bless you
Yours afftly
Eliz Eastlake
Kind Mr. Webster[5] in this same house with me is a great comfort to
me.
All is [sic] possible measures are now being taken to enable Tucker to
start with his precious charge on Saturday next. British and French
ministers are giving all assistance – Tucker will not leave his beloved
Master day or night. My return is delayed by this as I hope to join
Tucker at all events at Paris.
Again good bye.

  1. William Boxall (1800–79), painter and Director of the National Gallery

1866–74. See Michael Levey, 'A Little Known Director: Sir William Boxall', *Apollo*, 101 (May 1975), pp. 354–67.

2. John Prescott Knight (1803–81), painter and Secretary for the Royal Academy between 1847 and 1873. Knight was also Professor of Perspective 1852–60, which accounts for George Storey's anecdote of a conversation with C. R. Leslie and his daughter Harriet: 'we were one night speaking of Lady E., and saying what a fine handsome woman she was – she was nearly a head taller than her husband. "Yes", said Miss Harriet, "but she is quite out of perspective; don't you think," addressing her father, "that little Knight could do something for her?" Little Knight, as he was called, was then Professor of Perspective at the Royal Academy'. See G. A. Storey, *Sketches from Memory* (London: Chatto & Windus, 1899), p. 64.

3. Robert Browning dismissed her actions in a letter to Isa Blagden on 19 March 1866: 'I am thankful that there is no ground for Lady Eastlake's nonsensical fears or pretence of them – and that the ground will be preserved'. See E. C. McAleer (ed.), *Dearest Isa, Robert Browning's Letters to Isa Blagden* (Edinburgh: Thomas Nelson & Sons, 1951), p.133. Browning's sly reference to her 'pretended fears' echoed those who thought that her real motive for disinterring Sir Charles' body was to secure a publicly funded state funeral.

4. The news of Eastlake's disinterment was carefully outlined in *The Times*, 15 January 1866, p. 5, col. F.

5. Thomas Webster (1809–96), English genre painter, etcher and Royal Academician, who was present at Eastlake's funeral in Florence. Elizabeth later wrote an article about him, 'Thomas Webster, R.A.', for *Murray's Magazine*, vol. 2 (July–December 1887), pp. 222–31.

Letter to A. H. Layard   *NLS Ms.42169*

7 FitzRoy Sqre
Janry 10. 1866
Dear Mr. Layard

I reached this sad home last night. I should not trouble you so immediately but that there is one thing which has been much in my mind in my journey & for wh: I am anxious to work by any means in my power.

My Beloved one always thought that there was no one so like himself in mind, taste & education of art as Boxall. He is the man to succeed him in the National Gallery. He had the true feeling for the Old Masters – he has the knowledge of the literature belonging to

them. He has that peculiar – & as Sir Charles thought more & more
– indispensable requisite for the highest commissionship – he being
himself a refined painter who has always looked to the Old Masters for
guidance. And then he has those pure & upright qualities as a gentleman
without which no one could be fitted to succeed him.

I think you know enough of Mr. Boxall to know that this is no mere
view of personal friendship. Will you do all in your power with those
with whom the appointment rests & if permissible I may say how Sir
Charles thought of him.

Personally Boxall & you were the two men he most loved.

This needs no answer – I should not wish to see you until after the
funeral here. I expect our faithful Tucker & his precious charge tonight.
I met him at the Lyons station at Paris at 4 o'clock Saturday morning.[1]
Always yours truly
Eliz Eastlake

1. *The Times* gave regular bulletins in the lead-up to the funeral. The funeral
   took place on 18 January when a large procession of 22 mourning carriages
   drove from Trafalgar Square to Kensal Green, with almost as many more
   private carriages following, in front of a crowd of several hundred. It took
   almost three hours for the procession to arrive at Kensal Green, where more
   mourners were waiting. See *The Times*, 18 January 1866, p. 9, col. B.

Letter to A. H. Layard   *NLS Ms.42169*

7. FitzRoy Sqre
Janry 24. 1866
Dear Mr. Layard

I am unhappy without know.g anything about the Nat: Gallery – not
about the arrangements regarding his successor, but whether certain
pictures have arrived. The Carpaccio for instance, wh: was sent by
land – & others. You will advise me perhaps to address myself to Mr.
Wornum – but till Saturday that flegmatic [sic] man had not addressed
one word of the commonest condolence to me on the loss on one who
gave him his situation. Yesterday he sent me a rather bald expression of
the Trustees sympathy without so much as naming which Trustees had
met. Much business wh: was going on was necessarily in my hands. But
I will not harrass you. Would you be so very kind as to enquire about
the Carpaccio, the Giovanni Santi &c. & if you think it best to consult
Mr. Wornum as to what should be done with the many letters relating
to the Gallery (offer of pictures &c.) addressed to my Beloved which I

found here, will you kindly do so. But I feel that whatever passes into his hands will get no proper attention or answer. Therefore exercise your own discretion & if you would prefer to see me first I will see you whenever you feel inclined to come. I know no one like yourself who will take trouble for his dear sake. I am anxious, perhaps needlessly so, to have evidence that his immediate work is at all events being carried to completion.

Kindly send me a line to say when you could most conveniently come – & do not let me hurry you.

Your's very truly

Eliz Eastlake

Letter to A. H. Layard   NLS Ms.42169

7 FitzRoy Sqre

Janry 26 1866

My dear Mr. Layard

Many thanks for your most kind letter. I am glad to hear of the Carpaccio & shall be anxious to see it when I can bear seeing anything.

I do truly regret that the proposal which Lord Russell made to you & wh: you would have so disinterestedly accepted proved impracticable. That arrangement would have been excellent in itself, & would have given me great consolation. I regret also much that excellent Boxall has no chance.[1]

I will see you with pleasure on <u>Tuesday</u> afternoon any time from 4 to 6 & will have letters & questions ready.

What you quote from Morelli's[2] & Molteni's letters is very sweet to me – indeed the world can do no more in tributes of respect than it has done. But this cannot ease sorrow. God alone can do that.

Your's ever truly

Eliz Eastlake

1. Layard was approached to become Director of the National Gallery on 28 December, although his position as an MP precluded the appointment. See Jonathan Conlin, *The Nation's Mantlepiece: A History of the National Gallery* (London: Pallas Athene, 2006), p. 83. On a not unrelated matter, Lord Russell had written to Lady Eastlake on 1 January 1866 to assure her that she would be granted a pension from the Civil List of £300 per annum (see letter from Lord Russell to Lady Eastlake, Public Record Office, PRO 30/22/16A). The subject clearly caused some public conjecture because on 13 February 1866 (p. 9, col. D) the *Times* announced: 'We are requested to state that the grant

of a pension to Lady Eastlake was entirely spontaneous on the part of Her Majesty, whose pleasure in the matter was communicated by Earl Russell to Lady Eastlake'.

2. Giovanni Morelli (1819–91), Italian politician, writer, collector and art historian.

Letter to A. H. Layard　　　*NLS Ms.42169*

7 FitzRoy Sqre
Febry 2. 1866
My dear Mr. Layard

Many thanks for your kind letter & all you take interest in for his dear sake.

I subjoin a memorandum for Mr. Russell – of the pictures most present in his intentions. Still, it will be better for Mr. Russell to use me, as he knows nothing of the agents through whom the treaties were proceeding – & can have no help from Wornum – who can't write his own language far less a foreign one. For writing Italian letters in the most regular & official manner my Dear One, however able himself, employed an old Italian friend of great cultivation of mind. This was merely an excuse to give him payment out of his own pocket. But if Italian letters are requisite – as we know they are – Mr. Incoronati has the advantage of having been accustomed to Sir Chas' forms.

I will not bore you again about the benefits of it would be to the Gallery to have someone in manner, fitted to take his place & to use his materials – such as Boxall – but I trust still that Ld Russell may be brought to see that.

Wornum writes me that "the picture ascribed to Geo: Santi I have paid for, & read it off as a purchase at the last meeting"! That was not the way intended.

As to the letters on Nat: Gallery business I will put them into Mr. Russell's hands – but with the stipulation that he returns them to me to fold & docket with the stores that be here.

There can be no hurry on these points, & I do not feel at liberty to give up the stores of letters & notes which are a mine of information either to a Trustee, or to Mr. Wornum, whose irregularity & confusion were always a trial to him.

The Paris Bordone to which you refer is at Brünn in Austria. Mündler was to have purchased it at his own risk I believe. Sir Chas had not seen it.

I am reminded by Mr. Chas Eastlake of whom I spoke to you that you have the Queen's Messengerships in your gift. I don't know if this be true. He has long desired to obtain one of those, & I merely mention that he is well qualified in modern languages.[1]

I see I have written you a worrying confused letter. Tho' I send you this memorandum I will myself send a copy to Mr. Wm Russell, & ask him to call. So do not take any trouble, except to continue taking to heart the wants of the Nat: Gallery. I spoke to Fonter of them also.

Ever dear Mr. Layard you very sorrowful

Eliz Eastlake

I find books & papers have to be corrected before I arrive at precision about pictures proposed to be purchased – therefore the memoranda are delayed – but they shall be done.

> 1. Charles Locke Eastlake (1836–1906), nephew of Charles Lock Eastlake. Eastlake trained as an architect and in 1868 he published *Hints on Household Taste in Furniture, Upholstery and other Details*, which became highly influential in the United States in promoting what was called 'the Eastlake style' of interior decoration and furniture-making. Eastlake became Secretary to the Royal Institute of British Architects in 1866 and Keeper at the National Gallery in 1878.

Letter to A. H. Layard   *NLS Ms.42169*

7 FitzRoy Sqre
Feby 7 1866
My dear Mr. Layard

The very little hope that you are so kind as to give me about Boxall – which I shall keep to myself – is a great comfort to me. I shall wait patiently for more information, & trust it may confirm the hope.

You overlooked a few crossed words in my note saying that I had not enclosed the memorandum about the pictures. I did not remember whether the subject of the Abbazia Cornia was Tobias & Angel – or Pilgrims to Emmaus. I can find out – but that involves looking through things for which my nerve has failed at present. But that is of no consequence for you – who probably know the subject. And as to the Trustees the more I have considered the more am I unwilling to give the subject into their hands. They know not who to employ – they can't write an Italian letter – in short I cannot bear to entrust it to them, the more especially as there is the slight hope of better hands. The financial year terminates I believe on 31st March therefore there is no hurry.

Meanwhile, busy as you must be, I am sure you will find time occasionally to look in & see what Pinti is doing to the Carpaccio – & that he is doing it well.

It has struck me that I might undertake the 'Register' which <u>he</u> had so much at heart. He often said to me that I could help him do it. I believe Wornum <u>began</u> it – but all questions upon it are best <u>deferred</u>. To me the work would be an unspeakable consolation, & as my dear One has left the <u>form</u> there would be little more than mechanical work. But we will say nothing of this at present.

Your's ever truly

Eliz Eastlake

Letter to A. H. Layard   *NLS Ms.42169*

7 FitzRoy Sqre

Feby 9 1866

My dear Mr. Layard

This is the first sense of pleasure I have known for long. How thankful I am to your for it! For I am quite sure that good Boxall owes the appointment to <u>you</u>. Now indeed with you as Trustee, my Dear One's plans & views will be reverentially carried out – I shall so gladly make over all he has left into such good & kind hands.[1]

Your's gratefully

Eliz Eastlake

1. Boxall's appointment was approved by the Queen on 9 February 1866 and Layard became a Trustee of the Gallery on 13 February – the same day as a Treasury warrant officially appointed Boxall.

Letter to A. H. Layard   *NLS Ms.42169*

7 FitzRoy Sqre

Feby 16. 1866

My dear Mr. Layard

It has been a great consolation to me to see Boxall several times & to being to make him acquainted with the methods of work & the materials of information wh: he has left. The latter so far exceed my expectations – are so clear & full, & embrace so much that is is generally as well as specially interesting that I am lost in sorrowful admiration.

I shall make it my pleasing duty to carefully index these note books.[1] I am inclined to think – on the first feeling of admiration – that there is much that would be valuable to the public as well as to the managers of the N.G. But this, time will show.

I find that the Portalupi Cavazzuola is among the engravings from his works. Mr. Boxall, on the first meeting of the Trustees, will have the work with him so that they may see the subject – at the same time it will rest with his judgement whether to wait till he sees the picture some day himself.

An offer has reached him from Mr. Eastlake of Plymouth – a very unworthy nephew who gave him much trouble – to sell a small full length early picture by Sir Charles of the Emperor Napoleon, which is unfortunately in his possession. It is I believe the study for the picture which first gained him repute – taken from incessant observation of the Emperor when on board the Bellerophon in Plymouth. It must be seen first. I saw it alas! more than 16 years ago but I merely remind you that it is a very interesting specimen in all ways. The large finished painting is I believe in America.[2]

The proving of the will is suffering some delay owing to the ill advised proceeding of the same Mr. John Eastlake who has entered a caveat. But it is not apprehended that he will take further steps to obstruct his uncle's intentions. When that is done I shall be very thankful for Mr. Murray & your good offices in the portion committed to your trust & also in advice to me.

May I mention another subject – on which I am interested tho' ignorant. Are you aware that Lord Strangford is very desirous of succeeding Panizzi in the Librarian department?[3] It is out of the question for him to send in testimonials, & it must rest with his friends to have it, if possible, offered to him. In my limited means of knowledge it appears to me that it would be honorable to the country & to the Nobility to have a nobleman of his real ability & knowledge there. I knew his wish when at Pisa – & mentioned it my never forgotten one. He said he could give no competent opinion "but he appears to me to be the highest name & fittest man". I recorded those words. It is not for me to be writing to any one on this matter. I should be much obliged to you to tell me whether Ld. S'. wish is known, & whether you & theirs are seconding it.

Your's very truly
Eliz Eastlake

1. Eastlake's travel notebooks are in the Library of the National Gallery. See Susanna Avery-Quash, 'Sir Charles Lock Eastlake's Travel Notebooks (1852–64)', *Journal of the Walpole Society*, forthcoming in vol. 73 (2011).

2. *Napoleon Buonaparte on Board the Bellerophon in Plymouth Sound* (1815) is in the National Maritime Museum in London.

3. Sir Antonio (Anthony) Panizzi (1797–1879), Principal Librarian at the British Museum Library until 1866. He was succeeded by John Winter Jones (1805–81).

Letter to A. H. Layard   *NLS Ms.42169*

7 FitzRoy Square
March 14. 1866
My dear Mr. Layard
I feel much kindness for your letter – & you may be sure that I think often of one he so much loved, & that I should have applied to you, could you have done anything for me. But the stop put to all settlement of affairs by a nephew undeserving of his name precludes me troubling you yet to undertake the office the he laid upon you. I cannot help believing that the unworthy nephew will find it more to interest to stop short in the course he has entered – a day or two – I am assured will now decide.[1]

You have already done very much for my comfort in assisting the appointment of Boxall. He is almost discouraged by the <u>standard</u> of work which my Beloved One has left, but do not despair of Boxall's keeping it up. He has a happy time before him in increasing his knowledge of matter – the feeling for excellence he has already.

I am not actually engaged yet on the Register. There is so much for me still to look through – <u>nothing</u> to put in order, for all is exquisitely orderly, & I am still far from fit for any mental application. I fear the sorrow is not come to its full growth evern yet!

It would be interesting to compare you Gentile inscription with our's here. This is in stiff latin letters 'Opus Gentilis Bellini egritis Veneti"

Today I have put aside for Boxall a monogram of Alonso Cano which Waagen sent to my Darling & which I think will be found to correspond with the letters on the '<u>Roland Mort</u>'.

How grieved I am to hear of Mrs. Curzon's death! I had a very great regard for her, but the world cannot be emptier for me than it was already.
Ever dear Mr. Layard your's truly
Eliz Eastlake

1. Eastlake left the residue of his personal property (valued at £40,000 at probate) in two moieties: one to Elizabeth and the other to be divided between three nephews – William, Henry and Charles Locke Eastlake. The 'undeserving' nephew John Eastlake had attended him in Pisa during his illness and made a claim on the estate for expenses.

Letter to Hannah Brightwen[1]   *Private Collection*

7. FitzRoy Sqre
March 15 1866

If you cd know, dearest Hannah, how soothing your kind words are to me, you wd be rewarded for yr thought of the suffering cousin. No human words soothe me except those which are supplied by the experience of intense sorrow – all others fail to reach <u>my</u> sorrow.

"Words weaker than my grief but make my grief more strong". May you indeed never know <u>this</u> greatest of all human woe! Still we will not measure sorrows – your's was indeed as much as yr poor heart cd bear, <u>even</u> with full desire to lay it upon the Cross, wh: dear dear Hannah! we pay dearly for our very strong & tender affections. My heart, like yours, is one which does not leave a drop untasted of that bitter cup. I am always <u>struggling</u> <u>upward</u> – importuning the Father, claiming the Saviour, till the very body is weary. I <u>know</u> that is the only way to Rest. Divine Comfort can <u>alone</u> assist me – I cease not from my crying – I am, as it were, <u>forced</u> upward – to look on my Beloved as he was – as I have loved him here, upsets all my little fortitude – to <u>follow</u> him is my only resource & then we meet in Christ. But oh! the flesh is weak – the heart – poor heart! is treacherous – I was thrown off my guard – one dear association brings back a host – the floods go over me, & breathless I crawl to the nearest shore. Can my beloved One see me? This is a question beyond us, tho' there seems no interdict absolutely on the possibility. I know that there is no need for <u>him</u> to to <u>help</u> me, for Christ is all sufficient – but I feel that his love for me can as little cease as mine for him. Well, let me be patient & faithful, the conviction of God's Love & Wisdom is the answer to <u>every</u> question – in time I trust yr words will come true & that I shall be able to say <u>from my heart</u> 'Thy will be done'. I <u>say</u> it with my lips over & over again now but the heart does not entirely join.

But I shd deserve to be forsaken were I not to acknowledge that I <u>do</u> obtain gracious Help – imperceptibly a sort of calm succeeds to earnest prayer which I know is not of <u>myself</u>. The days pass – I am carried through them − heavy, weary, weeping, sighing, falling down, struggling up − but I do not <u>lose</u> ground, & I forbid myself even to <u>think</u> that I shall. Looking forwd is as dreadful as lookg backwd. I live but for the sad present. I try to occupy myself − have had much heart breakg work in lookg through sweet <u>stabbing</u> things − but they occupy my thoughts by slow degrees. Last night even I read to my sister Anne one of his essays from Contributions to the Literature of the Fine Arts − <u>gloating</u> over his dear occasional pencil notes in the margin. I feared it was a <u>suicidal</u> pleasure, but it soothed me. I know I must manage to keep constantly occupied, but that is the difficulty − most of my habitual pursuits are <u>too</u> deeply associated with my too dear companion. Again you will say <u>Time</u> <u>Time</u> − I will be patient. I am indeed thankful that <u>he</u> is spared the agony I know − that eleven such weeks of mental torture never passed over his beloved head. God gave him alas! physical sufferings for more than that time. How I longed to bear them on <u>my</u> body for him! Ah! he is at <u>rest</u> now − yet <u>living</u> − with his dear loved mother, whom I never knew, but who he often told me he felt approved his choice & rejoiced in his happiness − & with <u>our child</u>. Thus he <u>waits</u> for me, & shall I not be patient & <u>wait on the Lord</u> as long as he pleases me to continue my lonely pilgrimage! my constant ejaculation is 'Christ to Thee I commit my <u>Treasure</u>. Christ! to Thee I commit my life. Christ! to Thee I commit my Cross.

You have brought on yourself a sadly selfish letter dear sympathisg Hannah. To you, as to dear Mary, my heart flows over − I must not talk of loneliness, I have the kindest sisters − & friends, one at a time are with me. I have not been alone yet. Dear Anne is all sympathy & kindness − a letter from her Caroline from Malta today has cheered her. We are lookg <u>anxiously</u> for tidings of our Roger. May our aged mother be spared further strokes − mine has been hard for her, but fortunately the memory of sorrow is not <u>persistent</u> with her. She is wonderful − but cd she feel sorrow as she once did her feeble thread of life wd soon fail.

I need not <u>say</u> dearest Hannah how thankful I shall be for yr handwriting − how the opening of <u>your</u> heart to me consoles mine. Yr sorrowg but most affte
Eliz Eastlake

> 1. Hannah Brightwen (1808−82), daughter of Dawson Turner and Elizabeth's first cousin, married to the banker Thomas Brightwen of Yarmouth.

Letter to John Murray   *NLS Ms.42176*

7 FitzRoy Square
3 May 1866
Dear Mr. Murray

I receive with gratitude <u>for him</u>, the 3rd & last vol: of Cavalcaselle's work – I shall read it with great care & I am personally also greatly obliged to you for it.

But I am rather surprised to find that this volume is made the subject of another dedication – viz: H. Layard. No one is more entitled to such a dedication – but I always felt that the work ("these volumes") were dedicated to Sir Charles. It is the old story – Cavalcaselle & Crowe turn to the <u>living</u> one who can help them – & are doubtless wise in their veneration.[1]

I have refrained willingly from troublg you with any allusion to business – everything having been suspended by the shameless suit that had been raised against the Will. Last week the proposal was made by Mr. John Eastlake's lawyer that if I wd pay the expenses Mr. J.E. had incurred he wd withdraw the suit. Of course but one answer was returned to this & last eveng I received the tidings that the suit <u>is withdrawn</u>.

I therefore propose to fulfil the duties my beloved one has assigned to me as promptly as possible & shall hope to lay before you & Layard all necessary amounts preparatory to yr undertakg the trust. That is whenever, after ten days or so, it may best suit your respective leisure.

I regret to see that dear Menie has lost a little more of her never abundant flesh. I hope Wimbledon will soon restore her again. Dear Hester is looking well.

Ever dear Mr. Murray
Yrs very truly
Eliz Eastlake

1. *A New History of Painting in Italy from the Second to the Sixteenth Century* was commissioned by John Murray and appeared as five volumes between 1864 and 1871.

Letter to William Boxall   *NG14/4/1866*

7 FitzRoy Sqre
May 10. 1866
My dear Mr Boxall

Your kind letter from Turin of the 6th reached me on the eveng of
the 8th here & had a very sincere welcome. My only complaint is that
you did not tell me enough about yrself, & how yr health & strength
stand the traveling, but you may be quite sure that you can never tell
me too much about pictures. I am not surprised that the collection of
Dutch pictures at Paris was rather disappointing – they had no great
name. The Delessert Raphael[1] my Darling had seen, but not I, which
I much regret, as I shall scarcely see it now in the altered remainder of
my life. I conclude that it was the Père Delessert who showed it to you
& I am not surprised at his gratification at yr appreciation of it, which at
all events was not influenced by its supposed market price. Delessert the
son is I believe too ill to appear.

I am so glad that you had at once seen good old Orlandi – rather a
bore, but a dear & thoroughly reputable old man. He was so faithful
& kind during our dreadful time at Milan that I am really attached to
him. His Gaudenzio Ferrari is all you say of it, the little St. John below
quite charming. My dear Sir Charles always admired it, but the price
was out of the question, & also he thought that one figure, especially
– the legs of (I think) St William (in armour I fancy) – were too much
much [sic] rubbed "ever to be brought about" as his expression was. My
recollection was that Orlandi even asked 30.000 frs – 'un prix fou'. I shd
fancy that yr ultimate determination wd depend upon his abatement.
There is no doubt that it is a charming specimen of a charming & little
known master. I remember no worthy specimen of him out of Italian
galleries. That in the Brera – Martyrdom of St Cath: – has beautiful
things in it, but also great extravagances of form & colour. One in the
Accademia Carrara (public gallery) at Bergamo is very sweet, but not so
important as Orlandi's. Both of these are in Piannazzi's [sic] engravings
of Gaudenzio's works[2] which we have. Mr Holford has a very pretty
Gaudenzio you may remember – Nativity with Mad: & Joseph & angels
adoring. You will doubtless feel that it depends on the price, & on the
practicability of restoration. That Sir Chas admired it is quite certain,
but he felt that at the price it wd keep. Now perhaps with this dreadful
war pendg poor Orlandi may abate considerably – all in Italy ought to
do so. You will find in my little books of notes, that I have mentioned
this Gaudenzio under Turin.

I need not say how interested I shall be to hear yr impressions of the different pictures for sale at Florence. Meanwhile the Times will have probably given you the impression that the R.A. dinner went well, & that Grant got through it better than anyone expected.[3] I can but deeply feel the many touching allusions to my perpetually lamented one, also the slient health! – tho' that may be usual towards each deceased President. But I hear through Richmond's daughter, my little neighbour Mrs Farrer, that there was a great feeling of depression observable, that in short it was an altered thing! I hear in a note from Lady Grant that Sir Francis was & is far from well, tho' nothing of consequence.

The Exhibition is considered a good one. I have not read the report of it. Tom Taylor instantly found an ill natured thing to say of the motto of the Catalogue, wh: however I hear is properly appreciated by others.[4] Praise of yr two has reached me. Good Mrs Austen (Layard's aunt) no mean judge, writes me that yr full length of Mrs Peto "strikes me as one of the very fineset portraits I ever saw". My sisters say that yr John Moores looks gloriously. Goodall's Hagar & Ishmael appears to strike the public as the most attractive subject picture.

My good sister has been suffering severely with an attack she is subject to & wh: required much morphia, wh: fortunately does not disagree with her. But she is better & up & on the sofa with me to day & will take a drive in a little open carriage which good Tucker has picked up for me, & wh: gives us both more air. I have also a guest, kind Mr. Greene the clergyman at Pisa,[5] who had to come to London on business, & who deserved to be entertained in my beloved one's home.

I must tell you that the disgraceful suit is dropped. This step was prefaced by a proposal to do so if I wd pay the expenses he had incurred. Of course our lawyer did not listen to this, & it was withdrawn a few days after. Now I have given a cheque for Probate duty & hope that all will be settled very shortly.[6] Meanwhile I am thinkg much of the necessary monument to my Darling – in Kensall Green. I gave Charles Eastlake the commission to make the design, but I fear his abilities are mediocre – & that I will have to depend upon my poor judgement. I shall therefore mature my ideas very slowly & shall be thankful for your opinion when you return.

I fear this approaching & horrible war will greatly interfere with yr object, tho' it may be favorable as pulling down prices. But you must not mind what people ask. Italians always expect an offer from us, & then split the difference. Good bye dear Mr Boxall, take care of yr health & tell me about it. My sister's kind regards yr's afftly Eliz Eastlake

1. Jules-Paul-Benjamin Delessert (1773–1847) bequeathed his collection to his brother François-Marie Delessert (1780–1868). The sale following his death was held at the Hôtel Delessert, Paris, 15 March 1869. Boxall purchased a de Hooghe.

2. Silvestro Pianazzi, *Le opere del Pittore e Plasticatore Gaudenzio Ferrari* ... (Milan, 1835).

3. Sir Francis Grant (1803–78) succeeded Eastlake as President of the Royal Academy. See John Steegman, 'Sir Francis Grant PRA: the Artist in High Society', *Apollo*, 79 (June 1964), pp. 476–85.

4. Tom Taylor (1817–80), playwright, journalist and later editor of *Punch*.

5. Mr Greene was the chaplain at Pisa who had witnessed Eastlake's last will and testament two days before his death.

6. Probate was granted on Eastlake's will on 10 May 1866.

Letter to A. H. Layard   *NLS Ms.42169*

7 FitzRoy Sqre
May 28. 1866
My dear Mr. Layard

I was much obliged by your kind note before starting for Paris. I am told you are now back. I have heard from Boxall once – from Turin – I also hear from Mr. Penry Williams that he had not arrived in Rome (where he was going on Gibson's will business). I conclude that Florence is giving him much to see & something to do.[1]

I have not required to trouble you & Mr. Murray regarding your trusteeship but look forward now to doing so very soon.[2] And also to forwarding to you a cheque for the amount of legacy due to you. Meanwhile it is possible that you might feel it advisable to take advantage of the present state of money matters in case you & Mr. Murray should contemplate any change of investment in the money which will soon be committed to your trust. I therefore think it right to inform you that the greater part consists in consols – Reduced 3 per cent & New 3 per cents – which amounts to, I believe, above £10,000 stock (namely the half which will be in your trust) & the rest chiefly in Egyptian bonds of 1862 & 1864 – & something in Turkish Scrip.[3]

I would also be much obliged by your advice in case of <u>my</u> making any change of investment in that half which becomes absolutely mine. I have no wish for English railways or Colonial bonds. Would you advise any foreign stock at present depressed prices? Or do you think that a transfer of a portion from Consols & Egyptian Loan would be a safe measure? In that case is there any preference for the 1862 Loan over the 1864 one?

I feel doubly scrupulous in asking any questions of one so occupied as yourself – & especially questions which only concern my own share, but I know you will be indulgent.

Your's very truly

Eliz Eastlake

1. Penry Williams (1802–85), Welsh painter, living principally in Rome. See Derrick Pritchard Webley, *Cast to the Winds: The Life and Work of Penry Williams (1802–1885)* (Aberystwyth: The National Library of Wales, n.d.).

2. Eastlake had foreign investments amounting to some £13,000 to be held, under English law, in the names of his appointed male trustees, John Murray and Austen Henry Layard. For an account of the responsibilities of trustees see Chantal Stebbings, *The Private Trustee in Victorian England* (New York: Cambridge University Press, 2002).

3. Scrip is a provisional certificate entitling the holder to a fractional share of stock.

Letter to John Murray   *NLS Ms.42176*

7 FitzRoy Sqre

July 9 1866

Dear Mr. Murray

I had hoped before now to claim yr kind services as Trustee. As that business, however, must still be delayed I will no longer postpone sendg you the small legacy – namely £50 – which Sir Chas bequeathed to you. I enclose you therefore a cheque for the moment – I should be obliged to you for a receipt.

The causes for the delay in finally settling matters are firstly a claim made by Dr. Eastlake for his attendance on his uncle in Italy – & 2ndly the necessity (I understand) of converting the foreign securities wh: form part of the property, with other forms of investment. I have written to Layard for his advice on this point.[1]

Believe me dear Mr. Murray ever yr's truly

Eliz Eastlake

1. See letter to Layard, 9 July 1866.

Letter to A. H. Layard   NLS Ms.42169

7 FitzRoy Square
July 9. 1866
Dear Mr. Layard

I find that further delay is unavoidable before committing to Mr. Murray & you the trust you have kindly undertaken. I therefore delay no longer to send you a cheque for the small legacy namely £50 – which Sir Charles bequeathed to you & for which you will be so kind as to send me a receipt.

The impediments of the final completion of business are firstly the claim of Dr. Eastlake for a fee of £36, 7s, 10 & secondly the necessity for converting the foreign securities before putting the property in your hands.

Dr. Eastlake threatens an action against me & much as that will distress me I have no means of avoiding it. It is the opinion of our legal adviser that the claim is not legal – so that I am not at liberty to pay it from the estate – & I am not inclined to discharge it from my private means. Thus he must take what measures his chooses – though I am not without hope that his own solicitor – on knowing all the circumstances – will dissuade him from an action.

Then as regards the foreign securities they consist chiefly of Egyptian loan of 1864 – & Turkish 5 per cent of 1865, I understand from our legal adviser that these would not require to be converted for some months. Meanwhile I shall be glad of your advice on this point. I fear under my circumstances there must be a loss on that property.

You have doubtless much to do – but if you could name any day & hour when it would suit you to call I would be sure to be at home. Believe me always your's truly
Eliz Eastlake
Only from 4 to 6 tomorrow (Tuesday) am I engaged.

Letter to A. H. Layard   NLS Ms.42169

7 FitzRoy Sqre
July 16 1866
My dear Mr. Layard

I was at the National Gallery for the 1st time on Friday last. I went with good Mr. Penry Williams who is staying here. We remarked a circumstance that rather surprised us. Some pictures had been uncovered for the convenience of copyists & we saw a common police man with a feather brush wiping pictures & then putting on the glasses. A feather brush is very inadvisable under any circumstances to be applied to the surface of a picture. Sir Charles did not permit it to be done to our own pictures also, I imagine, a police man is not the right person to entrust with any operation of the kind.

I mention this to you but I would be sorry to have any name appear as the informer. Some of the officials were new & old Wildsmith was not there.

I know that Wornum generally took his holiday in the country in June or July – is he away now? You are probably aware that Sir Charles never left town whilst Wornum was away, nor allowed him to leave during his absence.

You will excuse me for giving you this trouble – you have the right to enquire with these things.

Should you be able to give me any advice as to Turkish matters I should be glad to have it if possible before the 1st August when I leave London – also I should be glad of further intelligence regarding Hudson's Bay Company before that time.

If I make any transfer from the funds I should wish to do it at the close of this month. But I am in no hurry unless it should be deemed advisable to profit by a comparative high price of funds (Government Funds).

Any advice you can give me I shall be very grateful for – but I am not going to torment you on these matters.

Your's always truly

Eliz Eastlake

Letter to A. H. Layard   *NLS Ms.42169*

7 FitzRoy Sqre
July 17. 1866
My dear Mr. Layard

I am much obliged by your letter. It is true that you leave me unavoidably without precise advice – but I feel that you have done your best. Your friend's advice to sell the Turkish Loan now is probably the best that can be given. I shall endeavour to see our honest old broker tomorrow & commission him to watch, & however unwilling, I fear I ought to direct him to sell at all events the amount in which you as Trustee are interested in case any further fall is imminent. This old gentleman will probably confirm your friend's advice.

The question is into what securities I may transfer the proceeds? Does dear Sir Chas' will permit of East India (Great Indian Peninsula) Railway Debentures – or even E. Indian Railway shares? Or may I purchase "Metropolitan St. John's Wood Railway Debenture" which are now advertised for at 6 per cent for three years?

I have not yet done with my report of National Gallery. A friend who paints there from 11 to 4 every Thursday & Friday tells me that all taking off & putting on glasses is left to the policemen – that the attendants come late – old Mr. Wildsmith not till 2 o'clock – & that since Easter she has not seen Mr. Wornum in the Gallery any Thursday or Friday. I am sure you will enquire into this. I trust you will not think me ill natured when I warn you of Wornum's exceedingly indolent habits.

Believe me your's always truly

Eliz Eastlake

Letter to A. H. Layard   NLS Ms.42169

7 FitzRoy Sqre

July 19 1866

My dear Mr. Layard

I am very glad that you & Mr. Murray propose taking these measures. No step has been taken by me as to the sale of any foreign security. The broker yesterday advised <u>waiting</u> as regard the Turkish 5 per cent bonds. He thinks they will rise in some measure with other securities.

I have not a copy of beloved One's will which perhaps I ought to have, tho' my judgement is not required.

Your's always truly

Eliz Eastlake

Letter to A. H. Layard   NLS Ms.42169

Cranbrook, Staplehurst, Kent[1]

August 6. 1866

My dear Mr. Layard

Just before leaving London for this quiet place I received a letter from Signr Orlandi of Turin. He is very anxious that you should visit his studio in Turin, & see his Gaudenzio. Should you therefore be now on the way for (to me) sad Italy, pray make a little memorandum in favor of old Orlandi. The picture is is some respects a very fine one, tho' not sufficiently intact for the N.G. He asks a great price, but it is worth a good one, & it is possible that you might covet it for Sir John Guest. Orlandi has other things too, & he is an honest man tho' little else.

I am here, with a sister. In a pretty Vicarage which I have taken for a few weeks in very pretty country. Webster, the painter, is my only acquaintance & I wish for no more. He is my Cicerone in the pretty walks – as far as the bad weather has permitted. And I even find myself talking a little about <u>art</u> with him – with mingled pain & pleasure.

I am glad to hear that Boxall has secured the Schönborn Rembrandt. We never saw it – but such notices as I have found of it in our Library are in high praise. I remember that there is a meeting of the Trustees today.[2]

Ever dear Mr. Layard

Your's truly

Eliz Eastlake

1. Elizabeth rented a house from the Vicar at Cranbrook. See letter from Thomas Webster to Elizabeth, 25 June 1866, National Art Library Victoria & Albert Museum volume marked Letters to Sir Charles and Lady Eastlake 1823–1882 86.M.4 MSL/1922/416/46.

2. *Christ Blessing the Children* is now attributed to Nicholas Maes. For the details of the purchase see Frances Suzman Jowell 'Thoré-Bürger – A Critical Rôle in the Art Market', *The Burlington Magazine*, vol. 138, no. 1115 (February 1996), pp. 115–29.

Letter to William Boxall   *UNC Elizabeth Eastlake Letters* #11,617

7 FitzRoy Sqre

January 31. 1867

My dear Mr. Boxall

I received the last sheet & your subsequent note – many thanks for both. I regret much to hear of the old fashioned cold.

I want rather to speak with you, & I wd come to you, only that when I leave home you are also usually absent from yr's – hoping that you are to be well enough – so I had better perhaps write you a few words which you can turn over in your mind.

As time passes I begin to feel the <u>duty</u> of doing something – by way of plan regarding the pictures & library left in my hands. I know how the N.G. is situated as regards want of space – & I shd certainly not like to see these pictures driven up to the ceiling (if hung at all) in case the Trustees should argue to purchase them. Thus I <u>am</u> not disposed to hurry this matter & it will depend upon further conversation with you, & the advice you may kindly give me, whether the terms on which I am inclined to part with this small gallery to the N.G., be communicated soon to the Trustees.[1] The same considerations apply to the Library – tho' I do not say that I shd bribe the N.G. (as in the case of the pictures by lowness of price) to purchase that. They have no <u>space</u> at present. But it has struck me that in the event of a <u>surplus</u> in your hands before the <u>Treasury</u> year terminates, you might think it expedient – with the concurrence of Trustees, to request Government to allow that surplus & any future one for the next year or two to be <u>retained</u> for the purpose of purchasing the Library – wh: wd in part at least obviate the necessity of applying for a grant expressly for that purpose.[2] You may like to consult Layard about this. I may add that as regards the volumes of engravings (Galleries) Sir Charles once told me that he wd wish them offered to the N.G. at the price he gave for them. The receipts for them still existing I believe, &. to this once expressed wish I shd adhere, believg that the N.G. would thus obtain them on lower terms than if present market price were ascertained. However, this wd not be reduced to a certainty, & if the gain were to be the other way then I shd feel at liberty to depart from <u>his</u> direction. I have to think of these matters a little & let me at your leisure see you.

All evengs we are at home at 8 o' clock – except today when we drive to my mother's to dine.

Ever yr's afftly

Eliz Eastlake

1. These are the so-called 'Director Pictures', paintings bought by Eastlake during his tenure as Director of the National Gallery. Elizabeth began to attend to the terms of her husband's request that the paintings should be offered to the National Gallery for the same prices he had paid, by sending a list of 15 eligible pictures to the Trustees. Boxall selected nine and she disposed of the remaining six by public sale. See David Robertson, *Sir Charles Eastlake and the Victorian Art World* (Princeton, NJ: Princeton University Press, 1978), pp. 274–85.

2. The Eastlake Library of around two thousand volumes was sold to the National Gallery, forming the basis of its library, in 1869. See G. M. Green, *Catalogue of the Eastlake Library in the National Gallery* (London: Eyre & Spottiswoode, for HMSO, 1872).

Letter to William Boxall   *UNC Elizabeth Eastlake*
Letters #11,617

7 FitzRoy Sqre
March 25. 1867
My dear Mr. Boxall
    I send you herewith my personal letter, which I beg you to lay before the Trustees. You have much <u>relieved</u> me by telling me privately that you will not sanction the purchase of the <u>private</u> pictures <u>collectively</u>. You will wonder perhaps that I shd still submit this question to you in my <u>official</u> letter, but I do so because yr official answer will be necessary for the satisfaction of certain parties who <u>insist</u> on my not breaking up the collection. What I shall do further – when I have rec.d your answer declining to advise the Trustees to purchase the private pictures in a lump – I need not trouble you with yet – even if I knew it myself!
    I have mentioned the reason for Sir Chas' havg purchased the "Director Pictures" for himself, & not in the first instance for the Gallery, as the Trustees may naturally ask the question.
    I shall rely on yr kindly obtain [sic] me answers on the different heads as soon as you conveniently can.
Hoping to see you soon
I am yr's afftly
Eliz Eastlake

Letter to William Boxall   *UNC Elizabeth Eastlake*
Letters #11,617

7 FitzRoy Square
April 11. 1867
My dear Mr. Boxall
    You will have seen the decision I have come to regarding the private pictures. Be assured that if yr visit yesterday influenced me at all, it influenced me in the <u>right direction</u>. The responsibility & the decision must be <u>mine only</u>, & I believe that this course will ensure me most peace of mind in the end, as protecting the honoured name I bear (which is all I care about) from any possible imputation.
Yr's afftly
Eliz Eastlake

Letter to John Murray   *NLS Ms.42176*

7 FitzRoy Sqre
May 31 1867
Dear Mr. Murray
The final transfer of the trust money will be made into your &
Layard's name today. I trust that the complete legal winding up will
very soon follow.
The half of the property will be assigned to yr trust entirely in
the form of Government stock consols, New Threes, & Reduced
Three's. I am aware that in giving the trust into your hands & half
the property, I have no further power nor claim to interfere. Altho'
some time I venture to hope that should the value of government
funds rise considerably, some would possibly admit the expediency of
realising a portion & investing it in some other way permitted by the
will. I feel myself constrained to say this in the interest of the legatees
– any thought of increasing my income is not the inducement & havg
discharged what I feel to be right in mentioning this I can only add that
you are in no way barred to give me an answer.
Foreign securities were sold a fortnight ago & the proceeds connected
with Govt. stock at the then price. The amount of stock which now
stands in your names is upward of £13.000.
I am expecting Dr. Waagen to come to his old quarters before long
– he is now in Paris.
Believe me to be my dear Mr. Murray
Yr's very truly
Eliz Eastlake

Letter to A. H. Layard   *NLS Ms.42169*

7 FitzRoy Sqre
May 31. 1867
My dear Mr. Layard
This morng I am going into the City to make the final transfer of
stock into John Murray's & your names. You will, I hope, before you
start for Paris, be called upon to do whatever is necessary to complete
this business. The half of the property will be assigned to your trust
strictly in the form of Government Stocks – Consols New 3 per cents
& Reduced 3 per cents. I am aware that having once made the transfer

to the Trustess I have no further power or right – at the same time
I continue to request that, should the funds rise to a height unlikely
to be kept up, you & J. Murray may consider the expediency, further
benefit of the legatees, of realising the high price & of placing part
perhaps of the trust property in some other investment mentioned
by the will. I say this in the interest of the legatees. As regards any
difference in my income that is not worth the consideration. I only say
this now to discharge a sense of duty towards his nephews – but there
is no need to pledge yourself by my answer.

If you have time to call before you leave London I am generally at
home till 4 o'clock & always of an evening & our Tucker will never
turn you from the door.

Should you not be able to call will you give me a line, & tell
me whether you still think well of Hudson's Bay Co. for a small
investment.

Always dear Mr. Layard

Your's truly

Eliz Eastlake

Letter to William Boxall   *UNC Elizabeth Eastlake Letters #11,617*

7 FitzRoy Square

June 5. 1867

My dear Mr. Boxall

There is no one whose judgement I so much rely on as yours & no
one who gives it me so honestly.

Theed[1] is now so far advanced with our simple monument as to
require the inscription. I have long thought over that solemn point –
unwilling to say <u>nothing</u> beyond the needful dates – & yet fearing to be
too much guided by feeling, & yet know.g that no one will <u>really</u> care
what is said & done (for how few will see!) except myself. Therefore to
please self seems the only sad guide, but I wd fair not displease others &
especially not <u>his</u> kind & honored friends.

I therefore venture, dear Mr. Boxall, to enclose what I contemplate
for the inscription. If you think it may be thus – well – if not you will
not fear telling me.

In a few days I will ask you to kindly go to Theeds where the
monument is soon to be set up. Tomorrow I go to see it – & I know he
will want the inscription.

Yr's afftly
Eliz Eastlake

1. William Theed (1804–91), English sculptor noted for portrait busts
   and monuments. Theed had been responsible for a marble bust of Lady
   Eastlake, exhibited at the Royal Academy in 1854. It passed to her nephew
   Charles Eastlake Smith following her death but its present whereabouts are
   unknown.

Letter to Louisa Harford[1]   *BRO 28048/C/117*

7 FitzRoy Square
June 7 1867
Dearest Mrs Harford

I have been rather busy or I should sooner have sent you the
promised little sketch (tracing – or rubbing) of the olive wreath which
is to occupy the centre, low down, on our monument, of which you see
the indication in the tracing with you.

I have just put it together for you in a hasty way, & I have ventured
to indicate a suggestion of your united initials – the relief is not deeper
than a penny piece – if so deep. It is in itself a very beautiful thing
from its simplicity. It is indeed what our beloved ones would both have
admired – pure Greek. It will be very inexpensive to cut.

Our monument is now placed up in Mr. Theed's studio. I saw it
yesterday, & found a sad pleasure in its simple beauty. The proportions
are very nice, & the highly polished white columns give a grace to it.
The rest is only half polished. Now they are awaiting the inscription.
It has long been in my mind but I hesitate still. I fear I have said too
much, & too feelingly – perhaps I shall end by having simple names
& dates & nothing more. The wreath requires good artist feeling to
execute it. Mr. Theed's workman has twice failed to please me – he
makes it mechanical & gives nibs & lines to the leaves which vulgarise
it. I require it be simply like the original & have now got a squeeze
in moist clay from the original & am doing the very little it needs
myself.[2]

I have seen dear Lady Inglis, one of her first questions was for you, &
you may believe how fondly & tenderly you were spoken of. The dear
lady is able to drive out now – but is dwindled to the tiniest little being
that ever had a <u>large heart</u>. Also I have seen good Mrs. Cockerell – she
<u>brightened</u> at hearing of Blaise Castle, so associated with her dear one,
& enjoyed my admiration of the gallery & space that leads to it. She

too loves to hear something of <u>Art</u>, now a silent theme in her deserted house. But she has one of the sons with her, & it was a comfort to see the dining table laid for <u>two</u>.

You will miss your dear companion – I do not forget that she leaves you today. Before long I shall hope to make my way to her but good Dr. Waagen has not yet written – tho' his proposed time of arrival is past. I suppose his King & Queen keep him in Paris.

My kind sister remains with me till he comes, so I care not how long his coming is delayed.

Now dear Mrs. Harford continue to give me your prayerful thoughts. I need them much. Sometimes the heart's thermometer is very low – just now rather oppressed. I need all my too little faith. I do try to fight the good fight against my over depression.

Ever your grateful & affectionate

Eliz Eastlake

1. Louisa Harford was the widow of John Scandrett Harford. See letter, 2 January 1856.

2. Enclosed with the letter is a sketch of the wreath and a note of the proposed inscription for the bronze relief on the headstone.

Letter to **William Boxall**   *UNC Elizabeth Eastlake*
Letters #11,617

7 FitzRoy Square

July 16. 1867

My dear Mr. Boxall

In return for your kind note I now make you the offer of the Rembrandt old woman for twelve hundred pounds.[1] At the same time I repeat my intention to <u>present</u> the <u>Pisano</u> picture to the Nat: Gal: & my readiness to do that & to make over to you the nine other Director Pictures which you & the Trustees have selected as soon as you desire, that is before you leave England.[2]

I wish to make a few trifling conditions with the gift of the Pisano picture, but which I am sure you will not object to.

Always yr's truly

Eliz Eastlake

I have written this so that you can, if you please, make use of it

1. Rembrandt's *Portrait of Aechje Claesdr* NG775 was sold to the Gallery for £1,200 in 1867.

2. Now in the National Gallery (NG776), described as by Pisanello, *The Virgin and Child with Saint George and Saint Anthony Abbot*. 'Presented by Lady Eastlake in memory of Sir Charles Eastlake P.R.A., first Director of the National Gallery, 1867.' Inexplicably, the painting was declined as part of the Director's Pictures deal.

Letter to **William Boxall**   *UNC Elizabeth Eastlake Letters #11,617*

7 FitzRoy Square
July 19. 1867
My dear Mr. Boxall

I received your kind words last night, & I do hope also that in time I shall feel comfort in having thus placed one of <u>his</u> treasures.

Now comes the question when to give it up? I shall be going into the country the first week of August. It wd be a great favour to be allowed to defer the <u>parting</u> until then, when all the other works will come with it. You will let me know.

Now as regards the Library – a subject which has been revolving in my mind of late. Of course <u>I</u> do not wish to throw up the semi-agreement (for I have had no real notification of the Trustees' desire to purchase it) which has transpired between you & myself, tho' the length of time before any decision wd perhaps warrant my doing so. But I must say at once that until I see that there is a fitting accomodation for the extensive Library & the sumptuously bound illustrated works I shall be unwilling to make them over to Mr. Wornum's tender mercies, & that <u>at all events</u> the delay in the answer (from whatever cause) having been so great – I shall not give up the Library during the ensuing winter, as I have much need of it myself in editing certain of Sir Chas' MSS. All access to it on your part is, as you know, always understood.

You will inform me when you wish for a note stating my desire to present the Pisano picture & the conditions therewith. For I shall not consider the offer accepted until the considerations are accepted also. If the Trustees wish for the one they must bind themselves to comply with the other. I have had a kind letter from Layard.

Ever dear Mr. Boxall yr's afftly
Eliz Eastlake
This is <u>not</u> official.

Letter to A. H. Layard   *NLS Ms.42169*

7 FitzRoy Square
July 23. 1867
My dear Mr. Layard

Yr letter was truly kind & has done me good service in keeping up
my courage through a transaction which, though in many respects what
I have desired, yet costs me many a pang. But whenever I die, I know
that I shall be thankful that some of his treasures are for ever in the
Gallery which is so especially of his forming.

I do not like to hear that you are not & have not been well. I should
like much to see you before we go different ways – I, probably, to some
quiet country retreat – but I know well how occupied are your hours
– & so are mine also – so that I would beg you not to come without
giving me the chance of an appointment.

Meanwhile – in order to save you further trouble – this being
I trust the last of the kind – I enclose you two more powers of
Attorney, authorizing our Banker to reserve dividends from the two
& the Government Stocks. Will you kindly take some opportunity of
requesting Mr. Murray to sign with you.
Believe me your's very truly
Eliz Eastlake

Letter to William Boxall   *UNC Elizabeth Eastlake*
Letters #11,617

7 FitzRoy Square
Aug: 1. 1867
My dear Mr. Boxall

I send you the accompanying note, to lay before the Trustees. I have
also written to Layard the conditions I affix. If you & he can let me
know before I start tomorrow whether they will be <u>generally</u> accepted.
I do not stickle for the <u>exact letter</u> (tho' I should be sorry to have it
departed from) & if you feel that they can be accepted generally in the
spirit they are meant why then I wd send the Pisano with the other
pictures on Monday mg. otherwise I shall wish it to stand over until my
return from the country.

As regards information concerng the other pictures I shall be anxious
to supply all that Sir Chas has left. But I have been so occupied with

our monument & with many <u>harrasses</u> & in getting this place in the country, wh: is very desirable for my dear mother & sisters, that I literally have had no time.

I <u>trust</u> that no fresh edition of the N.G. catalogue will be issued before my return – 6 weeks hence – when I shall gladly send Mr. Wornum all I can collect of information.

I add a few notes – my address will be after 11 o'clock tomorrow
"Brasted, Sevenoaks Kent"

Ever dear Mr. Boxall
(hop.g to hear from you)
Yr's affty
Eliz Eastlake

Letter to William Boxall   *UNC Elizabeth Eastlake Letters #11,617*

Brasted, Sevenoaks, Kent
Aug: 3. 1867
My dear Mr. Boxall

I had heard neither from you nor from Layard when I left London yesterday. I therefore conclude that the matter of the Pisano will stand over until my return.

Why I now trouble you with these lines is to beg that you will kindly interdict Mr. Wornum's sending a notice of the purchase to the Times. I believe that you are not <u>obliged</u> to publish in this way every picture you purchase, or that is presented to you, & I shrink from its being done in this case. Therefore dear Mr. Boxall be good enough to prevent the possibility of this.

We (my sister, Madame de Wahl, & I) drove over here yesterday afternoon – a cloudy quiet day, through much beautiful country. We are here in a nice house with plenty of pretty garden & lawn, larger than Cranbrook Vicarage – tho' not so <u>sympathetic</u> to me. I wish we could see you here, but I know that cannot be. This afternoon we expect our aged mother & my sister Miss Rigby – & I hope for the sweets of <u>Peace</u>.

Ever yr's afftly
Eliz Eastlake

Letter to William Boxall   UNC *Elizabeth Eastlake*
Letters #11,617

Brasted, Sevenoaks, Kent
Aug: 9. 1867
My dear Mr. Boxall
    I had been anxiously lookg for you letter which only reached me this
morning – having been posted in London yesterday. I had however,
heard from Layard yesterday.
    I am cheered & comforted by the assurance you give me that the
Pisano – or rather the offer of it – received a cordial welcome, & that the
conditions were accepted. One omission only I made (I believe) which is
that I wish P.R.A. to be inserted on the label after Sir Chas' name.
    I write to Tucker today to say that the Pisano should be delivered to
Critchfield whenever you send him for it.
    As regards the sum of £1885 – I wish it to be paid in immediately to
my account at Robarts & Lubbock's Bank – 15 Lombard Street.
    This morning a request reached me from one of our English magnates
to know whether I would part with the Art Library & with the Palma
picture, & to name the price. As regards the Art Library I shall never
depart from my desire (because it was Sir Charles') to see it attached to
the N: Gallery – tho' at the same time, as you are aware, I am glad at
the delay of your official answer occasioned by Chanc: of Exchequer, as
I do not intend to part with it yet.
    But as to the Palma, though as yet undecided whether to part with
it at any price (& I shd ask a private individual a very high one) yet I
know that it is one of those pictures in Sir Chas' collection which you
would not recommend to the N: Gallery, & that therefore any reference
to the possibility of its purchase by the N:G: is superfluous.[1]
    Will you kindly send me a line by return of post – so that I have it
on Saturday m.g – merely for form's sake, to confirm my knowledge
that, in the possibility of disposing of it, I shall be committing no
breach of deference towards the N:G: or rather towards you.
    Any information about your plans & your health will be acceptable at
same time.
Ever dear Mr. Boxall
Yr's afftly
Eliz Eastlake

    1. Palma Vecchio's *Madonna & Child* was sold to the Earl of Dudley. The
    painting is now in the Metropolitan Museum in New York and attributed
    to Bonifazio Veronese (Bonifazio de' Pitati).

Letter to William Boxall   *UNC Elizabeth Eastlake*
Letters #11,617

Brasted, Sevenoaks, Kent
Aug:12. 1867
My dear Mr. Boxall

Just a few words to answer your kind notes. I am sure you will never misunderstand me with regard to my Dear One's pictures. I knew those which <u>you</u> wd consider eligible for the N:G: & with my consent they will never go elsewhere. But I trust that there is no need for hurry – which wd embarrass you & <u>excrutiate</u> me. Shd I die <u>soon</u> why then there will be the opportunity of getting them by public sale – but I trust that I shall be able to bear to part with them – the Landscape Bellini, the Steuerbout, & the Mantegna – even during my life, as I think I shd die happier if I knew they were already safe in <u>his</u> N. Gallery. You may also be sure that I shd never allow the nation to pay the price that rich individuals would offer – the nation wd not thank me, I know, for the delicacy, but that wd not matter.

Now I shall be glad to have the money safe in our bank – & then the transaction will be over.

I had the pleasure of seeing Rich.d Boyle here the other day – he had come on a visit to some friends (Wells) who live here. He was full of kind feeling & gave a good account of the dear Nelly who was so ill at Florence, & of Ella herself.

I don't at all like your going away alone – & doing all kinds of imprudent things – standg about & over fatiguing yourself. I trust Sacchi[1] takes care of yr necessary comfort.

I rely on hearing from you. Ld Elcho is a horrid sneak. I never forget his calling the P. Veronese a <u>copy</u>. He is a very dishonest man but he did you no harm. I smiled at John Coleridge rushing to the rescue.[2]

Ever afftly yr's
Eliz Eastlake

1. Federico Sacchi, Boxall's secretary.

2. In the House of Commons Lord Elcho had accused the National Gallery of resuming the practice of picture cleaning that he had condemned under Eastlake's regime. John Coleridge had replied that 'any unbiased person who carefully studied the works of the old masters in the National Gallery would come to the conclusion that they resembled nature much more closely than they did when they were seen through the cloud of linseed oil and varnish

which it was formerly the fashion to put upon them. (Hear, hear.) Every one who knew Mr. Boxall ... must be aware that he was a most conscientious, careful, and reverent worshipper of the works of the old masters'. *The Times*, 10 August 1867, p. 6, col. D.

Letter to William Boxall   *UNC Elizabeth Eastlake Letters #11,617*

Brasted, Sevenoaks, Kent
14 Aug:1867
My dear Mr. Boxall

I return you the money order duly signed & beg that you will have it conveyed to Robarts & Lubbock, Bankers – 15 Lombard St., to be placed to my account.

I truly wish that I could give you God speed, viva voce but you know that I shall be very anxious about you & I beg that you will remember to take as much care of yourself as possible. Above all things avoid walking & engage a carriage for a day or half day wherever you may be. In your taking great care of yourself the Govt. will be best served. And whenever you are kind enough to write to me tell me where a letter from me will find you. Tucker writes me that you are going by Bruges. If you want help there apply to Mr. Weale[1] – a young Englishman, a Catholic, who lives there, a great archaeologist, & who was of use to my dear One in opening convent doors &c. Anyone will tell you where he lives and our name to him will be enough.

Then at Brussells [sic] look at the great Steuerbouts in the Gallery. They are genuine, tho' beyond the master's scale. A dealer at Brussels Mr. Le Ray was useful to us (Etienne Le Ray). He obtained us admission to two private homes. M. Le Comte de Ribeaucourt (rue d'Aremberg) where there was or is a magnificent family portrait by Rubens, & a Comtesse de Beaufort, where there are two fine portraits of a Seigneur de Lordes & his wife, also to other places.

Perhaps you will go to Berlin. Waagen is back there now. I have a letter from him this morn.g. I am glad you are taking the northern part of your journey first. Even Brasted is oppressive in this glorious heat!

Now God bless you dear Mr. Boxall, I shall miss you much
Every yr's afftly
Eliz Eastlake

1. See letter to Cosmo Monkhouse, 10 June 1887, n. 3.

Letter to William Boxall   *NG14/18/1867*

Brasted, Sevenoaks
9 September 1867
My dear Mr. Boxall

I was very glad to see your handwriting tho' it lost a day in coming to me here. I know all your ground so well that I follow in my mind's eye everywhere. Antwerp Gallery is very interesting – though the Ertborn part rather overestimated.[1] You will do as we did, & by degrees feel how all foreign galleries need <u>weeding</u>. This is no loss of pleasure, for one enjoys real excellence the more. I wonder whether the little delicate looking goldsmith who owned the houseboat at Ghent be still alive. The man himself made an impression on my memory. I shall be anxious to hear your feeling about the Cologne Gallery – it interested me much & the 'Master of the Bartholemew Altar' the name by which a particular crucifixion with gilt engraved background is known was one my Darling examined very closely. There is picture by the same hand in the Louvre. You will find something about his in Sir Chas' notes. The Tenniers – by the by – at Antwerp I do not remember that we saw – but I am not sure. Your account of Louvain will be interesting to me. The <u>Steuerbouts</u> in the cathedral there corroborates the belief that <u>our's</u> is by him. Those colossal pictures by him in Brussels Gallery will have interested you too, but they were beyond the master's scale.

I send this to Berlin – enclosed to dear old Waagen – & in your next letter tell me where to write. I shall conclude always <u>poste restante</u>.[2]

I shall be very curious too to hear your impression of sweet Cassel Gallery. I feel <u>drawn</u> to that gallery more than to any other, & I think I could <u>bear</u> to see that again – but perhaps not. Let the future take care of itself – the bearing of the present is quite enough for me.

I am here with my dear aged Mother & my sisters Madame de Wahl & Miss Rigby in a very comfortable house & pretty place (ah! I told you all that before). I will only add that the late rather cooller weather has made me feel stronger. I abandon the little open carriage to the use of Mamma & my sisters, for it does me more good to walk a little, & I find in our good cook, Mrs. Anderson, who is now here as a guest a kind humble friend ready to walk with me & <u>bear</u> with me. We talk much of <u>him</u> together, for next to his wife, his servants could do him most justice.

I am sorry to say that <u>Lord Dudley</u> (for that is the art magnate of whom I wrote to you) has willingly acceeded to the high price I put on the Palma Vecchio, & which I did partly to deter him. He is to pay £1,500 & it will be in a gallery, <u>now entailed</u>, in company with

Raphael, Fra Angelico & others. When I die I shall be glad to think that it is permanently & honourably placed, for the Gallery is fine, whatever the present owner of it may be. But do not speak of this for the present tho' I shall mention it to Waagen.

I heard from Layard the other day from Switzerland – the 'Bell Alps' – dated September 1. He was walking from 8 to 10 hours a day, & enjoying it – he talked of crossing into Italy in ten days & to be in Venice first week in October.

When you are at Venice – tho' I hope to hear from you before then – let your Sacchi get me three sponges – rather large & coarse, a handfull. They are cheap – about 2 francs a piece. They will not take room in his box being dry & light. I have always had my supply from Venice so please be my agent. Layard writes me that good Signora Molteni's present address is Milan "33 Via Principe Umberto" in case you should require it.

I return to London on the 13th (next Friday) & remain there. I have heard nothing of Penry Williams yet.

Glad you feel better

Ever your's affectionately

Eliz Eastlake

1. Ridder Florent van Ertborn Collection, now in the Museum of Antwerp, of Flemish and Italian paintings.

2. *Poste restante*, French: a postal holding service in which letters are kept until collected.

Letter to A. H. Layard   *NLS Ms.42169*

7 FitzRoy Sqre

4. Octr 1867

Dear Mr. Layard

It is now just a month since I had your kind letter from the Bell Alp – & as you mention your intention of being in Venice the first week of this month I venture a letter to you there.

I was truly glad to hear that you were enjoying fine air & plenty of exercise. The sky & warmth of Italy will have been all the more delightful after such invigoration. I am much obliged by Madame Molteni's address. I had been sending sympathizing messages to her through good old Sgr Orlandi of Turin. He had written to me to know whether I would purchase a small Borgognone, in private hands in

Milan, which he hopes to get for a not unreasonable price. It was the last picture which Sir Chas really admired. We saw it together in the short interval of his apparent convalescence. I had been rather <u>longing</u> for it, & I immediately wrote to Orlandi to obtain it for me. I have not heard since, but I trust he will succeed. This, & the Napoleon (which I never showed you that day) & the picture by Sir Chas of his mother, which I trust to obtain, will I think be the limit of the pictures which I shall buy.

I am sorry to say that the bidder for the Palma has accepted my price which I thought might deter him – namely £1500. It is <u>Lord Dudley</u> (will you keep all this to yourself) & I must be content that the beautiful thing goes into a first rate & now entailed Gallery.

I have Penry Williams staying here now & his is making a water-colored drawing of it for me which promises to be very nice indeed.[1]

Some of those fine sketches by my dear Sir Chas are framed & glazed & look <u>exquisitely</u>. The <u>reserve</u> of works of art in this house is so abundant that it is but too easy to fill up sad empty spaces. I have not had the courage to go to N. Gallery since our treasures moved there. I shall not go until either you or Boxall return, & will go with me. From him I only heard more than a month ago from <u>Brussels</u>. He is rather a <u>slow coach</u> in those things, good Boxall! But I have heard of him since as at Vienna. I trust he & you are together now, or will be soon.

I saw your aunt on Sunday last. She kindly came here. She looks very fragile, & her bodily disabilities seem only to increase. I can but admire her perfect cheefulness under all circumstances. I can't say much for <u>mine</u>, dear Mr. Layard. It is of no use you hoping to find me "in good spirits" for I shall never be that again. But I think I am stronger, though my stay in the country was not as conducive to health as I had hoped. We were in a charming place, but it was very relaxing.

I was with the good Hardwick's the other day at Wimbledon. They have a beautiful little place & their son has devoted all his experience to making the house as perfect for his infirm father & tender mother as possible.[2] Mr. Robert Curzon called yesterday. He too does not yet get over the ever permanent sorrow.

If you have time let me hear from you once more before you return & tell me how the Abbazia Cima stands. State N.G. secrets may I think be told to me.

Ever your's truly
Eliz Eastlake

1. A copy of a Palma Vecchio by Elizabeth and Penry Williams was sold at Christie's sale in 1894.

2. Philip Hardwick (1792–1870), architect and father of the architect Philip Charles Hardwick (1822–92).

Letter to William Boxall   *NG14/19/1867*

7 FitzRoy Square
8. Octr 1867
My dear Mr. Boxall

    I had yr kind long & interesting letter on Saturday evening – 5th
Octr – & was glad to see your handwriting & to hear what you had
been seeing. It is a sad pleasure to go over the well known ground with
you, & I shall indeed be glad to talk of the charming <u>Cassel</u> Gallery.
I have never known anyone – any English person – who had so much
as heard of that very exquisite collection.[1] I feel as if I <u>could</u> revisit
that gallery without too much pain, & were my dear mother not so
aged I shd seriously contemplate taking up my abode for a few summer
weeks there – for the place seemed so pretty too. But at Mamma's age
I could not go 50 miles away from her even in England. I was with her
yesterday at Norwood, & found her charmingly well. My good sister
Miss Rigby watches over her with the tenderest care. My sister Mdme
de Wahl is also with them now, & I have good old Williams for my
inmate. He is not a lively companion precisely, but he is company more
than good enough for so dull a companion as his hostess. The little
Tilghman ladies have been here to dine quietly with him, & so has
Incoronati. You will have heard of the death of old Miss Tilghman –
little Caroline was alone with her, the other sister living in the country.
It has been a very wearing time to the excellent but delicate little lady. I
saw her soon after the sad event, & they were cheerful when they dined
here. Caroline assures me that their means ensure them <u>comfort</u>, tho'
it will be necessary for them to leave their present home. She thinks
of hiring an apartment for a time. I hope near me, as I long to be of
some use to them. Their sister Emily seems to be hopelessly <u>insane</u> in
Paris. Incoronati is not very well – much troubled with boils, which
he <u>describes</u> very minutely! If he could have a good dinner every day I
think he wd be cured. He is rather excited about Garibaldi & Rome.
    Williams is, by my request, kindly mak.g me a drawing of the Palma,
which is still here. Ld D: being in Scotland. I prepared the outline for
him & have had a sad pleasure in going thus through the beautiful
thing. I fear Ld D: has it too <u>cheap</u> (you will think me most rapacious)
but in truth now that the picture is taken down for Williams' better
convenience, in a fine light, it is very beautiful & so little touched, that
I <u>grudge</u> it unspeakably. However such an effort to place one of <u>his</u>
treasures in the appropriate gallery seems to help me on with <u>winding
up</u> of life. Also I have such beautiful things of <u>his</u> to put in the vacant

places that I ought to be ashamed not to be glad to make room for
them. Merritt[2] continues to clean batch after batch of exquisited sketches
& copies of pictures for me – delighting in them himself. I have had his
fine Coliseum sketches framed & glazed & they look exquisitely.

I have been reading to Williams some of Sir Chas' professional MSS
of which there is a large collection. When you return I shall beg you to
look through them, as I think a selection of them should be appended
to the 2nd vol: of Materials of Oil Painting.

I trust that Layard & you will meet or are now together at Venice.
I am deeply interested in the fate of the Abbazia Cima, & hope that
will find its way to the N.G: – also the Verona (Count Portalupi)
Cavazzicola.

I am living very quietly. I get on so best but I shall be sorry to lose
the good, dry old bachelor. He begs to be most kindly remembered to
you, & enquires whether you had a letter addressed to you at Vienna.
I grieve for dear old Waagen. I shall write to him soon. Take care of
yourself dear Mr. Boxall. The Darmstadt Holbein I thought more highly
of than Sir Chas did. It struck me as richer in colour & more vigorous
than the Dresden picture. The Dresden Gallery is very ill kept.
Ever dear Mr. Boxall yr's afftly
Eliz Eastlake
Don't forget my sponges!

1. Cassel Gallery is the Old Master Gallery, formerly the Hesse Collection, at
   Schloss Wilhelmshöhe Staatliche Kunstsammlungen, mainly of Dutch and
   Flemish seventeenth-century art.

2. Henry Merritt (1822–77), a picture restorer and art critic, employed to
   restore Eastlake's sketches. See also Basil Champneys (ed.), *Henry Merritt:
   Art, Criticism and Romance, with Recollections and ... Etchings by Anna Lea
   Merritt*, 2 vols. (London: C. Kegan Paul & Co., 1879).

Letter to A. H. Layard   *NLS Ms.42169*

7 FitzRoy Sqre
31 Octr 1867
My dear Mr. Layard
    I have been very remiss in not thanking you for your kind letter
sooner. It took me by surprise with its English date. I am amused at the
Morolin inventions. They require no answer on my part. I am glad that
two persons I much like – Morelli, & R. Brown remembered me.

I have not been to the N: Gallery, & shall not go until <u>helped</u>
by Boxall or you. I am therefore the more obliged by your kind
description of the whereabouts of the dear old friends. I am well aware
of the press for room & that is one argument for not letting you
have any more of his treasures for the present. I have plenty of other
arguments beside.

Yesterday I received from Mr. Wornum his proposed notice of the
Pisano. It would have been difficult to have made it more illiterate &
vulgar. He describes St. George as wearing a kind of "Panama hat".

I should be glad to see his notices of the other pictures, if not
asking too much, for it is trying to have them made the sport of Mr.
Wornum's English & style.

Just now I am not very well, & am writing to you with only one eye
– having a bad cold in the other.

Little Hatty Hosmer is staying here now. She has been visiting at all
the <u>Dukeries</u> in the land & is glad of a little quiet with me.[1] If you were
in town I would beg you to come & dine one day.

Ever dear Mr. Layard

Your's truly

Eliz Eastlake

I have heard nothing further from Boxall

> 1. Harriet Hosmer (1830–1908), American sculptor who had been a pupil of
> Gibson's at Rome.

Letter to A. H. Layard   *NLS Ms.42169*

7 FitzRoy Sqre

18 Decr 1867

Dear Mr. Layard

Your kind sympathy is very acceptable to me for the great loss
sustained by my poor sister is shared by all of us. Her son Captain de
Wahl was a most distinguished young officer. His services are sufficiently
proved by his having obtained his front rank at 31 years of age without
any interest. My dear Sir Charles esteemed him very highly & would
have deeply felt his death. I reckon up all the troubles from which he
has been taken.[1]

I am sorry to hear that you are going away, tho' I trust the
expedition will be good & pleasant for yourself. When your return I
shall have a large & beautiful collection of Sir Chas' oil sketches to show

you – increased by many that have come to light since. They are being appropriately framed, & I shall be happy when I see them all well placed in these rooms. Also a very early portrait by him of his mother I must show you, for it is the image of his dear self.

And now with many apologies I will give you a little, very matter of fact commission to do for me at Venice. Will you kindly get me 4 or 5 sponges, thick & round, about the size of two fists. They are light & will take but little room – but their worthlessness will show you that if prevented getting them I shall not take it to heart. And at all events remember me to Rawdon Brown.

And now I wish you well & wish I could do anything for you more than remembering you very faithfully.
Ever your's truly
Eliz Eastlake
Pray excuse an oversight in the side of my sheet [*she writes on the wrong side first*]

1. Captain Thomas Alexis de Wahl RN, late of HMS *Cordelia*, died following an outbreak of yellow fever on board the Royal Mail Steam Packet *Douro* on 14 November 1867 sailing home from the West Indies.

Letter to John Murray   *NLS Ms.42176*

7 FitzRoy Square
9 Janry 1868
Dear Mr. Murray
I have been forwarded by mutual friends of the late Mr. Gibson (sculptor) & myself, to assist in putting together a Life of him. The Materials are sufficient – he has left a very quaint & interesting autobiography & also his friends have preserved many letters.[1]

I have been engaged in looking through both of these sources. I am giving them a practical arrangement. Also I have penned what I feel to be a necessary preamble in order to prepare the reader for the character, before introducing the man.

Would you be inclined to undertake the publication of this? I know that his friends would be thankful that it shd come before the world under your auspices. I think one good volume wd be filled or two slender ones. And I wd let yr reader see my preamble & a portion that I have arranged – only bespeaking time to have both copied – if you would like. The life is very naïve & pretty but has to be treated with a little discretion.

I hope this trying weather is not bringing any suffering to you, or to
Mrs. Murray, to whom I beg to be remembered.
Believe me yours faithfully
Eliz Eastlake
I am writing in <u>darkness</u>.

  1. This and subsequent letters refer to her edition of *Life of John Gibson, R.A.,
     Sculptor* (London: Longmans, 1870).

Letter to John Murray   *NLS Ms.42176*

7 FitzRoy Sqre
15 January 1868
Dear Mr. Murray
   I am not surprised at yr opinion of Gibson's autobiography. I was not
aware that he had submitted it to you. I told him frankly in 1862 that
I considered it entirely unfit for publication. Any more favourable view
of a life of him is now founded not only on a second perusal of this
autobiography – with a mental execution of a large portion of it – but
also on other remains of many letters which I have perused. I have
been so much urged to assist in this task that I would not refuse. I do
not think that a very readable work can be put together by a judicious
stringing of materials. There is no doubt that Gibson's character &
conversation had a great charm for all who came in contact with him,
& wherever I trace his character in his writings. I cannot but believe
that others will be interested. Also it was his own wish that his Life shd
be given to the world.
   I send you my preamble, founded on a very sincere admiration &
affection for him. And also such portions of the Life as I have put
together from the various materials – but chiefly – as regards this early
part – from the autobiography (much cut down): I remember the great
interest with which I read years ago Hans Anderson's life by himself in
wh: the early part, however egotistical, was something in the same style
as Gibson's. Furthermore there is much that is interesting about Canova
& especially about Thorvaldson. I will promise to strip it of its egotism
& apparent vanity as much as I can. His letters to Mrs. Sandbach are
<u>very</u> beautiful in parts, but so high flown that they will have to be used
with great discretion. But the life is <u>uneventful,</u> as an artist's life must,
or should be.
   I know that Lady M: Alford[1] has formed a very high opinion of what

the autobiography could be made – I find a letter from Lord Lytton to
Gibson giving excellent advice how to handle it.
I must leave it to your judgement. Believe me yr's faithfully
Eliz Eastlake
I have stopped just on the eve of his departure for Rome. I have no
other available copy but what I send you.

> 1. Lady Marion Alford (1817–88), née Marion Compton, one of Gibson's
> patrons.

Letter to Henry Sandbach   *PCA M/D/SAND/8/232*

7 FitzRoy Sqre
28 January 1868
Dear Mr. Sandbach[1]

I have been wishing to write to you for some time, but I have had
interruptions of a very sad kind in the loss of a very valued nephew, &
in the work that had to be done. Also I felt it better to defer troubling
you till I could tell you something definite regarding the proposed Life
of our dear old friend Gibson.

And first let me thank you for the valuable letters & documents
which you have entrusted to me, & which I have perused with deep
feelings of admiration & respect. Gibson's letters to your dear first wife
are a monument to her, tho' one of wh: I can only avail myself with
discretion. No one who knew her can ever forget her, but these papers
– memorandum book &c have, if possible to me, invested her memory
with a still more loving reverence.[2] I cannot say how much I feel in
this respect. The portion of the Biography also penned by her from his
dictation is superior to that he afterwards penned for himself.

Now my object is, as you will readily believe, to put together these
materials into a form which will suit a commonplace but critical public.
I have to word for those who did <u>not</u> know the man as we did. The
Biography as it is wd not be understood – very much <u>mis</u>understood
– the letters as they are, wd be liable to the same danger. My idea is
to gather what I feel to be rightfully <u>public</u> property out of each &
to make it if possible <u>more</u> concentratedly <u>Gibsonian</u>. The life is so
uneventful, & the form of an autobiography so unavoidably egotistical
that some pains must be taken to get the <u>essence</u> of the man so as
to make it interesting to the public. This is my <u>aim</u>, whether I shall
succeed is another thing.[3] I have felt that it is necessary to <u>introduce</u>
such a peculiar character as Gibson before letting him speak for himself.

I have therefore concocted a preamble in wh: I have endeavoured
to describe his rare qualities. But before going much further I asked
Murray whether he wd undertake such a Life. He answered that G: <u>had</u>
submitted the Biography to him, & that he had (as I cd have told him)
found it utterly unsuited for publication. But he allowed me to send
him this introduction, & also a portion of the Biography which I had
somewhat modified & rearranged. I enclose you his answer, which is a
proof to me that he is not sanguine as to the success of any efforts to
make it a <u>saleable</u> work. This does not affect my desire to make those
efforts. But I feel that I do not stand <u>alone</u> in this matter – yourself,
Miss Lloyd, Boxall & others have equal interest in it, yourself perhaps
the most. Now I find from Miss Lloyd whom I have seen since I recd
Murray's answer that she is much disappointed at the result, also much
disappointed that I shd consider it necessary to make <u>great</u> omissions
& general minute alterations (as to English &c) in the Biography. Shd
you in any way share this feeling I shd willingly resign the task. Also
shd you feel with her, that Murray's verdict is not what you wish to be
accepted & that another publisher shd be sought, on the <u>very slender</u>
chances of better terms I hope you will tell me.

I have the <u>Aurora</u> – given to me by yr dear first wife. But I do not
find in those pages an ode to Thorwaldsen of wh: G: makes mention.
Can you allow me to see that?[4]

And now pray present my kind regards to Mrs. Sandbach.[5] I can
never forget the kind words she & you have written to me whilst I trod
that dark Pass of Sorrow from which I am scarcely emerged yet. I am
thankful however for feeling gradually better. Pray believe me dear Mr.
Sandbach yr's very truly Eliz Eastlake

I must tell you, what distresses Miss Lloyd much – namely that I
do not intend to give my name to this work. People are welcome to
know that I have assisted in it & you may believe me that it wd gain
nothing from the name on the title page. The <u>Reviews</u> will all tell that
is ascribed to me.

1. Henry Sandbach (1807–95) of Hafodunos Hall, Wales. Much of Sandbach's
   collection of Gibson's work is now in the Walker, Liverpool.

2. Sandbach's first wife Margaret (née Roscoe) (1812–52), poet and novelist.
   She had begun writing Gibson's autobiography from his dictation in 1851
   and their correspondence is a significant source of Elizabeth's biography.

3. Frances Power Cobbe had read Gibson's original manuscript: 'If my good
   friend Lady Eastlake had not thought it fit to prune his extraordinarily
   quaint and original Autobiography … to ordinary book form and modern-
   ised style, I believe it would have been deemed one of the gems of original

literature, like Benvenuto Cellini's, and the renown of Gibson as a great
artist would have been kept alive thereby'. See Frances Power Cobbe, *Life
of Frances Power Cobbe*, 2 vols. (London: R. Bentley, 1894), vol. 2, p. 29.

4. *Aurora*, a poem by Margaret Sandbach, was inspired by the statue of the same
name which was commissioned for Hafodunos.

5. His second wife Elizabeth (née Williams).

Letter to Henry Sandbach   *PCA M/D/SAND/8/233*

7 FitzRoy Square
31 January 1868
Dear Mr. Sandbach

I received the two valuable little volumes yesterday morng, & am
now in receipt of your most kind & encouraging letter, which would
have given me the greatest mental assistance in my task. But I am sorry
to tell you & Mrs. Sandbach that an obstacle has arisen since I wrote
to you which compels me to resign the task. Miss Lloyd had much
disturbed me by her strongly expressed opinion as to what might to
be done with the materials, & still more so by venturing to me since
I wrote to you the Introduction & a portion of the Biography which
I had arranged & begged her to read without a comment, this tacitly
showing her disapproval. I waited however before deciding whether
I could continue the work under such circumstances till I shd have
heard from you. And certainly your most reasonable & judicious views
wd have made me set aside those of Miss L: But last eveng I received
a letter from Mr. Murray saying that unless I gave my name his
confidence in the success of work was so small that he must withdraw
from the publication. I feel that I have been under a false impression
from the first, having believed that it was my work that was required by
the mutual friends of Gibson. As to my name nothing shall induce me
to give it to the biography of G: or any one, while work of so much
nearer claims remains apparently not done. I do not say that I intend to
write a Life of my beloved Husband. I am sure he wd not wish that,
but he has left a large amount of MSS which, till I took up Gibson's
materials, I have been sedulously engaged in arranging, copying &c with
a view to editing such portions as he had designed for publication. To
this I may possibly prefix a short memoir – but all this requires mature
deliberation, & advice which very few can give me. Having done this
I shd have no objection, if required, to give my name to Gibson's

Biography, but I cannot do so beforehand. I have therefore no course left me but to withdraw from the task, <u>not</u> grudging the time I have given to it, for it has made better acquainted with Margaret Sandbach, & still better with Gibson. I have written to Miss Lloyd my <u>resignation</u> but have assured her that she or any friend who may undertake the Life shall be welcome, if they desire it, to the Introduction I have written, in which I have endeavoured to embody Gibson's fine character.

I can only thank Mrs Sandbach with your for your reiterated kind wish to see me. It is <u>possible</u> that I may come into yr part of the world after Easter in which case I shd be only too happy to come & thank you in person for all your kindness.

I am the more sorry to retire from my labour of love for Gibson because I feel how sorry it will make both of you.

Believe me dear Mr Sandbach

Yr's very truly

Eliz Eastlake

I need hardly add that all the materials in my hands shall be carefully returned. Miss L: has the biography in G's handwriting

Letter to John Murray   *NLS Ms.42176*

7 FitzRoy Sqre

31 Janry 1868

Dear Mr. Murray

I am in receipt of your letter of yesterday afternoon, which has taken me a little by surprise, tho' I entirely bow to your judgement. I have been under a false impression from the first, for in my innocence or vanity, I had imagined that it was my <u>work</u> that was required to give the proposed book a readable form. I attach no importance to myself in one sense, to my name, & refused to promise to give it when Gibson's friends first beset me to undertake the task. Now some of them are as dissatisfied with my refusal as you. I see that I was quite mistaken as to <u>what</u> it was they wanted from me. I could not dream of announcing to the public that I had been occupied on G:'s biography while <u>other work</u> is apparently not done. But I was literally pestered into promising to do it & did not grudge my labour, believg that it wd not take me long.

Now, however, I am as glad to retire from the task as you can be from the undertaking. I must add in justice however to Mr. Sandbach that he was perfectly satisfied to have accepted my conditions of work, & yours of publication.

Before long I will venture to submit to you a proposal concerning some of Sir Chas MS.S.

Believe me yr's faithfully
Eliz Eastlake

Letter to A. H. Layard   *NLS Ms.42169*

7 FitzRoy Sqre
21 Febry 1868
My dear Mr. Layard

I was truly glad to receive your kind letter & to be assured that you were back safe, & had enjoyed your time in Venice. The sponges arrived soon after. They are beauties, & I can't thank you enough for executing so impertinent a commission.

I hope dear old Rawdon Browne [sic] remembers me. I think of him as one of my very few true friends – some day I hope I may see him again.

I have been having Venice much before my mind's eye lately, having been occupied in reading old MSS & journal books which contain Sir Chas' first impressions of Venice in 1828. Never very enthusiastic but with so much refinement of thought. These, & other papers of an early date which I am gradually reading & copying occupy my mind much with a view to some ultimate purpose. I am in no hurry to edit anything, for I feel that there are so few who can advise me on such matters (& of those how few will!) that I am anxious to let time & deliberation supply as far as possible the lack of other help. You are too much occupied to give your attention to these matters, tho' I neither doubt the power or the will but I shall certainly not decide what to do with these MSS without giving myself the chance of obtaining advice.

I am always at home of a morning – that is before 2. I have many things to show you having necessarily made great alterations in the disposition of the pictures in the drawing rooms – & placed many of the beautiful oil sketches. But the arrangement is in some respects temporary for Ld Dudley has not yet taken our Palma – the negotiation papers through Christie's hands. And the longer the picture is left with me the better I am pleased.

I shall be glad to see your Bonifazio sketch. We have somewhere a good watercolour drawing of the picture, but I have not yet been able to put my hand on it.

Ever dear Mr. Layard
Your's truly
Eliz Eastlake
I had no idea you had never had my letter!

Letter to Louisa Harford   *BRO 28048/C/68/17*

7 FitzRoy Square
February 27 1868
My dear Mrs Harford

I grudge not having answered your kind & always welcome note sooner, but I have literally taken advantage of your words, & seen Mr. Smith at my leisure which was not till yesterday. They have not yet received both blocks of marble – only one – but the other is expected next week, & he assures me, & I know from experience, that no time will be lost in Mr. Theed's studio in executing the work. The delicate columns – which are done on a turning lathe – are the only difficult part. I shall not omit to enquire again in a short time. Meanwhile I was beside our grave yesterday. My iron screen is nearly completed & it is necessary to place the stone foundations for it. I took a careful plan of these with me, & on Monday our good servant, Tucker, will be thus early in the morning superintending the work. I long to get the screen up, & to plant my little rose slips, which have kept alive in my care – & also a honeysuckle. If you should have a few seeds of any creeping annuals, grown at Blaise Castle, I shall thankfully put them in, but that will not be for a fortnight or more. But I would like a nasturtium – or a convalootus or canariensis from you.

I continue to be alone, dear kind Mrs. Harford & if I need God's gracious Help the more I can only say now that I find it more. Prayer is like an imperceptible anodyne when the heart sets about acting which mine does very often.

It is forlorn to sit alone in his dear place, at his Library table, but he is gone before, & must have left me, or I him, & I hope I can now begin to feel that I would rather have my thoughts with him in his heavenly home, than his dear earthly self here at my side.

I have had a great loss in Lady Cranworth's death. It was all that a Christian could aspire to – so peaceful & so sustained. She had been a shining light in the high station, & numbers will miss her help & her sympathy. Poor Ld Cranworth. 18 years older than she! Now 78! But that tells two ways.

I feel for you much as regards the difficulty of an <u>inscription</u>. My heart had made a very long & loving one, trying to do justice to the sweet union of qualities. But I am <u>satisfied</u> now that by the advice of a <u>dry</u> judicious friend, I cut it short, & reduced it to little more than facts. "To the loving memory" & "by his sorrowing wife" are all the <u>feeling</u> I indulged in. No length can do your dear One justice – one line as to his <u>perfect</u> Christian life & character will <u>tell</u> more – pardon me for saying this, where you have so many kind relatives & friends whose excellent judgement is at your service.

I am interrupted, so farewell dear Friend
Your truly affectionate
Eliz Eastlake

Letter to A. H. Layard   NLS Ms.42169

7 FitzRoy Sqre
11 March 1868
My dear Mr. Layard
I have to thank you for two kind letters – & for the return of the M.S. I can't tell you how gratified & comforted I am by your opinion of these writings – the entire sincerity of which I am persuaded of. My dear One often quoted to me Bacon's aphorism "the secret of good writing is sound & abundant knowledge". I am so glad that you feel that he has exemplified these words. And this knowledge & this conviction on art were the first of comparatively early investigations – for what you have read belongs to 1830 – I & I have the same clear principles in letters & fragments much earlier.

I have nearly completed copying another, & last, chapter of 'How to Observe' with which I shall venture also to trouble you. I assure you that I shall be only too grateful for your judgement & advice in preparing & arranging an edition of these Remains. I do propose publishing a selection whether as a 2nd vol: to his "Contributions to the Literature of the Fine Arts" (which vol: is out of print) or as a separate work, remains to be considered. There are also his Discourses before the R. Academy – first rate in their way – which are printed, tho' not published, & of which I will send you copies. I should also be very grateful if you would at you leisure read certain chapters which he had prepared for his 2nd vol of the "History of Oil Painting". They come down to the best time of art & show a combination of philosophical, historical, & technical knowledge, to which I humbly

believe no one else has so thoroughly attained. Unhappily there are
few besides yourself who can appreciate this. My object would be to
be ready to publish in the spring of next year, &, if encouraged by
my researches meanwhile, to arrange an Exhibition of his chief works
at the same period. Meanwhile I shall pay Mr. Bellenden Ker[1] – who
edited the essays – the compliment of connecting him, if I can get at
him.[2]

Now to the other subject of your letter, which robbed me of sleep
last night. I have not yet heard from Boxall – but no matter. The offer
requires mature consideration on my part. I am aware that it is a fair
offer to one so deeply interested in the concerns of the N. G. as I. At the
same time it must be my question whether your offer can be set against
the fact of eliminating one jewel from a now very small collection
& one to which I am peculiarly attached. For it welcomed me to the
drawing rooms where it hs ever since been the prominent ornament. I
must take a little time to think. In truth Mr. Boxall should have taken
my advice, founded on your experience, & when you made the selection
of the low priced Director pictures, you should also have bid for some
of the others – which, one with another, as I impressed on him, would
have appeared a small sum to the public, & which was always Sir Chas'
way of proceeding.

However I can only be glad that he placed me in the position
towards the N: G: which I now occupy – tho' it was a bad play of his
cards for the acquisition of the higher priced pictures.

You must kindly allow me a little time.
Believe me your's very truly
Eliz Eastlake

1. Charles H. Bellenden Ker (c. 1785–1871), legal reformer and an early patron
   of Eastlake's work. He had lived in Cannes since 1860.

2. Eastlake's two published works were *Materials for a History of Oil Painting*, 2
   vols. (London: Longman, Brown, Green & Longman, 1847) and *Contributions
   to the Literature of Fine Arts* (London: John Murray, 1848). John Murray
   undertook to publish a second edition of *Contributions to the Literature of Fine
   Arts* with Elizabeth's memoir.

Letter to John Murray   *NLS Ms.42176*

7 FitzRoy Sqre
14 March 1868
Dear Mr. Murray

Your letter of the 11th required a little consideration & also I have had sudden & severe illness in the house, now happily over, which took up my time & attention.

I cannot hesitate to accept yr scheme & proposition regarding the remodelling of Kugler's Italian Painters, by the absorption of new information as Cavalcaselle's labours have brought to light. It is a task which will deeply interest me, & also contribute to increase my small knowledge of the History of Art.[1] At the same time I have much work now in hand preparatory to submitting to yourself & to Mr. Longman – as publication of Sir Chas two works – a more digested scheme for additions to each of those works. Layard has been kind enough to read & give me his opinion of a portion of MS belonging to so early a period as 1830–1, but, with trifling exceptions, more wanted, as a corrective of present art & criticism, now than ever.

I have also Gibson's Biography in abeyance, but that, when once I devote myself exclusively to it, will soon be got through. At all events I cannot have too much occupation, or prospect of occupation – & therefore I shall hope to be able to give my attention to the remodelling of Kugler as soon as you would find it desirable.

I will retain your letter on this subject, as a scheme on which to proceed.

Believe me yr's faithfully
Eliz Eastlake

1. Franz Theodor Kugler (1808–58), German art historian and chair of art history at the Universität in Berlin. Although no letters have come to light to document the fact, the Eastlakes had prepared an edition of Kugler's *Handbook of Painting in Italy, Part I: Italian Schools, Translated by a Lady. Edited with notes, by Sir Charles L. Eastlake ... Second Edition, thoroughly revised with much additional material*, 2 vols. (London: John Murray, 1851). The commission to remodel Kugler in 1868 was in response to recent connoisseurship, partic-ularly the reattributions of Crowe and Cavalcaselle, that had rendered Kugler outdated. As subsequent letters reveal, this bitter and protracted commission occupied Elizabeth intermittently over the next six years, before appearing in 1874 as *Kugler's Handbook of Painting. The Italian Schools ... Edited, with notes, by Sir Charles L. Eastlake ... New Edition. Fourth Edition. Revised and Remodelled from the latest researches, by Lady Eastlake*, 2 parts (London: John

Murray). Thereafter Layard edited further new editions of Kugler in 1887 and 1891, this time incorporating the scholarship of Morelli.

Letter to Florence Nightingale[1] *BL Nightingale Papers*
Vol. LXIII 45,801 f.6

7 FitzRoy Sqre
8 April 1868
Dear Florence
    (For that is always your name <u>within</u> me). I have been much interested by your letter & the Regulations, & am glad to have such chapter & verse in my knowledge. Wd that the Labourers were more for such a harvest! I do not doubt that the ladies of All Saints & other sisterhoods drain away a good many volunteers from you & setting aside periods of <u>fashion</u> & impulses of romance – which are always for evading the real battle of training – I fear that the standard of devotion for such service will always be lamentably low. From my very small experience in such matters, I find that it is the authority & matter of fact regulations (divested of the varnish of romance wh: the Ritualists give them) which deter volunteers – an objection which is the most proof of unfitness.[2]
    However, wherever opportunity offers I shall gladly canvass for you. And in time I hope we may see our fellow countrywomen wiping off, as a race, the blot which in other matters also I have had occasion to detect on them – that of not being <u>earnest</u> in anything – not even in <u>gain</u>, where the French woman so greatly beats them.
    I shall not readily forget yr portrait of the sweet <u>Una</u> you have lost. What more blessed career could an Englishwoman – with idle hands & unsatisfied heart – desire![3] I must not say what portrait I could draw of <u>you</u> – you wd not care for the best of pencils there!
I have indeed known sorrow & know it, & I crave to know its <u>uses</u>.
Ever dear Florence
Yr's affectionately
Eliz Eastlake

   1. Florence Nightingale (1820–1910), pioneering nurse during the Crimean War who established the Nightingale Training School and Home for Nurses at St Thomas's Hospital in 1860. Evidently Elizabeth and Florence Nightingale had been acquainted since 1846. See letter, 14 July 1846.

   2. Presumably in response to a letter from Florence Nightingale dated 5

April regarding the possibility of a Lady Superindendent for the Nurses of Liverpool Workhouse Infirmary. See the Auchincloss Florence Nightingale Collection in Augustus Long Health Sciences Library, Columbia HSL Special Collections C–89, Columbia University, New York.

3. See *Una and Her Paupers: The Extraordinary Life of Agnes Elizabeth Jones by her Sister* (Liskeard: Diggory Press, 2005). Jones took charge of the Liverpool Workhouse Infirmary; she contracted typhus and died in 1868.

Letter to John Murray   *NLS Ms.42176*

7 FitzRoy Sqre
18 May 1868
Dear Mr. Murray

On my return from Cannes[1] I have found yr enclosure of Mr. Ruland's letter about Kugler.[2] I trust that in due time yr renewed edition will supersede all others. I shall be very glad to do my best for that purpose.

For the present, however, I have to request your attention to the subject of Sir Chas MS.S. They may be classified under two heads – philosophical & technical (or professional), & my idea is to attack them respectively to the works by Sir Chas, published by yourself & by Mr. Longman, assigning to you the philosophical writings, & to Mr. Longman the technical.

I am anxious to know how you would be disposed to enter into such as scheme for a publication of a selection of these MSS. I think I understood you to day – when I first returned from Italy – that you would contemplate a reprint of the "Contributions". Supposing this to be the case, I would suggest an enlarged edition, consisting of the volume as it now stands, & of one or two more. To this series I should be disposed to prefix a short memoir of Sir Chas chiefly founded on letters written during his boyhood & growth to his parents, & to Mr. Harman. You will best judge how far such a scheme of which I give this crude outline be feasible & desirable. A prominent portion of the philosophical pages consists of a fragment omitted "How to observe". I find from Mr. Bellenden Ker that this was intended as part of a contemplated series of Essays, on different subjects to be undertaken by Mr. Chas Knight, of which only two were published, viz on geology by Sir Henry de la Beche & on travel by Dr. Martineau. The project went no futher. Sir Chas' discourses to the students – already printed – 6 in number – are rather doubtful in classification, whether under

philosophical or technical. At all events, should you desire your reader
to look through such MSS as I have set apart as eligible – the greater
portion of which I have copied, & which only require the additions
of notes, which I shall be ready to supply according to the indications
given. I shall be ready to send the to you.

Believe me dear Mr. Murray

Yr's faithfully

Eliz Eastlake

I heard with great concern of the alarm caused to yourself & Mrs
Murray by your son's accident. I trust that he is quite recovered now.

1. She had visited Bellenden Ker at Cannes in preparation for her edition of
Eastlake's *Contributions*.

2. Carl Ruland, Prince Albert's German librarian at Windsor Castle.

Letter to Florence Nightingale   *BL Nightingale Papers*
Vol. LXIII 45,801 f.55

7 FitzRoy Sqre

24. May 1868

Dear Florence Nightingale

A Norfolk lady, a Miss Wright, whom I have mentioned before to
Lady Verney, if not to you, has a great wish to join the small band
who devote themselves to the sick. But having some experience (I
believe in the Norfolk & Norwich Hospital) & havg spent many
weeks in the University Hospital here she feels unwilling, while
untruly admitting the excellence of the rule, to go through a whole
year's training at St. Thomas'. She is anxious to know whether this
could be remitted – under the circumstances – & whether she could
be admitted for a shorter period than a year. "Long enough (she
writes) for Mrs. Wardroper to decide if I am fitted to fill a responsible
position I am deeply interested in such work & wd put my whole
heart into it".

I give you her own words for I know nothing personally of this lady
except that hav.g seen her in the wards of University Hospital where her
kind face & benevolent manner much prepossessed me. I wd say that
she is about 35 years old. Her testimony of her own experience may be
therefore the more safely admitted.[1]

I am just returned from Cannes & Mentone where I have been for a
month on an errand of duty. It was the season of the highest poetry of

that Nature – the air fragrant with a harvest of orange blossom more than normally profuse. But I am glad of my dull Square again! & of the sad, & un eloquent house!

I hope Miss Wright's petition may not be a desperate one. Believe me ever yr's affectionately

Eliz Eastlake

1. Florence Nightingale's reply dated 25 May agrees that Miss Wright should be given an interview. See the Auchincloss Florence Nightingale Collection in Augustus Long Health Sciences Library, Columbia HSL Special Collections, Columbia University, New York.

Letter to Florence Nightingale   *BL Nightingale Papers Vol. LXIII 45,801 f.61*

7 FitzRoy Sqre
6 June 1868
Dear Florence

I feel sure that the "good words" to wh: you have contributed & wh: have reached me, come from you. You have indeed blown a trumpet in Sion which I trust will call many hesitators to yr ranks. I am so glad & proud that you have spoken in your own name – you never, to my knowledge, spoke more eloquently – inspired by both a general principle & by an individual sorrow. Either one enough to make one cry aloud.

My Miss Wright, whom unseen you put faith in, had been hitherto in Norfolk, but was to come to London as this last week. I have not heard or seen anything of her yet. But in answer to my last she wrote "I do desire during the rest of my life to be a useful worker". May she be fortified in this wish! And may you see more of your travail accomplished. The subject is never forgotten by me where I see any chance of a word in season.

A little woman in Norwich is doing beautiful things – for the tempted & the convalescent, in part continuing Mary Stanley's work. She is a Miss Crosse – she deserves that you shd know her name.

Ever yr's afftly
Eliz Eastlake

Letter to William Boxall   *UNC Elizabeth Eastlake*
Letters #11,617

7 FitzRoy Square
22 June 1868
My dear Mr. Boxall

I have a letter from dear old Waagen in which he trusts me to obtain some important information from you, & that soon. He is occupied about a Dictionary of Modern Painters & as <u>B</u> comes early on the list he is anxious to obtain from you the date of your birth(!), an outline of yr education, & a list of yr most important works. You will think this is a <u>bore</u>, but probably you have had to supply a similar little sketch before now, & I trust that you may be able to satisfy the old friend. I came to you Saturday, hoping to obtain it all vivâ voce but you were wisely gone into the country.

Waagen writes very depressed – he is bullied and ill treated by those above him in position, & below him in knowledge.

How glad I am this world is <u>not</u> our Home!
Yr's afftly
Eliz Eastlake

Letter to John Murray   *NLS Ms.42176*

7 FitzRoy Square
5 July 1868
Dear Mr. Murray

It appears to me that it would be best to retain the original title chosen by Sir Chas – calling this fresh volume, if it come to be published, "Second Series of Contributions to the Literature of the Fine Arts".

I hardly understand in what way you would propose to announce such a volume in the Q.R. If by regular advertisement, or by an incidental allusion in some article – in that latter case I should request to see the allusion before it appears, for there are many who will attribute it to my pen.

But I am not yet prepared to accept the proposal of thus announcing the work. I have submitted it, as far as printed, to a few friends whose verdict I have not yet recd. And I should which for more time before committing myself definitely.

I am preparing further MSS to be printed in this temporary form, so as to obtain opinions upon them, & I will venture to send them to you in a few days.

I think that the printer has taken more pains.

Believe me your's faithfully

Eliz Eastlake

Letter to John Murray   *NLS Ms.42176*

7 FitzRoy Sqre

9 July 1868

Dear Mr. Murray

I see no objection to the announcement as you have submitted it to me, merely in yr book list, as it does not bind me either as to time or quantity. I have added a P, before the R.A. as, if Sir Chas' connection with the R. Academy be inserted at all, his real position shd be given. Either let it stand as P.R.A. or omit all designation.

I have no objection, therefore, I repeat, to this little announcement appearg as soon as you please.

Yr's faithfully

Eliz Eastlake

You did not answer my query as to whether Cavalcaselle has proceeded so far with his next vol: that I could in my way profit by his forthcoming account of Ant: da Messina. If this be impossible pray do not trouble yourself to answer.

Letter to William Boxall   *UNC Elizabeth Eastlake Letters #11,617*

7 FitzRoy Sqre

22 July 1868

My dear Mr. Boxall

I know you will be deeply grieved to hear that dear Dr. Waagen is no more![1] I have just recd the sad tidings through his daughter, who was at Malvern & is now on her way to Berlin. He died at Copenhagen of inflammation of the lungs in the home of the Russian chargeé d'affaires. Alas! we can ill afford to spare such as one – I least of all. I had written to him just before he left Berlin. I had always the highest opinion of him, judgement & integrity & <u>work</u>, & he was − <u>is</u> − deep in my affections.

I was sorry to miss you yesterday. I want you to dine quietly here one day next week − but am kept unsettled as to day.

We are but few left of the old happy party! & shd draw more together.

Ever yr's afftly
Eliz Eastlake

1. Waagen died during a visit to Copenhagen on 15 July 1868.

Letter to Mrs Sandbach   *PCA M/D/SAND/8/336*

Blaise Castle nr Bristol [1]
11 September 1868
Dear Mrs. Sandbach

As time has passed on you & Mr. Sandbach have been much on <u>my mind</u>, for owing to circumstances wh: I could not prevent I find my holiday time so shortened that I have no chance of enjoying the pleasure of a visit to you this autumn. Friends to whom I am bound by many ties, & who were to have come to me by the middle of August never arrived (from France) till the end of the month, & did not leave me till last Tuesday. Nor can I mend the matter by extending my 'leave of absence' for Messrs Longman will require me to lose no time in prearing for them, & I have also an <u>auction</u> in view in November which will take me some time to be ready for. Having therefore friends to visit near London I must make this the farthest point of my travels. I hope you & kind Mr. Sandbach will not quite lose patience with me, but let me look forward to an <u>Easter</u> visit, shd that time suit you, & all be well. By that time I have every reason to think that my Gibson task will have been resumed, for I trust before then to have satisfied Mr Longman & Mr. Murray, &, if possible, <u>myself</u>, in what concerns the MSS & other remains of my dear Husband.

I trust therefore to yr kindness to forgive me for what <u>seems</u> a very ungrateful return to all yr kind invitations.

I am here at a very beautiful place,[2] with a delicate old lady − Mrs Harford. This is my first taste of country air since I returned from Cannes. If you should read the Life of Bunsen, which, knowing him & his family, has interested me deeply, you will find allusion to this place, & to its late excellent owner Mr Harford.

With kindest regards to Mr. Sandbach believe me dear Mrs. Sandbach
Yr's most truly
Eliz Eastlake

1. The home of John Scandrett Harford's widow.

2. Blaise Castle was noted architecturally and had gardens laid out by Humphrey
   Repton.

Letter to John Murray   NLS Ms.42176

7 FitzRoy Sqre
8 Octr 1868
Dear Mr. Murray
    You will be expectg to hear further regarding the work in question.
I am also anxious to tell you that I have now decided to defer the
publication which will emanate from your hands until the Spring. The
principal cause is that I cannot be ready so soon as you gave me reason
to think you wd desire. The preparation of the portion of the 2nd vol:
of the "History of the Materials of Art & Painting" for Messrs Longman
– with other technical matter which is is proposed to insert in the 2nd
vol: has occupied me longer than I expected. I hope however that this
work will be published in the course of next month. You will be able
to tell me at your leisure for what part of the Spring of 1869 you would
wish the Philosophical Essays to be ready.
    I trust that your stay in Scotland has been beneficial to Mrs. Murray
& all your family.
Believe me yr's faithfully
Eliz Eastlake

Letter to Florence Nightingale   BL Nightingale Papers
Vol. LXIII 45,801 f.128

7 FitzRoy Sqre
19 October 1868
Dear Florence Nightingale
    I am tempted to trouble you again regarding a lady who is anxious
to enrol herself under your auspices. I am not acquainted with her, but
she is described to me by one of the ladies at the University Hospital as

gratified by nature for nursing work & anxious to learn it. I have sent her your rules & have rec.d in return the assurance that she wd be ready to conform to all but one – viz: that it wd not be in her power to <u>pay</u> the small sum required at St. Thomas' for the board etc. The question is whether in certain cases where means are failing such payment wd be waived. It is a Miss Taylor – a <u>free</u> woman – not very young – living with sister near Seven Oaks.

I grudge giving you the trouble of answer.g this – but I only beg you to send it to those who can answer this question for you. You must attribute my addressing you to my anxiety to encourage volunteers. I have my eye upon another lady, but much younger, who is doing volunteer work at University Hospital – & doing it with a brightness which is a very tonic to her charges. I will secure her for you if I can, for she has <u>no</u> All Saints proclivities.[1]

I trust you are less suffering. Pray accept my love & believe me yr's afftly

Eliz Eastlake

1. All Saints Hospital in London had links with an Anglican nursing order, The Society of All Saints of the Poor, established in 1851, which assumed the responsibility for nursing there in 1862. See Susan Mumm (ed.), *All Saints Sisters of the Poor: An Anglican Sisterhood in the Nineteenth Century* (London: The Boydell Press/Church of England Record Society, 2001).

Letter to A. H. Layard   *NLS Ms.42169*

7 FitzRoy Sqre
10 Decr 1868
My Dear Mr. Layard

I must send you a few words not only for my insignificant self, but for the one who would have been so happy to have seen you in the Office you now hold. You are climbing the tree & will go higher still, & I hope you will find sunshine at the top.[1]

Your's always truly

Eliz Eastlake

Boxall tells me he shall keep in 3 months longer now! You will not disdain good Tucker's rejoicing at your appointment – you are a hero of his.

1. Layard was appointed a member of the Privy Council and Chief Commissioner of Works in W. E. Gladstone's government.

Letter to William Boxall   *UNC Elizabeth Eastlake*
Letters #11,617

7 FitzRoy Square
26 Janry 1869
My dear Mr. Boxall

I find I have omitted to ask you a question from Mr Ker recd in a letter from him a little while ago. Namely "whether a miniature of an officer in uniform by Cosway (R.A.) would be acceptable. It is very finely painted. Webb (late of Bond Street) says it is very fine".

I am writing to him today so that I shall be glad of a line as to what to say. He either means it as a gift or bequest – probably the latter.

This will be left when I send for the Academy petition.

Layard's engagement gives me pleasure. I trust the young lady[1] will be mistress of the situation.

Ever yr's very truly
Eliz Eastlake

Your messenger is just come & gone, before I could catch him to send back this. Many thanks for the signature, I now think that <u>Knight</u> has signed that poor woman's paper before, but he took my word for the case, wh: you have kindly done & safely so. Pray put it all on my shoulders. I wish they have nothing harder to bear!

1. Mary Evelyn Guest (Enid) (1843–1912) married Layard on 9 March 1869.

Letter to John Murray   *NLS Ms.42176*

7 FitzRoy Square
27. April 1869
Dear Mr. Murray

I am tempted to intrude upon you again in the matter of Gibson's biography, for a reason which I will explain. You declined it some time last year on the score of my refusing to give my name as the author. But circumstances have changed since then, & I am now willing that it should appear as "Edited by Lady Eastlake". Such being the case I feel it right to give you again the option of publishing it.

Though quite aware that, at best, it can be a matter of very little importance, yet I may add that having completed by far the larger portion of the work I have reason to think that it will be more interesting than was at first believed. Should you care to submit this portion to your reader I will send it you.

Believe me yr's faithfully

Eliz Eastlake

Letter to John Murray   NLS Ms.42176

7 FitzRoy Sqre

29 April 1869

Dear Mr. Murray

I can have no wish to induce you to publish Gibson's Biography against your better judgemt. At the same time the autobiography you saw forms the smaller portion of the work. Indeed I am quite as convinced as yourself (& always told him so) that what he had written wd not suit the public taste. I was quite unaware that Longman's had announced the work. This was without my sanction, but may have arisen from letters between them & Mr. Sandbach. I shall now offer the work to them.

The Essays on the Fine Arts you refer to are already, as you are aware, in the slip − therefore thus far almost ready. It will be a question whether the Discourses − six in number − should be included in the same vol: − This question will be for yourself to solve. I am at this time engaged in preparing a comparatively brief memoir of Sir Chas − drawn from numerous letters − I reserve the decision as to givg this memoir to the public − as a kind of introduction to the vol: in question − until I have proceeded further with it. At all events I see not the slightest doubt of being amply in time for yr annual Sale in Novr which I have long kept in view.

As to the revision of Kugler I have not touched it yet, nor can I, until these pending tasks are accomplished, which I hope will be the case in early autumn. I see no urgent reason for troublg you to come & speak personally on these matters, tho' I shd be sorry you shd think that I am not always happy to see you & Mrs. Murray whenever inclined to come.

Believe me yr's faithfully

Eliz Eastlake

Letter to A. H. Layard   *NLS Ms.42169*

7 FitzRoy Sqre
6 May 1869
Dear Mr. Layard

I wish to renew to you in writing the assurance that I shall be perfectly satisfied to receive the payment for Sir Chas Art Library in any instalments & at any time that may be convenient to the Trustees of the Nat: Gallery. At the same time I must repeat a condition which I have more than once mentioned to Mr. Boxall – viz: that it should be called "The Eastlake Library". Should this condition appear to you inconsistent (& I speak now privately & as a friend) with the fact of its being a purchase I beg you to tell me so. At all events I shall print upon the title page of each work the letter E, or some other small & unobtrusive sign of its having belonged to Sir Chas.[1]

I did not tell you yesterday that I have long had a private offer for the entire Library. This would have reconciled you to leaving it in my hands – but you have quite convinced me of the Trustees' real desire for it.

I have been thinking over the subject of Boxall's successor. I believe Richmond to be a most worthy man & thorough gentleman, but to the full as nervous & as little a man of business as Boxall. His sitters complain terribly of the impossibility of getting answers to letters.[2]

But I have been struck with his son – the young painter W.B: Richmond.[3] He was here the other day, & his intelligent enthusiasm over the Bellinis & other pictures was very remarkable. He is young – well acquainted with Italy – & too delicate for the exclusive anxieties of a Painter's Life. A very gentlemanly young man. Should you think it worthwhile to obtain privately any information about his capacities I could easily procure it for you through a safe channel. This only for your consideration.

When you answer this – at your leisure – tell me whether I may own to Boxall that I know of his resignation. Many thanks for your kindness yesterday.

Your's always truly
Eliz Eastlake

1. Elizabeth's condition as to the name of the Eastlake Library continued to be met until the early years of the twentieth century, but since the 1930s the library has usually been known as the 'Gallery Library'. Eastlake's library is still distinguished by the letter 'E' printed onto the title page of each of his books.

2. George Richmond (1809–96), portrait artist.

3. Sir William Blake Richmond (1842–1921), precocious artist, later Slade Professor at Oxford and Professor of Painting at the Royal Academy.

Letter to A. H. Layard   *NLS Ms.42169*

7 FitzRoy Sqre
12. May 1869
Dear Mr. Layard

Your question about the landscape Bellini has made me take a little time to consider. To the Nat: Gal: I would part with it for two thousand guineas. I tell you this in confidence & with no <u>positive</u> pledge to part with it even if the Trustees were inclined to give me that sum. Still, I am quite sure that I would rather see it there than anywhere else at any price.

Many thanks for your kind letter of the 7th I trust the affair of the Library will run smooth now. Whenever you have due accomodation I shall be ready to give it up. One other condition will be my own admission to the Library whenever I may reasonably desire. I think you will have to combine the office of Librarian with that of Director. Mr. Wornum will never undertake this in addition to all he does <u>not</u> do, altho' for such services as he renders he is much overpaid. As I said before, if it should thought [sic] desirable to obtain information about young Richmond, I have it in my power to get it.

I believe you & your Enid are going soon to Paris, & much pleasure. Your's ever truly
Eliz Eastlake

Letter to A. H. Layard   *NLS Ms.42169*

St. Leonard's Cottage, Slough[1]
25 July 1869
Dear Mr. Layard

My attention has been called to your kind & judicious letter in yesterday's Times. I thank you cordially for it. Engrossed as I now am with painful duties I had unfortunately not seen Mr. Bentinck's question & insinuation.[2]

I wrote to your Enid the other day on the subject of introductions to India for Mr. Ralli – a young man who will do no introductions discredit. I have since that had a kind letter from Lady Northcote saying that Sir Stafford will gladly furnish him – under these circumstances, knowing your over occupied time, I am glad to relieve you of any thought or trouble on this matter.

Still, there is a subject which I know you have kindly at heart – namely the materials for an article on the life, art & writings of dear Sir Charles. I told you that I was compiling a memoir from abundant early letters. I have completed it up to the time of his leaving Italy – 1830 – I have had it printed in the slip for better convenience of its few readers. I wish to submit this portion to you – & to Forster & to Reeve – before deciding on making a memoir public. I have a strong feeling against publishing a biography unless it <u>really</u> advance the reputation of its object, & though the boyhood & youth of my husband seem to be irregularly interesting yet I confess to being no possible judge in this case. I must trust to you & those I have mentioned for reading the portion I have ready very critically, & giving me an impartial opinion as to whether I should honour his memory by completing the life & making it public. It will not be long – not a vol: & my plan would be to let it head those more philosophical essays on which your favourable opinion so much encouraged me. At all events whether the memoir be published or not it may be acceptable to you as a contributing material for your proposed article. I think you said it was to be in the <u>Edinburgh R</u>.[3] I have the slip here, & will send it you whenever you foresee a leisure hour or two. I am sure your Enid will answer this for you.

Ever dear Mr. Layard
Your's truly
Eliz Eastlake

1. St. Leonard's Cottage, the home of Anne de Wahl, who died there on 3 August 1869.

2. Layard's letter to *The Times* refutes Mr Bentinck's claims that the Director's Pictures were being sold to the National Gallery for a higher price than Eastlake had originally paid for them. *The Times*, 24 July 1869, p. 8, col. E.

3. 'Eastlake and Gibson', *Edinburgh Review*, 131 (April 1870), pp. 392–417.

Letter to Mrs Sandbach   PCA M/D/SAND/8/251

7 FitzRoy Square
30 Aug: 1869
My dear Mrs. Sandbach

I have recd our friend Penry Williams this morning & he has told me of yr & Mr Sandbach kind expectation of hearing from me. I am quite grieved that you should have expected anything which you did not do, but I concluded you wd have seen the announcement of my beloved sister's death in the Times. This was not quite right of me, but probably you did not know her name "Anne de Wahl, daughter of the late Dr. Rigby of Norwich" She died on the 3rd August after sufferings which only increased as the end neared. I was with her entirely for the 3 weeks preceding, & almost entirely for many before that. Her daughter & her son in law had arrived on the 26th June & her only remaining son came from Petersburg for 3 days before she departed. I though I had written to you or to Mr. Sandbach from Slough, during her illness but I have written so many letters to a large family circle & to numerous friends before & since we lost her that I may be mistaken.

Now I can only say, dear Mrs Sandbach, that I am still fettered by duties which but for this sad episode wd have been completed before this time. I fully anticipated being free to come to you, but this has necessarily changed all, & both my sorrow & my work compel me to remain quiet. I still hope to be free about the middle of October, but it is quite time to set you at liberty & therefore I beg you will not let me give you another hospitable thought.

These events so shake all human plans that I almost shrink from any except those of completing duties. My dear sister is an unspeakable loss to me, as to us all, to her daughter especially. She was strong & tender, & I feel that another stay is gone. God's will be done! I can only be thankful for her, for her sufferings were terrible.

Gibson's Life is now printing. I am correcting & supplying headings &c. We are as far as about 160 pages.

My niece and nephew are with me now – anxious about his sister – I fear dying after her confinement! Thus my heart & hands are full. I rejoice amid all this to know that Mr. Sandbach is making a good recovery. Williams is welcome to come to me in about a week.

My kind regards to Mr Sandbach
Ever yr's truly
Eliz Eastlake

Letter to William Boxall   *NG14/31/1869*

7 FitzRoy Sqre
20. Septr 1869
Dear Mr Boxall

I have felt much from your kindness in remembering my troublesome
wishes about the 'Report on the Raphael' at the time of your hasty
departure. It has interested me <u>deeply</u> & confirms your belief that it
was the unfinished Fra Bartolommeo which Mr. Baring purchased
many years later as the Trustees in old times objected to purchase the
unfinished M.Angelo belonging to Ld Taunton – on the score of an
unfinished picture being uninteresting to the public. I was slow to
believe that they cd have denied to do so in this case. The Report is
worthy of my Dear Sir Charles – accurate & exhaustive.

Williams remained with me till Friday last, & I got good Newton
to come & drive one day otherwise he had only my company. If this
was a trial to either it was only to <u>him</u>. But I found the dear old
friend much eager & more talkative than of old. Perhaps <u>I</u> was more
so, for which I cannot be too thankful. He is now with two 'ancient
dames' (an expression borrowed from Lord Winchilsea!) near Seven
Oaks, but I expect to see him before he finally starts. I got him to
read through all the proofs of Gibson's Life, & he found no fault with
it.

Now I am just back from my Mother's at Slough. She quite well, but
feeling the burden of that which no one would covet – her very great
age, but it happily blunts me to the loss of that dear & useful life we
have so lately lost. My niece & nephew are now with me & leave me
only to sail to their Eastern home. It will be hard to part, but I now
feel nearer the land where there will be no partings.

I had a kind letter from Layard a few days ago, & shall write to
hime to Florence, where I suppose you will meet. I am afraid you may
miss the sight of Lord Winchilsea's letter to the Times – forsaking <u>you</u>
for <u>Byron</u>.[1] The letter is worthy of the noble writer & of the noble
subject.

Did I tell you that Tucker is going to forsake me! Reasons of health,
which a London life does not suit. I grow callous to <u>secondary</u> griefs,
tho' this is no common one.

I trust you are getting much good from change of air & having "a
feast of fat things" in the way of pictures. Ever dear Mr Boxall

Your's affectionately
Eliz Eastlake

1. Lord Winchilsea's letter to the editor in *The Times* (Saturday, 18 September 1869, p. 6, col. D) comments on the press interest in Harriet Beecher Stowe's book *Lady Byron Vindicated*. In previous months Lord Winchilsea had attacked some of Boxall's purchases for the National Gallery.

Letter to John Murray   *NLS Ms.42176*

7 FitzRoy Sqre
2 Octr 1869
Dear Mr Murray

I send you now the Essays – corrected – tho' perhapas slight emendations will yet be added even in the way of omission. I also add the Lecture on the distinction between the language of Poetry & Painting of which I spoke. I send it as it is, but it will require the opening passages referring to the students to be expunged.

I think still, as I expressed before, that the collective title for this proposed volume should be as you suggest – "second series of Contributions &c – to which is prefixed a memoir &c by Lady Eastlake."

The allusion to a title in my last note was directed only to the 2 chapters of "How to observe".

I am still kept waiting for some materials which will complete the last portion of the memoir. The gap however is so immaterial that, if you should desire, I can send you the the [sic] MS which terminates the memoir – more especially if you want to show it to any one. I shall be glad to hear what is thought of the Essays by the individual to whom you may submit them.

I shall be thankful to have all this business settled now as soon as yr leisure may permit, as I shall be leavg London probably on the 15th. Meanwhile I am ready to give my entire attention to the business. Shall I inform Mr. Bellenden Ker that he may send you his proposed preface for the reprint of the "Contributions"?

Believe me yr's faithfully
Eliz Eastlake

Letter to John Murray   *NLS Ms.42176*

7 FitzRoy Sqre
6 Octr 1869
Dear Mr Murray

I am glad to hear that some competent person is reading the memoir
& the Essays. At the same time, since I sent you the memoir I have
made an alteration in the introductory paragraphs which were thought
by one reader to be too tame & obscure. Also I have dele'd more than
one long letter of Sir Chas' & of his brother John. I would like your
literary friend to know this much.

I can have no objection to the terms you propose of dividing the
profits of every edition, if you think them the most fair towards yourself
& me. If you could send me a copy of the "Contributions" before
reprinting the vol: I would insert some marginal corrections made by
Sir Chas in the copy he has left. I will immediately let Mr. B: Ker
know that he may forward to me the addition he desires to make to his
preface.

I will let you know my address when I leave London so that proofs
may be sent me.
Your's faithfully
Eliz Eastlake

Letter to A. H. Layard   *NLS Ms.42169*

7 FitzRoy Sqre
6 Octr 1869
My dear Mr. Layard

I have been much longer in acknowledging your kind letter of the
12th September from Venice than I intended to be. But the various
work that attends the winding up of two tasks (Gibson's Life, as well
as my other work) has kept me very busy. Also I have had partings &
distresses which have made me more dull & depressed even than usual
– & not at all fit to be inflicted upon a kind correspondant. And first let
me tell you that the letter you enclosed me for Lady Strangford has been
received by her.[1] I had written to her the day before to a place near St.
Galle & I posted this letter to the same address & she has acknowledged
it. I believe she is now at a place called Goritzia, to which I am about
to write, when I have made out where it is.

I trust now that your wife has weathered the fatigues of traveling &
the heat of Venice in early September and is able to engage much under
your guidance. But she is too tall and beautiful to be very strong.

Your little allusion to Bergamo and to pictures set my mouth
watering (and I fear my eyes too!). It is like hearing of dear old friends.
I am glad to hear about Madame Molteni, and am thankful that you
made time to pay her a visit. I trust that Boxall has turned up safe and
has inspected the Carpaccio and others. I hope he may make another
attempt for the Bellini altarpiece at Pesaro.

You will be glad to hear that I have completed the memoir
– the later part will be less interesting to you, as containing fewer
of Sir Chas' letters (tho' not without them) but it will be suited to
the public as giving something of the society of the time. You will
like what he says about Sir R. Peel. I go a little with the history of
the Lawrence Collection of Drawings which it is only just to the
R. Academy, and to Sir Chas individually, to revive. It was a great
opportunity unpardonably lost, but shows at all events, that we are
more enlightened in such matters now. Sir Chas strived Heaven and
Earth to get even part of the Collection purchased for the Nation.
This last part of the Memoir is not yet in print, and will probably not
go through the slip state. But I have no doubt that it will be in proof
when you return, and will be immediately at your service. Mr. Murray
proposes to make one vol: of this memoir and of the Essays "How to
Observe" which you have read. He offers me half profits and I accept
any conditions.

My Life of Gibson is now almost fledged – I think it is readable
– and to those who knew the dear old man it will be interesting. You
shall have a copy, and I hope some one will be moved to review it
tenderly.

The Grotes have been at Hamburg for his health.[2] They hated it at
the time, but she reports him as now quite restored. They have been
back for a week, and I am going to see them this evening in Saville [sic]
R: where they are for a day or two. Then on the 15th I am going for a
little fresh air and rest into N: Wales to friends and relatives, and shall
be back the beginning of November.

Your will feel for me when I tell you that I am about to lose our
excellent Tucker! His long life with us in London has undermined
his health – and he has varicose veins of a threatening kind on his
legs, but he is only 48, and it is hard to lose such a universal helper.
However I am not without hope that after a while he may return,
especially if circumstances allow me to live more in the country for
which I long.

Now dear Mr. Layard goodbye. My kind love to the dear Lady, and
best wishes for both of you. I send this to B. of W.

Ever your's truly

Eliz Eastlake

1. Lady Strangford, née Emily Anne Beaufort (d. 1887), wife of Lord Strangford,
   travel writer and humanitarian. Following her husband's death in 1869 she
   trained as a nurse and established a hospital for Turkish soldiers in 1877
   during the Russo-Turkish War.

2. Harriet Grote (1792–1878), biographer and writer; and George Grote (1794–
   1871), historian. Elizabeth first met Mrs Grote at a dinner-party in 1854:
   '[Mrs. Grote] begged me to come and see her, which is so far a compliment, as she eschews all stupid women, and declares she seldom meets with
   a sensible one. She is herself the cleverest woman in London, only of a
   masculine and not feminine character' (J&C1, p. 323). The pair remained
   very close until Mrs Grote's death.

Letter to John Murray   *NLS Ms.42176*

7 FitzRoy Square

13 Octr 1869

Dear Mr. Murray

I have recd your letter with the enclosed remarks of the friend whom
you requested to the memoir – you misapprehended my meaning in
thinkg that I denied its perusal by any other than by your "reader" – for
your satisfaction not mine. At the same time, I could have no objection to
yr submitting it to a literary friend & to acceptg yr offer to send me his
suggestions but yr doing so can hardly be construed as a compliance with
my wishes. Still, I can be glad that I have thus been made acquainted with
adverse criticism in time to pause before giving a memoir of my Husband
which I have compiled with considerable samples, to the cold public.

I do not how the same individual who characterizes Sir Chas'
metaphysics as "confused and contradictory" and his logic as his
"weakness" can find any value in Essays which especially illustrate
his powers of reasoning & forms of expression. But as the Essays have
obtained his approbation I do not see on what other evidence he has
formed his condemnatory verdict, unless on the private letters & journals
contained in the memoir &, if he be right in his opinion, I would not
for the world subject Sir Chas' fame & memory to further criticism of
the kind. I will therefore take a short time to consider, & let you know
whether I wish the work to proceed.

I wrote you that I had rewritten the opening paragraphs, & I begged you to let yr literary friend know that fact. Still, the rewritten part equally maintained that combination of the reasoning power & the aesthetic sense which I venture to assert was Sir Chas' characteristic. If Raphael, Titian & M.Angelo possessed the same powers of reasoning & expression they have left no proof of them.

I trust that your new paper may prove as successful as you can desire.

Yr's faithfully

Eliz Eastlake

Letter to John Murray   *NLS Ms.42176*

7 FitzRoy Sqre

14. Octr 1869

Dear Mr. Murray

I leave London today and return tomorrow Friday for a few hours and then leave for good by 8 o'clock on Saturday mg. I shd hope to find the slips of the last part of the memoir tomorrow, so as to take them with me. I will only request you not to share one word of it to the person whose criticisms on Sir Chas you thought it right to send me.

My only object in suggestg the perusal by yr "Reader" was to obtain your views & plan with regard to the work wh: I had repeatedly asked for without any answer. But I cd have no objection whatever to your showing it, as you yourself proposed to "a literary friend". Unless, however, you concurred with such criticisms on Sir Chas as your friend entered into, I hardly see what object was answered by your giving me the distress of reading them.

As to panegyric, it wd be difficult for anyone, not hostiley inclined, to write a life of Sir Chas without panegyric – nor is there nearly so much in what I have said as in Leslie's Life of Constable, or from Taylor's of Leslie. Even in my life of Gibson I have been more unrestrained in generous laudation, than I have been, or would be in that of one so near and dear.

Should I not find the sheets tomorrow I must beg you to send them by post to me at H: Sandbach's Esq, Hafodunos, Llanewot, [sic] N. Wales.

Believe me yr's faithfully

Eliz Eastlake

I shall be at Hafodunos till the 23rd.

Letter to John Murray   *NLS Ms.42176*

Hafodunos Llanwert N.Wales[1]
21. Octr 1869
Dear Mr. Murray

I send you by this post a portion of the memoir, including the opening paragraphs which I have further remodelled, tho' in a sense entirely opposite to that suggested by yr critic; since my knowledge of the object has led me to dwell especially on his clearness of thought & expression. I conclude that you will desire to have the memoir divided into chapters. I therefore send it you up to p.24, where I have indicated the end of Chapter 1st.

I think you told me some time ago that the proofs would admit of some correction even <u>after</u> your Novr. dinner.[2] I am anxious to know whether this will be the case, as I have a short remark by the Duke of Wellington to insert which I cannot get at here – and if the proofs cannot be corrected and changed after your dinner I would return home the sooner in order to supply little things which I had not foreseen, or which have suggested themselves to me since I left home.

It will be safer to send me your answer to "Captn Strange Butson's, Plas Llandyffnan, Llangefni, Anglesea", where I remove on Saturday.

Shall I use the proofs by degrees? If so they must be sent to my niece's (Captn Butson) in Anglesea.
Your's faithfully
Eliz Eastlake

I conclude that you will require the <u>Essays</u> and the <u>Lecture</u> also in the course of a week. I am not sure that M.S. may come by book post. I therefore enclose the opening paragraphy here.

1. Hafodunos was the home of Henry Sandbach. It is situated close to the village of Llangernyw.

2. The annual Murray sale dinner was held at the Albion Tavern in Aldgate Street. See G. Paston, *At John Murray's* (London: John Murray, 1932), pp. 70–71.

Letter to John Murray   NLS Ms.42176

Plas Llandyffnan, Anglesea[1]
27. Octr 1869
Dear Mr. Murray
    I am anxious that no further proofs should be sent me here after
Friday i.e. none dispatched from London after Monday. If there be any
need to communicate with me on Friday, on Saturday, my address will
be at 'Bishop of Chester's,[2] Chester". I return to FitzRoy Square on
Monday the 1st Novr.
    I enclose you the first proof, on which I have made numerous
corrections. But this will not be the case further. I was anxious to
improve the first paragraphs as far as possible, and since I sent you the
M.S. of them I have received suggestions from a critical but kind friend
some of which I have in part adopted. I have submitted the concluding
part of the memoir with the same friend who has not yet returned it
to me. I am anxious to put it into your hands in its final state. When
I return to F. Sq. I will send the catalogue of Sir Chas' works which
will come after the memoir and before the Essays. I do not know yet
whether you wish to have the Lecture I sent you.
    I am not much pleased with the type and page. I hoped it would
have been the same as that of "the Contributions" but I conclude this
was necessary.
Believe me your's faithfully
Eliz Eastlake

  1. Plas Llanddyfnan was the home of Amelia (née Rigby) (1841–1923), Elizabeth's
     niece, and Captain William Strange Butson.

  2. Elizabeth's cousin, Eleanor Turner, was married to William Jacobson, the
     Bishop of Chester.

Letter to John Murray   NLS Ms.42176

FitzRoy Sqre
21 Decr 1869
Dear Mr. Murray
    I have just recd the enclosed title page (but one proof of it). As it is
in some respects not what I should wish. I venture to trouble you with
it. To call Sir Chas an "R.A." seems absurd when the line beneath

is considered. I feel that the initials I have inserted wd be more in
keeping. Of course more initials indicating membership of more learned
societies cd be added, but it appears to me that F.R.S., D.C.L. &c or
even F.R.S &c is sufficient.

I have also altered the sentence that refers to myself. Shd you see
any objection I beg you will express it. If not I trust that I may have
an immediate revise. I can only regret that the work has been so
pertinaciously delayed.
Believe me yr's faithfully
Eliz Eastlake
Is is time to trouble you with a few names to whom I shd wish copies sent?

Letter to John Murray   NLS Ms.42176

FitzRoy Sqre
22 Decr 1869
Dear Mr. Murray
     You will have received my note written yesterday. Meanwhile I have
recd your's of the same date. I am much distressed that the publication
of the work should be further delayed. It has been my especial object
since I took it in hand that the publication of Gibson's Life shd not, for
obvious reasons, precede that of my Husband's. Gibson's Life has now
been out for a month while my unremitting endeavours to expedite the
other work have been all frustrated.

As to the "detriment to its good appearance" nothing can well injure
so wretched a form of type & page as has been selected for it. In a
work which so deeply concerns my feelings, & to which I have devoted
no common labour & anxiety I surely might have been consulted. It is
obvious too that the 2nd series should at all events have been presented
to the public in the same form as the 1st series. Had I foreseen how this
valued work wd have been delayed I shd have stipulated that, at my own
expense, a more appropriate type shd have been substituted.

Now I earnestly beg that the quality of paper may be of a kind so as
in some measure to counteract the ordinariness of the look of the print.
You will oblige me much by allowing me to see a sample of the paper
chosen – also of the binding, which I should wish to be somewhat of
the same dark colour as that of the "Materials". I shall be here at home
until the afternoon of Friday.

As Messrs Bradbury & Evans have stipulated for a week's delay, and
your note is dated the 21st I beg that you will hold them to their own

conditions and that I may see the vol: issued on the 28th of this month.
Believe me yr's faithfully
Eliz Eastlake
If by extraordinary exertion the work cd be reprinted so as to match
with the 1st series, <u>in a fortnight from this</u>, I put it to your own
judgement whether it ought not to be done?

Letter to John Murray   *NLS Ms.42176*

FitzRoy Sqre
23. Decr 1869
Dear Mr. Murray
    You are aware that I <u>did</u> object to both the type & page at the outset
– when you assured me that it would look better when finished. The
remarks of others upon the meanness & indistinctness of the crammed
pages have since increased my sense of the wrong done to the work.
Printing is not a matter of "<u>taste</u>" but of legibility, & all the supposed
taste in the world – of which I see no evidence in Messrs Bradbury &
Evans – will not avail against the commonplace facts of distinctness &
legibility. Anxious not to give you trouble I concluded at first that the
<u>quantity</u> necessitated the cramming of the matter. But the vol: only
amounts to 344 pages (which an intelligent printer could have completed)
whereas the 1st series amounts to just 400 pages – so that there was every
reason for, instead of against, making the 2 vols correspond in type. You
have not replied to my request to see the paper & colour of binding, &
as I leave town to-morrow I have written to request Messrs Bradbury &
Evans to send me immediately samples of both.
Your's faithfully
Eliz Eastlake

Letter to John Murray   *NLS Ms.42176*

FitzRoy Square
23 Decr 1869
Dear Mr. Murray[1]
    You must also do me the favour to remember that I have been
unaware of any necessary connection between the <u>slip</u> & the finally
printed page. My only experience of the slip has been in the service of

the Q:R: where I had not observed the identity of the type & breadth of line. Under these circumstances I sincerely apologize for my supposition that you were answerable for more than the final choice of the type.

But I never concealed from you my intention to give only a <u>brief</u> memoir, fitted to head the Essays (of which you knew the extent – indeed the Discourse has been added since) & therefore I can only regret that you should have imagined any similarity between my modest volume & such works as Stanley's St. Paul & Lyell's Geology.

I am much obliged by the sight of the covers. I have put a X within the one I prefer, & would suggest that the words "with Memoir" be added on the back. At the same time I leave this suggestion entirely to your judgement.

Lastly, I beg to remind you that it was yr own letter that gave me the assurance that the type was a matter of the Printer's taste. Believe me I do not desire to give you the slightest cause for offence – my only consolation under sufferg is that I have never done so.

Let therefore my apology suffice for my warm feeling about the type, & let it be forgotten.

Your's faithfully

Eliz Eastlake

1. This letter was docketed at Albemarle Street as the first of a batch of 'surly ill-tempered letters'.

Letter to John Murray   *NLS Ms.42177*

FitzRoy Square

1 Janry 1870

Dear Mr. Murray

I am much obliged by the two copies forwarded to me yesterday. I conclude that they somewhat precede the general issue, for which I am the more grateful.

Her Majesty wishes me to present a copy. May I therefore ask you to have one copy plainly bound in purple morocco. I would wish to have the back lettered thus "Memoir of Sir C.L. Eastlake – compiled by Lady Eastlake".

With 2nd series of Essays should this be too long then the word "compiled" might be omitted.

At the same time I ask all this in ignorance, not knowing whether it involves too much expense or trouble. If it does I must have the back remain as it is.

I think a couple or so of plain gilt lines – somewhat like the black ones – on the sides of the volume, will be advisable, but I wish for no indication of its destination.

I shall be greatly obliged by your having this executed as early as will be conveniently possible. If you wish me to give any further suggestion about the binding I shall be ready at any time for I am not leaving London again.

Believe me your's faithfully

Eliz Eastlake

Letter to John Murray   *NLS Ms.42177*

FitzRoy Square

11 Janry 1870

Dear Mr. Murray

I now send you the vol: of the 1st series of Contributions with such corrections as were left by Sir Chas on the margin of his copy – & with a few more which the interval hs suggested. For this purpose I have been going thro' the vol: carefully which must account for & excuse a delay which I much regret. But these corrections hardly amount to editing, & I see no reason for any allusion to that fact. Mr. B: Ker wishes his preface to be returned, & I will add a few words by way of explanation of the reprint. But this all in good time. I am afraid you may think it necessary to make this reprint in the same form as the 2nd series. If not, I shall be glad.

I observe what you mention regarding the binding or rather non-binding for the Queen. But as the vol: in question has been put in hand I shall thankfully await it – as if I err in the better binding it will be on the safer side.

I find that our German edition of Kugler – 2 vols – is 1847. If there be a later one I shall be glad of it. I will apply to Mr. Mündler to know what other works besides Cavalcaselle will assist to bring the History of art down to the latest discoveries.

I must trouble you to send 6 more copies of the Memoir – for which, as further 6, you can send me the account if you think that arrangement the best.

I hope by assiduity to make rapid progress with Kugler. I am not aware that you have published any edition since that of 1857.

Believe me your's faithfully

Eliz Eastlake

Letter to John Murray   NLS Ms.42177

FitzRoy Square
15 Janry 1870
Dear Mr. Murray

I fear you will think me very troublesome about this work but I am
more deeply interested in its success than I can say, tho', I need hardly
add, not in any mercantile sense further than that it should entirely
repay you its costs. I find that on friends applying for the work at more
than one of the large London circulating Libraries, the answer has been
"not known", "not heard of". I am aware that it is far too early to judge
from any opinion of its popularity – at the same time I cannot help
fearing that its title is misleading. I ventured to suggest to you that the
fact of the Memoir should be signified on the back, which I see you
have kindly complied with. Still, I think that if the back were lettered
"Memoir of Sir … &c with 2nd Series … &c" it would attract a larger
number of readers. Why I presume to say this thus <u>early</u> in the stage
of publication is because I believe that in an edition of a thousand your
binder has not yet completed his task, & that there would be time to
alter the lettering at the back.

This is for your consideration & at all events I beg that you will
excuse the liberty I take in making this suggestion.
Believe me your's faithfully
Eliz Eastlake

Letter to John Murray   NLS Ms.42177

FitzRoy Square
18 Janry 1870
Dear Mr. Murray

I am much obliged by the receipt of the vol: for the Queen. It is
bound quite as I wished, & I am particularly pleased with the title on
the back. I wish (barring the allusion to me) that could have been the
title on all the copies. I am glad that you will in this respect alter the
tenor of the advertisements. I have not seen any, but Sir Chas' nephews
have called my attention to the circumstance that in the advertisements,
R.A. is placed after Sir Chas' name. This is hardly consistent, & had
better be omitted.

I have not received any information concerning Mudie, for one, from

those who would in the least be expected to purchase the vol:. There seems to be some some [sic] misunderstanding as to "the Memoir". Believe me your's faithfully
Eliz Eastlake

Letter to John Murray   *NLS Ms.42177*

FitzRoy Square
20 Janry 1870
Dear Mr. Murray

I am very reluctant to trouble you again on a subject which I know is objectionable to you, but I have a duty to perform which must supersede other motives. The type and page of the proofs just received distress me much, and I feel that they can hardly fail to be prejudicial to the reprint. Is it <u>absolutely</u> necessary that these two works should be alike? They are far from being two volumes of the same book. I venture also to look forward to the possibility of a time when the Memoir and other Essays may assume – at any sacrifice on my part – a more pleasing form.

The 'Contributions', like all that was bequeathed to me, are very sacred in my eyes, and I feel a serious self reproach in allowing them to be thus reproduced, if such as result can be possibly averted.

Your entire indemnification is the first object in this matter, and if that can be secured without an exact outward conformity between these two works I hope that you will give my present suggestion a favourable consideration.
Believe me your's faithfully
Eliz Eastlake
I write this at once before the printer proceeds further.

Letter to William Boxall   *NG14/361870*

7 FitzRoy Square
22. Janry 1870
Dear Mr. Boxall

I have a favour to ask, & perhaps a claim to put in regarding the Nat: Gallery, which I put before you in <u>writing</u>. Our Tucker who has left me about 2 months ago is now anxious to obtain employment & has asked me to endeavor to procure for him a place in the Nat: Gal:

staff. Mr. Wildsmith's age will probably lead before long to a vacancy.
Tucker would wish to obtain the vacancy which would be occasioned
by Wildsmith's death or retirement. I am sure that you will not require
me to say anything in <u>recommendation</u> of Tucker. You know his entire
trustworthiness, & something of his excellent sense and habits of business
& order. He is also accustomed to treat pictures with great respect, & is
well used to cleaning glasses etc. Indeed there can be few men, if any,
so peculiarly gratified for such a post as he.

Will you kindly give this subject yr attention. I am ready to write
to the Trustees or to do anything that may promote the entering of his
name upon the lists of the Gallery service. I feel that as Sir Chas' long-
trusted servant & faithful friend he has, for Sir Chas' sake, a claim for
consideration – besides being so excellent an article himself.

Will you kindly dine here on Wednesday next (26th) at 7 o'clock.
You wd meet your admirer, Lady Fred: Beauclerk and I shd be truly
happy to see you.[1] You will also find good Mr. and Mrs. Williams
whom you may remember at Milan.

Yr's affly

Eliz Eastlake

Posted at Slough whence I return tomorrow only.

   1. Lady Frederic Beauclerk (née Jemima Johnstone) (d. 1877), a friend from her
     time in Edinburgh.

Letter to William Boxall   *NG14/371870*

7 FitzRoy Sqre

11. Febry 1870

I return you the Demidoff Catalogue with many thanks.[1] Certainly
it is not worth my spendg a guinea & half upon. The 'Nani' <u>looks</u> a
beautiful thing.

I think you said yesterday that there was a meeting of the Trustees
at hand in which the subject of the Library wd be mentioned. It is not
<u>for</u> me under the circumstances of its purchase by the Nation to make
<u>conditions</u>, but I have mentioned to you I think before – & I wrote to
Layard long ago – that I greatly wished it shd be called "The Eastlake
Library."[2] This was strongly urged upon me by our dear old friend
Waagen.

I must leave this in your hands, being quite aware on my own part
that <u>sellers</u> like <u>beggars</u>, must not be choosers. I will only add that

Layard quite agreed with me in the desire that it shd be called as I propose. If the Trustees see no objection to this it will be an additional inducement for me to add to the Library at some future time.

Yr's afftly

Eliz Eastlake

1. Prince Anatole Demidoff's art collection was sold in Paris in 1868 and 1870. Many paintings were purchased by the Marquis of Hertford for the Wallace Collection in London. Boxall purchased two paintings by Carlo Crivelli for the National Gallery.

2. See letter to Boxall, 31 January 1867, and letter to Layard, 6 May 1869.

Letter to A. H. Layard   *NLS Ms.42170*

7 FitzRoy Sqre

13. Febry 1870

My dear Mr. Layard

I have always, & with very good reason, given you credit for being as good as yr word, but this time your impediments have been so formidable & numerous that I am as astonished as grateful at what you thus early report. I shd like very much to see yr article before it is finally printed, or even in Mrs Layard's fair & beautiful writing. But in the 1st place your non consent to giving me such a privilege would have to be obtained, & 2ndly from authority of Reeve. I leave this to yr discretion & kindness. I am sure to like all you have said, & at the same time I am more sure to detect any trivial blunder than Reeve wd be. He has been very kind all along, & he let me know also that you had announced part of your task.[1] The memoir is slow in gettg known – owing I find entirely to the mess Mr. Murray has made of the advertisement & title page. I hear however that he goes about prais.g the book & he has lately altered the form of advertisment, putting the memoir more prominent. The Queen has sent me a gracious message, acknowledg.g both books & assuring me of the deep interest & sympathy with which she shall read them. Gibson's life goes on attracting far more notice than I ever expected, & I can conceive nothg more grateful to the dear old man's shade than this popularity of his biography. It appears to be a favourite both with old ladies & young ladies wh: is sufficient to make a book's fortune.

The other eveng I heard Professor Ruskin's lecture at the

R. Institution. He was so much in request that above 300 persons were
turned away from the door. I have little doubt that these consisted
mainly of young ladies, who were his great supporters within. Before the
lecture began he was going about benignly among their ranks & parts of
the lecture were graciously suited to their comprehension – some parts
were beyond <u>mine</u>, but upon the whole it was a brilliant, ridiculous, &
interestg performance. I believe afterwards the horses were taken off his
carriage & he was dragged home to Denmark Hill in triumph by his fair
bearers, but I did not stop to see. One part particularly pleased me & that
was an allusion to our landscape Bellini now in the Exhibtion which he
selected as an illustration of the perfection of Belllini's time. By the way,
Boxall has been sounding me as to parting with it, to wh: I replied that
I wd not undergo the pain of parting with another picture. But I added
what I see no objection to tellg you – namely that I will <u>leave</u> it to the
N.Gallery. I will add a codicil to my last made will to that effect, & let
you know when I have done so. Meanwhile I intend to put that picture
into the principal place in our front drawing room, where I shall have it
perpetually before my eyes. I expect it to be returned to me in less than
3 weeks. The success of the exhibition has been <u>great</u>. I have enjoyed
yr Savoldo much, not havg seen any specimen of that grand painter for
some years now.[2] Your Bramantino – so called – also looks to very great
advantage.[3] It stands on the line, with two others on one side of a door
– Lord Lothian's Albert Dürer & our Mantegna. The Albert Dürer is
surely as ugly as a fine thing can be.[4]

Boxall & I are now quite agreed about the Library, he is preparing
to receive it, I to give it up. I am therefore going through the books
carefully, & am struck by their multifarious character, as regards the
speciality of art. All my dear one's varied studies in art, technical &
philosophical are reflected in them. Tomorrow I begin to stamp a small
E [*a circular cartouche drawn around the E*] in each. This keeps me happily
busy. It is a prick to part with them, but I am thankful to do so as
now arranged. If you can tell me at yr leisure what best to do with the
money I shall be grateful.

The weather is now <u>biting</u> cold, with a storm of east wind which
apparently keeps the snow from coming down. I sit so close to the fire
that I run the risk of getting burnt before I get warm. The old & the
feeble will perish before this dreadful wind. Your aunt has been ill again
as you probably know, but writes me that she is recovering.

Mr. Grote has been suffering with bronchitis at Ridgeway, & the
Historian has been taking a hot bath & she assisted at his toilette, wh:
I only tell you as a proof of the renewal of happy relations! She is the
best of possible wives to him. He is now about to sit to <u>Millais</u> for his

portrait. The students of the London University have subscribed for
it. Millais' ugly but capital picture of an engineer has made Mr Grote
prefer him, & we went to him together & beat him down a little![5]

I can't succeed in getting anythg for our Tucker. He is above the age
for admission into Nat: Gal: or any governmt employmt. I know you
won't forget him & you know that he is a prize.

Give my love to yr Enid & tell her that I think of her with much
affection. Tho' I have said so little of her I am so glad she & nice
Mdme Riano foregather so well. Boxall tells me that his Marco
Marziale is coming out beautifully in the lining.[6] Now dear Mr Layard I
won't try yr eyes any further. Yrs always truly
Eliz Eastlake
I have two recent letters from Lady Strangford from Naples. She is
<u>rather</u> better in health & spirits.

1. Layard wrote 'Eastlake and Gibson' for Reeve's *Edinburgh Review*, vol. 131
   (April 1870), pp. 392–417.

2. Giovanni Girolamo Savoldo (1480–1548) was also known as Girolamo da
   Brescia.

3. Bartolomeo Suardi, known as Bramantino (c. 1465–c. 1535), Lombard painter
   and architect.

4. *The Virgin and Child with the Goldfinch*, formerly in the collection of Lord
   Lothian and now at Berlin; 'our Mantegna' is the *Holy Family with Saints
   Elizabeth and John*, now in the Gemäldegalerie Dresden.

5. Grote's portrait of 1870 by Sir John Everett Millais is now at Senate House,
   University of London.

6. Marco Marziale (active c. 1492–c. 1507). Henry Critchfield supplied the taber-
   nacle frame on Marco Marziale's *Virgin and Child enthroned with Saints* (NG
   804) in 1869. See Nicholas Penny, *The Sixteenth Century Italian Paintings*,
   vol. 1, *Paintings from Bergamo, Brescia and Cremona* (London: National Gallery,
   2004), p. 127.

Letter to A. H. Layard   *NLS Ms.42170*

7 FitzRoy Sqre
22 Febry 1870
My dear Mr. Layard

Last evening by yr kind permission, & Henry Reeve's concurrence,
I recd the slips of yr article.[1] I did not sleep till I had read it carefully

through. And my immediate impression of it, which I hasten gratefully
to report to you, is that I think it a most admirable performance. As
regards the dear object of the memoir your tone of praise & admiration
is in such excellent taste that, (tho' I have throughout the pen of a
loving private friend,) I feel that all you have said is eminently credible
to the cold public. At the same time the article abounds with a deep
& subtle criticism of your own, unsurpassed by anything you have
hitherto written on art subjects. I cannot thank you enough, dear Mr.
Layard. I have found kindness & fidelity to an old friend & much rarer
than the reverse that I cannot prize them too much when they are
displayed to me. As to the conditions under which you have executed
this kind task it would seen from the result that the more bothered &
interrupted you are the better!

I am especially grateful for the way in which you have brought
forward Sir Chas' views on the Philosophy of Art, so opposed to the
spurious & empirically shallow notions which now prevail in precept
& practice – by which Art properly speaking, would cease to exist
– by which things are attempted to be represented not so they seem,
but as they are. I wonder the Pre Raphaelites admit of perspective
at all.

I do not shrink from noticing your estimate of Sir Chas' art. God
knows how dearly I love it. Still, I have long felt that it was not his
highest power – & as my estimate of his intellect, & good moral
balance grew, it involuntarily rose above that of his art. Whether I
agree with you altogether in particular instances is of no consequence.
What you have said makes me the more pause as to whether to
attempt an exhibition of his works. I shall be grateful to you for advice
on this matter. I am inclined to think that it will be wisest to let
the R. Academy bring forward the best of his works in some future
Winter exhibition. But to return to your article, I am glad you have
combined the Life of dear old Gibson, tho' the comparison is most to
his advantage, for thoughtful & sublimely simple as he could be, he was
essentially incapable of cultivation – illiterate to the last, in this there
was great contrast between him & Sir Chas. But dear Sir Chas can well
afford not to have the comparison looked into too closely, & Gibson is
welcome to the advantage of it.

Then again I am so glad you have said what you have about Maclise's
frescoes. I have always felt the same. They are true works of the time
– the others are more or less imitations or failures, exceptg Herbert's &
that especially in his landscape background.

I have been interrupted writg this hurried letter, & Boxall has been
here, unburdening his great soul, & also comg to some arrangement

about the Library. I meanwhile have got forward with stamping, &
otherwise going through the books.

I am looking forwd to the pleasure of making your brother Col:
Layard's acquaintance on Friday eveng, when he will kindly come here
with his wife & daughters. Hooker & Reeve & Newton &c with ladies
will be driving here.[2] Such things are a great effort to me, & I wish you
& yr gentle Enid were here to give me courage.

From yr aunt I heard yesterday – still confined to her room with bad
cough wh: yields to nothing.

I have not yet succeeded in getting employment for our Tucker, &
meanwhile he has begged me in his last letter, if not too great a liberty,
to send his "duty to Mr Layard".

My kind love to yr wife
Yrs always truly
Eliz Eastlake
I have read the article again this morng with same result. I shall return
it to Reeve soon with a few unimportant suggestions.

1. Layard's article 'Eastlake and Gibson', *Edinburgh Review*, 131 (April 1870),
   pp. 392–417.

2. Her cousins Joseph Dalton Hooker and Henry Reeve; and perhaps Alfred
   Newton (1829–1907), the naturalist and friend of Hooker.

Letter [to Jane Rigby] copied to Hannah Brightwen
Private Collection

Mar 23. FitzRoy Sqre [1870]

I was putting up books in the Library when a telegram came. Of
course I took alarm thinking it came from you – but immediately I
saw it was from Lady Stanley[1] "will you come at 4.40 & meet the Lady
to whom you gave your 2 books" – The messenger waited for a reply
telegram which I sent – I felt the great kindness, though I rather dreaded
being upset by meeting Her whose sufferings I know so well – I had
also to take the Ensor girls a drive, but I managed that easily. I did not
give a thought to dress, having really all that was necessary for morning
costume, & I of course was at the Deanery in time – tho' servants told
me the Dean & Lady A were in the Abbey with her Majesty,[2] but that
I would find Prof. Owen & Mr Froude in the drawing room. We were
soon joined by Prof. Tyndall, Sir H. Holland & Mr Leckie [sic][3] – I
the only Lady – the drawing room is an inner room, entered through

another, no door between. Soon we saw the Queen enter with Lady
A. where she took off her cloke [sic] &c & noticed 2 little Bruce children
who were running about – Then she came in, – the gentlemen stood
nearest. She bowed smiling to them, & then came straight to me &
shook hands, telling me the deep interest with which she had heard
every word of the memoir. I said "I cannot thank your Majesty enough
for your kindness in accepting it". She said "I like it very much" & I
answered over-spontaneously "I knew you would." She added that she
was very glad to see me, & I thanked her for permitting me to have the
honour of seeing her. The Lady A seated her at a little tea table on a sofa
& poured out tea – mixing a little green with it, which she said "I know
yr Majy likes". The Queen took off her shawl & unpinned her bonnet,
& took off her gloves. Lady A turned away for a moment, & the Queen
quietly began to pull the little table close to her. I instantly assisted her
then Lady A. made me sit at the same little table & take tea too. Before
that the Q. said to Lady A "Introduce Lady Eastlake to the Princess".
The Princess & the Duchess of Roxburgh were her only companions,
the Pss was standing & shook hands kindly & said immediately "I have
so often heard of you dear Lady Eastlake" & then spoke of Sir Charles,
& I spoke of the Prince & of the older times. Then I sat down at the
Queen's table, & the Pss & Duchss sat at another little one – I asked
H.M. if her neuralgia pains were better. She said "I can't say they are
– if they are not in one part they are in another, but I suffer more from
bad sick headaches – & Lady Eastlake I am bitter in cold weather". I
answered that "I feared, however, that the Abbey had been too cold".
She said "No, on the contrary I told Lady A that is [sic] was too warm"!
Then Mr Froude came on her other side & I heard them speaking of
Don Enrique de Bourbon the Queen said " It was quite a disgrace the
funeral – no religious service at all – the freemasons took possession of
the coffin & played revolutionary tunes over it – but he was a terrible
scamp, & a thorough mauvais sujet in every sense".[4] She speaks with great
animation taking interest apparently in all she hears, & somthg was sd
about Ireland – & she laughed & blushed & said "they are unmanageable
indeed". Then Sir H Holland was had up to tell H.M. something about
the Sun which has been discovered – & Lady A. playfully alluded to
where he had been last summer – the mouths of the Mississipi – & the
Q said "O yes, I know how Sir Harry flies about". Lady A said that a
revolution was sure to break out immediately after a visit from Sir Hy.
& the Red Indians had been up in arms since he was among them – I
said to H.M. "it is fortunate Sir Hy does not cause such effects in your
Majesty's dominion" – At which she laughed screwing up her eyes as
dear Sir Charles has often described to me – Then there was a little

stir, & I moved to the Princess' table & sat near the Dss the Pss being opposite – & the talk was of various things – & I told H.R.H. that the new Jewish Synagogue near me was the the most beautiful building in London, & she expressed a wish to see it – & the little Dean joined & nice Prof. Tyndall – meanwhile the little children were about, the Queen nodding to them, & they handing her things. She set to work at her tea table like a hungry person, but shook her head at the cake & said she was obliged to be very careful. She looks very well, with fresh sweet colour – as for her expression it is perfectly <u>lovely</u> – the eyes so sweet, the smile is bright & sometimes so sad – so <u>natural</u> & unconscious she was in everything. She was there more than ½ an hour & then she rose, & Lady A went to fetch somethg, & she said –"what have I done with my little brooch, I know I had it" & the gentlemen began to look about the sofa, but I recollected the table havg been drawn close to her, & it drew back & there lay the brooch which she picked up for herself before any one could help. Then she stood & said a few words to the gentlemen, – then again came to me & shook hands, & the Princess the same, & so it was over. When Lady A came back from escorting her to the door she said to me "How do you like her"? – I said slowly, "I am <u>in love</u> with her" – "I never saw such sweetness & simplicity". The tears came into Lady A's eyes. Truly she is a <u>sweet</u> <u>woman</u> winning in look & way, with that sweet gentle attentive manner & perfect ease that made others at their ease. How different to the <u>prècieuse</u> Queen of Holland! <u>Our</u> Queen is the real <u>thing</u>. I said to Froude when she was gone "that Lady may defy <u>Historians</u>". He hummed & ha'ad & said we should all be gone before her History was written – but then acknowledged that it wd be difficult to put a hole in her – adding "I really think the Salic law should be <u>reversed</u>, & <u>no men</u> allowed to reign in future". I begged the Dean to let her Majesty know this. The Dss of Roxburgh told me she had been the reader to the Queen of the memoir.

1. Lady Augusta Stanley (1822–76), the wife of Arthur Penrhyn Stanley (1815–81), Dean of Westminster, who held regular salons at the deanery for Victorian intellectual society.

2. Queen Victoria's record of the meeting is more abrupt: 'Went to the Deanery for tea, where, as last year, were assembled some celebrities: Lady Eastlake, tall, large, rather ponderous and pompous'. See G. F. Buckle (ed.), *The Letters of Queen Victoria 1862–1878*, 2 vols. (London: John Murray, 1926), vol. 2, p. 12.

3. John Tyndall (1820–93), physicist, mountaineer, and Professor of Natural Philosophy at the Royal Institution; Sir Henry Holland (1788–1873), writer and physician; W. E. H. Lecky (1838–1903), historian and politician.

4. Don Enrique de Bourbon's funeral had taken place on 15 March in Spain.

Letter to A. H. Layard   *NLS Ms.42170*

The Ridgeway
8 April 1870
Dear Mr. Layard

It is long since I had yr last kind letter which deserved my thanks but the winter has found me so very busy that I have not troubled you with any tidings of myself. Now however I think you will be glad of a line from this hospitable little home, where I am truly enjoying the society of our kind friends, & also the first burst of warm Spring weather. The bad season has not been confined to Madrid, & I do not remember a more wearing winter than this has been. But now the thermometer is at 60 in midday, tho' still sinking below the freez.g point at night, so the poor buds are getting alternately encouraged & snubbed like many of their betters.

Mrs Grote ties up her face & talks of hoarseness but I hear & see no signs of anything but the utmost vigour of mind & body, so I trust the handkerchief is only for the becoming. Indeed she is exhuberant with wit & thought, & asserts the usual prerogative of walking me off my feet. The de Salis' have been here 2 nights – he always a most interestg man – & Professor Tyndall came yesterday, & seems the happiest & lightest hearted of men – albeit wifeless.[1] Yesterday we lunched at Albury Park, with the D: & Dss of Northumberland. I cannot say much for his Grace's social powers. I had known the place in yr old friendly atagonist Henry Drummond's time – it is a most lovely spot. Mrs. Grote & I walked through the Park yesterday under a glory of ancient trees. I stay on till Monday, keepg Mrs. Grote company, for other guests have dispersed today & I think she will add a scrap to this letter, with her usual weakness for you!

You will be glad to hear that the transfer of the Art Library has been made. The necessary preparations on my part were rather tryg & fatiguing. The Nat: Gal sent me an able expert to identify the volumes, & he spent the greater part of 5 days in that occupation – docketing the catalogue & handg over the books to the packers. Twenty five huge cases gradually left their old abode, & now that all is over I can truly say that I am very glad & thankful. Great treasures came out, & it appears that the appraiser recommended by Christie's was not quite up to the mark in knowg the value of books. But this, or rather the result – is just what I cd most wish. I consider the privilege of keeping Sir Chas' library together & placing it in such a position so very great that I cannot be grateful enough. This sense of obligation will probably

find expression on my part by my <u>giving</u> the Landscape Bellini <u>now</u>.
I have been takg time to make up my mind to such a step, & have
been consultg a few judicious friends. I must own that their advise
is all <u>against</u> this step, but I think my own desire to be <u>free</u> of any
imputations of picking the public pocket – such as were leveled at me
last summer, which you kindly answered – will carry the day. Of course
as a <u>Trustee</u> you must encourage my giving it now.

I have not seen Boxall very lately. I rejoice that Lord Taunton's
unfinished M.Angelo is secured for the Gallery.

Of modern works for the Exhibition I have seen none, except
Millais', wh: are a large exception. His portrait of Lady Huntly, yr
relative, is first rate, with that luminous treatment of <u>white</u> dress wh:
I admired so much in his picture of his three little girls. Also a knight
releasing an undraped lady who is bound to a tree is in some respects
<u>magnificent</u>. The knight's head, & hands, & armour make one think
of Albert Durer & Giorgione both. But he is not a <u>Correggio</u> in the
undraped lady!²

I find that owg to the kind energy of Mrs. Grote, who does all her
friends true & faithful service, there will be also an article on Sir Chas'
Life & Writgs in the Q.R: She has seen it, & approves – so that I am
now doubly gratified.³

I have had the honour to meet Her Majesty quietly one afternoon
lately at the Deanery (Westminster). She has been readg the memoir &
was most gracious & kind about it. I fell very much in love with our
thorough bred Lady, who seemed all attention to others & unconscious
of self. A few notable gentlemen – Froude, Tyndall, Leckie [sic] &c
– were there & nobody, after she was gone, seemed ever to wish for a
<u>King</u> again.

Now dear Mr. Layard I hope you are better & are not conscious of a
stomach! Tell your Enid that I think of her often, & rejoice to hear that
she is so well. I hope Madame Riano's troubles are over & that all is
right. With love to both of you I am ever yrs truly
Eliz Eastlake

1. John Tyndall had a proposal of marriage rejected.

2. Respectively refers to Millais' portrait *The Marchioness of Huntly* and *The Knight Errant*.

3. Francis Turner Palgrave, 'Sir Charles Eastlake and the English School of Painting', *Quarterly Review*, vol. 128 (April 1870), pp. 410–32.

Letter to William Boxall   *NG14/421870*

7 FitzRoy Sqre
18. April 1870

Your tidings, my dear Mr. Boxall, about our old friend & companion
in <u>art</u> have quite overpowered me! I did not know I loved him so well.
We exchanged most kind letters last summer & I asked him to come
and stay with me, wh: he could not do. May God, for Christ's sake,
receive him into His Kingdom. Who shall go next! Not, I assume, that
either you or I wd recoil from the summons – but while here I am
anxious to <u>cherish</u> the few that remain to me.

I have been much occupied or I shd have called in Welbeck Street
before going to my Mother at Slough. Now will you kindly come &
dine here on <u>Friday the 29th</u> (Private View day) at 7.30. You wd find a
small number, including Mr & Mrs Grote. Please send me an affirmative.

I shall be anxious to hear more about dear old Mündler, & if I cd
get a few particulars such as date & cause of death I would send a little
notice of him to the Times.[1]

I had a charming letter from Hatty Hosmer the other day – one of
those letters in which she indicates her higher & better nature, speaking
too most kindly of you.

Ever dear Mr. Boxall

Yr's afftly

Eliz. Eastlake

    1. See following letter.

Letter to William Boxall   *NG14/42/1870*

7 FitzRoy Sqre
21. April 1870

My Dear Mr. Boxall

Just a word – havg been interrupted – to thank you for your kind
letter. I had also rec.d that same sad form of summons. It receached me
on Friday just as the funeral must have been going on. You may believe
I joined in spirit!

Hav.g thus the requisite date, & aided by your previous letter, I sent
the little <u>dry</u> notice to the Times which appears here this morng, over
<u>Julian Fane!</u>[1] I have also written to de Trigneti, & shall doubtless hear

soon. I begged my sympathy to the brothers of whom we had seen one. There are also sisters – good creatures I believe living at his native place Kempfen in Bavaria (where Thos a Kempis came from.)[2]

I am truly glad that I shall see you the 29th at dinner, tho' I trust we shall meet before then. Remember me to Mrs Lloyd [sic] Lindsay who I trust is being gradually released from her <u>bonds</u>.

Ever dear Mr. Boxall yr's afftly

Eliz Eastlake

1. *The Times*, 21 April 1870, p. 3, col. B: 'There are many in this country who will receive with regret the tidings of the death of Mr. Otto Mündler ... Mr. Mündler held the appointment of travelling agent to the National Gallery for two year – an office which was abolished by the House of Commons. He continued to render excellent service to the National Gallery as an occasional coadjutor to Sir Charles Eastlake, whom he accompanied several times to Italy and once to Spain'.

2. Thomas à Kempis (c. 1380–1471), priest and writer.

Letter to William Boxall   NG14/431870

7 FitzRoy Sqre
4 May 1870
Dear Mr. Boxall

It has been my intention, as you are aware, to bequeath the Bellini landscape, lately exhibited, to the Nation. And you are also aware that I have for some weeks entertained the desire to present it during my life. I feel that the present time is, for two reasons, opportune. 1stly because its merits have been publicly acknoweldged; & 2ndly because I deeply feel my obligation to Her Majesty's Government in their recent purchase of Sir Charles' Art Library. Accordingly I beg you to state to the Trustees my wish to present this picture now. Sir Charles considered this landscape by Gian Bellini & the small picture by Pisano the most interesting and valuable ornaments of his collection, & it will therefore be the greater pleasure to me to see them both occupying places in the National Gallery.

The inscription I would wish attached to the picture is merely "Presented to the Nation by Lady Eastlake 1870".

Believe me dear Mr Boxall

your's very truly

Eliz Eastlake

Letter to William Boxall   *NG14/431870*

7 FitzRoy Square
5 May 1870
Dear Mr. Boxall

I am sorry that I did not know of the intention to give in the Times a list of all the pictures purchased by the Nation for the last few years. Perhaps you did not know of it yourself. I mt have wished to anticipate it by the presentation of the Bellini. However, you are aware that my mind was made up to that step or I may rather say I knew that my mind was made up – for I had the picture taken down from its long held place in these rooms about 10 days ago. But now I wish the gift to be formally accomplished & I subjoin a note to you wh: you will be able to submit to the Trustees, if that be necessary. Meanwhile will you be so kind as to have the picture fetched on Saturday afternoon – any time at 2 o'clock or after, when I shall be away. Critchfield knows that it stands covered in the Printing room.[1] I make no condition for this other than the inscription "Presented by Lady Eastlake to the Nation –1870".

But I particularly request – indeed condition to be consulted before any paragraph is put into the paper. Will you make Mr. Wornum understand that. I shd like the place (now occupied by the Beaucousin Titian) but I make no condition of that kind. I send the coachman with these letters, & if you have time I wd beg you to come here, & tell me whether you approve of my official letter to you – wh: need not be considered as irrecoverable if you do not. I shall be here until 3 o'clock.
Yours affyly
Eliz. Eastlake
Send a verbal answer to say whether you can come.

   1. Henry Critchfield, framemaker, frequently employed by the National Gallery.

Letter to William Boxall   *NG14/431870*

7 FitzRoy Sqre
6 May 1870
Dear Mr. Boxall

I enclose you a fresh version of my official letter – subject again to yr judgement. I have endeavoured to do better justice to the magnitude of

my gift & also to express myself in a manner so as to <u>secure</u> it to the
Nat: Gallery. The word 'inalienably' is subject to yr expunging – tho' I
think it may pass as a little womanly exaggeration in a lady's letter.

I conclude that the last paragraph about the Trustees is <u>formally</u>
necessary.

I have still adhered to my two reasons, & even to my expression of
gratitude towards H.M.'s Government since that has really been my
chief support in the painless resolution I have come to.

I depend upon your hav.g the picture fetched in a proper van.
Critchfield will know best whether to remove it with the glass <u>on</u>. The
R.A.'s fetched it with the glass <u>separate</u>, but returned it (driv.g very
slowly) with the glass on. I will leave the keys for him & shd be glad
to find one word from you on Saturday even.g say.g that it has arrived
safely – or to see you at any time on Sunday eveng.
Yr's afftly
Eliz Eastlake
I can now "speak with my enemies in the Gate".

Letter to John Murray   *NLS Ms.42177*

FitzRoy Square
17 May 1870
Dear Mr. Murray

I have been unwilling to trouble you with frivolous matters, tho' well
knowing that business is a necessity and a solace.

I have been in intervals of unavoidable interruption, engaged in
endeavouring to amalgamate the tangled fullness of Cavalcaselle with the
more barren order of Kugler – placing however the latter, in my own
feeling, far above Cav: in all but mere novelty and abudance of matter.
This abundance of matter is however not in itself desirable and involves
much which is superfluous and would be wearisome to the Kugler class
of readers. It will be I foresee a work of no ordinary difficulty to keep
the popular form which is so necessary.

In the first place I would wish to know whether you desire the work
to be kept within its present limits, i.e. 2 vols.

Also I shall be glad if you will tell me whether you wish the
amalgamation with Cav: to be openly declared – not only in title
page, but in such direct quotations from Cav: or I may find it desirable
to make. In most cases I shal <u>not</u> make direct quotations, but simply
embody his information in a briefer and more sane form. Of course I

allude to him by name, when signaling a distinct change of master's name, but my query is whether in case of quotation I should give the reference to Cav: vol: and page in notes?

I hope to derive considerable help from Sir Chas' numerous notes on pictures, but I have not yet advanced far enough into art proper to recur to those.

I anticipate that the task will be somewhat long but I look forward to periods of entire quiet when it will progress more uninterruptedly.

The German last edition seems as far as I have collated it with the English edition to contain very little that is new.

I was much obliged by the half dozen copies of the 1st vol: of "Contributions to the Literature &C".
I remain your's faithfully
Eliz Eastlake

Letter to William Boxall   *NG14/431870*

7 FitzRoy Sqre
18 May 1870
My Dear Mr. Boxall
I remark this morng the paragraph in the Times about the Bellini.[1] You remember the condition I made on presenting the picture that no paragraph shd emanate from the Nat: Gallery without my previously seeing it. I must conclude, as I am sure you wd observe my condition, that you cautioned Mr. Wornum regarding my condition.

If this paragraph emanates from Mr. Wornum I can only beg you to call the attention of the Trustees to this want of good faith towards me on the only point which I was anxious about. I was anxious not to be startled by the sight of my own name & anxious especially not to see the fact stated in the bad English in wh: it now appears. But whatever my motive, you will agree with me that my condition shd have been complied with.

If Mr. Wornum has done this in defiance of yr instructions I am perfectly ready to write to the Trustees & complain for myself.
Yr's afftly
Eliz Eastlake

1. The following notice 'On the Presentation of the Death of St. Peter Martyr' appeared in *The Times* on 18 May 1870, p. 11, col. B: 'This noble work of art is the munificent gift of Lady Eastlake. It may be remembered that on a former occasion she presented the National Gallery with a most valuable and

interesting picture by Pisano of Verona. This continued generosity will serve to associate the name of Eastlake more closely with the rise and progress of our fine national collection of pictures'.

Letter to A. H. Layard   *NLS Ms.42170*

7 FitzRoy Square
9th Octr 1870
Dear Mr. Layard

It is so long since we have exchanged letters, that tho' of course I am sorry to forego the pleasure of finding fault with you yet I fear I cannot do so this time with my usual justice, for I forget who wrote last. I felt for long that you were too much occupied with very weighty matters to be interrupted, & tho' I trust your hand is more relieved, yet your thoughts, like everybody's, must be engrossed with the tremendous history of the last two months. I don't think that the late ruler of the French was a hero of your's (tho' being a tremendous scamp perhaps he was!) but I do not doubt that you now share the prevalent feeling about him here. He has even lost the credit of being a clever knave, & the attribute of that folly which the Gods bestow on those they wish to lose is all that is left him. I give myself some credit for never havg given him a good word – even in the zenith of his successful villainy. He always appeared to me as little great as good, & that he could have held resolute sway for so long only shows what materials the French are made of. The cession of territory by France is necessary for the welfare of Europe, were it only as a precedent to show that she may be dismantled without the world coming to an end. The very vanity with whch the French stickle for a prerogative of which they have robbed so may other nations makes it necessary to break that spell. You are aware of old how little I like Germans, & especially <u>Prussians</u>, & their successes do not alter my opinion of them. We run the risk of exalting them to the skies now because they are successful – just as the Emperor was exalted while believed to be the same. There is great talk here of superiority of the Teutonic over the Latin races. At all events I doubt whether Prussian successes over decrepid Austria & rotten France suffice to prove the fact. & I hope that your knowledge of the Italians & even now the Spaniards may lead you not to give up on the Latin races.

I have been wandering about England for more than 6 weeks, & am only recently settled again in my lonely home. I started in the middle of August by joining the Grotes – Mr., Mrs & Miss – at Chatsworth, at the

nice Inn at the Park Gate where we were very comfortable & inspected
the treasures of the Great House at leisure. Sir James Lacaita was there
& opened everything to us.[1] Especially did Mrs G: & I enjoy the study
of the Liber Veritatis, which is a wonderful vol: just as it came out of
Claude's hands, with his handwritg on the old fashioned mountings,
usually telling in ill spelt French who the picture, wh: the drawing
represents, was for. The drawings are the result of years of the knowledge
of Nature – till only the permanent & therefore grander & more familiar
qualities seem to have been precipitated like a precious virtue on his
mind's sight. They illustrate much of my dear Sir Chas' pure philosophy,
& are preeminent for taste. Great <u>breadth</u> is the prevailing characteristic,
& the most graceful lines. You know the facsimiles, but the difference
between them & the originals is incredible.[2] Chatsworth is a perfect
museum. Some glorious pictures (I had Waagen's treasures with me),
some of them neglected, & an immense collection of drawings, with
a Mantegna among them of matchless beauty. The place itself too is
princely, & the woods of the grandest character. We drove about much
& Mr Grote was so happy in pouring over some old editions of rare
books as we over the Claudes. Then we drove to Matlock – ten miles of
great beauty – & that too enchanted me. I left them for Bolsover Castle
which is perfection in its way, & after that I was in Wiltshire with the
De Salis',[3] & then at Aylesbury with your friends the Tindals'. I found
them in great prosperity & happiness. All three young men & much (too
much for me) company going on. The sons are all promising, especially
Gifford who <u>must</u> be a remarkable man. Nico sticks to his art & <u>really</u>
has done things in the way of clever caricature which place him very
near Leach. His kind parents gave him a year more to consider well
whether he pursue out as a professional. Acton himself owned to me that
it was useless putting him into any office. I have never encourage the idea
of art as a profession, but I own now that I think him competent to be
the first in that line. He has much refined his taste, & is studying animals
carefully, & on a large scale. The horse he knows by heart.

   All were well there, the little girl only looking very seedy & delicate
& not brought up so well as I cd wish. Charles, the younger lad, has
left Eton & is now going to Oxford. They spoke (Mr & Mrs A.T.)
most kindly of you. I need not say that the Grotes did the same &
often. I went to them for a week at the termination of my holiday &
you will not wonder that I enjoy the Ridgeway more than any other
place. I am always more & more astonished at the richness & variety
of her gifts, which I admire the more from the <u>soundness</u> of her mind.
Her society is a perpetual feast to me. I am very fond of the fine old
man & that without any danger of giving the lady uneasiness!

Their way of life too has a charm scarcely found elsewhere in these luxurious times, for all is plain & fulfils my motto "the best of common things".

Now I have resumed my London life, & have taken up Kugler's Handbook of Italian Art with the firm intention of working hard at it. The object is to amalgamate such parts of Cavalcaselle with it as shall bring it up to present times. There never was such a wretchedly put together & expressed work as Cav's, & many of his opinions are crotchety. But I adopt his facts, & these give me plenty to do. I have also dear Sir Chas MS notes at hand, wh: I have arranged alphabetically & I draw also upon these. I hope to finish my labour by Xmas. I miss my old connoisseur's society more than I can say. In good Mündler I have lost a regular encyclopaedia of art learning. But the late events reconcile me more to his death. He wd have had to leave Paris. In good Boxall I find no substitute. His feeling is always excellent, but he has not energy to acquire the lore of art history. I have not seen him for some time, but he returns from the country tomorrow. Before I left London I met him at the Nat: Gallery, & he showed me the Porto Guaro [sic] Cima. I am enchanted with it. It is the finest possible specimen (now that no end of repaint has been stripped off) & moonlight was never so finely expressed. It is a glorious picture.[4] The two Marco Marziales also look finely, especially the one with numerous figures.[5] Boxall perseveres in the same grumble about leaving the position next Spring when the 5 years will be up. I shall much regret that. I know no one fit to succeed.

The Memorial in Hyde Park is becoming exceedingly beautiful, & Newton is quite a convert to it. He wants me to give an article on it, when finished, in one of the Quarterlys, but this is between ourselves.[6]

Had I been more at the Ridgeway Mrs Grote wd have written it with me. She was deeply interested in yr report of Spanish improvement. I trust you may have reason for continual hope. My short time in Madrid interested me much in the race. I hope you have had time now to do justice for the Gallery & I shall look for some ravings about Velasquez.

Your aunt called today whilst I was out. She wrote on the card the pleasing intelligence that she was "unusually well". I shall go to her soon. The Mohl's are in London. She has been ill, but is better & I her an airing yesterday. You may guess how full & profound she is on French matters.[7]

Now I have not mentioned your by far better half yet! Not because I do not think of her, for that I do most afftly & frequently. That

you shd be with the Spaniards in this difficult time, & she with you
is indeed happy for all. My most kind love to her, & some of it to
yourself

Yours always truly Eliz Eastlake

1. James Lacaita (1813–95), Anglo-Italian politician, writer and authority on
   Dante. He compiled a *Catalogue of the Library at Chatsworth [Compiled by Sir
   J .P. Lacaita]* (privately printed at the Chiswick Press, 1879).

2. Claude Lorraine's *Liber Veritatis* is a book of around 200 drawings recording
   his work. It has been in the British Museum since 1957.

3. William Andrew Salicus Fane de Salis (1812–96), businessman and barrister
   and brother of Henrietta de Salis. He lived at Teffont Manor, Teffont Evias
   in Wiltshire with his wife Emily Harriet.

4. Cima da Colegniano, *The Incredulity of St. Thomas* (NG816), an altarpiece
   made for the church of San Francesco in Portogruaro, north of Venice. It
   was acquired by the National Gallery in 1870. The protracted and complex
   circumstances surrounding this acquisition are detailed in Boxall's letterbook
   1866–70 in the National Gallery Archive NG14/25.

5. The National Gallery acquired Marco Marziale's *The Circumcision* (NG803)
   and the *Virgin and Child Enthroned with Saints Gall, John the Baptist, Roch and
   St. Bartholemew* (NG804) in 1869.

6. She did not provide an article.

7. The Mohls were Julius von Mohl (1800–76), orientalist and scholar, and
   Madame Mohl (1793–1883) (née Mary Clarke), whose salon in Paris was
   meeting place for French and English intellectuals. See Kathleen O'Meara,
   Madame Mohl, her Salon and Friends (London: Richard Bentley, 1885).

Letter to Mr Robinson   *NCM uncatalogued*

7 FitzRoy Sqre
9. Novr. 1870
Dear Mr. Robinson[1]

On my return from the country where I recd your kind letter, I find
the valuable vol: of which you have spared me a copy. I assure you that
I add it gratefully to a remnant of works on art which have remained
to me from my dear Sir Chas' Library. I have already read yr admirably
written introduction & remarked the note compromising the mention
of Sir Chas. As I had thus recently searched into the history of the
Lawrence drawgs I am the more interested in yr catalogue of the two

great masters. A fine oil sketch by Rembrandt in my possession – upon mill board – was among the Rembrandts of the collection. Christ before Pilate.

I am sorry the South Kensington has lost the benefit of yr services. They have been invaluable there, &, in yr admirable catalogues, <u>abiding</u>. Believe me yr's very truly

Eliz Eastlake

1. J. C. Robinson, curator at the South Kensington Museum until 1863. He remained in the service of the museum until 1867.

Letter to A. H. Layard   *NLS Ms.42170*

7 FitzRoy Sqre
Christmas Day 1870
Dear Mr. Layard

I have been writg to you often and for long in <u>intention</u> but now I will beguile a lonely eveng (for my Xmas day has been solitary) by calling myself to you. A kind letter from Enid which Mrs. Austen let me see, interested me deeply by the account of the Escorial visit, & unexpectedly I came upon a kind remembrance of myself at the close for which pray thank her with my love. But especially I must thank you for your long & interesting letter of the 23rd October, even tho' it kept you <u>unwillingly</u> from church! I did get the No. of the St. Paul's which you mentioned & read it with deep interest & appreciation of the writer's sagacity & presience. I read some of it to Mrs. Grote. Of course we were inclined to give <u>you</u> the credit for the authorship – but somehow we missed the <u>wickedness</u>, & thought it not clever enough, & too wise! The more so considering that the happy event had then not taken place which has since crowned the edifice & made it all it ought to be! But you know that you are in very partial hands between us two, though Mrs. Grote calls you many more names than I venture to do.

I have been at the Ridgeway two or three times since I wrote to you – always more & more enjoying the company of two such first rate minds. Indeed I cannot be thankful enough for the solace which their friendship has afforded me. It has been one of the means for helping me <u>up</u>, for some depression & disappointment & exhausted strength had made me lose all self confidence. Few can know, as I do, how excellent our two friends are.

And I have been getting acquainted with another friend, or rather acquaintance of your's. Good Mdme Mohl. She is here, as you probably know, having come for her annual London visit in June, never dreaming that a fallen Empire would obstruct her return. M. Mohl had to follow her in due time, having had immediately after the declaration of War a conversation with the Duc de Gramamont wh: is too long to tell, but which sounds now incredible. Mdme Mohl fell very ill with distress of mind, & I first found her in a little home in South St & gave her a few airings in open carriage. Since then she has slowly been regaining strength as was good enough to give me ten days of her company – a pleasure which I hope she will soon repeat. M. Mohl puts up at a certain Mdme <u>Schwabe's</u>, but sees his wife daily, & so I saw much of him too. Mdme M: is a most delightful companion – imperishably <u>young</u>, but with a fund of experience & knowledge of the world which have not in the least impaired her heart. I do believe she would stand warmly by a friend unjustly accused, & this is indeed rare. She tells me that you came with your Enid & saw her in Paris, but that she does not know you as she would wish to do. We talked too about the <u>latin races</u>, & having an insufferable objection to taking even any credit to ourselves in which Germans would share we endeavour to persuade ourselves that it is the <u>Roman church</u> & not the latin race which is in fault. If we could see the one tried without the other I think no race would deserve better justice. Such men as Père Hyacinthe are encouragement to that hope. That good man is now at the Deanery (Westminster). Kind little Arthur & Lady Augusta looked him up at an hotel – a stranger to them – & carried him off to their comfortable home.[1] I met him there the other day & had a little conversation with him. I had read some of his "Conferences de Notre Dame", <u>noble</u> things, & struck upon the string of 'La Famille' which the good father expatiated as most glowing in theory (in those Conferences however little he may know it practically.) He told me how terribly domestic life has declined in Paris under the Empire & that <u>Haussmann's</u> houses were a positive hindrance to it. Then I heard him lecture the other day to an immense audience of French understanding people, on France & Germany & the present struggle, from a moral point of view. I have had no opportunities of knowing what <u>eloquence</u> is (since I never attend the H: of Commons!) but I suspect that the good father came very near to the best sort.

Of course people talk & read of little else but the war, & it is something terrible to feel that the very <u>sameness</u> of the horrors is becoming wearisome. I retain my <u>definition</u> of feeling towards the combatants. I condemn the French, but I <u>abominate</u> the Germans. I have no fears of their meddling with us, or even with others for long, but a great military despotism in the heart of Europe represented

by a people who have never fought for the <u>own</u> national freedom
is a terrible thing. I attribute their success in aims to two things, to
the <u>incapacity</u> of the French (as of the Austrians) & to the enslaved
condition of the German soldier. The slave makes an excellent fighter,
to wit the poor Russian, & the Germans think much more of serving
than their pharisaical King than of serving their country. It will be
deeply interesting to watch the working results of their unity. I have no
confidence in it as regards the real dignity & independence of man.

I saw something of Dr de Mussy, who attends Mdme Mohl. He is
<u>miserable</u> & only attends misery now in his numerous patients among
the refugees. He sees the Orleans princes frequently, suffering intolerably
in their enforced inactivity. He tells me that they receive hundreds of
letters entreating them to come forward, but the volcano will have many
more eruptions before it cools down for them.

I quite agree with you about Velasquez, tho' he is a <u>king</u> in his way,
& we <u>miss</u> nothing in him. His aim & forte was individual character, &
therefore he always failed in the ideal. His Apollo & Vulcan is a most
unsatisfactory specimen, but his <u>dwarfs</u> are each a type, & even in the
crucifixion he gives the <u>character</u> of <u>death</u>.

I hear from Boxall (who is hanger) that the exhibition of old masters
at the R. Academy will be <u>magnificent</u>. The Private View will be on
Saturday. I lent the Bellini Holy Family & Saints, & the two small Cima
single figures. Their chief strength is from Lord Ashburton who has made
them welcome to all they wished for. His glorious Rubens Wolfhunt is
alone an exhibition. Also I easily persuaded Mrs Culling Hanbury to
lend her fine things (the Eardley pictures) – two <u>first rate</u> large Murillos,
a grand Vandyck & a Balthazar Gerbier family by Rubens.

Also we have got an old master exhibition for the benefit of the
French Peasantry, to which the Duke of Wellington has lent his <u>gem</u>
of a Correggio (I had no idea that it was so exquisite) & his many
Velasquez's. Also Miss Coutts has lent her little Raphael – a predella
picture, formerly Mr. Rogers, & three more pictures from these walls
are gone there. There are also drawings & pictures on sale, & several
by French refugee artists, for the same purpose, & the first day £1000
worth were sold.

I have seen Boxall frequently lately – a mixture of enthusiasm &
misery, enthusiasm for the pictures England contains & misery for his
fatigue in hanging them. The Reeves have also dined quietly with
me. I coolly asked him to tell the truth about that article attributed
to Gladstone. He affected to be surprised that people do not attribute
it to himself! I am inclined to believe that <u>possible</u>, for I do not see
Gladstone's long sentences in it.

Millais has finished the portrait of Mr. Grote. It is a strong likeness, but I think he might have done more for it as a work of art. But the head is finely painted, especially the brow. Mrs. Grote is not satisfied, but I tell her wives are too vain! I make no doubt your Enid is! I hope you & she will see it at the R.A. Exhibition & I hope we shall see her's by Palmaroli there.[2] Meanwhile I am in love with Madrazo (shut up I hear in Paris) & if I had the slightest excuse for increasing the works on these walls I should treat myself to a picture of a black browed, sultry lipped Spanish girl now in the French Exhibition.[3] By the by Boxall loses no opportunity of trying to clear up the question about the prices of the Chas I pictures sold to Spain. I am afraid he has not succeeded yet. We all get as far as Vertice's Catalogue but no further.

My dear Sir Chas was much struck with that Flemish picture in the Formento, but he gave it no name beyond 'School of Van Eyck'. I have looked at his works in order to confirm the impression.

I am working at Kugler, having just got through the first vol: I have had the greatest pleasure in rereading your histories of Ghirlandajo, Gio: Santi, & Pinturrichio. They are masterly, & I have cribbed a good deal.x

I do not feel the Duke & Duchess D'Aorta interesting enough to ask you about them, tho' I shall be very glad to have your impressions. Sir Jas Lacaita tells me she is "ugly & ill mannered".

I have not seen your aunt lately, & have had but poor accounts of her. Old Mr. Hardwick is believed to be really dying now. He has indeed suffered long. I won't apologise for the length of this letter for I know you will forgive that.

Ever your's truly

Eliz Eastlake

xDid you not do another for the Arundel Society?[4]

1. Père Hyacinth: Charles Loyson (1827–1912), French preacher best known for opposing the doctrine of papal infallability. The reference to 'little Arthur' is on account of Dean Stanley's short stature; the Queen referred to him as 'the little Dean'.

2. Vincente Palmaroli y Gónzalez's portrait of Enid Layard is in the British Museum.

3. She is referring to the painter Raimundo de Madrazo y Garreta (1841–1920).

4. The Arundel Society was founded in 1848, ostensibly for the purpose of preserving a record of the colour and appearance of early Italian frescoes in what seemed to be the likely event of their destruction at the hands of negligent Italian officials. Funded by public subscription, it issued engravings

and chromolithographs after Italian frescoes and paintings. Layard was an active member, identifying works for copyists and making his own tracings of frescoes presumed to be in danger. He wrote several 'descriptive notices' for the Arundel Society, including *The Frescoes by Bernardino Pinturicchio, in the Collegiate Church of S. Maria Maggiore, at Spello* (1858) and *Domenico Ghirlandaio and his Fresco of the Death of Saint Francis* (1860).

Letter to William Boxall   *NG14/52/1871*

7 FitzRoy Sqre
10 Febry 1871
Dear Mr. Boxall
    Will you, before you make my heart very heavy by vacat.g yr position, give me an order of admission to the Library at the Nat: Gallery. As I know the look of the books so well I shall not be hindered by the absence of a catalogue. I only want permission to have access to the books unrestrictedly – so as to take a few notes necessary for my present Kugler work.
    I have had a long & interesting letter from Layard since we met. He never writes a hurried or an ordinary letter, however illegible the writg. I make it all out tho'.
I hope you continue to get better
Ever yr's afftly
Eliz Eastlake

Letter to William Boxall *NG14/54/1871*

7 FitzRoy Sqre
25 March 1871
Dear Boxall!¹
    I am surprised at my audacity in calling you thus – the appellation familiar between my Beloved one and myself – but I cannot quite yet fashion myself to your new name. Tho' it is in one sense as gratifying to an old friend, and more so, than it can be to you. Indeed I am quite proud for you and grateful to our Queen for thus giving distinction where it is due. I only wish for you that yr dear sister or some one dearer still were at your side to take pride & pleasure in the honour or share it.

But you have many friends to whom it will give sincere pleasure, & as for yrself I know well how justly you value, or rather despise the transient favours of this Life.

It will all be over soon for both of us.

Many thanks for your company last evening.

Your's affectionately

Eliz Eastlake

1. Boxall had received a knighthood.

Letter to A. H. Layard   *NLS Ms.42170*

7 FitzRoy Square

2. April 1871

My dear Mr. Layard

My last letter to you was written on Christmas Day 1870, your kind letter came to me on Febry 1 1871. So it is high time for me to trouble you again, the only hesitation being that I have so little worth narrating. Your letter was very interesting – despite the rust that your fancy is accumulating, & therefore you can always keep me alive by contradicting me – a good old habit which I am delighted to find you have not left off. Meanwhile we have been kept alive here partly by the misery & the folly abroad, & partly by ceaseless exhibitions of pictures at home. The last fillip being the knighthood of dear old Boxall who yielded to temptation & forsook the ranks of the Great Refusers. But of him more further on. The Exhibition of Old Masters at the R. Academy was almost as fine as the Madrid Gallery, tho' somewhat differently composed, yet comprising a few grand Venetians & the stupendous Wolfhunt by Rubens (Lord Ashburton's). The fashionable criticism was that there were too many good things, wh: meant that people who wanted to do the whole in a January afternoon's visit found themselves not half way thro'. Interesting works turned up from unheard corners. I reported all I knew of my native county (Norfolk) & others did the same. The riches of England are incredible in the way of art & one can trace different strata of taste or fashion according to the period of collection. Having seen so much myself I am pretty sure that what is new to me is the same to the public. Of course there were no end of misnomers & indeed the catalogue was a disgrace to a body of Printers. Great names were taken in vain, all the nameless Quattrocentisti were the Lippi or Bellini, & in more than one instance where they happened to be right by mistake in the first edition of the meagre catalogue they corrected it wrong in the second. Lord

Dudley's collection was almost all there & much disappointed was I with
it. I had not seen his pictures for years. Many of his pictures are merely
poor school works – his Perugino, his Bellini, his Francia &c some of
his Greuzes false. His Salamanca Murillos coarse & black, while his true
masters are laden with dirt & old varnish, the fine Fra Angelico Last
Judgement especially. Indeed the great drawback in the exhibition were
the many neglected & almost perishing works – Vandyck so dry that the
surface is all obliterated, precious small pictures left without a glass, or if
with one so close & so dirty as entirely to obscure. I fancy I recognized
Morelli's 2 angels by Moretto, in the possession of "John Samuel Esq".
I understand that the Royal Academy are repenting themselves of their
original announcement not to appropriate any of the profit from the
Old Masters Exhibition to R.A. purposes. They seem a very divided
discontent body, & no R.A. comes near me without assuming that I must
be a willing listener to the pecadillos of their President. My invariable
question in return is "why does not the Academy call him to order?"
As I was poring over Cavalcaselle's 4th vol: while this exhibition was
open I was the more interested in his remarks on a picture or two which
happened to be true. Mr. Baring's so called Van Eyck, "a philosopher in
his study" is pronounced by Cav: to be Ant: da Messina & I think there
is no question of it. That life has particularly interested me, & I am glad
to have his rectification of the supposed date of the Berlin Antonello –
1445 – which has been quite a puzzle, also the impossibility of his having
learnt his art from John V. Eyck, tho' of course in Flanders. This vol:
of Cav: interests me much, the enormous influence of Mantegna is not
exaggerated, but it gives me a tremendous deal to do in bringing Kugler
up to present time – indeed I can't help making it almost a new book.
Cav:s indefatigable research is beyond all praise. I am amused at the way
in which he melts 2 or even 3 painters down into one. As Cordelle Agli,
[sic] alias Previtali &c. He does not admire Mantegna, or Carpaccio, or
Cima eno' for my liking, but he does justice to old Gio: Bellini & to his
wondrous power of landscape in his latter days. I have been pursuing
this task thro' much interruption & have been quite hindered for the last
fortnight by long letters & much business, & too many engagements.
There has been no end of dinners, & I have been insensibly drawn in
more than I like. But people are kind, & I have no longer the privilege
of seclusion. Also our excellent friends the Grotes have been all along
in Saville [sic] Row, owing to the anxiety about him of wh: you have
doubtless heard. Great care & prudence have apparently arrested a
formidable disease, but I greatly fear that nothing will cure it. The dear
old man is much pulled down & is kept a close prisoner to a few rooms.
A few warm days allowed him to venture out, but a little too much

exercise set him back. I dined there quietly on Friday but he was not able
to be at table tho' we went up to him afterwards. Now Mrs Grote has
had a bed put up in his little library thro' the dining room where he will
have his books about him, & see his friends more easily.

Boxall's return to office will have interested you. It relieved my
mind greatly. Mr Gladstone had employed all his persuasion to induce
Richmond to accept the office, & R: came to me to hear how far the
duties were compatible with the profession of a popular painter. I felt it
my duty to urge him to accept, for I knew him to be eligible in some
respects, & succeeded, as he subsequently told me, in making him very
miserable by shaking his objections. But the arguments of a family of 14
childn, & the fear of disturbing a profession of more than £4.000 a year,
& his <u>peace</u> beside, triumphed in the end. I wonder yr beloved friend Mr.
Cole did not bid for it![1] The purchase of the Peel pictures is just what the
Gallery wanted. Boxall seems to have conducted the business with great
tact & courtesy & to have added Sir Robt P: to his numerous friends. He
can manage everybody, except Mr. Wornum! However, I believe he trusts
to the power of a title for keeping <u>him</u> in better order. I hardly know
what other inducement our good friend can have had! The Peel pictures
are now being carefully washed by Bentley, & Boxall reports them as
expected. He tells me he has written to you about the Trusteeship. I
conclude you must give it up for a time wh: I shall regret much.

The Buchanans have been in England, she for some time, he only
a month. They lunched quietly with me & were much interested in
hearing about you & yr Madrid doings. They are excellent people &
have no "crowned-head ways" as Mrs Grote calls fashionable follies.
One of his daughters is about to be married to Sir Geo: Bonham. They
left for P.S. last Saturday.

I have taken no part in either of the great <u>home</u> events – the marriage
of the Pss, & the opening of the Albert Hall. Both are in some respects
<u>experiments</u>. The Hall looks ill at a distance, being low & formless in
outline, but seen near, it has much to commend it, & is both sumptuous
& elegant. Much depends on its keeping its agreeable colour, wh: I
believe is warranted by Mr Cole, whose latest offer is to pull down all
<u>London</u> & build it again in his particular terra cotta! The other day I had
a visit to the female classes of art at S. Kensington. The young ladies have
all the advantages that their seniors went without. There are no less than
300 female pupils & Kensington is filled with boarding homes for their
accomodation. The only pity is that the fruits are so small & that the
young ladies do not draw near so well as their unfortunate seniors. They
are certainly not efficient pioneers of <u>Woman's Rights</u>. One object of my
visit was to find one of the great 300 who could make a copy of a crayon

drawing, but the Superintendent, Mr. Burchett, could not recommend
one, & I am obliged to put up with a male hand!²

I have seen your aunt lately, & found her as well as usual – always
much cheered by a letter from you & yr Enid. She looks quite as well
as usual. I hear from her of yr projected visit to Toledo in Passion week.
(this week). I was there for a day, & felt that it was truly Spain, & that
the landscape view from the town had supplied – or rather recalled –
Velasquez's tawny green backgrounds. There was much to sketch if I cd
have been there long eno'. The Cathedral, like all Xtian architecture in
Spain, is late, but just not too florid, as Burgos in Cavalcaselle mentions
a Pietà by Bellini in the Sacristy. I hope you have looked it up.

I shall envy Morelli his visit to Madrid & shd seriously think of one
(during your reign), did not my mother's great age prohibit all thought
of my going anywhere out of England, & ever of taking a country
place & growing beet or sugar or some other mercantile agriculture
wh: I shd dearly like. Last week I spent two days at Aylesbury with our
Tindal friends who are very flourishing, & where I was favoured with a
perusal of yr letter to her. Meanwhile they have heard 2 or 3 times from
Nico, who was greatly struck with the excellence of the beefsteaks &
splendours of the ladies' dresses at New York. The young ladies in Bricks
are very forlorn at his loss & valentines were very active before he left &
wonderfully worked slippers wh: mt not suit a miner's life have come to
hand since his departure. Gifford & Charlie were at home, both ardent
students & were fine fellows. Giff: especially is of no ordinary stuff. Your
friend Acton is very sanguine about his silver mine venture wh: is to
return his capital in no time. Meanwhile Nico has telegraphed for £4.000
more "immediately". I have perfect confidence in Tindal's good sense, &
for a word, he wd be off to America himself. Indeed he seriously thinks
of a trip to New York. She, on the other hand, hopes that next winter
may be spent in Italy & rebels about New York! They are most excellent
people & it is a great pleasure to see them in ever increasing prosperity.

I don't venture as to the question of Latin & Teutonic races! But
to the Roman church not succeeding with the Teutonic races I fear
that the predominance of that, to me, most unintelligible of all forms
of worship – the Anglican High Church – is a sad instance to the
contrary, unless it comes under the category of dissent, where I venture
to place it. I have been going deeper still, and have broken my head in
following Wallace's volume 'On Selection', a colleague & fellow thinker
of Darwin's, but less cruel. Perhaps the High Church are derived from
the lowest organisms!

You have not sent me a photograph of yr wife from Palmaroli's
portrait. I shall be most glad to possess one. I admired a head of her,

with a rose in hair, sent to Mrs Tindal. An equestrian picture of poor
Prim struck me much at a French Exh:, by one <u>Regnault</u> – since killed
at Paris.[3] It was an imitation of Velasquez, somewhat like <u>Matinzo</u>
whose art I admire much. Are you not glad I have only brought in the
name of <u>Paris</u> at the very end of this selfish letter! My kind love to Mrs
Layard, ever yr's most truly
Eliz Eastlake

1. Sir Henry Cole (1801–82), arts administrator and superintendent at the South
   Kensington Museum. See Elizabeth Bonython and Anthony Burton, *The
   Great Exhibitor, The Life and Work of Henry Cole* (London: V&A, 2003).

2. Richard Burchett (1815–75), artist and art teacher at the South Kensington
   Schools.

3. A painting of General Juan Prim by Henri Regnault (1843–71).

Letter to William Boxall   *NG14/59/1871*

Slough
21 September 1871
Dear Sir William
    Your kind letter of the 19th has followed me here, where I have
been with my dear Mother since the 9th. I can assure you at once
that she has so <u>marvellously</u> recovered that we have really no present
anxiety. She has a wonderful constitution, and there is no disease. We
have been watching her very carefully, and my sister's devotion to her
never flags – <u>she</u> seems sometimes the most fragile of the two. Under
the circumstances I am thinking still of venturing abroad. I feel rather
bound, now that our anxiety is removed, to fulfil a plan for which
good Miss Lane had prepared herself with such <u>delight</u>, and which
gave her father so much pleasure. I have not great <u>steam</u> on myself, but
should wait for that in vain!
    As for the Holbeins they are or were rather the pretext for a little
refreshment, and picture seeing. I have been very fagged this summer,
and my servants are taking holidays – and coach, home and stables are
being painted &c. So that I am rather turned out.
    I am glad you are with kind M. Baring, and I trust the country air
and <u>fare</u> will do you good.
    I you should be in London on Saturday, would you let Sacchi bring
me <u>Waagen's</u> little pamphlet on the Dresden Gallery which is among
those you kindly lent me. You shall have it safe on my return. If I go

I hope to see Berlin, Brunswick, Cassel and Frankfurt as well – all for their galleries!

I am only grateful when I see your handwriting at all – and never had yet "a poor letter" from you, tho' you are not such an incorrigible scribbler as I! Ever believe me your's affectionately
Eliz Eastlake
Your catalogue shall go to Crowe at Leipsic whom I hope to see – anything else I should be glad to do.[1]

1. Joseph Archer Crowe (1825–96), co-author (with Cavalcaselle) of the *History of Painting in Italy*. Crowe was British consul at Leipzig until 1872.

Letter to Hannah Brightwen   *Private Collection*

Berlin Hotel d'Ingleterre
9. Octr 1871
I am glad to take up my pen to you, my darling Hannah – I have been writing to you <u>all along</u>, only not on paper! – for you know how constantly you are in my thoughts giving me that 'fellowship' wh: is one of the few sources of comfort to a mourner. And yesterday I made my way to young Harriet Hooker, & ascertained that you are still with dear, suffering Maria. I know that you take it all as part of the Divine <u>plan</u> that she shd thus approach the gate of the Better Land & that you shd minister to her within sight of it. Life (<u>mortal</u> life) becomes fuller & fuller if such scenes & duties as we advance all helping us to forget our <u>transitory</u> state & to realize that our <u>turn</u> to go Home will surely soon come. As for the physical that may still try us, let us leave it all in His Hands. I am sure that you & I have known the <u>worst</u> that mortal hearts can go thro' – <u>all</u> comes comparatively light after it. Sorrow & pain we still must have, but agony comes but once!

I pray for yr dear Maria – that He "may spare the pains of the body & grant the comfort of His grace".

You will be glad to hear that I am thus far in tolerable comfort – all has gone smooth & my companion is truly suitable in unselfish thought, & intelligent sympathy, but "still I know – whe'ver I go – that there has passed away a glory from the Earth". I have been able in a limited sense to enjoy those things which <u>he</u> taught me to love – to bear to be in galleries which recall him at every step. & I am most thankful to have this <u>capacity</u> again. Only <u>Time</u> has brought it. You know how long that time has been. In truth I care for <u>nothing else</u>. Of course

I love sweet nature, but there is little of that in German wastes. Our crossing was smooth & tranquil – & we go on to Brussels that night. Then next day all was rain & puddle. I drove about a little to show my companion the exterior of the sumptuous Hotel de Ville &c, & then we got on to Cologne. There a day was spent, & a letter from dear Jane made me quite envy to go on. There we were hours in the Gallery, also well known to me. & with <u>his</u> notes on it in my hand! very interestg was that gallery to me. The early Cologne School havg certain affinities with that of Murano, wh: proves contact as quite possible. Then there was solemn Cathedral where we sat & rambled, & other older & grander churches of which we saw the exteriors. Then off next morning at 7.30 for <u>Brunswick</u> – a good 8 hours journey – but such a pretty place! A kind of Nuremberg – old carved houses with projecting stones & fine gothic churches & <u>RatheHaus</u> – & then there is an interestg gallery, with examples of Rembrandt & his school, showg how often & not ignorantly the scholars pass for the master. Too many of them are very fine painters. Brunswick was really a <u>pleasure</u> – & Clara Lane delighted in it. Then to odious Leipsic – little to be seen there but the <u>fair booths</u> which gave the hotel keepers the excuse of charg.g every thing double![1] Finally to Dresden on the Saturday eveng (Septr 30th) – the chief end & also reward of my exertion. That was deeply interestg – & Holbein Exh: & gallery gave us enough to do & think but the weather was very bad – cold & rainy – & I was not well, took cold & got pain my teeth, & then a swelled face. However I gave myself rest, & <u>quinine</u> & have done very well. The rival Holbeins were the great objects of talk, & of my thoughts. & we met intelligent English acquaintances – a Mr Atkinson & a Mr Nattali – both slightly known to me – the last Sub Librarian to H:M: at Windsor. I examined both pictures very minutely – the question is a <u>puzzle</u>. The Darmstadt picture is the first – & in many repects the finest, in some respects also the <u>inferior</u>. In short the Dresden picture being an <u>improvement</u> upon the other in certain portions & in its altered proportions connot be called a <u>copy</u>. But the question is made one of <u>party</u> now – & quarrels run high, & people scream & voiciferate before the two pictures which stand side by side. It was curious to look into pictures so much alike, & yet differing in minute & very significant particulars.[2] The Dresden people are very sore, for <u>Prussia</u> has no mercy & Berlin people call the Dresden Mad: abominable names. Well if they cd do no worse to poor subjugated down trodden Saxony! who [sic] King is a mere puppet now moved by wires from Berlin which is <u>hated</u>.

Here in Berlin we have been since Friday eveng – & spent all Saturday on the Gallery. To day it is shut! under pretext of cleaning! – so I have decided to remain all to morrow – for the Gallery is more interesting to me in its Italian Schools than Dresden. All the more recently formed collections have a higher standard of knowledge evident. To day we have been seeing other collections – with Anna Waagen the daughter of our old & dear friend the late Dr Waagen.

We leave this on Wednesday – & get to Cassel in 8 hours. There a splendid gallery awaits us, & perhaps we shall stop two days – thence, on Saturday to spend Sunday in Frankfort. Then probably on Monday to Mageme & down the Rhine to Cologne, & so by Bruges to Ostend – gettg back, I trust on Thursday or Friday week – 19th or 20th.

Meanwhile several letters from Jane have comforted me. The dear aged Mother is as well as normal. Keeping her bed, however, till 3 in the afternoon which is a very wise arrangement.

Now, dearest, farewell. I am glad to find myself getting quite too old for traveling, tho' still able to care for that study wh: helped to bind us together. God give you & me grace for that study which is alone worth living for, & in which all minor sources of interest are included. In Him are all creatures & all things – Seeking Him first, all things will be added, & that grace will come to yr bleeding heart with time, patience & trust. May He especially support dear Maria in this hour & give you strength to commit her entirely to His Love & Wisdom thro' our blessed Saviour.

Ever yr loving friend & cousin

Eliz Eastlake

I found Ht Hooker a modest gentle girl – quite happy & interested in gettg on in German &c.

1. Three annual fairs in Leipzig, especially for the sale of books, crowded the city.

2. The Holbein Exhibition at Dresden brought two versions of the Madonna – the Dresden Madonna and the Darmstadt Madonna – together for the first time.

Letter [to Jane Rigby] copied for Hannah Brightwen
Private Collection

Cassel

12. Octr 1871

Dearest Jane

"I felt I ought to make use of the rare fine weather to leave my name with our Pss at Wilhelmshöhe. I felt this to be a duty, tho' of course

an unwilling trouble. So I had a good carriage & laquais de place &
drove out – it is about 3 miles – thro' a straight avenue after which the
road rises & we wound to the right, & came in by the garden front. I
enquired for the Gräfin Brühl, her lady in waiting, whom I had met
in London. Both Pss & she were out, which I was glad of – so I left
my card to be delivered to the Pss, in case she had any commands for
England. I heartily trust I shall hear nothing further for it would bore
me dreadfully to drive out again. As it was, we drove to the usual
sights of Wilhelmshöhe – a fresh gigantic building at the top of the
wood, quite a climb – surmounted by a Hercules, 36 ft high – whence
all the waterworks issue – the view was splendid from it, & Clara has
enjoyed the day beyond description. Cassel is a most pretty place, & new
villas are building in all directions, so it appears to be flourishing. The
Empress of Germany was to be a Wilhe yesterday – I cannot say that I
thought much of its <u>late</u> occupant!

Friday 13. Octr. After leaving off here, last night & half undressed,
there came a knock & a <u>telegram</u>. It alarmed me <u>lest</u> it shd be from
you, so that the alternative of its being from the Pss was a relief. It was
to beg that I would come at 1 o'clock to day! That did not much alarm
me & this morng we were early at the Gallery & home in time to start.
But there was another telegram. H.R.H. begs Lady Eastlake to come
to dinner at 7.30 to night, instead of at 1 o'clock – signed "Countess
Brühl" – <u>What a bother</u>! & I without even a long dress! It was past 12
when I got it, so I thought it better to drive out all the same & try &
see Ctsse Brühl, & explain how entirely unfit my <u>toilette</u> was for such a
purpose. So off we set again, & found the Ctsse, who would not admit
the excuse – said H.R.H. was quite alone – that she would not mind it,
& that she would <u>tell</u> her the state of the case. This she <u>promised</u> to do,
so go I must & am greatly bored – but if she is as simple as she seems
& if <u>she</u> does not <u>care</u>, I shall make the best of it. So I will finish my
letter tomorrow after the bother is over. I fancy the Crown Prince is not
there just now, nor the Empress! Saturday 14 Octr. Well! dear, nothing
could be more charming & more interesting. <u>Both</u> he & she there, & he
by no means the least interesting of the two.

I drove out in good time, for on asking Ctsse B: in the morning, if
anything were necessary as to etiquette – she said "only punctuality" –
So I was there first – was shown through an ample hall, & up a grand
double branching stair, into a large lighted room – very stiff & German,
without any furniture but what was glued to the walls. Yellow damask
sophas – mirrors &c. Then there came in an elderly officer, covered with
orders, who attempted a little English – then other officers out of
uniform, & a smiling Count Seckendorf – a kind of chamberlain. Also

Ctsse Brühl, & Baroness Schenk whom dear Sir Charles, as I
remembered, had known. She was in a short black dress. Then Madme
D'Harcourt, the french governess, & a Miss Byng – a plain old person,
&c. Ctsse Brühl a chatty, lively, middle aged woman. I asked her whether
any traces of the late occupant had been found. She screwed up her face
& said, that certain traces unfortunately had been left in abudance!! – that
the dish was dreadful – that the stoves had been heated till they burnt, &
that all the wood work near them is scorched – that the french officers
had been most rude, but that the Emperor had been decorous in manner
& had thanked for what was done for him – then the door into a side
room opened & in came the little Pss – striking me as so very pretty –
she came straight to me with her open hands, saying, how glad she was
to see me. I thanked her for the privilege, but regretted I had not "a
more appropriate costume". She said in the prettiest way "what does it
matter Lady Eastlake – I have put on a short gown on purpose to keep
you company – don't you see?" & sure enough there was a commonplace
gown silk under a pretty white china crape upper dress, high & long
sleeved – her hair turned up, & a red bow. I was so occupied with her
that I did not remark that any one followed her, till I suddenly found a
splendid looking man – half a head or more above me – in full uniform
– light beard & beaming handsome face opposite me with his hand out,
giving me a most warm shake. It was the Crown Pe. "He was so glad to
see me – somebody had mentioned that I was in Germany he could not
for the moment remember who. He should never forget Sir Charles
Eastlake, nor "the Academy dinner" – where he had the pleasure to sit
next him! [sic] & he added pleasantly "I remember well too that it was
the first speech I ever made". I assured him I remembered his speech &
its affectionate tone. Then dinner was announced & Count Seckendorf
whispered "you follow next & take the chair next to H.R.H. So the Pss
lookg for her husband's arm, walked before into the dining room, & he
instantly looked back & pointed to the chair by his side. The pair sat side
by side. He began telling me what he could remember of the Holbein
which belonged to "my Grandmother" – then we spoke of the memorial
in Hyde Park, which he had not had time to look close into – "as I was
obliged to go to Munich for the entry of the troops" – Then he
remembered it was Mr Cole who had told them I was in Germany &
mentioned Mr Cole's idea to cover the monument with glass. I said, that
was "an old story", & then we talked about polished granite columns &
how they resisted even London smoke. I wanted very much to speak on
more important subjects – but felt my way! Some allusion was made to
"English Journals", & I turned full to him & said "does your R.H.
consider that the English papers give a full & fair account of the

incidents of the War?" He looked as full at me with his fine honest eyes
– "perfectly so" he said – "especially the Times & Daily News" – then
he told me that "Russell & Skinner" the correspondents of each had
even accompanied him to Berlin for the entry of the troops. I said
archly "then we are indebted to your R.H. for those interesting
accounts" – at which he bowed & smiled – then we spoke of
Pemberton, "killed 2 days before Sedan" – & he told me, his body has
been found & conveyed home. Then about Lloyd [sic] Lyndsay, & what
a noble fellow he was, and how welcome the English money had been
"for our sick & wounded", & that he & the Pss has lunched at Ld
Overstone's, whose name he could not at first remember! I can't go on
thus minutely. I told him I had heard in Berlin that an old German
friend of mine had been appointed to some post in Elssass[1] – her turned
& said "what sort of a man is he?" I said "a most upright, just man".
Thank God" he said we need such sorely for such an appointment, to
conciliate hearts" – "it will be a long & difficult work to convert people
to Germans who have for 200 years been french". He told me that the
population of the Vosges mountains were still so German as that only
the children who had learnt french in school could speak it a little.
Then he asked further who this "Horn" could be – I explained "a Jurist,
high in position Carl".[2] He turned & asked the Pss, & she said "here is
some mistake, your friend Horn is still at Königsberg – a most excellent
move, President of the Province" – "we could not give him so good a
position in Elssass – nor spare him from Königsberg" – I said my
authority had only been in the hotel at Berlin. He then talked warmly
about him "2 sons in my regiment – the eldest killed – I was so grieved
– the 2nd with typhus fever – but recovered" – "[illegible] on Horn's
cheek & spectacles?" – "that's the man" I answered. He spoke of french
Cathedrals, their beauty – Chartres, Rheims, St Ouen. I ventured to say
"your R.H. has taken away one of their finest". He smiled & said, "Ah,
you mean Strasburg, but Lady Eastlake, that was German", which I
assented to. I can't go further into minutiae, for we start soon. You may
see how interesting he was & how great a privilege it was to meet the
Hero of 100 fights. He mentioned a Dr Innes & said "I have this day
obtained the Iron Cross for him". I mentioned Dr Frank, & the Pss
caught the name & said, she knew about him, "he worked at Essernay"
– The dinner was simplicity itself – we were 16, there were 2 men in
livery & a butler – only one sort of wine, red, each glass filled, &
another glass filled with a kind of seltzer water – & 1 fish, 1 soup, 3
meats, sweet, nothing more but a few pears. On the other side of me
Kaulbach, a painter whom I remembered, & who was painting the
Prince's portrait. We all rose from table & returned to the stiff room.

Then the Pss spoke long & sweetly with me – told me much about the Queen's illness – feared that it is <u>gout</u> – one foot so swelled & much pain all over her, obliged to be lifted out & in of bed – but begged me not to say "in our family" that she had mentioned "<u>gout</u>". Spoke much of her own life – perhaps a little <u>too</u> frankly – so I will keep her Council. Then about Anna Waagen & the new Institution. I said I had a little cousin at a school in Berlin, "who? where? I will go & see her"! I smiled at her sweet eagerness & told her who and where, but said "your R.H. can have no time, but I will let her parents know your kind feeling". I asked for "commands". Oh! dear Augusta Stanley "this & that," & tell Mr Boxall how sorry I was I could not come to the Gallery" – I said "Sir Wm" & she laughed, then after coffee we went thro' a fine suite into an inner room. The Pss's with a wood fire on the hearth. "This was the Emperor's room – I write at the table he used" – "whence that pamphlet emanated"? I said "yes & yes" – The Pss then wanted to hear about a Raphael in London for which the owner asks £40,000 – I said "<u>we</u> can't afford it, yr R.H." "If you can't afford it, I should like to know <u>who can</u>?" he said. We then were called into another room to look at his portrait – a very tolerable picture by that Kaulbach – hair & eyes too dark – his are really <u>blonde</u> & <u>blue</u>! Then Pss then took for departure saying kind things to me & giving me a pamphlet she wished me to read – about the Holbein – saying also, "I am not well, & go early to rest". He remained & said more, & then shook hands & went too. By that time my carriage was waiting. Good Ctsse Brühl put on my wraps & I returned.

Yrs affectionately
Eliz Eastlake

1. Alsace.

2. Carl Wilhelm Heinrich Georg von Horn (1807–89), Oberpräsident of East Prussia, 1869–78.

Letter to A. H. Layard   NLS Ms.42170

7 FitzRoy Sqre
19 Decr 1871
Dear Mr. Layard
 I recently indicted a note to you introducing Miss Wright & Mr. Augustus Hare – who are old & good acquaintances of my own. I am now asked to do the same service for a young gentleman whom I

have not the pleasure of knowing, namely Mr. Abercromby, eldest son
of Sir Geo: Abercromby of somewhere I believe in Banffshire – head
of the Clan Abercromby! His mother a daughter of Lord Kilmarne. I
am petitioned to give this introduction by my old friend Lady Fred:
Beauclerk, so – as your see – the provienenze are perfectly aristocratic,
& in addition, I am assured that Mr. Abercromby is personally agreeable.
I feel quite sure that when he turns up with this in his hand you will
show him any kindness in yr power.

I spent last week chiefly with Mrs Grote, she, quite recovered in
health & apparently in spirits. She took me some charming walks & had
much the best of it in speed & breath.

I returned home to receive a few friends at dinner – chiefly on
Gregory's account, as I have relatives in Leghorn whom I wish him to
know about.[1] Boxall & Hooker came to meet him – both in great force,
especially Hooker.

I have just recd from kind Forster his 1st vol: of Dicken's life – done
con amore. How well I remember some 16 or 17 years ago (not so much
on 2nd thoughts) the generous kind way in which, sitting next Dickens
at his own table, you not far off, he spoke to me of you. This life has
nothing better to offer than a true friend – & such are very few. After
this morality you will be glad to hear that I am with love to your Enid
your's always truly
Eliz Eastlake

1. Sir William Gregory (1817–92), Anglo-Irish writer, politician, and Trustee
   of the National Gallery, 1867–92. See Brian Jenkins, *Sir William Gregory of
   Coole: The Biography of an Anglo-Irishman* (Gerrard's Cross: Colin Smythe,
   1986).

Letter to William Boxall   *NG14/62/1872*

7 FitzRoy Square
3 January 1872
My dear Sir William
    In the first place I hope my messenger will bring me word that you
are better.
    Secondly I have to ask a favour of you for my nephew Charles
Eastlake. Dear Sir Charles proposed him for the Athenaeum & this
spring his Ballot will come on. Millais has volunteered to 2nd the
proposal but Charles tells me that another good & popular name should
be added to that of the original proposer. Both he & I will be very

grateful if you will give your name & I feel that you will not object to place it next to that other dear name on the <u>nomination</u> paper. When you are well enough to be at the Athenaeum you will kindly remember this. Meanwhile, at your leisure, let me know that you <u>consent</u> & perhaps will additionally enlist votes in his favour. He is likely to be a popular member, for he is gentle & well conditioned.

I wail your time with regard to seeing the little Venetian pictures in my temporary keeping which I mentioned to you.

Saturday I dined quietly with Mrs. Hardwick at Wimbledon – & not venturing into the air.

Ever your's affectionately
Eliz Eastlake

Letter to A. H. Layard   *NLS Ms.42170*

7 FitzRoy Sqre
8 February 1872
My dear Mr. Layard

Yr very welcome & interesting letter of just a month ago (7th January) deserved an earlier acknowledgement – indeed I had long been makg myself reproaches for not beginng a letter to you, & with less excuse than in yr case, for you are supposed to be much more busy than I, tho' I manage to occupy a lonely life, & to be very tired by 11 o clock <u>p.m.</u> Whatever the lack of intellectual life in Madrid yr letter, beginng from yr leavg London, is full of interest to me. I had heard of you from yr aunt, & sometimes seen yr handwritg.

I ventured across the water in the late autumn – too late for travellg, but a slight illness on the part of my aged mother detained me. I did not know who to take as a companion. Boxall would not be induced – Wornum I believe being about – but doubtless the real reason was his <u>propriety.</u> I could have had a pretty young girl, but knew she wd be unpunctual, & not care enough for galleries. & so at last I fastened on the very best person, Miss Lane, daughter of Richd Lane the artist, herself a charming artist – not spoilt with luxury & indulgences, fond of nature & art, & new to & delighted with everything, & very kind & useful to me. So I started one beautiful morning at the end of September for Ostend & made galleries over stages. First Cologne, then Brunswick, Leipsic, Dresden, Berlin, Cassel, Frankfurt, Bruges. My ostensible object was the Holbein exhibition at Dresden – a poor exhibition in itself, the one interest being the comparison of the two Madonnas. No one,

without closer & longer & minute inspection than was possible to a
traveler cd thoroughly interpret the relation in wh: the two rivals stand
to each other. But I did examine with tolerable care & came to a very
different solution to that which you report to be Morelli's. There is no
question that the Darmstadt one is the earlier, & in that sense, & in a
very genuine sense, the original. But there are circumstances evident in
the Dresden picture wh: entirely removes it from the category of a copy.
In all accessories it is an excellent copy, but there are many deviations
from & improvements upon the Darmstadt one, & those evidently by the
hand of Holbein in his later & matured time. The Madonna herself & the
Child are so far finer in drawing & expression, & so different. The old
Meyer, so much older, contains things also exquisitely painted, wh: do
not exist on the Darmstadt picture, that I can hardly conceive any close
observers coming to Morelli's decision. Many minute reasons wh: I noted
cd be given why it is impossible that any but the master cd have presided
& particularly painted over the Dresden picture, but I need not enter
into those. As an impartial observer his opinion is entitled to all respect,
otherwise the question is now made one of one party – Prussia versus
Saxony, & the most ignorant & outrageous abuse, in German epithets,
wh: I shd be shocked to translate, heaped on the poor Saxon picture.
As to being a hundred years later, by an Italian, the very cracks in the
surface show the same vehicle & no Italian painter, except one perhaps a
century earlier than Holbein, cd have executed the so called copy. Poor
Gruner was quite glad to hear my opinion, such as it was, for this abuse
of their honored picture is the last straw which breaks poor Saxony's
back. The account of the humiliations they receive from Prussia are very
distressing. I met Motley & Mrs Ives in the same hotel at Dresden – it
was amusing to see his indignation at being milorded by the waiters &
porter.

At Berlin I studied the Gallery as closely as time permitted. There
are a great many interesting Italian pictures, large Cosimo Tura, Sandro
Botticelli &c. Many of the cinque cento misnamed, many curious or
guesses. Altogether a gallery wh: does our dear old friend very great
credit. A specimen of German misrule & red tape remains in the person
of an utterly ruined but originally splendid A: del Sarto, wh: was
scrubbed by some military order in Waagen's absence, & which broke
the dear old man's heart. I saw much of his daughters – most intelligent
& handsome women. The one who had been in England had been
appointed to conduct an Institution founded by the Queen of Prussia
for the education of the daughters of officers fallen in the war. Miss
Waagen was preferred for this appointment, & I found her full of plans
& preparations. But in a moment the orphans & the Institution were

sent to the winds! A gentleman, hearing of the scheme, was suddenly
overwhelmed with the fear of losing his chance, & came forward.
The lady owned that she wd rather be his wife than the mistress of
any institution, & so they are married & settled for the present at St
Germain en Laye. He is the only son of M: Hittorff the well known
architect & writer on architecture, who lived in Paris. The fathers were
well known to each other, & in short it is all that can be wished for our
dear old friend's daughter.

I much enjoyed the pretty gallery at Cassel & the charming country
round. Also I had several visits to Wilhelmshöhe, where I had the
honour of dining with our Crown Pss & her hero. They were both
most gracious & kind & I was delighted with his humane & frank talk
on subjects connected with the war. He is a splendid looking fellow too,
& you know how far that goes with me!

I was glad to get back at the end of October & to set to work on
a job I had in hand. I have been obliged to lay aside my new edition
of Kugler, as drawn in great measure form Cavalcaselle. Mr. Murray
reproached me two years ago with keeping him waiting, but now he
keeps me delayed, for till Cavalcaselle give out fresh material I cannot
proceed. Still I have done so much & it is, I fancy, so interesting that I
think even this part might appear. However, Mr. Murray has taken no
notice of my last letter. I saw Crowe at Leipsic, & he went through the
little gallery with me.

I have been pretty quiet since my return with the exception of guests
in the house, & of a visit to a grand, & to me a very new place, viz:
to the Meyer Rothschilds, at Mentmore.[1] What a palace it is! And
filled like a museum with every form of art & virtù. The furniture
alone fit for an exhibition, & I wonder your beloved Mr. Cole doesn't
get hold of it. I don't believe the Medici in all their glory were so
grandly lodged as these people. While it is very probable that some of
the minute & precious objects which filled cabinets in Baron Meyer's
own room may have played the same part with the Medici. I have not
seen such exquisite work, in crystal & jewelry since I saw the collection
in the small room at the Uffizi. My hostess Madame Meyer interested
me much. She is a very clever woman, thoroughly versed with social
questions of the day. I was quite beshamed by the endless proofs of
liberality of mind & openness of hand I saw. She is the leading friend
of all the clergy around, & enters into school & parochial questions
with an impartiality which must be as refreshing to some of these much
worried men as her liberality. The only daughter – only child – Miss
Hannah, is a Jewish looking girl, with a splendid voice for Handel,
whom she interprets magnificently. The Anthony Rothschilds are also,

as you know, in that neighbourhood & I paid them a visit. There are
two intelligent girls there. You see I am getting as <u>lax</u> as you cd wish.
I fear that a time of great sorrow has not shawn me [sic] of professing
Xtians to great advantage!

Of dear old Boxall I see something. He has been long sitting over
his fire with bad cold & cough, with his little bull dog between his
feet, but I beat him up occasionally, & listen to his groans & grumbles.
Just now he is very indignant, for Government seems to have done
in his department exactly what they shd have left undone, & vice
versa. Wornum's removal from the rooms of the Gallery on the score
of economy is a very <u>expensive</u> affair, & meanwhile Boxall has not a
shilling to lay out for pictures. Also Mr Cole is behaving in his usual
pleasant way about the N: Gallery at Kensington & Boxall gets no
redress from the Treasury. He wd like to set his little bull dog on yr
friend! However he is going to dine with me next week & the week
after & I hope to cheer him up.

You will have heard & seen accounts of the Old Masters at the Royal
Academy. It is a very partial affair. They cd not well go amiss with the
English painters, but their Dutch & Italian specimens do not exhibit
much discrimination in choice or great knowledge in the Catalogue.
Great Italian names are taken in vain, & copies are paraded in the best
places with the utmost complacency. I am ashamed to see the R.A.
body (Boxall took no part this year) do not know even so much as I do.
Every separate R.A. I meet lays the fault on the President, who appears
to have been the principal chooser & <u>namer</u> this time. As a specimen
of his connoisseurship he summoned an exceeding poor copy of our
Rembrandt old lady from Hopetoun, where I had long known it, in
order to prove to the public that our's was in the N.G. is a <u>copy</u>! Thus,
instead of mortifying me, wh: was his object, he has only mortified his
relation Lord Hopetoun. Now Mr Hart tells me that the President does
not intend to have any more of these exhibitions, he thinks they are <u>bad</u>
for young painters!

I saw Mrs. Millais the other day – she very near her confinement
with a 9th scion of the name of Millais. Your aunt I have not seen of
late, tho' I have called, but I had a kind note from her last night.

Mrs. Grote is just come to London, & I shall see her this eveng. She
is much better, & I hope wound up for a good while longer. She is the
kindest of friends to me. She is always glad to hear of you.

I have given you a sufficient dose I think now & I will only add my
best love to yr Enid, & thanks for yr kind message thro' Mrs Austen.
Ever dear Mr Layard, yr's truly
Eliz Eastlake

1. Mayer Amschal de Rothschild (1818–74), member of the wealthy family of merchant bankers. The Rothschild home, Mentmore Towers in Buckinghamshire, was one of the most magnificent of the Rothschild country houses. Rothschild was married to Juliana and his daughter Hannah later married the 5th Earl of Rosebery.

Letter to William Boxall   *NG14/65/1872*

2 Upton Villas Slough
30 Aug: 1872
Dear Sir William

I know that you have kindly inquired for me in FitzRoy Sqre, & that you know the sad reason that fixes me here – sad, not because my aged Mother must quit this earth, but because the illness which slowly heralds her end is more intensely suffering than I could have believed it possible at 95. I have been here above 5 weeks now. At first I thought that every day wd be the last, but I have learned the <u>cruel</u> tenanting of life wh: so much prolongs the struggle. We watch and pray and minister all that love & skill can suggest. I think the struggle will last still a while![1]

All my thoughts centre here, & here I remain until our dear Mother is released. My good sister Miss Rigby keeps up tolerably well. The nursing is very arduous but we have plenty of help.

This is all a sad story. I hope you are better, and have been able to enjoy something of the sweet summer season. I have the little open carriage her & we occasionally seek refreshment in drives. I am always in raptures with the beauty of forest trees. They & the sky at Eventide are soothing to heart and eyes.

Last evening I found my way to <u>Huntercombe</u> – the Richard Boyle's new place. She was alone there & gave me a sweet welcome. We spoke of you. She has had much sorrow. May it bear blessed fruits![2]

Ever yr's afftly
Eliz Eastlake

1. Anne Rigby died on 2 September 1872 at Slough.

2. Richard Boyle and his wife Eleanor (née Eleanor Vere Gordon) (1825–1916) lived at Huntercombe Manor in Buckinghamshire.

Letter to A. H. Layard   NLS Ms.42170

7 FitzRoy Sqre
31. Octr 1872
Dear Mr. Layard

I have been writing & long.g to write to you for some time. But now
I am only just <u>settled</u> at home again, & have indeed not been sure of
your whereabouts – tho' concluding that you were long ago back to yr
post. Now I have obtained all requisite tidings from yr aunt & have also
received thro' the kind Mm: de Gex[1] the volume of the new catalogue
for wh: I am greatly obliged & to the subject of which I will return.
You & yr Enid know meanwhile how the anxiety I was under when
I last saw you has terminated & that I have had much sad occupation.
I was glad when the last duties were over, to take my sister to a quiet
sea side place in Suffolk where we applied ourselves to <u>do nothing</u> &
obtained necessary rest. Since then I have been paying a few visits to a
friend at <u>beautiful</u> Tunbridge Wells, & to Mrs Grote at the Ridgeway
&c. I took the Q: Review with me & very much enjoyed the article on
Velasquez which is solid & dignified & <u>most interesting</u>. I never learnt
so much of the great master before, & for all yr superior love for Titian,
you have done the Spaniard justice.[2] I write Boxall how much the article
interested me (I have read it twice) & he answered that with all respect
for Velasquez "& you know how much I love him" he knows nothing
by him that can compare with Titian's Charles V on horseback, thus
anticipating yr comparison. The result was that I had to lend him the
number, which I very much grudged! However he has quite satisfied me
in his approbation of the article tho' he has not yet returned it. Thus I
have it not at hand to enter further into, but there are <u>words</u> & <u>allusions</u>
in it wh: you know well I do not require to have at hand to remember!
For which I thank you heartily. I am glad that <u>the notes</u> have been of
any use.

I have been spelling my way a little into the new catalogue. I see it is
most on the model of the Louvre Cat. & a great improvement in point
of information on the old one that we have. The change of title at a
certain page is a curious memento of the Revolution. Madrazo mentions
a Petersburg (Hermitage) Catalogue, but he probably knows nothing of
Waagen's edition of it.[3]

Last Tuesday little Hatty[4] dined quietly here with only Boxall, and
kept us alive with a perpetual firework of sparkle and fun. She came
late to England, and has been absorbed by great ladies not particularly
famed for punctuality, so that I have not known where to find her. She

leaves England for Rome – <u>so she says</u> – next week but as she waits for
Lady Ashburton to accompany her, she will probably miss the train, or
the steamer. At all events mt start when fixed. Hatty made great love
to Boxall, which he accepted very graciously. But occasionally she gave
him a rap – as when I alluded to his "immortal youth", she added "yes,
immortal with the <u>t</u> left out"! Terrible slander! In truth poor Boxall
is looking very ill – with constant cough. He returned from Milan
almost dead, and has required no end of <u>egg flip</u> and port wine &c.
to wind him up. He took no care of himself and went without meals
on the journey and could hardly stand when he reached home. You
know doubtless that he went to Milan partly from yr description of a
Boccacio Bocacini, Lowe giving him <u>carte blanche</u>. But he did not fall
in love with the picture, & he did not <u>believe</u> what they told him there
that <u>you</u> had offered £1.000 for it. He was delighted with some things,
& especially with a MS with miniatures which he thought worthy of
Leonardo.

Hatty intends to bring the statue of the Queen of Naples to London
next Spring and to exhibit it separately.

Now give my love to yr Enid & tell her that I have not forgotten
the promised <u>lace</u>. I am afraid to send it by letter, & therefore shall
await some means of getting it safe to her. She knows that my <u>pearl</u> of
a governess is with the Du Cane's & I hope they are <u>worthy</u> of her!
When they return to Roehampton I hope to go & see her. I believe
that Miss de Setan is much interested in the childn.

I must tell you a little of Mrs Grote. She has been far from well, &
no wonder, for her habits of hospitality far exceed her powers of health.
Her home has been full "to the last crib" all summer & autumn. She
has had an exciting, however pleasant, visit from her Swedish sister with
two nephews, & she forgets that she is 80 years of age. My visit, or
rather my <u>sobriety</u>, calmed her a little, & I was even one day alone with
her. She has made much progress with the "Biography" & I read part of
it in the slip. <u>Entre nous</u> I am not perfectly satisfied with it. Her art of
writing does not come up to her powers of conversation. She consults
friends, but it is difficult to speak plainly on such a subject tho' she has
kindly modified a few things to which I objected. She was in good
spirits upon the whole, & we had an occasional bout of whist. I have
been lately entreated to join a party to spend the winter in the Nile,
but, there are plenty of impediments besides my chronic want of spirit.
I am left executrix to my Mother's will & am particularly anxious not
needlessly to delay business.

Pray assure Enid that the lace is <u>bona fide</u>, <u>point d'aleneon</u>! very
brown, & in 2 or 3 pieces. If I may send it to Foreign Office I will.

Now dear Mr Layard wishing you all patience for another Madrid winter believe me yrs always truly
Eliz Eastlake

1. A. H. Layard, 'Velasquez', *Quarterly Review*, vol. 133 (Otober 1872), pp. 451–87.

2. Wife of Edward De Gex (1812–79), solicitor.

3. Pedro de Madrazo y Küntz, *Catalogo descriptivo e histórico del Museo del Prado*, 1872.

4. Harriet Hosmer.

Letter to John Murray   *NLS Ms.42177*

The Ridgeway, Shire
3rd Janry 1873
Dear Mr. Murray[1]

Your letter has followed me into the country, which must excuse the delay of my reply. It was at the end of September or the beginning of October 1871 that I wrote to you saying that I had proceeded as far as my materials – i.e. Cavalcaselle's work – permitted, and that so far my labours were ready for press, excepting a slight overhauling. I waited for your instructions, but you did not acknowledge my letter.

The amount of my progress in the new edition is therefore the same now, as it was then. I am not aware that my further vol: has emanated from Cavalcaselle – and till that is the case I do not see my way to the continuation or completion of the work. It must rest with yourself whether to employ my labours, as far as they go. In the small edition of Kugler you wish to issue. Very considerable changes have been made by me – so that the work is almost new, and, I hope, would be more popular.

I kept no copy of my letter to you of the date I mention, and therefore I may perhaps here have repeated what I said there.

As to the German edition you are aware that the very few corrected or added portions are really insignificant and worthless. There is therefore no advantage to the German public superior to that which the English Kugler presents as it is.

I return to town tomorrow and shall be glad to know your further wishes.
Your's faithfully
Eliz Eastlake

1. John Murray's Letter Book, containing copies of outgoing correspondence, records two replies (NLS Ms.41914). The first, dated 2 January 1873, suggests some urgency: 'The time has come round when I must send to press a new edition of Kuglers Italian Painting – and I write to ask whether your corrections and improvements are so far advanced that you could commit them to the printers hands. If not, I must do as I have of late – print off only a small edition. It is a pity however that the book should go forth imperfect to English readers while the Germans have the advantage of a revised edition. All must depend upon your convenience and the state of progress you have made with the new notes'. The second, dated 4 January 1873, suggests that '[as] you have already done so much for the improvements of Kugler, I see no reason why your copy should not go to press at once. When I originally proposed to you the revision I expected that Crowe and Cavalcaselle's work would have been completed (Titian inclusive) long ere this. As it is, it seems to me there is no use waiting for them. I had forgotten how little of good matter you had found in the German reprints of K'.

Letter to John Murray   *NLS Ms.42177*

7 FitzRoy Square
17 Janry 1873
Dear Mr. Murray[1]
I have just completed all that I can conveniently do without the 4th vol: of Cavalcaselle – so that I shall be glad of it even if only in the sheets.
I remain your's faithfully
Eliz Eastlake

1. This is the last letter addressed 'Dear Mr. Murray'; ten days later he is the recipient of a the first in a series of letters addressed 'Dear Sir'. See note to following letter.

Letter to John Murray   *NLS Ms.42177*

7 FitzRoy Square
27 Janry 1873
Dear Sir[1]
I am now glad to send you the result of my labours – as far as the first vol: of Kugler is concerned. I send you that volume also, to which perpetual reference is made, and which contains numerous corrections and changes. After the <u>ten</u> insertions which I have numbered in the

M.S. the printer has only to stick to the M.S. and turn to the book as directed – returning to the M.S.

I have marked three of the plates in Kugler to be annulled. The two heads are entirely fake, and that facing p.15 had better be replaced by a woodcut from a circular ceiling in Bottari vol II. p.CXVIII – the same as the woodcut in "History of our Lord in Art".

I have marked wherever it would be well to introduce a plate from Cavalcaselle. It would be as well also to introduce the Entombment of St. Francis by <u>Giotto</u> in the Bardi Chapel Florence, engraved in Layard's Life of Giotto for the Arundel Society. A drawing of my own of St. Ambrose in the Ognissanti, Florence, by <u>Ghirlandajo</u> – not hitherto engraved – will be at your service if you desire it. Also a figure in the picture in the Brera by <u>Mantegna</u>.

I have underlined all names of painters where they are <u>exclusively</u> the subject. It will remain with your to decide whether to print them in such cases in small capitals as in "Waagen's Treasures", or in italics. When mentioned incidentally, as Raphael for instance in account of <u>Perugino</u>, the name may be printed in ordinary type.

I much object to the small and <u>indistinct numbers</u> for notes. I think the asterisks might be used up to xxx and after that (which will be seldom needed) such other + forms as may be usual.

I have considerably shortened the earlier part, which is very incorrect. Believe me your's faithfully
Eliz Eastlake

1. This and subsequent letters to Murray are addressed 'Dear Sir'. The form of address 'Dear Mr. Murray' resumes on 23 March 1880. The following letters document the deteriorating relationship between the pair as the editorial disputes escalate. There are no surviving letters from Elizabeth to John Murray between 22 February 1876 and 1880.

Letter to A. H. Layard   *NLS Ms.42170*

7 FitzRoy Sqre
5 February 1873
My dear Mr. Layard

I had a kind letter from yr Enid the other day in wh: she gives me a message from you, remindg me of a fact in which you are far too accurate – namely that I am in yr debt for two letters. I beg to say that I shall be happy to be in yr debt for any number! However it is a true pleasure to write to you, only that I have little to tell you worth

reading. The world forgets me, and I forget that. Many have departed
this life who formed part of my circle of friends and some have departed
from me without the excuse of a change of state. One grows accustomed
to these things, tho' at one time I was so foolish as not to believe such
things possible. But then I was in prosperity – or was supposed to be so.

I sent you a note the other day by a very roundabout route. Friends
of mine (& true ones) Sir John & Lady Orde with their daughter
are spending the winter in Egypt. They hope to take Spain on their
homeward journey, & asked me for a line to you. I hope they will be
able to fulfil this plan, or rather that the state of poor Spain will allow
them, & I am sure you & Enid wd like Lady Orde. The telegrams about
Spain are not very enlightening, but they always make it appear that the
Govt. is gaining ground, or rather its troops. I wish it may be so, for
my heart is with the young Italian King who so nobly does his best.

My chief visits out of London have been to the good Tindals and to
Mrs. Grote. In December I spent a week at Aylesbury. All well & happy
& all three fine young men at home. Nico not long returned from
Utah, looking more manly & full of American stories. He has grown
fond of the wild life, & talks of taking land out there, & growing
horses, also shooting buffaloes. The silver mine which good Acton has
embarked in has stood still for want of Galena, & capital, but I hear
that their prospects are very promising now. Nico probably going out
again. I must own that yr friend Acton is beginning to look older &
heavier, but he still leads a most active life, is up & out while the boys
are sleeping, & makes breakfast for everybody. She is unchanged in the
bloom, & is always an interesting woman. The little girl is tall & slim,
& I think will turn out pretty. Gifford is still at Cambridge, Charlie
at Oxford. All three are a pleasure & credit to their parents. The great
subject in the neighbourhood was the engagement of Annie Rothschild
(Sir Anthony's 2nd daughter) to Elliot Yorke – Ld Hardwicke's son. An
arrangement which seems to please no one but the young lady & the
young man & his family. The young man attached the young lady's
affections by his spirited acting in amateur plays & the young lady
wrung the consent form her father & mother by her continual crying!
Her pillow every morning was found "sopping wet", & no tender
parents cd resist that. He professes to love her for herself, but it must be
difficult for him to know whether that be really the case. I dined there
one day with the Tindals, & was amused to see the number of Liddell
& Hardwicke connexions who were there, buzzing about the honey.
Generally speaking the Rothschilds – both the Meyers & the Anthonys
are the great topic of the neighbourhood.

With Mrs Grote I have been several times having now the prospect

of owning a few acres within sight of her domain. I have long wished
for a country summer nest. The London season has no attraction for
me. I was brought up in the country, and love it. I like plenty of sky,
and an orchard – the first I am sure of in that vicinity for the land is
high, and the second I shall have the pleasure of planting. Also I have
to build a small house, and so I laid out for myself plenty of trouble,
and also of interest. I intend to employ no architect, but to go to
work with a fine old builder, who has built several good homes in the
neighbourhood. Mrs Grote enters warmly into the scheme – indeed she
has not rested till she found some one who wd part with a few acres,
which are difficult to be had in part of the world almost entirely held
by large proprietors who will not let anyone squat. I believe I am sure
of my 6 acres – for 96 guins – but at present I have not signed a paper
or paid a shilling. I probably go to Mrs Grote next Monday for a few
days. She has been in London, but is sure to fall ill here, & has given
some anxiety by reasons of the heart. On such occasions she reverses the
usual custom, & sends for her country Dr. whom she trusts more than
all London ones. She is pleased with a match lately arranged in which
the families of Grote & Lewin will again be united. Her nephew Captn
Henry Lewin – a very worthy intelligent young man – royal engineers
– to Mary Grote, Mr. Grote's niece & one strikingly like him in face,
a charming girl. Mrs Grote & I often anticipated this dénouement, &
brought it on by leaving it alone.

You wd be much interested in the Exhibition of Old Masters now
going on. I was there on Private View day, & again early & quietly
with Boxall, when we looked closely at the Italian pictures. Two
great galleries have been compelled to contribute their treasures. Ld
Radnor's (Longford Castle) & the Duke of Hamilton's. The first sends
the great Holbein called "the Ambassadors", a very noble picture with
minutely painted accessories, mathematical & scientific instruments,
exquisitely coloured like those in the pictures at Berlin. But the picture
is dreadfully dry & starved. Also, what my dear Sir Chas called "the
finest head by Velasquez" – the portrait of Pareja, V's assistant – quite
a marvel. Then a striking Moroni portrait, called a Titian. The
pictures from Hamilton Palace are grander still. The great Botticelli
Coronation of the Virgin with all the host of Heaven in successive
planes. The numerous seated angels as exquisite as anything Italian art
has produced, tho' the picture much injured, & from its size needing to
be placed lower, the upper part being the most minute. Also a fine Luca
Signorelli, a large picture, Mad: Child & Saint, an then the great Daniel
in Lion's Den by Rubens, known to be entirely by the master's hand.
Many of the Italian pictures are misnamed & more than one are difficult

even to suggest names for. Then there are glorious Cromes & Turners
& Reynolds, & especially <u>Romneys</u>. There they have this time a room
of water colours. One wd think they were <u>Cole's</u> supplying for they
are ill chosen & generally poor specimens! A Shipwreck by old John
Cristall one of the finest there. In the catalogues one learns who are the
<u>nouveaux riches</u>, further names are sure to be there, as proud to lend
pictures, & a set of queer names these are.

Boxall is pretty well, having by dint of eggflip & port wine quite
recovered from his Milan journey. He has but little to do. He wd
be very glad if the D: of Hamilton wd or cd part with some of the
pictures. The Luca Signorelli especially attracts him.

This morning I have seen Philip Hardwick, his mother well, his wife
better. She has lately lost her father, & was much upset. He seems well
satisfied with his choice, & I think him a fortunate man. Little Mrs
Philip is no commonplace little girl – indeed she is superior to him in
intellect, & at the same time looks upon him as a sort of Divinity, so
that the combination is much in his favour. His good mother is also
very fond of her.

I saw yr friends the de Gex's on their return form Spain when they
kindly dined here & met the Hardwicks & Clare Ford. Since then I
have heard thro' yr aunt of the severe illness of Ed de Gex, from wh: I
trust he is recovered. But she begged me not to enquire at his door. Of
yr dear aunt I have heard & seen very little. She has been out when I
have called, which was a tolerable sign, & a long letter I wrote to her
last week has not yet had an answer.

My task of pouring Cavalcaselle into Kugler has laid long
uncontinued, for want of any continuation of Cav:'s vols: Now suddenly
Mr. Murray calls for what I have completed as if I had kept him
waiting. So it is in his hands, as far as it goes. Meanwhile he has sent
me the proof sheets of Burckhardt's 'Cicerone' – the English translation.
This forms "The Handbook of Art in Italy" and is printed like the
other Handbooks in two columns. I have not had time to look closely
in it, but it strikes me as rather confused, and not translated by one
conversant with technical English terms.

I have seen Newton occasionally. He dined here quietly with
Boxall not long ago. Of course I questioned him much about you &
am thankful to hear from Enid that you have recovered from what I
was sorry to hear of. Not long ago Mrs Du Cane called & found me
at home. She & I have become a little acquainted on account of the
excellent lady I recommended to her. Mrs Du Cane does know that she
has a treasure, but she works the willing horse so desperately hard that I
fear Miss de Setan's health will not allow her to remain.

Now dear Mr Layard I am glad to put you in my debt again – at all events as to quantity. With love to both of you I am ever yrs truly Eliz Eastlake

Letter to Hannah Brightwen   *Private Collection*

The Lodge. Shere
Guildford
19. March 1873
My dearest Hannah

My new address will show you that I have been moving & so far account for the silent return alone made to yr two dear & full letters – also to the subject of <u>Inglis</u>. I came here exactly a week ago – on the 12th & as you will guess, on business connected with my country house scheme. <u>Scheme</u> it still remains – for at present I have no formal possession of the land, & I will not stir a sod until I have that. I hear from all who have travelled this road before me, that hindrances & hitches & delays are inummerable & my experience hitherto tells me the same. My land – 6 ½ beautiful acres – lying to South & West – is <u>leasehold</u>. <u>96</u> years to be taken of Sir Geo: Hewett, Bt an honorable gentleman – an <u>Irvingite</u> – he leaves his lawyer to draw up the little lease that is required, & <u>of course</u> the lawyer makes delay – & meanwhile Sir Geo: is gone to Holland on Irvingite business. I bear the delay very patiently, as I happen not to be ready myself! I have no architect – no contractor – but a fine old man, a builder – renowned here for his thorough knowledge – & upright dealing. & much employed by the late Henry Drummond – much by the Duke (his son in law) – in short a capital man & moreover descended in a straight line from Sir Anth: Browne master of the Horse to Henry 8th!! This, you will say will not help my house much – but really a noble blood seems to run in the grand old fellow, who himself is "Anthony Browne".

My house is to be of <u>red brick</u>, a <u>double</u> wall will be required, for Southwestern winds & rain are no joke on my height, so first a 4 ½ inch wall – then a space of 2 ½ – & then a 9 inch wall are to keep me <u>dry</u>. All good houses are so built here. And I wish for a good honest square house – with no <u>dormers</u>, or <u>gables</u>, or <u>angles</u>, or <u>high roof</u> – for all of wh: I have no taste – but a straight wall, & a cornice, a parapet of moulded bricks. A South wide front – just 53 ft long – a west front of about 34ft – ground floor & first floor – no more – not a step up & down except back & front stairs. Kitchen level with dining room

– lower rooms 11 ft high – bedrooms 10 ft high – windows 2 ft 8 in: from ground 7 ft high below, 6 ft high above, 3 ½ ft wide. Large garden glass door to the South front – entrance door to the North. House to stand on a terrace – with steps down to grass plots & garden – beyond wich is a lovely grass meadow of about 4 acres. Slate low roof. Thus all is low & wide. Ground shape this [*drawing of floor plan here*]

This gives me plenty of room, perhaps over much. Drawg room will be large, 23 ft across to projection 18 ft otherwise, with glass door in corner onto terrace. The decorations are the bother. I wanted white terra cotta – but the companys of terra cotta who have homes in London & painted books &c have vile cockny [sic] taste. So now I am turning all attention to burnt moulded brick of wh: there are beautiful specimens – both modern & ancient hereabouts. I have coachman & open carriage with me – driven over viâ Dorking, from London – & so I am independent. I am in the home of a Revd Sir Emilius Bayley – officed to me for a low price – a wretched cold place with steps up & down wh: threaten to break my neck. I find dearest cook here – "Caroline" from the village does house maidg. I have coachman & my maid & want for nothg. Mrs Grote is about a mile off & I may dine with her every day if I will – she is so kind.

Thus you have my present life- wh: will last till next Tuesday the 25th. Meanwhile I have plenty to do – writg letters, drawg plans & suggestions, conferrg with Anth: Browne. Indeed I have not an idle minute.

When I return to London I will make a point of seeing Henry Reeve. His manner is always grand & pompous & is much against him. But he is kind,& sensible, & I am quite sure ready to esteem such merit as Inglis'. I see but little of Reeve's – we are too far off each other. They in an ever increasg vortex of society – I in an ever decreasg. But we meet as friends & cousins when we do meet, & dine together about once a year. The Economist's praise is an undesirable tribute.

I could have done much for Inglis, in times when Mr Murray thought it worth his while to pretend friendship for me. All is altered now. His wife has pulled down all that was generous or fine in him. She was always most jealous of my fancied superiority of position (wh: I never felt) & now that that is – also as suppositiously – considered over, she has got rid of me by the rudest & most heartless conduct. He unfortunately goes with her – as he must, & all communication has long, by her industry, ceased between us. I have a little business communication with him now & then, connected with some work I am doing – & wh: I cd not take from him without puttg myself in the wrong (& I care now for little else but to avoid that) but that is on the most formal terms. I shd be ashamed to own the long pain wh: their conduct, at such a time, has cost me – for I was attached to them, – but

now I now I have made a <u>sacrifice</u> of it to God, & so obtained <u>Peace</u>.
When a thing <u>preys</u> on me, & oh! how much of that my poor heart has
had! – I find <u>that</u> a way to tranquillity [sic]. & God knows I have reason
enough to <u>sacrifice</u> my will to One, who gives me still so much.

How beautiful is that article on the Sonnet! The writg is itself
imbued with poetic thought. I trace Tennison & Shelly [sic] in passages.
I will try & make out who it is by.

Did I tell you that the Pss Charlotte article (I thought it very poorly
done) proves to be a Lady Rosa Weigall.[1]

Now dearest you will hardly make out my writg, it is such a scribble.
I require all my energy to plan this house &c – but I think when once I
am <u>settled</u> in that respect I shall enjoy the work.

I have had Annie Butson with me for the last 2 months. Her good
husband brought her. Her state has given me great anxiety. Dreadful
spasmodic swoons with clenched hands & teeth – much shriekg & loss
of strength – in short a gradual failure of power have pointed to some
mortal cause. I trust she is slowly betterg – but Dr Burrows wd not let
her return home – nor go to her sister's wedding. And so I have left her
in F.Sqre under the charge of my good old Anderson. Annie is <u>a very
sweet love</u> – full of affection & deep thought – very congenial to me.
& giving me much <u>love</u>. Dear Jane is just now with Bessie Woodhouse
havg – last Saturday – wound up all affairs at <u>Slough</u>. She probably
returns to me when she leaves Bessie.

Now again I must slack rein, & am ever dearest as you will know
Yr ever lovg friend & cousin
Eliz Eastlake
I am delighted at Joseph's appointmt – it gives me two pleasures – a
good one & a bad one – the latter, over Ayrton![2]

1. Lady Rose Weigall (1834–1921), diarist and author of *A Brief Memoir of the
   Princess Charlotte of Wales* in 1874.

2. A reference to Joseph Hooker's long-running battle with the MP, Acton
   Smee Ayrton, over the management of the Herbarium at Kew.

Letter to A. H. Layard   *NLS Ms.42170*

The Lodge Shere Guildford
24 March 1873
Dear Mr. Layard

I hope that other friends have earned their interest in you & Enid
since the break up in Spain more promptly than I have done. But I have

thought of you much & for your sakes read many a puzzling paragraph
which otherwise my disgust at the Spaniards wd have made me skip. All
this must be & have been an immense trial to you. I fear that Amadeo
has few who regret him so sincerely as you. I rejoice that he is safe back
in dear Italy.

I date my letter from a house where I have been livg alone for the
last fortnight, havg hired it per week. I daresay I told you in my last
letter that I was in treaty for a few acres on the same height with Mrs
Grote & within sight of her home. My treaty has been so far successful
that I am planng and preparg to build a small house. And as I repudiate
an architect almost as vigorously as I wd a lawyer, I am planning it only
with the help of a clever, experienced & most honest builder. Also I
must add of Mrs. Grote, who is very learned in many things that lie out
of sight. I am not going in for a crooked cottage with angles & gables
& bow windows – which is not my taste – & what I am going in for I
had better not talk about till it is really begun. Meanwhile my ground
landlord – a certain Sir George Hewett (one of the Irvingite colony
here) does believe in lawyers & so of course there is much delay, & I
am not yet formally in progression, &, till I am, I will not stir a sod.
At all events the preparation gives me plenty to think of, & when I do
begin I shall probably take a home on beautiful Albury Heath for the
summer. You will believe that the pleasure of being near Mrs Grote is
one of my inducements to have a summer rest here. When I said I was
living alone here, I shd have excepted the fact that I have dined & slept
almost every alternate day with her. The weather has been the climax of
this trying winter since I have been here, & now hail, frost & all with
it. Now however the change has come & a South wind blows, or does
not blow, & everything is starting into leaf. This change has revived
Mrs Grote, who suffered much from the East wind, & she is as well as
you cd wish. Her nephew Captn Henry Lewin, & Mrs Grote's niece,
Mary Grote, took it into their heads to marry about 3 weeks ago, & I
found the happy couple at the Ridgeway when I first came. I think the
arrangement will answer.

Our Old Master's Exhibition was quite as fine as ever. I daresay I
told you all about it. It has further exalted the name of "Old Crome", &
there has been a discussion about a large & doubtful picture attributed
to him, in the Times lately, conducted most positively & pompously by
Robinson.[1] You may have seen the letters between him & a Mr Cox.
I feel sure that Robinson is wrong for I remember nothing so strongly
about J.B. Crome (the son) as his execrable art. Boxall & I looked much
at the picture in question. It approximates to Cotman (of Norfolk too)
but Cotman was not so familiar with the use of oil. Wonderful Sir

Joshuas have been selling recently at Christie's (Mr Noel Desenfan's pictures) & for wonderful prices. Indeed Christie's sales become more & more wonderful, & show something of the wealth of a nation who spend 26 millions a year in duty on spirits!

I return to FitzRoy Square tomorrow. I saw yr aunt about a long fortnight ago walking with a stick around the rooms, but alert & full of interest in all friends.

Boxall has been suffering with the bad weather, & has lost a young relative, wh: affected him much. He thought himself beyond all such vicisstudes! Who is! Lady Strangford at Cannes, Hardwicks flourishing & a scion expected.

Now dear Mr Layard this does not deserve an answer, but I shd be very glad to hear of you & of yr prospects. With kind love to Enid, ever yrs truly
Eliz Eastlake

1. Letters between J. C. Robinson and William Cox, *The Times*, 14 March 1873, p. 10, col. E; 17 March 1873, p. 10, col. A; 20 March 1873, p. 11, col. A; and 25 March 1873, p. 4, col. F.

Letter to John Murray   *NLS Ms.42177*

7 FitzRoy Square
13 June 1873
Dear Sir
I have received your notes & the woodcuts. The St. Euphemia & the Catacomb ceiling will pass muster – but I fear that I cannot say the same regarding the St. Ambrose which appears to me no improvement on the first attempt. The lines which ought to be the tenderest are the hardest – such as the outline of the head, & the glory above. However, I should be sorry to give any further trouble. Mr. Whymper is mistaken in thinking that any of the drawings were detached – but that is of no consequence. If the line of the glory be made a little less salient I shall be satisfied. The head may be left alone.

I am about to leave England for a few weeks which, as Messrs C. & Cavalcaselle make no signs of bringing out another vol:, will not I conclude be of any importance as regards the progress of the work.

I do not remember in the conditions respecting this edition of Kugler that you stipulated for my name as Editor.
I remain your's faithfully
Eliz Eastlake

Letter to Hannah Brightwen   *Private Collection*

Wiesbaden
Maison Black
23 July 1873
My dearest Hannah

The want to write to you has been upon me for the last few days,
& now here is yr dear letter just come! It is true that I have not recd
your first letter, which ought not to be detained at the Post Office, for
I enquired there myself for more than the first week, since which my
address has been known. I have often wished for you here with us,
for in point of comfort we have every thing we can wish, tho' as to
benefit that has still to be proved. I fear you & I have the same Palgrave
inheritance. I am so stiff when I rise, even after a good night, that I do
not know how to set my joints working. It is the same with Jane. I do
not sit for half an hour without havg as it were to unlock my joints. Jane
is absolutely lame, & I much fear that an early accident is answerable
for that, & that no waters waters [sic] will relieve that. But she also has
knots in her poor fingers which I trust may be benefited. I summoned
the Dr the morng after our arrival & we got our several orders – Jane to
bathe daily – I every other day – at 10 o clock – my little girl to drink
the Hamburg waters (brought to her bed side by 7 o clock) & my good
old Anderson both to bathe & to drink. And so we have continued to
do. The Dr also recommended me to an Hotel Garni in the best part
of Wiesbaden – which is more reasonable than the Hotels – & infinitely
more comfortable than any hotel I ever was in – every thing supplied
à la carte & everything excellent. We have four excellent bed rooms
– sitting room & balcony for about 5 gui: the week. It is true we are up
on the 3rd storey, but we gain in air & views. The place is very pretty
surrounded with villa & hills, & these again with wooded hills – with
beautiful public gardens, band playing, fine company & all that. You may
believe that I do not care for the amusement part of the place, which in
truth strikes me as partly vulgar, & partly disreputable, but the gardens
which include many acres of fine trees are a great resource to sit in. My
little girl is never tired of sitting by the lake, listening to the Band, feedg
swans & fishes – & wonderg at the queer men who smoke all day long in
the heat, & the queer women who trail about long trashy dresses in the
dust. My good Mrs Anderson is also like a girl takg her holidays – never
tired of the air, wh: is the best thing for her, & often acting Duenna to
the little Minna Lewin. But the heat is awful. We had one bout of it
at first, which yielded to three thunder storms – & now we have a 2nd

shorter bout – so that even the shady gardens are intolerable, & a drive
from 8 to 10 – or a seat in the gardens at the same time is all we can
do. We persue our writing, looking, reading &c in doors, & with Mrs
Anderson as 4th, occasionally a game of very innocent whist. The nights
are dreadfully hot, the house is so quiet & respectable that I can lie with
my door wide open (window too) but even that gives me little relief.
We have come fully late. The Wiesbaden season begins in May, & I shd
advise any one to come then. You see I can give you all encouragement
as regards comfort, & pleasantness, & I have no doubt that such strong
alkali baths must be efficacious. We take them about the temperature of
the skin (92,°) or sometimes cooler, & they are very agreeable – about
1/6 each.

I subscribed to a Circulating Library on comg, hopg to find some
modern German Literature wh: reflects the present political state of
United Germany, but no such thing exists, & I have tried to get at
such books as have been written on the War. I find only very ordinary
works, tho' of course none can be devoid of interest. The letters of a
Military Chaplain who accompanied the troops are very touchg in parts.
Soul harrowg scenes almost unmanned him – & tried his faith, never
shaking it. Much too there was in the resignation of the poor sufferers
to fortify it. All the sad roads only led to greater & greater execration
of the imperial monster, & his vain, frivolous, bigotted wife, who
have merrily brought a great country to this pass. Some one quotes a
definition of Louis N: wh: is ascribed to Lord Cawley "Lorsqu'il parle,
il ment, – lorsqu'il se tait, il conspire".[1] I do not think that France
will rise again in our time – tho' they may have, as the Germans fully
expect the madness to challenge War again. I am no admirer of the
Germans – very much the reverse – whether in their looks or their talk
I miss anything like principle – but their national & political structure
has roots, the French has none. Also I remark a great increase in activity
– much buildg going on, & signs of prosperity.

I get "the Times" every day – bringing the business, the follies, &
the sorrows of the world. The awful death of Mrs Archer Clive whom
I knew well weighs upon me. She was familiar – not fascinating – but
good & true – & the patience with wh: she bore most exceptional
infirmities always impressed me. And now such an end![2] All is mystery,
unless we are staid in God. Only that faith wh: ascribes to Him all
things can sustain the heart under puzzlg dispensations – & then after a
time all comes clear. Today the death of the Bp of Winchester is another
blow. How awful for Ld Granville! I knew the ground well, & "Fred
Leveson's" beautiful house, & Mr Farrer's home at Abinger where the
body of that most remarkable man now lies.[3] He was a puzzle to me.

I cd admire him, but I cd not repeat him. Lord Westbury's wife of 6 months is also known to me – she thought herself <u>very happy</u>.[4] I said something about "a brilliant position" & the ardour with which she rejoined "were he plain Mrs Smith I shd have him as well" has dwelt in my recollection.

Well, dearest, you are doing all the good you can with yr sweet Fritton. I like to hear of Effie & her daughters.

Heidelberg is full of pathetic recollections. Sisters sacrificed to a <u>dream</u> – "some have died, & some have left me, all, all gone, the old familiar faces" (Chas Lamb). Being so near I go (havg been several times since we lived there) to see an old German friend. I have a sad knack of being <u>faithful</u>! my Hannah. It has brought but little faithfulness in return! I shall hope to be home on the 2nd or 3rd August.

Now God be with you dearest

Ever yr lovg

Eliz Eastlake

Jane's love to you.

1. French: 'When speaking he lies, when silent he conspires'.

2. Caroline Archer Clive (1801–73), author, was disabled by two accidents and a stroke. She died after her dress caught fire in her library.

3. Samuel Wilberforce, Bishop of Winchester was riding with Lord Granville to visit Edward Frederick Leveson Gower, when he fell from his horse. He was taken to the home of Mr Farrer (the secretary of the Board of Trade), Abinger Hall.

4. Richard Bethall, Lord Westbury (1800–73).

Letter to John Murray   *NLS Ms.42177*

7 FitzRoy Square

25 Aug: 1873

Dear Sir

The printers have now completed all my material for the 1st vol: of the new edition of Kugler – which brings the work to the first period of the Venetian School – <u>Gio: Bellini</u> and his followers.

I have already, as I informed you in the Autumn of 1871, worked up all the hitherto published material of Crowe & Cav: available for the 2nd vol: of the new edition of Kugler. I am not aware that anything has proceeded from their hands since their 2nd vol: of North Italy issued in 1871.

Such masters as <u>Fra Bartolommeo</u>, <u>And: del Sarto</u>, of the Florentine
School, and <u>Giorgione</u>, <u>Sch: del Piombo</u>, <u>Palma</u> and many other
of the Northern Schools are ready, but the greatest names still fail
– <u>Michelangelo</u>, <u>Raphael</u>, and <u>Titian</u>, and their followers. It will remain
with you to decide what to do. Should you have reason to know that
Crowe & Cav: will soon be ready with these, and, in short, with all
the rest, I will apply vigorously to the work as soon as I receive needful
material. You expressed an opinion in a note in the summer that it
would be best not to wait further for Crowe & Cav: In that case would
you retain the 2nd vol: of Kugler as it is, only introducing the newly
worked matter which I have prepared?

The 1st vol: with the exception of Burckhardt's preamble on Early
Christian art, is almost entirely new, and the labour has been far greater
than I anticipated. It would have been impossible for me, however, to
have retained Kugler's somewhat antiquated sentiment and style. It is
possible, however, that you may prefer his to mine.
Believe me your's faithfully
Eliz Eastlake
I see that in my notice of Giorgione I have alluded to an illustration of
a very fine picture at Madrid – intending to offer you a drawing of it
for a woodcut. If you wish for it you are of course welcome to it.

Letter to Hannah Brightwen   *Private Collection*

7 FitzRoy Sqre
13 Septr 1873
My dearest Hannah

It is always a pleasure to see yr handwriting & I only wish it cd
have told me that you were more free from your pains. I fear <u>our</u>
constitutions are not amenable to mineral baths! Jane does not get rid of
her pain & lameness, tho' she is generally so much better that she carries
them more lightly. As for me I have no pain except that of <u>unlocking</u>
my old joints after long sitting – or after sleeping. I do not find that
<u>using</u> them helps – a few times in & out of my little open carriage quite
sets me fast. But I have health & my lonely days pass – & I dwell on the
only Future – where joints will be pliable, & all will be <u>true</u>.

I <u>trust</u> however, that you will tell a better tale before long, & I
hope the same for my Jane. She took me for two days on her way
from Anglesea, to Yarmouth, looking fat & well. She has great faith
in <u>sea bathing</u> & has always obtained more relief from that than even

hot salt water baths. She is comfortable in Yarmouth, near George &
Sophy Simpson – & I know that she will gladly come to you in due
time. She has just been forming a decision as to her future home. I
had proposed to build a country house where I wd be all spring &
summer, & she all the year round. Not in a lonely place either, but
surrounded with neighbours to whom I had introduced her. But she is
afraid of winter loneliness, & altogether prefers to set up a little home
for herself at Windsor, where she has a few friends, & where she is
known. She is very wise & prudent, & thinks my country home will
take too long to build &c & so it certainly will now – for I cd not dig
the foundations for myself only. Her decision has caused me to abandon
the idea altogether (I had the offer of a lovely site), & I need no pity for
so doing. I set my heart on nothing, my Hannah, except on a quiet &
as far as possible, straight course. A little place – to build & form – wd
have been a great expense, & I can always hire for summer months. So
my little Castle in the air is blown away, & I am content.

I am just now working a little hard – getting on with a 2nd edition
or rather an entirely new revision of Kugler's Italian Painters. I was
stopped in my progress after the 1st vol: by my rather brutal publisher,
Mr Murray – who has only shown me his teeth & his heels since my
bereavemt. But the book is his – & I had long ago engaged to do
it anew, & oh! how glad I am to fill my days with work! I am now
pouring over Leo: da Vinci, & there is a question I want to ask you,
dear – did you not go with us to the Brera? that happy time – & am I
right in my impression that you asked my Beloved what he thought of
that drawing of the Lord's Head (for the Cena) which is there. Did he
not say to you that he thought it an inferior thing? I may be wrong,
& some one else may have asked him, but I fancy it was you. Can
you bring it to mind? I really do think that he thought it so – I know
I did. The Life of Leonardo is extraordinary – a mixture of depth &
shallowness. Gifted enough for 100 men, but without any real sign of
greatness.

I hear that the French Church article is by Dean Stanley. I have
not read it yet – but I heard Mrs Grote pronounce it to be so. The
Beaumarchais by Hayward.

I have just settled to go to Edinr on the 23rd in order to see what
kind of small tombstone my dearest Mrs Jones' grave will admit of. She
lies next her husband, a strange man but most dearly loved by her – &
I understand that his monument precludes anything but a footstone to
her. I shall judge for myself – order what is compatible – then probably
go into Argyleshire to Sir John Ordes' – Lady Orde being a kind friend.
Perhaps to Mr Pender's in the same neighbourhood, & then back to

Edinr & home altogether in about a fortnight. This will be quite a
holiday, tho' I leave even solitude unwillingly.

I am so glad that I have succeeded in hooking dear Ellen's poor Lady
– on to this Establishmt on Harley Street (for such Ladies). A temporary
vacancy has occurred & I saw her there today happily installed. It will
depend on the <u>sense</u> whether the situation become permanent. It is a
very honorable & interestg one. I am quite satisfied with the excellent
character & she has a gentle & agreeable person & manner. Wd that it
were always "like me", dear, to manage such things! But generally there
is nothg more difficult to get than work & home for a poor, tried, lady.

I have heard of Mrs H. Coleridges flattering notice of me.[1] I look
back across a gulf, as it were, on those times. I have had sad experience
– the friends in Albemarle St have all turned into haters of me, & I can
lift my heart to God & say "<u>without a cause</u>". It has been & is a heavy
trial – but it is from God for He knows I have done nothing to deserve
the cruel disrespect & worse I have recd at their hands. It is has [sic]
been for <u>years</u> now. I cd not <u>speak</u> of it when with you!

The article on Mr Grote's life is by <u>Henry Reeve</u> the editor. It is
much better than the Q. Review.

Now dearest God be with you!

Yr loving cousin

Eliz Eastlake

1. Sara Coleridge, *Memoirs and Letters, edited by her daughter (Edith Coleridge)*, 2
   vols. (London: Henry S. King & Co., 1873). Here Sara Coleridge describes
   her impressions of Elizabeth in 1848 in a letter to Edward Quillinan: 'She
   is perhaps the most brilliant woman of the day – the most accomplished
   Crichtonian. She draws, takes portraits like an artist, and writes cleverly on
   painting; she plays with power, and writes most strikingly on music; she
   speaks different languages. Her essays and tales have both had great success,
   the former as great as possible. To put the *comble* to all this, she is a very fine
   woman, large yet girlish, like a Doric pillar metamorphosed into a damsel,
   dark and striking. No, this is *not* the *comble*: the top of her perfections is, that
   she has well-bred, courteous, unassuming manners, does not take upon her
   and hold forth to the company – a fault of which many lionesses of the day
   are guilty. At this moment no less than *four* rise up before me, who show a
   desire to talk to the room at large, rather than quietly to their neighbour on
   the sofa. Miss R— is honourably distinguished in this respect. She is thoroughly feminine, like that princess of novelists, Jane Austen' (pp. 224–25).

Letter to John Murray   *NLS Ms.42177*

7 FitzRoy Square
23 Octr 1873
Dear Sir

I am favored with your friend's corrections of Kugler. They seem to
me chiefly curious as showing how much labour can be devoted to very
small purpose. It is too late to insert the few instances – as for example
a prophet, instead of an apostle – or 15 medallions instead of 13 in early
mosaics in which he may be correct. And it is consoling to see the the
Public will not be great sufferers.

In criticisms on later art he dwells on what every connoisseur knows
– tho' unknown in Kugler's time.

I retain the sheets for the present, but will carefully return them.

He must have consulted a different edition of Kugler to that in my
use for misprints of dates he includes are not such in my copy.

I am resuming the work now, but both the labour and the
responsibility entailed by the absence of Cavalcaselle's researches are
much greater.
Yr's faithfully
Eliz Eastlake

Letter to A. H. Layard   *NLS Ms.42170*

7 FitzRoy Sqre
21. Decr 1873
My dear Mr. Layard

You must not measure my gratitude for your kind letter of the
12th November by my slowness in acknowledg.g it. In my lonely
life the few old friends who knew & loved my dear Sir Chas, &
also are <u>true</u> to me, are very precious, & the sight of yr handwritg
(however illegible!) is always a pleasure. It is true I have no need
to be lonely, but I lack the spirit for company & find <u>work</u> a more
congenial filler up of my days than any amusement. Your description
of yr present life is no way entitled to any compassion – a comfortable
home – an honourable position, & dear Enid reading aloud Grote's
Greece to you of an evening offers a picture which many would envy.
Mrs Grote, who shared in yr letter, was greatly interested, & praises
your perseverance in what she calls "wading" thro' the two first vols,

which are a tough hill to climb. I shd like to be reading that work too.

Soon after our parting in Saville [sic] Row I made my way to Scotland, having business in Edinburgh & then into the hills & lochs I had not seen for many a year. My chief stay was in Loch Gilphead – close to Crinnon [sic] Canal, at Sir John Orde's, whose wife is an old friend. I fancied I was coming to the world's end but no sooner did my steamer touch the little remote pier than the Duke of Argyle stretched out his hand, then Mr. Motley, then Mrs. Ives then Sir Bartle Frere, & lastly the Archbishop of York, & I found myself among the great of the earth. Soon after Mr Pender made his appearance, which completed the constellation. Your old flame – or one of your old flames – Mrs Ives, has gone the way of all American beauties, not anything improper I beg to say, but only she has lost her good looks. The Freres are cousins to the Ordes & were returning by the steamer that brought me. The others were all guests of the Duke & of Pender. As I am no walker & fond of staying indoors, I was rather amused by the <u>incessant</u> rain. Of course it rains <u>every day</u> in those Western Highlands, & often all day long. The consequence is that those once barren hills & sheep walks are being turned into a luxuriance of rhododendrons, <u>bamboo cane</u>, fuschias like trees, & heaths like shrubs, which I have seen nowhere else. No fruit ripens but the most astonishing flora flourishes. I enjoyed my stay at Kilmory (the Ordes) where there was a succession of visitors, among them a young Major Euan Smith who reminded me of a certain Layard of 25 years ago, <u>in spite of which</u> he interested me much. He is not unknown to fame, having been appointed to settle some boundary questions in Persia, having had important charges in the Abyssinian War & lastly having accompanied Sir B: Frere to Zanzibar. Also he is the youngest Commander of the Victoria Cross. We made rather friends & he has been dining here, & I hope to see more of him. From Kilmory I went on – 12 miles further up Loch Fyne – to Pender's. He has a <u>beautiful</u> place, where Mrs P: condescends to spend 6 weeks in the year. He is an interesting man, & I have long known him, but she has such high stilts that I cd not attempt to reach her. He was full of a plan for utilizing the endless accumulations of dust coal, by a form of compression, & blocks were burning in their grates which I shd be very glad to get for a pound a ton, wh: is the price he hopes to put them in the market for. I returned her the end of Octr & have been stationary since. Mrs Grote has spent a month in London, talking her best <u>all day long</u>, till she was worn out, at last she became too <u>hoarse</u>, wh: tho' a loss to us was a blessing to herself, especially as it did not prevent her playing whist. I hear that she has quite recovered in the country, where I hope to spend a few days the beginning of January.

The other eveng, being out, I paid a visit to Lady Wm Russell, who spoke of letters she had had from yourselves. She was as well as usual but at the opposite end of her house.

I hear of the book of the Memorial in Hyde Park, but have not seen it yet. Mr Newton wanted me to write an article on it, & it wd doubtless interest me to do so, but I have at present too much to do. This new edition of Kugler's Handbook gets on but slowly, having now no materials from Caval: to work from. Yet I can't leave the old version wh: is in every way antiquated. Both Leonardo & M: Angelo I have recast entirely, but there is little now to be said of Raphael, tho' some things to be left out.

Mill's autobiography is still the talk. It is a most curious book – treating a poor child like a cucumber & putting it into a case in wh: it could grow only in one direction. It gives me great respect as well as great pity for him. You will be sure to quarrel with me about it when we meet![1]

Give my kindest love to yr Enid, & with some to yrself wh: my mature age excuses, believe me dear Mr Layard, your's always truly Eliz Eastlake

The Buchanans were in London a short time. We went together to Bethnal Green, the collection looked very splendid.

1. J. S. Mill's *Autobiography* was first published in 1873.

Letter to John Murray   *NLS Ms.42177*

7 FitzRoy Square
3 Janry 1874
Dear Sir

I have received the enclosed note from Mssrs Clowes which speaks for itself. I feel it would be unnecessary for me to explain to them the reasons for the delay in the progress of the work. You are aware that it arose from your failing to reply to my letter of Sept or Octr 1871 in which I appealed for instructions – having then gone as far as Cavalcaselle's work allowed me – which instructions I only obtained from you last August 1873.

The 2nd vol: involves, as I have said before, more labour than the first – not having the advantage of Cavalcaselle's researches. But I have made considerable way with it – at least with the more important painters. I cannot say when I should be ready. I fear not for three months.

I regret the long interval of inactivity, for I had then more leisure than I am able now to command. Will you oblige me by answering Messrs Clowes' letter.
Believe me yr's faithfully
Eliz Eastlake

Letter to Francis Galton[1]   *The Galton Papers,*
UCL Library Services, Special Collections 122/1B

7 FitzRoy Square
3 January 1874
Dear Mr Galton,
  I have recd yr note, & the curious and interesting questions regarding twins. I am <u>not</u> a twin, but my family, both on father's & mother's side, abound with cases of twins & upwards.
  My Father was Dr. Rigby of Norwich, my mother a Palgrave of the same county. She was his 2nd wife – 30 years younger than himself. Their first children were twins. Boy & girl (girl first). They both grew up beyond middle age – he Dr. Edward Rigby of Berkeley Sq., she Madame Anne de Wahl. No brother & sister were ever more <u>unlike</u> in mind, temper, habits &c, nor were they at all alike in physiognomy, tho' both equally large & tall. My mother had then six single childn, all strong – five of them still alive – and then she gave birth to <u>four children</u>, in 1817. These were all perfect & healthy – but did not live above 3 months. A sister now with me, older than myself, remembers that there was great dissimilarity in complexion, colour of eyes, of general size among them.[2]
  My mother's sister Mrs Powys, long dead, had <u>three</u> childn at a birth, two boys & a girl. They all grew up & we think that the two men are alive still. They were James, Secundus, & Letitia. I never saw Secundus but Letitia was as unlike James as possible. She had no palate to her mouth.
  My Father had two daughters by his first wife, both older than my mother – one of them had twins, who did not live.
  My cousin Sir Ed. Parry had two wives. The first a daughter of Lord Stanley of Alderley. She had twins <u>three times</u>. The first were boy & girl – not alike in person. The boy is the Suffragan Bp of Dover, Edwd Parry, the girl died, & all the others died I believe as infants. Then he married Mrs. Hoare, & had twins again – two girls – I have never seen them, one is married. Lady Parry (the mother) lives at Tunbridge Wells.

As regards the <u>Stanley</u> wife I may remind you that the late Lord Stanley & his only brother were twins.

None of my mother's childn have had twins, tho' all have had childn, who are married. But my niece in Russia Baroness Maydell had twins, boy & girl – unlike outwardly – the girl has died. Also my nephew Dr. de Wahl of Petersburg has had twins – boy & girl – girl dead. We know nothing of similarity or not. Bss Maydell & Dr. de Wahl are grandchildn of my parents.

I remember & know many other instances of twins. The late Lord Stafford (Sir Geo: Jermingham of Norfolk) had twin girls. Frances & Georgina, both grew up & were <u>strikingly alike</u> in person.

Mr. Wm Stark of Norwich, brother to the painter, had twin girls, most —-fully [*letter folded*] alike – both alive – & grown up. Their mother Mrs Stark's address is St. George's Plain Norwich.

I have a young friend with me now – Mrs. Elliott – her sister Mrs. Cane of Weston Rectory, Newark has twin girls – so alike as not to be distinguishable, except by an outward mark.

The late Mrs. Douglas Baird had twin girls, equally undistinguishable. Jeannie & Charlotte Baird. One married Lord Cole, the other a Villiers.

A curious instance of three girls at a birth occurred in Norfolk, & mt be heard of by applying to a Edward Simpson Esq Tombland Norwich.

I may add that my Mother belonged to a large family. Her eldest brother Mr. Palgrave had twelve childn, her eldest sister Mrs Powys eleven, her next sister Mrs Dawson Turner eleven, another seven, another 5. My own brother & sisters have not had numerous families owing to accidental circumstances – one sister alone had eight.

I have now given you a long chapter – in a desultory way.

I see the great interest of the subject & am inclined, rather hastily, to generalise in two ways – viz: that twins occur in large families, & that those of the same sex are most frequently alike.
Believe me yr's truly
Eliz Eastlake

1. Francis Galton (1822–1911), explorer and scientist. In 1873 he put out a circular for information on twin births in preparation for his 'History of Twins', perhaps for *Fraser's Magazine*, 1875.

2. The remarkable birth of the quadruplets to a couple aged 70 and 40 years respectively was recorded in *The Times*: 'Dr. Rigby is a great grandfather, and, probably, never before were born at one birth, three great uncles and a great aunt'. *The Times*, 25 August 1817, p. 2, col. E.

Letter to Hannah Brightwen   *Private Collection*

7 FitzRoy Sqre
26 Janry 1874

I think you must have felt, my dearest Hannah, that I was longing to
write to you – & preparg to do it daily – but am daily interrupted.
Your dear letter clears away all procrastination, & I am glad to tell you
at once how much my thoughts have been with you at this tryg season.
I begin now to feel that all anniversaries & New Year's Days begin to
run together, & go swelling in one ever stronger stream to the great
Ocean. I hope that I trust the Pilot more & more, & in that find all the
Peace I now can realize.

   Your day was peculiarly present to me, for yr fellow sufferer on
that same day, Lady Strangford, took my little brougham to visit her
Husband's grave, & then came back to me & took & gave comfort.

   It is true my life is full of occupation – & yet so lonely! It is true
I cd obviate that if I wd, but havg none that naturally come to me,
except dear Jane, I have so ordered my life as to need, & my Solitude
– little as I like it. Society – "full dressed" I can go to, & summon to
me. I take the first as it comes – but I am niggardly of the great effort
of entertaing. On those occasions the missing him, whom my sould
loveth, is peculiarly painful. Still there are times when I must make
the effort – old & kind friends come from a distance & challenge the
usual hospitality. Such are Sir Andrew & Lady Buchanan – from Vienna
– who are in Engld on a short congé, & dined here last Wednesday.
I had the Italian minister – old Chev: Cadorna – a most intelligent,
simple, gentleman to meet them,[1] & Baroness de Hügil – niece of my
much admired hero-friend, Sir Jas Outram, & Hayward, & the youngest
Commander of the Victoria Cross a Major Evan Smith – much in
Persia, Abyssinia, & (with Sir B: Frere,) in Zanzibar, remindg me of
Layard in his ardent, adventurous life. And my dear Annie Butson came,
& it went off well. And dear Joseph Hooker – last, tho' truly not least,
who, tho' he had had a ball at his own home, & had danced 20 times,
yet was as bright as a boy. The Buchanans especially wished to meet
him. Strange to say I have found people whom one fancies must be
worldly, true & kind & thoughtful of me in my desolation, when those,
far more humbly placed, have been utterly heartless & disrespectful.
Especially I have had this experience from the professors of religion!
– the harm such people do to the great cause is not to be told.

   Your account of Miss Maher – whom I well remember – is deeply
touchg. Often, when sick with my heart's solitude, I call up the image

of a lonely governess – <u>heart starved</u>, & needg indeed a great <u>Trust</u> not to look forward with <u>dread</u> to old age & failing means. I remember yr asking me about investments for her. I longed at the time to say I wd take her money, & give her 6 percent for it (& a full receipt) but I was afraid she might think it a liberty. I do so with the small savgs of another lady governess, & pay her half yearly the small interest. I wd that I cd get such ladies the <u>situations</u> they desire. I have always a number of worthy candidates on my list. And all this time I am commissioned to select a "model governess" for the Gd Duchess of Baden, & have not succeeded.

No article in the new Q.R: is by me. I have it, but have hardly looked at it. The publisher of the Q.R. is one who had been among the most heartless & disrespectful of those I <u>thought</u> my friends, & I shall never write in it again. The Edinr (edited by my cousin Henry Reeve) is open to me – but at present I am engaged on a dry task, which owg to causes over wh: I have no control, has been needlessly protracted – viz: a new edition of Kugler's Handbook of Italin art. It will be like the little boy's knife – what with new blade & new handle there will be nothing of the old edition left in it! I have about a <u>quarter</u> more to do. After that I hope to turn to things which need more thought of my own.

As to Holman Hunt's Shadow of the Cross I have of course seen it, but what to say of it is difficult.[2] The chief merit alleged in its favor is that it took him 5 years to paint it & that he went twice to Jerusalem so as to have every screw & shaving <u>correct</u>. Neither of which reason necessarily constitute good art. He is a man of great conceit & affectation, despising all traditions of art, & repudiatg its most obvious rules. Much as if an author writg a book shd insist on inventing a new alphabet, & a new printing press! It has the merit of <u>labour</u> – if such be a <u>merit</u> – it is exhibited under claptrap conditions of artificial lights, & it is advertised & puffed in all directions. <u>Still</u>, I prefer it to <u>Dore's</u> most contemptible parody of the old masters.[3]

I have run on dearest – & can only just tell you that Jane seems contented at Bath. The waters agree with her health, tho' at present she derives no benefit for the main purpose. She is longing much for a <u>home</u>, wh: I do not wonder at – but it is difficult to plan for her. I wd fain live together in the summer – but it is not easy to arrange.

Now dear this is a long yarn. I have been to my hospital to day, always learning somethg there.

God be ever with you dearest!

Yr loving cousin & friend

Eliz Eastlake

1. Chevalier Carlo Cadorna, Italian statesman and ambassador.

2. William Holman Hunt's *The Shadow of Death*, 1869–73, Manchester City Art Galleries.

3. The Doré Gallery opened in New Bond Street in 1867 to display Gustave Doré's paintings.

Letter to Hannah Brightwen   *Private Collection*

The Ridgeway
28 March 1874
My dearest Hannah

I came here to Mrs Grote on the 26th (till next Monday) bringing your dear letter with me, for the chance of a little talk with you. Well do I know that there is more difficulty in findg time when one is idle than when busy? But here I have some portion of the day to myself, tho' tempted out to violets & peach blossoms in a way that F: Square does not present.

Mrs Grote is 82 – with much feebleness – for her – stronger in body, however, than many of her juniors – & stronger in mind than most men or women. She is not even known or done justice to in her writings. She assumes a manner with her pen. Her conversation alone does her justice – in that is heared her wit, her wisdom, her soundness, fairness – knowledge & accuracy. And that I fear can never be preserved. Her life has led her much into the political world, & in this respect she is singularly weatherwise, & few foresesaw [sic] the late unexpected turn of the English expression of opinion so clearly as she.

I I get on to this chapter involuntarily. I study her much – I owe her much. I begin to be very critical (& have been since sad experience in time of adversity) as to the real meaning of belief in Christ. It lies sometimes between those who say 'I will' & yet go not, & those who say 'I will not' & yet go. But this is a terribly large question. Doubtless the real meaning of belief in Christ lies only between God & the soul, & will never be entirely defined too often it is a mere formula.

It is good indeed to see a highly cultivated man walking, as you say "simply in an earnest & sensible, & holy course". Work prevents over much reasong. "travaillons & ne refléchessons pas" was a wise say. g, tho' by Voltaire. Still I am sure that Christianity & a Christian's highest faith are the highest reason. But one needs to turn to one's Bible, & to the law of God in the soul to stand firmly & patiently

against the host of inanity & presumption which the present democracy
in religion pours forth. I know that I am very impatient at the trash
written upon art – the same must apply to the million who write upon
religion. I very much dislike that book you mention "modern Xtianity
a refined Heathenism".[1] I read it with many a sotto voce of irritation,
some months ago. I believe it to be false in its premisses throughout.
Brahminism is not what it suits the writer to represent. Also that
incessant terror of everlastg punishmt is rank treason to Christ – who
has died for the sins of the whole world, & who is better served &
rewarded by remindg his creatures of the duties He has entrusted to
them than by a perpetual worry & panic about the Salvation wh: He has
obtained for us. I expected all along that the writer was going (& from
his premises,) to demonstrate the impossibility of Eternal Punishment
– but he leaves us suspended in a sort of agony wh: can bear no fruit
but doubt. Such books to some minds wd almost destroy the belief in a
Creator – & such books much account for the so-called scepticism of the
day.

I am readg one much recommended by the Dss of Northumberland
"The Christ of History" by "John Young M.A." proving the Divinity
of our Lord from sources independt of miraculous intervention waiving
those for arguments sake. You do not want these proofs my dearest
Hannah – nor I – but to those minds who, from various reasons, are
not reached by dogma, such a view is most useful. I have not seen "La
femme forte".

As for my worldly matters I have not succeeded in getting the desired
little place either to hire or buy, & am come to a pause. Meanwhile
my ideas of inducg dear Jane to combine with me, which perhaps she
never cordially took to, have found their frustration in the fact that
she has suddenly found what she likes as a home for herself alone. She
came from Bath, not a fortnight ago, to lodg.gs at Windsor. There she
discovered that the house, 2 Adelaide Place, where our dear Mother
& she had lived for 10 years was vacant – new drained & new every
thinged. & the landlord haltg between two applicants for it, but
throwing them both over for her. So she came to me last Monday
full of this plan, & she liking it better than any other & not shunning
loneliness as I do, I cd see no objection. It is within her means – &
were it not, that wd matter little, as long as I have plenty. So she
decided the day before Lady Day & will be into it with her furniture
by next Thursday. So that is settled. & tho' sorry not to have her move
under my wing, I am content with what she prefers. I have meanwhile
taken a ready furnished house near here – on Albury Heath – for 4
months in beautiful air, tho' with only a sandy garden. But the Albury

Woods are close by & the ground is entirely to my taste. There I shall fix myself about the 20th May. With Jane I bargain that she spend at least a month with me in summer & a month in winter. Perhaps you, dear love, will come to me before the next 4 months expire.

I am glad to know the period of Dawson's Polly's marriage for I mean to send her a few words of greeting beforehd.

The Grote's heart & mine are bleeding for poor Hilda Bunsen (as she was) the Madme de Krause of hardly a year, with a child of five weeks old. Her husband killed by a fall from his horse! But the Cross is our necessary lot, & our best friend. I feel that more & more now that habit has worn away its sharpest edges. A great sorrow is a great endowment – that alone can make the wilderness blossom like the rose! The true mourner must get faith proportioned to her need. Nothing else but such sorrow requires such faith. The well to be dug is deep, & toilsome – but the waters are those of Life.

My dearest love to Ellen. We shall meet where there is no parting "if we faint not" & yet I feel the presumption of putting myself in the category with her!

Ever my dearest Hannah

Yr loving

Eliz Eastlake

I return home on Monday 30th.

> 1. Henry William Pullen, *Modern Christianity, a Civilized Heathenism* (Salisbury: Brown & Co., 1873).

Letter to A. H. Layard   *NLS Ms.42170*

7 FitzRoy Sqre

4 May 1874

My dear Mr. Layard

Your date of March 9th, and mine of May 4th, make me feel rather guilty, tho' the interval of time has not abated my enjoyment of yr letter, & my gratitude for it. I heard of you as being at Gibraltar, & this, with a wish to tell you a little about the Private View of the R.A: Exhibition have been my reasons for delay. But Boxall has just been in, pouring his grumbles into my ever compassionate heart, & from him I know that you have written to him from Madrid. I told him I was on the point of writing to you & am charged by him with a few messages to you. Like me, he did not doubt that you wd long ere this have known that

his resignation was a <u>fait accompli</u>. The reasons for it he manages to
ascribe in equal share to you & to Gregory! He feels that yr unsupplied
places at the Board, you both retaining yr seats, have been a great loss
& hindrance to business. For many months there have been as good as
no Trustees, Wm Russell long ill, good J. Baring dead, Ld Northampton
incapable, Sir Walter James away. So Boxall fell from depression, to
despair and could not bear the weight of the Gallery on his shoulders
alone. You will believe that I did my best to keep hime in office, and
I did keep him true for a time, but he grew beyond my management,
and was so evidently incapable of exertion that I could only submit.
Mr. Burton is, I may say entirely, <u>his</u> choice.[1] Of course I had known
his name as a watercolour artist, but I was unaware of anything further.
Boxall had no reason to know that he is a man of education – a good
scholar – a gentleman. He He had been of much service to B: in making
out the real subject of Mr. Virnon's fine Mantegna which required some
accurate and some classical knowledge – as you would see in the latest
N: Gal: Cat: Mr. Burton is also one of the few modern artists who had
devoted himself to the study of old masters. In short, tho' wanting that
technical knowledge and acquaintance with the diseases of pictures,
and modes of remedy, which I fancy will be indispensable (and which
I trust he may pick up) there was positively no one else in the shape
of a cultivated <u>gentleman</u> who could be found. Gladstone took a great
alarm because Mr. Burton is not an R.A. – supposing that the diploma
entailed a fitness for the Directorship of the N.G. – but Boxall overruled
that. As to your not being consulted about his resignation Boxall seems
astonished at the <u>unreasonableness</u> of your expecting such a stretch of
form on his part. As you could not discharge your duty to the Nat: Gal:
and to him, he argued that he could not discharge his to you, which he
feels was of far less importance to the public interests. He heaps no end
of responsibilities on your shoulders, and, being of a forgiving disposition,
no end of <u>coals</u> on your head! If you and Gregory would have resigned I
believe Ld Overstone wd have resumed his Trusteeship, whom Boxall <u>I
believe</u> thinks worth Gregory & you put together. However you may lay
this last impertinence to my unassisted imagination.

    I have made acquaintance with Mr. Burton and invited him
purposely to dine, where I had some talk with him, and assured him
of my readiness to supply him with any information from dear Sir
Chas' copious notes. He is a pleasant looking and mannered man – left
handed. He has made an expedition to Majence [Mainz] to see some
reported Mich: Angelo which turns out as might he expected, a rather
ordinary M: Venusti of the reputed Pieta. Boxall has rather resumed his
spirits since his emancipation from office, & I hope you will find him

much better when you come. When that does happen I fear I shall not be here to see for I have taken a house on charming Albury Heath for 4 months to wh: I go on the 20th this month. I wish you wd take 7 FitzRoy! I hope yr visit to dear old Sir Fenwick has refreshed you both, & made you better able to <u>endure</u> Madrid, for much as I admire the picture of Enid seated at yr feet reading the History of the Past, I can compassionate the lot of any one cast in that country.

I went and inspected the drawings and photographs form the tapestries of the Apocalypse of which you told me – at the Arundel Society. I am inclined to think them Mabuse – as Morelli did. But I do not think they would be popular even for the most frantic highchurch clergymen. They are too ugly in subject and treatment, tho' judgg from the photograph, full of a certain force. So I let my influence over Mr Maynard alone.

Meanwhile the Private View took place last Friday, I spent many hours there. The exhibition is extolled but I did not feel up to the usual standard. The older men have indeed gone off. <u>Cope</u>, <u>Frith</u>, and <u>Faed</u> all the poorest of the poor. The intermediate set of <u>Calderon</u>, <u>Marks</u> & <u>Leighton</u> in great mediocrity. <u>Prinsep</u> a horror. <u>Holman Hunt</u> unmentionable. <u>Ouless</u> very unequal. <u>Nicol</u> without his humour, which is his only quality. And of new ones not much – excepting a <u>Miss Thompson</u> in a very favourable picture of the "roll call after an engagement in the Crimea" & <u>Fildes</u> in Casuals waiting to be taken in. But <u>Watts</u> stands firmly. A head of Jas Martineau the dissenting preacher is a type of a grand, ugly, spritual head, contrasted with that is a head of J.S. Mill – quite fit to be a frontispiece to a memoir, compressed and even extinguished in feeling, & unnaturally expanded in intellect. The mouth tight shut, the eyes not loog at you, the cranium immense. Lastly <u>Millais</u> is in full force – a picture he calls "the North West Passage", an old navigator sitting with a fair girl at his feet readg to him (the allusion to the N.W. Passage very remote). The old navigator is painted from "Greek Trelawney" who, being an utter scamp, is, doubtless, one of yr intimate friends. It is his <u>finest work</u>, with a harmony of tone & line quite refreshing after the host of trash on the walls.[2] <u>Lewis</u> also stands well. There is no <u>Walker</u> & I missed <u>Mason</u> who has gone to his rest.

Mrs Grote is in town, & was there, partly under my care, not at all in a mood to be pleased with the pictures, but much in a mood to sit & talk with a <u>relay</u> of gentlemen at her side, & never more brilliant. It was the best position for the dear lady, for she is not fit for the fatigue of standing about.

I am now just concluding the edition of Kugler's Handbook I have had so long in hand – no fault of mine, but certain people in Albemarle are quite too grand to attend to any business of mine, and so I waited

a year and half – or more – for instructions. Crowe & Caval: have
made no further sign since the 5th vol: and so I have finished the
greater matters. Leo: da V., Raphael, Titian & Correggio unassisted
by them. Sir Chas' notes have been my chief resource. I am now
correcting proofs, & shd have been pouring over them but for this long
letter to you. I am looking a little into Leo: da V.'s nature & character
as connected with the state of Italy at this time, & I hope to make
something of it for an article in Edinr. But, London is full. I have two
young nieces staying with me, no end of interruptions & a very speedy
end of strength. I shall be thankful to be in the country.

Meanwhile I fear you will return me all my complaints upon yr
handwriting! I assure you I prize it too much to lose a word. I saw yr
good aunt about a fortnight ago, about the same as usual.
Now with kind love to Enid
I am ever yrs truly
Eliz Eastlake

1. Frederick Burton (1816–1900), painter and Director of the National Gallery
   from 1874 to 1894.

2. John Everett Millais, *The North-West Passage* (1874), Tate. The sitter, Edward
   John Trelawny (1792–1881), had not been pleased with the results of the
   portrait and alledgedly challenged Millais to a duel.

Letter to John Murray   *NLS Ms.42177*

Albury Heath, Guildford
29. May 1874
Dear Sir

I beg to acknowledge the receipt of your cheque for £210 upon the
completion of the new edition of Kugler. I also return the enclosed
paper with my signature. I hope that you will not in my lifetime, allow
any further alterations to be made in this work without giving me the
option of supplying them.

I have referred Messrs. Clowes to yourself for the form of the title
page but I should wish to see a proof of it before it is finally arranged.

I have also referred them to you for any additions to the list of
publications on Italian art – or comparing Italian art – besides Waagen's
Treasures, and Crowe & Cavalcaselle's work.
I remain yrs faithfully
Eliz Eastlake

Letter to William Boxall   NG14/77

Albury Heath
Guildford
9. June 1874
Dear Sir Wm

You are often in my thoughts, tho' you have not been bothered with my handwritg. Today, however, I must break silence, after reading the report in the Times of the Barker Sale, & ascertaining (for I have the Barker Catalogue with me) the pictures which Mr Burton has ventured to purchase.[1] I do not remember them all, & I am sure you wd give him yr kind advice, if he requested it, but I fear he has brought much that is second rate & much that is irrepairably injured, & for enormous prices. That Venus & Amorini by S: Botticelli seems to me to be monstrous in price – indeed almost all. I do not envy him, but doubtless his set will approve, & he must learn experience.[2]

I have been longing to beg you to come here, but I have not yet that freedom to ask you which I desire. I fear I shall not come begging till the beginning of July, for my sister is coming & maid, & I have not so many rooms as I wd wish to fill.

Let me know how you are dear Sir Wm. I am enjoying the sweet quiet, the flowers, birds, views &c &c & trying to get strong.

We hardly wanted more Crivelli's & I do not remember the Barker Crivellis – I hope they are fine.[3] Ever yrs afftly
Eliz Eastlake

1. Alexander Barker (d. 1873); his sale, Christie, Manson & Woods, London, 6 June 1874.

2. Botticelli's *Venus and Mars* (NG915) was purchased in 1874 for £1,050.

3. Crivelli's *Immaculate Conception* (NG906) and *Saint Mary Magdalene* (NG907.2).

Letter to John Murray   NLS Ms.42177

Albury Heath, Guildford
11 June 1874
Dear Sir

I have recd your note and the proof of title page. I have not the old one to compare it by, but it seems to me as if no alteration had been made

in it except the date, and the proposed striking out of the line alluding
to Scharf. I hardly can comprehend how Sir Chas' name can be left as
it now stands – most of your readers will be aware that he is no longer
in his place. Even if my preface did not mention the fact of my using
the valuable memoranda he has <u>left</u>. But at all events this is no longer a
"third edition" which my preface states to have been published in <u>1855</u>.

I can only repeat that I do not <u>understand</u> such a title page, and can
only conclude that there is some mistake, and by that you will do me
the favour to revise it. I return it to you.

Yr's faithfully

Eliz Eastlake

I am quite satisfied that the list of books shd be omitted.

Letter to Hannah Brightwen   *Private Collection*

Albury Heath

Guildford

11. June 1874

My dearest Hannah

I can truly respond that yr dear handwritg is always a "sight for sair
een" to me,[1] however much of sorrow & anxiety it may report. You see
that yr letter has followed me into my favourite part of the country, wh:
I have resorted to earlier than supposed. I felt the want of fresh air &
sweet Nature & took this house – near one I had last year – from the
21st May till the 21st Septr.

Now to yr letter, dearest, & first to the subject of the French journal
of which really I know nothing. But if you write to, or ask someone
to apply to "Rolandi's Foreign Library, Berners Street, Oxford Street"
I have no doubt they will furnish all information – or the journal itself
– & give the means of supplyg statistical French publications. People
can subscribe for a week – a month – or a year there – & they are <u>very</u>
intelligent people. I only fear that Inglis may say 'Oh, yes we know all
about Rolandi, & he has not got the work". & if he does say so, dear,
then let me know & I will turn to my good friend Mdme Mohl who
comes to the Stanleys (Deanery, Westminster) on to morrow. Shd you
or Inglis not know Rolandi, then you are quite welcome to mention my
name – tho' it wd not be necessary.

And now for that other <u>most</u> afflicting subject, which fills my
thoughts. Strange to say no whisper of yr poor brother's illness had
reached me (or Jane), except by a letter from <u>Rome</u> – dated May 31

– from Mr Hamilton, to whom I had commended the Woodwards & who, writg on some business alludes to Mrs Woodward's anxiety about her father. Ah! my Hannah! this is indeed hard for <u>him</u> & <u>his</u>, & for all of you to bear. His work has truly been always <u>superhuman</u>, & his holidays feats of strength. The falling off of the School is a sad trial for the ardent mind, which takes all labor by storm – & health giving way, as I know it is for long. Poor, poor fellow!² When a thing <u>preys</u> on an ardent mind & on an affte heart I know too well how akin that is to its <u>overthrow</u>. I have wondered that my own has stood. He has my deepest sympathy. And, dearest, if help be needed, do quietly dispose of £50 from me. It shd be ready in <u>July</u>. I <u>trust</u> that the need for his being where he is will soon leave – but I see all the distress – & God <u>only</u> is our Friend! & we know that we can trust Him! – & that sorrows are the highest proof of <u>honour</u> that He can bestow upon us. <u>But</u>, it is all hard for anxious human hearts to bear.

With yr letter came another wh: gave me great pain too – from my dear & good nephew Charles Eastlake – an architect & Sectry to the Institute of British Architects. He had had work to do for a person, believed to be a man of honor & property – wh: had involved Chas: in expenses he cd ill bear, taken up time, employed workmen &c. The man proves an <u>imposter</u> – & what is more & to me makes it worse he is brother, as it proves, to that unprincipled fellow whom <u>Justina</u>, in return for countless benefits, brought against all our <u>entreaty</u> into our family! This must not be mentioned further either, tho' I fear it will become public story.

My good Jane comes here on Saturday for a month. She has become so much more lame that I doubted the fact of rheumatism, & felt sure that she ought <u>not</u> to walk, wh: of late has given her <u>intense</u> pain. Her old & kind Dr at Slough has seen her & pronounces it inflammation of the socket of the thigh bone – interdicts all movement except on two sticks so as to give absolute rest to the limb – under wh: circumstances he gives her hopes that after a few weeks she will feel the benefit. I am the more glad to have her coming here, where she can have carriage exercise & every indulgence. I have the same dear little girl with me I took to Wimbledon last year. She is like a niece – & <u>waits on</u> both of us Minna Lewin – Mrs Grote's niece – so this will be congenial to Jane.

I am obliged to hurry this end of my letter being interrupted, & must speak of R.A. Exhibtion (<u>not</u> first-rate) next time.

Pray take my small offer for yr dear Dawson <u>au sérieux</u>. It shd be sent to you first week in July, & I can help my good Chas Eastlake too.
Ever dearest yr attached
Eliz Eastlake

1. Scottish, 'sight for sore eyes'.

2. See letter, 4 March 1865.

Letter to John Murray   *NLS Ms.42177*

Albury Heath, Guildford
15 June 1874
Dear Sir
   I consider that the publication of a work is the best judge of what
title page will most promote its interests in the sale of the work. I
therefore offer my suggestion with diffidence. I do not see how Sir Chas'
name can be retained on the title page of a work edited by him not
later actually than 1851. And I think that the mention in the preface
of the assistance derived from his notes in this edition is the only
form in which that fact can be made known. I therefore enclose a few
suggestions – though I disclaim any responsibility on a matter in which
I have no special knowledge.
Yr's faithfully
Eliz Eastlake

Letter to John Murray   *NLS Ms.42177*

Albury Heath, Guildford
19 June 1874
Dear Sir
   Your letter just recd is incomprehensible to me. In the first page you
state that it would never have entered your head to omit that Name
from the title page to which the work in question owes so much – &
in the next page you state that you will take good care that the present
edition shall be known to come from another Editor. I am therefore at a
loss to guess who the Editor is whom you propose bringing forward for
the present edition – as, in the same breath you regret my prohibition to
give my own name, which you have never requested me to give.
Yours faithfully
Eliz Eastlake

Letter to John Murray [1]   *NLS Ms.42177*

Albury Heath, Guildford
22 June 1874
Dear Sir

I do not see the possibility of retaining Sir Chas' name in any way in the title page of this edition. It is plainly impracticable to connect the name of One, long passed from this scene, as editor to a work of the present year, and one in which, moreover, not a tenth part remains as in his edition.

But the duty & privilege of embodying his labours in this quasi-new book have been thoroughly exercised by myself, as will be obvious to every reader, and as mentioned in the preface. By this means his identification with the present work is entirely secured, and was, indeed, my chief motive in undertaking the task. The desire, therefore, to insert Sir Chas' name on the title page or advertisement of the work can be of no further tribute to him.

Also it will be obvious to all who care about it that this edition can only have proceeded from me, for no other person could either have been imbued with his teaching, or had possession of his notes. But you have never requested my name as editor. You once alluded to a possible wish on my part to insert it, but you assured me that it was superfluous. Still, there can be no doubt that my name is, in every sense, the right one for this work, and that it also would increase its mercantile value. But the labour I have bestowed on it, greatly increased and impeded as it has been by your inattention to my letters, has been very arduous, and I do not see that you have any further claim upon me. At the same time the labour has been one of love, and I only wish it could have been more thoroughly complete.

If you still desire a different arrangement of the title page to that suggested by me I beg that you will submit it to my approval

Yr's faithfully
Eliz Eastlake

1. Copy of letter from John Murray to Elizabeth, 23 June 1874, in the Letter Book containing copies of outgoing correspondence (NLS Ms.41914), in reply: 'As I understand from you that your labour in editing Kugler has been greater than you expected and also that you attach a mercantile value to your name as Editor I will give you £50 more for the permission to insert it on the title page. I regret that I cannot comply with your suggestion of omitting Sir Charles' name'.

Letter to William Boxall   NG14/77

Albury Heath. Guildford
29. June 1874
My dear Sir Wm

I am longing to hear from you, & know how you stand this changeable weather. Mrs Grote is just back from ten days in London, & to my question whether she had seen <u>you</u> she pretends that she has no chance of getting at you except thro' me! I cd get at you myself! But I have still my good sister with me – with her maid – & till she is well enough to leave me I have not the requisite room. And I want to have you & nice Mrs Cavendish Boyle <u>together</u> wh: I trust will be some time next month. Meanwhile you have lost nothing, for the weather has been so damp & chilly that you are best by yr <u>own fireside</u>. I had fire in the drawg room yesterday here.

I have a letter from my dear little "Mary Elliott", whom I am sure you do not forget – at all events she does not forget <u>you</u>, for she says "pray tell me about that nice Sir Wm Boxall". The dear thing is in a very feeble & suffering state, havg had much to <u>overcome</u> wh: she has done bravely. I want her parents to entrust her to me for a time.

I have been corresponding a little with Mr. Burton in consequence of a few words I write Sir Walter James – as to Sir Chas havg originally purchased that P. della Francesca for himself. Mr Burton is quite welcome to state that. Robinson's malicious vulgarity, & his <u>mongrel</u> English must convince all worth convincing what he is.[1] Lady Alwyne Compton writes me that you brought Mr Burton & introduced him to Ld Northampton, who was pleased with him. Do you know what part Gregory has taken?

Let me know how you are, by the by I hear but sad accts of dear old Penry Williams from Rome. I you wd help me with him I wd ask him to come. Ever yrs afftly
Eliz Eastlake

1. The National Gallery had just purchased Piero della Francesca's *Nativity* from the Barker Sale for £2,415. J. C. Robinson wrote several letters to the editor of *The Times* (Tuesday, 9 June 1874; p.7, col. E; Monday, 15 June 1874, p. 12, col. D; and Wednesday, 24 June 1874, p. 13, col. F) outlining his role in bringing Piero's *Baptism* to London (purchased by Eastlake for £241) and castigating the National Gallery for missing out on the opportunity to purchase the *Nativity*, for presumably a similar sum of money, at the same time.

Letter to John Murray   *NLS Ms.42177*

Albury Heath, Guildford
28 July 1874
Dear Sir

After the long delay in preparing the index to the new version of
Kugler I was not a little surprised to receive yesterday the proof of
that which you have had drawn up. The old index of 26 years ago
was in every way troublesome and unserviceable. I am aware that
you thought so, and you are aware that I thought so. I am at a loss
therefore to account for your wishing to preserve the same form in
the present instance. A work compiled with the care that has been
bestowed on this not only requires but deserves a clear, full and
careful index.

In addition to this I now find that the contents of chapters drawn
up by me – of which I enclose you the 1st proof – is now reduced to a
mere bald list. It was unnecessary to give me the trouble of compiling
a careful summary of contents, when, without consulting me, it is put
aside. Between the index and contents of chapters, as now standing, it
is impossible to find the place of any subject or picture in the work. I
have placed a note to the list of painters stating that the index is not by
me – but this is very insufficient protection against my being thought
responsible and I must earnestly protest against the appearance of the
work in this state.

Messrs Clowes have been so inattentive to my directions and queries
concerning the illustrations that it is impossible for me to make up the
list. Till they return me the proofs last paged I cannot tell where to
place the Raphael Madonnas which they have omitted.

At the same time any one with common attention could have
inserted them.

I remain yr's faithfully
Eliz Eastlake

I trust you will do me the justice to have a proper index drawn up
– in which case I may recall to yr mind the index I put to Waagen's
Treasures – which is both simple and serviceable.

Letter to John Murray   *NLS Ms.42177*

Albury Heath, Guildford
30 July 1874
Dear Sir

As I remembered your objections to the lists in old Kugler, I cd not anticipate that you would forget them. I am sorry I left the compilation to you, tho' I cannot be blamed in feeling that such details were more familiar to you than to myself. I consider the evil of the present awkward and empty lists – for they are no index at all – so grave that I desire to be absolved from all responsibility for them. I therefore request that the note I have appended may not be omitted. Another proof, with that note inserted and the list of Painter's names, base and inadequate as they are, put first, will be all that I require.

But I do hope you will reconsider your determination not to have a proper index. Even this one must be ameliorated by reversing the plan. It is the whereabouts of pictures that is wanted by the reader – not the whereabouts of places. The place should be appended to the Painter – as in Waagen – & not vice versa as in these foolish lists of places.

Also Raphael's Madonna's – the plates of them should be inserted in the illustrations. Why a separate list of all his pictures is given I know not since not a single picture (except in the list of illustrations) of any other painter is alluded to in the lists.

For such mere lists as these you cannot surely have paid so much as not to be able to afford a proper index to a work of this kind. I have very little time, but I would undertake to have a thorough, simple and clear index made for 20 guineas. The pity is that so much time has been wasted.

As to Messrs Clowes they do not attempt to attend to my corrections or answer my questions and it is useless my addressing them. Fresh proofs of illustrations were sent me yesterday in which they have taken the liberty to insert superfluous words in the inscriptions, and have not answered a particular correction and question I made them more than a week ago regarding the Bartolommeo at Vienna. I enclose you the illustrations. Where their insertions are of no consequence I have left them – in order to avoid the incessant trouble. But I will not have those "in the"s inserted which I have struck out from all the rest. I cannot, however, answer for their not having altered my last proofs for press. And I feel that I may find myself answerable for alterations I have never made.

I remain yr's faithfully

Eliz Eastlake
I enclose two of my written inscriptions <u>to show</u> what Messrs Clowes
have inserted.

Letter to A. H. Layard   *NLS Ms.42170*

Albury Heath
7. Aug: 1874
My dear Mr. Layard

I am acknowledg.g yr kind letter from Langham House of July
13th. I could not <u>scamper</u> you off a note in return, as if you had
been in London, so I have waited till you cd receive something less
unworthy yr readg. Just now I am quite alone, but hitherto I have had
a succession of kind humdrum guests − as such suit me best − among
them dear old Boxall, and Mr. Penry Williams. The place I have taken
is shabby inside and out − but roomy and comfortable, commanding
charming views and the best of air, with a heath behind and a garden
in front, and swallows, and roses, and a cat, and a not bad Library, also
the advantage of Mrs. Grote's vicinity so that we meet very often. She
was in Saville [sic] Row at the time you wrote to me, but the heat
was such that, she bid me say, she could not look you up, tho' longing
to do so. She is much younger than I, & frisks backwards & forwards
to London to see friends, while I grudge a single day spent away from
this delicious landscape. This shows you that she is in good health, tho'
complaining of sciatica. But yesterday at Wootton Rectory, where I
accompanied her, she walked me tired. Still, there is no doubt, that she
is feeling in some measure the feebleness of her age − 82 − & does not
stand much company for long.

Among my guests has been Lady Strangford, who certainly is an
exception to the <u>humdrums</u>. As she wished to pay a visit to Mrs Rate
we drove to Milton Court, & I was almost as kindly recd by the pretty
hostess as Lady S: was. I was no little struck with the improvements
& additions to the fine old house, the slippery stars of which recalled
to me our visit to you there. Many kind things were said of you & yr
Enid, & the cabinet shown. Lady Strangford was tolerably well doing
a good deal of hard work, for she has thrown herself into benevolent
schemes, nurse-training &c & people find out that she can work, &
will take trouble, both of which are sure to entail employment. She
brought some of Lord Strangford's early letters to his father, from
Constantinople, to read here, of years 1845−6, at time <u>you</u> well know.

She let me look thro' a few. They are most sparkling & original. Her
collection of poor Mr Deutsch's remains, with her brief memoir of him,
have answered well. Albemarle Street sent her while here a nice sum by
way of half profits. Otherwise the occupation of her Cumberland Place
House – to which she has added a story, by <u>Schenk</u> – gives here much
trouble & small profits. He is a most unconscientious tenant & wd prefer
to occupy it gratis.

The other day I had tidings from good Acton Tindal wh: will interest
you. Good-looking Nico, the eldest son, has lost his heart to a young
lady of £4.000 a year, a Miss Carill-Worsley.[1] Or rather this young lady
has consented to take his heart, without which his losing it wd have
been useless – provided the Lord Chancellor allow her to do so. She is
ward in Chancery – 17 years of age, very pretty, fine figure &c &c. Her
fortune is chiefly in land, some of it building land in Manchester, but
all strictly tied up by will of Father, who was a lover of <u>Mrs Tindal's</u>.
Both have taken the epidemic very violently, the more so as, till the
Chancellor's consent be obtained, they are not allowed to meet or
correspond. At the same time they have settled to marry in February
next, when she will be 18. From all this exct Nico seems to be a lucky
young man, at the same time the young lady & her fortune will be in
good hands. All those three sons are very steady, tho' Nico has cared for
nothing so much as drawing, wh: of late he has stuck seriously to. Now
he will be able to indulge it to heart's content.

Altho' I enjoy the peace of the country yet I cd not exist without
some work. I have completed Kugler's new Hand Book, & unless
Albemarle Street bestow a copy on you I shall have the pleasure of
doing so. It has been a great labour. I have been so struck with the
many sidedness of Leo: da Vinci & the hollow nature of the times in
which he lived that I am trying to put together something about him.
I have a new compilation of his life, by a Mrs Heaton published by
Macmillan, a very poor thing, recently published, tho' with an excellent
chapter on his scientific & literary work, by a Mr. C. Black. Allusion
is made to important documents of his early time, said to have been
discovered. If you cd hear anything of them at Venice I shd be glad, &
if there be anything new published, & you will bring it to me, I will
promise to pay you! Also I shd be glad of the expected publication of
the M.Angelo letters if it be out.

I am much inclined to envy you yr sojourn at Venice. I sometimes
<u>dream</u> of coming there for 6 weeks or so, but it wd be chiefly to see the
old friend Rawdon Brown, who I hope you find is in unabated strength.
I am so bold as to send my love to him, but, it gets delayed & so never
done. You will tell him what you can of me & may add that I am

growing very old & infirm! & shall never, <u>could</u> never, cross the Alps
again, either outside or inside.

I trust that Enid is getting all the good you cd wish from the baths.
From you I shall hope to hear, when you return & come into this part
of the world, that Venice is looking up, & that the P.&O. steamers
contribute to her prosperity. Everything about Italy interests me.

You wd see how the P. della Francesca subject was treated in the
House. I have had some correspondence with Mr. Burton about it.
Now with my kind love to Enid I am every dear Mr Layard yrs very
truly
Eliz Eastlake

    1. Nicolas married Elizabeth Carill-Worsley, heiress of Platt Hall near
       Manchester.

Letter to John Murray   *NLS Ms.42177*

Albury Heath, Guildford
14 August 1874
Dear Sir

I beg to acknowledge the receipt of your cheque for £50 which has
reached me this morning. I was about to write to you at all events.
I devoted some hours yesterday to looking thro' the index & am
distrest [sic] to find that even in its present form of bareness it is <u>utterly</u>
<u>incomplete</u>. It is impossible to look thro' twenty pages of the letter press
without finding the strangest omissions of artists' names. I send you the
proof with a few (comparatively) of the names <u>omitted</u>. The compiler
has evidently not known which was the popular name in instances so
present of two names to the same painter [sic]. He[1] omits for instance
<u>Bertucci</u> whom no one will know under <u>Faenza Gio: da</u>. He gives no
reference, from the familiar name to the surname. When a painter's
name has been identified as <u>Bonsignori</u> instead of <u>Monsignori</u> as hitherto
called, he gives only the <u>Bonsignori</u> which will be no clue except to a
<u>very</u> few. Where there are two brothers – as with the <u>Grandi</u> and the
<u>Tucconi</u> he omits one. The two <u>Lendinara's</u> he omits altogether. These
are only <u>specimens</u>. He omits <u>Leon Bruno</u> altogether, and tho' but little
is known of him, yet his <u>name</u> has been a late and certain fact. I have
not pretended to go deep into the letter press, which would be indeed
to make a new index, but there are the results of a few hour's attention.

I have gone still less into the list of places – but I find no mention

of Ripoli where there is a celebrated R: Ghirlandajo nor of the Corsi
Signorelli, or the Lawrie Raphael – both at Florence. Nor of Monte
Uliveto – were I to go further I should discover plenty more.

It is true that the note appended relieves me from the responsibility
– but I feel the great injustice to the work no less. No one knows better
than yourself that for such a work the index is everything. Reviewers
are sure to find out how wretched the index is, in spite of its pedantry.
I can only hope that for your own sake you will have it revised by a
competent person.

Yr's faithfully
Eliz Eastlake

1. Evidently Elizabeth did not know that her estranged sister Matilda Smith
   was the indexer. In a letter to John Murray of 17 August 1874 Matilda
   Smith responds to the charges: 'Your letter caused me much distress, but
   when I read E.E.'s I took comfort – either through wilfulness or carelessness
   she has overlooked some of the names she complains of as omitted' (NLS
   Ms.43077).

Letter to A. H. Layard   *NLS Ms.42170*

7 FitzRoy Sqre
30 March 1875
My dear Mr. Layard

Your kind & long letter to me of the 13th was a very welcome
pleasure & reproach to me. For I am quite aware that the debt of a letter
was on my side. But tho' I sent you & Enid many thoughts & felt my
self very guilty, yet like most guilty people, I had a host of excuses ready,
all of which I now forget, except that I equally have been very busy. I
can assure you that I am quite well. I do not grow stronger, but much
the reverse, & begin to comprehend what is meant by the "infirmities of
age". But I have had a more cheerful winter than usual, having had the
society of my young friend – Miss Elliott, whom you saw with me at
Milton Court, & who is still with me, though, I much regret, leaving me
on the 15th April. She is a charming musician, & very intelligent, & very
pretty, which you know of old is a virtue in my eyes! We have had some
society & some quiet home reading, & we have attended some lectures
at the Royal Institution, Friday evengs, & I have heard Tyndall, Huxley
& Lubbock, all three deeply interesting. The first very complimentary to
"fair hearers" & very impatient & irritable (as I sat near enough to hear)
to his unfortunate assistant, as he showed the most to one conjurer's trick

of a gas flame jerking up & down as a particular note was sounded, &
even to a particular chirp from Tyndall's own lips. Huxley very grave &
rather dull sententious detailing the wonders of the red sand at both Poles
& green mud in the central parts of the globe or vice versa, wh: has been
picked up by the Challenger & found to consist entirely of minute shells
of defunct invisibilities at a depth of 2 miles or so which drop incessantly
from the surface as they die. And then Lubbock quite charming on
insects & flowers, & himself so good looking!! Then we have had Elijah
at Exeter Hall, & the Messiah at Albert Hall, & Saturday & Monday
Popular Concerts with Joachim &c &c.

You are the first person who agree with me as to the dullness of the
Greville journals. I cd hardly wade thro' the petty squabbles of Ministry
detailed by a man who thought himself wiser than them all, & who
never tells a story without taking the shine out of it. I hear that Disraeli
has said "Greville was the vainest man I ever met with, & I have read
Cicero, & known Lord Lytton". Doubtless the abuse of the powers that
be, & of people's fathers & mothers is not a thing to be defended, &
I wonder at my good cousin Reeve's want of judgement & discretion
as Editor, but the chief thing apparent in these memoirs is the harm
wh: his arrogance & vulgarity does to his own particular class. Even
such a red republican as you say you are supposed to be cd not prick
them more effectively. There is a great feeling against Reeve but he
bears it stoically, & I hope his friends stick to him as faithfully as I do.
Hayward's rather vulgar article in the Q:R: has certainly not increased
the prejudice against him but the reverse.

Since I recd your letter I have been risking my neck by climbing
up & among the new rooms of the National Gallery for your sake.[1] A
friendly policeman pioneered me over planks & under beams. They are
pretty much all in the same condition, ornamental ceilings & cornices all
finished, upper glass in the skylights, marble columns almost all placed,
walls close battened, apparatus for warming not yet laid, but a deep ditch
through each room for that purpose. I should imagine there is another
months work. The rooms – 9 in number – are very sumptuous, or will
be, but they are over lofty, which I consider a far greater defect than the
reverse. I cannot say that I anticipate much credit to the Gall: from Mr.
Burton's additions. I did all I could to help him last year, but on seeing
the pictures he has hung in conspicuous places in the Gall: I feel that
he has already vulgarized the general effect. The two school Bòtticelli's
are both very second rate, & one of them indecorous & the result of
an expenditure of more than £10.000 is most unsatisfactory. Cassone
pictures, pretty for a private room, but not important eno' for a great
gallery are still below, put into very fine frames. I have seen Mr. Burton

several times, & he has dined here. He is an intelligent agreeable man, but on talking with him on pictures I feel how utterly he falls below the level of what I have been accustomed to hear.

As to dear old Boxall yr mention of Heaven in lieu of Welbeck Street is not so far wide of the mark. For he has been so very ill, that I feared we shd lose him. A very bad attack of bronchitis revealed his exceedingly low condition, & the only prescriptions were I believe turtle soup &c &c every two hours. He is now better, & I saw him quite lately back again in his usual small den. I go often to see him, & have taken my young lady, whom he has a tenderness for, but his life is very lonely & desolate, tho' there are many who wd gladly welcome him to their firesides. He always kindly comes to me when I ask him & I want him very much to come to me in the country. For I have as good as taken (for the 1st June) the same house on Albury Heath I had last summer, where he cd be very happy. Somewhere he must make up his mind to go, for he has sold his Welbeck Street home & turns out on the 24th June. He tells me he has sold it well, so he will not want for means. As to dear Mrs Grote I have been to her in the country, & she has been off & on in Saville [sic] Row. She only left last week, & Miss Elliott & I go to her on Thursday next till Saturday. She has bought a beautiful piece of 4 acres almost opposite her gate, in conjunction with her neighbours the Misses Spottiswoode, & she has given her share to her niece & kind companion Miss Lewin. I let her hear some of the contents of yr letter, & she sends you her kind love – not at all pleased that you are going straight to Venice instead of coming to yr friends. But I can only envy you, & think you very wise especially when I imagine charming Morelli in yr home with you. I anticipate that yr Enid will make a fresh start in art. I do not forget the capital sketches I saw last year.

I have not seen yr aunt very lately, but I write to her, & I remark that her handwriting is sometimes steadier than of old.

I have seen but little of the studios, & shall be out of town on the 3 days that the R.As open their doors. But I saw Millais' performance some weeks ago, a fresh breezy Scotch landscape, but beyond that nothing wh: interested me, or promised much. Coutts Lindsay's things I saw yesterday, one out of three was pleasing, but in truth she draws much better than he. Her water colour copies from old masters, & also her large drawings of childn & others are very remarkable things.

You will like to hear of good Tindals at Aylesbury. True love is not destined to run smooth in Nico's case. He is engaged as you know, to a young ward in Chancery, only turned 18 last month. They had made up their minds to marry early this month, but were met by an interdict from Master of the Rolls. Papa & Mama Tindal were moving heaven &

earth to persuade Sir Geo: Jessel of the cruelty of this interfering, but at present with no success.[2] Nico is seriously attached, & for the first time. The young lady I have not seen.

You ask me about <u>Kugler</u>. I had almost forgotten him, for he was off my hands before Christmas. Meanwhile I had been a little studying Leo: da Vinci & his time & my ideas thereon appeared in January (present) number of the Edinr Review. I wd like you to read it & give me yr <u>criticism</u>. & if you have not the Edinr I will try & send you a copy. Next number I shall have an article on <u>Thorvaldsen</u> in. Thus I try to requite the time, tho' never ceasing to miss the one whom I know you loved, & who loved <u>you</u>.

My kindest love to Enid I am always yrs truly
Eliz Eastlake
I have not alluded to Spanish politics of wh: I know little & care less.
I have known Cabrera[3] as a most odious companion at dinner parties.
Of course I am interested in the young "Sandhurst boy" & am sorry his worthless sister has joined him.

1. For an account of the redesign see Christopher Whitehead, 'Architectures of Display at the National Gallery. The Barry Rooms as art historiography and the problems of reconstructing historical gallery space', *Journal of the History of Collections*, 17.2 (2005), pp. 189–211.

2. Sir George Jessel (1824–83), judge holding high office in the Chancery Courts.

3. Don Ramon Cabrera (1806–77), a general denounced as a traitor by Don Carlos of Spain in 1875.

Letter to Hannah Brightwen   *Private Collection*

7. FitzRoy Sqre
14. Octr 1875
My dearest Hannah
Your handwritg is always a welcome pleasure. I feel that I shd have written again after yr question about Leo: da Vinci's supposed "Salvator Mundi" wh: I tried to answer from Albury – but time brings daily claims, & the present overrides the Past. I left sweet Albury Heath on the 30th Septr – after a stay of 17 weeks, & singularly free from care, & with so many blessings & pleasures comprised in the time, that I was not afraid to acknowledge that I was <u>happy</u>. Or if I was not, it wd have been ungrateful of me. Calm happiness it is true – but perhaps the best.

I had scarcely been <u>alone</u>, & to my clinging nature absolute solitude is a great trial – one or the other of two <u>young</u> friends had always been with me – kind friends came for a few days – one or two at a time – & throughout I had plenty of <u>work</u>. Without that I cd not have enjoyed the idle social hours. Now I think myself settled for the winter – <u>please God</u>. I paid a short visit in Kent last week at Sir Walter James' beautiful place near Walmer Castle, & heard a great deal about our Pss Alice from Honble Emily Hardinge Sir Walter's half sister. The Pss, accordg to Miss H's acct, lives "for a purpose" hopes to <u>civilize</u> the Germans a little, is very attentive to duties, & makes herself liked. I saw a little of Lord & Lady Granville there – him I had known before & always felt to be one of the most <u>charming</u> of our noblemen – he married as 2nd wife a young Campbell girl of 18 – the marriage answers – they have 3 young childn. People talked of her beauty – but she is tall, fair & distingué lookg – nothing more.

But dearest I don't write to you about great people – whom I very seldom come across nowadays. Yr mention of the drawing of my father – made from <u>Sharpe's</u> small picture for yr dear Mother's etching, interests me much, & I shd <u>indeed</u> like to have it, & be very grateful to you. I can just remember Mr Edwards the engraver who left us a rather extraordinary collection of <u>eyes & noses</u> to copy. They are peculiarly imprinted on my mind's eye.

I am amused, dear, at yr impression of my article on Thorvaldsen, or rather at my remarks on his sculpture. I grudge that the 'talent' – i.e. the knowledge of art lies so useless with me. I had such an exceptional education in connoisseurship at my beloved One's side – & there is scarcely a creature with whom I can share it. I feel that <u>I</u> shd have been his best successor in the direction of the Nat: Gallery. Boxall was unimpugnable, but hated the employmt, the present man is totally unfit for it, & has introduced most inferior things. Without vanity I know I shd have been the right person, tho' the world wd be astonished at such an idea.

My summer's work is coming out in the now announced <u>Quarterly</u> Review. I shall leave you to <u>guess</u> what it is that has interested me. I am now beginning the review of a french work, & am driving as deep as I can into french life, – a far better thing – in the middle classes – than we generally suppose. It will be for the Edinr Review if it succeeds. It is a great comfort to me to have found my <u>pen</u> again – an infinite resource against the great solitude of the heart. Your occupation is better, dearest, but I do not quite relinquish my poor friends & am always makg new ones at my Hospital.[1]

Dear Jane is still at Buxton & has been there more than two months. She has enjoyed it much but I wish I cd report improvement. For the

present there is none. In addition to the waters – inside & out – she is
now being <u>shampooed</u> daily.

I am glad you are in snug quarters for the winter, tho' I can feel for
yr lengthened expulsion from Fritton.

Now dearest Hannah I am every yr lovg cousin

Eliz Eastlake

1. Springall mocks her hospital visits in verse form: 'To University she went
    / With regularity / And at the bedside hours were spent / The suffering
    for to see; / And cheering words to give to those / Who, racked with pain
    were there ...'; Stephen Springall, *That Indomitable Old Lady: A Romance of
    Fitzroy Square* (London: Henry J. Drane Ltd, 1908), p. 345.

Letter to Hannah Brightwen   *Private Collection*

24. Octr 1875
7 FitzRoy Sqre
My dearest Hannah

I safely received the drawg you had so carefully packed. <u>Very many</u>
thanks for letting me possess it. I have been lookg at it very <u>enquiringly</u>,
for, tho' I remember my father's tall figure & white powdered head, he
is in himself very unknown to me. Our Gertrude was doubtless most
like him of all his childn. I see that yr dear Mother <u>improved</u> both
likeness & art in her beautiful etching. Thank you also, dear for her
pretty, refined etching of Coltishall Church – the church itself does not
live in my memory.

I am amused at yr guesses as to the article, & very glad to plead
guilty to that which has interested you. An acquaintance I have formed
with Donald Dalrymple's widow led to my hearing many details; while
no one can live in London without being convinced of the terrible
power of the <u>Publican</u>. The Editor cut out some pages, on the real plea
of the article being too long – or you wd have read that in one square
mile of the East of London – for wh: our sympathies & our money are
from time to time so piteously invoked in wretched English by "Cath:
Gladstone" – there are 320 public houses which have a revenue of above
a quarter of a million! Alms giving <u>pauses</u> before such facts.

I am not aware that the Quarterly stands before the Edinburgh R: – I
have written in both since my Beloved One's death. But the Editor of
Edinr is as you know my relative Henry Reeve. The Editor of the Q.R:
is a prig, & a <u>parvenu</u> – Dr Wm Smith, tho' a full man.

I have been thinkg of Cotman but I cannot get hold of any date of his career. In 1824 I shd say he was under 40. But I expect dear Jane here from Buxton on Tuesday & she is a living chronicle.

Caroline Carver & husband are home from Russia. This visit had been terribly marred by the intelligence of his sister & nephew – Mrs Mainwaring & son – havg died at Heidelbg from eating poisonous <u>fungi</u>!

I am settled into my winter quarters, & have found something to work on. To day I have been to my Hospital – always very fatiguing to body & refreshing & edifyg to heart.

Ever my dear Han: yr lovg
Eliz Eastlake

Letter to Hannah Brightwen   *Private Collection*

7 FitzRoy Sqre
30 Decr 1875

I will not let this old year elapse without writg to you dearest Hannah, & acknowledging yr welcome letter. It has been several times before me to answer, but necessary letters have multiplied at this time, as you doubtless find, & day light is short & interruptions many.

I have <u>felt</u> the blank for you this Christmas in the absence of our beloved Mary.[1] She may be much <u>missed</u>, tho' she must not be <u>grudged</u>. She did much work for her Lord, & we know that she is <u>in</u> Him, <u>with</u> the Beloved Ones. May we only have grace to cleave unto our Lord with all our <u>hearts</u> – always renewing prayer & supplication. I feel more & more than I can do <u>nothg</u> of myself. Life gains on as now. I have felt the symptoms of <u>age</u> more this winter than ever before. With me it takes the form of hereditary rheumatism – impedg my <u>small</u> habits of walkg. I <u>deserve</u> rheumatism more than most, for I have been very inactive, & I can therefore bear it better. Still, I am makg a struggle against it by sundry rubbings. I have dear Jane with me now. She came before Xmas on wh: day I gathered together a few of the kith & kin on each side – Carvers, Johnny Simpson, Chas Eastlake, & a few waifs & strays who are glad to join in a family party. But these family parties have their attendant <u>skeleton</u>. I am thankful for those who are left, but they tell painfully of those who are absent, not from the Will of God – Death – but from the will of the flesh. My poor Matty is a perpetual sorrow & a perpetual prayer to me. She has broken off from us for <u>long</u>. I remember tellg dearest Mary, when I saw her last in 1871, that for no object in this world were my hands so <u>lightly</u> folded in prayer as for her. I never leave these supplications. They will be answered, I know, in some form

– either here or beyond. This is a chapter in my bereaved life wh: I don't think I have ever mentioned to you before. It began immediately on my sad return from Italy, & is a tangled skein over wh: I have no longer any power – unless by a constant love ever seeking for opportunities to show itself, & ever receivg the same repulse. My poor Matty has been ever my Darling. "Your Matty" as all called her – a difficult being to deal with, & more so since an ill assorted marriage. But I never thought the difficulty wd fall on me – & at such a time of anguish! I lay it at the foot of the Cross. & have peace within, tho' constant sorrow for her. These things have helped to make me doubly alone. Justina, as you know, has been no comfort to us, & has made a sorry return for all that was done for her. Her Eton life has been a series of mistakes & follies, & now the daughter of above 40 years of age, who kept her horse till the last day, comes to be a governess! Jane & I suffered much, & our Anne suffered the more from both Justina & Matty. I am the more glad, therefore, of the work wh: keeps my mind occupied in long lonely days. I have been busy since the Drink Chapter in wh: you take so much kind interest. A very different subject & one leadg me into french life of the last 60 or 70 years. All so different to our lives & ideas! but enviable in one way – the warmth & fidelity of their friendships. I fear my experience of English friendships (or rather I shd say Scotch) is not favorable. Certainly the Scotch, with a few exceptions, are too worldly to comprehend the sacred dress of friendship. My experience since my bereavement has chilled me to the heart – & I find I am not singular. But the french are beautiful in fidelity – more to that tie than to most others. You will find an article on "the Two Ampère's" – father & son – in Janry forthcomg Edinr R:

How glad I shd be dearest to send you a chaussure that mt comfort yr dear old feet, & remind you of me! I am trying to get the same sized pair of the very common boots that you kindly took. When I have done so they shall find their way to you. As for my old ones, they are too dear to be parted with to any one – besides being worthless. I too covet ready made old boots, & a new pair always costs a certain amount of misery to break in.

I am interested in all you tell me of the Bp's temperance league. There is no doubt that the attention to the subject is spreadg. I have a comical letter from Sir Wilfred Lawson – not to me – in wh: he says that the Bps are tumblg over each other to join his views. But I know from Ld Shaftesbury that the Legislature will do nothing to diminish the temptation to the Poor to a public cry is raised for it.

Jane sends you dear love. She is quite well, tho' sadly stiff. Still we too hobbled out together to [illegible] yesterday afternoon & performed the walk tolerably – a capital rubbing woman who lives close by comes

to Jane every mg at 7.30. I trust this may do good. If not I ponder over
a winter – 1876–7 – in the South.

Now dearest goodbye – may we find more & more love & good will
&c. Peace on earth in 1876!
Ever yr lovg cousin
Eliz Eastlake

    1. Marg Turner, Hannah's sister, had died in September 1874.

Letter to A. H. Layard   *NLS Ms.42170*

7 FitzRoy Square
9. Janry 1876
My dear Mr. Layard

I duly recd your kind letter with good wishes to me for this new year
from yourself & Enid. I most heartily return them. For you both I hope
& wish all the grand things this world can give – speedy promotion,
large legacies, honors & glories. For myself peace & quiet, & plenty to
do!

I said in my last letter that I would let you know in a few weeks
my decision about your home, so kindly put at my service, at Venice.
I have now decided <u>not</u> to take advantage of your generosity – at least
not this spring. I am not strong enough to do justice to so agreeable
a plan. But this winter has so tried my strength that it is possible that
I may avoid the next & seek refuge before the damp & cold set in in
some warmer climate – or rather a drier one. This would be for the
winter & spring of 1876–7. I am the more tempted to think of such a
plan, for my sister's sake also. For she is worse than I, & hitherto no half
measures, such as a month at Wiesbaden – 2 months at Bath – & three
months at Buxton – using the waters at each place have done her any
good. I would make an effort for no place short of <u>Italy</u>, but we have
time enough to consider which part we would choose. For the <u>racket</u> of
Rome I should not feel energetic eno! But all this is still too much in
the clouds for me to speak of seriously yet. Meanwhile, if I live, I shall
probably be found at Albury again this summer, as the two last, & shall
be quite ready to give you & Enid rendezvous there.

The new year opened here with the Private View of the Old Master
– which in many respects – or rather in respect of English masters of the
last century – is one of the best we have had. Sir Joshua & Gainsborough
appear in all their glory – especially the latter. The Queen has lent 25

pictures. A Gainsborough of Queen Charlotte in her young time is one of the most exquisite examples of his art. I was glad to find old Boxall, who knew it of old, say that he would go down on his knees to it. Then there are many pictures from Lord Radnor's collection – including the curious Rubens landscape with the Escorial. Of Italian pictures there are but few interesting or new to me. A dilapidated picture of Federigo of Urbino & the young Guidobaldo – called by Mel: da Forli, which Prince Albert bought at Christie's with Sir Chas' concurrence. A mere wreck, but with an ineffable grandeur. An odd Florentine picture – Adoration – circular, with an odd temple wonderfully harmonious, called Filippini Lippi, interested me. I fancy it is by the elder Pesello.[1] I had seen it before – it belonged to a Mr. Leyland. I was awfully interrupted by acquaintances, who came to see each other, & not the pictures. Nor did I find much sympathy or intelligence in Mr. Burton, who does not seem to have seen many of the fine things in Florence, so well known to you & to ourselves. I do much wonder at his writing to you. He has got much into society, country homes &c. I have asked his leave to see the Wynn Ellis pictures, when temporarily so arranged as to be seen at all. It is one of the few London collections that I do not know. From all description it seems to include just those Flemish & Dutch masters we most want. With these & the Peel pictures we shall have a really fine collection of the Netherlandish School.

Boxall I see often – the only difficulty is to get away from him, for he likes my picture chat. He is very feeble, & complains much of loneliness. Nor can I conscientiously recommend the experiment of a Lady Boxall so late in the day!

Your aunt I saw about 3 weeks ago – much as usual – lame, as well as deaf, but brightening up before I left. The little de Gex's called on me kindly one Sunday lately, & just as I was leaving the Old Masters they came it, it being then dark.

Mrs Grote has left London, but I hear often from the Ridgeway, & she seem to have gone thro' her Christmas hospitalities & speeches brilliantly.

You will have been grieved to see the death of M: Mohl about 6 days ago. It is a great grief to me. I once spent a fortnight with them in Paris, & thus knew his racy talk & kind ways. She, poor lady, is fortunately many years his senior. I cannot wish her to realize for long the unutterable void. His work, his subjects, his Library were all objects of the deepest interest to her. If I were stronger I would offer to go to her – but three flights of steps & slippery stairs would be difficult for me, tho' I would go 500 if she wished & if I could do her any good.

I have been very busy all 1875. The result of my last application has been an article on the Two Ampères, which will appear in the forthcoming Edinburgh R: What a rich & interesting groupe of French hommes d'esprit were collected in Paris in Louis Ph's time! Ampere junior, Tocqueville, & Mohl were close friends! Reeve says that on looking back at that time he is astonished at a brilliancy which is now quite extinguished.

John Forster I have not seen lately – but I occasionally find his good wife at Boxall's. It is always the same report of him – suffering & distressed. He kindly sent me his 1st vol: of Swift's life – the only one I fear likely to appear. It is done with peculiar minutia – wearisome in some respects – for he is anxious to refute the hitherto accepted ideas of Swift's heartlessness, but I think the work betrays a decline of power.

I wish you & Enid had a more agreeable life at Madrid. She has the more of your company, & the more leisure for her art in both respects – since I may venture to pay you a compliment at this distance – she is to be envied. With kindest love to her I am ever dear Mr. Layard

Your's most truly

Eliz Eastlake

I hear that Sir Fenwick is rather better. I ventured to enquire for him about a fortnight ago, but I have not seen him yet. I have sold my Turkish Treasury Bonds at less than half what I gave for them – but I am thankful to be out.

I admired M:Angelo's letters. Curious specimens.

1. Francesco di Pesello, early fifteenth-century Florentine painter.

Letter to John Murray[1]   NLS Ms.42177

7 FitzRoy Square

22 Febry 1876

Dear Sir

It would be impossible for me to accept the work you have forwarded to me. As I imagine it may have been sent with a view to some notice in the Quarterly R:, I may venture to say that I am now engaged in reviewing M:Angelo's Letters for the Edinburgh R: – I perceive that Mr. Wilson has added valuable matter to the Life by Gotti, which I have, & fearing that it might be difficult for me to remunerate you for this copy, I prefer to return it, & have ordered a copy from a bookseller.

Yrs faithfully

Eliz Eastlake

1. This spiky letter is her last to John Murray until 23 March 1880.

Letter to A. H. Layard   *NLS Ms.42170*

7 FitzRoy Sqre
9 March 1876
My dear Mr. Layard

I am always glad to see your handwritg, & am so far deserving of it that I never miss a word, however <u>hieroglyphical</u>. And I have been wanting to write in return, but do not find time every day, what with M: Angelo, & notes & drives, & visitors, tho' but few of the last. Today I am going to find Mrs Ball at home at 5 o clk. I think she is a nice woman, & is getting liked, & is perhaps better suited to him than pretty "Elise"!

I have been to the Wynn Ellis pictures – or rather to what Mr. Burton has selected, & am glad to talk to you about them. My impression is that he had selected far too many, but that he intends a further weeding. The collection, which has never been seen in its entirety, could never have been of a high class, containing no doubt true specimens, but of a very second rate kind. Several <u>large</u> <u>Tenier's</u> empty in character, several ditto by <u>Cuyp</u>. Of these Mr B: had selected far too many, for the Cuyps especially are ugly cows' backs, very ill drawn, however, he tells me he has discarded one of them. Among the few of a higher order is a Metzer, tho' rather injured, a nice Ruysdael, the little Memling of the painter himself wh: belonged to Mr Rogers, a good replica of the Duke of Bedford's glorious Teniers of a country feast with culdron's smokg & numerous figures. An Isaac Ostade, two tolerable Wouvermanns, a Paul Potter small & signed, & doubtless true, but ugly in parts, 2 Holbeins, one doubtful to me, Wynants, 2 or 3 Van de Capellas, very empty & with disagreeable skies, Van der Heyden, 2 pretty Greuzes, childn's heads, a pretty wood & figures by V der Welde, signed, 2 or 3 good Berghems, &c. I have thus instanced a few of the 140 (out of the 400 odd) wh: he had kept back, & these as you see, not very interesting. I did all I cd venture to do in suggesting that it was better to err on the side of fastidiousness. I wish I could see more title in Mr. B: to occupy such an important post! But his ignorance seems to me great. Nor does he know anything of the history of art, he did not even know that Wynn Ellis' collection was described by Waagen. It is a trial to me to see him there.

Meanwhile the Old Masters have closed. I went to them 4 times, always with increasing pleasure, taking Mrs. Grote once, & Boxall once. But other exhibitions have opened & closed too. One of <u>Walker's</u> works was very attractive. He was a fine colourist, & gave a charm to Thames

scenery. His village children & old women, dogs, sheep & geese,
delightful. He has been succeeded in the same room by an exhibition of
Pinwell's works. I had long lost my heart to some of his. His work is a
kind of distemper, highly favourable to his small heads which are quite
exquisite.

I think dear John Forster was not dead when I last wrote to you. It
came like a shot to me, for I had ever had kindness from him, & he
loved dear Sir Chas. He had suffered much & had been very weak, tho'
still up & moving from one room to another. I have seen the poor lady
twice since. They had been married 20 years & she is much afflicted.
The S.K. Museum accept his fine Library of books. I don't know
about his pictures, & Mrs. F. intends to sell the house in due time. His
collections of all kinds are numerous, especially of autographs, which she
is now cataloguing. She feels much the departure of Ld Lytton who was
as affectionate a son to him, & most kind & attentive to her.

Your good aunt I sat half an hour with a short while ago. You know
her feebleness, but she brightens up with an old friend like me. She &
Sir Frederick exchange notes about each other's state. I have called on
the dear old man but perhaps he did not see my card, for he has taken
no notice.

Of Mrs Grote I have seen much during the last three weeks that
she has been in town, but she has left to day. She has got thro' this
disagreeable winter wonderfully well, & shows no dimunition of power.
She decries her love to you, & is ashamed not to have acknowledged
yr letter, but long letters are rather an effort to her. She talked of
sending a little piece for me to enclose in this, but none has come.
Dear old Boxall is not is the least ashamed not to have written to you,
but pleads incapacity of every kind & that he cd no more write a long
letter – or any letter – than he cd walk a mile, "but tell him I can
think of him & his wife & that I do as affectionately as ever". He is
truly past all exertion, still he is thro' this winter, wh: has carried off
so many. I see him often, & occasionally go & take tea with him, old
honest 8 o'clk tea, & we talk over M: Angelo & look at the autotypes.
I think I told you in my last that I had got the Letters. They are more
curious than interesting, & go far to upset all ideas of the romance of
that period. It was indeed a most wretched period for everything but
Art, even for artists, who like M Angelo, were cheated by Popes &
Princes. The more I look into the Letters the more I detect the lies
of Vasari, & now I do not trust a word he or Condivi says. All the
story of the 20 months only spent on the Sistine Ceiling is upset by
these Letters, tho' they are edited so badly that the Editor tries to twist
the dates to suit the old story. I have also got Chas H: Wilson's first

published Life of M.A. a life professing to be founded on the letters, & a very respectable performance, tho' with no power. Indeed I have accumulated quite a new collection of recent works on him, including Aureleo Gotti, & Grimm, the last great twaddle.

I can't tell you anything about society, for I go but little into it. The Drummonds, Mrs & single daughter, I saw the other eveng at the Thompson Hankeys, & she holds out every Thursday as usual.

Lady Augusta Stanley's long sufferings, death & burial have been the great topic. Few are treated as they deserve to be, but that gentle & kind woman deserved all the sympathy & honour. She was good to high & low. I can speak for her ever kind thought of me.

This winter has tried my health much, & I creep about, partly from rheumatism & partly from feebleness like a still older woman than I am. I still contemplate going South next winter, to Pegli near Genoa, or some such place. I cannot stand Cannes or Nice, & I want, while away, to lend this home as it stands with servants, coachman, horse, carriage &c, to someone who can be trusted, & I shd ask no rent, but the incomer wd have to pay the wages, taxes, &c for the time.

People are talking much of the Queen's new title for India. I think "Empress" is a great mistake, unsuitable to a Queen, & snobbish in itself. She shd call herself "Ruler of India" which is the simple truth, & also neither masculine nor feminine. My chief political desires are for the repression of <u>Drink</u> wh: is becoming a very terrible question & will soon very an evil beyond modifying.

I see today that they pronounce the railway to Bagonne open & secure. It will soon bring you a lady who will not make Madrid more endurable.

Now dear Mr. Layard good bye. You may give my kind love to Enid, of whom I shd like to hear a better account, but summer & sweet Venice will soon come. Ever yr's truly
Eliz Eastlake

Letter to Hannah Brightwen   *Private Collection*

7 FitzRoy Sqre
4 May 1876

Your pretty handwritg is always a most welcome sight my dearest Hannah. It is associated with true sympathy in heart & head – with dear Ones gone before – with more than eno', even without the more than suff: personal love for your dear self. I am glad to write to you to

Chester, for I feel as if I were half addressg our dear Ellen. The fewer
we are left the closer we shd hold together. Dear Jane & I feel that very
much.

I will take your question as to best advice for Inglis Palgrave
first. Sorry that he shd need it for such an undefined grievance as
rheumatism, of the variety of wh: there seems to be no end. I have
lately resorted to Dr Radcliffe (25 Cavendish Sqre) He makes the
whole family of Paralysis, gout, neuralgia, rheumatism – his speciality.
He immediately pronounced my troubles not to proceed from
rheumatism. Most glad shd I be if a new denomination of it helped
to take them away! This is some proof, however, that good Dr
Radcliffe knows his business. Then I hear much of Dr Garrard, 11
Harley Street, for all neuralgic affections. The regular Dr for decidg
what foreign baths will do good is Dr Weber 44 Green Street,
Grosvenor Sqre. I will add his address before I finish this – for there
are two of the name. Not that his recommendation to Jane to go to
Wiesbaden did her any good, but either Wiesbaden or Wildbad are
easy of access – with good accomodation, & beautiful scenery. In
Wiesbaden I can give you further particulars as to Hotel Garni & I
make no doubt that change of air wd in itself help Inglis, & do you
good too, dear Love.

You may care to know what my complaint is – Dr R: only says
"nerves of the spine", "overdone" &c. If very intense mental suffering
for many years can have affected them I certainly am surprized at no
failure of strength. Certainly the brain has not suffered, but my lower
limbs seem sometimes on the verge of paralysis, without pain – except
that caused by trying to make stiff muscles do their work. However
Dr R: prescribed "as little walkg or standg" as I cd help – wh: with
an exceedingly liberal diet, especially in aliments I like best – make
up a very comfortable regimen. His advice is curiously opposite to
what one is accustomed to. "A great mixture", "chiefly made dishes",
little butcher's meat, unless very fat", plenty of milk, cream butter &c,
vegetables, fruit – what you like if but mixed enough". "Tea – poison".
I cannot say that I have yet felt decided benefit, tho certainly I sleep
better, & have less exhausting spasmodic twitchings of the limbs. I am
also taking phosphorus.

As for dear Jane she suffers infinitely more than I, wh: I believe is
an indisputable sign of rheumatism. Her last letters have made me very
unhappy – for the dear thing was driven to bed, & yet found no rest
there. She is takg the best medical advice of Windsor & that is good
– & Dr Harper insists on Aix les Bains, tho' not yet. Probably I shall
have her consult Dr Radcliffe before she decides to go. Perhaps I told

you before that, please God, we both intend to spend next Winter in
the <u>South</u> – probably the north of Italy – a place called Pegli – on the
coast – about 10 min: rail north of Genoa – dry, sheltered, & good
accomodation. Two parties I know have wintered there for consumptive
reasons, & I shall hear further. We shd not go till Novr, & so there is
time. Meanwhile I have taken my little nest on Albury Heath again,
from 1 June – & look forward to that mingled quiet, & sociability wh:
I have had before. Of course, dearest, I must take something <u>to do</u> with
me – or I shd "cut my throat" wh: is the alternative I usually startle
my friends with, & wh: is recd now with most heartless mirth. But as
you say in a former letter "the mind must have an absorbg interest, tho'
that does not prevent the heart from aching". I am most <u>thankful</u> to the
Giver of all, for the power to work. My M: Angelo has been rather a
tough job. I have not attempted a regular life – that I did pretty well at
my dear one's side in Q.R. 1858. I have gone in more for character of
himself & art – & for refutation of Vasari's & Condivi's stories of him.
His own Letters may be relied on – nothing else. They show a life of
persecution & misery, historians have been slow to admit. My article
will be in Edinr R. in July.[1]

You will care to hear a little about the R.A. Exhibition. I fear the
knowing ones do as I do – & pronounce it very ordinary. There are no
really first rate pictures. Leighton & Poynter are rivals in large pictures
of poetic subjects. Leighton's a classic procession of female figures
singing. Poynter's "Atalanta's race". The first has great beauty in many
parts – especially an Italian landscape of glorious stone pines & olives &c
– but the figures are <u>pretty</u>, wh: is a reproach in high art. & the whole
scene (with many merits) is too artificial, smooth, & theatrical. Poynter
is more powerful. The pictures are true to the men. Leighton will be
the next President. A refined, accomplished & voluble in all languages,
man. Poynter has succeeded the arch <u>Barnum</u> <u>Cole</u> in the direction
of S. Kensington – wh: has been a disgrace to us. The schools are all
changed, & have some chance now of teaching art.

I have an appointmt & must run away (<u>metaphorically speakg</u>!) I wish
there may be a chance of getting you to <u>Albury</u>, either going out or
comg home.

I see the death of a little "Ed Rigby" Taylor, Susan Rigby's child,
today in Times. 2 years of age is a sore loss. I had not heard of her for
long – for no <u>earthly</u> <u>kindness</u> can draw those nieces to us – but I shall
write my true sympathy to her.

And now dear, love to our Ellen. May she have joy & comfort in
those childn left to her. Tell her I feel more & more that trials are
<u>compliments</u> to us from our God.

Ever yr lovg
Eliz Eastlake

1. She had written 'Michel Angelo', *Quarterly Review*, vol. 103 (April 1858),
   pp. 436–83; now she reviewed 'The Letters and Works of Michel Angelo',
   Edinburgh Review, 144 (July 1876), pp. 104–47.

Letter to A. H. Layard   *NLS Ms.42170*

7 FitzRoy Sqre
16 Aug:1876
My dear Mr. Layard

I heard with very great pleasure of Enid's being in England before
I left Albury, & was comforted by the assurance that you were much
better, which I trust is true. As I had the pleasure of Riano's company
with me for a few days, I learnt how much you had suffered.[1]

This summer we are not destined to meet at Shere, for I gave up
my home in Albury Heath earlier than usual, & have returned here.
My health requires me to avoid & English winter & I am glad also
to tempt my sister, Miss Rigby, who is very rheumatic, to accompany
me. My own trouble is not, as I have thought it, rheumatism, but
something amiss with the nerves of the spine which renders me very
feeble & lazy.

And this brings me to <u>one</u> object of this letter which is to know
whether you could by any possibility allow me that occupation of your
Venice house which you & Enid were kindly willing to permit last
year. Shd it be free for the winter months I should be most grateful if
you wd let me hire it. That wd be in itself an immense favor, for I cd
get nothing else so comfortable. At the same time our possible going is
contingent on whether Venice proves (on further enquiring) to be, what
some assure me it is, decidedly <u>anti–rheumatic</u>. For me any place warmer
than Engld & tolerably bright will do, but my sister needs to be thought
of. I apply to you, before enquiring much further, for in case of there
being any barrier to yr kind willingness to entrust yr home to me, I
shd at once turn my attention in another direction – & still in <u>Italy</u>. I
cannot stand the English colonies of Cannes or Mentone.

I think of starting the end of October & should like to be in Venice
from 3 to 4 months.

I left Mrs. Grote much tried with the heat, & very ravenous to see
you. I grudged much not seeing the Rate's, tho' I would willingly have
braved the scarlet fever.

With love to Enid I am ever dear Mr. Layard

Yrs truly

Eliz Eastlake

Alas! I am not able to go to the Nat: Gallery

1. Don Juan Facundo Riaño (1828–1901), Spanish art historian, member of the
   Spanish Senate and an advisor to the South Kensington Museum.

Letter to A. H. Layard   *NLS Ms.42170*

7 FitzRoy Sqre

21. Aug: 1876

My dear Mr. Layard

Your kind letter from Eastnor Castle, anticipating what I had asked,
quite touched me. I can't thank you & Enid enough. Now I have yr
2nd this mg to acknowledge, both so very very kind.

Meanwhile the opinions about Venice I can gather seem curiously
divided. Ed Cheney talks of thick fogs, & some ice. Sir Jas Hudson I
hear considers the climate favourable to gout & rheumatism, not for but
against. I think it will end by my settling somewhere on Lago Maggiore
for the first 3 months of winter, & then begging you for yr Casa at end
of January. But I shall claim a visit from you from Blackheath all the
same, & shall store up all you tell me. Meanwhile I am enquiring about
Pallenza.

I have just been with Boxall who grumbles about the new rooms
at the Nat: Gal: as much as any one. He wishes much to see you. He
& I are going to try & visit the gallery this week. Boxall is nimble
campared with me!

I fear Hooker will have left you by this time, if not, give him my
kind love. He knows the interest I take in his approaching marriage. I
hear excellent things of the lady.

Give Enid my best love & tell her I don't like to hear of her fainting
fit & trust she is better.

You do not suppose that I much admire good Mr Wilson's M:Angelo.
He has taken pains but he has not the art of writing a book.

Ever dear Mr Layard

Yrs truly

Eliz Eastlake

Letter to A. H. Layard   *NLS Ms.42170*

7 FitzRoy Square
23. Aug: 1876
My dear Mr. Layard

We all know that you do not mind your p's & q's and now I find our that you do not mind your f's & p's. I am delighted now to believe that instead of "fainting away at Eastnor Castle" which you write as plain as possible, your Enid has been <u>painting</u>, which may not be so interesting, but is much more pleasant to hear. I trust that <u>yr</u> performances in that way will not renew.

You are most kind to give me the information about Baveno. I have sad associations with that place, for we were there when dear Sir Chas was ill, & while this very hotel was building & I know & much liked M. Pedretti. But I am assured that it is closed in winter & that Dr & Parson & all disappear. But this is easily ascertained. Since writing to you I have recd wonderful assurances of the anti-rheumatic influences of Venice. This chiefly form Mrs Hen: Walpole, who says that the Chaplain, Mr. Mereweather, went there a cripple, & was entirely restored, also that the air is good for gout, & even for consumption. I think it will end my becoming yr tenant from the beginning of 1877, & spending November & December on the Lago Maggiore where I am told the weather is often delicious. I knew Mr Henfrey in our old times & shall be sorry if he be absent. I am shocked to hear that Hooker was looking forward to the solemn estate of matrimony in such a frivolous state of mind, as you evidently succeeded in putting him in.

Ever dear Mr Layard
Yrs truly
Eliz Eastlake

Letter to A. H. Layard   *NLS Ms.42170*

7 FitzRoy Sqre
24 Aug: 1876
My dear Mr. Layard

Just a few words to say that I have heard from Mrs. Grote today, & that she begs me "to negotiate" with you & Enid to fix a day to visit her, for a day or two, "any day between now & the 3rd Septr". She includes me in the invitation, & I shd be delighted to have this opportunity of talking to you & Enid on the subject of the <u>house</u> & thus save you the trouble of coming here, tho' you know how glad I shd be to see you.

I have not yet cleared up the question as to whether Mr Pedretti keeps his hotel at Baveno open in winter, but I hear that the crowd of Germans (for whom my dislike is unabated) in summer at Pallanza is exchanged in the winter there for about 30 English inmates!

I was at the Nat Gal: to day with Boxall. It is truly a splendid collection & dear old friends look some of them to great advantage. Still, the arrangement leaves much to be desired. As to Mr. Burton I hope you are not prepared to <u>insist</u> that he is a properly qualified man as Director. If you are, we shall differ, <u>for once</u>! He has no business to be out of town now that Wornum is away, & no one to attend the Gallery. The decorations are most <u>theatrical</u>.

Nor can I say that the female portrait by Moroni deserves its place in the Gallery.[1]

Will you let me know as soon as you can whether you can spare a day or two for Mrs Grote, & then we will go together.
Ever yrs truly
Eliz Eastlake

1. Giovanni Battista Moroni, *Portrait of a Lady* ('*La Dama in Rosso*') NG 1023.

Letter to Hannah Brightwen   *Private Collection*

7 FitzRoy Sqre
15 Octr 1876
My dearest Hannah

I must be indeed over busy not to find time to write to you, dear Love, before I leave our common country. This solitary Sunday eveng I am glad of a little converse with you. It is true I am very busy in a <u>scrappy</u> way, arrang.g with one hand behind & with the other before – & often rememberg <u>your</u> dear Mother's rule to do a thing as soon as you think of it – or at least to make a note of it. My great searchings & emptyings have ceased, not ended, for I dare not attack some cupboards & drawers – <u>brimful</u> of papers – which will not be wanted. Upon the whole I am thankful to have destroyed the spell that hung over even the insignificant relics of the past. If <u>time</u> do not make the future life more real than the Past or Present we have not reached the due fruits of great sorrow! I feel now that 'Forward' can be our only motto.

I hope we may have a blessing on our move – dear Jane & I – &

the young things I hope to take with us. One, certain – a niece of Mrs Grote's who is quite a child of mine – the other I won't mention now, but I hope it will be managed for her to accompany us. I leave this home under comfortable auspices – lendg it & its staff to a thorough lady with only one daughter – Honble Mrs King Harman, sister to my old friend Mrs Hamilton Grey & Lady Fred: Beauclerk, & recently a widow. Jane I hope has also made a favorable arrangement for her little domain – tho' there was a hitch wh: I hope her tomorrow's letter will tell me is past – for I gave her yesterday the means to smooth it away.

We start on the 30th Monday. I hope & purpose to be at Pallanza by the Saturday if not Friday. We go straight to Paris in the day – remain a night & day, & proceed Tuesday eveng at 8 oclk & go <u>thro'</u> to Turin – arrivg there Wednesday eveng at 6. To Arona on Lago Maggiore is I believe a 3 hours' rail – & thence steamers go to P: 3 times a day. I take my excellent Anderson with me – who has lived with me 27 years & in this home 31. She has strong head & heart, robust health, ready resources in emergencies or illness, & a great devotion to me, & all who belong to me. Jane takes her maid – a good kind creature – very rheumatic & gouty herself. Jane is feeling this late rainy & disturbed weather very painfully & longs for the change. All look forwd to the expedition with delight – <u>present company excepted</u>! who is to have all the responsibility! Still, I am not afraid.

I shall bask at first on a sunny terrace under or out of our windows at P. & <u>rest</u> – threateng only to perfect myself in <u>knitting socks</u> which little Minna Lewin will direct me in. By the time we get to Venice I hope to be in <u>working</u> mood, for I have subjects in my head. All Italian matters interest me deeply. I think the Italians by far the noblest race in Europe – not even exceptg ourselves – but they need time & peace. Of course the Eastern question cannot be banished even from such a <u>scrappy</u> state of head as mine. I am <u>not</u> afraid of Russia, & I <u>detest</u> despised & cruel Turkey, & do not find myself singular. A most philosophical letter from Mr Hayward – all in this same direction – to Mrs Grote, deserves to be printed.

I paid Joseph & <u>Hyacinth</u> a visit a week ago,[1] & expect them to morrow to 2 oclk lunch. She impressed me very favorably, & I felt I knew her better in an hour than I ever did good Frances! I hope the marriage will thoroughly answer.

If dearest Ellen be with you give her my tender love. I hope she will <u>rest</u> in yr quiet haven. <u>That</u> is what we weary ones want. Rest, not from thought, but to think in sweet calm & quiet.

I <u>think</u> you will find my pen in this forthcomg Q.R. & I shall again leave you to guess it.

And now dearest friend & cousin may God be with you & us! Answer this to me at "Grand Hotel, Pallanza Lago Maggiore, Italy". Ever your true lovg
Eliz Eastlake

1. Joseph Hooker and his second wife Hyacinth.

Letter to A. H. Layard   *NLS Ms.42170*

7 FitzRoy Sqre
29. Octr. 1876
My dear Mr. Layard

I have been longing to write to you, & have felt quite ashamed not to do so earlier. But plans have not been entirely dependent on me, & all work of preparation has! So now I take the pen to tell you that I really depart from Charing X tomorrow morning at 6.30! I shall be in Paris comparatively early in the afternoon. Then next day by express thro' to Turin – so that I reach Pallanza possibly on Thursday the 2nd Novr or certainly the next day. I propose staying there exactly 8 weeks which will bring me to the 28th Decr – on which day I shd wish to move on to Venice. These dates may be near enough to enable you to prepare yr agent Mr. Malcolm for my invasion of your house – a circumstance, the kindness of which only grows in estimation with me. I shall go to an hotel for one night – perhaps preceding my party with my good housekeeper – & seeing that all is in readiness for them. And I must tell you that a very young cousin is added to my party – by the urgent request of a rich old uncle. I am prepared to find no bed for her, & shall therefore procure a small iron one & appurtenances for her.

I have had a kind letter of promised welcome from Rawdon Brown, who tells me that Mr. Malcolm is the man he likes best in Venice. I hope that R. Brown will not object to enter your home, for I doubt my capability to mount his stairs. My address will be Grand Hotel Pallanzo, Lago Maggiore where I shall certainly write to you.[1]

This has been written by declining day light in a way you have not, I hope, seen before. I have seen a little of Madame Riano since my return to London, who has given me news of yrselves, recd from Enid. I have also seen the new Mrs Hooker twice, & think her a great acquisition to the family as well as to good Hooker, who looks very happy.

And now dear Mr Layard I must attend to "straps & labels" &c & shall be very glad when my journey is over. With kindest love to Enid. I am always yrs truly
Eliz Eastlake

1. Elizabeth may not have known that her nickname was 'Lago Maggiore'. In 1879 M. Grant-Duff noted in his diary of meeting Lady Eastlake 'who has grown extremely stout and more than ever deserves her old name of Lago Maggiore'. See Mountstuart E. Grant-Duff, *Notes from A Diary 1873–1881*, 2 vols. (London: John Murray, 1898), vol. 2, pp. 112–13.

Letter to A. H. Layard   *NLS Ms.42170*

Grand Hotel, Pallanza
Lago Maggiore
13 Nov: 1876
My dear Mr Layard
Our letters have crossed. I fancy they were respectively written on the same day. I recd yours here two days ago. You know therefore already I propose leavg, & takg possession of yr home – or at least, going to Venice for that purpose – about the 28th Decr. I <u>may</u> perhaps make it a week later, but I cannot say you to yet. At all events I will write to Mr Malcolm (– "Malcolm Esqre Venice") will I suppose find him nearer the time [sic] – & I propose to precede my party, with one servant & go to an hotel for a night or two – & prepare for them. I am only sorry that carpets &c will be put down for me.

The life here, altho' very pleasant & comfortable will prepare us to enjoy the privacy under yr roof the more.

The journey here, began from London on the 30th Octr, was quite successful, tho' dependant solely on me for head and tongue. We had splendid weather. The descent into Italy – the country I have loved so much – was for me full of sad feelings, but it was new to my companions,[1] & soon the glory of the land under a radiant sun became new to me again. From Turin we took the rail to Genoa where a steamer awaited us, which coasted along the beautiful shores, touching at different places, till we came to the part I know – Stresa, Baveno – & finally this lovely Pallanza. Here we are domiciled comfortably in the great hotel, our rooms on a first floor opening on the great terrace to the South East, where I take the little exercise I have strength for, & bask in glorious sun. The view is also <u>perfection</u>. This little island of S. Giovanni within a stone's throw, with great masses of hydrangia in full flower. The last few days have, however, been very cold, & one day it snowed for several hours. I have just begged the Landlord to let us have a stove, with a flue up our chimney, for no expenditure of wood & no effort of bellows, which my young companions use vigorously, suffice to warm us when the sun is off. The public rooms are warm & light – & all the papers of all the people in the world may be seen there. We have pretty much the same assortment of fellow residents – French, Italian, Russian, American, monsters of Germans, & quizzes of English, & a lady with an unfortunate lap dog wh: she holds by a string, just out of reach of tempting bits which my young ladies throw to the wretched little brute – to their infinite amusement. In spite of the cold I find the climate justly represented in one respect – its perfect dryness. It is this which I think will benefit my sister & me. As to Venice, it seems to my companions too bright a dream to be realized. I cannot express how I feel you & Enid's kindness. Someday I shd like to put FitzRoy Sqr at yr disposal! if you wd have it.

The death of the Duchess d'Aosta will, I know, affect you much – poor lady! She cannot have known much happiness.

I have had kind visits from our appointed neighbours Mr Henfrey[2] & Bp – & must try & return them with the first milder day. With my kindest love to Enid, believe me ever dear Mr Layard yrs most truly & obliged
Eliz Eastlake

1. Her companions were Jane Rigby, her housekeeper Mrs Anderson, her cousin May Woodhouse (later Grimston), and Harriet Grote's niece Emma Catherine ('Minna') Lewin (later Anderson).

2. Charles Henfrey lived at the Villa Clara in Baveno.

Letter to A. H. Layard   NLS Ms.42170

Ca' Capello[1]
14 Janry 1877
My dear Mr Layard

It is well I do not write to you or Enid as often as I wd wish – for I long to do so every time I find myself rejoicing in the comforts & pleasures we experience under yr roof, & that is many times by day & by night too. There has been no change except for greater comfort – the rooms have become warm – our fire in yr drawing-room is

charming – Antonio waits upon us & provides for us with unflagging
civility – my servants are contented – the two young ladies are in
ecstasy from mg till night – I feel myself decidedly stronger – my sister
alone, I am sorry to say, has become more suffering. She took severe
cold, & is so set fast with lumbago that I have kept her in bed, whence
I trust she will soon rise & resume her usual habits. Her rheumatism is
so chronic that Pallanza with all its bright dryness gave her no relief –
Since we left it I hear that they have had more rain & fog than we have
had here. Also we can but remember how <u>drowned</u> our own country
has been – especially round Windsor – my sister's home – & how still
worse she mt have been there. In short my sister is determined that
Venice shall not be blamed for her present condition, & I really believe
that this month hitherto here has been finer than in most places. We
have had fog rise at about 10 oclk a.m & last for a couple of hours – but
the rest of the day has been free from it, tho' quite cloudy. Yesterday &
today we have bright sun, & everything looks beautiful.

Meanwhile we have seen a little more of Mr Malcolm – tho'
he is by no means recovered from his severe cold – but he has given
me two long visits, & submitted to no end of questions from my girls
about Venice. So kind has he been that I told him I shd complain
of him to you! Your silver – whatever the quality – he pronounces
not to be forthcomg – being at the bottom of the chest – & so he
has sent me over complete sets of his own – spoons & forks, & I feel
daily covered with confusion to use them. Then half a dozen of his
<u>Val Policella</u> has come across & in short he overpowers me. Dear old
Brown also is all fidget & kindness – sendg me books & extracts from
archives, & announcing a sack of potatoes! So you see me rejoice in
the best of neighbours. I manage to get in & out of a gondola better
than I did & go out for a couple of hours about three times a week. I
have entered into no contract – but have allowed Antonio to indulge
a natural nepotism – by havg some relation of his – a young man – to
pump water, hew wood &c for part of the day – & to play gondolier
with another whenever we wish. This does very well – also the young
<u>Donna di faccenda</u> is daily here & begins to understand our ways. I
make occasionally an excuse to go into the kitchen to look at her pretty
pouting face – as fair as any English woman's, & with splendid light
hair. But the soul of all our quiet comfort is Antonio. He shops, & I
make no doubt he cooks too – tho' he pretends that the young Donna
does it. Occasionally my good woman, Mrs. Anderson, goes out with
him to show him what kinds of fish, or cheese or vegetables we prefer
– Their mutual attempts to understand each other are funny in the
extreme.

A few days ago I went to Salviato's – on the Gd Canal. I remembered him in London of old, & he has never forgotten some kindness my dear Sir Chas did him. He almost upset my equaniminity with his grateful remembrance. I was delighted to go thro' the rooms with him – I need not dwell on the exquisite objects – some not yet known in St James St. Nor may I venture to repeat what he said of you. It wd have done dear Enid good to hear the enthusiastic man – & in her absence it did me good. Now I must talk to you a little about yr pictures, which are a constant pleasure & interest to me.

Your <u>Bramantino</u>, wh: I knew in London continues my great favourite. It is truly <u>original</u> in colour & design. I know nothing like it. I am sorry to see it without its glass – tho' it can take no harm in this dry room.

Your so called <u>Bono Ferrarese</u> is also most novel & pathetic – as far as I can see it. I know no other representation of the Saviour like it. I shd like to see it in the place of the truly <u>so called</u> <u>Lorenzo Costa</u> below it wh: is not worthy of its companions – still less of its name. Then yr <u>Cosimo Tura</u> is <u>capital</u> – the very essence of the fantastic master – a perfect curiosity in its way. What a strange man the painter must have been!

The female Saint by <u>Garofalo</u> is a very pretty specimen of the master.

The delicate & very pretty Ferrarese picture picture beneath it which I fancy I remember in the Constable Gallery (I wish yr catalogue contained also the <u>provenienze</u>) – you have called <u>Ercole Grande</u>. As there were two of them I can't dispute the name – but I fancy that the <u>monkey</u> was the sign of the master & gave him a name – cd it be <u>Bertucci?</u>

Your <u>Pedrini</u> is most charming – the master all over – I regret to see it much injured.

Your Flemish Magdalen is not by <u>Rogier van der Weyden</u> – it is <u>very</u> interestg – the head of fine colour.

Your little Ferrarese picture under it I can't recall the name of – but of course we know it well. It is a most genuine specimen.

The <u>Montagna</u> John the Baptist is again most true – with the peculiar brillancy of eye & low colour

The large <u>Moretto</u> portrait is of fine colour – but I shd venture to criticize the arrangement.

The two <u>Moroni</u> heads are both interestg & the older one of charmg character.

I make no doubt that the name <u>Previtale</u> is right, as attached to the christ blessing.

The portrait attributed to <u>Ant: da Messina</u> is very curious. I have a strong resemblance to the master in one of the hands.

Mount Parnassus by <u>Romanino</u> I can't judge about. I shd have fancied rather <u>Bonifazio</u> or <u>Schiavone</u>.

Your <u>Buonsignori</u> over fireplace is very interestg. What curious traces of Mantegna in the Childs' head, & Virgin's hand! I don't know the master except in the Nat. Gal. portrait wh: identified his name.

Now I have been presumptuous enough & will not go further for the present – tho' the <u>Ercole Grande</u>'s in the middle room are most interestg – & so are several others. Your <u>Savoldo</u> in the Gallery I never saw before – it is most true.

But I must tell you how well the copy from Paul Veronese looks on ceiling of centre room – it is charmingly executed. The room itself is beautiful with its red silk hangings, wh: Mr Malcolm are only recently put up. The Boudoir is beautiful & the <u>Carpaccio</u> & others attract me much.

Little perraquet refuses to make our acquaintance & blunders & flies about when we show ourselves.

I must tell you that I heard from Morelli when I was at Pallanza – he had got my address from young <u>Frizzoni</u> who lives in the same home at Milan, & who by the bye has written a pamphlet on Morello & Moroni.[2] Your friend kindly sent me a big <u>panettone di S. Ambrogio</u> for Christmas, wh: was excellent.

Now I must bid you goodbye – only begging you & Enid to employ me, if there be <u>anything</u> here I can do. & pray believe that we have plenty of <u>everything</u> & are incessantly feeling how much we owe to yr extraordinary kindness,
Ever yrs most truly
Eliz Eastlake
I have asked Mr Malcolm what shd be Antonio's full pay for board & service weekly – he promises to tell me. I shall beg Mr M: to continue to be paymaster.
I expect Swinton in Venice about the 20th perhaps he will come into yr lower room.
I was at the Belle Arti yesterday. The <u>Carpaccio</u>'s & <u>Cima</u>'s, & <u>Paris Bordone</u> were lookg their best – there are many additions since I was here!

1. The Layards' home in Venice was a fourteenth-century palazzo at the corner of the Rio di San Polo and the Grand Canal

2. Gustavo Frizzoni (1840–1919), connoisseur and friend of Morelli's.

Letter to A. H. Layard   *NLS Ms.42170*

Ca' Capello. 4. Febry 1877

It is high time for me, dear Mr. Layard, to repeat to you what I
am always feeling afresh – viz: that we only become more & more
comfortable here. I, for my part, more & more astonished that my friend,
however true & kind you have ever been, shd have bestowed on me so
great a favor as the loan of this beautiful house. I have to rub my eyes of
a morng to know where I am! And now let me thank you for yr most
delightful letter of the 19th. I am thankful my letter served to correct
Mrs Grotes' – I can testify to my party having been in the best of spirits
since the beginning, especially the young ones & if I did not manage at
first to give them the usual allowance of 7 meals a day, & spoons & forks
were scant, they only thought it the more fun – & at all events young
cheeks are rounder & easier than when we arrived. I ought to have had
my party photographed before I left, so as to prove how well they have
profited by the sufferings wh: Mrs Grote reports, or you invent! I may
say at once that this winter is more than usually dry & bright here.
We had slight fogs of a morning in the very first days – I suspect that
Novr & Decr are the fog months here – but we have long forgotten that
existence. One day in ten may be cold & dull, but all the rest are cold
& bright – or even mild & bright – the sun warming the whole home
as nothing she can do, & streaming into yr corner room in the most
cheery way as it now does. It is this brightness from early to late that has
settled us in this room – due care being taken that the sun shd not touch
yr pictures. Enids' charming boudoir with its balcony is not so <u>light</u>. I
must own too that I preferred <u>not</u> littering with our daily books work
& meals such a beautiful apartment. We turn the balcony, however, to
account which, as long as the sun shines is a delicious hothouse – the
girls sit there & read, & even have their Italian mistress, & when we start
in the gondola my old housekeeper Mrs Anderson fondly looks down
on us from that altitude, & then turns her attention to winning <u>Polly's</u>
affections. By this time our cooking has become a curious cross between
Venice & FitzRoy Sqre. Antonio & Mrs. Anderson dispute over dishes,
they have however first to determine what they are to be made of, &
to agree as to <u>definitions</u>. It always ends, I remark, by her insisting on
the supremacy of the English tongue – which she presents to his ears, if
not true & undefiled, yet without the slightest attempt at any glossary.
Yesterday he came to me in despair "che vuol' dire "<u>arve</u> soss"?[1] Upon
the whole we fare delightfully, & with all sorts of heterodox mixtures.
I find the meat excellent, & cheap, the vegetables the same, but the

fish disappoints me. They tell me it is less good & much dearer at this
season. <u>Soles</u> I have relinquished – they are poor, & much dearer than
in London – oysters also are not the thing. "Pappalini" – sprats I think,
fried – are very good & quite reasonable, tho' Anderson informs Antonio
"I could get more for 2d in Tottenham Court Road". <u>Turbots</u> are my
resource, small "chicken turbots" are excellent, but otherwise, after
many experiments I give up depending on fish. <u>Pigeon pies</u> will deal in
much & also comparatively fine fowls. I think you will find Antonio's
marketg talents improved under 'Ellena' wh: is his nearest approach to
'Anderson'. Yesterday he returned uncommonly proud of a fine chicken
at comparatively low price, but submitted immediately to <u>return</u> it
– Anderson pronouncing it "a grand papa". Nothing can equal Antonio's
civility & good humour. He is always at work for us in some way & we
give him no little trouble. <u>Luigia</u>, the beauty – with her bushel of fair
hair – is turned by this time into an efficient kitchenmaid – understandg
all that is wanted, & Federigo begins to say "yes" sometime, instead of
the eternal "per ubbidirla".[2]

About ten days ago Swinton arrived, as he will have reported to
you, quite astonished at the dryness & brilliancy of the climate. He
was much tempted by your lower room – wh: I think quite charming
– but he has a man with him whom I shd decline taking in even were
it possible & so he takes himself to his hotel at night – generally spendg
the best hours of the day here. He does not know <u>much</u> of the old
masters – still, as an artist himself, he is one to admire what is really
good. I went out with him a little too much at first, & now limit
myself to enterg a church or gallery to about 3 times a week. We have
studied the Academia together – always to me with increasg interest
learning to appreciate the great <u>Assuntà</u> better. I hate the subject of the
Virgin ascendg – with a dozen great men in frantic action turning their
backs on the spectator – & therefore one must search for the resources
the painter showed in overcomg such conditions, & in this sense I
think the picture deserves <u>any</u> reputation. Ed Cheney, in a privately
published work on Venetian painters, thinks Titian's treatment of the
<u>Padre Eterno</u> unfortunate in this picture. On the contrary I feel that the
foreshorteng of the figure was an intentional & clever device to reduce
so unrepresentable a figure to the minimum of size. You mention in
yr letter to 'Brown' that you had read Cavalcaselle's just published Life
of Titian. Of course I look forward to getting it – & am hoping that
careful examination of the great master <u>here</u> may assist me in treatg the
Life. Havg done Leo: da Vinci & M: Angelo, Reeve begs me to try
the last of the great trio. I fear there are but few materials (as in M.A.'s
letters) furnished by Titian himself.

This brings me to Brown. I am sorry to say I am beginning to think
him more & more <u>odd</u>. As an <u>original</u> he is perfect in his way – &
sometimes refreshg for in this age of philanthropy one is almost glad
to hear someone profess that they do not care one snap of their fingers
for their fellow "creaturthe".[3] And I can forgive him being delighted at
Genovese's (Daniele's) smash – for 2 million francs they say – Genovese
had been setting up soup kitchens or something. "Fanthy a Pot houth
keeper going in for benevolenthe". But I begin, like Enid, to get tired
of "his musty archives." He has been ridg some passage in the Pesaro &
Gradenigo family history ever since I have been here – till I have it by
heart – & this morng a long note began it all over again! There is no
relaxation of kindness however, but I feel it all depends on the view I
take of the Pesaro & Gradenigo chapter! He professed not to know who
Swinton was, & then to have a particular dislike "to the fellow" – but
he belies his words, by being exceedingly kind to him, & gettg him
on invitation to the Grovanelli great ball. By the bye I do not venture
to ask Brown to introduce me to anyone, & so I let Ctess Marcello
in peace. My physical powers, altho' so decidedly better here, are still
too low for me to make acquaintce except with those who will be
very indulgent. I wish I cd hit upon a few young girls to talk & laugh
alternately in Italian & English, to mutual advantage, with my girls. But
I have not succeeded at present. Meanwhile Swinton brought Madame
Pisani – née Milligan – to call, & I like her much, but she is leavg
Venice shortly. I fear Burrano is too far for me – but I shall find my
way to the Lace shops here, & get some specimens. As to Mr Malcolm
I am out of his books, for he has hardly called since I wrote to you.
Antonio occasionally tells me that he is not well – but my girls who
occasionally accompany some kind American people to the Opera have
never failed to see him there. So Enid need not be uneasy or jealous &
I only feel that he is over occupied, & that if I wanted anything he wd
do it.

I quite enjoy yr chapter on yr pictures here – I wander often among
them. I must leave yr Flemish Magdalen – she is too high for me
– tho' I admire her from below. As to the strange Baptism of a Duke of
Alexandria I quite agree that it is by <u>Paris Bordone</u>. It has that peculiar
rosiness of his features & extremities, & the curl & colour of hair. But
it is slighter than anything I know by him – <u>very</u> pretty. Your "old
Tryptic" hang.g under the <u>Moretto</u> I have admired from the first. The
finish & delicacy are worthy of any first rate name – & there is but one.
The child indeed is better formed & grown than Van Eyck's little <u>rats</u>.
Its limbs, & the Virgin's hands quite beautiful. I have almost deciphered
the inscription – the flourishes of which are charming.

I ogle yr so called <u>Ant: da Messina</u> as I pass from this into yr centre room – always admiring its force & character. I intend to look closely at some Vivarini heads & convince myself whether that name be justifiable. In truth I have not seen an <u>Ant: da M:</u> so large & fully carried out.

But now let me tell you that I entirely concur in the praise of the Queen of Sheba & Solomon. It is a <u>most exquisite</u> thing. Solomon himself (the old Doge) & the figures around him – with that of the Queen, & the graceful maidens, most beautifully executed – with lightness & sparkle that reveals the most practised hand. Also the architecture is beyond all praise. At present I do not know enough of the <u>Bonifazio</u> to identify him. Bonifazio I know in his old men's heads – in a peculiarly velvetty green – in a fine tawny landscape – & in a reputed incapacity to draw feet, wh: makes him hide them – but none of these peculiarities do I find here – but plenty of better things, which the stage of unfinish makes it only more charming in my eyes with the lines of the architecture seen thro the figures, & thro' the beautifully indicated red canopy.

The small <u>Moretto</u> in Enid's boudoir is a prize. It must have been for some small rich altar. I have never seen him so minute & finished – but his <u>blue</u> & other indications are indisputable. What is called <u>Bissonolo</u> is a very pretty picture. The S Veronica is charming – & all is agreeably coloured.

Now dear Mr Layard I must stop – for the light is going off, & I want to send this off this even.g. I can't even enter into the Eastern Question! except that much as I know & detest Russia, the Turk is to me too abominable to be spoken of with patience. Under all that wickedness – in wh: I grant past European history shows him not to stand alone – there is nothing developed, no progress, no learning, no arts – nothing but what depends on the misery of those he oppresses, or swindles, & which <u>must</u> tumble to pieces in spite of treaties. He seems to me simply a cunning, cruel, superstitious sensual <u>fool</u>. The reports in the Times of the discussion in their grand Consul are like the <u>Palaver</u> of a north American tribe!

I trust Enid is quite well again. Tell her with my kindest love, that she is not to write to me till she has nothing better to do. Pray give my love too to my little Mdme Riano – & ever believe me dear Mr Layard Yrs most truly & gratefully
Eliz Eastlake

1. Harvey sauce.

2. Italian, 'to obey you'.

3. An imitation of Brown's lisp.

Letter to Hannah Brightwen   *Private Collection*

Ca' Capello. Grand Canal. Venice
25 Febry 1877

I look back on yr kind & long letter my dearest Han: & see that I
recd it at Pallanza (the very last day of our stay there) I wonder how
it comes that I have not given myself the pleasure of acknowledge.g it
sooner, but − words or not- every day seems to bring its fulness [sic]
or sometimes its tiredness, & my 3 foreign stamps − "Franchi bolli per
l'entero" are always being ordered by the dozen & always comg to an
end! Your letter was & is deeply interestg to me, dearest. The time
at which you wrote was that of my just passing anniversaries & of yr
approaching ones. Mine made up the full 11 years! I look back & marvel
how I have borne them! & yet my present calm is a proof how <u>many</u>
they have been − & how much too of intense anguish has been needed
before such waves cd subside. By what the sorrow has <u>left</u>, we can guage
what it has been. I marvel sometimes at the importance people set upon
a few years more or less of this transitory life − & yet how shd those
who have not been scorched to the quick do otherwise! Perhaps the
abiding feeling is the conviction that suffering is the greatest boon God
can bestow on us. He <u>will</u> have us for His childn & there is no other
certain way. I speak confidently − & some mt be shocked − but a sense
of <u>utter</u> unworthiness may or must coexist with the conviction that He
will never leave me or forsake me. He is <u>my Father</u> − I cannot fear. The
other world grows very rich − so many are added to <u>him</u> who is my
chief deposit there!

I was exceedingly interested in yr vist to Dr Andrew Clarke − &
do very much like that his prescriptions have borne fruit in yr greater
ease. Judg.g by my feelings I fancy I cd digest "a temporary nail" nor
have for long felt lighter within & without than since I left Engld. Still,
I cannot report any great improvement. The days are better − I can
bear necessary standg better − & I get in & out of <u>gondola</u> better, &
occasionally manage a church − or rather the pictures in a church − but
still <u>stick</u>, & sometimes arm too is necessary. But I am not rheumatic,
or not in any degree like Jane − & my nervous affection tells most
in the night when spasmodic movements keep off sleep. I wish I cd
report better of dear Jane but neither Pallanza nor Venice have done
any good. She was <u>ill</u> there with her enemy − obstinate diarihea [sic]
− & has been the same here. I feared I must unwillingly summon an
Italian Dr but my old Anderson & I have brought her thro'; & for the
last month & more she has been regaing her usual health. Still I can

say that she enjoys herself in her quietness here. She has a comfortable
arm chair by a bright fireside & the Times comes every day. My young
ones create an atmosphere most acceptable to both of us. Both are very
dear, intelligent, & trustworthy girls. Minna Lewin at 26 taking the
lead of course – & very good as leader to young May Woodhouse of
16. Their fan about every thing & any thing, is like a gentle stimulant
to my weary old heart. But there is plenty of sense & industry too.
Italian is worked at well – I have no longer regular lessons for them,
but I have engaged a nice Italian lady as "Parlatrice" twice a week who
talks & makes them talk. Thus we are all getting much more fluent. It
is very different here with an Italian manservt & other servants to what
it was at Pallanza. All speak some venetian – wh: consists in leavg out
every possible consonant – so that this house is Ca' Capeo – but we
make them out & Antonio the man is very intelligent, & we extract
some information from him. I have this house, from my kind friend
Mr Layard, on the same terms on wh: I lent my own – I pay & keep
his servants, & pay the taxes for the time – only his servants are much
fewer, being only 'Antonio' & his wife, who keep the home in Layard's
absence.

We moved here the 28th of Decr – a bitterly cold day, stopping our
train at Milan! The English consul kindly met me, & carried off the
girls just so see the Cath: We reached this with bright moon at 8 p.m.
the line of railway from Mestre was a great excitement – sea on each
side – but when we issued from the shelter of the station here – & saw
moon & stars – Palaces & Church reflected in the quiverg waters of the
gd Canal, my party were utterly dumbfounded! I went on to an hotel
– on an open part of canal & lagune opposite the Salute church – &
came here the next day with old Anderson to inspect. It felt like a home
at once for the two servants were standg in the porch to welcome me,
& soon took us thro' the beautiful hall & up stairs to the first floor. All
was much larger & more sumptuous than I had expected – not a palace
accordg to the grandest Ven: type – but still with its grand gallery & 3
beautiful reception rooms off it. All walls hung with satin damask, &
with Layard's collection of the old masters – many of wh: I had known.
Many precious objects too about – indeed all left as if they had been
here. The open fire places had been long guiltless of fires – but bonfires
were made in all we selected to inhabit & after 2 days at the Hotel we
got in, & soon became comfortable. The house stands at the corner
of one of the subsidiary canals – & manages to catch every ray of sun
– east – south – & west – & with the sun on one can be miserable
in Italy. My little household was soon made up – a beautiful young
woman – with a wealth of fair hair – 'Gigia' acts 'donna di faccenda'

– or maid of all work under Anderson. Federigo, a nice young man, comes in to chop wood & pump water & run errands – & acts chief gondolier. Neither of them get any food, but I pay princely it is thought wages to Gigia in a lira (at most 9⁰) a day) & Federigo 5 lira a week. As gondolier he gets pay by the train. besides These with Anderson & Jane's maid make us quite comfortable. Antonio markets, & is as honest as an honest Italian. Anderson speaks to him in native cockney at the top of her voice – & at all times asserts the supremacy of the English tongue. Antonio listens with the most buffo expression – as good humored as a boy – still occasionally resorting to me. The other day he was in great perplexity. "Signora – che vuol' dire "Arve Soss"? but the Harvey Sauce was soon got, as everything can be got here.

You will wonder what our winter has been here. Certainly the very reverse of yours! English friends write in commiseration of the damp they suppose us to suffer – & I answer with a just retort. I did not venture to Venice without testimony as to its dryness from all thoroughly acquainted with its climate. And our experience more than confirms their report. We have been here above 8 weeks & have not had above 3 days of rain – 2 of fog – & 1 of snow. All other days have been dry & most both bright & mild. Nor have we had wind – the beautiful white gulls come in when the Adriatic is strong, & soar about the Canal – but the wind seldom reaches Venice. Indeed this beautiful water with its exquisite olive green colour – breakg up into flashes of luminous green with the stroke of the oar – is like a living creature, all light & motion. People rave about the palaces & architecture, & I have done the same & shall do again, but the water is the thing that grows upon one – & must be most fondly remembered. I am never tired of watching it from one of the 4 big windows of the room we inhabit – as it sparkles & gambles round us – & we are surrounded by it on 3 sides. I believe nothing conduces more to health than this salt, tidal body perpetually rushing to & fro – & when at the lowest giving us the scent of forests of sea weed wh: the Drs pronounce to be very salubrious, as containing bromine, iodine, ozone &c &c. As to damp it rather bears it away than leaves it. Add to this all the trafic of a great city – gliding silently on its beautiful surface – & you may guess how fascinating our position is. I venture you a poor photograph of a poor pen & ink sketch I made on my visitg card.[1] The photo make it much coarser – but it will give you the idea of one of the great masses that float opposite us. White marble originally – but blackened by centuries of exposure to weather, sun, & salt – for the corrosion by the salt is what people mistake for damp.

I have an old friend here – Rawdon Brown, employed by our govt

to collect all historical notices of Engld from the archives, who has lived
here 43 years. He plies me with books about Venice, for I am anxious
to get all the information I can. <u>Modern</u> information it is hopeless to
expect from him – he lives in the Past – but I can see for myself how
<u>revived</u> Venice is – how many palaces are tied up – while, as a little
sample of the custom of the Pen: & Oriental steamers wh: come here
twice a week, one of them carried off <u>600</u> pigeons last time.

All yr family news interests me deeply. You know how heartily I like
Frank & wife, & Reggie & wife too – only I see less of them. Deeply
did I feel & do I feel for dear old Lady Turner, who has ever been kind
to me. I wrote to her, & recd a most touchg & kind answer. I shall be
glad to go often to her on my return – wh: I expect will be at end of
April. You ask me about <u>Herkommer</u> [sic] as an artist, whom you met at
yr brother's in law. He has only appeared (to my knowledge) for about 3
years – but is <u>capital</u> – peculiar in colour, but fine in expression.[2]

Now, Jane sends you her best love. She is patience itself – but I fear
she will never <u>walk</u> again. She grows so like our Mother! Give my love
to dear Ellen when you write – & ever believe me dearest Han:

Yr most affte cousin
Eliz Eastlake

1. Enclosed is a photograph of a sketch. Written on the reverse is 'Palazzo
   Spinelli – Corner, Janry 1877'.

2. Hubert von Herkomer (1849–1914), German-born British painter.

Letter to A. H. Layard   *NLS Ms.42170*

Ca' Capello. 11. March 1877
My dear Mr Layard

Yr kind long letter of the 23rd ultmo was truly welcome – I have
been daily longing to write in return – but truly were I to write to
you every time that I thank Enid & you in heart for the comfort &
pleasure we enjoy here, my pen wd never be quiet. I fear indeed that the
advantage I take of yr house will even go beyond yr hospitable bidding,
for I propose not leaving before the latter days of April. My own <u>locum
tenous</u>, Mrs. King Harman to whom I have lent 7 FitzRoy Sqre leaves it
on 2nd April, & then there are domestic furbishings necessary which will
occupy perhaps 3 weeks. Mrs. King Harman & her twin sister Lady Fred:
Beauclerk (old friends of mine from Scottish times) come straight <u>here</u> on
their way to Athens, where Lady F.B.'s eldest son is <u>attaché</u>. They will

put up at the Victoria Hotel, but I expect to see much of the good ladies.
Mrs K.H.'s eldest son has not long been returned to Parlt for Sligo.

We continue our very happy domestic life here – the two young ones
studyg Italian hard, & now beginning a few lessons of a singing master.
I think I have got hold of an excellent man – a Sgr Buscovitz – who
gives me references to all the Duchessina's & Contessina's in Venice &
seems thoroughly to know his business – only complaing that English
women will never open their mouths.

We have had a period of cold weather since Swinton left – & of late
more wind & storm than we had seen before. The canal today is of
a deep green & furrowed with waves, so that the reflections which I
delight in have vanished. But I enjoy almost any aspect of this living
water which rushes thro' every vein & artery of this wonderful place.
I have no patience with correspondents who pity me for living in "bad
smells & filthy water." Certainly at this season no description can be
more false. On the contrary the water – all light & motion as it is
– seems to me to bear health on its surface, & far from having damp
– another benevolent concern with friends – provides the surest means of
carrying it away. Nothing is damp in your home – least of all yr rooms
nearest the water, wh: I sometimes saunter into on returning from the
gondola – & wh: always feel not only dry but warm. This cold weather
– for today a north eastern is blowing (with bright sun & careering white
gulls) – has kept us in of late, except one of the girls who delights in
walkg & goes out with a maid. Meanwhile I am glad to read all I can
about Venice, & Brown has supplied me with 3 big volumes published by
the Society of the 'Dotti' which each weigh about a stone – but furnish
me with curious information. I have also Ruskin's Stones of Venice –
from Brown – which I have not read for years – They incite for the most
part, I am sorry to say, the same evil passions in me against him which
time has not mollified – or rather I acknowledge my extreme ignorance,
for I have no conception of what is meant by the moral forms of dolphins
& of arches. You, who admire him, have doubtless the key!

Brown continues to come most kindly – not always in the best of
humours when he enters, but generally placable & urbane before he
leaves. I perceive he has the not uncommon weakness for young ladies,
& takes to my two young companions, one lively & the other pretty.
He has asked me to bring them to see him tomorrow – if a fine day
– only sending word beforehand, which gives him time to light a fire. I
am only asked as a chaperon!

And now to that painful subject of Dr Salviati – your account of the
real state of the case has grieved me deeply – not for the man, in whom
I can take no further interest – but because, like yourself I have very

distressg experience of ingratitude, & there is nothing in this world so detestable. [*illegible*] ingratitude is there is <u>no</u> really fine quality – & vice versâ. But it is as old as man – how true the words of Christ – "were there not ten cleansed, but where are the nine"? Even one in ten is I fear an overstatement.[1]

I know that Dr S. is gone to England – he left the two papers on Mosaics with me, which I have read. I shall see what I can say in a contemplated article of <u>scraps</u> connected with Venice – I <u>enjoyed</u> yr lecture, & not the less for longing to fight you on some of the sentiments – but which those are I shall not trouble you with yet!

I see in the Times of 9th, arrived today, the marriage of Mr Guest & Lady Theo: I wish them heartily well. I have liked her in former days very much. When Enid writers to her sister-in-law will she kindly assure her that I have not forgotten Lady Westminster's & her kindness in old days, & that <u>Mr Guest</u> has my best congratulations.

I cannot say that that <u>other</u> marriage in high life has the same from me. I am ashamed of Stirling Maxwell – as for his <u>bride</u> I won't throw away even any good shame upon her – I hear that she was too ill to go to any church, & that the happy man started immediately after the ceremony <u>alone</u> for Scotland. I benevolently wish she only mt recover! Those promising boys will not be the better for her teaching.[2] I am sure this occurrence will have given great pain to dear little Mdme Riano – Pray give her my best love, & tell her I condole with her upon it. I am delighted to hear that you sometimes talk of me when you are together. I leave my character in yr hands without much fear.

You will be sorry to hear that dear old Boxall is <u>very</u> ill. He has had a threateng of paralysis, sufficient to take away all strength, & to render him very excitable. To day I have a card from a mutual friend which reports him as still worse. I <u>much fear</u>. He is one of the oldest & certainly one of the truest friends I have had since I came to FitzRoy Sqre. & of late years that have seen him so much shut up I have finished my daily drives at least twice a week with a short visit to his little room. It is only about a fortnight ago that he wrote me a better letter than usual. He too had read the Life of Titian – glad of much information – but wishing many things had not only been better said but not said at all – I know too well the senseless affectation of Crowe's art-vocabulary – & he has heard so much about it in sundry reviews that it is double affectation to keep it up. Dear old Boxall tells me of some discovery Ruskin has made of the greatest perfection in Venetian art in the Carpaccio's in S Giorgio dei Schavoni – with a description of which he intends to exalt the minds & purify the lives of the Sheffield workmen! I will go & see them as soon as the wind is less cold. I have no doubt that Carpaccio will always charm me – tho' I may not be so capable of moral reform as the Sh: workman – still I hope I may find something to quarrel with Ruskin about even in him.

I can assure you that the green silk in Enid's boudoir is <u>perfection</u> I never saw a more beautiful green – & it is quite the right thing for your pictures. If Venice were to revive in all respects as well as in this <u>brocatello</u> she wd soon be as great as ever. I continue to take the greatest delight in yr gallery. The sketch of the Ricco Epulone I soon <u>spotted</u>,³ & the light from the morngs sun so illumines the room – & my eyes are still so good that I have no need to take the picture down. It is a capital specimen of a great master's first thoughts. One dark day I was with Swinton at the Pal: Reale & saw two grand pieces of Bonifazio – the real man – which I intend to revisit. Also I <u>adored</u> the Tintorets in the Libreria – the Stealg of St Mark's body – however preposterous the height of the camel – & many of the single figures in niches – one especially with outstretched hand which is <u>stupendous</u>. Your "Musica" I see is taken from that ceiling. As soon as it is really mild I intend to work rather hard in churches & galleries again. I have been in the Pal: Giovanelli which dear Sir Chas & I <u>last</u> visited with you. There are fine things there – I shall be curious to look at his notes of them again when I return. A great S. Rocco with angel descendg, & fine landscape is called <u>Titian.</u> I know who else it can be.

As for Burano lace I have had a little experience of it from an old soul, called the "Buranella" who made her way to me. I took a little of the old coarse furniture lace – but her specimens of the Burano cushion were not tempting.

The other day I had a long letter from Mrs Acton Tindal – herself very suffering & entirely kept to the house, & even sometimes to her bed – Nico & young wife had set up housekeeping about 15 miles from Manchester & were very happy. That was all prosperous & promising but poor Giff: is a sad subject. His derangmt is of a singular kind, & one on wh: Dr Forbes Winslow – in whose Retreat he is placed gives but little hope of cure. As in many cases, he has turned most against those he loved best – especially against his mother! Few things wd grieve me more than this sad state of one of the cleverest & best young men I have known – & so handsome too – for wh: you know my weakness.

Your friend – Ctess Morny – has not yet made her appearance – but shall have my best <u>accueil</u> when she does.

I won't give you any more handle for perverse interpretations as to the Eastern Question – not that you need any! But I think I love the Turkish people better than you do, for I heartily wish them better rulers – & the Sultan <u>more toothache.</u>

To return to yr pictures – that over the door leadg from boudoir to middle room is I think by <u>Polidoro</u>. I forget what name is given it in yr list – for Antonio has taken it to Mr Malcolm for some purpose.

This will reach you before you leave for Cadiz – I hope it will do you both much good – especially the sea air in an English vessel.

You see in the Times Mrs Grote's transfer of £6.000 to the University College – left by Mr Grote at his death. It is like that generous lady. I have good accounts of her health.

Now dear Enid & Mr Layard goodbye till yr return to Madrid I already feel the "lightening chain" of my expiring time here. I have not been so happy since that Decr 1865! & am glad to owe it to you two.

Ever yrs affectly
Eliz Eastlake.

1. Dr Antonio Salviati (1816–90), a glass and mosaic manufacturer in Murano whose pieces were exported all over the world.

2. Stirling Maxwell married Caroline Norton. The 'promising boys' are his children from his first marriage.

3. 'Il Ricco Epulone' is an allegory of Lazarus and the Beggar.

Letter to A. H. Layard   *NLS Ms.42170*

Ca' Capello. 1 April 1877
My dear Mr Layard
I conclude that this will find you returned to Madrid with Enid – & both I trust much the better for yr holiday & change of air. I fear, however, that with all the regal & naval entertainments of which I have read in the Times yr holiday must have been rather hardwork. I rather hoped to have heard from Swinton about you – but I do not yet know whether or when he has found you in Madrid. So aristocratic a gentleman ought to have made one of of the Regal <u>Cortegé</u>! I heartily wish you such weather as we are now enjoyg – tho' I fear my wish is in vain. For the last week we have been without fires, & with wide open windows – & if your house was <u>comfortable</u> in colder weather it is <u>delicious</u> now. The more I enjoy it the more am I glad that it belongs to you two. I cannot conceive a more enviable home to fall back upon – in the intervals between future missions to Rome, Constantinople &c!

And now I must introduce the enclosed lady to you – wh: I beg you to accept as the <u>last</u> that will ever be intruded on you – for Vianelli's art has so flattered my venerable physiognomy, that I will never risk to have

the truth more undisguisedly told.¹ All my party have also been taken &
equally flatteringly.

Venice is filling more with travellers, & this morng at church – which I
climbed successfully – there must have been 100 people present – among
the rest Dean Howson (Chester) & Richd Boyle.

We go on much the same – seeing somethings over & over again
– & a few new ones – to me. I forget whether I told you of my first
acquaintce with the little church of S Giorgio dei Schiavoni – which is
full of Carpaccio. I conclude you know it. Boxall – who is I am happy
to say – much better, wrote me word to find the church, wh: was easily
done. I delight in the pictures – & fancy them earlier than the S. Ursula
scenes. All are naive, but the calling of Matthew rises with higher
feeling. Much as I abused Ruskin last time, I find his "Stones" very
useful. Yesterday, being gloriously bright, I spent some time in S. Mark's
where every corner & height were lighted up. The columns & their
capitals are the most curious I know.

I expect friends to be comg to Venice in this month who will
necessarily take up my time – therefore I already look at every beautiful
object with a rather sad goodbye feeling. And again I assure you that my
heart has been lighter here than it has been for years.

And now I want to do a little business with you. I have preferred
to have Antonio receive his monthly pay from Mr Malcolm – but I
know what he gets per diem, & therefore I shall have no difficulty in
reimbursing Mr M: in yr name for that. But Mr M: is so busy that we
have not seen him for many weeks, &· as he is also too busy to answer
notes, I have ceased troublg him in that way. I have therefore not been
able to obtain from him the little account of putting down these nice
carpets &c &c, & I must rely on yr supplyg me with that when you
receive it – in case I fail to extract the desired information from him,
which, before leavg, I shall make one more attempt to do. But you, dear
Mr Layard, know what are the taxes & outgoings on this home – &
therefore will be good enough to let me know what the 3rd of the year
amounts to – for I shall have been here 4 months & shall be glad to
know my debt, altho' you have made them so out of all proportion to
what I have recd.

I have ventured to look into yr great portfolios – one empty, & the
other with the numerous photographs from tapestries. Those from Albert
Durer, van der Weyden &c or called, are curious – I had seen some
of them by yr suggestion at the Arundel Society (I think) before. But
the photographs from Raphael's cartoons are especially interestg to me.
They must be the best tapestries ever worked from them – & in addition
they have most exquisite borders – with arabesques & figures – Raphael

all over – which were new to me, & I fancy are so to most. I am quite glad to have seen these.

Good Brown continues very faithful – & findg that I prize the various books he lends me, & really read them, he is ready to take any trouble in that way. He comes in about twice a week – lisps furiously, & is comical beyond description. But I am glad this intercourse with the old friend has answered so well. He forgives me for not fulfillg his prophecies of taking awful cold in the open gondola – or of not getting a sun stroke!

I think of starting to return on the 28th – & getting home by the 2nd. My sister is so lame that except for rest I can make no delay on our journey, & shall thus be back in time for Royal Academy Private View – for which our Eastlake nephew always joins me. It is not till the 4th. You will have heard from Swinton perhaps more about Coutt's Lyndsay's "Grosvenor Gallery".[2] Could he not find another name! You are such a radical that perhaps you think the Roy: Academy shd be superseded but I hardly think he will do that – indeed I doubt his finding unexhibited pictures suff: to attract the public. We shall see. Coutts L: himself or rather his art will not turn the scale. Now dear Mr Layard this is to welcome you both back to Madrid. My love to the Rianos. I am glad dear Mr Ford's handbook is in their hands Ever yrs gratefully

Eliz Eastlake

1. A *carte de visite* photograph taken by Fratelli Vianelli in Venice.

2. The Grosvenor Gallery was founded by Sir Coutts and Lady Blanche Lindsay in 1877 to exhibit the work of contemporary artists. See Susan P. Casteras and Colleen Denney (eds.), *The Grosvenor Gallery: A Palace of Art in Victorian England* (New Haven and London: Yale University Press, 1996), and Christopher Newall, *The Grosvenor Gallery Exhibitions: Change and Continuity in the Victorian Art World* (Cambridge: Cambridge University Press, 2004 [1995]).

Letter to A. H. Layard   *NLS Ms.42170*

Ca' Capello
26 April 1877
My dear Enid & Mr Layard

We are now preparing to leave your delightful home, & to bring the happy times we have enjoyed within to an end! Your sudden removal

from Madrid has placed you so far off that I feel the more the leaving
the Ca' Capello & the certainty of not seeing you again for an uncertain
time. Under any circumstances I can but feebly express how I have felt
& even shall feel as to yr kindness in entrustg so much to me. This
home has been like a happy home to us all, & especially to myself, who
have enjoyed all within it & without it more still than my sister, or
my young friends could possibly do. I wish I cd say that my sister had
benefitted by Venetian air – but I believe her rheumatic enemy is too
hereditary & chronic to yield to anything. On the contrary her maid – a
martyr like herself – but happily young has improved wonderfully. My
young ones too are the better for this air & life, & I can only truly say
that it has agreed charmingly with me. I have not even had a cold.

We have not been so quiet of late as at first – for sundry parties of
friends have found their way here & Venice is now full of travellers. At
an American acquaintance's house, where rank & fashion, & of course
title, abound, I am astonished at the number of English I meet.

Dear old Brown deserves the best character from me – I must not
pretend to have tamed one who has resisted you, dear Enid – but
my spells have been more of his own sort perhaps – This morning I
took back a gondola full of books – the last importation havg been in
doglatin. He has been here 2 & 3 times a week – has come to call my
young friends "my dear" & we have parted like old friends – as we are.
But Mr. Malcolm is proof to all such charms as I can offer! & we have
never seen him since the first fortnight or so. And this brings me to a
little business, which you, dear Mr. Layard, must endure from me. As I
know the amount of Antonio's wages (3 ½ lire per day) I have just sent
the amount (420 lire) to Mr. Malcolm, begging him to send over an
accountant to inspect the articles of linen, glass, china &c according to
the inventory. I have also thanked him again & most sincerely for the
loan of his spoons & forks! But it is useless for me to bore him anymore
for the bill of laying down & removing these many carpets, taxes, rates
&c &c. I therefore adopt this mode – by cheque – of meeting some of
the expenses at all events which belong to me. I can only trust to your
kindness & honesty to tell me, if, & how far this sum falls short of my
liabilities.

I must tell you of a nasty accident, of which yr servants & we have
been guiltless. The other day we heard a smash in your centre room
– a broken window I thought – but on hurrying to the scene there was
the Ercole Grande, wh: hangs over your piano, with its rope broken, &
lying part on sofa & part on piano (which latter had been turned against
the longer wall). The glass was showered into a thousand pieces. In its
fall it had broken the glass of yr silver eagle, & I regret to say gone

through part of the picture of <u>yourself</u>, the part that can best be spared
– on the left hand. No one was in the room – it was just after breakfast
– the fault was in a weak cotton cord – not fit to hang a picture by.
Antonio let Mr Malcolm know & begged him to come or send to
inspect – but after waiting some days – he wisely picked up the pieces
& removed both that picture & its fellow opposite & now they stand
against the wall in the Gallery. The picture itself took <u>no</u> injury.

Now, dear friends, I must say good bye – <u>crying</u> has already begun
in the kitchen! & I will not answer for its not being catching when the
time of departure comes. Venice is <u>beautiful</u> the canal quivering with
light. The <u>Bosphorus</u> can't be so lovely? – wd that yr mission there were
more successful! – the prospect fills me with sorrow. Ever yrs afftly &
gratefully Eliz Eastlake
I shall be in London on Wednesday the 2nd May

Letter to A. H. Layard   NLS Ms.42170

7 FitzRoy Square
10 June 1877
My dear Mr. Layard
Yr kind long letter of the 6 May deserved an earlier thanks, but even
in my small way, there has been a good deal to do in getting back to
old quarters & recovering the <u>épouchemens</u> of the few friends who
are left to me. And then our English weather gave us such a barbarous
welcome that I feared I was losing all the good the Ca' Capello has
done me. However I am better again, that is when not too dissipated
– tho' I cannot say much of my walking powers.

In the first place I am glad to tell you that Mrs. Grote is well & with
no sign of abated mental energy. I think I have dined with her 4 times
– meeting Newton, Dean Stanley, Geo: Howards &c &c. The Dean &
Newton contending for the talk, but the little man was very sad for all
that. Then Mrs Grote has been staying at Oxford with Jowett – taken ill
in the night with good cheer, but none the worse next day. I told her of
your intention to write to her, even at the sacrifice of another day from
church, which she <u>appreciated</u>.

Then I saw your aunt again yesterday & was suddenly worried that
her memory has passed away! You & Enid must have perceived this
– or you would be apt to be misled by her letters. If it be true that she
writes to you so often as she told me she did. She was as well as usual
in health & cheered & brightend up before I left her.

I have seen something of dear old Boxall, who actually comes out to me – & once was coaxed to come & dine tête à tête – but he had the grumbling to himself. He thinks he should like to live in the country – but I know what it all comes to. I made enquiries for him last summer & found a charming little place, but he had not the slightest intention of taking it.

I did manage the Private View as I doubtless told Enid in a letter I wrote about a week after my return, & which I trust she has had. And I have been again since, & am rather better able to tell you about the Exhibition. It is a very mediocre one. Millais' pictures are not up to his usual mark. An old Halberdier in red coat & black cap is one of his strong effective pictures – the head very vigorous – but a Scotch landscape is half filled with old wood or old rock – something unintelligible & uninteresting, which is like so much dead weight in the future. The same may be said of a large picture of a young man & a young woman standing opposite each other, called "Yes", so you may guess the tender moment. Fortunately for him his face is averted, so his inexpressible <u>spooneyism</u> is concealed. His chief expression is an immense ulster coat & half a leather portmanteau, brought in for two purposes, to fill the picture & to indicate that he is on the point of departure. She is a lady of the accepted decided type, who looks as if she could say 'no' too when occasion requires. <u>Watts</u> is not seen to advantage in two portraits – Lord Cowper & a Miss Somebody. Then he has an extraordinary picture called "The Dove returned not any more". Simply a forked tree [*she draws a tree & dove here*] & the dove nestling in the cleft. The tree is apparently in the <u>Isle of Wight</u>, with nice English ivy twining about it & a view of the <u>Needles</u>. <u>Poynter</u> has a well drawn but very ill coloured portrait of a beautiful woman, Mrs. Archd: Milman who has by nature the quantity of hair, & the golden coloured hair, & the complexion which some ladies endeavour to create. But he has done her no justice. <u>Leighton</u> has an exquisitely finished picture – child & mother – called "The Music Lesson", with all his beauties & all his faults – but a charming thing. Then his bronze statue of a man & snake which has great merit. The snake is coiled round him strongly, but the man holds it at arm's length by its throat, & it is supposed will strangle the animal before the animal overthrows him. But Prof: Owen enlightens the world by stating that you cannot strangle a snake & that therefore the man will have the worst of it, which I do not think Leighton intends. At all events it is a most meritorious work. Painters supposed to be rising do not shine, & wherever I see the A.(associate) I am sorry to say I found a weak picture. Three children by 'H. Holiday' are <u>beautiful</u> as Luini. <u>E. W. Cooke</u> is much as usual, rather

feebler & minuter. Hook full of air & freshness, Calderon poor, Eyre
Crowe not himself. Cope quite himself! Ditto Grant! Peter Graham not
so fine as usual, but your friend Hart still exhibits, & so does Weigall!
With this consoling assurance must leave you!

As to the Nat: Gallery I have not yet ventured. I get tired too easily.
You shall hear about that another time.

Now will you please forgive me if I ask you if you can get me any
information about the Ottoman Bank. I have a few shares, but a friend
of mine has a good many. I believe the annual meeting is soon to be
here. I shd have thought your beloved Turks' extremity wd have been
the Bank's opportunity – We shd be glad of any encouragement to hope
for better times.

Pray tell Enid with my love that she can do nothg for me at
Constantinople – except take care of you, for wh: I know she needs
no prompting. I trust she has really recovered all the great fatigue, & is
enjoyg.g yr beautiful Therapia.

I have seen Lady Strangford – who is none the worse, & longs to be
back again – but I have only seen her once.

I am amused at yr grandeur in calling the Ca' Capello yr "little
home". I shall ever think of it with gratitude & affection. I wrote to
Antonio reportg the safe arrival of the party he had so well served – but
the good man does not venture to write to me. Brown has – & most
amiably – the more so as I had to confess the unintentional abstraction
of his books! I trust this will reach you safe by post. I forebear my
remarks upon yr Turks. So good & wise a government must carry
everything before them!

Ever dear Mr Layard yr's most truly
Eliz Eastlake
I like Hooker's new wife very much – his daughter is just about to
marry, & then they (Hooker & spouse) to the Rocky Mountains on a
scientific excursion.

Letter to A. H. Layard   *NLS Ms.42170*

7 FitzRoy Sqre
19 Aug: 1877
My dear Mr. Layard

When I wrote to your Enid last – about 3 weeks ago I think – I
was unable to give her my account of your aunt. I had been very busy
with a house full of old friends, & I had not been able to go & see her.

But the other day I found her at home & sat with her. She seems to
me as well as usual, & not more failing in memory. She dwelt much on
Enid's kindness in constantly writing, & she showed me your pencilled
conversation with her on that day in May when you were in London
– It was no betrayal of confidence, & I only mention it to show how
lovingly she has kept it. I see no great decay in her physical powers
– tho entire deafness – the rheumatic hands & the necessary stick are
the same – but she occasionally drives out & leaves a few penal words
on the card here. She spoke much of Ed de Gex's failing health – but
that his brother had taken him abroad in the hope of some restoration.
I will shortly enquire at their home in Hyde Park Square, for I have a
great respect for those little gentlemen,

As to Mrs Grote she is now in London & I had the pleasure of
dining with her last evening. I shd say that she is gaining rather than
losing her faculties! for I never remarked her memory to be clearer or
her mind to be more acute & stored a good many subjects were talked
of – for she likes to tell me what she has been reading & thinkg, & I
tell her what I am doing, She is enchanted with an article on Comte in
the Encyclopaedia Britannica the authorship of which she has traced to
Mr Morley. She remembers Comte some 40 years ago, & had made a
clever pencil sketch of him from memory – somthg like Sam: Rogers.
I talked to her a little of Titian whom I am thinking about just now &
she told me the delight with wh: Mr Grote wd stand before the Bacchus
& Ariadne which seemed to animate all his pagan proclivities. I stood
or rather sat before it 2 days ago in perfect amazement of admiration.
Titian seems more entirely at home in such a world of fiction than in
any other class of subject. His Saints & Madonnas are exquisitely acted
– his portraits are what his sitters wished to be thought – quite true
to old Gibson's definition, 'Men thoughtful & women calm' – but the
Bacchus & his rabble rout are realities. It is a very curious study how
far the intensity of fancy in one mind can commend itself as truth to
another – like Motte La Fouque's Undine. Perhaps Milton saw this
picture & wrote his Comus the easier for it.

I am indeed rather immersed in thoughts of Titian, who appears
to me the most complete of the old painters – running his course
unchecked, & working out his own art from beginning to end. I
am puzzling myself also with ideas about 'colour', which cd not but
occur to me in my deeply interesting time under yr generous roof in
Venice. That expanse of fine neutral tones, always seen around the city,
& rushing thro' it, must have intensified the sense of colour to her
artists & I fancy may be credited with their preeminence as colourists.
I doubt the grand old man's being of a high type of taste in life: his

'compar' Arentino was not much to his credit, unless Arentino can be whitewashed or, wh: is probable, was an irresistibly good fellow. I am hunting for his letters to see, without touching any pitch, whether I can make him out. Mrs Grote & I talked much of Voltaire who is being whitewashed by modern analysis, & whom I often heard vindicated by Mr. Grote.

Blackwood (Edinr) is employg known writers to form a series of Lives of Celebrities. It is being edited by Mrs Oliphant, who has herself undertaken <u>Dante</u>, with, I imagine, questionable power – & Reeve is doing <u>Petrarch</u>, – & Hayward <u>Goethe</u>. For no writer have I so little sympathy as for Goethe – shd we fight upon this? I read his '<u>Wahlverwandtschaften</u>' not long ago <u>patiently</u>, & came to the conviction that I never read such unmitigated trash – alike bad & stupid. Hayward did not disagree with me in this verdict.

You see dear Mr Layard I am taking for granted that you will not object to being taken off to other subjects than those which press so painfully around you. It is quite eno' for me to read the Times everyday to feel the world of anxiety & difficulty in which you live. I wish the Turks better governors, & I wish the Russians better Generals. Grand Dukes with no particular brains & no experience are not to be trusted with lives of me.

Long before this you will have had Lady Strangford with you. I conclude she will venture no further than Phillipopolis. Her report of the winter's doings is well drawn up.

A few days ago I had an affectionate letter, tell Enid, from Rawdon Brown. He enclosed me, by way of a treat, a signature traced – which he says is that of Margaret of Anjou. Why it shd interest me, except as a specimen of how not write one's name, I cd not guess but yesterday appeared a proof sheet of his preface to one of his large Calendar vols: in wh: she is mentioned. He makes these prefaces very interestg – but it is well that Miss Agnes Strickland has departed this life for he has no mercy on some of her rather slip slop history – nor does he spare Froude.

Tell Enid that I recd her kind note of 23 July from Miss Isabel de Matiago[1] [sic] & the pretty little lady appeared shortly after. She assured me that I pleased her very much. I hope I gave her to understand that I thought her pretty. I shall be happy to anything in my power for her, but I am leading so quiet a life & am so little able to move very freely about that I fear I shall be very useless. I found that her father had seen nothing beyond the N. Gal: I wd have done my best to get him to some private galleries but he was leavg London.

I am glad to find that a sprig of ivy is growing in my little conservatory which my good housekeeper Mrs Anderson stole from your's at Venice. It has many a loving look from me. I cannot too often repeat what a time of enjoyment that was to me, & how deeply grateful I am to you & Enid for it. I have written twice to Antiono but I cannot extract a line from the good man. I wanted to hear of Carolina & him. Now dear Mr Layard forgive this most humdrum letter wh: comes from a recluse & with kindest love to Enid

Believe me yrs most truly

Eliz Eastlake

Mrs Grote begged particular love to you both

1. Evidently Isabel de Madrazo, connected to the family of Spanish painters.

Letter to John Blackwood   NLS Ms.4358, no. 121

7 FitzRoy Square

26 September 1877

Dear Mr Blackwood

We communicate but seldom, but I always address you with pleasure, for the remembrance of Auld Lang Syne, & of many kindnesses from you.

I have been wishing to ask you a question & will no longer delay doing so. I hear from Mr. Hayward – from my cousin Reeve, & others – that you are compiling a work of celebrated characters in the history of literature. If you have not already engaged all yr labourers for the whole alphabet I shd much like to have the privilege of assisting. I cd refer you to Gibson's Life by me, but I have also treated graver names & more of the past.

In the Edinburgh Review of later years you will find rather exhaustive lives of Leonardo da Vinci, & Michel Angelo, with other topics, such as "The Two Ampère's". I shd not wish to repeat either of these two painters, but if you admit female notabilities, such a life as Mdme de Stael's wd much interest me to compile. But, if, as I say not already promised in all respects, I shd like to see yr list of characters to be treated.

I employ myself willingly in literay labour, for Life is lonely with me. I hope on the contrary, that it is full with yourself, & fertile of all home happiness.

Believe me yr's very truly

Eliz Eastlake

Letter to A. H. Layard   NLS Ms.42170

Marine Parade Brighton
12. Octr 1877
My dear Mr Layard

I have been payg a few visits and am now landed here for a few
days, carryg always with me the great longing to write to you, not
easily indulged till I shd find a little leisure. I have not only yr kind
& interestg & long letter of the 5th Septr to acknowledge, but also to
tell you how deeply I sympathise in the untimely loss of your excellent
nephew Lt. Layard and how truly I feel for his parents. The thought
of the many mourners in this frightful war terrifies me as deeply as
that of the many sufferers. I have also a nephew – a very excellent and
intelligent man, Dr. de Wahl, at the head of the Russian medical staff at
Sistowa – encountering great perils to his personal health, while doing
endless good professionally to others.[1] I fear you cannot have patience to
hear anything about <u>Russia</u>, but I cannot help feeling that, apart from
all issue of the war, this trial of her powers will go far to show those
corruptions which must be exposed before they can be reformed. The
Crusades of the Middle Ages were neither wise nor just, but they did no
end of indirect good to those who undertook them.

I was glad to find that you and Enid had taken flight to Besika Bay,
which must have been a welcome change from the perpetual strain on
your strength and sympathy at Thesapia.

On leaving home I went first to Mrs. Grote, whom I found a
little depressed with a cold, but forgetting it from time to time in
animated talk. Prof: Jowett arrived whilst I was there and I renewed
my acquaintance with the kind little man. He and Arthur Stanley
seem to be of the same class of reputed "Atheists", and most real and
loveable philanthropists. I fear I must confess a very scandalous liking
for 'Atheists' of this sort. After leaving Mrs. Grote I went on to Wm
de Salis' in Wiltshire and was rejoiced to find that they had succeeded
in getting any one to meet me, for my host does not readily do himself
justice in a large party. They took me lovely drives into the Wilton
woods, and Fonthill grounds. Here I am rejoicing the finest weather
which seems banished from every other part of England. And I hope to
gain strength to encounter London darkness, also to return to such work
as I can do. For I am working at Titian for the Edinburgh Review, and,
which is doubtless my own fault, do not find the subject so full and
varied as that of his great compeers Leo: & M.Angelo. You mention if
his realisation in art of what Greek painters would have been confirms

me in some timid ideas I had in that respect and I find the suggestion
as fertile as all true ideas are sure to be. So you may expect to see that
I have expanded on this topic, tho' without venturing to look up your
article in the old Quarterly – which I will not do till I have finished.
I fear my article will be dull to the world, for there is no avoiding that
sort of analysis of art which borders on connoisseurship. I have a little
theory about the causes for the development of colour in Venice without
admitting, as Ruskin insists, that they are borrowed from the East. I am
proud that you do me the honor to like my 'Venice Defended' and I
should like nothing better than to gather all possible information about
Present Venice, bringing in your pet subject of the modern mosaics.
Rawdon Browne also writes me that he has a few "historical playthings"
all ready for me – certainly no <u>modern</u> information could be captured
from him. Indeed I should like of all things to go to Venice again in
the early spring if strong eno'.

Here I have made acquaintance with Mr. Spencer Baines (Professor)
who is editing a new edition of the Encyclopedia Britannica, as you
probably know. He kindly wishes I should undertake a few biographies
for him. I have thought of <u>three</u> which form rather a jumble – viz: Mrs.
Jameson, the Medici and Madame de Stael! But as he is only as far as
"Em" there is plenty of time.[2]

I am doubly discreet as to your confidential remarks on Lady
Strangford's doings in Adrianople, for I saw too much of her in her
sorrow not to be attached to her, and therefore jealous of her reputation.
But also no one knows better than I how the poor little woman lacks
discretion. A letter of her's from Adrianople is printed and sent about to
her friends, in order to raise money. You know I am <u>not</u> a Turk (<u>you
always</u> were!) and I have my ideas that (unhappily) one can no more
interfere between an iniquitous government and its wretched subjects
than between bad parents and their unhappy children. But my practise
is not so wise as my principles and therefore I have sent a contribution
to your fund. Indeed I should contribute to the old gentleman himself if
you were to ask me! But I have not sent it under my own name!

I am amused at your remarks on Titian's choice of companions. I
suspect that his art was the best part of him. The more I look into
those 'glorious' times the more I am disgusted with the greed, the
baseness, treachery, and adulation. Every letter of Titian's and certainly
of Aretino's is directly or indirectly to beg for money or place. The
poets and the sonnetteers[sic] who surrounded Princes only thought
of the <u>cento ducati</u> they expected to receive – and were ready to sell
themselves to the nèxt bidder for the same. I am aware that we went
thro' something of the same phase ourselves, but that does not mend the

matter, nor have we been so much extolled. I have to admire the native Italian character the more – of course I mean the best of them – when I see the vile times and influences they have come thro'!

Now I fancy we agree in this dear Mr Layard, & so I had better have done & let well alone. Pray tell dear Enid with my best love that I don't intend to leave troublg her with my letters altho' I have deserted lately from you. I return to FitzRoy S: on Wednesday next.

Ever yr's most truly
Eliz Eastlake

1. Dr Eduard von Wahl (1833–90) was the only surviving son of Anne de Wahl. He was a military surgeon during the Russo-Turkish War of 1877 and later Professor of Medicine at Dorpat University in Estonia.

2. Professor T. S. Baines edited the ninth edition of the *Encyclopaedia Britannica* (Edinburgh: Adam & Charles Black), the so-called 'scholar's encyclopaedia', between 1875 and 1887. The final volume was published in 1889 with contributions from 1,100 'scholars'. In the event she did not write the entries for the Medici or Madame de Staël but she did write the entry for Anna Jameson (vol. 13, pp. 562–63) and for Lockhart (vol. 14, pp. 762–64).

Letter to A. H. Layard   *NLS Ms.42170*

7 FitzRoy Square
27 January 1878
My dear Mr Layard

Your last kind letters belong to <u>last year</u> (Decr 11th), & considering how little time you can have for writing private letters you must think me very ungrateful for not sooner acknowledg.g it. One never has a good excuse for delay, & so I won't attempt one – tho' I can truly say that you & Enid have never been more constantly in my thoughts. In the great distress & misery that surrounds you you are working & ministering for all of us, & there are thousands who feel thankful for such representations at this dreadful time. Whatever be the difference of opinion on the origin & conduct of the war there is but one opinion as to the noble part that you & Enid are playing – & I listen with emotion to the terms in which I hear you spoken of. I only trust that her & your strength may stand the strain. Though the blessed tidings of a signed Peace have been recd, yet your labours & those of the noble workers in all parts of the late scenes of war will be long needed. But that you may be glad to think of other topics I shd hesitate to talk of such comparative frivolities as Exhibitions, parties &c – still more of my own doings.

The world here has been much shocked at the death of Sir W. Stirling
Maxwell. I knew him well eno' to be truly grieved. So little has been
known as to the particulars of his untimely death at Venice that I have
written to Rawdon Brown – who was pretty intimate with him – for
information. He must surely have known that he was there, & ill.
Meanwhile I hear from a sure source that his last days were tended by
kind Aimée Wingfield – Ld Castletown's daughter – whom I daresay
Enid knows. She & her mother are spendg this winter at Venice, & Mrs
Wingfield no sooner heard of his illness, than, tho' a stranger before, she
was at his bedside, recd his instructions about his boys, closed his eyes, &
placed seals on his things. He could not have had a gentler voice & hand
to soothe him. I hope I may hear from Brown before I close this so as to
give you some further acc^t. The enigma of this shrewd and remarkable
man's life was his late marriage. I must not comment on one who is
gone, & I shd indeed find it difficult to define the mingled admiration &
its opposite which I felt for Mrs. Norton – we women may be allowed
some grudge against one who might have been the glory of our sex, and
was not. Anyhow among the many of yr sex whom she enthralled there
was no more remarkable a man than "Wm Stirling". It is even said that
he died of her loss. He had taken her granddaughter – young Charlotte
– to Naples, & was on his way back. Two boys of 10 & 11 remain to
divide his wealth & I hope inherit his abilities & kind qualities. I have
stayed with him at Keir & liked him much.

By this time you know from the papers the Old Master's Exhibition
is open. I was there on P. View day and have managed a 2nd visit since.
It is smaller & in some respects choicer than usual. The first room
devoted to what is called 'the Norwich School'. "Norfolk" would have
been the better word. The two prominent masters Crome and Cotman
totally represented, both so fine that people are astonished even with
what I know to be mediocre specimens. I mean especially as to size
and importance – but two small pictures of the low parts of Norwich
next the river are equal to, tho' not like, anything Dutch. These are by
Crome, whom the R. Academy wishes to call "Old Crome" – his painter
sons having been worthless as artists, and I fancy as men. At all events
two of their widows have been constant applicants for artist charity.

There are the usual proportion of Reynolds' and Gainsboroughs – and
beauties by each. A portrait of a gentleman skating – a very fine thing
– all in black, full sized, called Gainsboro' but imputed to be Raeburn.
A Romney of Wm Pitt as a boy, stretched full length at the foot of a
tree – quite "the father of the man". A few good portraits by Rembrandt
– one of himself, cetat: 28 the youngest I have yet seen, but the curtains
of a blue bed perfectly exquisite. A tolerable collection of Italians – some

curiously misnamed – a late Venetian paraphrase of a triumph called
"Mantegna". Wm D. Bromley's Death of the Virgin by Giotto which
you probably remember heads a room, and renewed all my admiration.
It seems to me to contain all the painter's qualities, & therefore the germ
of all that succeeded him. There is a copy or replica of the figure of St
Michael – the left hand compartment of our great Perugino in the N.G.
– belong.g a Revd Fred: Sutton, & called 'Raphael' – at all events a work
of the time, & deeper in colour than the Perugino. A portrait of a young
girl – in profile – something like the 'bella Simonetta' by Botticelli – is
here called Ginevra Benci by Ghirlandaio. It is very pretty, & genuine as
to time, but flat. It has a pretty Latin inscription about her perfections &
is dated 1488. Several rooms are filled with the large mezzotint portraits
of Reynolds, I have not the strength for them yet.

Of course my deliberations on Titian are now in the Janry number of
E. Review.[1] I think them very dull, & so I am sure will you – but they
are liked by artists. I am now thinking of taking up a subject which you
may think more suitable to my powers – namely "Female Education"!
There is quite a literature upon the subject now – the worms have
turned! & insist on knowg more & better. Considering that we have
no marriages de convenances <u>nor polygamy</u> & that therefore a good
man ladies in default of either resource are left to starve, or to maintain
themselves, I think they have every right to break through that ideal of
feminine helplessness which gentlemen deem so attractive, & prepare for
the possibility of helping themselves. If every single gentleman would
maintain a single lady – or every widower a widow – the need for better
female instruction wd not exist. But there might be some difficulty in the
<u>rating</u>. I fear the poor ladies themselves can't be acquitted of blame. I am
always ashamed of their low grade in art – & unhappily our Government
Schools of Art are not calculated to raise them. South Kensington and
Miss Gann continue to practise on this ignorance of the young – to fill
their classes and ruin the taste & hands of their pupils.[2]

Of Mrs Grote I heard a few days ago – not very well, & remaing in
the country till about 8th of next month.

Good Acton Tindal paid me a visit lately. Nico's wife comg of age
in March & therefore into her large fortune, wh: Nico will manage
prudently. Poor Giff: who has been so long away from them, now able
to return with every prospect of no relapse. The Rothschild-Rosebery
marriage to come off early in March – he not allowg her to settle a
sixpence on himself. She is a fine honest girl & I think it is a marriage
of real affection. Now dear Mr Layard I have kept you away from duty
too long! Now that Enid is as busy as yourself I cannot even ask her to
write in yr stead. You will believe that the season (tho' not the weather)

reminds me daily of Venice, & I am more & more astonished at &
grateful for the kindness that admitted me to the dear Ca' Capello, &
gave me months of such peaceful enjoyment.

　　With kindest love to Enid ever dear Mr Layard yr's most truly
Eliz Eastlake
I shall probably call on yr aunt today.

　　1. 'Titian', *Edinburgh Review*, vol. 147 (January 1878), pp. 105–44.

　　2. Louisa Gann. See F. Graeme Chalmers, 'The Royal Female School of Art.
　　　Louisa Gann: A Humbler and More Cooperative Servant', *Women in the
　　　Nineteenth-Century Art World: Schools of art and design for women in London and
　　　Philadelphia* (Westport CT: Greenwood Press, 1998), pp. 49–74.

Letter to A. H. Layard　　　*NLS Ms.42170*

7 FitzRoy Square
17 March 1878
My dear Mr Layard
　　If I have not written again or sooner it is because I have feared you
should think I wanted an answer, & so hurry you into what you have
now time for. My wonder is that with all that is upon & around you
& dear Enid you can either of you find time for old friends – & those
old friends wd be very unworthy if they expected it. But it is a pleasure
to write to you & tell you from time to time how the world goes on
here – little as I know of it. Now, however, I have two rather pressing
reasons. I daresay I have felt the debate in the H: of C. more than you
have, & yet I need not have felt it at all, for it was evidently directed
at the Govt <u>through</u> you, while the majority was as much due to you
personally as to the Govt. But Mrs. Grote & I could not help being
a little unhappy. You have not a stauncher friend than she, & by this
time I trust her intended letter has reached you with a copy of certain
passages in Ld Derby's letter – if she has not sent it you entire. She said
she shd have a good night after that letter. It is hard that two great men,
who have much in common – even to their <u>imprudence</u> – shd become
enemies – but distance has lent <u>confusion</u> to the scene, & I shall not
despair of a clearing up in time.

　　The other pressing reason for writing was that I met yr brother Col:
Layard the other day at dinner at the de Gex's. He sat next to me – &
havg a very pretty woman on his other side he turned his broad back
most persistently on me for more than half the dinner. At last I managed

to mesmerize him – one operation I am not so dexterous in as of old! & I was glad to hear 'the voice of Jacob" – for his voice is the same as your's – tho' little like you in other respects. He told me an anecdote of a little french prig of a boy who said he wd like best to be "un soldat anglais" – & on being asked why, & yr brother expectg a flatterg reply, lisped out "parce qu'ils ne se battent pas"! Yr brother expressed quite a Layardlike wish to throttle him. He was only in Engld for a short time or I wd have tried to tempt to come & see me. Poor Ed de Gex managed to sit at the bottom of the table – but I hope he did not eat much of the dinner, for it was so sumptuous an one that it required a stout digestion to do it justice. As I find that he likes a visitor I called yesterday & sat with him – he was sitting alone, reading <u>Gibbon</u>, & tho' very weak yet very pleasant. Then I went on & paid a visit to poor Lord Coleridge – you may have observed the death of his wife about a month ago. She was invaluable in a dreamy, talky Coleridgian house – being a woman of great sense & simplicity. Her loss has almost <u>unColeridged</u> him. She was a magnificent artist – her large chalk heads some of them <u>really</u> as grand as Watts! One of himself is the finest of all – not quite finished & a most touching memorial.

Since I last wrote my nephew Chas Eastlake has received the appointment to the Secretaryship of the Nat: G: which is a <u>very</u> great pleasure to me. I believe your beloved Ld Beaconsfield did it off his own bat – & I have expressed my gratitude to him. I have the satisfaction of feeling not only that an Eastlake is connected with the Gallery again, but that there cannot be a better man for the post. He has had thoro' business experience at the Architect's Institute & has by nature much of the organising power & love of order and accuracy that distinguished dear Sir Chas. The number of congratulations that I have personally received has been very gratifying. At present he is in the position of not being off with the old love before he is on with the new – for the architects have still need of him. So I will give Dizzy a good word for this!

I have been to a good many dinners lately, for I dine often with Mrs. Grote – but otherwise I live quietly eno'. For all that there are no end of interruptions & a great difficulty in stickg to work. The subject of female education – here in Engld – still engages me, & will for some time – for it has bearings which make it intricate. The higher the education of course the better. The wonder is that England should be in this respect so much behind other countries where universities, as in Italy, are thrown open to women, and classes instituted for all grades, and mixtures of grades. But the question is not education for itself, but for the bread & cheese purposes to which it can be turned. The number of single, destitute and helpless so-called ladies is so great as to become a very sad & depressing matter. And the great object is to give this class the power of maintaining themselves – at least in the rising generation – but while it is so difficult to secure profitable employment for our boys it seems in vain to expect it for our girls. But I must do your sex the justice to say that they do not deserve all the abuse levelled at them by some lady writers. In the movement for improved female education the gentlemen have been most liberal – both individually & as the University authorities. From all I read I am sorry to shock you by saying that I find <u>Russia</u> very forward in promoting the education of her ladies – so much so that on the marriage of our Duchess of Edinburgh several Russian towns presented her, by way of acceptable present, with endowments for girls' schools. Talking of Russia I shall horrify you further by acknowledging that I am thinking of paying a visit to the Baltic Provinces this early summer. Married nieces there put great pressure on me to come – having all husbands and too many young children to come to Engld themselves. So I am thinking a little seriously of spending 3 months – June, July, and August – there, taking only a servant with me, & perhaps going by sea, which, as I am a good sailor will try my small strength much less than a long and in great measure uninteresting land journey. But I shall be writg to you again ere that, altho' you are too much shocked at my even thinkg of going to such barbarians.

We are now in rather a transition state as regards exhibitions. The R.A. Old Masters & the Grosvenor Gal: both closed to open again with renovated splendour. Tho' how this is possible with "the Lindsay Folly" as Ld Overstone calls it is difficult to say – i.e. if they only receive pictures wh: have not been exhibited before. After many cards of Lady Lindsay 'At Home' on Sunday afternoon I at length made a rush there last Sunday, which was a very bright one. I wished much to have taken a companion but scrupled & went along. I need not have been so particular, for host and hostess had royalties on their respective hands, & did not notice any other guests. These last were a medley of artists, actors and actresses, and grandees. I saw Gregory there who has been but a short time in England & is going off to Cannes tomorrow. He writes me a note (not having found me at home) saying how much he would like "a talk with you, National Gallery, Layard &c".

I return to Mrs. Grote, she is really well tho' she had a shock lately in the death by an accident of her only remaining brother – much younger than herself, being only 68. His horses ran away with him down Blackheath Hill, & he was thrown from the carriage & died 2 days after. She is too old to feel this deeply & had not lived in much intercourse with him, but for a few days her nerves seemed shaken. She had been readg Reeve's <u>Petrarch</u>. One of Blackwoods series of "Foreign Classics for English Readers" & her enjoyment of it made me get it too, & I am enjoyg it much.

If Lady Strangford be with you or near you in Constantinople pray give my kind love to her. I fear she will never <u>settle</u> again to peaceful life!

Now dear Mr Layard & Enid I must have compassion on you. My thoughts go much to the <u>Ca' Capello</u>, & remind me of the very great happiness (if I can use such a word) your incredible kindness gave me last year. I have not heard from Rawdon Brown very lately.

Believe me ever yr's most truly
Eliz Eastlake
Will Enid forgive me for enjoyg <u>Punch</u>![1]

1. Layard had been caricatured as a bull in a china shop in *Punch*, 2 March 1878.

Letter to Hannah Brightwen   *Private Collection*

7 FitzRoy Square
24. March 1878
My dearest Hannah

I feel ashamed by yr kindness as I see <u>two</u> dear letters of your's lying by me, proving how willing you have been to give, & how tardy I have been in giv.g in return. One always thinks there is some impediment at the time – & one invariably forgets what it has been! Some work & much interruption are my two pleas, & I like to feel at leisure when I write to those I love like you – which I seldom do. It is more than three months since I wrote & told you of the species of operation which dear Jane had undergone. Alas! I have had nothing cheer.g to say of her since – except the fact of her unalterable patience & content. Yet I am not so <u>anxious</u> about her as I was. She left me after Christmas – but before New Year, hav.g her 2nd servt. about to marry, & feeling the need of being at home – but before January expired she was suffering so much that I hurried to her. I was greatly alarmed for I found her with immensely swelled legs – both equally so – & I spent a night of sad forbod.g, but the next day I saw the Dr. & medicine she had begun before my arrival began to take effect, & I left her much reassured. Since then the dropsical symptoms have not returned – but she had had a fit of lumbago of the severest kind from wh: she has risen more set fast than ever. She has a very intelligent Windsor Dr. – & kind too. He is at his wits ends what to prescribe – but advises her when the weather is warmer to have recourse to some warm <u>electric</u> baths at Leamington – administered by a regular physician – Dr. Maberly – which have done good to some extreme cases. Poor Love! She wd rather not incur the pain of journey – still I think she will like to make the trial, & I will take care that she is enabled to do so. We write to each other about three times a week, so that I know all – as to <u>loneliness</u> she prefers it. The maids, the cat, the 'Times' &c are all she wishes for. Kind Bessie Woodhouse wd go to her, but Jane feels her a fatigue tho' she does not tell her so. I shall probably go for 2 or 3 days soon – but <u>my</u> feebleness renders me only fit to <u>sit</u> by her.

I cannot say that I am better or worse – very well in health – & feeling a little stronger on my feet after much rest, & vice versâ. I pace about a little, & <u>stand</u>, I think, rather better – but back soon gives me <u>intolerable</u> notice if I attempt too much – & knees strike work altogether. But our beloved Father in Heaven cd not have laid a lighter physical trial on me – I suffer so very little – & I have all other faculties in usable state! All January I had my young friend Mary Elliott with me – but so delicate that except in her bed I hardly saw her till lunch time. Then I have been alone since & trying to work thro' the hustle of a full London which even reaches my quiet life – & now to morrow comes an Eastlake great niece who wants to study at the Slade School art university College near here.[1] She has like most of the sisters a strong instinct for art – two of her pretty sketches of boy & girl – something like Old Hunt – are in the Dudley Exhibition.[2] I have my fear that the Slade School will not help a student of real feeling but we shall see. Her father – a very good nephew to me – wished her to come & I cd but offer to take her in. However I shall make no stranger of her, & go on with my tack – for which I usually take forenoons & evengs.

I don't wonder my 'Titian' rather puzzled you. I thought that in trying to bedeck I had only been dull – but from Editor (Henry Reeve) & from two painters – the one not know.g the authorship & the other guess.g it – I have had more praise than I sever rec.d before. In due time I hope to do <u>Raphael</u>, of whom Cavalcaselle in preaparing materials – & then – if I am alive – Longman wishes to put the four painters together in a separate work.

Meanwhile I have a difficult subject in hand – "Female Education" – as connected with the immense movemt. of the present day. I daresay you know a little of the wretched old private schools for girls – & of the present advanced public ones as I did three months ago. The old state –

present still in many schools – was incredibly bad. The question is now
an urgent one from the terrible number of destitute & helpless so-called
ladies, who have nothing, & can earn nothing. There is an immense
preponderance of single women in Engld & the same of single men in
our colonies, & meanwhile the women starve here – i.e. those above
domestic service & trades. It is one thing to raise the standard of female
education – & another to make it bread-earning for ladies – there is the
difficulty. One thing, however, seems already certain – viz: that women's
brains are as good as mens' – ceteris paribus[3] – & women are by nature
better teachers than men. These are verdicts which men have given after
a careful school enquiry commission. But the subject is intricate – &
it will be long before it gets beyond the experimental stage. The male
sex are divided as to two opposite parties – the one little better than
'tradesunionists' – the other most noble, generous, & fair.

Last even.g Joseph & Hyacinth dined here. I was obliged to have
what I destest – viz: a dinner party – & I am always glad to include
them. London is not for friendship – one must visit in dinner society
to have any society at all. I can now drive out without the intolerable
depression of comparison of Present with Past, & I meet interestg people
– but to give a dinner is what I never shall do without great pain. The
blank which is never absent is more present then. But I must return
hospitality to friends, & also I had a nice French couple, related to dear
people in Paris, particularly recommended to me – & so I made a great
gulp & had 16!

Otherwise I often question myself as to how I can live without him,
as I do. I never cease to miss him – his Library – his no end of things
– stir the tear & the sigh – but increas.g age & infirmity change me too
much to wish him back to this instable scene. All things are so changed
within that I care less for what is without. The world & life seem of
so little value except as a trial place of Faith & Love. Gods holy spirit
can make up for all things! & that is closer now! Before I was afflicted I
could not have felt thus. Where I am not changed is in the sympathy for
the bereaved. It is the privilege of my life to be allowed to visit those in
affliction, & for that I am quite strong enough.

I have my most kind & noble friend Mrs Grote in London now for
a short time – her great fault is that she is 86. But the heart & mind
seem beyond the power of time to weaken. I talk over my subjects
with her, & her vast read.g, fine memory & long intellectual & political
life have given her a wisdom as regards great public questions which
is rare even in men. On Thursday I sat next Gladstone [sic] at a small
dinner of 8 at her table – a great Enchanter he is – I know no higher
intellectual pleasure than meet.g him. My small society are almost

all <u>Russian</u> in feeling & I am strongly so. Still I think the Turkish <u>people</u> need rescuing from their rulers as much as the Christians did. Gladstone thinks that <u>Midhat</u> will still play a part – & an unscrupulous one – accord.g to our notions – incorruptible himself – but ready to get rid of bad rulers in any way. Gladstone's heard is one of the largest possible in circumference – without having a deformity – certainly it seems to hold every thing. The slightest seed of a subject starts with him into life – leaf, bud, & flower follow in quickest succession. He seems to enjoy his own ideas, by turns grave & witty. I am regretg the passages between him & <u>Layard</u>, the last the one to blame, & get so fine a creature that I expect he will get upon his injustice. The two men are something alike – even in their "imprudence" – wh: I ventured to tell Layard in my last letter.

Now dearest my light is failg & I am sure yr patience must be. Give my tender love to dear Ellen. I am glad you are together. I did make an essay to write a supplement to "Fellowship" but I fear I shd be thought a heathen – my ideas of the Better Land are so material. Now I shd find it difficult, as you say, to work down to that deep aim where those feelings lie. Ever my Han: yr attached

Eliz Eastlake

The Carvers have let their London Home & taken one at St Leonards. I was with them a few days. She is very delicate, but better there.

1. The Slade School of Art was founded in 1871. It was also the first art school to allow female students to draw from the life model.

2. The Dudley Gallery opened in 1867 as an alternative exhibition venue to the Royal Academy.

3. Latin, 'all other things being equal'.

Letter to Hannah Brightwen   *Private Collection*

7 FitzRoy Sqre
16 May 1878
My dearest Han:

I have been longing to write to you & tell you my plans – but these latter have been kept so uncertain, from <u>public</u> reasons, that I have hesitated to speak of them. When I tell you that I think of pay.g a visit to my old quarters on the <u>Baltic</u> you will understand how all this war suspense interferes with positive decision. All I can say is that I will go if I can, & that in the first week of June. I have no less than four dear

nieces there – out of the <u>five</u> left by my beloved Gertrude – the fifth
being in Poland – & they have been so lovingly importunate for a visit
from me that I have determined to make the effort. It is no small one
at my age, & so strengthless on my feet as I am – but you know how
strong is the love for the Dead, & Gertrude was & is ever the tenderest
love of my heart. Her child.n too feel that I shd represent her – that her
eyes wd see <u>their</u> childn thro' mine, & their rejoicg at the prospect of
my coming touches me profoundly. It is true it wd sound more possible
for them to come to me – but young childn & husbands & means wh:,
tho' ample there are not so, measured by our standards, keep them away,
for the dear girls were dowerless, tho' I trust at their father's death they
will not be fortuneless. So I go, if I can, & am gradually making
ready.

In this Eastern question I am out and out <u>anti-governmt</u>. From the
first I have been <u>ashamed</u> of Dizzy's insincerity – I think we have been
exceedingly unjust to Russia – I of late we have been both brutal in our
language & deceitful & thoroughly ungentlemanly in our acts. I have
been with Gladstone all along. I read "Crown & Cabinet" early after its
publication – & my copy is always being lent, for it is not easily had.
I am sorry to say I concur in every line, & so do all whose opinion
I value here. It seems as if our charlatan Premier had <u>bewitched</u> our
Queen – that cravg for the Indian <u>Imperiality</u> being the first symptom,
& that title you may be sure is the real <u>spur</u> to bringing over Indian
troops. All that remains for Dizzy to do is to put himself at their head
when they come in green & gold uniform. If that won't intimidate
Russia what shd!

But people think that the country is slowly rousing, & tho' the
dissensions among the Liberals have lamed their action, yet the people
will speak.

That 3rd vol: of the Pce Consort's Life is one of the strangest &
most indiscreet of books. The abuse of the aged Ld Russell is most
unbecomg. We do not want to hear secrets at the expense of honored
names – & it is unfair to the Prince's memory to make it unanswerable
for such indiscretions. With his admirable sense I doubt if the Q: wd
ever have gone in for the Indian title, or gone against Russia as she
has done had he lived. Her very <u>adulation</u> of Louis Nap: had better
have been kept to herself. It wd have been ungenerous not to say some
kind things, but to lay bare her extreme admiration for a man who
has been already condemned at the bar of History, is incomprehensible.
How women <u>want</u> the guidance of the beloved Ones who are gone
– even in the manner of doing them homage! If you wish to read a 3rd
indiscreet work, the first being the Greville journals, & the 2nd the 2nd

& 3rd vols of the Pce Consort's Life, read the memoirs of the Viscount Strangford.

Talking of family memoirs I had the opportunity last week of lookg thro' the proofs of the Palgrave Genealogy.[1] Our cousins, Thos & Chas P. have as you know pleased themselves in employg "Croix Rouge" at the Herald's Office − a Mr. Ernest Tucker − to draw up the tree for them − & there we all are, figurg with great circumstance. But one thing I noted as regards the Turner family wh: I told him I wd ask you about. It is stated namely that yr father's youngest uncle James Turner (brother of Dean & of Richd T.) was married to a daughter of "John Cotman" "of a good Yarmouth family". I never heard of Cotmans, except our good haberdashers in Norwich & that gifted brother John Sell − not of any connection with yr family. Will you clear that up, & I will convey yr answer to Mr. Tucker. He has, of course, a passion for pedigree.

I have been idle for the last 3 weeks or so, havg been rather occupied before with the subject of 'Female Education'. This occupies a larger share of public attention than is suspected by many. What is going on is quite a revolution − or as some wd call it a rebellion − but the more I have looked into the subject the more I feel that it is one of those movements which cannot be stopped − & shd not be, until fairly tried. You and your sisters had good instruction. What wd I not have given to have had the same! I believe it will come out in July Quarterly, if not, in the October number.

From my Jane I hear often. She has now a galvanic battery of her own − & her servants have been taught how to administer it & she is hopeful − for her nights are better − & this cheers me much. Of course I did not take up this plan of going away without her concurrence − & indeed her advice, for she thinks I ought to go, whilst I can. I shd go by sea, much the shortest & least fatiguing at this season − but I have not yet been able to ascertain by which line of packets.

I have had a young great niece (Eliz: Rigby Eastlake) with me for the last two months, attendg the Slade School close by − a gentle, tall, delicate woman − daughter of my eldest nephew Wm E. All his family are imbued with interest for art − or rather all his girls − 2 of whom are married − but still exhibiting beautiful flowers &c − & gettg them sold.

Now dearest Han: I shall be grateful to see the well known handwritg. Give my dear love to Ellen when you write.

Ever yr lovg friend & cousin

Eliz Eastlake

1. C. J. Palmer and Stephen Tucker (eds.), *Palgrave Family Memorials* (privately printed, 1878).

Letter to A. H. Layard   *NLS Ms.42170*

Estonia

3. July 1878

Altho' no one can take deeper interest than I in all distinctions that fall to your share, yet it is not without a little pang that I take leave of the old dear & familiar address & greet you by what I conclude is your present designation – dear "Sir Austen"![1] May you long enjoy it! At all events, however indifferent you make be to all sublimary titles I know dear Enid will doubly enjoy every honor you receive & I rejoice in it for her & with her.

You see I have fulfilled yr hope that the fact of no war might enable me to make good my journey hither. Many a kind friend expressed anxiety at the prospect of my venturing among these 'Barbarians', at which I laughed in my sleeve, but promised to be very circumspect. I wish they could have seen the welcome with which I was recd – how all Russian Custom House regulations were suspended in my honor! how there is no chance of my being killed except with kindness, and how as my old Mrs Anderson says "they could not treat you better if you were the Queen herself". I started just a month ago – the 4th June, preferring to come by Sea at this time of year – had a roughish passage to Hamburg, but made good Emmerson's (the American's) dogma that "great minds are never sea sick"! – thence a short rail to pretty Lubeck, & so three days & nights passage to little Reval upon a perfectly smooth Baltic. There you wd be quite happy, for Turkish officers are seen at every street corner – walkg about in perfect freedom & evidently enjoyg themselves. At present they have not murdered anybody, & the peaceable inhabitants begin to look upon them with less apprehension. I only hope Russian prisoners in Turkey may have fared no worse, that is, if allowed to live at all.

Shortly after my arrival I went into the country to one of the old country houses of my relatives – an elastic structure, which took in at least 40 people & where we sat down to dinner 27 every day, all related to me except one. Four kind & pretty nieces, with most amiable husbands, contend for my company. I am now at 2nd country house of the same hospitable kind, & next week I move to a third, where I remain till I leave, towards end of August. The 4th niece lives in Livonia, & I declined to journey thither. I see much of a third generation – great nieces & nephews – all really very civilized in looks & manners, & some among the boys who I hope may make themselves a name in the world. Reval has an excellent public school where generations of Estonians have been educated, & Petersburg or Dorpat are the universities for which they are subsequently bound. Of the effects of the war I see nothing. The land is one flowing, if not with milk & honey, yet with milk & cream, & every other good thing. Everybody eats three times as much as we do in England, & is none the worse for it. This year the crops promise to be magnificent, & if the taxes promise to be high in proportion at all events they will be met without difficulty. Of course I hear what I knew before much good of the Russian people, much bad of the government, no complaints of cruelty – that they leave to your <u>friends</u>, & indeed they complain that the laws are morbidly humane, & that rogues and villains do not get their deserts. But it is the caprice & uncertainty of the Govt that is the real tyranny. It is the interference with freedom of commerce which is the short sighted folly, for a wonder they have a low postage & desire a proportionally increasing revenue from that source, but they apply the same principle no further.

Of course I am delighting in readg the forbidden books – of course upon Russian matters, and have thus the better chance of getting at some truth. What I did not hear of Schouvaloff before leavg London! There was no name that my good cousin Reeve did not call him, provg him to be quite as much fool as rogue. Here, he is the highest object of the highest respect. His governorship of the Three Baltic Provinces proved the wisest & justest they had ever experienced, & he is looked upon as one of the few Russian officials who can be trusted for truth & honesty. These Provinces are allowed great independence, they have their own administration of police, roads, church, schools, post &c, & their Barons may be really compared to our average country gentlemen, fulfilling the magisterial posts gratis, & being at any rate not exposed to bribery.

4. June [sic] This letter has laid a day & no I must quickly finish. I am without public news for the last week, for my 'Times' has failed. I only hope that no disturbances in Constantinople have complicated matters & given you fresh trouble. I cannot say that your Sultan gives me much evidence of the sense & good feeling for wh: you give him credit! Your acct of your conversation with the Sultan in his Summer Palace sounds like a page from the Arabian Nights – his ideas about marriage & ladies in general being just as credible! I heartily wish yr next promotion might be to be Sultan in his place – tho' with the strictest guarantees for only <u>one</u> Sultana.

You tell me of Gregory writg to you on Nat: Gall: matters. We do sadly want both more "go" & more judgement in them. Burton's Feraroli pictures (at the price given) are not fortunate. Now I see by the 'Times' that he has bought that charming S: Botticelli of the Nativity &

the dance of angels above from Fuller Maitland's Sale, wh: I rejoice at.
Of course I miss a good deal of picture-seeing in London now. But I
am hardly strong eno' for such sights now! Here I am as completely out
of the way of art, as you must be in Const: Nor does the fact that one
of my hosts here <u>paints</u> supply the deficiency! My politeness is put to a
severe proof to know how to look & what to say!

You kindly make me welcome to a 2nd occupation of the Ca' Capello.
At all events it is a great pleasure to feel that I may, if I <u>can</u>, renew that
great privilege. Whether I may be able to beg for it early next spring
is a question. After comg <u>here</u> I may fancy myself strong eno' to go
anywhere, but in truth my day is over, & I am contented it shd be so.

I saw yr aunt a day or so before leavg London, but I did not tell her
that I meditated this journey.

I remain her till towds end August. Shd you come to Engld & have
any time my address is "Chez Baron de Maydell, Schloss Felks, par
Reval et Jeddefer,[2] Russia. I hope we may meet in Engld.

Now God bless you both. Yr's ever truly
Eliz Eastlake

1. Layard was knighted in June 1878.

2. Jeddefer is modern Jädivere in Estonia.

Letter to A. H. Layard   *NLS Ms.42170*

7 FitzRoy Square
10 November 1878
My dear Sir Henry

The last time I addressed you, tho' not precisely by the same name,
was from a country house in Estonia. As you are not <u>very</u> popular
among the Russians it is possible that the letter never reached you – tho'
I consider it more probable that you had no time to answer thither, &
are perhaps now uncertain whether I am safe at home or not. I am most
glad to say that I am, for in dark days & coming winter there is truly
"no place like Home" – but as long as the summer lasted I was very
happy. It is not often that ladies my age can expect to be <u>worshipped</u>
as I was there – so I made the most of the last opportunity. Of course
I stayed longer than I had intended and my relatives got nervous about
my leaving by sea, & there happened to be no moon – & so I made this
the excuse for going to Petersburg & returning by land. I had visited
Petersburg twice before in early days, but dear Sir Chas had never been

there. Thus I went through pictures at the Hermitage with no pangs of association – only wishing for Boxall or for you to share in the pleasure – or as Mrs. Grote expresses it "for someone to pinch".

It is a glorious gallery, tolerably well furnished in the schools we like. Some of the later acquisitions from Italy well known to me, such as the so-called Leonardo from the Litta house in Milan – & also the Costabili Raphael. I was enchanted with it, & with the Alba Madonna, wh: I had seen almost before you were born, in Mr. Coesvelt's house in Carlton Terrace. The last is the ne plus ultra of Raphael's perfection in this class. But the strength of the Gallery lies in the Rembrandts, chiefly from the Houghton collection, above 40 in number, including every phase & subject of his brush. They are quite sublime, & one acknowledges as indubitable all but two, wh: I don't remember. A small picture of 'the Lord of the Vineyard' is one of the gems of the world. The Gallery terminates in the pictures executed by Reynolds for Catherine II – & it is well they are placed last. I think I shd have pronounced them horrors even in Engld, or standg alone – but, after the feast of Rembrandts, they were simply intolerable – bad colour, bad composition, egregious affectation. "Cupid loosening the girdle of Venus" wd make you sick – & of the 'Infant Hercules', which is a pile of theatrical men & hysterical women, it is truly said that it matters not which way upwards it stands.

Petersburg left no pleasing impression tho' the weather was fine, and the streets full – at least the principal one – but when you have streets as wide as the Neva there can be no effect let the houses be ever so large. As for architecture, it is the most wretched mixture of all styles & no styles, all plaster, & that painted. Here and there a truly Russian church – the Isaac's Church especially – & the Admiralty, show you where you are.

I can't pretend to have gained much information about Russia, even were you desirous or deserving of knowg it. The natives themselves know nothing. I had Wallace's book with me which is worthy of all respect, & found that told me what they were perfect [sic] ignorant of & indifferent to. In truth they have not come to the reasoning period. They hear nothing and read nothing (nobody reads anything more than a novel) & have nothing to reason from. The emancipation of the serfs, a fine thing, but most dishonestly executed, has affected the condition of the peasantry throughout the Empire. Thus the peasant of the Baltic Provinces, tho' long emancipated had not hitherto been able to purchase land. I don't know how it may be in Russia proper but in these provinces, where there are only two classes, this liberty to land has begun to work a kind of revolution. The upper classes who are all a German noblesse, giving, as in Germany their paltry titles to every

man and woman of the family – & dividing their property equally
– have by the logic of such a system, come down to utter poverty.
Estates come into the market which no one can buy, & the peasants
who have been thrifty, come forward as purchasers. Formerly none
but a noble could purchase an estate, and I witnessed much fruitless
indignation at the cessation of their privileges. I am still inclined to
think the Russian Govt: much more agreeable. There is the same panic
at the attempts at assassination. No one thinks himself safe in Germany
since old Emperor's life was attempted, and the attempt on Tressoff, and
the murder of Mesentzoff in Prussia has had the same effect. No one
trusts to the laws to protect them and ensure justice, but all is terror and
suspicion and arrests and imprisonments. I fear they thought me very
wicked for sleeping soundly when I went to bed instead of lying awake
with terror – or getting a nightmare.

Novr. 11th. It is fortunate that I did not finish this letter last eveng, for
this morng has brought your kind letter of the 4th – evidently penned
under the irritating sense of a doubtful cause, but which I can afford to
excuse! Russia has enough to do to reform her ways – but I think she
will do it – which is more than you can say for yr beloved Poste. I often
wonder where the Philo turks are to be found here – except in rabid
newspapers & in the two Quarterly reviews. Wherever I go I hear but
one voice on the Turkish misdeeds, ill faith, & incapacity – but this you
will say is only a proof of the bad company I keep. It is well we have
the delightful field of Art to adjourn to, in wh: I believe we never did
quarrel! I have been wanting to tell you of the new acquisitions in th
N. Gallery, not new purchases only but things which have cropped up
I know not whence – which now help to fill the additional space. Of
this category is a large & curious & very grand picture by Old Ward
who was decidedly a great painter. It is an enormous picture of some
rocky pass in Yorkshire – an unpromisg subject most grandly treated. I
am quite fascinated by it. Then there are the Fuller Maitland pictures
– the enchantg Nativity with dancing angels above, & the odd Greek
inscription – by Botticelli – & another Nativity wh: Burton has not
decided how to name. I believe it a Lippi. The Gabrielli Raphael, a small
Holbein & a Gerard David – new in every way to me, fit to rival Jan van
Eyck and also Fuller Maitland's pictures. The Gallery is full of interest,
surpassing almost every other in selection & accuracy of baptism. Burton
is still in Italy – from what I hear doing little that I' shall approve, for I
am far from agreeing with you as to the difficulty of obtaing more fine
things. I am glad to say that my good nephew Chas Eastlake is happy
in his position & I am sure working well. On my way home I spent a
day in Berlin & of course visited the Gallery. The old pictures are truly

interestg, but the new acquisitions struck me as ill chosen. They have the Signorelli of Pan & other gods wh: is engraved in Cavalcaselle but it is much ruined & horribly black. I endeavoured in vain to find a Director – there being apparently three of these gentlemen – one of them a Count. As there is no new catalogue since Waagen's time – tho' I believe one is on the point of appearg – I was anxious for a little information.

My much diminished strength does not allow me to haunt galleries as of old which is perhaps as well – for the visit to the Berlin Gallery was more pain than pleasure. I am sorry to assure you that the Russian railway & carriage are <u>excellent</u>. I spent 24 hours between Petersburg & the frontier more comfortably than on any other line, but this you will perhaps attribute to my having a delightful young nephew – tall & handsome wh: you know are weaknesses of mine – whom I carried off from Petersburg as my courier & Russian interpreter. It ended by my bringing him here where he spent a month with me & left a fortnight ago. I had become even reconciled to his <u>cigarrette</u> which shows what a weak aunt I was.

Of Mrs Grote I can give you only a tolerable account. She is feebler & slightly deaf now, but I see no diminution in mental vigour or readiness. I bought her a little present from Russia, & recd as clever a copy of verses as she cd have written at any time. She is <u>invaluable</u> to me – all I read or write I talk over with her. I shall never have such a friend again but while her powers of mind remain so fresh we may hope still to keep her. How different to yr good aunt! I found her the other day, but her failing mind & memory are melancholy to perceive. She does not look more ill.

I have felt much for Mrs Kay – & write to her, but have had no answer. The successor to Sir F. Grant will be appointed this eveng. I wish it may be Leighton, but old Richmond is talked of as not being likely to last long – other approved candidates such as <u>Horsley</u> & <u>Redgrave</u> horrify me.

Much do I thank you for your kind offer of the Ca' Capello – if younger & stronger I shd not hesitate so dearly do I love yr home & Venice – but I fear I must not think of it [letter torn] never fails to persuade, wh: is no small compt. By the by yr tenant Mr Sullivan who is in London came to me to offer his remaining year of lease & the furniture all on cheap terms. I cd only decline.

Pray give my love to Enid & congratulate her on her <u>Order</u>. Meanwhile I congratulate you on yr <u>wife</u>.
Ever dear Sir Henry yr's truly
Eliz Eastlake

Letter to Hannah Brightwen   *Private Collection*

Adelaide Place
Windsor
29. Decr 1878
My dearest Han:

I have to thank you for two letters now, & as I sit by dear Jane's side
this quiet Sunday afternoon I can write. All yr words are sweet & true
to me. There is hardly a greater trial than when we see "our loved ones
faint & die". & my heart is so prone to realize all beforehand, & rehearse
sorrows, which come only too soon. I was <u>very low</u> on first coming for I
found the limb much more distended, & the water evidently risg with the
body. For it is not our terrible family sourge wh: I am fearing, but the
sure but slow progress of dropsy! This can only be arrested by punctures
– <u>rather</u> painful, but she who suffers so much makes light of them, by
which the serum is made to flow off. For the last two days the flow has
been <u>immense</u>, &, in the same proportion as the system, & the breathing
relieved, & Dr Harper assured me this morng that immediate anxiety was
over. As for her she is as ever placid & patient – wondering what this odd
complaint can be – & by the Drs wish I do not yet enlighten her, for to
know the truth wd be to receive the sentence however deferred the end
may be. On the general great questions of religion dear Jane's mind is
made up, & as for <u>duty</u> few can have done it better.

Still, I stay on here for the present. Kind Caroline Carver was over
yesterday & is ready to come for a week of so when ever I have to
return to London. But as I accept no invitations there is no need of my
return yet – or only for a few days.

This mg by telegram I recd the tidings of my very dear Mrs Grote's
death! who passed away early in the mg. The family – (only nieces &
nephews, but wrapt up in her) have so long made me one of themselves
that I have offered to join them at the funeral. I was at Mr Grote's – in
Westminster Abbey, where I conclude she will also be laid. I have had
no kinder or truer friend than Mrs Grote since I stood alone – & life
will be still more lonely <u>within</u> without her – but death is no longer
the <u>sorrow</u> & surprize it was – the mind has entered a road which leads
beyond it. A most attached niece has lived with her during her last years
– for <u>her</u> I feel – & hope to draw her much to me. Mrs Grote was a
very great woman – generous, courageous & decided beyond the highest
average of woman – with so <u>large</u> a mind & tenacious a memory that
it was a privilege to submit questions of interest to her, sure of a <u>sound</u>
solution. & I cd always submit such to her. She has formed one of the

<u>epochs</u> in my mental education. And she did much more for she helped me out of my hole of despair – she & dear Mr Grote by their persistent kindness – stimulated me to recover the use of my mind.

Now dear you may be sure that I shall write to you with any change. May you report an abatement of yr pains.

Jane's dear love to you, ever yr lovg Eliz E:
Dear Jane won't let you be troubled to send anything to her.

Letter to A. H. Layard   *NLS Ms.42170*

Windsor
29 December 1878
How kind of you, dear Sir Henry, to write to me at a season when we are thinking of some friends, & <u>missing</u> others! Your letter of the 17th reached me here on the 26th & was much prized. I am here for a sad reason – the illness of my sister, Miss Rigby, whose state of health has long given me uneasiness & great grief for her sufferings. She is a little better in the last few days & her Dr assures me that anxiety is over for the present. By his suggestion I have had Dr Wharton Hood over from London, & I am satisfied that medical help can do no more.[1]

And now I have been reproaching myself for not having written to you sooner to tell you of the illness of one valued by us both – namely dear Mrs. Grote! Her health gave way soon after I wrote to you, & I have gone thro' an interval of hopes & fears. This morning alas! I received a telegram, saying that she had passed quietly away in the early hours of today. I fear you may receive the announcement earlier by some telegram, but at all events it is a comfort to me to write about her to one who knew her as you did, & was loved by her as you were. For the strong, largeminded, gifted & most generous woman has a tender affection for you, & you can never lose a truer friend. To me her loss is very great. No one has been so truly kind to me since I stood desolate as she. Mr Grote & she more & more since he died. To many she might seem removed from the sphere of such sympathies, but I can bear witness how she practised them to me. In her death we shall feel his loss renewed, for her large interests & fine memory had preserved much of his mind to the world. Nor would Mr. Grote have been so great without her. She knew what he was, & helped bring him forth. He would have been as learned with a commonplace woman at his side, but few would have known his merits. It is a great privilege to have known this distinguished couple – we shall not know such another. I don't know whether it was agreed that she was to lie in the same vault in Westminster Abbey. Wherever the funeral may be I have written to beg to join the family, who have long associated me in their joys & sorrows. I was at Mr. Grote's in 1871. Should they allow me to be present then I shall send a tender thought into the grave for you & dear Enid. How glad she was to know you happily married!

I believe that Lady Strangford is by this time back in England, & I left a note to greet her in Chapel Street. I have much indulgence for her, but, I fear, I have too little difficulty in believg all you tell me. She is a woman if not a fair one "without discretion". I know how kind you can be to a wife of a friend you have loved, but I fear she has now even sacrificed that claim to your kindness. But I have not seen "Truth", which seems to be a propagator of lies.

We have an intelligent German connoisseur in London now – a Herr Jean Paul Richter. He is going deep into the nomenclature of pictures – with true German research, boring dear old Boxall sometimes who is too easily bored now & mystifying Burton. I had a letter from Morelli introducing him & whenever he calls, whether I am at home or no, he walks up, by my leave, to the pictures.[2] He writes me today that the Duke of Newcastle has a splendid picture by Vandyck – figures large as life – to which the small grisaille in our back Drawing room "Rinaldo & Armida' is the sketch. They ask for it for the Old Masters Exhibition this January & of course I am happy to lend it. It came from Sir Thos Lawrence's sale to a dealer & thence to Sir Chas – & the pendant to it is in the Peel Collection in the National Gal:.[3]

I had a long letter from Giff: Palgrave the other day. He seems well pleased with his position & strange to say with Russians & Bulgarians also! I am astonished you should pay the Russians such a compliment as to give them credit for having taught the Turks immorality? What a clever people they must be!

Like you I begin to believe that all people are interestg, were they but well governed – many, at all events more interesting than common people.

It is true that the little gem – the Conestabile Raphael – was broken in its transit to Petersburg. You know that panel & frame are all one. I believe a slight portion of the edge was injured. Fortunately there has been no attempt to burnish up that graceful portion even. The pictures in the Hermitage are in excellent condition, being much let alone in comfortably warm apartments.[4]

And now dear Sir Henry let me wish you & Enid all good things in & out of season. I should be glad to see you in England & hope it may come to pass. Two days ago I had a most hearty letter from Brown, he says his last tidings from you was in a letter from you by Mr Kennedy. Brown's chief topics to me were divided between records of a <u>Grimani</u>, & intelligence of more modern grandees such as Hamiltons, Comptons, Barringtons, & Dorchester! With best love to dear Enid ever yr's truly Eliz Eastlake

1. Dr Wharton-Hood was a noted bone-setter and chiropractic physician.

2. Jean Paul Richter (1847–1937), German art historian, collector and dealer. Richter moved to London in 1877 to research his *Italian Art in the National Gallery* (London: S. Low, Marston, Searle, and Rivington, 1883) and *Catalogue of the Pictures in the Dulwich College Gallery, with Biographical Notices of the Painters* (London: Spottiswoode, 1880). However, his principal work in this period was the *Literary Works of Leonardo da Vinci* in 1883.

3. Antony van Dyck's sketch of *Rinaldo & Armida* was sold at the sale of Elizabeth's paintings after her death at Christie's for £73 10s. It is now in the Musées Royaux des Beaux-Arts, Brussels.

4. The *Madonna Conestabile* was bought by Alexander II and bequeathed to the Hermitage in 1880.

Letter to A. H. Layard   NLS Ms.42170

7 FitzRoy Square
[undated c. July 1879]
My dear Layard

I am ashamed to see the date of your last letter – May 28 – which referred chiefly to the death of our mutual old friend Mrs. Tindal. I have seen him several times since & am glad to say that he steps in here without scruple, & is not ashamed to show his natural feelings before one who can so well understand them. I have seen also something of the youngest son – Charles – who appears to be a great comfort to his father & sister. Late as it is for me to thank you for the description of yr short stay in dear old Venice I do most sincerely. It must have done old Rawdon Brown good to be pulled out of his shell. Particularly was I struck & grateful by yr rememberg my question to him about Nuremergers havg any right to the title of Patricians! I am delighted that he disdainfully poohpoohed it. It was what I wanted.

My time since I recd you letter has been pretty well taken up in receivg & entertaining Russian relatives. I am now getting the <u>return</u> visits to mine to the Baltic of last summer. I had one party all June, & now have another – 4 strong – since July 2nd & till August 4th. With my

feebleness as to locomotion I have required <u>relays</u> of young lady friends
to help me in showing them about etc – having first enlisted Miss
Lewin – our lamented Mrs. Grote's companion & niece – who was most
useful. But her health has so broken down with anxiety & sorrow that
she has wisely taken a journey to Switzerland, & is now enjoying the
bracing effect of Pontresina, & will descend into the Italian lakes before
returning. I hope to have her much with me in future. She does me
the compliment to think that I come nearest in way of life & modes of
thought to Mrs Grote, & my life is so lonely that it will be a great boon
to me if her parents can spare her sometimes to me.

My Russian guests are always a study to me. They belong to a phase
of society & history thro' which we have passed long ago. They are
better than the pure (or impure) Germans, in dislike of whom I believe
you & I agree (for once!). They are not so vulgar. At the same time not
so instructed. One of the party – a niece's husband was <u>alive</u>, & if he
had a chance would be a remarkable man – seeing far & clearly – but the
general character is a certain degree of <u>torpidity</u>, accompanied by a good
appetite! The <u>live</u> man sees how much the Baltic might send us than it
does – especially in cattle – for they could feed any number – the soil
being so productive & so much land unredeemed. But our precautions
against the <u>RinderPest</u> at present interfere. Which is stupid for the Pest
has only existed in the South of Russia which is as far from the Baltic
as the Baltic from us. One never has any <u>politics</u> from Russians – they
know far less of their own country that [sic] <u>we</u> can tell them. You know
I am no fanatic against Russia like somebody, on the contrary I only
abominate the Government, & lament that they have no statesmen, &
very injudicious patriots, but I fear they may repress the growth of the
Plant of Liberty <u>too long</u> – so that it will only grow crooked – if at all.

The other eveng – my Russians being a night in the country – I
ventured to a great soireé at the Grosvenor Gallery, not having seen
it at all. It was beautifully lighted. Lady Lindsay herself is grown
unpicturesquely fat, & is not anxious to conceal her goodly proportions
– but she is <u>very</u> clever in art. An oil portrait by her of Piatti, the
disreputable violoncellist is <u>capital</u>. Watts has some of his best worst
there – i.e. two exquisite portraits & some very queer allegorical
subjects – neither fine in composition or colour. Whistler, I generally
defend, were it only out of hatred for Ruskin – but this time he is too
unattractive even for me. The usual aberrations of Burne Jones, &c &c
are there in force, & I acknowledge some beauty in them, which is
saying much. Coutts Lindsay has a remarkably forlorn & passé looking
<u>Ariadne</u> there, looking over her shoulder on the seashore. <u>Lawson</u> is a
landscape & sky painter only recently known to me, & perhaps not at all

to you. A very fine artist – with the breadth of a Bassano in treatment
of foreground. He is a little high headed man who will survive I think.

I have again been interestg myself with the case of good Mrs Finn,
with wh: I troubled you.[1] I have been instrumental in submittg it
to Lord Selborne, who has looked patiently into it. His opinion is
<u>favourable</u> & <u>unfavourable</u> – helpg her in some respects & discourag.g
her in others. There was a talk, I heard, of the F: O: referring the
matter for further investigation, wh: were made & settled in her favor 15
years ago, & wh: therefore cd not permit of fresh enquiry, since many of
the actors in it are dead.

Enid & you will remember Miss Meyrick who wishes to come to
see her brother's grave at Constantinople. The impediment has been the
want of means, but I am raisg a small fund unknown to her & therefore
I fully expect she will make her way thither by the end of August.

I saw Boxall yesterday – as well as usual. Now dear Layard with my
kindest love to Enid believe me always yrs truly
Eliz Eastlake

1. Mrs Finn was Elizabeth Anne Finn (1825–1921), the wife of the British
   consul at Jerusalem and writer, photographer and campaigner. See Elizabeth
   Anne Finn, *Reminiscences of Mrs. Finn, Member of the Royal Asiatic Society*
   (London: Marshall, Morgan and Scott, 1929).

Letter to A. H. Layard   NLS Ms.42170

7 FitzRoy Square
6 Novr 1879
My dear Layard

I ought to beg your indulgence for not sooner acknowledging
your kind letter of 13 August, but you have been more favoured by
the breach than the observance – for while you have been makg yr
triumphal progress thro' Eastern lands I have been leadg a dull & quiet,
tho' not quite an idle life, with very little to tell. I felt, however, that
you & Enid must expect to hear something of Miss Meyrick – about
whom I troubled you. She was with held from attempting to journey
to Constantinople by the warnings of Drs, who prophesied fever, &
what not, from the Bosphorus in hot weather. The Committee of the
Institution – of wh: I am one – made her up a purse & she was ready &
eager to start. Now she proposes coming in the Spring.

I was amused at your congratulations on my Russian visitors. One
may have too much of a good thing – even tho', as you say, they are

not quite "the genuine article". It was rather severe on me to sustain a party of 4, who could not speak English, nor venture anywhere alone, nor take right tickets for themselves even for the Crystal Palace! And just before they left me I knocked up & for 5 weeks after enjoyed the quiet & rest of a sofa in my bed room more than I can say. I made up my mind that the invalid state is the happiest in the world. You are petted & made much of – see only those you like, & have time to <u>read</u>. I have been diving a little into the French Revolution – for I think I told you that I was thinking of editing some interesting letters from my Father to his first children (older than my mother) from France, he having entered Paris just at the outbreak of the tumults i.e. in the beginning of July <u>1789</u>. This sent me to <u>Taine</u> to <u>Tocqueville</u> – <u>Lanfrey</u> & to <u>Arthur Young</u>, till I could hardly sleep at nights with the sense of the iniquities, not of the Paris rabble, but of the <u>ancien régime</u>. I am not inclined to make light of "Terror" but the horrors of a century & half of oppression & the starvation of millions seem to me to be a blacker page. I am afraid you will pull me up for being "Rouge"! No works of late times are more remarkable than those on the causes of the Revolution. After readg some of them, I opened J.W. Croker's Essays on the Revolution, & they made me sick!

I am glad to remark that you are getting a little less of a <u>conservative</u>, & are venturg to suggest that the Sultan shd mend his ways & perform his promises. You will have to charm very wisely if you succeed in making him do so! His dinners must be worth attendg, but what of the poor bakers & butchers who are not paid!

As soon as I cd leave my room I went to my suffering sister at Windsor, & drove about in the splendid Old Park which did me much good. Thence I ventured into Devonshire & paid a visit to Ld Coleridge & his daughter at beautiful Ottery St Mary. Altogether that part of Devonshire is most lovely – a splendid vegetation & tremendous hills. I went on to Sidmouth for a few days – a <u>charming</u> place & climate.[1] Then I paid a visit to my cousin Reeve at his new country home in Hampshire – built on high ground & overlooking Christchurch & Isle of Wight. They are delighted with their new abode & Reeve after looking hitherto like an <u>Alderman</u> now begins to look like a <u>country squire</u>. He took me some beautiful drives. After all England is a lovely country. There is no rival to it in my heart except <u>Venice</u>!

I finished my humble wanderings a fortnight at Hampton Court Palace with a friend – visited the pictures of course, many of them wrong named, & a few very good.[2] A Dosso Dossi is not be mistaken.

I returned home to receive Madame Mohl who remained a week with me. Dean Stanley dined one day, & Newton another – both old

friends of her's. I could not persuade myself to invite <u>Fergusson</u> – he
is <u>too</u> ugly. You know my old foible. Madame Mohl is only 87 – her
baptismal register is in St. Margaret's Westminster, so Dean Stanley
knows all about it. She is a most intelligent companion as lively & also
as nimble as a girl. M: Mohl's Reports of the Asiatic Society (of which
he was President) have been gathered into 2 vols with an introductory
memoir by Max Müller. She wants also to do something with his letters
which are very remarkable. She wishes me to visit Paris & look thro'
them & talks of "next summer" much more securely than I do!

You ask about Boxall – alas! I grieve to say that the mind is going
before body! He is as well as usual but full of delusions – all of an
innocent kind, but very trying to those about him. He thinks & says
that he has not seen me for 2 years tho' I go certainly twice a week.
Still, a painter's name will bring him to himself, & I am sure your name
would do the same. "When the brains are out, the mare should die".
And I am glad to know him at rest. I have not been at the Nat: Gal:
since Burton's last purchases haved arrived. A good German connoisseur,
introduced to me by Morelli, shakes his head at them. Altogether I am
getting disatissfied with the present <u>reign</u>.

I have not seen your aunt yet since my return home – but shall soon
– nor little Mr de Gex.

I hear that the Edinr Review has run thro' 2 editions on account
of an able article exposing the Germans – root & branch – financially,
morally &c &c. Of course I have sent for it – as you know they are
favourite aversions of mine.

Now dear Layard I wish this letter were more your & Enid's reading.
With my kind love to her I am ever yr's truly
Eliz Eastlake

1. Maria Justina lived at Sidmouth.

2. Rose Cavendish Boyle lived in one of the 'grace and favour' apartments at
   Hampton Court Palace.

Letter to A. H. Layard   *NLS Ms.42170*

Windsor
22 Decr 1879
My dear Layard
I have yr kind letter of the 8th Decr & I am glad that you accept
my sympathy in the death of yr mother. We grudge those we love the

more if taken in full possession of their faculties, & yet how sad it is to
see them outlive them! My writing again so soon is, as you will guess,
for another sad reason – to give you a few particulars about the death
of dear old Boxall. He was already gone when you were writing to me
– for he died on the 6th. I had seen him three days before – findg him
feebler but quite calm, & with no delusions. The last words he said as
I left the room were "Lady E: I am weary of life". He might well be,
for the weakness & unrest were great. Still, he loved to see his friends,
& the time before last when I called – taking Miss Lewin with me
– he said jokingly "I wish you would both stay till you eat yourselves
out". The notice in the Times was kind & just – but the writer (no
one I know) knew him more as an artist than as a man. But as a man
he was quite as <u>remarkable</u>. He had a rare independce of thought &
judgemt & a nobility of <u>soul</u> wh: was very grand. His nervous nature
& physical weakness & his mental force & inflexibility were curious
contrasts & very rare ones. When dear Sir Chas first introduced Boxall
to me he said "I want you to like him for I think we are rather alike".
And it was so, & especially in the physical & mental contrasts I have
instanced. But my Darling went beyond him in general mental power of
concentration. Dear Boxall's death was easy – a night of mumbling with
his niece & kind maid watching, & a placid death in full consciousness
at 7 next morning. They let me know in the afternoon & I went to
the sad home soon after. The poor blind day upset me terribly – lying,
<u>listening</u>, in the old place. He leaves all his property – about £10,000
to his niece Mrs Longland – who has been a faithful relative to him.
She is very anxious to carry out all his known wishes & I am glad to
hear that you already <u>have</u> the copy of the Presentation. She has brought
me the interesting portrait in a beautiful frame by Boltraffio.[1] I have an
<u>embarrass de richesse</u> with pictures – but I shall find it a good place.
He had no money cares – for he had £400 pension from N.G. & £100
from R.Academy. No man cared less about money. He is buried in
Kensal Green cemetery as near to Sir Chas as a place could be found,
which is a comfort to me. Ph: Hardwick is executor & writes that he
shall consult me as to his many half begun things. I wish you were here
to help with your counsel. Lord Coleridge & his daughters have proved
themselves true friends to him. I shall miss him <u>much</u>.

Otherwise I have little new to tell you. Miss Lewin was with me
for three weeks & we went thro' some of the journals & letters of
dear Mrs. Grote. There are most powerful & interestg things in both
– especially in a few letters of her's to Tocqueville – returned after his
death. Altogether her correspondence with & friendship for him forms
a most interesting instance of friendship between minds of different

nations, but similar calibre. Tocqueville, it appears to me, was one of the few foreigners who stood on a level with the distinguished Englishman of the higher middle class – independent both in thought & purse – a landholder, living in an old family place, a member of Parliament, a scholar, with general culture & enlightened views. I do indeed know his 'Ancien Régime' which seems to me a master work. Mrs Grote conversed much with him at St Cyr, near Tours, while he was engaged on that work, & in Senoir's Conversations with Tocqueville, wh: I have just been reading, are introduced some of her recollections, wh: are intensely interestg to me.

I am here with my suffering sister (rather easier in state now) but return to F. Sqre tomorrow – & Miss Lewin soon returns to me & we shall prosecute our investigations of the journals & letters. Certainly her marvellous powers of conversation did not come by chance. The pains she took to record passing events, & to generalize what she [word missing] were such as few wd undertake. At the same time her powers were of the highest order, & she had a magnificently educated companion. It has been a great help in my lonely life of the last, soon 14 years, to have gained her friendship & known her so well. I cannot be too grateful. If – as I hope – I undertake some account of her mind & character it will be difficult for me to please myself. Even her journals, & letters to Tocqueville do not give an entire idea of her powers of conversation – tho' they do of their more solid parts. Nothing tells the humour – but I have a few notes of that.

I was at the N: Gallery lately to see the new Perugino – with Chas Eastlake & Mr. Burton soon at my side. The Perugino – belonging to some Baron at Rome – is very fine in colour, most deep & golden, & the character of the Virgin & Ch: sweet. She is standg with Ch: in arms, St. Jerome on one side, St. Francis on other – two angels inn corners above. These angels are the blemish. They are wretched wooden things, nor is the head of S. Francis fine. I admire the picture much, but I am not sure that Sir Chas would have bought it.[2]

Then there are three fine Turners new to me, added. And Lor: Lotto, himself & family, presented by Miss Solly, placed on a standg frame in room – interestg but not first rate.[3] But the gallery itself strikes me more & more. It is full of jewels.

In speakg of foreigners as comparable with Englishmen you will doubtless instance a few Italians – & there I agree with you. But the German, or Russian, & scarcely a Frenchman can now be found.

Now dear Layard I will let you off all remarks upon yr Sultan – & remain with kindest love to Enid, & all the wishes you can wish for yrselves yrs ever truly

Eliz Eastlake

I saw a little of Giff: Palgrave here – and was glad to hear direct of
you & Enid. His wife is amiable & in some respects intelligent woman
– tho' an immense adorer of him! She is also my cousin.

1. Boltaffio's *A Man in Profile* was sold at Christie's following Elizabeth's death
    to Ludwig Mond for £378. It is now in the National Gallery (NG3916).

2. Perugino's *Virgin and Child with Saints Jerome and Francis* (NG1075) was
    purchased in 1879.

3. Lorenzo Lotto's family group *Giovanni della Volta with his Wife and Children*
    (NG1047) was bequeathed by Sarah Solly in 1879.

Letter to Hannah Brightwen   *Private Collection*

7 FitzRoy Square

7. March 1880

I have two letters of yours, by my side, my dearest Han: which shd
have been acknowledged long ago. I feel even that I take <u>too</u> much
advantage of the kind allowance you are always makg for my many
occupations – for tho' hindrances look very formidable at the moment,
they shrink into nothing in retrospect. All I know is that there is no
one to whom I write with greater pleasure & sense of sympathy. It is
not the real work, but the many interruptions to it that bother me.
I fell as dear Mrs Grote used to say "all sorts of things go thro' my
turnstile". I have had more than usual writing to my Russian ones – for
death has fallen among them! Dear Gertrude's second daughter Cessy
de Rosenthal's <u>husband</u> died suddenly on the 10th January, & the poor
darling is in the grip of that sorrow we know too well. <u>Nine</u> childn
are left – eldest 20, youngest 2. She needs the sympathy which none
about her can give, for they are happily ignorant of the great anguish.
He was a kind & intelligent little man – very fond of her & of his
childn – a bad manager of his property – 54 years of age. His death
makes no difference in means, for nothing dies with him. His brother,
& her brother in law, Otto Lilienfeld, Ebba's husband, undertake to look
after the estates, & my poor Cessy has employment enough at home.
Rosenthal had an edifyg death, which made a great impression on some
disposed to be careless. There is much more attention to religion than
there was when I first visited that country.

About the real state of Russia they know nothing – no one reasons
on what they call <u>politics</u>. They only feel that the pulse of the country

is in a depressed condition, for the <u>rouble</u> sinks lower & lower in value
– all <u>paper</u> money – I never saw a morsel of gold. The Emperor is
always right to them – the attempts on his life incomprehensible, & fillg
them with terror for <u>themselves</u>, for they have no confidence in their
own laws or forms of justice. Above all, they never read, & so take no
warnings from the antecedents to the French Revolution.

The upper classes will never wish for a constitution, for no
constitutional monarch can give them the <u>Backsheesh</u>[1] they are always
needg. To my sense, however wicked these attempts, they are inevitable.
They are the <u>symptoms</u>, & while the poor wretched Czar thinks only
of repressing them, the disease obtains more & more. Still I do not
apprehend a <u>Revolution</u> – there are not the materials for it yet. If you
can get "Russia before & after the War" you will find parts of it very
significant. Especially the <u>soldiers</u>' tales of the late Turkish War. It will
show you that the country is more advanced than the govt – wh: is
certainly not difficult.

Another book, wh: has more engrossed me are "Memoires de Mdme
de Rémusat".[2] Charmingly written. She was for years <u>Dame de Palais</u> to
<u>Josephine</u>, & the revelations concerng Buonaparte & his family are <u>what
me mt have expected.</u> For a wonder Tallyrand gains by being better
known – at least relatively.

Now let me tell you about my poor Jane. The suffering has
been very heavy of late, & she has again been laid in bed – intense
rheumatism in right hand, arm & shoulder is added to her other ills,
& she knows not <u>how</u> to <u>move</u>. But there is always the same sweet
unforebod.g patience – forgettg the pain that is past, & not dreadg that
wh: is to come. I was with her before Xmas, & again about 10 days
ago – & dear Caroline for some time in the interval. I do not pretend
to predict what turn this most strange illness will take – nor does her
Dr allow me to have any cause for real anxiety. She & I have had
a pleasure lately. You know our poor Matty Smith has been a great
trial to us – keepg the childn from knowg us. What was my surprize
therefore about two months ago to get a letter of the kindest, tenderest
kind from her 2nd son Charles.[3] He had long had my special prayers,
for owg to an accident 2 ½ years ago the fine young fellow now 29
has become all but <u>stone deaf</u>. But even in that condition a young
lady of great attractions & some fortune has taken to him, & he wrote
to tell me of an engagement which has <u>illuminated</u> his silent world.
Since then I have seen them both more than once here, & also have
met them when they went to see dear Jane. He is a fine handsome
young man with the gentle look of one who bears a cross – & he
fills by heart to the brim as he sits next to me, & I speak slowly &

lowly into his left ear – too thankful even for that slender means of
communication. He is most loving to me. She is a bright little thing,
who seems to have weighed the cost of what she has undertaken – but
he is quite a creature to love most devotedly, & his gratitude to her is
most touching – he does not underestimate her sacrifice. So this is a
fresh source of interest in my rather lonely life – tho' only lonely as to
available family ties.

You speak of my father's Letters. They are now printed, & should
be soon out. The introduction & a few notes are the only parts for
wh: I can claim any credit. They required much reading wh: was most
interestg to me. Frank Palgrave who gave me a long foreworn visit the
other day tells me there is a favourable anticipation of them in the Daily
News! I have of course given my name – as it was my <u>privilege</u> to do.
I seem to know my Grand, intelligent, warm hearted Father as I never
did before. How much our lives have needed him!

Now I am attempting to draw up a character of <u>Mrs Grote</u>. Not a
biography, but characteristic description & illustrations of her remarkable
mind & powers. Nothing she has <u>written</u> has done her justice – or
given an idea of the brilliancy & profoundness of her talk. I shall submit
what I have done to one or two of her friends before decidg whether to
publish. Her niece Jessie Lewin is with me now, with all letters, journals
&c. She has many spheres – Art, Literature, politics, <u>France</u> – Buckle
called her the first of conversationalists, & the French with their superior
art of conversation appreciated her perhaps more than English society
did. Next Friday Jessie Lewin & I are thinking of going to Brighton for
a few days – we both want a little fresh air. I cannot <u>walk</u>, but I long to
sit on a bench in the sun & look at the sea!

I have been havg a little correspondce with Gifford & Kath: & rather
expect they will engage an excellent governess whom I recommend.
I undertake to recommend each party to the other – wh: is rather a
responsibility!

My love to <u>dear Ellen</u>. Ever my dearest Han's loving friend & cousin
Eliz Eastlake

Alas! poor Mrs Orde!

Vol: of Pce Consort all right.

1. A tip, a perk or fringe benefit.

2. Madame de Rémusat, one of Empress Josephine's ladies in waiting. *Memoires
   de Madame Rémusat 1802–8* (Paris: C. Levy) was published in three volumes
   in 1880.

3. Charles Eastlake Smith (c. 1851–1917) was the second son of James and
   Matilda Smith. He was a noted athlete, playing football for England in 1876

and playing for Crystal Palace, perhaps leading to the 'sad accident' that left him deaf. Elizabeth regarded him as the most intelligent of her nephews and made him her literary executor. He subsequently edited the *Journals and Correspondence of Lady Eastlake.*

Letter to John Murray [1]   *NLS Ms.42178*

7 FitzRoy Square
23 March 1880
Dear Mr. Murray
   May I trouble you with a little business, before leaving London on Thursday. You are aware of my deep attachment to Mrs Grote, & the opportunities I had of studying her character. It has been my wish to draw up a sketch of her <u>mind</u>, & of the various spheres of interest, politics, art (of both kinds) French society & friendships, which she combined in her long & full life, <u>not</u> a biography, for on that there is little to tell & that is already comprised in her biography of Mr. Grote. Having access to her entire journals & to portions of her correspondance – for she destroyed the greater part – I have been drawing up a sketch of one I have so much cause to lament. Would you consent to read part of what I have done? with a view to publication in a small vol:? I could easily make ready about 50 pages of M.S. for your perusal. I have no intention of making it long. I feel the more desirous of paying this tribute to her memory from the fact that her own writing – tho' occasionally very masterly – gives no adequate idea of her powers.
   I should be ready in a few days to send the small packet – I conclude to Wimbledon – from Windsor where I go on Thursday afternoon.
   Miss Lewin has entered very warmly into my work on which I have been principally engaged during her stay.
Believe me dear Mr. Murray
Yr's very truly
Eliz Eastlake

   1. This is the first surviving letter to John Murray since their rift of 1876. Since the letter coincides with the renewal of Elizabeth's ties to the Smith family and to Charles Eastlake Smith (see preceding letter) it is likely that Elizabeth's rancour towards John Murray was also connected to her estrangement from her sister Matilda.

Letter to John Murray   *NLS Ms.42178*

Adelaide Place, King's Rd., Windsor
29 March 1880
Dear Mr. Murray

I am as good – or as bad – as my word now, & send you a rather weighty packet of M.S. You will see that it is no biography, but that I have endeavoured (as I told you) to carry out as far as I can the analysis of the character, as exemplified in the various interests which occupied her remarkable mind. The first chapter is mere analysis of the mind. You will find five chapters, one short chapter only failing, which I intend should rather sum up her <u>deeper</u> portion, but which will be very short. I have drawn much upon my own recollections, & also upon jottings I privately made while enjoying her society.

You will observe that the <u>pencil</u> numbers in centre of page are the real pagings. I have to ask your indulgence for a fragment ("over") when you will turn over & then come back again. And also for some over minute writing in one instance, which I fear will try your eyes.

Of course to my feeling the intellectual & reflective part of my late friend's mind is still more interesting than her liveliness. Accordingly I trust you will approve of some rather lengthened passages from her journals on subjects of political & rural interest. And also the same from the letters to Alexis de Tocqueville – <u>his</u> to her have been published, but not <u>her's</u> to him. Of course, as I am a liberal in politics, & a great detester of both the Napoleons, I feel the soundness of her philosophy.

Should you feel inclined to publish this it would make only a small, rather large printed vol: If not I think I should offer it to Macmillan, but of course I should prefer your name attached to a work on <u>her</u>.

I am glad to think that you & yours – & everybody – are enjoying such holiday weather. I find my sister rather easier again after a fit of suffering.

Miss Bird's book is no common work, however allied to Munchhausen, but the descriptions of scenery are charming.[1]

I return to F. Square on Thursday afternoon, till then my address is here.

With love to Menie, believe me dear Mr. Murray
Yr's very truly
Eliz Eastlake

1. Isabella Bird, *A Lady's Life in the Rocky Mountains* (London: John Murray, 1879).

Letter to Hannah Brightwen   *Private Collection*

7. FitzRoy Sqre
7. April 1880
My dearest Han: You don not often get the <u>retort</u> so soon – but
today is an idle one – between two jobs, & I am glad to <u>thank</u>
immediately for the always welcome handwritg. Also I have found up
the Report of last year's Charity Organisation & hasten to send it you. I
fear it will not help to provide for an old servant, but I am glad you shd
have this opportunity of seeing what it can do.

My Father's Letters are not yet out. They have long been off my
hands, but I suppose, like all publishers, they (Longmans) were tardy
before Easter, & now they wait till the hurricane of the Elections is
over. Nor do I yet know what Murray intends to do with my attempt
to make people understand what sort of a woman Mrs Grote was – tho'
he bespeaks the disposal of it. I have no idea what will be thought of it.

I have been with dear Jane for a week, returning last Thursday. I left
her with a less anxious feeling. It was a good turn of the wheel with
her. She was in her chair, & that next the window where the beautifully
budd.g trees of the Long Walk, & the trafic [sic] of a busy road interest
her. Also she is always read.g. I looked out partially for some country
home near Windsor, but only saw what was <u>too</u> large, however, her
neighbours are lookg for me in & close to Windsor. I must be somewhere
near her, & this home needs doing up outside so that I must be away.

I have been busy negotiating for a governess of my acquaintance
with the Giff: Palgraves – & they have engaged her. I think they
will be satisfied tho' she is not "certificated" & has therefore neither
the pretensions not the mannerism of that condition. She is to go
direct from Lpool to Alexandria in first week of May & will pay me
a short visit first. She is a lady, & a person of culture her name Caux
– pronounced <u>Cawkes</u>.

I have only seen Millais' pictures – never more <u>splendid</u>. One of
himself for the portrait was at the Uffizii [sic] (Florence) wh: will make
the Italians stare. The fact that they have invited three English painters
to send their portraits is mentioned in todays Times. And they are all
three (Leighton & Watts beside) handsome men.[1] His pictures this year
cannot have brought him less than £72.000 – so he may well live in a
literal <u>Palace</u>.

I won't be called a 'Democrat'! You dear 'Aristocrat' – on the
contrary I think a constitutional Monarchy the best form in the world
– & within that the most opposite parties oscillate within narrow

bounds. I am glad the late ideas of the <u>prestige</u> of Engld will be stopped for awhile. The underhand annexation of Cyprus was to my mind quite a prestige of the wrong sort! I never knew what it was to feel ashamed of my country till I first denied & then had to acknowledge the fact when I was on the Baltic.

It is said by, or <u>for</u> Beaconsfield that his success with ladies is owing "to his laying it on with a full brush – while, with Her Majesty he lays it on with a trowel".

I am enjoy.g the 5th vol: if the Pce Consort. He does not spare Louis Nap: – & indeed I find I can follow him with ardent approval in all his political principles. He made himself an Englishman in the best sense of the word as regards our Laws & Constitution. He criticized our modes of <u>Education</u>.

I go on seeing my dear deaf Charlie frequently, & hearg from & writg to him oftener. He interests me deeply. In <u>May</u> <u>Macmillan</u> you will read a letter from Matilda's eldest boy Donald – caught in the late cyclone in the Fiji islands, & preserved from <u>20 deaths</u>. I will not give you details beforehd. God's most merciful hand in all, & that I think he feels, & expresses in a way of his own.[2]

Now my dearest Han: this talk is quite an extra treat for me – & dear Ellen is joined with it in thought. My tender love to her.

> Ever dear yr lovg cousin
> Eliz Eastlake

1. An exhibition of *Portraits of Painters* in the corridor of the Uffizi Gallery in Florence included self-portraits by Millais, Leighton and Watts.

2. 'An Escape for Life From a Fijian Cyclone', *Macmillan's Magazine*, no. 1877 (5 June 1880).

Letter to John Murray   *NLS Ms.42178*

7 FitzRoy Sqre
8 April 1880
Dear Mr Murray

I am <u>very</u> much obliged to you for your criticism & other remarks on my attempt to portray the character of Mrs. Grote. She was so kind & wise a friend to me, & that thro' a time when I had very little to offer her in return, that I have far more eagerness to do her justice than cool judgement in doing it. The "extreme epithets" are easily corrected. As to her <u>conversations</u>, not having the art of Mr. Senior,[1] I must say that it would impossible [sic] to supply a fair specimen & I deeply feel

that deficiency. I noted her sayings – odd expressions – opinions, & her
ways, & those I have endeavoured to reproduce. As to letters those to
M. & Mdme. de Tocqueville strike me as very remarkable, & I have
cited passages from others. But it will be easy for me to cite more. I
have a large collection myself, but they are very private, with here &
there a striking passage. Some I have quoted one to Mr. Stanley, as the
Dean has kindly supplied me with a small number. But in quoting I
want her to be understood & not misunderstood. I have some intention
of applying to Mr. Hayward, & to Ld Justice James – perhaps to your
good Editor, of whom I rejoice to hear a safe account.[2]

Miss Lewin comes to me tomorrow, in order to have the pleasure of
dining with you. She is as anxious as I to court criticism on this to[sic]
absorbing subject – & I am sure she will be glad of your's.

To your liberal offer of the mode of publication I readily assent.
Believe me dear Mr. Murray
Yr's very truly
Eliz Eastlake

1. Nassau W. Senior (1790–1864), English economist and intermittently Professor
   of Economics at Oxford. Harriet Grote's correspondence with Senior (1844–
   59) is in the National Library of Wales.

2. Abraham Hayward (1801–84), essayist and translator of Goethe's *Faust*.

Letter to A. H. Layard   *NLS Ms.42171*

7 FitzRoy Sqre
15 April 1880
My dear Layard

I am very behind hand in my correspondce with several friends for
which I have only the excuse of having been over occupied, but this
excuse of all others is the least fitted to be offered to you, who, with all
your occupations manage to write to distant friends. Perhaps old age &
laziness have something to do with it. I love work, & can't live without
it, but I can't get thro' so much as of old. May it be long before you feel
the same!

And now in the sudden reversal of political prospects, I feel that there
may not be much time to spare in finding you on the Bosphorus! It is
quite an anomaly that you should not rejoice in the advent of a liberal
Ministry – & an unfortunate one too – but I feel sure that your powers
will be recognized & yr services needed in some other part of the world

– & people are already saying that your instructions are to blame & not
yourself for the small progress the Turks have made towards fulfilling
their pledges. I am too old to be much moved by such changes. The
utmost extremes of party under a constitutional gov^t cannot happily to
the harm, or even good, which the change of one Despot for another
would create. The laws are above all parties, & their common ground
& interests are great. Of course my feelings are against the man who
ministered to our Queen's vanity by the title of 'Empress' & who
annexed Cyprus in an unEnglish underhand way. I never felt ashamed
of my country till that fact came out beyond all denial whilst I was in
Russia. The next few months will be very interesting for us at home
to watch – but the team of the nation cannot suddenly be driven in an
opposite direction. Meanwhile nothing will interest me more than your
& dear Enid's destination.[1]

How our old friend Mrs Grote wd have taken part in all this
bouleversement![2] I have been spendg my time very much with her
– havg devoted all the leisure I can command, wh: is not much, for
I am far too good natured to interruptors. She did herself no justice
by her journals, tho' of course there are interestg things in them &
they were evidently made the means for working out large questions
for her own improvement. Nor can I command many interestg letters.
Dean Stanley has put his & his mother's collections at my service, also
Hayward, a few of 1873–4. My plan has been to give typical letters on
certain points, so as somewhat to show the range of her interests &
sympathies. I have loved her even more than before, in going through
these documents. Sydney Smith, on first meeting her, said that "the basis
of her mind is rural, but whatever it may be she is an extraordinarily
clever woman" &c.

I see the truth of his first impression, there was so much common
sense & fresh air about her. What I have put together will not be long –
one small vol: at most, analysis of character is not a fertile subject, for its
strength lies in being compressed, &, as I have said, her letters are few.
I have had Miss Lewin with me for some weeks, to my great assistance.
Mr. Murray will publish, but he does not seem much to relish.

Your last letter – 6th February! – was much about dear old Boxall, &
was most charmingly just. He was truly "a gentleman in the best sense
of the word". My Darling when he first introduced him to me said "I
want you to like Boxall because I fancy he is like me". He meant as to
sensitive nerves, but they were of the same type in higher things.

I have been in the Nat. G: since I last wrote – much dissatisfied with
a Borgognone [sic], placed on a separate stand in the centre of the great
gallery, a picture in three parts & a very poor specimen of a master who

is only beautiful at his best. £1200 was a very needless outlay when we have a fine specimen already.[3]

I went about no studios before the pictures were sent into the R. Academy, only to Millais' who particularly requested me to come, & he never had a finer roomful. Two children in a wood listening to a cuckoo are splendid in force, freedom & colour. Right is a fine quiet portrait, his own head with just a hand & palette, for the Uffizi portrait room is really magnificent – the Italians will stare at it. If Leighton & Watts send as fine versions of their respective heads our painters will be thought a fine race.

Now dear Layard I must say goodbye. Perhaps the world is wrong in thinking you are to leave your post, perhaps you & Enid will not be sorry to quit so arduous an one. You may not find me in London – for I propose taking some little pied à terre at Windsor for part of the summer, to be near a suffering sister. But somehow we shall meet.

With kindest love to Enid I am ever yr's truly
Eliz Eastlake

1. Layard had been appointed by Lord Beaconsfield ambassador at Constantinople in 1877, where he remained until Gladstone's return to power in 1880, when he finally retired from public life.

2. French, 'overturning'.

3. The National Gallery purchased three panels by Ambrogio Bergognone in 1879; the 'fine specimen' referred to is the altarpiece purchased by Eastlake in 1857, *The Virgin and Child with Saint Catherine of Alexandria and Saint Catherine of Siena* (NG 298).

Letter to Hannah Brightwen   *Private Collection*

7. FitzRoy Sqre
28 May 1880
My dearest Hannah

I can but have one answer to Mrs Herbert Jones' flattering desire for my acquaintance, wh: is that I shall be happy to exchange it for her's. I shall probably here all June & if she will kindly send me her address when she arrives I will give her a choice of days when to find me at home. We shall have plenty of subjects in common.

I saw that announcement of dear Ellen's fresh trial, & have been longing to send her my sympathy thro' you. It must not be said that we get used to trials – but we know better how to set about bearing them.

Dearest Ellen has had sad experience! I hope she can say, as I do, that
the Cross is the highest form of God's blessing – but we only say so
"after a while" when things settle into their right moral perspective. The
mystery of such struggle & suffering as you describe is great. If we could
believe that they help to fill up the measure of our Lord's sufferings for
this world, it wd be a great comfort. A writer of the name of James
Hinton, now dead, made that theme his reverent thought.

I enjoyed the Private View of R. Academy in a wheel chair – & was
there for hours. There is much that is interestg – tho' the Academy as
a body do not contribute much that is good. The President's works are
terribly namby pamby,[1] but there are rising men – & some fine things
by foreigners – especially "Women stringing beads at Venice by one Van
Haanen", the best thing there.[2]

Yesterday my dear <u>deaf</u> Chas Eastlake Smith (Matilda's 2nd son)
married a good girl with sufficient fortune.[3] They came & lunched here
on their way thro' London, & dear Caroline Carver & Jessie Lewin
came & helped me. He is a very interestg young man – bearg his Cross
bravely, & feeling the devotion of a young heart such a compensation &
gift from God.

I shall not forget that Mrs Herbert Jones is sister to poor Mrs Orde.
How this "depth of sorrow" is known to you & me, my Han! Now
God bless you – dear Jane no worse perhaps rather less suffering. Ever
the same gentle unmurmerg patience. I hope to spend July with her.
Ever yr lovg
    Eliz Eastlake

1. Lord Leighton was President.

2. Cecil Van Haanen (1844–1914) Dutch painter, active in Austria.

3. Charles Eastlake Smith married 'Lizzie' Cooper.

Letter to A. H. Layard   *NLS Ms.42171*

7 FitzRoy Sqre
3 July 1880
Dear Layard

I have today seen a picture which I think wd interest you. It is
by no means perfect as a work of art, but is believed to be an early
Correggio.[1] Dr. Richter – the best connoisseur we have now in England
pronounces it to be a Correggio. It's in the care of Mrs Lyell (sister of
late Lady Lyell) who has recd it from three Italian sisters to whom it

belongs. She lives No.9 Cornwall Gardens, & would show it, or have it shown to your & to Sir Wm Gregory whenever you could call. We are too well represented in the Nat Gal: by Correggio to desire an immature specimen however interesting – but it is worth the attention of collectors.

I leave London on the 8th & am far too well aware of the demands on your time to expect to see you again till a quieter time.
Ever yr's truly
Eliz Eastlake

1. *Saint Catherine of Alexandria*, c. 1515–30, now attributed to Garofalo, but proposed as an early work by Correggio (NG3118, Layard Bequest, 1916).

Letter to John Murray   *NLS Ms.42178*

Adelaide Place
[undated, 1880]
Dear Mr. Murray

It is more than time to place the M.S. of "Mrs Grote" in your hands for I feel that all delay now is upon my head. Within the last fortnight I have recd a packet of Mrs. Grote's letters from Mdme Léon Faucher, some of them very interesting, which I have now incorporated with the rest. M. Léon Say also writes me that he has "one letter admirable" from her in her last days, bidding him farewell. But it is in the country & his post at the Senate keeps him in Paris. He hopes, however, to send it me soon. I have, however, not waited for it. If inserted at all it would be at the end, to which period it belongs.

I return to London at end of this week, but merely to pass thro' on my way to a little place in Albury "Weston Lea – Albury, Guildford" where I shall be all August & September, & where I shall be most thankful to receive the proofs.

I have not written to any one on James Smith's death, except my dear boy Chas. It would have been impossible for me, & also it was needless. Peace be with him! there where I hope all may meet.[1]

Hoping that you are all well, & enjoying your pretty place, I remain dear Mr. Murray your's very truly
Eliz Eastlake
I send the packet to Albemarle Street.

1. James Smith, Elizabeth's brother-in-law and father of Charles Eastlake Smith.

Letter to A. H. Layard   *NLS Ms.42171*

7 FitzRoy Sqre
18 Octr 1880
My dear Layard

Considerg that you found time to write to me from the Ca' Capello
as early after your arrival as August 30th, you must have thought me
(or, at all events, I have thought myself so) very ungrateful for sending
you no acknowledgemt. It is a pleasure to know you installed in a home
which your never forgotten kindness enabled me to know so well – a
home plus 2 stories – & the contents of 264 cases, on which I wish you
joy!¹

I feel often that I have too many worldly goods – & am sometimes
so ungrateful as to forget where or <u>whom</u> little objects come from, but I
am a pauper in comparison with you. I can't wish you a more delightful
home to retire to, when the time comes to pass.

I delayed writing because I wanted to announce to you the
publication of the little sketch on our dear old friend – but Murray still
gives no sign. However, one of the first copies I receive shall find its
way to you.

I have also been busy giving a few raps to my favourite aversions
– the Germans, & I begin to think that hatred is as potent in its powers
of work & inspiration as love, perhaps you will say more. I have ordered
a copy of the Edinr Review to be sent (today) to Rawdon Brown, who
is so kind as to care for what I write, & I daresay he will lend it to you
if you care to be bored with it, or if you do not receive it regularly.

I left my pretty country quarters with regret. My nine weeks in
Albury were very successful & I bade goodbye to two french maids
who had waited on me & to a little dog who had taken to me, hoping
to find the same established at some future time. Neighbours had been
very kind, but I could not get to Milton Court again, nor Mrs Rate
(nice woman) to me. Ladies, with daughters who are out, I know by
experience to be unavailable for any other duty than the young ladies
give them, & that is generally pretty hard. Milton Court, with all its
improvements, seems to be as fascinating in its way as the Ca' Capello.²

Your last account of the sad story of pillage & ingratitude under
your roof grieves me to the heart. Those two were so attentive &
honest to me when here that this terrible finale is a real pain to me. I
still reserve some doubt about Carolina – it is the old story of putting
the blame on the weaker, from the beginng of the world "The woman
tempted me & I did eat"! I always felt that to be an <u>excuse</u>, & Adam

a <u>sneak</u>! But with your very orthodox ideas I fear my sentiments will shock you![3]

I have not been anywhere, nor seen anything, & hardly anybody but my nephew Chas Eastlake, just returned from the Continent. Longmans have employed him to draw up short accounts of three principal Galleries – the Louvre, Munich, & Dresden – illustrated from good engravings, & he has made it the occupation of his holiday.[4] Chas E: is a very happy man in his position & it is a constant pleasure to me to know him in it. He kindly proposes to submit his notes to me before final publication. What a profitable thing the publishers make of art! An article in January (1880) Edinr R: on Hamerton's Life of Turner strikes me as a new & intelligent hand. I must get Reeve to tell me who it is. I have got Hamerton's work itself & I hope to find time to read it.[5]

I have been going a little into Göethe's works – strange extremes of power & puerility! I am sorry he is a sealed book to you. But of all the great men of the world he is the most <u>detestable</u>. Hayward's Life of him is fair, admitting his utter egotism but pronouncing him in his last page "the most cultivated intellect" that the world has perhaps known.[6]

I am now going to bury myself in <u>Madame de Stael</u>, & see how she strikes me – character & works.

Give my kind love to Enid, & if Lady Westminster be with you, or coming to you, pray make my regards palatable to her. I retain no common impression of her.

I suppose you will soon be starting for the Nile.
Ever dear Layard yr's most truly
Eliz Eastlake

1. The Layards' possessions were transported from Constantinople in 264 cases.

2. Milton Court in Surrey was enlarged by William Burges in the 1870s. Mr Rate was Lachlan Mackintosh Rate, a lawyer and director of the Imperial Ottoman Bank.

3. Two of Layard's servants, the gondolier Antonio and his wife Caroline, had stolen household items from the Ca' Capello in their absence. See Enid Layard's journal for 7 June 1880 (BL Add MS 46162).

4. Charles Locke Eastlake published a series of notes on European picture galleries: *Notes on the Principal Pictures in the Brera Gallery at Milan … with Illustrations* (London: Longman & Co., 1882); *Notes on the Principal Pictures in the Louvre Gallery at Paris … with Illustrations* (London: Longman & Co., 1883); *Notes on the Principal Pictures in the Old Pinakothek at Munich … with Illustrations* (London: Longman & Co., 1884); and *Notes on the Principal Pictures in the Royal Gallery (R. Accademia di belle arti) at Venice … with Illustrations* (London: Longman & Co., 1888).

5. *Edinburgh Review*, 151 (1) (January 1880), pp. 40–67.

6. Abraham Hayward, *Goethe, A Biographical Sketch* (1877).

Letter to A. H. Layard   *NLS Ms.42171*

7 FitzRoy Sqre
2 Janry 1881
Dear Layard

I have had the excuse of not knowg precisely where you were – but
now I have heard that you are back in the dear old Ca' Capello, & I
will not delay send.g Enid & you all good wishes in & out of season. I
hear too that you are soon starting for Egypt, & shd like of all things to
be in your company for a Dahabia must be just the place (on a smooth
stream) for a lame lady, & with plenty of books, a delightful climate,
perpetual interests, & dear companions there wd be nothing left to
desire. But I have come to the end of my wanderings in the world, &
am thankful for the comfortable home.

All the world, as you may guess, are talking of Ireland, & Gladstone
is as much abused as you could wish – even I give a man up who could
not forgive atrocities in Bulgaria, & yet encourages them in Ireland.
Up to now he seems to have looked on with "le coeur leger" but I
understand that Mrs Gladstone now reports her Wm's rest at night to be
broken with anxiety. I never remember Society – so far as I hear & I
see & hear – so unanimous in condemnation, the lawyers especially so
& his commissions equally disapproved. It is believed that the Cabinet
intend makg Lord Cowper their scape goat. You must long to be in the
turmoil that is approachg.

It was a pleasant change to turn one's mind to <u>art</u> yesterday, which
was Private View of Old Masters at Royal Academy. Fortunately
it was very fine & I spent the greater part of the <u>light</u> hours there.
It is a magnificent collection, chiefly supported by the Hope & the
Panshanger Galleries, both as you know full of jewels. I think I was
chiefly enthusiastic over <u>Paul Potter</u>, <u>de Hooghe</u>, & <u>Raphael</u> – however
discrepant the names sound. The two Raphaels are a world in
themselves. The first, hardly of the earth earthly – not even the <u>mother</u>,
but a young girl, holding the babe in a reverie of solemn wonder. The
later picture, with every adornment of the ripest art, a fair Lady with a
beautiful child. Of course in the sense of art the last gives me the most
pleasure.

There is a glorious male portrait by Andrea del Sarto – hitherto called the painter's portrait – but an Andrea in the Nat: Gal: disproves that – nor does the head look like that of a painter. Then the well known Fra Bartollommeo Holy Family is a splendid picture, & the grand Vandyck as big as the side of a room of the Count of Nassau with Ctss & family is one of his finest.[1]

I was in the Nat: Gallery the other day, & Chas Eastlake showed me the Gatton Park Leonard Holy Family & angels – the counterpart in most respects of that in Paris. I missed a hand of an angel wh: I always adored in Paris, but there is a head of one of the angels here wh: I hardly think is equalled in the other picture. It is an immense addition. Chas Eastlake is studyg the gallery very carefully, & qualify.g himself for connoisseurship.

The catalogue – to return to the "Old Masters" – is as poor & inaccurate as usual, a good opportunity of disseminatg a little knowledge lost – ridiculous dates & absurd christengs. A portrait of Petrarch's Laura from life by Andrea del Sarto!

You may be glad to hear that my little vol: of "Mrs Grote" has gone into a 2nd edition. But I don't hear of its going further. I have had many pleasant letters about it. I wish it might do that good to modern young ladies which you rightly say is wanting.

I have had a German work send me anonymously upon the Italian masters, translated by a Dr. Wh: Schwarze from the Russian of Ivan Lermollieff.[2] I have not had time yet to read any of it. At this season every body is sendg everybody Christmas cards, & the amount of note writg required to requite the civility is a perfect burden. As soon as I get a little free I want to prosecute my readg & think about Madame de Stael whose "considérations sur la Revolution française" strike me as equal to any of the later works upon it, & as anticipating them. I am fascinated with her writg wh: seems to me a compound of the solidity of Johnson & the brilliancy of Macaulay – & a compound which is better than either. I am deeply interested in Necker's character too – a man who never took a salary for all his work. But his daughter has strong nerves & decision which he failed in.[3]

Now, dear Layard, it is time to relieve you. I shall not expect to hear from you till you reach Phyle – the wonderful inland with the endless columns &c., nor even then if pressed with letter writg. People are askg whether you are going back to Constantinople. Perhaps you do not know yourself. Ottoman Bank shares have risen much lately but I hear of no div.ds this January.

We have queer weather. Yesterday a brilliant sun as long as it was up, & today an Egyptian darkness – with fog, so that pedestrians carried lanterns in the street, & the windows in the church were like slabs of black marble.

I trust this year begins happily to you & Enid to whom I beg love. Every yr's most truly

Eliz Eastlake

The "Manor House" at Aylesbury broken up, & all out door things sold. Chas & the young girl going abroad soon.

I do not cease to think of unhappy Antonio & wife – I trust he is tried by this time & she released.[4]

1. Group portrait of John, Count of Nassau and his family (1634), formerly in the Panshanger collection but now in Firle Place, Lewes in Sussex.

2. This was Giovanni Morelli's pseudonym, a near anagram of his name. See n. 2 to letter, 26 January 1866. 'Lermolieff''s essays, *Ein kritischer Versuch*, were 'translated' from the Russian by Johannes Schwarze, another pseudonym. Elizabeth was unaware of the conceit at this point, although a letter of 14 December 1881 shows that she was later made aware of it. Morelli's pranksterish motive for sending her the work without an acknowledgement of his authorship is mentioned in a letter from Morelli to Layard, 21 November 1880 (BL BM Add MS 38963 fols 276–79).

3. Jacques Necker was Madame de Staël's father.

4. Antonio, the Layards' gondolier; see letter, 18 October 1880.

Letter to John Murray   *NLS Ms.42178*

7 FitzRoy Sqre
24 January 1881
Dear Mr. Murray

Is it possible among the stores contained in your warehouse you may still have original coppers of the etchings to the old Baltic Letters? They would belong to you of right. Mr Seymour Haden[1] – the great etcher – asks me for proofs as he is setting up a rather important exhibition in the spring. I can find no proofs in this house – but he offers to print fresh ones himself if I can lend him the coppers. These I have <u>not</u>.

Happy those who have comfortable <u>homes</u> now! I hope you & yours are holding out against this inclemency. I do not stir out & find the absence of interruption very welcome – but shall willingly compound for less leisure & better weather. Meanwhile my good old housekeeper

knows the <u>anatomy</u> of all the pipes in the house – so much Greek to
me! & watches jealously over them.

With kind love to Mrs. Murray who I hope keeps well I remain yr's
very truly
Eliz Eastlake
An old friend Mr. Willinell is I hear hopelessly ill!

1. Sir Francis Seymour Haden (1818–1910), collector of old master prints and
   founder member of the Royal Society of Painter Etchers in 1880. See
   Catalogue of Engravings and Etchings (London: Fine Art Society, 1882).

Letter to John Murray   *NLS Ms.42178*

7 FitzRoy Square
25 Febry 1881
Dear Mr Murray
I feel that I owe you a little further explanation about my so called
'patronage' of Miss Bennett. I am always glad to assist in art matters,
especially when connected with the employment of my own sex – & as
I refused her my name I, the more willingly, promise my guarantee for
£25. Of course sincerely hoping that her success would never require it!
But perhaps the real reason for my readily listening to a lady & a plan of
whom I knew so little was the hope that it would enable me to throw
some work into the hands of a niece who depends upon her fingers for
all pocket money. At all events I am glad that you know so much of
Miss Bennett & that my small encouragement will do good to somebody.
Believe me yr's very truly
Eliz Eastlake

Letter to Rawdon Brown   *NOTT PWM235*

7 FitzRoy Square
16 March 1881
Dear Mr. Rawdon Brown
I have yr kind letter of 13th January & Luigi Pasini's pamphlet at
my side – both mutely reproaching me for <u>neglect</u>.[1] I make no defence
except that it has been work, not idleness, wh: has kept me silent. From
the beginning of the year I have been rather pressed, endeavouring to
draw up a suitable article on that remarkable woman, Madame de Stael.

A new book on her has appeared by an American, wh: collects all that can be well known of her. It led me to read her chief works & I must say they have inspired me with astonishment – their merit is so great, & just as great at this day as when they were written. I don't know yet whether I am to appear in next month's Quarterly, or in that of July. At all events I have had no rest till I was out of the wood. I am never happier than when I have rather too much to do! So now I trust I have exonerated myself in your eyes. Whether I shall bore you with the article on its appearance is another question!

"I Navigatori al Polo Artico" are personally interesting to me. For as Parry was my first cousin, however more fitted image to be uncle – I was brought up as a child to hear of the "North West Passage". The name of 'Rigby' is also attached to a bay on the map of his discoveries & baptisms. I have met McClintock too – the real solver of the question.[2]

My winter has passed quietly. The excessive cold kept me to the home for a fortnight – & emptied the streets wonderfully. I never had such delightful leisure! Since then the world has been particularly sociable in the way of dinners, of wh: I have had to eat an unusual number. It is after all the best form of Society – for English people – at least in London – to understand good talk, tho' not quite in Madame de Stael's style! It is only fair to judge her as a frenchwoman, as one English one we should have quoted her overpowering.

From Layard I have several kind letters. He is the best & kindest of correspondents. He will be very soon in London, if not here already.

Of yr old friend Mrs. Millais I see very little, & at this time she is at Cannes for her own health. It is whispered that Millais enjoys her absence! Somehow they do not harmonize. I have long thought that poor Effie never mentally recovered from her great trial. Her great present love of pleasure & excitement of manner were not formerly natural to her. As to fame & fortune Millais carries all before him. Time already shows that his pictures improve by it. There is now a small exhibition of his works alone – a series of about 20. I can only say that in his realistic way no past painter stands higher, & no present one so high.[3]

I suppose even Venice has felt the shock of the Czar's murder.[4] It could not fail to be. The son of Nicholas, & descendant of such monsters as Cath: & Paul, could not expect to die in his bed. Still, it has taken me by surprize. The fault of these muscovite rulers is their utter ignorance! They, & all the higher Russians have only 2 objects & occupations. Playing at soldiers & playing at cards. When a man assumes the responsibility of the government of 80 million of people he ought to have time for neither! He did a good act in empancipating the serfs

– tho' he did it badly – but other classes need enfranchisement as well. V. good example, Russian society is a barbarous "ancien Régime" – & no Russian reads history. Poor man! His dread of assassination is over now!

I don't like to hear that you have had even a hint that your interesting office is to cease. It wd be a link the less with Venice – a great public loss – &, feeling as I do about the solace of work, a great daily loss to you.

I hope next time you kindly write you will not confirm this hint. Ever dear Mr. Brown

Your sincere old friend

Eliz Eastlake

The fate of the two servants, who were so kind to me, can but give me pain however deserved.

A long letter from Lady Castleton from Ireland the other day. I have to answer it!!

1. Luigi Pasini, *I Navigatori al polo artico. Comprising an Italian translation of an article in "The Manual of Dates" by George H. Townsend; an account of the voyage of the "Vega"; an article by Edward Cheney on John and Sebastian Cabot; and a letter on John Cabot from the Diary of Marino Sanuto* (Venice, 1880).

2. Sir Francis Leopold McClintock (1809–1907), British arctic explorer who wrote the popular *Voyage of the Fox* (1859). Admiral William Edward Parry (1790–1855), Arctic explorer of the northwest passage. See Ann Parry, *Parry of the Arctic: The Life Story of Admiral Sir Edward Parry, 1790–1855, with portraits, a facsimile and maps* (London: Chatto & Windus, 1963).

3. See *Notes by Mr. A. Lang on a collection of pictures by Mr. J. E. Millais, R.A. exhibited at the Fine Art Society's rooms, 148, New Bond Street* (London: J. S. Virtue & Co., 1881).

4. Tsar Alexander II was assassinated on 1 March 1881.

Letter to A. H. Layard   *NLS Ms.42171*

7 FitzRoy Sqre

12. April 1881

Dear Layard

Is it very presumptuous of me to ask whether you think that Turkey & Greece will come to terms or to blows? My motives are most low & mercenary – Ottoman Bank shares are higher than they have ever been, the question is whether to sell. I don't ask you to resolve that question, but to kindly give me, if <u>possible</u>, some grounds ny which I may resolve it myself. If you desire I will promise not to let your answer go any further.

I was glad to see your Enid today, & much enjoyed a talk with her – partly upon the Russian govt about wh: I know you & I shd agree, & partly about <u>lace</u>.

Yr's always truly

Eliz Eastlake

Letter to Hannah Brightwen   *Private Collection*

7 FitzRoy Square

24 April 1881

I had your last letter before me dearest Han: from days ago in order to indulge myself in answers when other more pressing came in the way, & now I am ashamed, & yet <u>glad</u> to be deeper in your debt. A letter from Chester is the more acceptable as including tidings of dear Ellen. Your <u>vorlezter</u> letter is of Janry 20. Your <u>vorvorletzer</u> of October 18.[1] So you see I <u>have</u> them. Your January one included one from Lucy Boyd & was written with deep snow around you & perplexity how to get at food for sheep & bullocks! The change of season is indeed grateful – tho' not not [sic] yet warm – but when did I ever know a Private View of Royal Academy except in winter clothing! This next will be on Friday the 29th.

But I must go back to your January letter. I have just read Lucy Boyd's again. I fear she did not obtain that Matronship to the Bexhill Convalescent Home, for I have heard somehow that her Ernestine has taken a situation, which was to be the alternative of her <u>not</u> succeeding. If I am alive next January I have no doubt I shall be able & willing to send her the same little sum – thro' <u>you</u> dearest – tho' you have so considerately abstained from committing me. She seems to have well doing children, which is more than money's worth.

You asked me what I thought of "le recit d'une soeur"? I read it several years ago – before my dear Mother died – which was in 1872 – for I remember reading it as I drove from Slough to London after being with her in my little open carriage. My heart was still so sore as to feel the <u>intensity</u> of Alexandrine's grief, tho' I could not echo one sentence 'Je pleure mon Albert gaiment'. That was not a grace given to me! Nor is it yet, tho' there is something better I hope in place. But she had the better too. Although this is a curious book as a picture of

a French family of a high class & high aims. I have heard, however,
that the father M. de Ferronays was a worthless man. Nor did I hear
good of Mrs. Capel.[2]

How kind you are, dearest, to be interested in what I am doing, or
have been doing. I did not begin to apply at all seriously to work till
about the middle of January. I had had friends with me & had been for
the Christmas week to dear Jane etc etc but then I attacked Madame
de Stael – the character, life & writing. Which a new work on her
by a Dr. Stevens, an American, has brough afresh before the public.[3] I
had hardly been reading her before. I can't tell you how I have been
struck by the glorious <u>mind</u> of that wonderful woman. The clearness,
the fairness, the great resources & especially the power of <u>thought</u>.
She seems to me – with all the fame – not to have been sufficiently
esteemed. Her 'Allemagne' & her 'Considerations sur las Revolution
Française' are splendid works. With my <u>detestation</u> of the German
character & manners, I have been enchanted to find how well we
agree about those barbarians – only that she is all gentleness in her
modes of expression. Of course the Germans disliked her – as they
now do our Pss Royal. When did a German ever tolerate a woman
of intelligence!

I believed that I was wanted for the Q.R. of April & was well ready
with a long & tough article in the middle of March. But the good
editor asked me as a favour to stand over till July – as Russia & Ireland
(& now Carlyle) are taking unexpected room. So I am quite content
to 'open the ball' as he tells me I shall do, then: I conclude Hayward's
article on Carlyle is delaying the Q.R. in this unprecedented way. I
generally get mine about a day before the general public, but none
has come yet. Meanwhile I have not yet been able to get the 'Carlyle
Reminiscences' so am much behind most people. But the notice on
them in the Times & elsewhere has sufficiently showed me the wretched
malice of the writer, & the abominable indiscretion of the Editor.[4]
The sneers at most of those who were most kind to him have created
an immense condemnation here. The characters of Mr. & Mrs. Basil
Montague [sic], Lord Jeffrey & wife, & Mr. Wishaw [?], all foremost in
kindness to him from his earliest boorish years, are all <u>vilified</u> by him.
Mrs. Bates (stepdaughter of Basil Montague) has taken up the cudgel for
him & her mother – printing letters of the same date as his scurrilous
entries in his journals, full of praise & adulation & worth a remarkable
little introduction by herself. For she is a very remarkable woman of 80
years of age. The article in the Q.R. is to be most unsparing, with such
paternity & maternity as Heyward & Mrs. Proctor there is no fear of
the offspring being milk & water!

The Edin: R: has let Carlyle off very mildly, but then Henry Reeve's own indiscretions as Editor of the Greville journals have given him a fellow feeling for Froude. Indiscreet publications have been the order of the day. That is why Mrs. Grote destroyed most valuable letters – tho' she did not interdict – or would not have interdicted – the little "Sketch".

Of course we knew Carlyle, & I even had met him before I married. But one could never trust him.[5] He was too unequal in manners & temper – & was often very rude & quarrelsome – so as to be banished from some homes. Mrs. Grote used to say 'You can always tell a man who had not been brought up in the parlour". The chief sign is the giving way to temper. Poor Mrs. Carlyle was a very 'hadden down' woman. With no beauty & a great deal too good for him. I hear that the subscriptions for his statue have all ceased! His real fame will now be estimated when his ingratitude & slander are forgotten.

You will believe that the murder of the Czar shocked me as it did every body. Tho' it could not surprise me. In vain is History acted & written if the poor man himself, or anybody else, could expect the descendant of two such monsters as Catherine & Paul & son of Nicholas to die in his bed. The sins of the fathers are visited to the 3rd an 4th generations. And he had sins enough of his own – as Czar – to answer for. His private morals were between his God & himself, but his sin to his people was that he undertook – as all despots do – what he could not perform. What man in his senses would undertake, one would think, to govern single handed, 97 millions! Such men must pay the penalty of a responsibility they do not choose to share. People who talk of Russia little know what that Imperial family of the higher classes are! A mixture of modern luxury & ancient barbarity – their lives divided between playing at soldiers & playing at cards. I expect nothing better from the present man. They are all educated in frivolous & profligate ignorance. Nihilism as it is called, (but I never found any one in Russia who could tell me what it meant.) is a terrible symptom of a terrible disease. But all the Czar thinks of is the repression of the symptom. It was the same before the French Revolution. What does a peaceable sovereign want with a million & a half of soldiers! – or a respectable sovereign with a Secret Police! Or a wise sovereign with an army of underpaid officials – all grasping at bribes – hiring informers from few kopecks![6] A reformation on these three points would alone work wonders.

You ask about the three R.A. portraits. Millais' is now exhibiting at 148 New Bond Street with other works of his – a most interesting room full. It is a superb portrait. Watts' I did not care for – tho' finely painted

– but he had not done himself justice. Leighton's is still to come & I
conclude will be in the forthcoming R. Academy. He can paint a good
portrait. Tho' now very weak & poor in other subjects. And he too is a
striking handsome man. So the Uffizi people will think well of English
painters' looks as well as works. You see the pictures have not yet found
their way there.[7]

Now, dearest, to the closer subject – my poor darling Jane! I was
a week with her about 3 weeks ago. I can only say that she suffers
more & more! She is immensely increased in size, tho' rather stringent
measures have been taken to carry off the fluid by the natural means.
At all times, while sitting up by day, it flows immensely thro' one
poor ankle. Then ulceration takes place & she is obliged to go to bed.
She is in bed just now. As the Dr. rather wished her to be seen by
Dr. Wharton Hood again I have fixed for him to go over next
Wednesday, when I will meet him there. It is only with the hope of
his suggesting some alleviation to excessive pain – I know he cannot
avert the end!

Justina has been making us anxious with internal inflammation – but
Laura's Saturday's card gives a better account. Still I look anxiously
upon her state. She is over burdened with cares & penalties that no
one can prevent. Each fresh mistake in life entails fresh distress & truly
no one can prevent her making them. Jane & I try not to think of her,
for we are hopeless. Jane has been indefatigable in kindness & advice
for – gd daughters, but nothing helps. The elder gd daughter is now
expected from Russia next month, as penniless as she went for Russo-
German relatives won't pay! And she is no nearer doing anything here.[8]

I am owing a letter to Katherine Palgrave at Siam.[9] Like you I
mistrust a foreign governess for English children – especially a German.
And those boys require a very specially good English governess. And
this makes me ask you of dear Ellen to remember that good Miss
Caux is in need of a situation. She had been in Ventnor & is now in
Bournemouth. Kept free in both by a benevolent woman. But she wants
to work now & is most capable. I can recommend her in every way.
Modern languages & Latin included – except as a walker, of which she
can do but little. But she helps poor children to overcome faults & bad
habits in a wonderful way – as is a thorough lady.

How glad I am that you & dear Ellen are together! This letter is
for her also in thought, tho' not in form. Now dearest this letter is a
tremendous dose for you but your dear precious love will swallow it.
Ever yours attached cousin
Eliz Eastlake
Not a word about Beaconsfield!

1. I.e. her last letter but one, and the one before that.

2. *Le récit d'une soeur*, a semi-fictionalised account of the life of the Ferronays by Madame Craven, translated into English in 1868.

3. Abel Stevens, *Madame de Staël: Study of her Life and Times*, 2 vols. (1881). Elizabeth's review appeared in the *Quarterly Review*, vol. 152 (July 1881), pp. 1–49.

4. James Anthony Froude edited Carlyle's letters, but his editorial approach was considered to be rather indiscreet at the time. Thomas Carlyle, *Reminiscences, edited by J. A Froude*, 2 vols. (London: Longmans & Co., 1881).

5. She met Thomas Carlyle (1795–1881) in 1844 (see J&C1, pp. 116–17). Their initially cordial relationship deteriorated so that later Carlyle referred to her as 'that termagant of a woman'. See G. H. Fleming, *John Everett Millais: A Biography* (London: Constable & Co., 1998), p. 192.

6. Kopecks, a Russian monetary unit.

7. See letter to Hannah Brightwen, 7 April 1880, n. 1.

8. Maria Justina de Rosen, now living at Sidmouth; Laura de Rosen (later Murchison), her daughter. Her other daughter, Leonie Jervis, had a daughter, Alice Jervis, listed as an artist/painter/sculptor in the 1891 Census.

9. Katherine was married to Elizabeth's cousin William Gifford Palgrave (1826–88).

Letter to A. H. Layard   *NLS Ms.42171*

7 FitzRoy Sqre
11 Septr 1881
My dear Layard

Ever since receiving your kind letter of the 23rd from the dear old Ca' I have been longing to acknowledge & answer it – but have somehow been too busy or too idle, havg been visiting a little about, & now this letter will arrive just as your thoughts are engrossed with the King & Queen &c even more than with geography. However, that is of little consequence. I quite foresee the many picturesque scenes that are before you & hope that our 'Special Correspondent' will do them justice. I rejoice in all that makes Italians & English better known to each other, tho' a King & his court are not the best side of a nation. But don't you be calling me anti monarchical for this! I only hate Despots, especially in a German skin – more even than in a Russian skin.

My doings have not been very excitg. I went first (after being a
month with my sister at Windsor) to my friend Miss Elliott's wedding.
You must remember her more than once with me at Milton Ct. Well,
she had made up her mind at last, & accepted a Cambridge Don
– Principal of the new Ridley College – a clever, good man, whom I
approve. & both bride & bridegroom are so popular that all Cambridge
shared the excitement. Such a shower of presents fell upon her that
there were hardly tables enough in the house to hold them. I counted
above 150!¹

Then I went to yr friends the Thompson Hankey's at Shipbourne
Grange. Kind people! She is much stronger – & as for him, with
auburn hair & cheeks like roses, & powers of walking & unfailing
spirits he seems to enjoy immortal youth – the only condition on
which 80 years – for such I am told is his age – can be acceptable.
They are most excellent people & the house most pleasant. Among
other guests there were two daughters of Sir Ed. Thornton – pretty
charming girls, with a certain piquante American frankness, learning
Russian with all their might. Then I went on to Ph: Hardwick's
country home about 4 miles off. His little wife & four fine noisy
children make the house very gay. He is rather venerable to have
commenced the office of a Paterfamilias – but he seems to enjoy it.
We had Jenny Lind there. I was prepared to be very much snubbed,
but she was in so gracious a mood that I quite enjoyed her company,
& contradicted her two or three times without fear. Her knowledge of
the world is not slight – her own caprices seem to have given her the
key to other peoples'. And she had some curious tales to tell. She aught
to write her life, & so I told her, & as she talked exclusively of herself
I don't see why she shd scruple. So gracious was she that more than
once she sat down to the piano voluntarily – preluded a little (very
finely) on the keys, & then burst forth into song. Had I gone on my
knees to ask her she would not have done it. The voice is as good as
ever, for a room – & she has the same perfect justness of time. Indeed
she interested me & if I live this winter I think we shall become better
acquainted.²

You remember my dining with you in Saville [sic] Row before you
went to Norway. Why on earth did you attack me about my fake
judgements on my sex generally! It has dwelt in my mind ever since,
& so now I will give you my simple answer. I judge my sister women
in a very matter of fact way – as to whether, namely, they are good
daughters, wives, or mothers, & there are none of them hardly who do
not fill one of the characters. I have no other test of character. If you
fancied me censorious about fast ladies I beg to say that they are not in

my line, & I still less in theirs – so we do not come across one another.
You had a fascinating woman next you – in the evening – at the Ball.
She was not in my line, however you might be in her's.

Yesterday I climbed up to your Aunt's bedroom in Montague Place.
She was seated by a comfortable fire which I rather envied her. She
knew me as kindly & affectionately as ever – & said I looked 'so well',
while I could hardly look at her without emotion, so greatly is the dear
lady changed. But she was cheerful & happy & said much in praise of
her kind maid who stood by. This last told me that Col: Layard & his
wife often came, also the de Gex's.

It is most good of Enid & you to offer me your home again – more
than good eno' would it be for me now! My four months of spring 1877
under your roof were the happiest I had had for long, or have had since,
or shall have again! I had my dear sister, & two young things (one since
married) & we had all the comforts of home & family life & all the
excitements of novelty without. The memory of it is only dashed by one
thing! (But I shall never leave England again)

Poor old Rawdon B: I hope is recoverg & will be able to use his hand
again. Pray, dear Enid [sic], give him my love when you next go. I am
sorry he bored you with the Q.R. but that is the price one must pay.

Tomorrow I think I must manage to go to the Nat: Gal: I hear
that S. del Piombo has turned out splendid. Perhaps you have seen the
correspondce about M.Angelo's Pietà. Robinson's vulgarity & pretensions
never were more conspicuous.

Now dear Layard wishing you well thro' all your troubles & with
kindest love to Enid I am ever your's truly

Eliz Eastlake
Kind regards to the Balls

1. Mrs Handley Moule, wife of the Principal of Ridley Hall at Cambridge and
later Bishop of Durham.

2. See letter, 1 October 1847, note 5.

Letter to A. H. Layard   NLS Ms.42171

7 FitzRoy Sqre
14 Decr 1881
My dear Layard

What must you think of me as a correspondent to have left yr two
long & kind letters of the 18th Octr & 28th Novr unanswered! You are

certainly the best correspondent in the world – & I did not think myself the worst, but I have been very remiss of late. I have had much anxiety, some sorrow & very much to do. & I have neglected those who I knew would not unkindly take offence.

The death of my nephew – Mr. Wm Eastlake of Plymouth – has been both a loss & grief to me. He was dear Sir Chas' eldest surviving nephew – very attached to his uncle's memory, very fond of art – chiefly modern, & truly affte & dutiful to me. I of course thought that a man ten years younger than myself wd not be taken & I not left, & had made my arrangemts accordingly – but God has pleased otherwise. A sudden failure of the heart carried him off. He leaves nine fine grown up creatures – the sons in the Colonies, the daughters married & marry. g – some of the girls are very interest.g to me. And so there is another gap in the few still remaing to me. Chas Eastlake of the N. Gal: is a much younger brother – also a very excellent & dear fellow. He is feeling this death deeply.[1]

My sister, Miss Rigby, is a very great sufferer, & sometimes I take a panic of anxiety & rush over to Windsor to her. I am only lately returned from a stay of some weeks with her, having taken advantage of a little easier period to leave her. But I shall go for the Christmas week, before which I shall hope to have shaken you & Enid by the hand. My occupation has been the preparing of an article for Q.R. on the late works by Taine & others on the interminable subject of the French Rev: It is not yet 'lu et apprové' by good Dr. Smith. But I fancy he will pass it. At the same time the task has been rather above my powers, & I have felt anxious about it. I am not so strong as I was, I cannot expect to be, but I hope my head – such as it is – does not show signs of decay. A definite object of occupation & a definite subject to read about & think over, is a great resource & comfort to me – now that my powers of locomotion are so small & that a lonely life inclines me to great pensiveness! When I see you I shall venture to ask you to enlighten as to how to prevent any use being made of my sundry writgs – or any other such use as I may permit. I don't believe such trumpery will be wanted further, but I should like to guard against any foolish use of them.

I can but rejoice that many reasons have conspired to bring you to England, you are arrivg just in time for the worst weather we have yet had! Yesterday was thick fog & this eveng I fancy I shall have some trouble in gettg to Swinton's home in Warwick Square, where I dine.[2] Just now there are many of those quiet dinners wh: are most pleasant. The other day I met your beloved friend Gladstone – who has so little to do that he invites himself to dinner in some places. This was at Ld Coleridge's. Gladstone was lookg ghastly, but in usual force. He certainly

is the best abused man of the day. I never hear a creature give him a
good word, nor see any periodical do it either & yet! ... Hayward is his
only defender.

I am ashamed to say that I am only at last going through M:
Lermollieff & doing him justice. It is truly capital in stuff, & charming
in style – more German in some respects than the Germans – that
young life of his in Munich sunk deep into his mind & memory. How
well I remember his comg to see us at Bellaggio, when Mündler was
with us – & we all talked German because as I remarked "one Italian
was with us", but really because he cd not speak English, nor I Italian.
I quite envy you his company. No amount of Burtons can make one
Morelli! But this you will keep to yourself, for a make a point of never
writing how little of a beau idéal either of a man or a Director Mr B. is!
(to my mind!)

It is true that there is a society for doing Mr Browning posthumous
honor in his life time & nobody is more delighted with the institution
that good Browning himself. I was invited to join – but I pleaded
too great stupidity, & was excused. Dryden, Milton, & Pope are I
understand quite commonplace on comparison – that I am inclined
to believe! But I like Browning himself & his son is getting on as a
painter.

I trust you have some cast of Enid's bust to show me, & then I shall
hear who Costalazzo is, wh: is quite a secondary point. What you also
have been doing, tho' not in the way of art, will I trust be open to
yr friends in some form. I wish they would send you with unlimited
command to Ireland. I think you wd manage to put down the upper
knaves, & lower brutes, & rally the honest men about you.

Now dear Layard I hope soon to welcome you both. You say soon
after the 15th.[3]

Your's always truly
Eliz Eastlake

1. William Eastlake (1820–81), solicitor, Admiralty Law Agent, and Deputy
   Judge-Advocate of the Fleet, died 12 October 1881 at his home in Plymouth.
   He was also an amateur watercolour artist. See obituary in *Law Times*, 5
   November 1881.

2. James Rannie Swinton had built a house at 33 Warwick Square, Pimlico in
   1859.

3. See Enid Layard's *Journals*, Vol. 7 (BL Add MS 46159), Wednesday 18 January
   1882: 'dined at EE's met Mr & Mrs de Gex, Mr & Mrs Wm Fitch, Dr. and
   Mrs. Flower, Mr Norman, Mr Beaufort (Lord Strangford's brother) and a
   Mr S Cavendish Boyle and Mr and Mrs Simpson frere senior'.

Letter to Rawdon Brown   *NOTT PWM237*

7 FitzRoy Sqre
4. March 1882
My dear Mr. Brown

I recd a registered letter last eveng from yr friend or secretary
M. Pasini of the Arctic discoveries, expressing yr anxiety about the
collection of cuttings with which you favoured me more than a month
ago. You are perhaps rather too mistrustful of the safety of all entrusted
to the post. At the same time there was another reason of an inexorable
kind. Your letter & packet found me laid by with illness (from which I
am now slowly recoverg) & quite unable to give attention to anything.
Your packet shall be returned to you in a day or two – & had I died
– as I calmly contemplated I <u>might</u> – it would have found its way to
you all the same.

It is most kind of you to have written to me. I see by you
handwriting the effort it cost. Still, I am thankful that you have been
able to resume the pen at all.

We live here in a din of politics – Ireland – the Jews – Bradlaugh[1]
– & over, & through, & round every subject the incarnation of all
political evil – Gladstone!

By the by I am assured that Bradlaugh's outer man is so ugly &
forbidding that no one in their senses, assuming to be a physiognomist,
wd trust him.

I saw the Layards a few days ago – they have most kindly been to see
me in my warm invalid room. They are much in request – dining out
every day.

Our weather is now sharpening & our deluded shrubs in the Square
which have put forth their green feelers will be checked from going
futher at present.

I have looked in vain for further accounts of Lord Houghton – there
have been none in the Times these last days. What a glorification of old
Severn – the vainest of men – this committal to Keats' side! Everybody
flattered everybody.[2]

I trust you are resumg yr activity though not your daily visits to the
Lido! & have never lost your health.
Believe me ever yr faithful old friend
Eliz Eastlake

1. Charles Bradlaugh (1833–91), atheist politician elected to Parliament in 1880
   who refused to be sworn in as an MP by an oath on the Bible.

2. In *The Times* in January and February 1882 there were regular notices about
   the reinterment of Joseph Severn's remains in a grave adjoining Keats' in the
   Protestant Cemetery in Rome. Lord Houghton was to have presided at the
   ceremony but became ill and his place was taken by J. A. Trollope.

Letter to Rawdon Brown   *NOTT PWM239*

7 FitzRoy Sqre
9. March 1882
My dear Mr. Brown
    I write again a few words to assure you that the interestg vol: which
you kindly sent me returns to you today by book post as securely fenced
from injury (I hope) as it was when it reached me. I have read the
cuttings from the Athenaeum with great interest – for themselves – &
for the talks – sometimes under <u>moonlight</u> – which they reveal. I am
sure my dear Sir Chas did far more for you by letter than I did.
    Our Parliament goes in wrangling, & the Irish brutes go on
murdering & maiming, & there has been no unanimity except in the
loyal fuss about the attack on our good Queen – who appears to have
thought less of it than anyone else.[1] I have no patience with German
papers which compare the attack upon Her with those on two certain
Emperors, who deserve but ill of their subjects. From all reports only a
spark is needed to fire as atrocious a persecution of the Jews in Germany
as now in Russia. How little they know their own interests in those
countries. The Jewish community is the most benevolent, as the most
peaceable and loyal, as well as wealthy class in our country.
    Your suffering hand did not spoil your handwriting, dear Mr. Brown.
I hope the act of writing is costing you less & less pain. Ever yr sincere
old friend
Eliz Eastlake

1. Roderick McLean fired a pistol at the Queen at Windsor (the seventh attempt
   on her life), missing her. He was arrested and found 'not guilty, but insane',
   a verdict to which the Queen responded by encouraging the implementation
   of a new verdict 'guilty, but insane' the following year.

Letter to A. H. Layard   *NLS Ms.42171*

7 FitzRoy Sqre
7 May 1882
Dear Layard
My mind is so full of horror at this awful Dublin atrocity that I
must brim over to an old friend like you – who can go along with me
in indignation and beyond me in power & knowledge.[1] There is not a
right thinking man in England who ought not to make it his duty to
protest against the governmt which has brought our country to such
as pass. An <u>immediate</u> change of measures may arrest the evil, but
nothing can redeem our character. Engld is disgraced & humiliated, &
has allowed herself to be so. She has looked on with apathy when the
innocent mother of young childn was murdered. We can only hope
that there is more distinguished, but not more innocent victims may
elicit more manly feeling. What can be done? Cannot any leading man
call a meeting & petition the Queen to dismiss her counsellors! I do
not venture to say that <u>you</u> shd do so, though you were meant to be
the leader of men. But you will hear the feeling of the country gentry
around you, & most thankful shd I be to hear that they kindled into
some patriotic action against the real authors of this foul crime. What
is the good of our freedom when our perverted use of it only turns the
laugh of despots against us!
    What a Nemesis the brother of one of the members of this wretched
Cabinet appointed doubtless as a job, shd be sacrificed the first day of his
landing on Irish soil! But the more distinguished the victim the better. I
wish they could have chosen a <u>guiltier</u> one! You see I am chafing under
the trammels of my sex, & shd like for once to possess <u>your</u> prerogative
of redressing injuries.
    Thank you for the information about Sir Chas Layard. He was very
kind to do me the honour to call, but I shd like to know why.
    I own that Morelli is very troublesome, tho' I shall forgive him for
keeping you longer in town.
My kindest love to Enid. I hope she is better. Tell her she may read all
this letter!
Ever yr's truly
Eliz Eastlake
You see I have written in my horror & heat

1. The Phoenix Park murders of 6 May 1882.

Letter to A. H. Layard   *NLS Ms.42171*

7 FitzRoy Sqre
15 Octr 1882
Dear Layard

I recd your letter of Septr 21 while stayg in Yarmouth (Norfolk) where I have taken a home with a friend. I was truly glad to hear from you & think you were very kind for givg me yr time. I have since then seen the good Chas Eastlakes who can't say eno' of their pleasant dinner with you. He told me a few days ago that Burton had not started & that he appeared to fear that the floods would begin over again on purpose to trouble him. We will hope therefore that Mr. Burton's absence will arrest a recurrance of that calamity. I grieve much over the damage done at Verona no part of which one can afford to lose.[1] The seasons have been strange. From the Baltic I have heard of an unprecedented summer in warmth, steadiness & produce.

My stay in Yarmouth was very agreeable. I joined a friend who had daughter & grandchildn with her, & all three generations suited me well. I had also Jessie Lewin with me, whom I consider a kind of legacy from dear Mrs. Grote, & who is with me still, but goes, alas! tomorrow. Yarmouth is one of the most picturesque seaside places in the world. One sees old Crome & Cotman at every step. It is a place in full activity – the sea too is alive with shipping & has a magnificent roll of wave one is never tired of watching. Yarmouth has been full of Palgraves – my mother's family – & the name appears to be held in high esteem for no end of coal merchants & herring salters are "Palgrave Smith" or "Palgrave Brown". Artists shd go there but I heard of none. Then I returned by Cambridge & spent a few days with my old, young pretty friend, Miss Elliott, now wife of the Principal of the new Ridley College. This put me among tutors & masters & showed me a little of college life. I saw a fine picture by young Richmond of Darwin, which hangs in the new museum.

I was not sorry to get to my comfortable home. For to own the truth, I had been getting so much lamer as to be a nuisance to myself & to my friends. I have been to the first doctors & one looks me in the face & says, "it is all your nerves" & the other looks me in the face & says "it is all your muscles" & one tells me not to walk a step, & the other, to walk as much as possible. So now I have been to a quack, whose cures I knew of. I think he is going to do me good. But I have only tried him for one week. If I am able to welcome you next time you come, with something like my old step, I will tell you what his recipe consists in. meanwhile I sleep better, & feel altogether better. If size be a sign of skill I am in good hands for my Dr is about the size of the Clairmont [?].

I did a little work in Yarmouth with Lermollieff's book. I have made it the peg to hang something about Raphael upon, & as Morelli teems with new & original ideas I hope to make it interestg. Meanwhile the character of Raphael's art comes more & more clear before me. I find I had given a slight definition of it in last edition of Kugler's Handbook & shall venture – as it was my own – to prig some of it. Your account of my much admired Crown Prince & Pss is most interestg. I rejoice that they were seen by you & Enid in their domestic colours. She is a most intelligent well read woman, & of course it is eno' for me that he is good lookg!

Now I want to ask you a most humdrum service. Young Chas Tindal has been here, giving me an account of themselves. Nico & wife very flourishing with 3 fine boys, & an estate which they are gradually selling at £1,000 an acre. When they have parted with the last bit they intend to come & inhabit the home at Aylesbury & try to get l& in the neighbourhood. Poor Gifford is well in health, but no better in mind, the young lady is well. Something in their father's will entails changes, but these seem happily to be to everyone's gain. But Charles – a nice, long nosed young man – wants to come to Venice for a few weeks, & wd be glad to know of a boarding home or lodging where he cd have 2 bedrooms & sitting room & decent cookg. Does yr Major Domo, or groom of the chambers, or Ld High Chamberlain know of any such respectable home, & wd you kindly let it be sent me on a post card, with terms. Chas Tindal wants to leave England on the 23rd so there is not much time. He was modest about applying to you himself. I am sure you & Enid would like him for his own sake as well as his dear parents.

Now a hasty goodbye & kindest love to Enid
Ever yr's truly
Eliz Eastlake
Not a word about Egypt!

    1. There was a severe flood in Verona in 1882, when the river rose by eight
       metres, damaging many buildings.

Letter to John Murray   *NLS Ms.42178*

7 FitzRoy Square
20 Novr 1882
Dear Mr. Murray

I have to thank you for the 4th packet of Crowe & Cavalcaselle's
Raphael arrived today.[1] One sheet of the proof has been inadvertently
omitted from pages 144 to 161. I wish I could give you a hopeful
impression of this work, but their system of telling a tale is not improved
– nor is their language. I should think the public will puzzle over "the
root of Mary" by which they mean "the Genealogy of the Virgin".
I should be glad to hear that Mrs. Murray is better.
Yrs faithfully
Eliz Eastlake

1. J. A. Crowe and G. B. Cavalcaselle, *Raphael: His Life and Works, with Particular
   Reference to Recently Discovered Records, and an Exhaustive Study of Extant
   Drawings and Pictures*, 2 vols. (London: John Murray, 1882–85).

Letter to A. H. Layard   *NLS Ms.42171*

Windsor 29th Decr 1882

You never forget an old friend, dear Layard, & I pride myself on
the same & was intending to find time before the year shd expire to
send you & dear Enid best wishes for the coming year. This letter
will probably reach you on the 1st. I cannot expect many more New
Years – but am thankful for those given, & for the old friends still left,
especially for those who knew dear Sir Chas. I wish your Enid had. He
would have dearly liked her.

You are certainly makg the dear old Casa the most hospitable house
in Venice. I only wonder you find time for any business of yr own. I
am here in Windsor & have been for the last fortnight with my sister
– who alas! cannot come to me but she has been comparatively at ease
since I have been with her. Nor do I see any cause for alarm as to her
life tho' from time to time I take panics about her. As for my own
health the Quack has for the present done me more harm than good.
I was decidedly better but he wd not be persuaded to let well alone, &
carried his measures too far, & I am lamer than ever. However, as no
regular M.D. will give me the slightest hope of amendment the Quack
still promises real benefit. I shall try him once more.

Meanwhile I have been very busy, with Morelli's book & with the
subject of Raphael generally, & the result appears in January's Edinr
Review. Dear old Dr. Smith would not hear of the article when I
proposed it to him, but Reeve readily concurred, & tells me I have
a chef d'oeuvre. I wish I thought he knew much about the matter,
but you may have found out also that good Reeve is a very lenient
Editor. It was difficult to say anything new about Raphael – except
what Morelli supplies. Certainly in looking up photographs & prints,
of wh: there are plenty still in the old house, my admiration for the
artist has waxed higher & higher. The <u>man</u> was doubtless very nice, but
he does not come up to a high standard, & I hate the courtier – like
characters of the time. I hope you may like parts of the article, but
some of it, I may assure you beforehand, is mere twaddle! I think you
get the Edin R: regularly, or I wd be glad to send you the number. As
to the "recently discovered records" about Raphael which Cr: & Cav:
advertise, there is not a sign of them in this first vol: but a series of
<u>conjectures</u> wh: lead to nothg. I have not shown them up <u>much</u>. It wd
have exasperated Mr. Murray, & he hates me eno' without my doing
anything to deserve it.

I am much interested in your new application of Murano glass, &
shall be glad to hear when we meet how it is disposed of, & whence the
demand. Old Palace windows in Venice don't often get broken! I am
glad you have succeeded on stirring up some of the old families – the
commercial faculty should be latent in them, but they have vegetated so
long that you must be a kind of phenomenon amongst them. I am sure
there is much still to be written about old Venice, if anyone cd get at
records & take the trouble. I wish that I had the doing of it!

I was glad to hear from Chas Eastlake how he approved the careful
restorations that had been going on in St. Marks. I grieve to hear
that the Italian govt have paid attention to the ignorant outcry. As for
Ruskin's "St. Mark's Rest" I have the first number, but have never
heard that it has been continued. Who attends to the cross, crazy old
man now?

I am not surprized at what you say of Chas Tindal. He is steady &
well conditioned, but has eno' to live upon, which is a condition fatal
to some young men. How that family whom we have known in the
hey day of the good parents' prosperity has changed now! Poor Gifford
shows no sign of recovery, but pores over his classics by a kind of
mental habit.

Your home must be a temple of the muses, with Enid's clever busts
& bas reliefs – & with your Wednesday concerts.[1] After all the arts are
the last worldly solace we can have for the disappointments of this life!

Happy those who love the best music. I hope you admit Mendelsohn [sic] in your repertory. He bewitches me almost the most.

Our weather is extraordinary – wet for ever & just now over warm. The thermometer at 56 early in the morng.

And now let me refer unwillingly to a sad subject – namely that of your two unwilling servants (or at all events one of them) Antonio & Carolina. Is he out of prison? And can he get his living? Few culprits interest me more than discharged prisoners, from the difficulty they must find to obtain employment. Pray don't think that I would wish you to do anything. But he has written to me lately – 20 November – not begging, tho' I can see that he wd gladly have the little present I used to send him for Christmas – namely a sovereign. He has given me his present address, it looks like "Fondamento da Severo" No. 5016 S. Zaccharia". I wd send him again a sovereign if you think it would not be misapplied – & yet I do not like to give you the trouble of answerg this. But a few lines on a postcard would do. It gives me pain to speak of the subject to you.

I return home for the New Year's Day & dine with the Chas Eastlake's & I shall tell them how kindly you mention them. I rejoice to hear that you may be in Engld soon.

Now with kindest love to Enid, & very anxious to see her medallion of you, I am always yr's truly
Eliz Eastlake

   1. A circular bronze plaque of Layard by Enid Layard is now in the Government Art Collection.

Letter to A. H. Layard   *NLS Ms.42171*

14 January 1883
7 FitzRoy Sqre
My dear Layard

It was very good of you to answer ever so soon as you did & I in return have taken my time. As I may look forward to seeing you & Enid so soon in England, it is hardly worth while my troubling you with a cheque or postal order for £7. I will therefore take the liberty of asking you to advance me £7, & deposit it with Mr. Malcolm, for Carolina. I think you will be safe to find it again in your pocket the first time we meet. This will be a great relief to my mind, & I shall be very grateful to you.[1]

Meanwhile I have ordered the forthcoming number of the Edinr R: to be sent to yr address, & hope you will find more than one article that may interest you. Last Sunday good old Dr. Wm Smith came in & told me he thought his forthcomg Q. R: would be found interestg. He is lookg thin but well. He & I swore eternal friendship on dear Mrs. Grote's death, & I always see him with great pleasure – next to real & original friends are those which friends bequeath us. And this brings me to that allusion to "J.M" which I ought not to have made to you. I fear alas! that your proof of his "not hating" me wd not stand a moment before mine. But you know I have never uttered a word to you on this sad subject – & beg yr pardon even for the few words in my last letter.[2]

I have kind Jessie Lewin with me now, & hope to keep her for the month. I have not been feeling strong enough to indulge in any hospitality tho' I trust I may be well eno' by the time you & Enid come. I have perforce to trust to a Quack, for regular Dr – & I have tried the best in London – won't look at my case, or rather only look at it as hopeless. Don't be alarmed at my owning that I have gone back to my Quack – he did me much good before & I will take care he shall not go too far again. And really – after only a week of his remedies which are very simple – I am sleeping better, & movg a little easier. Indeed I could hardly move at all. I have seen but little of the world, for I have refused all dinner invitations, & so know no gossip or scandal – except about Coutts Lindsay, which is unfortunately no scandal. Nor have I seen any exhibitions as yet. The other day Jessie Lewin & another friend staying here mounted up dear old Gibson's works in the R: Academy, & were enchanted with them, also with the Diploma pictures wh: are in the same apartment, you must see those if you have not done so already.

I have Villari's Macchiavelli on my table, have read the introduction, & I hope now that I have finished the long job of arranging my year's accounts! to set to work & finish the book. Mrs Ball was here the other day in great spirits & owng a strong <u>penchant</u> for Morelli. I have not seen him yet.

With kindest love to Enid & thanks in advance for the kind office I have suggested at your hands I am always yr's truly
Eliz Eastlake

1. Money given to Layard's dismissed servants Antonio and Carolina.

2. Layard's response rejects the idea that Murray 'hates' Elizabeth but does nothing to counter her perception of their chilled relationship (NLS Ms.42340).

Letter to A. H. Layard   *NLS Ms.42171*

Hotel Venat et Bristol
Aix les Bains Savoy
6 June 1883

I seem to be so near dear Enid & yourself here, that it is doubly
unnatural not to try & communicate with you, dear Layard. But the
life here is idleness without leisure, & fussiness without work. Quite
a new experience to me! It is exactly a month now that I have been
living thus, & while there has been much enjoyment in it I cannot
report any improvement! I have had my share of 'Douches' &
'Vapeurs' & all the usual course of treatmt & not without effect of
some kind, for I feel considerably lamer & feebler than when I came.
This, however, I am assured is the usual result. You must be worse
before you are better & this part of the program I have
faithfully performed.

But it has been a great interest to me to witness for the first time
the burst of Spring in a Southern climate, & most wonderful it has
been. This hotel lies in a beautiful garden, with plenty of seats for the
dowagers, & a lawn tennis for the young – surrounded with no end
of flowerg shrubs & trees, plenty of glorious things for wh: I have no
name, & such as I know ten times more beautiful than with us.

The hot springs here are marvelous. The chief one sends forth
more than a million gallons of sulphurous water daily, of which my
unfortunate person receives a full share, for a <u>douche</u> means the
application, through different fire engines of a thousand concentrated
showers of rain, till you can neither see nor hear, your attendants on
the occasion being a cross between water nymphs & opera dancers.
I cannot say that it is unpleasant, but it is very exhausting, & a long
siesta is the next act. Then there comes much eating & drinking, &
driving & lounging, & so my usual share of letter writg has been much
curtailed. Nor can I say much of the reading. I brought <u>Gil Blas</u> with
me to peruse, but have not yet got through him. While a French novel
lent me by my very sedate & respectable Dr., disgusted me so much at
the end of 30 pages that I decline proceedg further. A book by Emil
Montegut – "L'Angleterre et ses Colonies Australes" – has given me
more information on this subject than I ever possessed, tho' chiefly
taken from Trollope's work.[1]

Our companions in this hotel are some of them agreeable, & some
<u>good looking</u>. The only swells are Lord Monk [sic] & a deaf & dumb
daughter, & Lady Ely who makes herself generally amiable. She seems

to be a partisan of your's, for I heard her express great indignation at yr usage by the present government.[2]

I cannot say that I have been much interested by the Moscow doings. I cannot say whether I most pity or despise the old man who lets himself be thus deified, & assumes to govern 90 million of his fellow creatures single handed. I cannot conceive of course of history in such as country – with no one fitted to govern.

We remain here probably till the 14th, when, if the weather promises to be steady, we are advised to seek a little bracing at Monnetier – on the Salève about 1½ hour's drive from Geneva. I shall be very glad for a little coolness – at 23000 ft above the sea, for the heat has been great.

I hope you have enjoyed our Crown Princess' good company & have had the pleasure of increasing her enjoymt of my beloved Venice. She must be a very good woman as well as an exemplary daughter in law not to be impatient for that wretched old Emperor's death!

As my sentiments are so unbecoming about <u>Emperors</u> I had better bid you good bye, & with kindest love to Enid beg you to believe me yr's always truly
Eliz Eastlake

1. *Gil Blas* by Alain-René LeSage was an eighteenth-century French picaresque adventure translated into English by Tobias Smollett. Emile Montegut, *L'Angleterre et ses colonies Australes. Australie – Nouvelle Zélande – Afrique Australe* (Paris: Paul Brodard for Hachette et Cie., 1880). Anthony Trollope, *Australia and New Zealand*, 2 vols. (London: Chapman & Hall, 1873).

2. Sir Charles Stanley Monck, fourth Viscount of Monck (1819–94) and Canada's first Governor General. From 1874 to 1892 he was Lord Lieutenant of County Dublin, Ireland. Lady Ely was Lady of the Bedchamber to Queen Victoria between 1851 and 1890.

Letter to Sir John Savile   *NASDRO SSSR 226/24/100a*

Upper Norwood
10 Aug: 1883
My dear Sir John

Your letter has followed me here where I have been seeking a little bracing air – of which indeed we have rather too much, as it is positively cold.

I am delighted to hear that you have presented your most interesting Velasquez to the Nat: Gal: – I hope Mr. Burton is duly grateful but that does not necessarily follow as he is rather peculiar in his views of pictures & of their value. At all events I trust, indeed I am sure, that the trustees will do your generous gift justice. Unfortunately Layard & Sir Wm. Gregory – the men of highest taste – are both absent. I shall gladly remind them both by letter how highly Sir Chas estimated that picture. I hope you remember that there is a fair etching of it in Mrs. Jameson's work "the Life of our Lord in Arts".[1]

I enjoy good health, but am become very lame from a species of rheumatism. I sought some benefit from the waters of Aix les Bains this spring – but found none! I enjoyed my stay however in a beautiful region.

I see Lady Buchanan often in London. She feel's Sir Andrew's death very deeply, & looks paler than ever. She & her widowed sister Lady Seafield live chiefly together, but all this I daresay you know.

My pretty niece Mdme Manderstjerna has long queened it in Warsaw, where her husband is General of Division. If it depended on him there atrocities against the Jews wd be soon prevented.[2]

I visited my relatives in the Baltic Provinces a few years ago. I returned thro' Petersburg where I greatly enjoyed the collection at the Hermitage – seeing for the first time the Conestabile little Raphael, & renewing acquaintance with the Alba Madonna. What glorious Rembrandts they have! But my time for seeing pictures is over – for I cannot stand about.

Believe me dear Sir John
Yrs always truly
Eliz Eastlake

1. *Christ after the Flagellation* (NG1148). Presented by Sir John Savile Lumley (Baron Savile), 1883.

2. General Manderstjerna was aide-de-camp to the Russian Emperor.

Letter to A. H. Layard   *NLS Ms.42171*

Eagle House. Eltham
19 Aug: 1883
My dear Layard

You must not judge my deep interest in yr letter from Potzdam by my delay in acknowledg.g it – for I see that I am past the middle of the month, which you mentioned as the period of yr return to Venice. Indeed it falls to few to have the opportunity of writg or receivg such

an interestg account of yr visit to our Crown Pss as you were kind eno'
to write me. There are few people who interest me so much. Certainly
no royalty! I feel very grateful to her for rememberg me, & to you for
doubtless helping her to do so. I remember hearg from Sir Jas Clarke of
the total absence of the commonest comforts which had awaited her in
Berlin, & of the necessity of sendg her over an English housemaid! I fear
she has had many trials in living among my particularly hated Germans,
tho' I believe the Crown Prince is an exception to his race. At all events
I could not condemn such a <u>fine lookg</u> man! I am sure yr & Enid's visit
must have been a great pleasure to her.

It is indeed long since I wrote to you from Aix, & much has
happened which makes me feel the time all the longer. For my mourng
paper[1] is a tribute to the truest friend I ever had – namely to our old
& faithful housekeeper – Mrs. Anderson, who lived first <u>with</u> dear Sir
Chas & then with us together 38 years. She accompanied me to Aix &
was feeling great benefit, when only 10 days after our return she broke
a blood vessel & died in a few days. Her great attachment to Sir Chas &
me helped to make me feel F. Square a home, even after I stood alone.
But she has imbued all the little household with her devotion to me, &
I am not allowed to miss her more than can be helped, wh: is, however,
very keenly.[2]

I am sorry to own that the waters of Aix have done me no good
whatever & I am come to the conviction that my rheumatism is of a
kind that nothing can help. I was medically advised on my return to go
to some bracing place. I can't take a long journey again so I hesistated
between <u>Hampstead Heath</u> & <u>Upper Norwood</u>. I found a house at the
last. It did not suit me, however, tho' I had my open carriage & took
charming drives. So after a fortnight there I have come on here, where
my friend Miss Lewin has secured me a nice, large, old fashioned house
with glorious lawn & garden, which I am enjoying much. Here I shall
be until 4th Septr & then return for good to F. Sqre. The time is fast
coming I feel when I shall not be able to move at all, & then I have
made up my mind to live entirely in the two drawing rooms – among
the pictures.

And so you discovered the dear old Mantegna at Dresden! It has been
there since the autumn of 1876! Just before I went to Italy – old Gruner
coaxed me out of it & Boxall had told me that it wd not be eligible
for the Nat: Gal, I felt tempted to place it in a grand Gal: like that of
Dresden. They gave me £2.000 for it – but for all that it was a severe
pang to let it go.[3]

You will have been hearing of Lumley's generous gift of his Velasquez
to the N. Gal. He wrote to me to beg me to confirm to Mr. Burton the

assurance of Sir Chas' great admiration for it which I can readily do. I am not sure that you know it, or that the picture remained in Madrid when you were there. I hear various reports of the small Mantegna Mr Burton has bought lately for the Gal: Tho' all accounts agree as to its enormous price. At all events Mr. Burton's reign has inaugurated a great rise in prices.

I hear from a relation of the late Mdme Mohl that she has bequeathed an unfinished Greuze – a young girl, bust length, with a lamb – to the N.G. I remember it as a pretty thing. This relation had not heard whether it was accepted.[4]

I don't wonder at your delight at the Vienna Gallery. Several of the pictures are imprinted on my memory – especially a Titian with the Child giving cherries to some one. The Albert Dürers also – upstairs – I can never forget.

I am afraid that the decline of the cholera will allow for your voyage to Bombay. I say 'afraid' because it will place half the world between you & your friends.

I believe Longman has just begun to print my "Five Great Painters". He makes two small vols of them which I think a pity. Nobody cares to read more than one vol: of anything. I think I shall venture to send a copy to our Crown Pss.

I suspect that the short remainder of my life will be devoted to reading only – I am rather sick of writg – except letters to a few! My habits have become necessarily rather recumbent, in wh: position I am writing now, which must explain a great deterioration in my handwriting!

I hope you are safe & well in delightful Ca' Capello now – with fresh store of thought. With kindest love to Enid I am ever yr's truly Eliz Eastlake

1. Writing stationery edged with a black border, the width of which was determined by the relationship between the letter writer and the deceased person they mourned, and also by the time that had elapsed since the bereavement.

2. Elizabeth Anderson was the Eastlakes' cook and housekeeper. Elizabeth placed a notice of her death in *The Times*.

3. Andrea Mantegna, *Holy Family with Saints Elizabeth and John*, Gemäldegalerie Dresden.

4. Greuze's *A Girl with a Lamb* (NG1154) was presented to the National Gallery by Madame Mohl in 1884.

Letter to A. H. Layard   *NLS Ms.42171*

Eagle House. Eltham
1. Septr 1883

I have both yr kind letters, dear Layard, & thank you much for them.
I have written to Mr. Chenery[1] to ask whether he will allow me to
contribute the notice of dear old Brown – wh:, with the assistance &
the cutting you enclose – I think I could do. If he have [sic] provided
elsewhere – or however that may be – I have offered to send him the
cutting. He is rather a <u>grumpy</u> man, but I hope he will answer me
without loss of time. I return home on Tuesday – 4th – & shd set to
work immediately.

And so the old friend is gone! like so many others. My only wonder
is that I am here myself! He well deserves a tribute to his memory. He
was a man of purpose, one of those Englishmen who adopt a foreign
home & devote themselves to a particular vein of history. I have known
him for more than 30 years & he was particularly kind to me. And I
hope I was never impatient with his hobbies, but walking with him in
old days about Venice, I sometimes did not know whether we were in
the 19th or the 16th century! The money he has left to that detestable
Geo: Bentinck is like coals to Newcastle![2]

I am thankful you will still turn yr steps to England perhaps in time
to receive compensation for the Past. The few words about you in the
Times article yesterday were a welcome sight. Mr Gladstone wd do
better to encourage such researches than in listening to fine ladies in
favor of a monstrous injustice. In great haste but always with love to
Enid yr's most truly
Eliz Eastlake
So many thanks for sympathy about housekeeper's death

1. Thomas Chenery (1826–84), editor of *The Times*.

2. Her dislike of Bentinck stemmed from the aspersions he had cast on the sale
   of the 'Director Pictures' to the National Gallery; see letter, 25 July 1869.

Letter to A. H. Layard   NLS Ms.42171

7 F. Sqre
8. Septr 1883
My dear Layard

I have no doubt that you see the Times, & therefore have found out that I have done my best to follow out yr suggestion in a letter about our old friend Brown.[1] You will have seen also that yr cutting has materially helped me. I only hope you, & other few remaining friends, will approve what I have done. There is rather a grave misprint – an omission of a word – but the meaning is obvious. I knew dear old Brown in his time, when his oddities were softened, & when he was always so kind & devoted to me – tho' pretending to quarrel with dear Sir Chas – that I had a real regard for him, & altho' rather tiresome when I was in yr Ca' Capello there was nothing to lessen my regard.

And thus old friends depart! One by one, or rather two by two, for, like as with good Tindal I have lost no end of well known couples.

I have left Eltham as you see – none the better in the main, or rather considerably worse. <u>Nothing</u> cures rheumatism, when once its implacable progress begins. I am not much disposed to try other Drs, & certainly not other countries. I can nowhere be so comfortable & well cared for as at home, even tho' I have lost my dear old friend & housekeeper. But other servants – whom she mainly taught – are all goodness to me.

I am correcting my "Five Great Painters" & see no reason to trouble you with proof sheets. I have no longer the energy to make any great alterations – so they must go as they are. I have taken Richter's Leonardo, & corrected my article by it, as far as I saw fit.

I hope to spend the short remainder of my days in the enjoymt of readg interestg books. I have more than once tried to induce Dr Smith to take an article on the Italian Emancipation. I read many details of the youthful heroism & lives that were expended in its early attempts. When I was in Italy Lord Broughton also wrote on it. But Dr Smith shakes his head. I have not seen him or anybody, but enjoy London to myself.

With kindest love to Enid, who I hope will also approve I am always yr's truly
Eliz Eastlake

1. 'The Late Mr. Rawdon Brown', signed 'E.E.', appeared in *The Times*, 8 September 1883, p. 6, col. C. A few days later in a letter to the editor George Cavendish Bentinck disputed her claim that Brown had demurred from a salary for his post in Venice (13 September 1883, p. 6, col B). Bentinck's letter ends with a swipe at Elizabeth for calling the Ca' Pesaro (visible across the

Grand Canal from Brown's home) by the 'tourist's' term 'Bevalacqua Palace', stating that the expression would have provoked Rawdon Brown to utter 'an expletive calculated to make the speaker's ears tingle sharply'.

Letter to A. H. Layard   *NLS Ms.42171*

7 FitzRoy Sqre
13 Octr 1883
Dear Layard

I have been wishing to thank Enid & you for yr kindness to my old friend Miss Clerk in lettg her see the Ca' Capello & yrselves. She is back in London & lunched with me yesterday. She had been also partly in yr track in the Fruili hills – at S. Martino & its surroundgs & seeing the woods which seemed all to belong to 'Signor Malcolm'. Now people are throng.g back before London is ready for them – for the chief streets are still much up, & even Hyde Park has been difficult to pass thro'. Today I have had a visit from Lady Loyd Lindsay who – with Lord Overstone – has not left London at all. He is now really failing at 87 years of age, havg had rather a remarkable life of comparative simplicity for a millionaire, & that by inheritance. He looked on the commonsense side of everything – not so much objecting to giving to charity, as to others receivg it.

But now I must condole with you on the death of Ld Somers.[1] My first acquaintance with his great drawings was thro' you. I have ever placed him foremost as an amateur, & superior to many professionals. His great eminence as an artist ought to have been mentioned in the Obituary. But those notices are very dull & colourless affairs. I don't know whether his union with the beautiful Virginia Pattle, whom you were all so much in love with, gave him much happiness. Their daughters certainly did not. I hear however of Lady Tavistock's ability in art. But Ld Somers himself was to me a very interestg man. He had lived long eno' however for a man with a weak heart. I think everybody shd die or be killed off at 70 – by that time we have had enough of this life, & people are getting tired of us. A kind friend of mine died the other day – Mr Moore Esmeade – brother of the Miss Carrick Moore's – & to my surprize I find he was 77.

My nephew Chas Eastlake & his wife are home from a tour chiefly confined to Dresden. He dwells on a fact which has struck me before that the race of modern German connoisseurs throw doubts on every picture of importance. He had met with some at Dresden who left nothing in

peace, & then pretended to make great discoveries of things which are
horrors. The truth is they learn their business irrespective of any exercise
of taste, wh: is not a quality of German growth. Nor are any of them
artists, without which no high place in connoisseurship is attained.
I wonder nice Morelli can stomach them. I hear of an exhibition of
photographs from Raphael's drawings – & Mr. Fagan wrote to beg me
to come & inspect them, which alas! I cannot do. I suppose he wrote
the notice of them in the Times, which curiously ignored all Morelli's
theory.[2] I conclude he can't read German. What has become of Madame
Richter's translation I know not. I have not heard a word about it.

I am readg a rather remarkable book. Nasmyth's life – rather egotistical
as all autobiographies must be – nor do I see what good Mr Smiles has
done in editing it – except to give it an ill-written preface.[3] But it is very
interestg & ought to fire the present youthful generation to follow his
industrious example. I know the man, & like him much personally.

I have been lookg into Emerson's Essays, strong, masculine,
exaggerated writing – truly American. I see he classes you with a
rather heterogeneous list of discoverers – "Denon, Beckford, Belzoni,
Wilkinson, Layard, Kane, Lepsius & Livingston".[4] I think I cd do better
for you!

As far as later morng hours, weakened strength & letter writing allow
me, I am enjoying more readg than I have long had time for. I have an
inexhaustible store before me. My powers of locomotion diminish every
day, & I seriously think I shall soon retire into the two drawing rooms
& never leave them. I might be much worse off. I stick to Dr. Gerrod
& will try no more quacks, tho' I have three kind friends who each
more urgently recommend a separate quack of their own. I answer with
three objections – "they take up your time, they spoil your things, &
they steal your money". I decidedly prefer my rheumatism to them.

I hear from Mr. Ed Cheney quite an opposite opinion of dear old
Brown's will to what you have given me. viz: that he has left his Italian
servant far too much.

The "Five Great Painters" will soon be out. When I have the pleasure
of seeing you in London I shall consult you – being the only thorough
Courtier I know – how to address our Pss Royal in requestg her to
accept a copy. She seems free from a failing wh: is rather disgraceful to
Royal ladies here – for Princess Christian & Princess Mary are 'criblees
dedettes"[5] – but then they have both German husbands without a penny.

Now dear Layard I have gone on unmercifully & will only beg my
best love to Enid
Ever yr's most truly
Eliz Eastlake

1. Charles Somers-Cocks (1819–83), Lord Somers, Liberal politician, married to the fabled beauty Virginia Pattle (1827–1900).

2. Exhibition of 152 photographs of Raphael's drawings at the British Museum. See *The Times*, 19 September 1883, p.7, col. A.

3. *James Nasmyth … An Autobiograpy, edited by S. Smiles … with illustrations* (London: John Murray, 1883). Samuel Smiles (1812–1904) was a prolific writer on self-improvement topics and a biographer.

4. Ralph Waldo Emerson's essay on wealth, which refers to Layard, appeared in *The Conduct of Life*, first published in 1860 and revised in 1876.

5. *Criblées de dettes*, French, 'up to their ears in debt'.

Letter to A. H. Layard   *NLS Ms.42171*

7 FitzRoy Sqre
10 Decr 1883
My dear Layard

It is more than time to acknowledge your kind long letter of Novr 2nd. But increasg feebleness & lameness are driving me into very lazy habits. I now live entirely – night & day – in the two drawing rooms & only crawl into the front room by noon. But my health is good, & that being the case I need say nothing more of self – except to assure you & Enid that I have the best medical advice & every possible comfort of luxury, but there is no cure for rheumatism.

It interests me much to hear of you trip to Florence, Siena &c. Siena must be much improved to boast of a good hotel. I remember a very rough concern when we were there for a few days, but I delighted in the old city, & especially with varied line of high horizon which surrounds it. Our mutual friends – the Hardwicks – have been or are at Florence. She writes me that many of the pictures look out of condition – "flaking off". You will have been sure to observe this – if it be true. But who my "conceited & self-satisfied friend H.C.R who collects rubbish from the stone maker's yard & puffs it in the Times &c &c" may be I have not a conception! I can't remember any one with those initials – except old <u>Henry Crabbe Robinson</u>, who has been dead ages.

I am amused at yr visit to my queer cousin Mrs Ross who never made herself very pleasant to her relations – nor was particularly fond of her husband, or of her only child – a very nice boy. But I know she was very fond of you! & I had heard that even the Stufa episode had not eclipsed you![1]

You will probably by this time have found out that I complied
with a pressg request from my cousin Inglis Palgrave to give him
an introduction to you. You have kindly encouraged me to use this
freedom, nevertheless, I always do it with a certain scruple – tho' in
this instance he & his wife are very nice & intelligent people. His elder
brother Gifford Palgrave has been sitting with me this morng – much
out of health & the very ghost of himself in appearance.[2] He is waiting
for an appointment, & meanwhile gaining time to recover. He talked
about Egypt, & seemed to consider England pledged at any price to
annex & hold it – & that the giving up of the Soudan [sic] wd rather
diminish the slave trade than not.

I have been seeing both Lady (Coutts) Lindsay, & her unworthy
husband lately – of course here, for I go nowhere.[3] She interested me & I
hope she will come again. He came to ask my intervention with Sir Chas
Bunbury to lend his fine Sir Joshua for the Grosvenor Gal: Exhibition.
It is to consist of Sir Joshua only – & he reckons on getting about 200,
the Queen is lendg hers. Sir Coutts Lindsay seemed fresh struck with the
glory of Sir Joshua. I have also had some visits from Lady Loyd Lindsay
– the late Lord Overstone's daughter, a very charming, unspoilt woman.[4]
I was fond of Ld O. he was exceedingly kind to me. I hear that Sir
J. Saville Lumley has been in London, but he did not find time to visit
me. His Velasquez is excitg some talk but upon the whole people do not
seem to relish it. I admire it exceedgly – Sir Chas did so.

I did send my "Five Great Painters" to our Princess Royal, havg got
the precise form of addressg her from Sir Theo: Martin. I hope old
Count Münster forwarded my note as well, but Seckendorf, who visits
in the Pss' name, does not allude to that. You know my opinion of
Germans, so I conclude it was only stupidity.

The translation of Morelli's book is very faulty in detail – tho'
the sense is tolerably given. But the translator has taken some stupid
expressions out of the Crowe vocabulary.

Christmas is fast approaching. I hope you will have some friends to
enjoy it with you. I probably shall have one old lady friend with me.
I feel much the not being able to get to my sister at Windsor, who
cannot come to me, but this is really my only trial in my confinement
to these two rooms. Meanwhile two days have elapsed – it is now Decr
12 – since I began this, when my handwritg I fear shows that I was
feeling unusually tired & good for nothing. I have my kind friend Miss
Lewin with me & only wish I cd keep her altogether, but her parents
can't spare her. I fear ultimately I shall have to get a hired companion
but I defer that evil day as long as I can. Meanwhile I have the kindest
of servants – but an old coachman has given me some alarm lest he too

shd give me the slip as our dear old housekeeper did! However he is on
his box again & is useful to my friends.

Some of my friends are in great trouble. Sir Jos: Hooker is in anxiety
for his daughter who has very threatening symptoms of the evil that
carried off her mother. Then Ld Coleridge has returned from America
to find his only daughter set upon a miserable marriage which he cannot
prevent, & wh: is unworthy of her in every way.

Now dear Layard – with kindest love to Enid believe me yr's every truly
Eliz Eastlake
You'll please tell me who H.R.C. is!

1. Janet Ross (1842–1927), Elizabeth's cousin, was the daughter of Lucy Duff
   Gordon and granddaughter of Sarah Austin. She lived at Settignano outside
   Florence, with her husband Henry James Ross. The 'Stufa episode' most
   probably refers to the gossip about the Ross's domestic arrangement with
   the Marchese Stufa, with whom they shared a villa at Castagno. See Sarah
   Benjamin, *A Castle in Tuscany: The Remarkable Life of Janet Ross* (London:
   Murdoch Books, 2006).

2. Sir Robert Harry Inglis Palgrave (1827–1919), Elizabeth's cousin, banker in
   the business of Gurney & Co, Great Yarmouth, and financial editor of The
   Economist; William Gifford Palgrave (1826–88), Elizabeth's cousin, Jesuit
   convert, diplomat and writer on Arab culture.

3. Blanche Coutts Lindsay was separated from her husband.

4. Lady Loyd-Lindsay (1837–1920) was the only child of Lord Overstone. She
   married Brigadier-General Robert Loyd-Lindsay, later Baron Wantage of
   Lockinge, in 1858.

Letter to A. H. Layard   *NLS Ms.42171*

7 F. Sqre
25 March 1884
Dear Layard

Many thanks for yr kind note. I think I am a trifle easier with new
remedy. "Canapis Indica" [sic] nearly related to 'Bang' I believe![1] And I
wd see you tomorrow (Wednesday) or the next day at any time between
3 & 5 if either be strictly convenient to you.
Ever yr's truly
Eliz E.

1. *Cannabis indica* was Indian hemp, introduced to British medicine in the mid-
   nineteenth century for the treatment of rheumatism.

Letter to A. H. Layard   *NLS Ms.42171*

7 FitzRoy Sqre
24 May 1884
My dear Layard

It is early to trouble you with a letter so soon after your return, & especially upon business, tho' that is my immediate motive. You are doubtless hearing about the conversion of 3 prct government stocks into a 2 ? or 2 ¾ one. You & Mr Murray are trustees for the govt stocks left by Sir Chas, consistg of Consols, New Threes, & Reduced Threes. I foresee much bother & some loss by this transfer – & I shd be truly glad if you & Mr Murray wd consent to selling these stocks at once, & havg realized their present high price, that you shd invest again in any good Colonial or Debenture stock at low interest of about the same price. I am sure my nephew Chas Eastlake wd give his vote for this exchange, wh: wd doubtless be for the benefits of the <u>heirs</u>, as well for mine. His elder brother – my nephew Wm Eastlake – who died two years ago was very anxious this shd be done while govt stocks were high. But there was no such change then in prospect as there is now.

Will you kindly talk this over with Mr. Murray. I think the aggregate sum amounts to £13.300. My life will be but short now, & at my death the sum will be divided between three of Sir Chas' family.

I hope you had a successful journey, & that the Murrays have joined you. I have been rather losg ground lately, but am getting better. I have had to wean myself from opiates – which has cost me some bad nights but the worst is over. And now that I can get natural sleep I hope strength will increase.

I enclose you a list of securities considered perfectly secure wh: my broker has sent me.

With kindest love to Enid & kind messages to yr guests I am ever yr's truly
Eliz Eastake

Letter to A. H. Layard   *NLS Ms.42171*

7 FitzRoy Sqre
30 May 1884
Dear Layard

I received yr kind letter yesterday afternoon in which you tell me that you & Mr. Murray see no objection to the proposal I laid before you, but that Mr. Murray has written to consult his solicitor. Meanwhile, I have written to my nephew Chas Eastlake – whose prompt answer I enclose.[1] With regard to railway debentures they are at such a high premium that I felt reluctant to propose them. Still, if they keep up the same price till my death there wd be no loss to those who come after me – indeed there may be a further gain to them. I quite agree with you in the policy of placing the money in two or three different stocks.

My broker, Messrs Ellis & Co. 2 Royal Exchange Buildings who are also brokers to Robarts & Lubbock, my bankers, wd transact the business, & I need not say that I shd take the expense of it.[2]

I shd suggest that the business shd not be delayed unnecessarily less Govt stocks with all this tampering shd lose their slight premium.

I have been hearg a little of 'Burton versus Mdme Mohl', & have seen a rather vulgar letter from him to Mrs Wynne Frick. If you have not been able to manage hitherto, there can be no chance now that he evidently thinks his Knighthood one of the most important events in Modern History. I only wish it wd inspire him with better taste in selections.

I am havg a fire again in these drawing room. I hope you have forgotten such a thing, & that you & your guests are enjoyg warmth. Meanwhile I am better & have succeeded in weaning myself from all opiates, wh: required a resolution which almost deserves the Victoria Cross! My kindest love to Enid, & every kind message to yr guests
Ever yr's very truly
Eliz Eastlake

1. Enclosed letter from Charles Locke Eastlake, 41 Leinster Square, Bayswater, dated 30 May 1884: 'My dear Aunt ... I can see no possible objection to the course which you suggest, especially if the trustees, on whom I suppose the responsibility rests, approve of it. I would have thought that the best English railway debentures would be safer than Colonial Stock but I offer this opinion in all deference to your judgement, and no doubt you will take the advice of your trustees on this point. It is fortunate that Murray happens to be at Venice, as he will be able to talk the matter over with Sir H. Layard'.

2. Robarts, Lubbock & Co., established in 1772, had premises in Lombard Street. The company was acquired by Coutts & Co. in 1914.

Letter to John Murray   *NLS Ms.42178*

7 FitzRoy Square
11 July 1884
Dear Mr Murray

My broker, Mr. Ellis & Co. writes me that he has now sent you the certificate for the Great Eastern Debenture. Standing in your & Layards' names. I now send you the certificate, for the Queensland & Switzerland stock – the Queensland in two papers. I hope now to obtain powers of attorney for my Bankers & receive the dividend in your stead. & then this rather troublesome business, which has caused you & Layard some trouble, will be completed & for which I am exceedingly obliged to you both.

I hear from Layard that you have requested him to reedit Kugler's Handbook of Italian Art. You can't have a better man. I will carefully look over the last edition & see whether there is anything I can suggest.

But Layard's friend Morelli is the best authority of all. The knowledge of the Ferrarese School had made some advance since my day.

Pray give my tender love to Mrs. Murray.
I walked part way downstairs & back again yesterday!
Ever yr's truly
Eliz Eastlake

Letter to A. H. Layard   *NLS Ms.42171*

7 FitzRoy Sqre
17 July 1884
My dear Layard

I have thought much about yr letter of the 7th telling me of the proposed new Edition of Kugler, & have been anxious to write earlier but tho' I am much better my strength is hardly equal to the demands upon it. I need not say that I am truly glad that this job is committed to you. I am attached to the work for reasons you will readily understand – feeling it to be imbued with dear Sir Chas' mind. I have been readg

the preface again, wh: is a very remarkable document. You may find
it necessary both to add & curtail, but I feel sure you will not banish
those thoughtful passages wh: only the experience of a thoughtful
painter dictated, as to the excellence of each art consistg in the qualities
peculiar to itself.

I think it wd not be desirable to add to the size of the work, wh:
John Murray appears to desire. Still, there must be much new matter
– & in this & every respect I feel how valuable will be the help of
Morelli. He dwells somewhere upon the importance of clearg up the
Ferrarese school, the two or more Grandi's &c. There was a little
whippersnapper of a German – a Herr Harck[1] – who called here 2 or 3
years ago with a circular introduction from Count Münster, who seemed
to have given particular attention to the Ferrarese painters. Doubtless
Morelli knows about him. Also I remember being dissatisfied with
the index, in wh: I detected many omissions – especially as to cross
reference, in cases of two names for the same painters. Murray would
not let it be improved at that time, & I therefore begged the note to be
inserted wh: states that the index was not compiled by me. I need not
say that I can give no new information – all my knowledge being now
rather antiquated.

So much for Kugler. Now another subject. Charles Eastlake tells me
that £100 annually is voted to increase the Art Library of the Nat:
Gallery. I am anxious to part with a splendid set of proofs of Toschi's
Correggio. They were selected especially by Toschi for Sir Chas, & have
Toschi writg in pencil upon them. I heard from Colnaghi's a few years
ago that their market value was 60 gui. I wd willingly know them in
the Eastlake Library for half that. They are all in their original numbers
& in perfect preservation. Then there are other books in my possession
– such as the two illustrated works (Arringhi & Bosio) on the catacombs
– which the S. Kensington people were anxious to purchase of me a few
years ago. I wd only part with them to the N.G., & at the same reduced
prices. There is no occasion for you to be troubled to propose them – I
only mention this subject so that you may know in case I shd make a
direct offer to the Trustees. The catacomb works are rare.[2]

I feel intensely with you as regards the Blenheim pictures – tho'
inclined to think that a little delay will bring down somewhat the
Duke's demands. Of course Gladstone sees no comparison in importance
between treasures of art, wh: wd add to our glory & culture, & the
millions squandered by his atrocious acts – both of commission &
omission. I see no further steps for him & his followers but to come to
blows with their adversaries. Language can supply them with no further
choice of mendacious & abusive language.

You are proposg a charming Alpine expedition & ultimate rest on Lake of Como with charming Morelli.

For my part I am ordered somewhere for change of air, & shall endeavour to get to the Pavillor hotel at Folkestone at the end of this month. But all letters shd be addressed to me here.

I fear you are to have a further claim on yr time & patience in signing a power of attorney for my bankers to receive the divds on the lately purchased stock, but this will be the last trouble.

My kindest love to Enid

Ever yr's truly

Eliz Eastlake

1. Fritz Harck, *Gli Affreschi del Palazzo di Schifanoia in Ferrara ... Traduzione di A. Venturi* (Ferrara, 1886).

2. Paolo Toschi, *Tutti gli affresco del Correggio in Parma e Quattro del Parmigianino disegnati ed intagliati in rame da P. Toschi e dalla sua scuola* [*With descriptions by P. Giordani*] (Parma, 1846); Paolo Arringhi, *Roma Subterranea*; Antonio Bosio, *Roma Sotterranea, opera postuma di Antonio Bosio Romano, antiquario ecclesiastico singolare de' suoi tempi. Compita, disposta, et accresciuta dal M. R. P. Giovanni Severani da S. Severino* (Rome, 1632).

Letter to John Murray   *NLS Ms.42178*

7 FitzRoy Square

26 July 1884

Dear Mr Murray

I am much obliged by your giving safe storage to my securities. One further trouble still awaits you – the signing power of attorney to empower my bankers to receive the dividends on these stocks. And that I trust will be your last bother.

I am realising the difficulty of finding sea side accomodation. What with the English keeping at home, & the French coming to us, every place is crammed. I have tried at Folkstone & at Ramsgate in vain – so now I turn to Eastbourne & my kind friend Mr. Williams goes over on Monday to inspect both hotels & apartements.

Can you give my love to Mrs. Murray without worrying her! I think often of her.

Yrs very truly

Eliz E:

Letter to A. H. Layard   *NLS Ms.42171*

3. Grand Parade Eastbourne
27 Aug: 1884
My dear Layard

Your kind letter of the 28th from Longarone reached me here in
due time. I was ordered to some sea side by my Dr. Garrod, under
the delusion that it was to finish my <u>cure</u>. And as I always do as I am
bidden, I took the trouble to come, accompanied by one of my kind
Lewin friends. Rooms had been taken for me in the gayest part of
Eastbourne – directly opposite the Pier & of course opposite the sea
– & for the first day or two I thought I shd go out of my mind, for
the space between the Pier & us is the resort of all the <u>din</u> of a bathing
place in the height of the season – bands, & organs, & Punches & every
form of itinerant minstrel, & childn roarg, & dogs barking, made up
an incessant concert which my nerves could hardly bear. However the
nerves have grown accustomed to the row, & I am rather shocked to
own that I now rather enjoy it. And I have discovered one vagabond
who has a tenor voice which sings the sixpences out of my pocket, &
with whom I communicate through my pretty maid, who delivers a
message to him to come nearer! All of which will shock the purity of
yr morals, so I had better change the subject. Meanwhile tho' I think I
am a little stronger I cannot say that the fine air has had any effect on
my powers of locomotion. I go out in a Bath chair, & look at my fellow
creatures, who are a most snobbish lookg set, tho' here & there I have
found an old acquaintance, & then I come in & write letters & read
novels. One by Ouida, the first I ever looked at, begun this eveng. Miss
Broughton I have tried, & Miss Braddon too – the one too vulgar, the
other (a most clever writer) too sensational for me. Ouida I hear I shall
find too improper! which will be worse still![1] I return to F. Sqre the
middle of Septr & hope then to set up some kind of carriage wh:I can
get into & out of, & not lead quite so confined a life, not that I ever
tire of my two drawing rooms.

I am glad you found time for one day in the Munich Gallery. It is
fortunate that Dr. Something – the Director – is not too ignorant to be
corrected. We have seen more than one Director of that Gallery – & all
apparently equally ignorant.

I rejoice to hear that the quiet life at Longarone gave you time to go
thro' the old Kugler. No one will be more interested than I in seeing
what you do. I am not afraid that you shd praise the so-called <u>Giusto da
Guanto</u> at Urbino. I know that Morelli quite endorsed Sir Chas' verdict

on it. I am sure also you will retain his <u>forms</u> in some respect. Simply S. Giovanni, or S.S: Giovani e Paolo &c. Others write Sta and Sto or Ste. Now that I feel stronger I shall hope to look my Kugler thro' more carefully on my return.

You know long ere this that the purchase of the Raphael has been concluded. Chas Eastlake writes me this in confidence from Ullswater where he is spendg his holiday. This is delightful news. Doubtless other heirlooms will now come forth. May I but be able to get to the Nat: Gal: again!

Many thanks for your willingness to back my offer of the Toschi engravings to the Gallery. I am in no hurry & shall wait till other Trustees return to London.

I was a little <u>enraged</u> the other day to hear from Mrs Vivian (mother of the Vivian who sold a Mantegna to the gallery) that it is given out that our old friend Rawdon Brown left his money to G. Cav: Bentinck because G.C.B: had kept him going with money, & paid his debts!! I cannot for one instant believe such a tale. Surely Brown was the last man to put himself in such a position – & such a story ought to be stringently contradicted.

The business of the transfer of the Funds is completed – thanks to you & Mr. Murray. The last named wrote me that he had placed the certificates in his strong box. I am deeply obliged to both of you. Many of my friends are making the same exchange.

Now with kind love to Enid believe me ever yrs truly
Eliz Eastlake

    1. Popular Victorian novelists: Ouida (Mary Louise de la Ramée) (1839–1908); Rhoda Broughton; and Mary Braddon (1835–1915).

Letter to John Murray   *NLS Ms.42178*

7 FitzRoy Square
9 Octr 1884
Dear Mr Murray

I am sorry not to have had the pleasure of seeing you yesterday, & you would hardly have expected to find me out in such weather. But I had accompanied my friend Miss Lewin to the station for Eltham, where her aged father is very ill.

I had been intending daily to write to your Marion for tidings of Mrs. Murray. I hope she can still give me something cheering.

I owe increase of strength to Eastbourne, which I am very thankful
for. Though my locomotive powers are but little increased. But at my
time of life I find they are what I can spare best.

I have been thinking much lately of our old friend Gruner, & have
been in active correspondence with her. She is anxious that his fine
engraving from the Blenheim Raphael shall now be more known. And
by her earnest wish I am now concocting a letter to the Times – the
only disagreeable part of which is that by his request & that of the
'Acting Editor' I am compelled to sign it with my full name. So perhaps
you will see it in a few days.[1]
Believe me yr's very truly
Eliz Eastlake
The impression from Watt's drawing of me is very popular with my
friends, but I do not pretend to have so many friends as you have kindly
given me proofs.[2]

1. Blenheim or Ansidei *Madonna* (NG1171), bought by the National Gallery in
   1885 for a record price of £70,000. Elizabeth's letter to *The Times* appeared
   on 14 October 1884, p. 2, col. E.

2. See letter, 1 August 1853.

Letter to A. H. Layard   *NLS Ms.42171*

7 FitzRoy Sqre
12 Octr 1884

Here is the 12th October & I have not yet acknowledged yr kind &
interestg letter of Septr 5th, dear Layard. I have no excuse to offer – one
never has, & therefore I had better leave that alone. The letter found
me, as you rightly directed, still at Eastbourne which I really regretted
to leave – my favourite tenor, singer & all! And the last ten days seemed
to do me more good than all the preceedg time. & this impression was
confirmed on my return to the familiar places & ways here. I can't
say much for general activity, but I do manage to creep downstairs for
lunch, & what is more to the purpose, up again, & I have tried a little
Victoria, lower than my own, & get a drive about every other day. My
good Jessie Lewin has looked very sharply after me, & has not allowed
me to shirk the drivg out, which I am rather inclined to do. I am sorry
to say that the sudden illness of her Father hurried her home a week
ago, so that for the first time for fully a year I was left alone – her
father is better. Now I have a young great niece with me, but I am no

longer afraid of encounterg solitude. I should be quite satisfied with the
attendance of my maid, who is very clever at nursing & very pretty, &
can be most amicable, but her temper is infirm, & I fear I cannot put
up with it. She has been 6 years with me – or rather I with her – & in
that respect is the youngest of my staff, who all reckon from 14 to 22
years, & make me afraid least they shd die before me! Wh: however is
not likely.

I have been compiling a letter for the Times about the Ansidei
Madonna, & Gruner. My old friend Mrs Gruner – his widow – asked
me so very earnestly to call attention in that way to his fine engravg
of the picture, that I cd not refuse, though I greatly dislike to make a
public appearance in any form. I wanted to give only initials & address
– but both Mrs. G: & "the acting Editor of the Times" (I only know
him by that name) made such a point for my full name that I cd not
decline to give it. So I expect the disagreeable sight of my own words
tomorrow![1] Gruner's engravg is very faithful & beautiful, but I question
whether the copyright of it will fetch what she wishes. Colnaghi's
are willing to treat with her for the plate, & for a number of proofs.
But there is one serious rival on the field, & that is the perfection to
which modern photographs are brought, so that the true relation of
one colour to another is preserved. A Frenchman, Braun of Dornach,
is now photographg the chief pictures in Nat: Gal: & when done you
will be able to have the whole set for £120! But single proofs perhaps at
15/. I foresee that this perfected photography will go far to drive even
the best engravgs out of the market. But people do not yet know of
these magnificent photographs, so I hope good Mrs Gruner will make
something by her good husband's plate & proof, before the rivals get
well known.[2]

And I have written thus far before tellg you how glad I am to hear
that yr full diplomatic pension has been awarded you, tardy justice! if
justice at all, for you are entitled I conclude, to the arrears of many
years. But tho' you have kindly told me of it yrself I had already heard
the pleasant news. The pleasure it was sure to give me was so well
known, that little Lady Gregory wrote it to me at once. I am truly
glad that this will give you & Enid a house in London, but I shall not
forgive Gladstone for all that. Still, with a beautiful residence at Venice
& a good house in London, & not least, a dear wife, you will have as
much as any mortal man should desire. I quite agree with you that it
is high time your flirting powers shd cease, altho' you longed to renew
the exercise when stayg with beautiful women (in spite of their voices)
at yr friends the D'Addas!! I quite enjoyed yr description of that house
& its guests. I greatly prize my knowledge of the Italian race, tho' so

far short of your's. I rejoice to have lived to see Italy united. I delight to hear of yr entire devotion to the next edition of Kugler, & that there will be more illustrations. There is, I am sure, no man living with the knowledge of Morelli.

One little task I have undertaken lately has been to compile a catalogue of the pictures & objects in these drawing rooms. I intend to have a few copies printed for benefit of friends. When I am gone there will be no one who knows their history.[3]

Now dear Layard with kindest love to Enid I am ever yr's truly
Eliz Eastlake

1. 'Madonna del Ansidei', *The Times*, 14 October 1884, p. 2, col. E.

2. In 1884 Braun & Co took over 300 photographs of works in the Gallery's collection. See Anthony J. Hamber, *'A Higher Branch of the Art': Photographing the Fine Arts in England 1839–1880* (Amsterdam: Gordon & Breach Publishers, 1996).

3. The information appeared as *Catalogue of … Drawings and Engravings, the property of Lady Eastlake, deceased, late of 7 FitzRoy Square, which will be sold by Auction by Messrs. Christie, Manson & Woods … Tuesday, June 19, 1894* (London: William Clowes & Sons, 1894) and *Catalogue of a small Collection of Objects of Art, the Property of Lady Eastlake, deceased … Which will be sold by Auction by Messrs. Christie, Manson & Woods … July 5, 1894* (London: William Clowes & Sons, 1894).

Letter to Frances Power Cobbe[1]   *HL CB399*

7 FitzRoy Square
13th January 1885
Dear Miss Cobbe

I lead a very idle life in my semi–invalid state – not doing the things I ought to do & tho' I hope not so guilty of the converse – or I shd ere this have followed the promptings of my feelings & have expressed to you my homage & gratitude for your late & present letters to the Times, in answer to that cruel & impudent liar F.R.S. who does well to conceal his identity. I am exceedingly obliged by the printed copy sent me of yr first letter.[2]

The courage & ability with which you enter the lists against this execrable practice & its heartless votaries are an unspeakable comfort to those who can only raise their voices, & those too often inaudible. You are fighting the good fight & the the reward cannot fail in the end, tho' all great victories over sin & wickedness are indeed slow of achievement & require that strong faith which the great & humane have.

I can't write to you without thinking of Mildred Coleridge. Where is her <u>mind</u>? to say nothing of heart, feeling & duty. It is one of the most painful incidents that has crossed my path. I hate the fashionable plea of insanity for crimes we can't comprehend, but a Coleridge mind thrown off its balance will account for much. It weighs heavy on mine![3]

Your's with true gratitude
Eliz Eastlake

1. Frances Power Cobbe (1822–1904) founded the British Union for the Abolition of Vivisection (BUAV) in 1898. See Sally Mitchell (2004) *Frances Power Cobbe, Victorian Feminist, Journalist, Reformer* (Charlottesville and London: University of Virginia Press, 2004).

2. Letter to the Editor signed *F. R. S.*, *The Times*, Friday January 2 1885, p. 10, col. C.

3. Mildred Mary Coleridge (1847–1929), daughter of Lord Chief Justice Coleridge, involved in a public row with her father about her marriage (1885) to Charles Warren Adams (1833–1903).

Letter to John Murray   NLS Ms.42178

7 FitzRoy Square
26 Janry 1885
Dear Mr Murray

You have kindly sent me a very pretty book, on a most interesting feature in art. In times gone by I should have requested leave to review it. But I am not strong enough now. At the same time I have dipped far enough to see that Gilbert & I do quite agree in estimate of landscape.

I showed the volume to Chas Eastlake yesterday who pounced upon it with great delight & lamented that there is little chance of his being able to order it for the National Gallery Library for which a grant of £100 a year has been allowed. But Gladstone's policy – evasive in all ways – consists, as regards the Gallery, in cutting off at one end what he gives at the other. The purchase of the Blenheim Raphael will deprive the Gallery of its allowance of £10,000 for seven years! Also the allowance for the library is to be stopped!

I wish the whole Cabinet & the old Emperor of Germany had been

placed in the rank of the weakest 'face' of that square of Abu Kea! [sic]
It would have saved us better men![1]

What villany is made possible by the newest inventions of science!
Believe me yr's truly
Eliz Eastlake

    1. The Battle of Abu Klea, at which a British force en route to relieve General
       Gordon at Khartoum were attacked and formed a square with the cannon
       on the north face to defend themselves.

Letter to A. H. Layard   *NLS Ms.42171*

7 FitzRoy Sqre
17 Febry 1885
Dear Layard

May I be allowed without presumption to tell you how much I
admire your letter to the Times.[1] You have filled up the measure of
indictment against our imbecile & perverse Govt by recalling acts of
their's which their numerous subsequent sins may have helped to bury
in oblivion. And you speak in all respects with a knowledge that no
other man possesses. How I wish yr Turkish govt were more worthy of
the race they groom! or that you were permanent Sultan, or permanent
English adviser! But the dog has a bad name & people can't get over
that. Accordg to my small light I heartily wish Egypt under our sole
administration, with no limit on our time. The narrow highways of our
globe ought to be in English hands since we are the only nation who
can be trusted to hold them for the benefit of others.

The Times is great today in its 2nd article – liftg up its voice with no
uncertain tones as it did in the mismanagemt of the Crimean War. How
well I remember a dinner at Dean Milmans when you sat next to me
& first gave me warning of the horrors of stupidity & red tape we shd
soon hear.

It is quite eno' that I trouble you with this note, wh: you are not to
acknowledge.

Regarding my proposed cheap sale of the Toschi Correggio's to the
N: Gal: library I am given to understand by Chas Eastlake that the small
fund is to be withdrawn this year – & that the purchase of the Raphael
is to cost in 10 year's grant![2] Our Premier prefers to spend the nations's
money in sheddg blood. My best love to Enid. Ever yr's truly
Eliz Eastlake

1. Layard's letter to the Editor, criticizing the Government for its foreign policy in Turkey and campaign in Khartoum, appeared in *The Times*, 16 February 1885, p. 7, col. D.

2. The purchase of Raphael's *Ansidei Madonna* for £70,000 in 1885.

Letter to A. H. Layard   *NLS Ms.42171*

7 FitzRoy Sqre
25 May 1885
Dear Layard

I have been distressed by a note from our little friend Sir John de Gex[1] telling me that Enid has somehow caught the measles, & is now laid up with them. I can only hope that they are of a mild kind, & that she may be by this time out of pain, & you out of anxiety. But at any age above childn they are not desirable. I hope you won't take them! Doubtless you are having summer weather, wh: is still far from us, supposed to be delayed by icebergs in the Atlantic.

Even at Venice you are not out of the reach of political weather! It is hard to see everyone powerless to break thro' the evil spells of that fiend Gladstone. (I have plenty of monosyllables to define him.) I know of some English gentlemen, & hear of more, who will not go abroad this summer, because positively ashamed to look foreigners in the face. What a new position!

As you see the Times you will have been amused (& of course shocked) at this discussion about nudities. They seem to me all wide of the mark, tho' I take part with the British matron usually. But it is really all a question of art. Really fine art will never raise a blush. It is also a matter of scale. Mulready's exquisite drawings were not above 9 inches high. Poynter's young lady – judg.g from the illustrated catalogue – has not a defence.[2]

A visit from Chas Eastlake yesterday acquaints me of a legacy of £10,000 to the Nat: Gal: from a Mr. Walker to be spent in 'a picture, or pictures'. This will give you one year's income for yr Director to spend questionably. A visit also from Enid's (& my also) aversion – poor Mr. Richter – tells me an odd story about the Sistine Madonna, namely that it does belong to the Saxon Roy family, & that they do offer it for £150,000! & further than that 150 English gentlemen have formed a Sindicate[sic] to give £1.000 each & present it to our N.G. I am afraid this may be told to "the Marines".[3]

A kind letter from Morelli, acknowledg.g my introduction of Frank Palgrave to him, tells me that he had the pleasure of seeing you & Enid at Milan.

I have not yet obtained my new carriage from the maker, & meanwhile am not impatient to go out, being very contented with books & kind friends. With kindest love to your dear patient ever yr's truly

Eliz Eastlake

1. John De Gex (1809–87), legal writer knighted in 1882. Brother of Edward De Gex.

2. The exhibition of Edward Poynter's life-size nude, *Diadumene*, generated numerous letters to *The Times*, one signed by a 'British Matron' of 20 May 1885, p. 10, col. A. See also *The Times*, 21 May 1885, p. 6, col. B; 22 May 1885, p. 5, col. D; 23 May 23 1885, p. 10, col. B; 25 May 1885, p. 10, col. D.

3. 'Tell it to the marines', a scornful expression of disbelief now rarely used.

Letter to John Murray   *NLS Ms.42178*

7 FitzRoy Square
9 July 1885
Dear Mr. Murray

I am induced to apply to you on behalf of a gentleman who has been long engaged on his life of S:T. Coleridge. He is a Dr Brandl (Austrian Tyrolese) with fewer demerits about him than most Germans.[1] He has had every English opportunity of increasing the materials hitherto known. He has read me a small portion of his M.S. & the style & the stuff seemed to me alike good. The question is whether you would consent to publish a translation of this work, which I am willing to undertake. It is not to exceed one vol: Your father, I believe, published the 'Cristabel', & you have I know the portrait of the strange old man. Of course Dr. Brandl has got from the family all they have to give & it is well thought of by Lord Coleridge – that much maligned man!

You can let me know at your leisure what you think of this proposal. I shall remain in London to end of month – perhaps longer. Dr. Brandl speaks English & is a presentable being.

I hope you are all as well as circumstances permit, surrounded with all the best beauty of the year.

Ever yr's truly
Eliz Eastlake

Please tell me in your answer how Robt. Cooke is going on.

1. Alois Brandl (1855–1940), Professor at Humboldt University in Berlin and pioneer of English literary studies in Germany. He was the author of *Samuel Taylor Coleridge und die englische Romantik* (Berlin, 1886). This and subsequent letters refer to Elizabeth's simultaneous translation, *Samuel Coleridge Taylor and the English Romantic School* (London: John Murray, 1887). J. L. Lowes berates Lady Eastlake's 'flagrant mistranslations' of Brandl's work: 'There are few more untrustworthy translations than Lady Eastlake's rendering of Brandl's book'; *Road to Xanadu* (London: Constable, 2nd rev edn 1951 [1930]), pp. 594–96, n. 128.

Letter to A. H. Layard   *NLS Ms.42171*

7 FitzRoy Sqre
12 July 1885

I owe you two interestg long letters, dear Layard, the one of the 1st June, the other the 1st July! I shall have no objection to your continuing to write on the 1st of each month! The first gave me the assurance of Enid's recovery from her too long delayed measles. She is very fortunate to feel no evil effects. I had a beautiful cousin who was deafened for life by late measles. Tell Enid how glad I am to find that not all beautiful women have the same fate & mind you don't alter my message!

I need hardly say how interested I am by the account of yr Kugler doings. The work must now be a mosaic of different styles. Tho', I am sure, not of conflicting opinions. I am not alarmed by your having retained my opinions as well as dear Sir Charles' for I am pretty sure that all mine were derived directly or indirectly from him. Of Morelli's connoisseurship I think so highly that I quite approve of yr havg given him the precedence above all others.

I honour you more than I can say for havg refrained from sayg anything uncivil about Messrs C. & C.! That is a self command wh: I fear I could not have practiced! Murray has just sent me their 2nd vol: of Raphael – & I have done no more than peeped into it or rather into the heads of chapters! & they have turned me sick! "Lionardo's Epiphany"! Isiah & John Goritz" "The Virtues, Justice & Comity!!" (pray what is comity? – I fear I don't possess it.) I know I shall be too much exasperated to read the book. There are good many people who ought to die! such as the old Emperor of Germany & Gladstone, & Crowe is another, & then poor

Cavalcaselle's arduously collected facts must have some chance of a decent dress.

But I fear it is too late for Gladstone's death to do any good, & he had better perhaps live now & fulfil the prophecy of his dying "in a madhouse", wh: wd be a powerful argument against the sanity of his late doings. & I consider this a very charitable aspiration on my part. For surely it is better to be <u>mad</u>, than <u>bad</u>. However little the Conservatives may have it in their power to do, yet there is a great sense of relief in feeling that the plots of G: & his gang against the <u>country</u> are for the present in abeyance. That they are plotting against their successors is true – but I am one who do not [sic] despond as to the results of the next general election. The agricultural labourer is dull, but not a fool, & makes his own conclusions in favor of the landed class. I hear of ladies who are willing to take bets as to the triumph of the conservatives – only findg it is difficult to find anyone who does not think the same.

I am much interested by yr account of the so-called Raphael sketch book. I hope the description of those drawings is well given in your new edition & don't you wish that drawings & pictures could speak! There would be strange revelations – all the more shd we honor those, like Morelli, who anticipate such revelations.

Speakg of pictures I have been havg those in this house carefully looked after by Dyer. Chas Eastlake pointed out to me that several – especially those not under glass – were over dry, as well as very dirty. Dyer took the two small Paul Veronese's over chimney piece in front drawing room away for a few days & has returned them in an exquisite state, & with a glass over each. Also he has been here for 2 days washing others & the large Bellini has come out like a new picture.[1] So I can die now with the consolation that they have not deteriorated in my keeping, & thankful for the happiness they have given me.

We are now havg, for us, <u>hot</u> weather – tho' still with a sting of East wind wh: particularly affects me. At the same time I am quite well, & just now getting out more. For a long ordered little Victoria – very low & easy – is with me now, & I feel it my duty to dine out 3 or 4 times a week, tho' a little regretting the quiet days when I used to lend my old Victoria to my friends & when I stayed at home & saw my friends who liked to call. This old Victoria – still in excellent condition – I am now parting with for a song to the coach builder. Had you been here I should have tried to persuade you to take it for £25 only. Perhaps you wd not have condescended to a vehicle for only one horse.

The other day I called to enquire for Mrs Drummond & she kindly came out to me, & we had a little chat at her door. Mary Kaye was away.

Kind old Sir John de Gex was here also a few days ago.

I have engaged a country house for a few weeks from the end of this month. That is if I can now get it for the old lady to whom it belongs has fallen ill, & whether she will be able to vacate by that time (& I don't wish her to die) is very uncertain. It is a house on Albury Heath I have had before – within sight of dear Mrs Grote's chimneys [sic], & the ground floor so flat that I can go in my wheelchair from the drive to the drawg room. I do not expect ever to walk again, & am quite satisfied with my past feats in that respect, but I shall enjoy to sit in the air, & to see beautiful English nature – never more beautiful than now.

You will have a house full I see on the 22nd for the launch of this "useless iron clad".[2] Lumley is an old friend, & therefore I beg you to remember me kindly to him. He is a real lover of art. I am glad his Velasquez is in the Gallery, tho' I can't see it.

From yr description of yr portrait by Mr. Vigor I fear I shd not recognize it! or rather you.[3]

I promise I won't answer you always at such length.
With best love to Enid I am ever yr's truly
Eliz Eastlake

1. Dyer was a picture cleaner employed by the National Gallery.

2. The launch of the battleship *Francesco Morosini* in Venice attracted enormous crowds to Venice.

3. *Portrait of Sir Austen Henry Layard* (1885) by Charles Vigor. British Museum.

Letter to John Murray   *NLS Ms.42178*

7 FitzRoy Square
15 July 1885
Dear Mr. Murray

I am much obliged by your note of the 10th & glad to find that you consent to undertake a translation of Dr. Brandl's Life of Coleridge. We must do our best to break the spell of non-success which attends your translations. He has written me word what passed between you.

I have also to thank you for the 2nd vol: of Raphael – a valuable

collection of facts, tho' unfortunately clothed in the peculiar
Crowe dialect. I was writing to Layard & gave him forthwith a few
specimens.

   And further I have to thank you for the new number of the
Quarterly. It looks most tempting, but I shall begin with the last article,
which is sure to gratify my conservative spite.

   I rejoice at the good account of Robt. Cooke, & wish you could give
me better home news.
Believe me yr's truly
Eliz Eastlake

Letter to A. H. Layard   NLS Ms.42171

7 FitzRoy Sqre
15 Aug: 1885
My dear Layard
   Considering how much you had to do in preparg a move to
Longarone on the morng of the 1st Aug: I am the more obliged to
you for the long & interestg letter you wrote me between yr packings.
I am surprized that no account of the launch, or the Royal visit to
Venice has appeared in any paper I have seen, but those are only
the Times, & our occasional Globe – & Punch. Old Morosini little
anticipated that a King & Queen of Italy wd be present at the launch
of a vessel named after him. I trust that the Arsenal sends forth vessels
of peace & trade alongside this ironclad, & that Venetian trade is not
suffering as our's is! When I was at yr Ca' Capello the English Consul
("Sn/wipes" as Rawdon Brown used to call him) told me that Venetian
trade had increased 75 per cent since the union with Italy. I often long
to make use of a work on Venice I brought home with me by the
society of I. Dotti, & to enlist also a curious work, printed by Ruskin,
with all the minutes of Councils from the earlier time – beginning
in Doglatin, & continuing in Venetian dialect – from which a true
history of early Venice could be drawn, & upset the inventions of
Count Daru.[1] I am too old now & not strong eno'. Meanwhile as I am
strong enough for some work, & therefore hardly know how to live
without it, I have undertaken to translate a forthcomg biography of
S.T. Coleridge by a Viennese man – Dr. Brandl – a good-lookg man
of course, who has been compiling it for some time. On the strength
of my assurance that it wd be worth readg Mr. Murray has undertaken
to publish my English translation. I urge upon Dr. Brandl to have a

portion ready for Murray's dinner, but he is not a man of business, &
I require to translate from a German proof, & not a wretched German
scribble.

I am glad to hear of Kugler's forwardness, & know well that I shall
have an early copy.

Meanwhile my old Albury landlady has neither died nor got better, &
all hope of my getting the house is over. However I have some chance
of getting a convenient old house at Beulah Hill Lower Norwood, with
all flat & plenty of ground floor accomodation. More chance than I
really wish, for the summer seems gone, the days are shortening fast, the
evengs are cold, & I am comfortable at home & so well that but for the
persistent bullying of kind friends who have looked out this house for
me, I wd much prefer remaing where I am. However I do not think of
being away more than a month.

Lately I have an interestg essay from M: Ravaisson – Conservateur
des antiques – on Louvre, upon a torso of a Hercules by Lysippus, very
like the well known torso M.Angelo studied. M. Ravaisson is the same
who set the Venus of Milo upright, on her coming unjoined at the hips
after being in a damp cellar during the Commune. This is learned,
but very interestg, givg as much the history of Hercules as of Lysippus.
Hercules, the Christ of the Pagan world, who converted savage tribes
from their ways, one tribe in particular who were accustomed to eat
their Dead, & to marry their mothers![2]

The land will have peace now from Parliamentary wrangles, &
we shall miss the excitement we have had for months. Meanwhile
the exposure of Chamberlain equally by friend & foe is very
refreshing. And I must own to a sneaking enjoyment of that impudent
Randolph's speeches.[3] I remember a certain gentleman who told his
supporters that if they could find a genuine live Tory he wd have him
put in the British Museum. Don't I remember Henry Drummond's
retort too – in Latin! So much for "Sir Layard" your cutting has
greatly amused me.

In my last letter I neglected to notice the new made Baronet. I
thought Millais wd have been wiser – but I suppose female influence
carried the day. At the same time I know that Gladstone called upon
him & urged it as a particular favor that he should accept the title – as a
compliment to art! Little does that false old man know of what is really
complimentary to art, or Poetry! It's a pity he did not raise Ruskin to
the Upper House! before his death, which is soon to be expected. As a
compliment to art too. I hope Enid & you are greatly enjoyg yr country
quarters, & that you will do both Baveno & Rome. With best love to
her I am ever yrs truly

Eliz Eastlake

I can't imagine Morelli either ill or cross! Not knowg yr Longarone address I direct this to Venice.

1. Comte Daru, *Histoire de la République de Venise* (1819).

2. Jean Gaspard Felix Ravaisson-Mollien (1813–1900), French philosopher, archaeologist and conservator at the Louvre.

3. Lord Randolph Churchill (1849–95), Tory statesman.

Letter to A. H. Layard   *NLS Ms.42171*

7 FitzRoy Sqre
8 Octr 1885
Dear Layard

I had yr kind & long letter of the 19th, & as you were crossing a mountain on the 1st I forgive you for not writg on that day. You have had a very interestg tour. I have gone over some of the same routes in my youth, & also with dear Sir Chas, but he was not in time to go through any Alpine tunnel, & I have only known the Mont Cenis one, wh: interested me intensely. Doubtless they will increase with the more & more restless generations, but he would be a bold man – or woman – who wd prophesy how much further the earth is to be subdued. I follow you two with some of yr acquaintances – the new Ld & Lady Monksworth (Monkbarnes I feel inclined to call him!) whose daughter is supposed to have had the same predilection for handsome men which I am credited, & of course proved to be – & I follow you, tho' rather with fear & trembling, into the presence of the formidable Mrs Fanny Kemble. How clever of Enid to tame her! I used to live in fear of being beaten. Switzerland is not precisely the country I shd go to for sketching, but in truth it is the easiest for the purpose. A mountain greatly covered with snow is like Monti's veiled busts, the snow & the viel are easier than the bare earth, or bare face. I think I shd prefer Holland to Switzerland, & Hobbema to Calame.[1] But indeed I have seen so much of the truest picturesque within drivg distance from London that I think I shd fix myself on Streatham Common if I were to begin life again! But perhaps the grapes are sour. I suppose "the crowds of mobs" which swarm over the old land wd be called the greatest happiness of the greatest number – a dogma I have no respect for, for in Engld it wd consist in unlimited beer, & freedom to beat your wife.

I remark that wherever you go you fall in with Princesses & pretty girls, wh: is of course accidental. Still, I rejoice whenever you come in contact with our Crown Pss, as you are sure to conjure out of her a kind message for me! Morelli & you together must be rare company for her after German stiffness & pomposity – & a good many worse things, but I fear you do the young Princess no good! Instead of exhortg them to walk in the ways of propriety.

Meanwhile I have been spendg a month in a very pretty place near that same Streatham Common wh: has so smitten me. It was within sight of the Crystal Palace, but for all that perfectly country, with fine trees & a beautiful view, & a garden full of plums & pears which was a great attraction to Miss Lewin, & other nice young ladies who were stayg with me. I drove out & sat out, & did all I ought to do, & I daresay it did me good in return. But in truth I am well in health tho' not more nimble. I was glad however to return to the <u>pictures</u>, some of wh: have been havg necessary repairs by Mr. Dyer of the Nat: Gal: & almost all hitherto unglazed, getting glasses, especially the Gentile Bellini. A propos of Nat: Gal: I have recently had a visit from M. Ravaisson – of whom I told you in my last. He was full of some grand antique figure – earlier than the Venus of Milo, & as fine – now in the Louvre of wh: he promises me a photograph. He also made some pointed but polite remarks on "Monsieur Burton" to whom he had written about some pictures wh: belong to himself, especially a small Correggio, but who had vouchsafed him no answer. I am not so sure that the lunatic asylum is the place to wh: I shd relegate the head of a great institution who is too lazy to compile a catalogue or to answer letters. I shd just put him into some <u>House of Correction</u>. Meanwhile you Trustees shd pull him up. M. Ravaisson is an accomplished gentleman, evidently well versed in the Italian masters. I said I wd call your attention, in case of yr being in Paris, to his little collection. He is "conservateur des antiques aux musées du Louvre". But with such a Director as Monsieur Burton I can understand such fine pictures as you tell me Richter has bought, not comg to our Gallery! But there are two meanings to the word 'fine' & the Richter meaning may not be the same as your's & mine, but on referring, I see <u>Morelli</u> has endorsed the 'fine' so I fear it is true.

I wonder whether we mean the same work by Ruskin. I don't remember that it was called a History of the Ducal Palace, rather it was a reproduction of all minutes & records of councils held there from earliest time of the Republic, beginning in doglatin, & continuing in <u>plat</u> Venetian – I deciphered some of both, especially about the prison's – in time of illness – which showed a humanity very great for the

time towards the sick prisoners. That vol: shd be the basis of a reliable
History of Venice. I fear I am far too old to undertake another "Venice
Defended" – but I sometimes think of lookg into the life of Fra Paolo
Sarpi & letting the English public know more about that man who was
so hated by Rome. In due time I may perhaps bother you to answer
questions. Meanwhile my handsome German keeps me without printed
text, so the translation does not progress. As regards Mr. Horatio
Brown's Life on the Lagoons' I have it & admire it, & I trust he may
now receive the appointmt dear old Rawdon Brown held. I detest that
man Cavendish Bentinck.

We have lost good old Ld Shaftesbury since I had your letter. The
initials G.O.M., so utterly misapplied in the first instance, shd rather be
given to him.[2] For his career of consistent philanthropy is unexampled.
I knew him tolerably well, & have seen his lively & most pleasant
side in society. On his last birthday – 16th April – he came her to a
sort of Meeting for the persecuted Jews. He had a little rough parcel
in his hand, & explained that he had just recd it from the "One tun
Ragged School" with a sheet of paper – he showed us – covered with
signatures of little boys & girls. The parcel contained some ha'pence,
but now end of farthings, amounting to 6/10 subscribed for his
benevolent purpose by the childn. We also had a present for him, for
the result of a little quiet circular by the Committee had brought in no
less than £740. He had been anxious about two of the Jew Colonies in
the Holy Land for which the funds had failed, he turned to me & said
"this will do me more good than all the medicine". He was then lookg
wretchedly ill. At this moment the service for him is going on at the
Abbey, & I have sent two friends to a window on the route to see the
procession wh: I suspect will be something unprecedented in amount &
material.[3]

I continue terribly anxious about the comg elections. A niece, whose
husband is canvassing for some place in Norfolk writes me that the
labourers seem to be all Liberals "and as they far out number any other
class the election is as good as certain". I am sorry to say her husbd is a
radical.

I don't wonder that Taine's Revolution supplies you with many a
foreboding, & yet how differently have the higher orders acted towards
the lower orders here! They have no right to reap the wind, for they
have not sown the whirlwind. The antecedents of England are different
to that of every other European nation. And tho' your correspondents
speak of the division of classes now here – yet in truth that is nothing
in comparison with what they are & have been in Germany, & of
course in Russia. But Germany is the stronghold of empty pride.

How glad you will be that my 2nd sheet is at an end! With kindest love to Enid ever yr's most truly
Eliz Eastlake

1. Alexandre Calame (1810–64), Swiss painter.

2. GOM stands for Grand Old Man, the title more usually applied to William Ewart Gladstone.

3. Elizabeth Eastlake, the Countess of Rosse, Lady Wingate, Lady Maria Forester, Mrs Colonel Ratcliffe and Mrs Kent Hughes formed a Ladies' Committee for the purpose of collecting and offering to Lord Shaftesbury on his 86th birthday (29 April) a sum of money for the Jews in Palestine. See *The Times*, 24 February 1885, p. 10 col. D.

Letter to A. H. Layard   *NLS Ms.42172*

7 FitzRoy Sqre
6 Febry 1886
Dear Layard

I mentioned to my cousin Frank Palgrave your wish for information about the Norwich School. He has sent me this work by the Redgraves, which contains notices on Crome, Vincent, Stark & Cotman. If new to you you may be glad & consult it. There is also allusion to Ladbroke another Norwich man, whom I only know by name. I fancy he was very inferior.

I wish we had a Cotman in the N. Gal! I always feel his affinity to Turner. He was an odd man – always on the brink of insanity, & I fear it is true that he deranged himself.[1]

What a scheching [?] pen I am treating you to!

I have a nephew in Parliament – Frank Taylor, M.P. for South Norfolk[2] – a horrid radical, but what he has seen & heard already seems to have greatly lessened his admiration for the Old Rogue.[3]

What a defiance to the world this appointment of John Morley! How can decent men join such a gang![4]
Ever your's truly
Eliz Eastlake

1. See letter, 10 November 1830.

2. Francis Taylor MP, who married Susan Rigby, daughter of Dr Edward Rigby Jr.

3. Namely Gladstone.

4. John Morley MP, editor of the *Pall Mall Gazette* and *Macmillan's* magazine. He was a supporter of Irish Home Rule, and was appointed by Gladstone as Secretary for Ireland in February 1886.

Letter to A. H. Layard   *NLS Ms.42172*

7 FitzRoy Sqre
13 March 1886
Dear Layard
At the risk of boring you I enclose you a little paper I was asked to write for an humble Periodical – upon – or rather to the present Female Art Students. It is only humdrum & matter of fact, but at the same time the result of some experience of the fruits of the present mania. You can put it into your paper basket.[1]

1. 'The Female School of Art', *Englishwoman's Review*, n.s. 155 (15 March 1886), pp. 102–104.

Letter to A. H. Layard   *NLS Ms.42172*

Albury Heath Guildford
6 Aug: 1886
My dear Layard
I am, as you see, in the country & so, still further from you & from yr kind letter of the 26 July, but I hope I have recd it in time to thank you for it. It is truly far from empty, containg something of every thing, especially accounts of yr life, & a few hits at Enid without which I shd be uneasy. I know nothing of fishing nor of Norwegian life. Nothing of the kind goes on in Russia, indeed no sport of any kind, that I know of, goies on – unless it be drawing lots for poor conscripts! No hunting, shooting, or fishing, only whist playing, & smoking, & worse things! But since I read Wm Davenport's "Sport" I have a good idea of what yr life now is. He made his wife so happy that the poor lady has had a paralytic stroke since his death which I fear she will never recover from. But even in that state her son's return fm some part of Cheshire has given her great pleasure.

I am always <u>bullied</u> by kind friends into leaving London in the summer & so I was bullied into coming here, just a fortnight ago – & immediately as I arrived it became so cold that I all but made a

vow never to leave London again. At the same time I am fond of the
place wh: is full of memories of the kind Grotes – & certainly our
English country never looked more beautiful. This, as you know is a
tree country, & the woods here nevermore magnificent. And now it is
warmer & I contemplate the sensibility of sitting out of doors. Meanwhile
I have not been alone – having had two married couples at once with
me – I was always making mistakes as to which lady & which husband!
I am glad they did not! Now I am alone – except a kitten – who will
make up to me, especially when I am writing – of which I have plenty
to do – for some little time ago I undertook to translate a German life
of the Coleridge. My Professor – for of course he is one – keeps ahead
of me & I get his proof sheets in succession. Upon the whole it is thus
far very ably done – all that great reading & a passion for the subject can
do – with a little playfulness too – not quite of such a cart-horse kind as
Germans generally indulge in – my fear is that it will prove too clean for
our English public – too much technicality as to poetic terms in parts –
all this will be delightful to a German reader – but I maintain that I can
best judge what will suit an English one & threaten to omit what bores
me! which puts him into a fright! The interestg part is the connection
between C's early modes of thought & the Revolutionary tendencies of
the time – he was born 1772. Also the analysis of his extraordinary mind.
I have known chief of the living Coleridges – a family which has gone
to ruin in itself, alas! & they have all a vein of clever address wh: must
come from the same source as his did. Not that I call young Bernard C
clever,[1] who being direct heir to a peerage, votes for the Abolition of the
House of Lords! In short he is a Gladstonian! I fancy no retreat wd be
secluded enough to isolate me from that subject. I wondered at yr moral
courage in leavg England while the great issues were pending. Now we
have a temporary calm, & with the Old Rogue[2] out of power – for good
– the worst a bad man can do is over – but what some will call worse
is doubtless still to come. Still, I hardly think more Irish rebels wd fight
– more than the Crofters of Tiree have done, if they saw that we were in
earnest. The future is doubtless full of incident & anxiety.

Of course I was not able to go to Christie's to see the Blenheim
pictures. I have been at B: & do not readily forget pictures. It is
humiliating not to have been able to buy any but one little uncelebrated
picture – not even the Teniers – a most interesting lot, wh: only
fetched something over £2.000. He mt copy whom he wd – he always
remained Teniers. I quite agree with you that for the next 7 years a
Director is superfluous!! especially one who is past his day (if he ever
had one) already. So I trust to hear that the Trustees have advised the
new Treasury to dispense with Sir Fred: – I am disposed also to agree

with Ld Thurlow that the purpose of the Nat: Gal: is to attract pictures
hitherto unknown – to draw them out of old places in Italy or elsewhere
– as dear Sir Chas did – <u>any</u> body can buy well known pictures from
<u>English</u> collections! – & to leave it to the generosity, ambition or vanity
of private individuals to present & bequeath at home. I am so glad that
you agree with me on all these points!! The sale itself, following that of
the Hamilton pictures & library is a disgrace to two English Dukes –
who date from <u>Palaces</u>. For all that I am not one to despair if in glorious
country – never higher in many high respects than now.

I shall be much interested in your article on the Nat: Gallery – there
is much to be said to a connoisseur public – & comparisons with other
galleries will not shame us. We have more <u>painters</u> represented than
most other galleries – far more than the Louvre. I suppose my good
nephew Chas Eastlake will have to supply the long wanted Catalogue.
He is preparing to go to Madrid, & I wd envy him that pleasure.

Now I must big you good bye – hoping to hear from you when
you are settled somewhere – for Italy seems riddled with cholera – &
Venice not yet free. Your three brothers having spent this time together
must have been charming & will be always so to look back upon. I am
glad to know a little of yr General brother. In short the quartett – for
all must be harmony where Enid presides – must be perfect – My best
love to her
Ever dear Layard your's truly
Eliz Eastlake

   1. Bernard Coleridge (1851–1927), a judge and Gladstonian Liberal MP.

   2. This remark is Bowdlerized in J&C2, p. 287 as 'Old Man'.

Letter to John Murray   *NLS Ms.42178*

Albury Heath Guildford
15 September 1886
Dear Mr. Murray
   I have for some time been wishing to report to you on the subject
of Prof: Brandl's Life of S.T. Coleridge, but have been interrupted by
causes you can well understand – not by him – for he has supplied
me with the German proof without delay. Indeed it is only a few days
ago that I received the last proofs from him. Since I began I have
wished to ask you whether you wish for more than one vol:? His now
complete German pages amount to 429 – excluding preface & index. I

can assure you meanwhile that the work is well done – in some parts
excellent. The thoroughness however which it displays is, at the same
time sometimes overdone. He stands too long occasionally, as I tell him,
on one leg, to suit the English public. Whatever may be your wish or
plan with regard to the size of the work I strongly recommend some
compression. I have from the first let him know that I reserve to myself
the right to decide what suits the English reader. I only wish to know
your real views as to whether to compress more or less. Certainly this
work exhausts the subject – everything that can be said of Coleridge
– & much of his contemporaries – is said here.

I think the work sufficiently fresh & full to warrant an article in
the Q.R. I wrote to Dr. Smith to that effect, some three weeks ago. I
conclude he is out of England (I hope not unwell) for I have recd no
answer.

I have been here in this part of the world, to which I have become
much attached, since the 22nd July, & leave it for home on the 30th
instant. I have a succession of guests who enjoy the heath & its air
heartily. I have heard of you & yours as not being at Wimbledon. I
hope, however, somewhere to the benefit of all, & especially of your
dear invalid.
Believe me dear Mr. Murray
Yr's very truly
Eliz Eastlake

Letter to John Murray   NLS Ms.42178

7 FitzRoy Square
5 Octr 1886
Dear Mr. Murray
I returned here last Thursday, & am working as hard at my translation
as an accumulation of business will allow me. I have, as you know,
the German publication now entitled "Samuel Taylor Coleridge & the
English Romantic School". I think the title of the English version had
better be the same – namely "Samuel Taylor Coleridge & the English
Romantic School, by Professor A: Brandl of the university of Prague.
Translated by Lady Eastlake" – for I feel that my name may be justly
given.

The Romantic School is a term I do not much like, the Germans call
it simply "die Romantik" but I know of no better. 'The Late School' is
very inadequate.

I receive <u>murmurs</u> from Dr. Brandl as to the <u>compression</u> of his pages
– which I lay on <u>you</u> – tho' entirely approving it myself. I can quite
promise him that nothing of real importance shall be omitted.
Believe me yr's very truly
Eliz Eastlake

Letter to John Murray   *NLS Ms.42178*

7 FitzRoy Square
17 October 1886
Dear Mr. Murray
I have been too busy at my translation, even to write to you about it, as
I had intended to do before this. I hope to get through the translating
part during this next week, & then to begin the work of compression.
Just now I am in a <u>metaphysical</u> vein which I shorten without mercy,
but hitherto I have translated all, & reserve the expungings for a general
summary of the work. I think <u>very well</u> of some portions, &, should
you desire it could prepare you a few pages for print for your publisher's
dinner.
    Prof: Brandl has overdone his German punctiliousness in always
giving, in brackets, the source where he has taken his facts, sometimes
two or three in a page – <u>needlessly</u> I think – tho' some might be
retained. But the omission of two thirds of these would in itself shorten
the work. At all events I hope to bring it down to your dimensions.
    I have mastered Layard's article in Q.R. which is well done, tho' I
demur at calling anything by Rossetti "exquisite"! The political articles
are also most able & interesting.
Believe me yr's very truly
Eliz Eastlake

Letter to A. H. Layard   *NLS Ms.42172*

7 FitzRoy Sqre
31. Octr 1886
Dear Layard
    It is more than time to acknowledge your kind long letter of the 27th
Septr which I found just arrived here on my return from the country
on the 20th. A letter from you is always a great pleasure to me from

the many subjects of common interest & memories of the same. And
now, for about a fortnight I have been in possession of the last Q.R.
in which I devoured your article, before lookg at another. There wd
be no doubt of its interesting me, but I find that it interests the general
reader also extremely. I need not say how entirely I concur with you in
the estimate of our treasures, & of the many features which distinguish
one Gallery smaller, & later information as it is from the larger galleries
which succeeded it. I suspect we have a far larger list of names, & those
more correct than one represented in the Louvre.

Nor need I say how I pounced upon your description of dear Sir
Charles' qualifications as first Director, greedy & insatiable as I am on
this topic I have not known justice so amply done him in so brief a
space before. I have not yet turned to yr old article of 1859 – but I shall
do so – as I have the whole QR in the house. Your tribute to dear
old Boxall too is not more generous than true, & very grateful to my
feelings. I don't see much agreeing with me as to your friend the present
Director! For you know I shd pack him off without much delay were
I the Trustees – but there is a meek little note in the first pages as to
the long delayed catalogue, which won't trouble his vanity, & which the
world will hardly interpret sufficiently. How glad he must be that there
is no money to spend except on such an item as his salary, that there is
no work to be done abroad, & that at home he succeeds in leavg all the
word[sic] to my good nephew – & without even allowing him to have
the credit of it! But eno' of that – only you wd not be sure that it is
I who hold this pen unless I were to touch on this subject! Altogether
I think it a masterly article, & one especially calculated to show the
advance of knowledge as to the Old Masters. I read yr remarks on the
pictures I know so well like annals of old friends – rather longing to see
those few wh: have come in these last 3 years – wh: I perhaps shall do
someday.

A few little remarks – hardly criticisms – I may venture to make
– differences in spelling – de Hooch instead of time-honoured de
Hooghe – but Chas Eastlake tells one that is the fashion now, & Frans
Hals instead of Franz or Frank. I go all lengths in praise of the Raphael
– tho' as you probably know, ignorant people – & such is the public
– wonder what there is to admire in it. But there is all the future
Raphael in it, tender tho inaffable grace of his early time. Then I am
glad you do justice to the two M Angelos – I like each of them better
than the awkward Holy Family in the Tribune at Florence. Then I
shd not call a real Van der Meer of Delft on the second class Dutch
painters. I shall never forget the impression made on Sir Chas & me by
a picture of his in a house at the Hague I think. We used to pronounce

that fine de Hooghe – (a woman readg at a window) at Dresden to be
a Van der Meer. Then I see you call that early German collection of
horrors bought by an evil genius, for the Gallery, on his own ignorant
hook, the Kruger collection – Surely the Minden was it not? Again, I
fancied the beautiful 'August Moon' (if we mean the same) is by Mason
not Lawson – Mr Something Smith has it. You do not deny Hogarth
technical qualities – but to my mind he has first rate ones, crisp &
beautiful in touch almost as Teniers.

And now only one more indictment – that must have been a slip of
yr pen when you mention "an exquisite youthful work by Rossetti!!! I
even remember that picture some 35 years ago when I did him the favor
to call on him – from early recollections of his gifted uncle Dr Polidori,
MD to Byron – & was surlily recd. The annunciation was then on his
easel, & I have ever retained the impression of its careful want of all
grace or beauty.[1] But I have done now – & you are very good to have
read all this.

I am still workg at the translation of my German Professor's Life of S
T Coleridge – which I promised him to do rather incautiously two years
ago, – but then he is a good looking young man! & you always said
that my proclivities that way wd get me into a scrape! And now Murray
wants me to boil down 429 pages of German into 329 of English text. I
quite approve of this – & am cutting out a deal about Kant & Schelling
– greatly to the improvement of the work. At all events it has taught me
something. & S.T.C. is a character to ruminate upon. It set me thinkg
how to define Genius, which I find very difficult – unless it be as a
disease. I have Coleridge, Göthe Burns, Gibson & your friend Gladstone
before me – & what five men can be more various! Göthe & Gladstone
the black sheep of the party – for selfishness & vanity. The last remark I
have heard of Gladstone is that he is a perpetual actor – but always plays
to the Gallery. It is useless to speak on politics. One has only to hope
that our present men will do their duty – wh; is principally to stand
firm at any cost. I feel that we ought as strenuously to oppose Russia
now, as we did old Buonaparte at the beginning of the century – no
matter what income tax or any other tax. The late history of Bulgaria &
its much sinned against young Prince wd hardly be believed in a novel
or drama. Your friend Mdme Novikoff is doing her best or worst.[2]

We are looking to the Ld Mayor's day with I won't say apprehension
– for "forewarned is forearmed" but one can hardly expect it to pass
off quietly. I am more anxious about the want – real & fictitious – that
is sure to be felt this winter. Last winter was bad enough – with hosts
of police guardg the soup kitchens. And yet Engld & especially London
never so earnestly sought to alleviate the condition of the poor.

Your real friend little Mdme Riano is in England. She managed to come & see me at Albury – stayg with Mrs Stuart Rendels not far off – & I have seen her again here. She is far from well – & indeed has been left here, as her husband had to go back to Spain, & I am delighted to see how attached she is to him. I find her much ripened in thought & very interestg. She desired her love to you – wh: I hope Enid won't take amiss. She is pretty well used to such messages to you!

The Chas Eastlakes returned from their holiday tour which had taken them to Madrid much refreshed, he as much impressed with the Gallery as I expected, and disgusted with the dirt & beggars of Spain. Now he is high busy at the Gallery, & tells me today, that Gregory is in town. I have been busy & quiet, & have not looked up any one – nor have the DeGex's been here.

High time to release you now – but I must give you one anecdote of an Irishman – "And sure the times are bad – here am I going on my honeymoon, & can't afford to take my wife with me"!!

By the by I saw Mrs Rate – who kindly came to me at Albury – with her eldest girl – & I shd have made the effort to go & lunch at Milton Court but she was hurried off to Folkestone – And I saw poor Miss Rolli – who came riding with her brother just before startg for Scotland. The sad event shocked me miserably – the brother writes me that she had "a defective heart" – she was certainly not drowned – He feels it deeply. Now dear Layard believe me yr always truly, with kindest love to Enid

Eliz Eastlake

1. Dante Gabriel Rossetti, *The Annunciation (Ecce Ancilla Domini)*, 1849–50, Tate.

2. Madame Olga Novikoff, Russian propagandist widely believed to have influenced Gladstone's thinking in his pamphlet 'Bulgarian Horrors and the Question of the East' of 1876.

Letter to John Murray   *NLS Ms.42178*

7 FitzRoy Square
9 Novr 1886
Dear Mr. Murray

You need not be in a hurry with the slip for me at this busy time. In truth I have been glad of a little rest after rather close application to S.J.C. I only hope the public may find him interesting eno'. The necessity for compression has got rid of some heavy parts – written for German taste. But I give the good Prof: credit for genuine pains.

Indeed I gobbled up Layard's article the first evening that I possessed the Q.R. & think it excellently done, & have written to him about it. He & I do not differ about the present Director – for I know he agrees with me entirely about him, tho' far more patient than I should be in his place, for Burton is a thoroughly incompetent man. It is true we should not know who to put in his place, but, while under late Gladstonian arrangements we really do not want a Director, for there is no money to spend.

Believe me yr's very truly
Eliz Eastlake

Letter to John Murray   *NLS Ms.42178*

7 FitzRoy Square
17 Novr 1886
Dear Mr. Murray

Your specimen page appears to me a very sightly one. Still I am disappointed to find that the pages amount to 380. I think I can shorten it a little more, but not sufficient to be of consequence. I have not seen the Saturday & should be much obliged to you to lend it me. Perhaps you know thro' Dr. Smith that he has sanctioned my reviewing the English work, & I am preparing to do so. He reminds me that Life & Review should appear almost simultaneously. I intended to tell you this in my last note but forgot it. I should make it rather an estimate of S.J.C.'s character than of his works.[1]

How grieved I am that his present chief representative should have had the insult & humiliation of another public trial!

Believe me yr's very truly
Eliz Eastlake
I hear that the Saturday also contains a paper of Layard's N. Gal: article.

1. 'Samuel Coleridge and the Romantic School', *Quarterly Review*, vol. 165 (July 1887), pp. 60–96. This is not the only instance of Elizabeth reviewing her own work. 'Treasures of Art in Great Britain', *Quarterly Review*, vol. 94 (March 1854), pp. 467–508 was a review of Waagen's work that she had translated; and 'Christian Art', *Quarterly Review*, vol. 116 (July 1864), pp. 143–76 was a review of Anna Jameson's *History of Our Lord*, which she had co-written.

Letter to John Murray   NLS Ms.42178

7 FitzRoy Square
10. Decr 1886
Dear Mr. Murray

I received you letter last evening & immediately forwarded your most kind & generous present to Mrs. Burton. As you requested me to do so anonymously I can only the more thank you for her in my own name. I have little doubt that your help & £2 I had sent will avert the disaster she dreaded. He is a painter who ought to maintain his family, for he has plenty of merit. He painted a picture many years ago – exhibited at R: Academy – a duel between a Cavalier & a Roundhead,[1] but he is odd & nervous – which is an expensive quality. I shall be much interested in seeing your "Murray Magazine"
Ever yr's truly
Eliz Eastlake

1. William Shakespeare Burton (1824–1916), *A Wounded Cavalier* (1856), The Guildhall, London.

Letter to John Murray   NLS Ms.42178

7 FitzRoy Square
11 January 1887
Dear Mr Murray

A letter from Prof: Brandl this morning tells me that a large vol: of Coleridge family papers is announced for publication – & that a small biography of Coleridge by "Hall Caine" (as well as I can make out the name) is also announced for this month.[1] Therefore he feels it important that our present work should, if possible, antedate those. I have corrected all the proof I have yet in hand, & if desired can very soon be ready. Meanwhile I am about to send what I have ready to Brandl's friend Mr. Herford at Manchester – who is an alter ego of his – for final supervision, but that shall be no delay.

I have been anxious to get on with my proposed article on Coleridge – as Dr. Smith wrote me it would be desirable that should appear about the same time as my translation. But I could not be ready yet, & if there be anything important in the other works announced I should like to profit by them.

Excuse haste, dear Mr. Murray, yr's very truly
Eliz Eastlake

1. Thomas Henry Hall Caine, *Life of Samuel Taylor Coleridge* (London: Walter
   Scott, 1887).

Letter to A. H. Layard   *NLS Ms.42172*

7 FitzRoy Square
23 Janry 1887

I am quite ashamed, dear Layard, to see the date of your last
unacknowledged letter. All excuses seem empty – but at the same time
there is something nowadays in Christmas & New Year which takes
away one's breath as well as time. We have caught all this folly of trees
& cards from the Germans who seem to have nothing else to do. &
then I wanted to work a little closely, & extricate myself from this
translation of the handsome young man's Life of Coleridge, & what
with visitors & the cold, & increasing age, I have not been so brisk as
I used to be. However I am now correcting proofs. There is no end
apparently to the public interest just now in Coleridge. Two more works
are announced, one taken from the family papers, & as I am preparing
for an article upon him I delay a little in order to include them. He is
a fertile subject, being one of the most extraordinary of men – with
character requiring no common care & thought to analyse – a most
excellent man, without any conception of duty & responsibilities. His
torrents of talk were like some great conjuring performance – nobody
knew how it was done! But all who heard it are unanimous as to
its wonder & charm. Carlyle is the exception in this respect, but his
impartiality is doubtful – dyspeptic men can't be impartial! One thing
Coleridge lacked, & that was <u>ambition</u>, and we can hardly compute the
difference that makes in the way a man shows himself to the world for
that is the moving principle with most distinguished men. One part of
his mind beats me. I cannot comprehend how the same man cd write
such <u>exquisite</u> poetry & such awfully dull, heavy, & clumsy prose, out of
which I can make neither head nor tail. People say it was the laudanum
– of which he is known to have taken a quart in 24 hours – but I fancy
it was all the German metaphysics. He was always groping into his own
mind, until he lost all measure of his neighbour's. Coleridge on <u>Art</u> wd
amuse you!

I have been living very quietly – Miss Lewin with me for a month

before Christmas – but since the New Year I have been alone. I am
glad to hear about the exhibitions which are just now legion, but I
do very well without them myself. I lent Coutts Lindsay the small
chiaroscuro Vandyke (Rinaldo & Armida) which people tell me looks
well. They ought to have put it beneath the large picture, for which it
was evidently a sketch.[1]

I am going slowly thro' Gambier Parry's "Ministry of Art" which
Murray has sent me, & perhaps you also.[2] It is written with great ease,
& with some eloquence – with a happy selection of words. The first
three lives of the work are the key to all, & he is so good an artist that
he speaks from experience. Like all of us, he is getting old.

I am exceedingly interested in your researches on the Massacre of St
Bartholomew, & the obvious desire of the guilty parties to stifle enquiry.
England did apparently nothing more than look askance at the French
Ambassador in the person of that old frump Queen Eliz: – (if you are
one of her admirers I crave pardon) – but she welcomed those who fled,
& the Huguenot Hospital still in our midst is a curious relic. When we
consider the refuge Engld has given to the persecuted form all parts
she deserves a better return than she had received. But the 'charge' by
one of the french bishops to the proscribed priests who fled, like him,
from the French Revolution – which I have read somewhere – filled me
with admiration for his noble courteous gratitude, expressed in beautiful
French. For some time after the Revolution the french works on Engld
are of a high & courteous order – but from about 1830 to quite recently,
indeed to the Filles de John Bull, they have been as scandalous as
mendacious. There is a collection of them in the London Library wh: I
have read.

I hope you will let me know how & where to find your two papers
for the Huguenot Society. I have some Hug: blood in my veins, from
some Martineau great godmother.

Of course here one can't repress the natural interest in politics.
Reeve who was here the other day tells me Ld Ashbourne is a failure,
& havg obtained his peerage cares for nothing else. I don't know
the present Sir Henry Holland enough to know whether he is an
acquisition to the Cabinet – but he is a good lookg man! I cannot
doubt that Goschen will get his election, & he will be a great ally,
power of speakg, habits of business, & some Jewish blood![3] The old
Emperor of Germany does not seem to grow wiser with years – or to
know better the part a Constitutional Monarch shd play. His laments
that the Reich's Tag will not consider <u>his</u> wishes wd be ludicrous if
they were not wicked.

I am always glad to hear that Enid is copying pictures – hoping
to see the results some day. I hear that you are expected not far into
February. Meanwhile we are gettg so many fogs that I hope we shall be
clear by that time! With kindest love to Enid I am ever yr's truly
Eliz Eastlake

1. See letter to Layard, 29 December 1878, n. 3.

2. Thomas Gambier Parry's *The Ministry of Fine Art to the Happiness of Life.
   Essays on Various Arts* was published by John Murray in 1886.

3. George Joachim Goschen (1831–1907), politician and businessman. In January
   1887 he needed a seat to join Lord Salisbury's ministry as Chancellor of the
   Exchequer.

Letter to A. H. Layard   *NLS Ms.42172*

7 FitzRoy Sq
17 Feb: 1887
Dear Layard

I recd the two beautiful volumes on Tuesday evening – <u>very</u> many
thanks for them – as yet I have only looked at the new woodcuts, &
read your preface. It gives me no common pleasure that your name shd
be connected with that of one who loved you well. Every kind & just
word about him goes to my heart. I ought to thank you too for what
you have said of me – only that I feel unworthy to take such a place.[1]
As soon as I have earned a little leisure I shall make it my holiday to
read the new Editioni through. Meanwhile some of the new woodcuts
are beautiful – especially S Augustin, from Vivarini. I am glad to see
two of the Glorious angels by Melozzo. How fine too are the group of
women from Gaudenzio!

I fear such a morning as this must make you hate London

I have read Morelli's <u>Opusculo</u> with much interest & amusement, & I
am perfectly willing to undertake the translation as soon as I get rid of
this translation for Murray, which I ought to do in about a week or so.
It wd give Enid more trouble than it will give me.
Ever dear Layard yrs truly
Eliz Eastlake

1. Layard's new edition of Kugler credits the Eastlakes for their work on earlier
   editions.

Letter to John Murray   *NLS Ms.42178*

7 FitzRoy Square
17 Feb: 1887
Dear Mr. Murray

Your urgings to Clowes make the printers give a spurt, & then lag again. However I have plenty to do between the proofs. I enclose you a letter to me from Prof: Brandl's friend – Mr. Herford – who is revising the slip sheets after my corrections.[1] He is quite an <u>expert</u>, & tho' his suggestions are not of <u>vital</u> importance, yet I recognize their value. You will see what he says about your desire for compression, for, tho' equally desiring it myself, I have laid the responsibility of it on your shoulders! I can only say now, as before, that I believe the work has had the gain of a loss, in the omissions I have made. But there are two classes of Coleridge's admirers – those who enjoy his metaphysics, & those who detest them, & the same work would find it difficult to please both. Still, I think that suff: metaphysical matter to content the one has been preserved.

As the "note book" to which allusion is often made in my text, & the quotations from which Brandl supplied to me in the original English, they seem to me very unimportant & trivial – even when not wild & confused, as of the emanations of opium. Brandl some time ago suggested that you might like to have the entire contents of this "note book" – hitherto unpublished – included in the Engl: vol: I felt this so little desirable, that I did not even consult you.

Now it is a question with me whether, in a preface, to make reference, as Mr. Herford suggests, "to the greater completeness of the original". In that case what would you wish to have said? I conclude also that I ought to translate B's preface, which I have not yet looked at. His headings & chapters I should not have been content with.

But, <u>au bout du compte</u> I can only repeat that I think B's work <u>very</u> good, with thought & felicity of expression. Hall Caine's work has nothing new, & sometimes an unpleasant tone.

I have a few words form Mrs. Wynne Frick – a great friend of Mdme Mohl's – asking me to interest my Athenaeum friends for her son – <u>Mr. Guy L'Estrange</u> – whose election comes on the 21st (next Monday). If there, will you remember him. His proposers are Ld Arthur Russell & Mr. Kinglake. Judging by his mother he must be an interesting man.

I am dear Mr. Murray ever yr's truly
Eliz Eastlake

1. Probably Charles H. Herford, scholar and critical writer, who wrote *Studies in the Literary Relations of England and Germany in the Sixteenth Century* (1886) and *The Age of Wordsworth* (1897).

Letter to John Murray   *NLS Ms.42178*

7 FitzRoy Square
27 Feb: 1887
Dear Mr. Murray

Prof: Brandl's friend, Mr Herford, has been in London & paid me a visit last week. I find that there is a little soreness as to the entailments of the book – doubtless exaggerated by him – as if it were unfair not to acknowledge the fact in some way. I quite agree with you that an acknowledgement of 'incompleteness' in the preface is out of the question, & would be ridiculous – nor have I any intention of adding a translator's preface at all. But one thing perhaps might be done, with your approbation. Suppose the words "slightly abbreviated" were added on the title page – in smallish print. I don't say that I think it in the least necessary, but I do not see what harm it can do. I am sending tomorrow the translation of the Author's Preface to Clowes, which is my last task, so that nothing impedes the work of the printer.

This has been a sad visitation on the beautiful Riviera! & as you have your eldest daughter there I fear you are suffering anxiety. I expect tomorrow morning will bring me tidings from S. Remo.[1]

Instead of returning to his bed, our Prince of Wales would have done better to have dressed & gone down among the frightened people, & assisted by his example to tranquillize them. He has lost a grand opportunity of being thought a hero for life.

I have to thank you for the 3rd No. of the Murray Magazine – but I must really interdict your kindness. If you are so liberal it will never pay!

It is well this anxiety cannot reach your dear wife!

Believe me yr's very truly

Eliz Eastlake

1. The French Riviera was hit by a large earthquake on 23 February, killing 2,000 people. The quake was also felt in San Remo, where Elizabeth's niece, Laura de Rosen, ran a boarding house. The Prince of Wales was in Cannes.

Letter to John Murray   *NLS Ms.42178*

7 FitzRoy Square
19 March 1887
Dear Mr. Murray

You are very kind to antedate your cheque even by a few days, for I hope it may not be much more before the Life of Coleridge is really out. And I hope still more that the public will like it. I really think they will, for Brandl has done his best, & so have I. I am progressing slowly with the article – no slight task, for there never was a stranger character or life. And no one can write about him so as to please both parties – each extreme of its kind. But from what I can gather from university men I am not inclined to echo the extravagant assertion that he has moulded the thought of England. In politics he did latterly much, but in theology & moral philosophy he appears to have been merely eccentric.

Believe me yr's very truly
Eliz Eastlake

1. 'Samuel Coleridge and the Romantic School', *Quarterly Review*, vol. 165 (July 1887), pp. 60–96.

Letter to A. H. Layard   *NLS Ms.42172*

7 FitzRoy Square
Easter Sunday 1887
My dear Layard

You kindly invited me, if I understand you rightly, to give you my opinion on "the new Reformation" by Canon Fremantle in the March *Fortnightly*. I have heard it much abused but havg just read it I am not disposed to join in the abuse. Nothing stands still in this world, & I have lived long eno' to see that good has become better. Still, it is rather startling to see liberties openly taken which a few only have been quietly holding, & wh: may give alarm to the many who are not yet ready, tho' another generation will be. The comfort & stay of a religion in wh: the holder has been brought up is hard to relinquish. Like as with the enfranchisement of serfs it is best to make it gradual by making only the newborn first free. This is my general view in such questions, individually, I have long held certain so called 'broad' ideas,

wh: the Canon defends; while others appear to me unimportant. I have
long scorned the idea of Eternal Punishment as more insulting to the
Supreme Being than cruel to His creatures. The value of miracles has
also long been decling. Christ Himself evidently not valuing them &
only impelled to them because "unless ye see signs & wonders ye will
not believe". But, as to who the books of the Scriptures are <u>by</u> seems
to me very unimportant. Their internal merit is the only question
worth considerg. That St Paul's Epistles are glorious things there can
be no doubting, nor that the <u>Saul</u> who was raging against the new sect
of Xtians can only have been so suddenly converted by a <u>miracle</u>. But
the Epistle to the Hebrews is too fine & helpful to poor human nature
in parts for me to care who it is by. Those who require further literal
inspiration of every word there is no argument at all with. A misprint,
if it be but 'in the Bible' wd be sacred in their eyes, & there have been
strange misprints – especially one in the Commandments, wh: I daresay
you know all about!

Dear old Milman gave me a little printed answer he had been obliged
to make to some one who charged him with unorthodox ideas – it
simply explains his conviction that things were not true because found
in Holy Writ, but Holy Writ was true because certain thing stand in it.
The command to love our enemies is one those things. But I have heard
Milman harshly censured by your friend Mr Murray years ago for the
religious unsoundness of his History of the Jews.[1] On readg that work
afterwards I was amazed at its beauty & piety. As the level of sound
truth gradually rises it is only the few who are uppermost, & they get
the kicks! Still, I am not disposed to approve of a Bradlaugh in our
Parlt.

I have not had time to read yr beloved Miss Robinson yet but I will
do so carefully.

I had a visit today form yr young friend Mr Reid, & rather take to
him now, wh: I did not at first. I suppose I did not think him good
looking enough! His sister is probably going to join Jessie Lewin in a
short trip to Italy, the week after next. Lookg to see you & Enid before
you take flight I am ever
Yr's truly
Eliz Eastlake

1. Milman's *The History of the Jews*, 3 vols. (London: John Murray, 1830)
   had been a controversial publication when it first appeared. There were
   subsequent editions.

Letter to Cosmo Monkhouse[1]   *Author's Collection*

7 FitzRoy Square
10 June 1887
Dear Mr. Monkhouse

Your little volume is a pleasing surprize to me, & I thank you sincerely for sending it to me.[2] Few works cd interest me more deeply, for, as you well know, Sir Chas Eastlake was the chief purchaser of the Trecentisti & Quattro-Centristi for the Nat: Gallery- & almost every one you mention takes me back into the past. He felt it necessary for the gallery to have there early masters, & most of them were supplied by the Lombardi Baldi Collection. The plates are perfect as to drawing, being taken from photographs, tho' much of them from that cause darker than the originals. Our old household God – the Annunciation by Fra Filippo – is charming.

I have read the little vol: through & find the style as attractive as it is unconventional. I see that you have greatly progressed in the study of art since you undertook yr delightful vol: in honor of Sir Chas. I see that you are puzzled as to the real master of Antonello da Messina. That has been solved by the gentleman who wrote the Handbook of the Netherlandish School – Mr. Weale[3] – Vasari interpreted 'Gio: da Bruggia' as Jan Van Eyck – but the real Gio: da Bruggia was Jan Memling, & he doubtless was Antonello's master. Indeed their styles have something in common.

I am sure the little book will be very popular. I am now going to send for 2 copies – one for Sir H. Layard, the other for Mrs. Richard Boyle (E.V.B.)

I am now an old woman & confined to a wheelchair, but I should be at any time glad to see you & hear your remarks on the pictures with wh: I am surrounded.

With renewed thanks believe me yr's truly
Eliz Eastlake

1. William Cosmo Monkhouse (1840–1901), English poet and critic and regular contributor to the periodical press. He wrote *Pictures by Sir Charles Eastlake* (London: Virtue, Spalding & Co., 1875).

2. *The Italian Pre-Raphaelite Painters* (London: Cassell & Co., 1887).

3. William Weale (1832–1917), art historian and writer on Flemish art and resident of Bruges.

Letter to John Murray   *NLS Ms.42178*

7 FitzRoy Square
June 24. 1887
Dear Mr. Murray

I have not seen the Athenaeum, & certainly have no wish to read it.[1] My conscience acquits me of even the slightest carelessness of work – tho' it might be easy perhaps to prove that the translation is not verbatim. I should only be sorry anything should injure the success of the work for your sake. If any gratification to you I can quote the following remarks by the author, in a letter to me on receiving the English copy. "28 May 1887. I have recd the English edition of my book, & must say it must have caused you a vast amount of thought & labour. It is excellent reading indeed, & often you have been wonderfully happy in hitting upon the proper English expression for some awkwardly racy German word. One fruit is certain the book cannot be ignored" ... & again "I should be proud if I had some day to offer you another book of mine to translate, & if you had again the courage to take it up". "Admiring your patience I am dear Lady" &c &c. Also he asks for my photograph "For may I betray to you that my parents & many of my friends have a strong desire to see the face of my clever & accomplished translator".

I attach no importance to compliments, but at all events these extracts suffice to prove that the man most interested in the fidelity of the translation is satisfied.

Just now the Athenaeum has arrived, sent, I know not by whom. I have set my niece Miss de Rosen – who is with me – to read it, & she reports that the writer abuses the author as much as the translator, decidedly it is worthy of no notice from you. Tho' of course I leave you to do as you think best.

How thankful the country may be that the 21st was in every sense such a success, & our brave Lady not overpowered with her enormous duties.[2]

Ever dear Mr. Murray
Yr's truly
Eliz Eastlake

1. Review of Brandl's *Life of Coleridge* in the *Athenaeum*, no. 3112 (18 June 1887), pp. 791–94. The reviewer itemizes numerous mistakes and remarks that 'the amount of blundering is incredible' (p. 79).

2. The Queen's Golden Jubilee.

Letter to Dr William Smith[1]   *NLS Ms.42178*

7 FitzRoy Square
28 June 1887
My dear Dr. Smith

I am much obliged by your kind letter. Also glad that you have decided to retain the article for next month. I had come too to the conclusion that, as all the petty criticism of the Athenaeum did not in any way impugn the sense of judgements of the work, & as my article in no way <u>puffed</u> Herr Brandl, my limited praise being entirely confined by the Athenaeum itself, there was no real antagonism between that article & mine. But I own myself much vexed & disappointed by the author's great inaccuracies. How many I corrected <u>en chemin</u>[2] it would be impossible to say!

Now I have written to Mr. Herford on some of the queries you have put in the revise. The quotation from Cowper about robbing "a poor bird of her young" I will answer for, only I must place it as I have done here above. "who could rob a poor bird of her young" is the literal line. I almost thought that he had a different version of Coleridge's poems to mine.

You tell me to expect another copy of this revise. I hope it will be that which I corrected about a week ago with my corrected proof – if not, perhaps you will direct Clowes to send it me. The additional extract from Brandl to which you refer is not included in the Revise (as far as p.20) which I revised this afternoon. I need not assure you that I gratefully adopt all your recommendations & shall do the same by all that are yet to come.

Ever dear Mr. Smith
Your's truly
Eliz Eastlake

1. Dr William Smith (1813–93), lexicographer and editor of the *Quarterly Review.*

2. French, 'on the way'.

Letter to John Murray   NLS Ms.42178

7 FitzRoy Square
6 July 1887
Dear Mr. Murray

I hope you have not been seriously annoyed by the review of Brandl in the Athenaeum. It seems to me much ado abouth nothing, or about very little, while in itself it is very ill natured & malicious, & also inaccurate – for I have detected two instances in which the translation is <u>right</u>, &, had more pages been given, should doubtless detect many more. Brandl also, in Athenaeum 2 July stoutly denies the reviewer's accuracy. Still I do not defend his own inaccuracies. He says also that he "carefully copied out the original words of all the quotations, trusting they would be as carefully inserted". I cannot tax myself with the slightest infringement of that trust, but I do not intend to disturb myself or him by any dispute upon the subject. All the proofs passed thro' his friend Mr. Hereford's hands & more could be done to insure justice to him.

I hear of favourable reviews & hope also that the forthcoming Q.R. article may a little undo the effects of the reviewer's malice. I cannot sufficiently say how kind & amicable Dr. Smith has been, for altogether the article has given him much trouble.

I hope the two showers of rain have done Wimbledon good.

On the 28th of this month I go to house at Windsor which I have taken for a few weeks, which will enable me to be much with my sister, who is not so well as I could wish.

Ever your's truly
Eliz Eastlake

I remember being told some years ago that no one attached any importance to the dicta of the Athenaeum.

Letter to John Murray   NLS Ms.42178

7 FitzRoy Square
8 July 1887
Dear Mr. Murray

I have written to Brandl – being glad of the excuse, & have enclosed the cuttings you sent me. I make no doubt that your suspicion about Mr. Hall Caine is true. I thought his a vulgarly written book, & we

know that the immense <u>business</u> nowadays of review writing gives
sometimes occasion for private pique. I read the reviews, which are a
fair specimen of better & worse.

The quotation of "The Coming Man &c" is from 'Paradise
Regained'. I met with it as a quotation. I have written to Dr. Smith.

I have this morning recd a proof of my Webster article from Mr.
Arnold.[1] He has inserted what I left out, viz: my signature. I hope you
will be satisfied with E.E. which is all I have given on several occasions
in the Encyclopaedia Brit: – & is just as identifying.

Your's very truly
Eliz Eastlake

1. 'Thomas Webster, R.A.', *Murray's Magazine*, vol. 2 (July–December 1887),
   pp. 222–31.

Letter to A. H. Layard   *NLS Ms.42172*

7 FitzRoy Square
14 July 1887
Dear Layard

My visit to the Nat: Gal: stands as it did for tomorrow (Friday), but
by Chas Eastlake's advice I am to come in by the back entrance in
'Hemming's Row' where there is a <u>lift</u>, which will transport me to the
Gallery level. I am only sorry to lose the help of my handsome Carter,
who unfortunately will not be required! But pray do you & Morelli
not give me a thought till you find me in the Early Italian room or
elsewhere.

It will be an immense treat for me. I shall have my maid with me to
drive me about.[1]

Ever your's truly
Eliz Eastlake

1. Enid Layard's journal records: 'At 12 Henry and I went in hansom to
   the National Gallery to meet Lady Eastlake, Mr. C. Eastlake, Morelli and
   Frizzone. It was the first time I had been there since the new staircase and
   rooms had opened and was very much struck with the excellence of the
   arrangements. Lady Eastlake was wheeled about in a chair and surrounded
   by her friends enjoyed herself very much. There were many of the late
   purchases she had never seen as for 3 or 4 years she has been unable to
   walk' (Enid Layard's Journals, Vol. 10, BL Add MS 46162, Friday 15 July
   1887).

Letter to John Murray   NLS Ms.42178

2 Park Street, Windsor
13 Aug: 1887
Dear Mr. Murray

I am much gratified by Sir W. Farquhar's kind opinion of my article on Coleridge – though I hardly expected that any admirer of his would think that I had done him justice, for I take small notice of his metaphysics, of which I can't make head or tail. I quite agree with Sir Walter that his letter to his godson is most touching & beautiful. I know it well – it is either in Mr. Traill's or Mr. Hall Cayne's [sic] life of him. I advised Brandl to wind up his work with it, but he thought it superfluous. It seems to pair with a letter from S.J.C. (in his most doubting time) to Lamb, at the time of the terrible Lamb catastrophe.[1] I should be very glad to see it embodied in a 2nd Edition – if you can get rid of suff: copies of the old edition.

I have not heard from Brandl since you were kind eno' to send him the Q.R. which doubtless was addressed to Prague, whereas he had gone to Innsbruck. But he returns to Prague after holidays.

I am in a comfortable house belonging to Mr. Holmes, the Queen's librarian – whom I knew in old times in the British Museum.

I had a letter the other day from from Sydney.[2] He describes the colony as in a distressing state, from the numbers of the unemployed. If things be so depressed he ought to get land cheaper, which I conclude he will try to do. He did not ask for a remittance which I am ready to send whenever he does.

I return you Sir Walter's letters, having made a note of Prof: Shairp's work – which is one I do not think I know, also the pages to which he refers.
Believe me dear Mr. Murray
Yr's very truly
Eliz Eastlake

1. Charles Lamb's sister Mary stabbed their mother.

2. John Murray and Elizabeth had given their mutual nephew Donald Rigby Smith £100 to assist him in settling in New South Wales. Letters to John Murray NLS Ms.42178 dated 24 December 1886 and 5 April 1887 discuss his prospects. Springall embellishes this story, telling of a relative seeking £1,000 to set himself up in Australia but becoming an actor and going bankrupt (Stephen Springall, *That Indomitable Old Lady: A Romance of Fitzroy Square* [London: Henry J. Drane Ltd, 1908], pp. 325–29).

Letter to A. H. Layard   NLS Ms.42172

7 FitzRoy Sqre
16. Octr 1887
My dear Layard

I was truly glad to get your kind letter, written from Queen Anne Street the day before you started for Venice, & I am rather ashamed not to have thanked you for it sooner. But what with getting home again, short as the journey was, & finding plenty to do here I have fancied myself very busy. I hope the monkey & the parrot & the other nobler animals arrived safe under yr escort at the dear old Ca' Capello, which I understand it now painted red & covered with creepers, till it has the prettiest front in Venice. My Windsor time answered very well in seeing much of a sister who lives there, in getting beautiful drives, & in having the spare rooms perpetually filled. One handsome young man was with me a month – the sketching of old houses being the attraction.

I shd indeed have liked to hear your experiences in Ireland. Surely the English people are the most patient, & the English govt. the most pottering, to go on dawdling with such a mass of crime & rebellion. These are the abuses of liberty & the follies of humanity. People talk of there being a traitor in the Cabinet, of that I don't believe a word, but there seem strange mistakes in their management. But English people have seen worse times than this, tho' none precisely like it. The outlook here in London is bad eno', with winter comg on, & even honest workmen out of employ.

I have not seen many friends yet. Lady De Gex came to me the other day, & told me much about herself. She mourns the kind little old man very sincerely, but does not refust to be comforted, & spent a few weeks in Switzerland. She seems to have recd much true respect & sympathy from many membersof the Bar, especially from old Vice Chancellor Bacon.

I am much interested in hearing that you are to join the Crown Prince & our Pss in the Tyrol. Alas! from two sources I hear depressing accounts of him. The one from Morelli, who writes to a young lady protégée of his that the Prince's altered appearance has made a most sorrowful impression on him. The other from Dr. Frank – the well known Cannes Dr. – who shakes his head at Dr. M. Mackenzie's hopes. One shrinks from carryg out these fears to their ultimate conclusions. What royal couple ever seemed more destined by Providence to bless a land which so much needs humane & liberal institutions! The blighting of such a prospect is a loss to the world. I shall be very anxious to hear

what you & Enid think of him, & of her poor Lady! Meanwhile I hope
your 'Scandalous Adventures' will be sufficiently forward for you to give
Murray a sample for his publisher's dinner. But I think the booksellers
might take them on faith. I should. I suppose you know something of
Morelli's protégée! A pretty young lady – a Miss Ffoulkes – with an
enthusiasm for Italian art, & some for <u>him</u> too I think.[1] He sent me a
German letter the other day introducing her, & I have had two visits
from her. She is bringing out an improved catalogue of the Dresden
Gallery, in which he has much assisted her. She has got a publisher of
the name of Allen to undertake it, for a rather stiff consideration. It is
too bad of Morelli to be engaging a young lady's affections under cover
of teaching her how to view Art! I am sure a hint to you to chaff him
on this point will be enough. Talking of catalogues when is yr beloved
Sir Fred: going to produce his?

I have no errands for you or kind Enid in Venice, except to bid
you undertake a real history of Venice, wh: at present does not exist.
I saw eno' under dear old Rawdon Brown's lead to convince me what
untouched materials there exist. If I were younger I shd like nothing
better than to undertake such a vindication. And you are a mere <u>laddie</u>
yet. With a little industry you might finish it before Sir Fred: his
catalogue!! I know you like this subject & only the end of my paper
prevents my continuing.

With kindest love to Enid
Ever yr's truly
Eliz Eastlake

1. Constance Jocelyn Ffoulkes translated Morelli's *Italian Painters* and co-wrote
   a book on Vincenzo Foppa in 1909.

Letter to John Murray   *NLS Ms.42178*

7 FitzRoy Square
25 Octr 1887

Many thanks dear Mr. Murray, for your faithful recollection of my
special infirmity, in the shape of finest Ripstone [sic] pippins![1] I had
some from the same tree last year, & am glad to see how favourable this
season has been to it. You are wise to be keeping still to Wimbledon, &
to postpone our fags as long as you can.

I have been intending for the last few days to write to Mr. Arnold.
That book of "Mit Heilungen" you sent me has created a revolution

in my article on Casper Hauser – making it more interesting & more – much more difficult. However I am working away, & fancy he will divide it between two numbers. I fear I may not be ready even for December but I will write & tell him. I have commissioned Rolandi to get me two more works on C.H: which I feel to be important.[2]

As to Lord Stanhope I should like to know in what way he showed his eccentricity in England, but I have not found any occasion to impugn his honour or liberality in his dealings with Casper Hauser. Though your friends the Germans abused him.

I hope you are all well

Ever yr's truly

Eliz Eastlake

1. There are letters to John Murray each autumn thanking him for the Ribstone pippins from his orchard at Newstead.

2. As source material for her article 'Kaspar Hauser', *Quarterly Review*, vol. 166 (April 1888), pp. 469–95.

Letter to A. H. Layard   *NLS Ms.42172*

7 FitzRoy Sqre

30 Novr 1887

It is high time, dear Layard, your last letter dated Octr 31, to acknowledge it. It was a very interestg letter, with its many subjects of importance, & I have often recurred to it. Foremost in interest is that engross.g subject in wh: I am sure our thoughts often meet – the state of the noble Crown Prince. He is truly cared about in his wife's country & the papers are eagerly searched for the accounts of him. One must be thankful for this delay in his symptoms, during which he & our Princess may be said to be almost enjoyg a period of rest, in each other's company. If ever one cd long for a miracle it is now, instead of which the world has to face a completion of ills in wh: the future for Germany appears darker than ever. Had the vain ignorant old Emperor – who I see has been admonishing the Reichsath to behave better than they did last year & vote his army more money – had the sense to abdicate 20, or at least 10 years ago, he might have redeemed the mistakes of his reign. A letter from the Prince Consort to him in Theo: Martin's life calls him to account for not performg his promises to his subjects. You & "Aunt Enid" doubtless hear often from head quarters. I was amused the other day by hearing from Mrs Hallam Murray, who had expected a guinea

from me for some charitable concert, that the Prince was busy readg yr
new Edition of Kugler! More in her line than his I shd think.

I sympathize with you in the completion of yr 'Scandalous
Adventures' for wh: the world is impatiently lookg.[1] The contents ooze
out a little thro' Mr Murray, whose enthusiasm & admiration make
him less reticent than usual. Kind old Dr. Wm Smith was here last
Sunday, & repeated some of the adventures wh: Murray has retailed to
him. They were scandalous in a way but I hope Enid has left us more
scandalous ones to come. I well know the rest after a great literary
execution, & I well know too that you will soon tire of it, & long for
further work & victories. I am experiencing just now rather the reverses
that I had got up, with the Editor's concurrence a thorough acct of
that mysterious being, on whom no light has ever been thrown, Casper
Hauser. It is a long story, & there are above 30 German works upon
it. I warned him that it wd be long but now after keeping it 3 weeks
he returns it me today, under the plea that it is too long. There is no
reason why he shd not cut in in halves, especially as he gives me a deal
of soft sawder upon its interest & excellence. So I am rather savage, &
must think wh: of the many magazines going will give it a place.

You don't in the least convince me by yr reasons for not undertaking
a history of Venice. Instead of being too old I shd say you are just the
right age, havg come now to those years of discretion wh: I shd think
you were long in attaining. As to young Horace Brown he is far too
young, & has not yet the grasp of mind necessary for such as subject, if
ever he reaches it.

You must be amused at the state of Trafalgar Sqre has been in of
late. The consequence is an immense enthusiasm for the Police force,
& now for "the Specials". I have several friends in it, & among them a
worthy General – not much above 60 – who chafes at inaction & takes
the command of a hundred men. He tells me there are some splendid
young fellows in it. Chas Eastlake, on the worst Sunday, took up a place
of vantage at the Gallery & witnessed the various encounters with great
interest. The next Sunday he took his wife, who was quite disappointed
to find the Square comparatively quiet. Your beloved Sir Fred: (what
on earth was he knighted for? for not doing the catalogue?) seems to
think prudence the better part of valour, & does not appear. I have been
greatly gratified of late by hearing of two houses from wh: his rude
ways have banished him. At each the conversation turned upon pictures,
& he seemed to think it a personal affront that he was appealed to.

I am now shut up for the winter, nothing loth, & have to depend
upon the kindness of friends who come to me. I have just parted with
Miss Martin, a grand niece of Mdme Mohl. If you have not recd Mr

Simpson's life of that original old lady, it wd interest you & Enid.[2] I
have just finished readg a rather old work – Hooker & Ball's Morocco.
Considering that I know nothing of botany I was delighted to find it so
interesting. But what a pity that so far a portion of this earth & such a
beautiful climate shd be worse than wasted on a brutal government! It
ought to be the sanatorium of Europe.

I am feeling interest in the conferences upon Fair Trade, & the Sugar
bounties, & have been much struck by an axiom of Sir Ed Sullivan in
a long letter to the Morng Post, that cheap living & low prices are no
sign of prosperity, but rather of the reverse – witness Ireland, & other
degraded parts of the globe. I am not a great consumer of <u>jam</u>, so I am
all for retaliatory duties on beet sugar. Indeed if I were a poor man I
wd far rather pay more for bread & earn more wages & have constant
work. I know too that Adam Smith does not advocate free trade for
the foreigners, & protection for ourselves. Dr. William Smith had lately
seen a rich Frankfort merchant who cd not conceal his astonishment &
derision at our persistence in benefiting the foreigners at our own grave
expense, tho' very glad we do persist in so doing.

Now dear Layard, I must have sent you to sleep, so I will only beg
my love to Enid & remain your's every truly

Eliz Eastlake

1. Layard's *Early Adventures in Persia, Susiana, and Babylonia* was published by
John Murray in 1887.

2. M. C. M. Simpson, *Letters and Recollections of Julius and Mary Mohl* (London:
K. Paul, Trench & Co., 1887).

Letter to A. H. Layard   *NLS Ms.42172*

7 FitzRoy Sqre
Christmas Day 1887
My dear Layard

Christmas cards & notes are flying about, & have been for the last
few days, & I have been too much interrupted to write you the long
'yarns' which have accumulated since I received your 'Early Adventures'.
I only wish they had been double as long, for after living with you at
every spare moment or half hour for a week I felt quite lonely when
I came to the end. Murray did not say too much, by this time you
know from the reviews how enthusiastically the work is recd. The
only wonder is that you lived to tell such tales. I was obliged to stop

& remind myself that you really had not perished by treachery, hunger
or fatigue or nakedness, but had to my certain knowledge been in a
flourishg condition for years, before I cd turn over the next page & see
what it brought. Wd that I cd have the same consolation regardg many
of those with whom you were thrown! Those sinning & sinned-against
fellow creatures, with their strong contrasts of good & bad – ruled by
such demons as Metameh! The poetry of yr work is the character &
fate of the noble Bachtijari's chief, & the poor Khanum! Nor did your
subsequent information about them relieve my mind. One can hardly
enjoy one's own liberty & laws while knowing what fair portions of
this earth & what noble souls languish under such tyranny. I am by no
means an enemy to Mahommedamism – but his followers no more obey
his teaching than too many Christians do that of Christ. Your generous
Jew at Tiberias refreshed my heart. I am glad it has thro' life given
you a kindly feeling for the race. There are plenty of pictures in yr
description wh: wd do for the R. Academy – but yr Lazarus condition
at the Gate of Bagdad is the one I shd suggest. Your adventures fit
in perfectly to those of Hooker & Ball wh: I had just been readg (in
Morocco) – all the same vile tale of wicked oppression & misrule. Of
course I am disappointed not to find anything in the shape of scandal –
but suppose that was Enid's fault! One finds plenty of one characteristic
wh: if you live to 100 you will never lose. Dear old Sir John de Gex
said to me once "Layard is always the boy" I am not sure that he did
not add "the naughty boy" but I won't vouch for that. And after all
yr adventures by mountain & plain your arrival & reception & time at
Constantinople are by no means the least interestg part. I knew Lord
& Lady Stratford – & if Mr Cartwright was afterwards our Minister at
Stockholm I have known him too.

I have only space to thank you for yr kind & immediate response
to my question about 'Temper' in Italian & Spanish. Your Italian has
helped me much. Spanish is I understand "corto di genio' wh: I suppose
I may translate as 'short of sense'.

I hear that Ld Lyon's supposed conversion to Popery is strenuously
contradicted by those who knew him best. Now let me congratulate you
on the approaching visit of Mr Gladstone to Venice! How he will talk
about Art when he returns!

I keep Xmas to-morrow when a few relatives includg Chas Eastlake
& wife dine with me. All good wishes to you & Enid, & my love to
her.

    Ever dear Layard
    Yr's truly
    Eliz Eastlake

Letter to Frances Power Cobbe   *HL CB400*

7 FitzRoy Square
12 Febry 1888
Dear Miss Cobbe

When I first read your "In the long run" in the September
"Zoophilist" (& I have read it twice since) I determined to take
the liberty of writing to you. But reasons which seem now of no
consequence came in the way, & I have slumbered on till now, when
the perusal of yr article in the Fortnightly leaves me no peace until I
venture to express to you the exceeding admiration with which both
these papers have impressed me. The subjects to which they are devoted
are calculated to inspire most good heads & still better hearts, but they
are treated by you in a style which seems the happiest now before the
public. The growth & movement of our Country goes on at such a
gigantic pace nowadays that we are doubly bound to be grateful to the
very few who are able to explain & direct them, & to explain & expose,
as it may be, the cruelty the sophistry & the mistake. Especially are the
questions of the education of our lower classes important.

I am delighted with the view you take of the moral evil of our
great hospitals – an evil which only drags them down into the most
indefensible debt, & which tends to weaken what appears to me to be
gradually disappearing for those already infected. With a hearty wish
that you may long have health given you to keep & teach us I remain
dear Lady your's very truly
Eliz Eastlake

Letter to A. H. Layard   *NLS Ms.42172*

7 FitzRoy Sqre
25. March 1888
My dear Layard

It is indeed long since I have troubled you with a letter. Your last
to me dated Janry 6 was very interesting – partly about your 'Early
Adventures', my enjoyment of which has not gone off. I was amused
by my cousin Reeve's remarks upon them. He was astonished that you
had not retailed them in London society for the general entertainment,
& was evidently greatly taken by surprise at yr <u>modesty</u>! Meanwhile as
I knew not where to find you I have not attempted to write, tho' my

thoughts have constantly followed Enid & you, especially in yr visit to
S. Remo. What a change has since occurred to the object of so much
interest & anxiety! wd that it were as favorable in health as in position!
However these two noble beings are now at last in their right place, &
brief as the term may be it cannot fail to do good. It has rejoiced me so
much that I have borne with the more patience the absurd mendacious
adulation lavished by our press upon the wretched old Emperor, who,
has he seen himself as many besides my humble self have seen him, wd
have abdicated in favor of his son 20 years ago. I knew a good deal of
him from our old friend Waagen. The two sides of the Times upon
him, printed between mourning lines, are believed to have been written
by a German, & translated for the Times. I follow every word that
proceeds now from the present Emperor, & perceive significant signs of
walking in the old paths but with a difference. It is an immense thing
for the new Sovereign & the new Empress to gain time. I can imagine
how Enid & you are engrossed with this subject.

Chas Eastlake tells me of yr kind mention of me in yr letter to him,
from Naples I think. I am sorry to say he has been very unwell of late
so as to be asbsent from the N.G. for some days. Our hopes delaying
long winter made many 'sick' [sic]. I saw him last Sunday & he & his
wife were hopg to go to Brighton for a week. I keep quite well, because
I keep strictly at hom but I am heartily tired of the monotonously bad,
raw, Eastwind.

I have been readg rather a jumble of books lately. Ld Shaftesbury – a
rather narrow man but a magnificent career going from abuse to abuse
& fighting them in turn with marvellous patience & persistence till they
gave way – the little shoeblack brigade remaining one of the monuments
to him. Then I have had Darwin's Life – I am sure I should have liked
the man, but I am not sure that I endorse his 'origin of species'. I had
my cousin Hooker & his nice wife with me last week. Darwin's Life
is partly his life, which may be the reason why he owned to being
heartily tired of it. Hooker with his simplicity & modesty is delightful
company. His first family were the dullest childn in the world, now
he has got two little clever boys wh: are the apple of his eye. When
here I made him look thro' a list of Venetian flora which I have in the
big work compounded 'I.Dotti' but he could find nothing peculiar.
I did this because good Dr. Smith[1] wishes me to write an article on
Venice, & I am anxious to read all that I can, as well as brush up old
knowledge. For this purpose you must prepare yourself to be asked
many a question en route, & shd you have or know of any historical 'tit
bits' which dear old Brown used to promise me if ever I came back to
Venice, I shall have time to procure them. Or if you have such, & will

entrust them to me, you might send them by the Hallam Murrays, who, I understand, leave London tomorrow to spend a fortnight at the Ca' Capello. Above all I want to beg or borrow, for it cannot be bought, that book containing the old Minutes of Council from the Earliest time, beginning in doglatin & merging into Venetian Vernacular which was printed at Ruskin's expense. Doubtless you know it. In the collection of dictionaries made by dear Sir Charles is a very grand 2 vols of the Venetian dialect. I have set my heart on the use of that vol:. One of the pegs for the article wd be Mrs Oliphant's "Makers of Venice", a rather flimsy tho' agreeably written book, the worst part of which is perhaps the title, for neither sailors not soldiers were the makers of Venice, but Liberty & Commerce, & Position.

You did not send me yr papers on the St Bartholomew Massacre, & the Revocation of the Edict of Nantes, but I shall be delighted to have them. Your account of the Ven: documents about the Jews interests me much. It wd make a paragraph in my article; even if it does not make an article of itself in yr hands. I am looking into my cousin Gifford Palgrave's work. "Ulysses" rather a presumptious title! It is written well, but rather too much like himself to interest me, no vain main is interesting in a woman's eyes.

You will be havg Miss Jessie Lewin soon for a few days in Venice, & she will be sure to make her way to the Ca'. A younger married sister, Mrs Howe, will be with her. I shd think they will be in Venice in about a fortnight.

Now, dear Layard, I have inflicted a long letter on you, & must bid you goodbye. With kind love to Enid believe me ever yrs truly Eliz Eastlake

1. Dr William Smith, editor of the *Quarterly Review*.

Letter to Bessie Rayner Belloc[1]   GC GBR/0271/GCPP
Parkes 9/133

7 FitzRoy Square
14 April 1888
Dear Madame Belloc,
Pray accept the assurance of my gratitude for your recollection of me, as well as for the capital notice of our old friend Mrs. Proctor. It is admirably written & has no fault except its brevity. I did indeed know & delight in that remarkable lady, tho' since my great lameness & her

increasing years we had not met. I wrote to her on Edythe's death &
she promised me a visit but did not come. But I echo all words on her
kindness to her friends of whom I was proud to be one. She was rare
in many respects. With deep feeling she had not a woman's ready &
dangerous resource – <u>emotion</u>. She had singular self command, nothing
threw her off her balance, & for this reason her <u>advice</u> was invaluable.

I am glad to hear of your interest in my Father's Letters from France.
They are unique of their kind, for there are no other private English
letters of that critical time, & Arthur Young had left Paris. The older I
grow the more am I surprized to have had a dear father, born in <u>1747</u>.
And that reminds me that Priestley – driven from England to America
by public violence – was my father's Schoolmaster! he was at Priestley's
Academy in Warrington, &, as far as I am aware, at no other place of
instruction.
Again thanking you I am your's very truly
Eliz Eastlake

1. Bessie Rayner Belloc, née Parkes (1829–1925), writer and journalist, granddaughter of Joseph Priestley. Madame Belloc later recalled: 'Lady Eastlake
   possessed a stalwart intellect, with no softening haze about it. She disliked
   the literature of passion, even on the nobler levels of Jane Eyre, and had a
   firm grip of the morals of Christianity; holding orthodox opinions, which
   always seemed to me to have been sincerely reasoned out in some past mental
   epoch, without penetrating the fibre of her mind'. Bessie Rayner Belloc, *A
   Passing World* (London: Ward & Downey, 1897), p. 11.

Letter to John Murray   *NLS Ms.42178*

7 FitzRoy Square
12. June 1888
Dear Mr. Murray
I have to thank you for the most beautiful flowers I have seen, & yet
kind friends have kept me well supplied. But your rhodadendrens beat
all others. Very many thanks. They are great delights to me.
I was intending to write to you today about a little point connected
with the history of Saml. Rogers. I hear that his 'Jacqueline' was
published in the same vol: with Byron's 'Lara'. The first edition of each.
Did that answer? & was there subsequently any ill feeling between the
two? Your Father told me once – & I forget nothing he said – that on
Lara's appearance in a single form, Mr. Rogers was calling in Albemarle
St & your Father gave him a copy. But that on leaving the room

Rogers dropped it & left it behind. Can you account for this act? Was it jealousy? Or pique that it was then published alone. I know that Rogers was proud of Byron's letters to him which lay in a case on his drawing table.

I have been looking thro' Claydon's [sic] 1st vol: of Roger's Life – not particularly well done.[1] & do you remember any instance of Roger's severe severe [sic] tongue? I must own that I remember nothing but kindness from him, & culture of taste.

You must be enjoying your country retreat. I hope to get to Albury next month.

Your's very truly

Eliz Eastlake

1. P. W. Clayden, *The Early Life of Samuel Rogers* (London: Smith, Elder & Co., 1887). Elizabeth reviewed the work in 'Reminiscences of Samuel Rogers', *Quarterly Review*, vol. 167 (October 1888), pp. 504–13.

Letter to A. H. Layard   *NLS Ms.42172*

7 FitzRoy Sqre

29. June 1888

Dear Layard

The death of Mrs. Austin [sic] of which I recd tiding this morning puts an end to my delay in writing to you. I feel that I want to speak of her to some one who knew & loved her. Mr. Harding the co-executor with your brother was kind eno' to write & inform me that she had passed away yesterday. Everest soon followed with a message left at the door – while the Times conveys the tidings to every one.[1] One can only be thankful that the long period of mere patient existence has terminated. She is preserved in my memory as a beautiful & brilliant woman, & no one could be kinder to me than she was, & ever to my aged Mother whom she used to see here. Altho' her mind has been so long eclipsed I know you will feel her death much, & so will Enid.

And then the Emperor's death! Inevitable as it was & a real mercy to a noble sufferer, but one had become accustomed to his lingering state, & while there was life one fancied there was hope. Those three months of power & pain in Berlin will hereafter appear like a dream to the bereaved Empress. You are doubtless in communication with her, &, if not too presuming or awkward, I should like her to know how deeply I mourn the noblest man of his place & time & how intensely I feel for her. He & she have had the prayers of the English nation,

& she has them still. Every word from the present young Emperor is closely scrutinized now, & I must say his proclamation & recent address to his Parliament have a confident & even braggish tone which jars on the minds of many. I am determined to take no interest in the coming history of Prussia under his rule, & so spare myself useless distress.[2] By this time you have perhaps seen Sir Morell Mackenzie, for the Times said that he was going straight to Norway to recruit after the double tension of mind & body. He can doubtless tell much which wd not improve our opinion of the upper German classes. I have been long crying in the Wilderness against them.

I have not much to tell you from my quiet life. Of course I have been busy, but not so exclusively upon Venetian subjects as I could have wished. I was tempted off from it to recall some reminiscences of Rogers, for a periodical which I won't mention for the present lest my article shoud fail to be approved. He ws an old friend of dear Sir Charles – & very kind to me but I only knew him in his latter years & never experienced anything but the most courteous kindness. His character has been vulgarly treated by writers who perhaps had no real opportunities of knowing it. I have been anxious to vindicate it on some points. Even Byron was vulgar about him – indeed however great a poet B: was a vulgar man – & Rogers returned good for evil in noble lines upon him after his death.

Last Sunday I had a visit from good old Dr. Smith. He & I swore eternal friendship after the death of Mrs. Grote whose kindness he repaid by true devotion, as I witnessed at her funeral. Murray is about to bring out a work in which I am interested as it concerns connections of my family. Your friend Mrs. Ross, as you doubtless know has been drawing up an account of the three generations who preceded her – at the head of which stands an old John Taylor of Norwich, who was my Father's first cousin.[3] I cannot say that I know the more of them from our connexion for the young children of an old father are not cordially welcomed by those of his generation. However, Dr. Smith threatens to impose on me the task of reviewing the book when it appears. So Venice will again go by the wall. My only feeling in the delay is that I shall be keeping the books you have entrusted to me. However, I shall soon be going into Surrey for some weeks, to my old haunts, & there I shall have more leisure, if such a thinkg ever fall to my lot!

I trust you & Enid are adding length to your lives by the side of your Salmon streams. I get salmon from the nearest fishmonger & think of you! I fear I may be still away when you return, unless the business entailed by yr Aunt's death deliver you in London. It is a full house to clear out, & must team with reminiscences for you of yr brothers. What a clearing out there will be of this house when the time comes! I have left Chas Eastlake one of my executors – no one is more fitted to the task. He was here last Sunday – but is not so well as I cd wish.[4]

I don't think I shall want to be reminded of the claims of yr English Church at Venice. I will send Enid 2 guin: or more if I can afford it. And now I must wish you plenty of salmon & goodbye. With best love to her.

Ever yrs truly Eliz Eastlake

1. Layard's aunt Sara Austen had died.

2. Frederick III died in June 1888 after reigning as Emperor for 99 days.

3. Janet Ross, *Three Generations of Englishwomen* (London: John Murray, 1888).

4. In the event her executors were Charles Eastlake Smith and Jessie Lewin.

Letter to A. H. Layard   *NLS Ms.42172*

Albury Heath Guildford
7th July 1888
My dear Layard

Your long interesting letter which reached me here on the 25th was particularly welcome – for knowing your kindly punctual habits I had begun to fear that my letter to you must have miscarried – & was thinking of firing you off another. Every part of your's interests me, & not least the particulars of your Aunt's will, which appears to me to be a thoroughly just one, & the more so as she has given <u>you</u> a certain preference. I had – as long as her mental power continued – good reason to know her deep attachment to you. It happens also that just before I left London (on the 18th inst:) that I turned up a few letters I had carefully preserved, among them on from your Aunt, at that time when there was a run against you in the H: of C:, speaking of you in terms which it was well worth hearing a little injustice to elicit. I have made up my mind to let Enid have that letter. I am sure she will treasure it. I had a great affection for your Aunt, & no wonder! For she ever treated me with openness & utmost kindness, & had I been able to mount stairs & go out & in of houses I may safely say that I shd have been among her constant & latest visitors. I shall be curious to know what letters she has left & can quite believe the influence she must have had when in her prime of beauty & mind. She has a <u>charm</u>, which attracted all. She occasionally found my aged Mother at FitzRoy Sqre, & quite fascinated

her. But who wd wish to live to a great age, even with intellect
preserved – not I!

I am amused at your description of Janet Ross. Even the very little
I know of her convinces me of the truth of it. I fancy she has no
charm! Though much cleverness. I have known something of all Three
Generations – the oldest, a representative of the moralist & Unitarian
of her day. Tho' both characters exceedingly valuable & the more
respectable at a time when society was lax, & our church worse than
inefficient. I must say I am extremely interested by Mrs. Austin's letters
(Janet's gdmother).[1] But Dr. Wm Smith has withdrawn his wish for
an article on the work. Having now read the proof sheets himself he
thinks them hardly suited to an article in the Q.R. I am rather sorry,
for I think my knowledge of Norwich 'blue stockings' (by tradition)
& my relationship could have made something interesting. However
I am likely to be much interrupted here by a sucession of guests – &
the little time I can claim will be given to reading & thinking more
of Venice. I am already doing more justice to your friend Mr. Horatio
Brown, who captivates you so much. It's well I am not exposed to his
fascinations, for just now I have not a vacancy even for a handsome
young man![2]

The sufferings & death of that noble Emperor will be a pathetic
thought to me as long as I now live. I am not surprized that you express
yourself as you do. Her grief will be rendered worthy of him I feel sure.
Thank you much for promising to let her know of my earnest sympathy
& my high respect for him.

You cd hardly do justice to Mr. Rogers at the latter end of his life,
when it was easy to see his foibles, but he had noble qualities, & it was
partly to vindicate those that I consented to write my few reminiscences.
They are worth very little, but I shall make you read them in August
'Fortnightly'. I don't like some papers in that periodical, so I have only
given my initials.[3]

I have Miss Lewin now with me here, & I hope for my whole
period of stay, & I have a handsome man too, & am expecting another
tomorrow tolerably good looking. This country is lovely, in spite of
rain. I hope I shall see Mrs. Rate. I shall indeed be still away when you
return. But I think I can send you the Fortnightly before then.

With kindest love to Enid I am ever dear Layard yr's truly
Eliz Eastlake

1. In a letter to John Murray of 1 January 1890 (NLS Ms.42178): 'As soon as
   the press of business at this season is over I shall be delighted to see what
   kind of book "Janet Ross" as I am accustomed to hear her called, has put

together. We are very good friends but I would not like her for an enemy!
I hear of her own memoirs being in course of writing – Layard wonders
what she will <u>omit</u>!'

2. Horatio Brown (1854–1926), historian. Through Layard's inflence Horatio
   Brown succeeded Rawdon Brown in the British government's commission
   to calendar the Venetian state papers relating to British history.

3. There is no article on Rogers in the *Fortnightly Review* and the contribution appeared instead as 'Reminiscences of Samuel Rogers', in the *Quarterly
   Review*, vol. 167 (October 1888), pp. 504–13.

Letter to A. H. Layard   *NLS Ms.42172*

7 FitzRoy Sqre
6. Decr 1888
Dear Layard
   Your kind & interesting letter of the 19th Novr has been much
enjoyed by me, only that I feel ashamed not to have anticipated it by
one from myself to you. But the occupation of my article about Venice,
the continual reference to yr books have kept my thoughts much with
you, tho' preventing my writing to you so soon as I wished to do. It has
been a difficult job, & perhaps good Dr. Smith won't approve it after all;
& I feel pretty sure you won't! I felt all the romance about Venice ooze
away the deeper I went into her history. It is more romantic now as a
historical <u>shell</u> than it ever was when the creature within it was alive.
No State was ever like it in varied interests, but its past history does not
touch my imagination as its present decay does. It is a wonderful <u>mosaic</u>
in character, partly Italian, partly Eastern, but as a whole like nothing
but itself. Plenty that was wise & judicious & eminently practical but no
salient noble & generous actions. & the wisdom belongs to the earlier
part of her history. After the 16th century there is not even that. Indeed
the last two centuries of her existence seem to me despicable. In her
earlier times she was better than her reputation – in her latter, worse. I
hope I have vindicated her from some of the accusations against her, but
there is no defendg her at last. I ascribe her decline to a mistaken caste
of noblesse, the greatest misfortune that can befal [sic] a nation. I have
seen society in Germany & Russia too closely not to be convinced of
that. Pride, poverty, & pretension always <u>crescendo</u>. Our dear Princess
must have seen eno' of that in Berlin. I have <u>a little</u> called [sic] Mr
Horatio Brown over the coals, for calling the self styled Patricians of

Venice "Nobility". But I like his writing much, tho' even he cannot make the <u>government</u> of Venice <u>interesting</u>.[1]

I am amused with your account of your former guest Miss de Bunsen. My dislike of Germans extends even to their affected <u>maniérées</u> girls, who are never like English ones, but with set manners & phrases which I know by heart. Nor has any Bunsen <u>son</u> that I have seen seemed to me worthy of the fine old Chevalier, whom I knew well, whose talk was delightful, tho' no one I believe ever read a word he wrote. I am glad, however, to hear that his son George is a liberal. I had a visit from Madame Ernest de Bunsen the other day (née Gurney, with a good fortune). She quite agrees with me in hating Germans, including her own husband I believe, whom she snubs from morning to night. She told me of much suicide among young officers who with their pretentions & their poverty get hopelessly into debt. She also volunteered to tell me how that noble Emperor, whom we all deplore, disliked the obsequious manners of the German Drs calling him "All Highest" at every third word, & how much he preferred the manly simple ways of his English Drs. I have been lately reading Murell Mackenzie & quite agree with you that he has made out his case, but it is a pity he did not make it out in better taste. Of course he is not a <u>gentleman</u> at heart. I hear nothing of the Empress except through the papers. Our Queen & she are most circumspect. They do not utter a word upon the subject that can be reported. The letter to Enid must indeed be touching.

I have been hearing from both Mrs Hardwick & Lady De Gex, about the Watts fresco, how doubtful (no not from Lady De Gex) it is that the mosaic can translate it agreeably or justly. The wish seems to be that Watts himself shd go over it & use the <u>Waterglass</u> so as to fix it. Hardwick says nothing can be done till <u>you</u> come to London. It wd be a pleasant work for Watts.

I hope you have read Janet Ross' "Three Generations" & perhaps will agree with me that Mrs. Austin's letters redeem the book. I can <u>just</u> remember the old great grandmother, Mrs. John Taylor, who looked to my young eyes like an old witch. Mr. John Taylor was my father's first cousin. I am amused at Janet's asking you to review the book (the bad writing above was done in the <u>dark</u>). Before it came out, or rather in the summer, Dr. Smith asked me to review it. Being related to the generation & of Norfolk origin he thought I should do it. But he had not then read it – when he had he wrote me that he did not think it quite fitted for an article. I shd have treated it in a local way & made old Norwich the <u>setting</u>. Then when she came to me at Albury she told me in the first ten minutes that Dr. Smith was going to review it himself! Now she applies to you – & you think of me! But I no longer feel inclined to try. You say truly what a strange bringing up Mrs. Austin, Lady D.G. & Janet all had – all allowed to do <u>as they liked</u>, well <u>instructed</u>, but no more. I see Allick [sic] occasionally. I hardly think a broker's profession the right thing for him. He loves books, & has a totally different class of intelligence to that required in the Stock Market. I am amused how he is "<u>lisping</u> in numbers". He is a nice boy.[2]

I only heard of Mr Murray's accident yesterday & have now sent to enquire for him, & have an answer from his son Hallam. I suppose you know that it was last Monday evening – running along the platform to catch the train he missed his footing & did not get fully in & was carried along till he fell on the platform, & cut his forehead slightly & bruised his face. He is doing rightly, & keeps quiet at Wimbledon.

I remember Countess Pisani well when I was in yr house, we exchanged visits, thro' dear old Browne. She was still handsome. Her life must have been a strange one. It is well it has ended as Padrona of an Italian Estate, than which I think few lots must be more charming.

One cannot help wondering how Prussia will go on. Unless they are still more abject & insolent even than I think them the Empress Fred: must have a <u>party</u> for her there. It has been indeed a tragedy of the deepest kind, but perhaps he is taken from the evil to come. They wd perhaps rather have upset the throne than have allowed those two noble creatures a seat upon it. They were indeed too good for such a people.

If you are kind eno' to write again before my article is finally printed wd you answer me 2 or 3 questions. Did Rawdon Browne [sic] live about 50 years in Venice? Is Lorenzo's Librarian of St Marks Library? What is the meaning of "vode senza collo di spetie" in 1504 the galleys returned so from Alexandria & Beyrout.

I have read Molmenti with the utmost care, & there is no fact or opinion I have stated which I have not gathered from him.

I expect Miss Lewin on Saturday to stay ten days or so, & shall read her about the English Church. The dignity of Churchwarden must be new to you!

My kindest love to Enid

Ever yr's truly

Eliz Eastlake

1. Pompeo Gherardo Momenti, *Venice: Its Individual Growth from the Earliest Beginnings to the Fall of the Republic*, translated by Horatio F. Brown (London: John Murray, 1906), 6 vols.

2. Alick Ross was Janet Ross's son, to whom she was notoriously indifferent.

Letter to John Murray   *NLS Ms.42178*

7 FitzRoy Square
3. Janry 1889
Dear Mr. Murray

I have to thank you for a very beautiful book. I delight in Caldecott's art which truly fulfils Sir Charles' definition of style "a form of art in which you miss nothing". I am glad to see our old ballads thus honoured.

A new year is rather an awful thing at my age. I can only wish for a continuation of my present health – fortunately I have no longing to be nimbler – all that has had its time. But I do wish that one dear to you more restored! I never miss her in my prayers.

You will think me very idle when I own that only this morning am I opening Miss North's MS.[1] The last two weeks are the busiest of the year to me, & Christmas cards are terrible responsibilities to acknowledge. I never send any.

With all good wishes to you & yours. I am ever yr's truly
Eliz Eastlake

> 1. Marianne North (1830–90), botanical illustrator. The manuscript is her *Recollections of a Happy Life* which she sent to Murray in 1888. In it Elizabeth would have read the following recollection: 'I was sent to school at Norwich with Madame de Wahl, one of the three sisters of Lady Eastlake who had committed the folly of marrying Russian nobles while students at Heidelberg. She had lived to repent, and escaped after much trouble, bringing home to England a son and a daughter, whom she had to educate and bring up by her own earnings. She was very handsome; it was impossible not to love her, but school-life was hateful to me. The teaching was such purely mechanical routine, and the girls with one exception were uninteresting.' Susan Morgan (ed.), *Recollections of a Happy Life, Being the Autobiography of Marianne North* (Charlottesville: University Press of Virginia, 1993), p. 13.

Letter to A. H. Layard   *NLS Ms.42172*

7 FitzRoy Sqre
18 Janry 1889

It is more than time, dear Layard, to thank you for your kind answers & solutions of my troublesome questions, which were in time for my purpose. Now that the Q.R. is just out & 'Venice' safe in it

I am the more anxious to acknowledge the great help in more than
one form which you have afforded me. Your books – Lorenzo, & Mr
Hor: Brown's 2 vols I have sent to your home today. The Molmenti
you gave me is in three pieces, & goes to the binder tomorrow. You
doubtless know the pleasure one feels to put away the evidences of
the labour that has been. But I shall not be quite easy till I know
that you not positively condemn my partially heterodox opinions of
the government of Venice, & that Mr Horatio Brown does not set me
down for a presumptious ignoramus – there is of course no such thing
as an ignorama. Good Dr. Smith has turned down a few expressions
rather more than I like, but I never quarrel with one so kind &
careful.

Of course I have not been able to see the 'Old Masters' – open about
a fortnight ago. Many of the Masters are not very old – especially poor
Holl who died the other day.[1] I hear diverse opinions about him, as seen
en masse. I trust Mrs. Richard Boyle's opinions most, & she is startled
at the rapid transition from Rembrandt, Watteau (a beautiful painter) &
Romney to what she calls Holl's 19th century photography. At all events
the poor man seems to have painted himself to death. She also expatiates
on the 'vulgarity' of Leslie, Etty & Mulready. Etty is welcome, but the
two others are only vulgar in subject. They have both fine qualities of
art. Now the Grosvenor Gallery opens tomorrow.

The chief excitement of late has been the elections for the County
Councils. I was sore pressed to go & put my mark – only a X – at a
house up high steps & down a dirty narrow lane in order to help to
bring in two gentlemen opposed by a billiard ball maker, & a green
grocer. But I am happy to say that the two gentlemen were returned
by a large majority, without my help. I hope the may help to solve the
pauperising problem in London – which puzzles me more than ever, &
which apparently one cannot justly judge without a certain hardening
of the heart. My hard-hearted opinion is that the evil will not be met
till the Poor of London bring up & treat their children better. As it is I
believe that most of them – mothers as well as fathers – would sell them
to the best bidder as soon as they are born! I hope Venetian parents are
not come to that.

I hope that you & Enid still hear of & from the Empress Frederick.
She is perpetually in my thoughts. I remark that the conduct of the
Prussians towards her & towards the noble Emperor has opened many
eyes to the real basesness of German way & opinions. I am quite
proud of havg been foremost in discovering their real character. I stood
comparatively alone in that respect for long. You I remember, soon
fraternized with me, & now I am no longer singular. Their doings in

South Africa are a proof of their overbearing ignorance, dishonesty & cruelty. Bismarck <u>catches</u> it now from our Press. Mrs Holford was telling me yesterday that she had met <u>Herbert B.</u> at the D: of Westminster's, & never came across a more insolent & conceited prig. I shd like to toss Herbert Bismarck & Herbert Gladstone in one blanket & the two <u>Papas</u> in another. I must not venture to say more, or I shall shock <u>even</u> <u>you</u>! You & Enid will soon be here I hope. London meanwhile has been detestable in atmosphere.

Ever Layard with love to Enid

Your's ever truly

Eliz Eastlake

From family reasons I am about to purchase a head of my Father by Opie, & having no room for it I intend to offer the small Vandyck – companion to one in the Peel collection – to the Nat: Gal to purchase. I have too many family claims to <u>give</u> it. I shd offer it for less than Sir Chas gave for it.

1. Frank Holl (1845–88).

Letter to A. H. Layard   *NLS Ms.42172*

7 FitzRoy Sqre

6 Febry '89

My dear Layard

I have been long.g to acknowledge your most kind letter – if I had not so many others to write, I should have done so by next post. In addition to wanting to thank you for the kind view you have taken of my "Venice" I <u>burned</u> to tell you that I found you out in the Q. Review <u>at once</u>. The general style set me on the scent, & then the adroitness with which you soon brought yr subject to Venice, & then to the Nat Gal:! Of course D'Israeli's intimacy with yr Uncle & Aunt was in itself a suff: testimony. I hear it praised by everyone – the public divided between you & Lord Lamington, that "it reads like a novel" &c. I am sure good old Dr. Wm. Smith is greatly obliged to you.

On my part I am only glad not to have given the young man who you say is so good looking, no offence. Had I seen him I daresay is shd have been more laudatory! As for "that little trickle of gall against the Germans" I was afraid I had toned it down too much! Nothing increases my self respect more that the steady, unflinching way in which I have talked & written against them upon every decent opportunity.[1] A great compliment has been paid me of late – of which alas! I am undeserving. That late article in the Contemporary about Bismarck has been attributed to me. Would that I could have written anything with such power! But I am sure it is my rather notorious dislike of the Germans that has obtained me the compliment. You must have seen the article – if not, you will when you come. & I trust our dear Empress has seen those concluding passages which encourage her to take 'a noble revenge'.

I sometimes wonder what will pull <u>our</u> England down and whether it will ever decline as other countries have done. Our antecedents differ from those of all other European states – present & past. Our higher orders have never oppressed the lower ones – indeed have protected them. There is no <u>chasm</u> between classes, we have an enlightened national church. Other causes seem to me trifling in comparison. With all mistakes, follies & stupidities, England never, to me, seemed to stand higher. There is one universal mania to do good, in some form or other. Not that I include your friend Gladstone in this sweep – all he thinks of is to do good to himself.

I am interested in what you say of Sir R. Morier. I have known him & considered him a vain man & a tuft hunter.[2]

I have mentioned my wish to part with the little Vandyck to Gregory, & have written to Sir Frederick Burton – who promises to call & look at it. Gregory told me a delicious anecdote about Burton which I shall not forget. But you are both bewitched by him! My Opie of my father I expect today.[3] With kindest love to Enid – ever your's truly
Eliz Eastlake

1. Letter from Austen Henry Layard to Elizabeth from Venice, 23 January 1889, NLS Ms.42338: 'I have read your Article with interest, pleasure and profit. My dear friend Horatio Brown is delighted with your kind mention of him, and as yet, I have heard no criticism from him. I did not tell him that you were the author of the Article, but he said at once "no one but Lady Eastlake could have written it". Why he should have said so I cannot tell you. I should not have had the slightest difficulty in tracing to its source that little trickle of gall, which is so copiously and so justly turned occasionally upon our friends the Germans ... I am quite ready to give a hand with you to the tossing in blankets of the Bismarcks and Gladstones, old and young. The German Prussian is a brute and has always been one – and Bismarck is the very type of the race'.

2. Sir Robert Morier (1826–93), diplomat with many German, Austrian and Russian postings. A tuft hunter is a toady, someone who tries to curry favour with the nobility for personal advancement or gain.

3. The current whereabouts of Opie's portrait of Dr Rigby are unknown. The painting was last traced to the possession of Claud Eastlake Smith (d. 1944).

Letter to Frances Power Cobbe   *HL CB401*

7 FitzRoy Square
18 April 1889
Dear Miss Cobbe

You have been so kind as to send me your collected writings on that dreadful subject which has occupied your mind so painfully & yr pen so bravely & powerfully for long. It is no slight thing to have produced such a work. Providence appointed <u>you</u> to do it. There is no one else who so combines the right thought & the right manner. Few women have the gift & humour – none, I ever knew or heard of, possess it in the degree that you do. Thus you command the weapons & argument at both ends. No candid mind can fail to be struck with the moral ingenuity as well as humanity & rectitude of your pleas. Painful only in one sense, as showing the depths of yr own tortured heart from which they have been drawn. Indeed next to the poor animals I find myself feeling for you who suffer so much for them! But you will not have suffered in vain – for it is as sacred a course as ever a noble philanthropist took up. How it helps to convince one that there must be another life both for the animal sufferers & his human defender. In reading Butler's analogy again just now I find to my surprize & gladness signs of his holding that hope for the animal. How I wish <u>I</u> were able to do anything! but at my age the pen is falling from my hand. I once suggested to kind Dr. Wm Smith to have the subject treated in the Quarterly. He negatived the idea, but said he had been struck on reading the Royal Commission with the utter absence of all feeling of humanity & compassion.

Nor can I close this epistle without a tribute to yr "Science in Excelsis" which is simply <u>perfect</u>.[1] But you will have better tributes than mine. All I can do is to speak the <u>truth</u> whenever I can as to the worse than uselessness, the <u>misleading</u> of the diabolical practice. The public aught to withdraw all support from the Hospitals where it is practiced.

With my deep & affte respect, believe me, dear Miss Cobbe
Ever yrs truly
Eliz Eastlake

1. Frances Power Cobbe, 'Science in Excelsis: A New Vision of Judgement', in *The Modern Rack: Papers on Vivisection* (London: Swan Sonnenschein, 1889).

Letter to A. H. Layard   *NLS Ms.42172*

7 FitzRoy Square
Decr 1. '89
Dear Layard

You say rightly in your letter of the 22nd Nov, that you do not think you owe me a letter – all the more kind of you to send me one so interesting & full. One of the many advantages I owe you in having allowed me to occupy you home is the power it has given me to <u>see</u> you & dear Enid there, & also the friends who visit you. I can vividly see your Princes & Princesses in the rooms I know so well, further beautified as they now are. All is most interesting. Did you succeed in making the Princess of Wales talk? I hear that the dinners given by the Duke & Duchess of Fyfe, are, in the language of the day 'ghastly dull'. I rather wonder what, beside an inanimate, ignorant young girl, he has got in his Princess.

Your account of our Princess Fred: interests me most of all. She is never long out of my thoughts. She says what must be quite true that some of her pleasantest hours are owing to you two. You know my opinion of Germans, & I can imagine the welcome contrast she finds in your company, especially in this time of sorrow & depression. She is brave to do all she does, & especially to have undertaken this voyage. I trust the young <u>Sophia</u> is in good hands. I am glad the remaining Psses keep up the tradition of 'Aunt Enid'. How it would shock the Germans! Altogether the chapter of the Empress' treatment in Berlin from the first day she placed her young foot there is a disgraceful one & will come out some day.

The torrent of rain that have flooded Italy have been unknown here. Upon the whole the autumn has been fine & dry, & gorgeous in tints. Now we are havg cold, tho' not severe, with find sun.

I have at last brought my Czartoriski article to a conclusion, & am improving the proofs at my leisure. I think I told you before that my reading for it has given me the lowest <u>possible</u> opinion of the Polish race – vain, frivolous, boastful, & cruel – they had not a single quality, unless perhaps a reckless bravery, which fitted them to rule. They richly deserve their subjection,& in the nature of things, were predestined to the position they now occupy, & will for ever occupy. Czartoriski was a poor thing, with no political capacity, to my view, he was no real patriot, but only one of a shortsighted caste, who wanted time to roll back & restore them to powers of tyranny. How ungrateful, too, to that real patriot, philanthropist, & hero, Alexander Ist, of whom his posterity

has made too little! He was a man after my own heart – a compound of
Prince Albert, the Emperor Frederick, & himself, & good looking too.
I have not heard from dear old Dr. Smith what he thinks of the article,
but have reason to believe he does not think it worse than usual.

Like you I am much grieved at the death of John Ball. He is
associated with pleasant hours in the Past. You & I have met at dinner
at his table. I have known both his wives – the little Italian soon after
she came. I have written to poor Mrs Ball, but forbade her answerg me
at least for the present. I hear that she felt utterly unprepared for his
death – most wives do! I can do little nowadays for old acquaintances,
but I shall endeavour to keep in touch with her.

In Lady Bagot I find unexpectedly an old friend of Enid's. I liked her
much, but unfortunately I don't know her address, or whether she lives
in London, so unless she is good as to come to me again I fear we shall
not meet.

Today I have had Chas Eastlake here, who told me some good news,
wh: I am not allowed to repeat. I see good old Thomson Hankey
occasionally, who kindly comes to me. He is a little deaf & suddenly
had become much worse, which distressed him. He was afraid he shd
have to give up his little dinners of six friends at a time. However, I
sent to enquire for him last eveng & received word that the deafness
had much gone off. He bears the loss of the dear good wife of 50 years
very bravely, but flinches from going back to the country house in Kent,
& assures me that remaining in London this autumn was very pleasant
& sociable. I shall perhaps try that if I live another year, for the move
into the country tried me much last time. I was much interested in yr
avant dernière letter of Septr. 22nd with your account of the Vaudois
Bicentenary, & your climb up the hill, & anglo-french speech. & this
reminds me of a dreadful loss I have had which you alone can repair.
I had taken the greatest care of yr pamphlet on the result of yr search
with the Venetian & Roman archives on the subject of the massacre
of St Bartholomew. I had it out for some purpose, & a friend coming
in, Lady Juliana Walker, took it up & became so interested that I let
her carry it off, adding as she took it, "I know I can rely upon you to
return it safe". The next morng she wrote me a heartbroken letter that
she had in some way dropped it out of her muff, & that it was gone
beyond recovery! Is there any hope that you can ever spare me another?

I shall be sure to send for 'l'homme d'autrefois'. I wd read anything
that dear, noble woman recommended.

I am sorry you have had to entertain yr beloved friend, the unworthy
Director of the Nat: Gal: It is just like him to get two Tuccarelli's
which he could just as well have picked up in England. He has never

obtained a 'capo d'opera' fro the gallery, only second rates at first rate
prices, wh: he considers the essential thing.

Give Enid my best love. I know how she must enjoy reading to you,
& believe me dear Layard

Ever yr's truly Eliz Eastlake

Tell Enid I see something of her friend old Mrs Hamilton.

Letter to John Murray   *NLS Ms.42178*

7 FitzRoy Square
8. Decr '89
Dear Mr Murray
Since I had the pleasure of seeing you yesterday I have been thinking
of this proposed tribute to Layard. From what you & Ph: Hardwick
have said & written I feel convinced that the bust in question is hardly
worthy of royal patronage, & therefore I have suspended my proposed
letter to Sir Theodore Martin. I make no doubt that the subscription
as now proposed is pretty well filled up by this time & the postion of
the bust in the Hugenot Hospital will be, as far as it goes, appropriate.
But his Hugenot descent does not embrace Layard' claim on his
English compatriots. You will judge whether it would not be desirable
to get Layard to sit, on his return here in the Spring, to some first
rate sculptor, raise a suff: sum among his numerous friends & present
it to the B: Museum for the Assyrian room. I hardly think this smaller
subscription for an inferior bust will stand in the way – tho' perhaps
rather unfortunate. But the scheme was got up without my knowledge
– & I was only asked to touché up a miserable sketch of a circular about
him, which I entirely replaced by the present circular, except the last
few paragraphs. I was assured by <u>non</u>-connoisseurs that the bust was
very fine, its not being so makes all the difference. At the same time it
is perhaps good enough for its Hugenot destination.

Will you kindly turn this over in your mind. It is as well to make no
mistakes & it will be no affront to good Mrs. Hamilton to have another
bust for another place.

Ever your's truly
Eliz Eastlake

Letter to A. H. Layard   *NLS Ms.42172*

7 FitzRoy Sqre
13. Decr. '89
My dear Layard

You are very good indeed. I received yr Massacre of St. Bartholemew
on Wednesday evening, & the photograph of Ca' Capello yesterday
morning. So I am rich & very grateful to you. Poor Lady Juliana
Walker had not forgiven herself since losing the first copy of the
Massacre which you gave me – so I immediately relieved her mind. Ca'
Capello looks charmingly in the new coat you have given her. I have
followed the line of windows with melancholy pleasure, knowing so
well the rooms they represented. I say 'melancholy' for all past pleasures
have a certain mournfulness, & my time under your roof was interesting
& peaceful, & I can't return again, tho' you are kind as to wish it. My
place for the small rest of my life is in this old home, which could tell a
good deal of weal & woe & where I have now been 40 years. I first met
you I think in 1851.

Your letter prepared me for the death of Browning which appears in
today's Times. I knew him tolerably well, & liked him better than his
works. He had a peculiar set of readers who adored him – Ld Coleridge
& his family were among those. There are always peculiar admirers for
peculiar writers, painters, clergymen &c. I suspect very few quotations
from Browning have got into general use. I don't know one. I knew
Mrs. Browning slightly – he certainly showed taste there. She was so
interesting a woman that half an hour of her company gave one much
to remember. His illness & death in the splendid Palazzo Rezzonico
shows how his son has got on in the world. Browning was happy not to
have lived to extreme old age – there is extra death in that.

I omitted to ask you in my last letter what your Q.R. labours were
upon. I shall get it out of dear old Dr. Smith when I next see him. He
was here last Sunday looking particularly well. Mr Murray was here
shortly before & expressed his opinion that Mrs. Smith was "fond of
champagne". I trust this is a calumny.

I have read the life of the "Grand Dame Polonaise" indeed I
have inserted it among my headings. That alone I think would tell
what Poland has been. The Poles – at least the caste which fancied
they represented the Country – may have been heroic, if rashness &
foolhardiness represent heroism, but they certainly were not 'patriotic'.
There are excellent articles on Poland in the Réone Francaise by a M:
Leroy-Beaulieu.[1] says, of their insurrections, "C'étad de l'héroisme;

ce on'étart pas du patriotisme" – but, however, I shall enjoy to get yr criticisms when you have read the wretched article.

You were sure to defend yr beloved Knight of Trafalgar Square.[2] But if pictures are so dear now that is exactly his <u>line</u>. Mediocrity at high prices are his special delight. I suppose the Lucarelli's cost thousands.

Pray thank Enid for me for Lady Bagot's address. I envy her reading aloud. You ought to sit & do some handiwork, as Lord Sherbrooke does when read to. I am happy in havg Miss Lewin's company now, but expect to spend a lonely Christmas.

Ever dear Layard with renewed thanks
Yrs very truly
Eliz Eastlake

1. Pierre Paul Leroy-Beaulieu (1843–1916), French economist.

2. Sir Frederick Burton.

Letter to A. H. Layard   *NLS Ms.42173*

7 FitzRoy Sqre
5. Janry 90
My dear Layard

The poor Postmen have never been so overpowered of late in bringing every form of good wishes – in the shape of picture cards, letters, notes, photographs, books, pamphlets, Devonshire cream, flowers &c. & the burden of acknowledg.g them all has been so proportionably great that I find your kind letter, & the photograph of the Ca' Capello still unthanked for. By dint of writing batches of letters & notes – a dozen at a time – I have diminished my debts & am thankful now to recreate myself by thanking you for both letter & photograph. The latter arrived a little battered but otherwise unhurt, & I am now sending it to a great place in Oxford Street to be mounted & also to have a small one taken from it – to send to a young lady, now happily married & settled in Ceylon, who was with me in your house, & much craves a picture of it.

I lost no time in getting from London Library 'L'homme dautrefois' recommended by our Empress Fred: I have been much interested in it. It follows well upon the books I have been studying of late. One remark in a letter from le Marquis Costa to his wife, being à propos of a young french officer of note, <u>qui s'appelle Buonaparte</u> about 1797. There is no end to the tremendous interest of that time & that of the preceding

decade. Mrs. Grote used to say there was no end to the History of
the French Revolution, & that remark is verified every day. Just now
I am reading "Englishmen in the French Revolution". My attention
was called to it from its including a notice (a poor one) of my Father's
presence in Paris at the taking of the Bastille, & I find it a curious
contribution to the times, tho' not well eno' done to be very absorbing.

Also just now I have read Morelli's book on the Borghese & Doria
Pamfili galleries. He is most kind to remember me, & I will soon write
him a German letter of thanks. But I have as yet done no justice to
the work. Being in German it is, I am sorry, a sealed book to you, &
I wonder more than ever at his complete command of the language. I
fear it wd not answer to translate – Murray, I am sure, wd not hear of
it, or I shd gladly undertake it. It is too special for English readers tho'
enlivened I see with several of Morelli's conversations with pigheaded
German would be connoisseurs. Also with one with a pretty young lady
who seeing a fine handsome man, artlessly asked him his opinion on
certain pictures, & was in no hurry to drop the dialogue.

As to your Knight of Trafalgar, I am in a worse humour with him
than ever, wh: is difficult! Mr. Carrick Moore – a fine old gentleman,
own nephew to the Sir John Moore – whom you may perhaps know,
has called my attention to two notices in Notes & Queries, one of end
of last July, the other of the other day, in which home questions are
very pertinently asked as to Burton's authority for displacing Oriosto
as the subject, & Titian as the painter of that fine portrait from M:
Beaucousin's Collection. It required no small self confidence to substitute
simply "Le Poet", by Palma "for the former inscription". Mr. Moore
asked me if Sir Chas had left any description of the picture, & I had
no difficulty in turning up his remarks of the time (1858) in which he
accepts both painter & sitter & gives an excellent description, adding
what is curious in a connoisseur sense that in the single fact of the laurel
leaves wh: compose the background it might be by Dosso Dossi. To me
it appears that Art is sure to tell her own age as much as all of us do,
& that no Palma, 2 generations later than Titian, can bear the stamp
of such vigour & sparkle as that picture shows. I daresay you will find
some excuse for your beloved friend, wh: if possible, will incense me
against him more still!

I did mean the gift by Mr. Tate of his collection of English masters
– certainly to be told that such as rich nation like the English cannot
afford a gallery large enough to receive such generous gifts is not
encouraging to those who have meditated leaving pictures to our Nat:
Gallery.

Dear old Dr. Smith seems much troubled just now to get the

forthcoming number of Q.R. ready – several of his contributors being
late with their articles, he cannot say that of ours'.

The English public have been doing all justice to good Browning
both as poet & man. I wish I cd do the same to the first of the two
'mea culpa' I have no doubt. With all hearty good wishes to Enid &
yrself I am ever dear Layard – apologising for this long letter,

    Your's very truly
    Eliz Eastlake

Letter to A. H. Layard   *NLS Ms.42173*

7 FitzRoy Sqre
9 Febry '90
My dear Layard

It is now more than time to thank you for your last most interesting
letter of the 14 January. This year the business – if deserving such a
word – which comes with Christmas & New Year, was so severe that I
only feel myself free of it by now. Writing for the Q.R. is less fatiguing
& more rewarding! It was late before our thirst was quenched, &
immediately assuaged mine upon the first article, which had a double
attraction for me. You have summarised a subject which is one of the
most significant of Italian history – when Italian States had become
rich & selfish & shortsighted enough to prefer to fight by proxy, &
thus to introduce elements of violence & danger highly detrimental to
themselves. I have been long interested in the question of Carmagnola,
& now I think you have solved it. It seems to me that there was no real
patriotism in the Italian character & that this basis of all public good has
only grown up thro' much tribulation & that during a comparatively late
time. Only a longing for Freedom can excite it, & only Freedom itself
develop it. A history of <u>Patriotism</u> would be curious – certainly the <u>Poles</u>
had it not. I wonder what you think of <u>my</u> ideas on that detestable race!

I have been alone for some little time now – my friend Miss Lewin
just started for Cannes where she will remain 6 weeks, then perhaps
go on to Rome. I am driven in my solitude to much reading, & am
just now deeply interested in the life of Stein – the Russian minister
in Napoleon's time by Prof. Seeley. I see that he shared my admiration
for Alex 1st of Russia. By the by I have had Mr. Murray here this
afternoon & he & I discussed your article, & did not differ upon it
– but agreed that in addition to the usual attributes of the "Layard style"
this article showed a temperateness which enhances them all. I suppose

you know a Duchess is one of our fellow contributors – the Duchess of Rutland in Haddon Hall. I have not had time to read it yet.

I regretted to hear from him that you at last had succumbed to the influenza. I have been more fortunate, nor has it touched one in the house.

Another book I am trying to read, because much talked of & recommended – namely "Journal de Marie Baskertschoff", [sic] a young Russian girl, who sighs for fame, becomes an artist, & dies at 24.[1] At present I find no attraction – I have waded through above 100 pages, & find only a vain & frivolous, forward young lady fancying herself in love with the Duke of Hamilton, when she was 12 years old, with tirades wh: she should never have been allowed to put in print. But I am assured that fine things are to come. I am sorry to say I have not advanced very far in Morelli's vol: which is my own fault. I am glad he did not entrust this work to Mdme Richter, who tho' speaking English fairly, could not translate ten German lines into readable English. I fear the length of the work wd be an insuperable object to Murray. It was different with dear old Waagen's work which concerned England & which I shd hope has answered his purpose.

I am rather interested in the vaccination question to which the poor shows as much sympathy here as you describe in Venice – as my father was a friend of Jenner's, & himself the most enthusiastic advocate & practiser of vaccination.[2] I have reason to know that the ignorance & brutality of the present generation of vaccinators is the real cause. They inflict 3 or 4 deep wounds on each arm, & cause such suffering illness that most parents – especially the poor in their limited space naturally resent. Nor are the Drs nearly careful eno' in watching the stages of vaccination – when the different phases of the pustule are right, one prick even with a needle is as efficacious as 6 gashes with a lancet. I often have watched the discussions in Parliament on the subject, & am surprised that the real reason for the opposition is not stated. And it is not only the Poor who complain. Joseph Hooker very nearly lost his youngest child by modern vaccination.

Your translation of Antonio Barbara's letters however fatiguing must be deeply interesting. I hope I shall have the opportunity of reading it. Altogether what heaps of interesting subjects could be found in these old Italian libraries. I envy the young who have such opportunities before them, & rejoice that your friend Horatio Brown has taken possession of such a line of study.

I think dear Enid's three nieces are much to be envied in passing this winter with you. I make no doubt you keep them in order & take it out in merciless chaff, but meanwhile it is an education which they can't

fail to profit by. I am thankful I led no idle life when in your house at
Venice. I often think of dear old Brown.

Your love of classic music is another point I sympathize. I have had
the same – tho' not able to indulge it now. I come down to <u>Mendelsohn</u>
[sic] & find beauties in him which are level with my generation, but
I go no further. The modern German only cares for the music of his
own time, as the old Italian only cared for the art of his time, & would
whitewash Giotto to make room for Vasari. I can conceive no greater
treat than the good rendering of a trio by Mozart – or still more by that
eccentric enchanter Beethoven, & as for a symphony by either it is a
feast not to be described.

Now dear Layard I must have done. I shall be thankful to know that
you have quite recovered. With kindest love to Enid.
Ever your's most truly
Eliz Eastlake
I have had the photograph of Ca'Capello mounted, & is perfectly right
now.

1. Marie Bashkirtseff (1858–84), Ukrainian artist whose diary was published in
   French in 1887.

2. Elizabeth's father Dr Rigby had been a friend of Edward Jenner and shared
   his friend's enthusiasm for vaccination, introducing vaccines into the city of
   Norwich.

Letter to A. H. Layard   *NLS Ms.42173*

7 FitzRoy Sqre
17. Feb: 90
My dear Layard

I have your letter of the 13th & need hardly say the pleasure that
every letter from you gives me. No one was more prized by my dear
Sir Charles. And now as to the request you convey to me from Morelli,
& possibly Miss Jocelyn. It is difficult to decided, except on one point,
namely that I wd <u>not</u> give my name. I have never done so except for
very exceptional reasons. Nor do I believe it wd do the work any good.
And then I am not satisfied that the work itself is destined to run a
straight course. It will require peculiar & careful translation – will be at
all events very long, & then has Morelli secured a publisher? These are
the questions wh: must be asked before an introduction can be thought
of. Next to doing anything for you, I wd do anything in my power

for Morelli. Willingly wd I undertake to look thro' MS or proof, &
suggest anything for their improvement. Nor wd I refuse to compose a
short introduction if convinced that it wd benefit the book. But that, if
it cd be shortened, wd speak for itself, but from my own experience &
from what you say I feel that it requires a careful hand to do justice to
it. I conclude you have consulted Mr. Murray – if not I shd be happy
to place the matter before him & to volunteer any trouble which cd
conduce to his undertaking it. As you are well aware an Italian's banter,
however clever, is not easily intelligible to our dull public. So for the
present I can say no more.

Have you heard of a book, a stiff one in 2 full vols "Le Journal de
Marie Baskercheff"? [sic] in french, wh: everyone is reading, & I fancy
praising here. If not, it will hardly reward you to read it. I have waded
through 300 pages & am ready to pronounce it the most detestable &
unhealthy rubbish I ever read. Very like what I have known of young
Russian girls in the School room. I have asked Dr. Smith whether he
knows about the book, & whether he wd entertain a thought of a short
article on it, combined with "Memories [d'une] Grande Dame". They
seem to me birds of a feather.

I have my little friend Mrs Anderson, née Lewin, who was with me
in yr house & we have read together the account of your ball, & greatly
enjoyed it – especially the remarks on "Sir Layard" & dear Enid. I shd
like to see her in her diamond coronet.

I am delighted that you like my article. I hear that your's & mine are
pointed out in the Morning Post as the best.

Of course I am not an anti vaccinationist. How shd I be when my
Father was one of its first & most enthusiastic promoters. The truth is
I know too well how the little operation shd be done. The poor never
object to it under reasonable conditions.

But no more now. I am interrupted.

Ever your's truly

Eliz Eastlake

Letter to A. H. Layard   *NLS Ms.42173*

7. FitzRoy Square

5 March '90

My dear Layard

You have doubtless been expecting to hear from me, & I have
been anxious to write, but this winter weather has seemed to deaden

my energy, & it has even cost me some effort to thoroughly read &
study Morelli's book. Meanwhile I have felt the possibility of hearing
from you not only what you think of the young lady's translation,
but of the work itself. I am sure that we agree in our estimate that it
is most original & striking in style, & exhaustive in information, &
to the few who wd care enough for Art to do it justice, wd be the
most valuable work on Italian Art that has been written – but alas!
those few are so <u>very</u> few, that I despair of any publisher undertaking
it. It may be perhaps owing to my present powers & opportunities of
judging being so lessened, but it appears to me that we have hardly
a thorough connoisseur now rising in England. In Germany, Italy &
France Connoisseurship is a <u>profession</u>, however limited in number.
Here your beloved Burton seems to have infected the world with his
suprise indifference & ignorance. Morelli's book is all alive with the
interest he has taken for years, who can you mention here who wd
respond to his enthusiasm? It is strictly a <u>special</u> subject, & always
a limited one, & what publisher wd invest a considerable capital in
producing it for English readers? I feel certain that Murray wd shake
his head. Crowe & Cavalcaselle have sickened him of such enterprises.
I know that their writing & our friend Morelli's are as different as
light & darkness but I much doubt whether the one wd succeed here
better than the other. I cannot bear to seem lukewarm in the cause
but these convictions are the fruit of my common sense. Otherwise I
wd ask Murray to morrow – also volunteering to go through the MS
of translation with the better advantage of being able to compare it
with the original German. Meanwhile I shall hear from you after yr
receipt of this & shall be curious to know how far you agree with me
as to the chances of success in our English public. To me individually
the book is delightfully original, & so like Morelli's self, full of point
& playfulness, & bearing on it such proofs of enormous study &
observation as ought to carry all before it. It has taken me back to my
old world, with the longing to be young again to continue & enlarge
that life. Of course it wd enrage the German Gallery Directors, as
well as Messrs Crowe & Cavalcaselle if still in existence. The other
day a french connoisseur, M: Emile Michel, begged to see our little
chiaroscuro Rembrandt, & took careful notes. He also paid great
attention to the Terburg, those two masters being his special study,
but I was struck with his <u>astonishment</u> at the two Bellini's. He spoke
of yr beloved Burton with a true Frenchman's shrug of his shoulders.
"Je parait que les tableaux l'eminent". I felt rather guilty (not on that
point) from my recent reading of Morelli, who has generally occasion
to differ from Herr Bode of the Berlin Gallery, who M: Michel quoted

several times, also instances from Dudok "archives", knowing how little
Morelli cares for either.

I am glad to hear that you are busy. There must be plenty of material
for articles in the Q.R. in Venetian annals & chronicles. I trust also to
find occupation too. Living alone as I do, & lame besides I cannot live
without an object, to employ thought & time, tho' it is high time to
give up such aims.

I have peeped into PS Lieven's & Lord Grey's correspondence, &
caught sight of sentimental passages wh: disinclined me fro more. The
<u>Prince</u> seems to have been nowhere in her life. Just now I am reading a
little about Tolstoi & Russian literature. I remember being much taken
with Tourgenieff tales at the Mohl's, & with Tourgenieff himself too! a
handsome man! Now with best love to Enid ever dear Layard yr's truly
    Eliz Eastlake

Letter to A. H. Layard   *NLS Ms.42173*

7 FitzRoy Sqre
3. May '90
Dear Layard

I had a visit from Mr Murray before your note came. But that made
no difference. We talked equally much on the subject of the translation.
I did my best to put Morelli's book in the most attractive colours, but
he seemed decided not to undertake it. But he said he knew a publisher
who would, &, I understood him, one of the name of <u>Bell</u>. It would
be as well to ascertain who he is & where. We were interrupted in out
talk so I did not get so far as that. The question remains between you
& me about the revision of the translation. I have thought it well over,
& I feel the young lady should herself undertake to go over her work &
improve it as much as she can. I will willingly revise <u>more</u> of it so that
she may see what it is, in my opinion, wants – summed up in the word
'compression', & with certain corrections. It would be a tremendous
work to revise & recopy the whole, & there is no reason why she
should not give her time & attention to it. But it requires practice &
judgement, & I fear she is a novice in both, but she would improve in
the course of the job.

I hope you are better – I hope to leave this note & hear.
Your's ever truly
Eliz Eastlake
There is too much pretence of art in England now.

Letter to A. H. Layard   *NLS Ms.42173*

7. F. Sqre
27 Septr '90
Dear Layard

I have your kind long letter of the 18th & I am much obliged to you
for findg time just now to write it. I was grieved not to have been able
to see you before you left London, but I shared Enid's anxiety on yr
account & was glad when you cd get safely out of London. You were
indeed very ill, & I will trouble you not to be so again – at least while
I am alive! The only consolation in our rainy & cold Summer was that
all the world seems to have had the same from Russia to Italy. Enid had
been afraid of the demand the Empress Fred: wd make on your strength,
but I am glad to hear that you bear it so well – indeed her company
must be a great pleasure & interest to you. Enid I know is quite
broken in as Lady in Waiting. Good Mr. Malcolm (tho' bad to <u>me</u>)
must be enchanted to have put his house at her disposal & meanwhile
to be your guest. I am thankful that she can take interest in people &
things, tho' opprest with the sense of her unspeakable loss. Morelli &
you will do her good & give her fresh ideas & help her to forget her
rhodomontade Son, to whom Punch has been doing justice.[1] I wonder
if H.M. ever speaks to you of him. I know that he is an exception to
most royalties, but I do not forget a Swedish Minister's definition to me
of Prince's – "Childn, with whom you must <u>not</u> play". I am sorry you
have to acknowledge that the Prince of Schaumburg-Lippe is a thorough
German.

I have not much to say of myself. I have spent a few weeks with
my Sister at Windsor whence I returned last week, & feel myself the
stronger for the change. I took no house this time, not feeling up to the
exertion, so I rested in Windsor, & read the old books in my Father's
good Library which has come down to my Sister. Among other thing
I read Voltaire's Life of Peter the Great. He has whitewashed him all
he could, but that has not succeeded in concealing the <u>brute</u>. A more
extraordinary character for energy & perseverance never existed, & this
combined with absolute power made him a tremendous man, he must
driven [sic] his attendants crazy. It is much doubted whether he did
not do Russia more harm than good, which is a favourite idea with
modern writers – but this is more easily said than proved. A veneer
of civilisation is better than no civilisation at all. Generations must
pass before Russia is honest or decent, & if you had read an article on
Russian morality in the 'Fortnightly' of this month, wh: your friend Mr.

Verschoyle tells me he toned down all he cd, you wd have no hope of
her for centuries. Altogether I have been readg a good deal on Russia,
especially a large work by Mr. Leroy-Beaulieu in beautiful french & in
a dignified style. The consequence has been that I have put together
an Article, for wh: I have no title at present, but good Dr. Smith tells
me he has made too many promises for the Octr No. & must defer
me to the New Year – even if he approves it wh: of course I am not
sure of. I have combined with it a mention of "Le Journal de Marie
Bashkirtscheff",[2] which Gladstone has extolled in the 19th Century. I
wonder whether the Empress has read it! I shd think she wd abominate
it, as I do.

I see dear old Thompson Hankey now & then. He is almost too
feeble to come to me, but as he lives on his Ground Floor I go to him
occasionally for 5 o'clk tea, for wh: he give me carte blanche. You see
the Times doubtless. I hope you liked Watts' modest letter on Galleries.
By the by Chas Eastlake is just back from Switzerland & I shall probably
see him on Sunday.

Goodbye dear Sir Henry – my best love to Enid. Ever yours truly
Eliz Eastlake
Also remember me to Morelli.

1. Kaiser William II.

2. 'Russia: People and Government', *Quarterly Review*, vol. 172 (January 1891),
   pp. 113–42. See pp. 133–34.

Letter to A. H. Layard   *NLS Ms.42173*

[undated c. 28 October 1890]
Dear Layard

I am requested by two young & ardent connoisseurs – friends of
Morelli – Herr Berenson & Sgr Costa – to give them an introduction to
you in order that they may have the advantage of seeing yr gallery.[1] Mr
Berenson wrote to me from Vienna, but he & his friend were on their
way to Venice. I fell rather in love with the two young men – both
speakg good English, tho' neither of the particularly good lookg! But
their enthusiasm delighted me. They know the pictures in this house by
heart.

I hope you have quite regained yr strength. The Empress Fred's
society was well worth a little fatigue. Now I believe you have a
housefull, with Lady Charlotte & others. I trust Enid is quite well.

I see there is an account of Sir Richd Wallace's will in this morng's Times.[2] I have not had time to master it yet.

Today we have the first real cold, & sharp frost in the night. I would rather be in Venice! where I often am in thought.

I know I shall hear from you before very long.

With kindest love to Enid I am yrs ever truly

Eliz Eastlake

1. Bernard Berenson (1865–1959), American art historian and connoisseur. Mary Costelloe, later Berenson's wife, describes visiting Elizabeth's art collection: 'Bernhard and I looked at each other with shining eyes that confirmed each of our secret resolutions to follow in our humbler way the example of Lady Eastlake'. See Ernest Samuels, *Bernard Berenson: The Making of a Connoisseur* (Cambridge, MA: Belknap Press of Harvard University Press, 1979), pp. 120–21; and Enrico Costa (1867–1911), a pupil of Morelli.

2. This dates the letter to 28 October. See *The Times*, p. 12, col. A.

Letter to A. H. Layard   *NLS Ms.42173*

7 FitzRoy Sqre

26. Decr 1890

My dear Layard

I received your most kind letter of the 16th & truly can I begin this as you did your's. I have also lost dear old friends in this 1890 – the more thankful I am to have so true an old friend left as yourself. My dear Sir Chas bequeathed me no one more faithful & kind than you. & your friendship and dear Enid's have been an unspeakable comfort to me since I stood alone. & I have lost more than friends, for one of the two sisters left me died last week – on the 17th, and I have but one left, & she too infirm to come to me tho' I manage in fine weather to get to her at Windsor. My late sister – John Murray's sister-in-law – had endured a long and painful illness, & the cold we have had snapt[sic] the feeble thread of life.[1] She leaves grown up sons & daughters, who I hope will wish for me & come to me. Her 2nd son – a fine fellow, deafened by a sad accident, has long been as a son to me, helping me with his sound judgement, & comforting me with his warm attachment. I have been unavoidably alone this Xmas week, but my nephew & his wife come to me tomorrow for a week.

I doubt whether you could bear such a winter as we have had. I do not recollect one so severe & so early. I am thankful never to leave the house, & with the exception of one desperate cold quite gone now, have kept quite well. You have had evidently a very charming time in Venice – increased doubtless by "mothers in law, & brothers in law" & by a lively daughter of Lord Selborne. He is so solemn tho' excellent, that I am glad to hear of a lively offspring. Lady Selborne was the best of women. All contact with the Empress Fred: must be <u>super</u>-interesting nor am I surprised at her partiality for Venice while Ca' Capello & its inmates are there I am thankful that the marriage of Enid's royal <u>niece</u>, tho' arranged by that conceited Jack of all trades "Willie"! promises to be happy. And always repress my contempt for petty German Princes when I think of our admirable Prince Albert. Doubtless you will be hand & glove with the Emperor in time, & I hope do him good. Mr. Macolm won't know whether he stands on his head or his heels!

Meanwhile I am glad to hear what you have been doing, & shall hope for a copy from the Hugenot society. Nothing can be more interesting than what you have already done in that line. Your <u>Cookery</u> article is a new subject for you. I hope Enid has tried some of the recipes. If Murray's Mag: gives them <u>in extenso</u> I shall try them. I have an excellent old Cook now.

Nor have I been quite idle. I dawdled leisurely through an article on "Absolutism & Russia" (so I believe it is to be named,) which good Dr. Smith did not want till January, when it is to appear. It is founded chiefly on a <u>masterly</u> work by M. Leroy Beaulieu "L'Empire des Czar & le Russia" one of those lucidly written french works in which the French excel. He calls no names, but all the more establishes his case. It is a work heavy in size which the Empress Fred: should read. Plenty of other works I have read, & also included some in the article. One you may have heard of – "le journal de Marie Baskörtscheff – over which some fashionable ladies have gone wild as an interesting "pyschological emanation" (psychological fiddlestick) – & even your friend Gladstone discoursed on it in his usual occult way in the 19th Century. Then also I have information, firsthand, from the Baltic Provinces, divulging the Czar's favourite way of governing the subjects whose liberties he is bound by a treaty to respect. It is really curious to witness a Despotism of the worst type of the 13th century, still alive (& kicking!) in our day. "A violation of all social laws" as Card: Manning wrote.

I have lately had a book "Rural Italy" sent me. It is by a young friend of mine Nelthorpe Beauclerk – long <u>attaché</u> in Rome under Paget, <u>Lumley</u> & last under Ld Dufferin – a very able man – tho' made up of statistical reports it is very interesting. I take the more interst in it because there is a work on the agriculture of Italy by a Mr. Chateauviaux – published in 1812 – which my father – a keen

agriculturalist – translated[2] & it is curious to compare them. I fancy
even that it might be worked up into a Q:R: article in which case
I may beseige you with questions as to modern changes in systems
of agriculture in Italy. Meanwhile I shall study old Italian history
– Muratori for instance which I have.[3] It is strange how little certain
writers suspected that Italy could ever rise again.

Now I am delighted to have bored you so long & to have put you
into my debt! The portrait I hope I may see, & also the clay model by
the lamented Böhm.[4]

I have seen Gregory – & dear old Hawtrey lately – both speaking of
you. Now with kindest love to Enid I am ever your's truly
Eliz Eastlake

1. Matilda Smith died on 17 December, her 75th birthday, at West-Hill,
   Sydenham.

2. Dr Rigby translated Jacob Frédéric Lullin de Châteauvieux, *Italy, Its
   Agriculture, etc. from the French of … Chateauvieux being letters written by him in
   Italy, in 1812 and 1813* (Norwich: R. Hunter, 1819).

3. Lodovico Antonio Muratori, eighteenth-century Italian historian.

4. Sir Edgar Boehm (1834–90), formerly Josef Böhm, Austrian sculptor who
   worked in London, most noted for his portrait busts of well known Victorians,
   including a bas-relief of Layard now in the Government Art Collection.

Letter to A. H. Layard   *NLS Ms.42173*

7 FitzRoy Sqre
3. Febry. 91
Dear Layard

I am late in thankg your for yr last delightful letter of the 21. Janry,
but I have waited for the number of Murray's Mag: & only had the
pleasure of readg yr 'Renaissance Cookery' yesterday eveng. I could
say a good deal about it, its simple, clear, intelligible writing, the art
with which it is put together, so as never to lose interest, but chiefly I
want to say that if the chief objects in writing of the Past is to exhibit
its manners & habits you cd have found no more thorough a way. The
part that eating & drinking has played in this world, from Heliogabalus
till now, is a most unerring tell tale. The economy of time wd seem to
be the latest as well as the highest improvement in civilisation, & that
exists chiefly among the English. My beloved friends, the Germans, have
not yet arrived at the art of conversing & eating at the same time. They

can talk with their enormouths [sic] full, & make a great noise, but they never converse.

I am delighted to hear that the subject of yr bust gives you all the pleasure we cd desire, tho' that was by no means our principal aim, but rather to pay a too long deferred debt. I am sure good Gregory never wrote at least 200 notes with more zest, & not short ones either. I shall try & see the clay model before it leaves Böhm's studio. It stands nearer the original than the best copy can do, & also can be easier brought to my little carriage. I hope there will not be another vacancy in the committee yet, but you may not have heard that dear old Thomson Hankey has had an accident. He was going to bed & stretched up his arm to reach a little clock to wind it up, lost his balance, & fell, breaking 2 of his ribs & injuring a 3rd & hurting his shoulders. It seems almost impossible that he shd have passed a long night in this painful state, but at all events he did not ring his bed till 8.30 next morng. He is however, doing well – sleeping much, & very submissive to his nurse, like somebody else I cd mention! He has a pretty woman taking care of him, some relation, a Mrs Harvey, & he orders all the cards of enquiry to be carefully kept so that he may drive round & thank his friends in person. I trust I shall soon be admitted to the dear old man, as he is on the ground floor. But that my coachman managed to break his arm in the slippery weather I shd have been with him before now.

I can't give a favourable account of any work of late, havg had no end of interruptions – chiefly in the way of lookg over & through old letters & papers with a view of saving trouble to my executors. So I have been conversing with those who have gone before me wh: has rather unhinged me for other work. So 'Rural Italy' stands over for the present tho' I hope to take it up with the help of that work by Luzzati wh: you mention & kindly offer. I will be sure to let you know if I attempt to concoct an article. Before doing so I may perhaps work up some spare scraps about Russia in the shape of an examination of the reign of Peter to be called 'Great'. I have been readg odd things about him. He was a <u>Great Savage</u>, that is indubitable, tho' not without remarkable qualities. One thing is certain that he must have been enough to craze his unfortunate subjects with his extraordinary pranks – they did think he was 'antichrist'. How far his total want of judgment & common sense contributed to bring his Empire down to its present state is a question which Leroy Beaulieu's work wd help me to answer. But this I shd do for Murray's Mag: if I do it at all.

I have been deeply interested in the accounts of the Empress' visit to Paris, & am glad it is safely over. If any one cd conciliate by manner & intelligence it wd be she, but I fear that detestable 'Willie' has undone whatever good she may have effected. Certainly if I were a french man or woman, I wd not send a picture to Berlin.

I have written to Mary Kay since her mother's death but have heard nothing.

I agree in all you say about Tolstoi. There is a difference between dirty & clean dirt. His is indefensibly dirty, but I soon had eno'. His 'Kreutzer Sonata' is I hear his chef d'oeuvre in that line.

With best kind love to Enid, & assuring you that the sun is shining on my paper – for a wonder, I am ever yrs most truly

Eliz Eastlake

Letter to F. R. Becheeno   *NCM Beecheno Collection (116.935)*

7. FitzRoy Sqre
15. Mch. 91
Dear Sir

You cd have hardly opened to me a subject more interesting than that of my old friend Ed. Daniell.[1] He is interwoven with my earliest recollections – & with my earliest attempts in that practise of art which he loved so well. Circumstances dating from 1829 took us from Norfolk, & me to distant countries,[2] but on my marriage to Sir Chas Eastlake I found that <u>his</u> friendship with Ed. Daniell greatly helped to fill up the blank. Very often have Sir Chas & I regretted that he had not lived to see us united. As a young girl I used to stay at his mother's house in St. Giles, on the last occasion meeting his friend Mr Blancowe there. To Ed. Daniell I owed my first instruction in the processes of etching, & all I did in drawg was submitted to him. I have two little early drawings by him, somewhere in the wilderness of portfolios which helps to fill this house.

In the society of artists which he frequented the names of Eastlake, & of Boxall shd be included.

As to the immediate cause of his death, Sir Chas has told me that on his going to sleep on his balcony the sun was allowed to reach him, wh: acted fatally.

I can hardly trace a resemblance in the little frontispiece. My recollection of his face was that of one of the <u>openest</u> that cd be seen – a superb forhead, & splendid teeth, which showed themselves with every smile, & no one smiled & laughed more genially.

His admiration for Turner inspired Turner with genuine affection for him. Boxall has told me that at an R.A. dinner, he & Turner sitting

with one between them, Turner leant back, & touched Boxall to attract
silently his attention, & then pointg to a glass of wine in his other
hand, whispered solemnly "Edward Daniell". He was indeed calculated to
inspire the warmest affection.

I have read yr memoir with the deepest interest (& am much obliged
to you for it) but I have nothing more than I have said here to tell
you about him. I wd give much to see the approaching exhibition at
Norwich – but beside being very old I am also so very lame, that I
live in a wheel chair, & have great difficulty in moving & being moved
short distances in the summer. In truth I have seen none of his maturer
works, & am astonished at the wealth of them wh: your memoir report.
I shall look eagerly forward to seeing the fresh catalogue & memoir.
Believe me yrs faithfully

Eliz Eastlake

1. See letter to John Murray, 16 November 1842, n. 2.

2. The removal of the Rigby family to Heidelberg is dated to 1827 by Smith,
   J&C1, p. 6.

Letter to John Murray   NLS Ms.42178

7 FitzRoy Square
12. April 91
Dear Mr. Murray

I am coming to the end of your Father's Memoirs which have
afforded me so much interest & pleasure that I cannot help telling you
so.[1] You are doubtless hearing the same from many, but few, or none,
who have lived until now, can have a more vivid recollection of his
kindness & liberality. I grudge approaching the end of the volumes – for
they have been delightful companions to me in many a lonely hour
during the last fortnight, & I shall quite miss my companions. I shall
turn to Byron's works. The fine edition which your Father gave me
– the history of them is perhaps the most extraordinary in our literature.
What a medley of the fine & the base he was! Alas! Besides the
memoirs of your Father these volumes contain a gallery of friends, never
forgotten. What an interest dear Hester would have taken in the work!

I am busy, trying to put together an article on a common friend of
Layard's & our's – Gio: Morelli, a very noble fellow inn every way,
& the best connoisseur that ever lived. He differed too often from
Messrs Crowe & Cavalcaselle, & from heads of galleries in Germany

not to excite their anger for saying so. I intend to steer clear of all connoisseurship wh: would not interest the public – but the subject of connoisseurship is so new & sometimes so curious that I think it can be made interesting & even amusing. This leads me to the history of the early days of the Q.R. which have interested me particularly. It is high time for me to cease my connexion with it, & I daresay this the last attempt I shall make. Dear Lockhart appears to great advantage in these pages. I am truly glad he should be done justice to.
Believe me yr's truly
Eliz Eastlake
I think your title very felicitous & so true

1. Samuel Smiles, *A Publisher and his Friends: Memoir and Correspondence of John Murray*, 2 vols. (London: John Murray, 1891).

Letter to A. H. Layard   *NLS Ms.42173*

2 Adelaide Place
Windsor
30 May 91
Dear Layard
    I venture to trouble you with the proof of my article as far as it goes for the present. Enid writes me that you have an article published some years ago on Morelli which you think may be useful. I shall be very glad of it. Meanwhile I am quite aware that I have done scant justice to the dear man. But you know the kind of limit to a Q.R. article. I determined not to make it controversial, or personal – or offensive to any one. At least not so in the eyes of the Public – tho' doubtess some readers will understand who the <u>mistakers</u> have been. I am promised a present catalogue of the Berlin Gallery, in which I hear there are changes of attribution openly owned as Morelli's. I was unwilling to allude even to my Sir Chas' name – but the imputation of having "improvised" two Giorgiones ought not to rest on him. Those two pictures were not of his time, as I daresay you will remember. I supposee they are your beloved Burton's.
    You will immediately see that the article is almost entirely made up from his own writings & that I have endeavoured to make it, not learned, but popular. I wonder what good Dr. Smith will say to it!
    I propose to make the headings of pages 'Giovanni Morelli' & 'Connoisseurship'. I shall be obliged to you to find every fault you can

think of – both as to matter & style, & to make any amendments.

I told dear Enid how much I feel for you in the death of your brother. He seemed to me a very manly, loveable man – & alas, Grief is in proportion to Love.

Ever dear Layard your's very truly
Eliz Eastlake
I return home on the 2nd June (Tuesday) in the afternoon

Letter to John Murray   *NLS Ms.42178*

2 Adelaide Place, Windsor
1 June '91
Dear Mr. Murray

I hear from our friend Layard that you are a little annoyed not to find any allusion to Messrs Crowe & Cavalcaselle's works in my article on Morelli. Little as I admire Mr. Crowe's literary style, I quite agree with you that this is an unjustifiable omission – & especially unjust to Morelli, who gives them most generous due. I have therefore at once drawn upon the enclosed paragraph, which will fit in perfectly on page 6 of the slip – & which, considering the limits of the article & subject, will I hope repair my omission.

I return to F. Square tomorrow (Tuesday) & shall doubtless soon see Layard, & ascertain what other suggestions he can make. Morelli was so noble a fellow that I am doubly anxious to put him in a right light to the English public.

I hope June will bring us the long pined for good weather, & I hope you & your's have not suffered from its delay.
Believe me ever yr's truly
Eliz Eastlake

Letter to Bessie Rayner Belloc   *GC GBR/02 71/GCPP*
Parkes 9/134

7 FitzRoy Square
1 July 91
Dear Mdme Belloc,

I return you the 'Review of Reviews' which has satisfied my wish to see Calderon's subject. I cannot say that it shocks me, absolutely – tho' doubtless if I were an adorer of the Saint it wd. Perhaps to the size of life may make a difference.[1] The Review itself itself [sic] is an odd mixture. The scurrilous picture of our Queen does shock me. I find myself very ignorant of much of the literature of the present, whether novel, or drama – a side of the present day I do not like to investigate.

I am now just reading Lord Grey & Ps Lieven. It appears to me unworthy of him. She was an imperious plotting Russian. I knew her character well through her family – the Benckendorffs.[2]

Ever dear Mdme Belloc

Yrs afftnly

Eliz Eastlake

1. Calderon's picture *Saint Elizabeth of Hungary's Great Act of Renunciation*, Presented by the Trustees of the Chantrey Bequest 1891 (Tate Gallery No1573). The painting caused a stir by showing the kneeling saint naked.

2. Princess Dorothea Lieven, wife to the Russian ambassador in London from 1812 to 1834, and mistress of, among others, Metternich, Lord Grey, the Duke of Wellington, the Earl of Aberdeen, and Lord Palmerston.

Letter to John Murray   *NLS Ms.42178*

7 FitzRoy Sqre

28 Octr 91

Dear Layard

I was glad to put my hands upon the "translated extracts" immediately, for I had taken care of them. How noble they are! & how vain addressed to Germans! There never have been those class hatreds in Italy or in England as in Germany. The man who could grapple with them would be the real Statesman. Bismarck had no conception of what was wanted. I have known more of the misery of Germans than he did. Nor will the young Emperor, with his 'paternal' admonitions effect any change.

I no longer see the Fortnightly, & so have not read Dr. Bode's impertinent ignorance. But I had the honor of a visit from him not long ago, & he looked like a sausage himself. I shall enjoy to see your castigation of him.[1] I hope Miss Ffoulkes' translation improved as she proceeded. I remark nowadays how bad translations are, evidently undertaken by young ladies who don't know grammar. Any young & lively hand could concoct an amusing article on the slipslop grammar of the day – my time is over for doing that.[2]

I was asked the other day whether that so called portrait of Cesare Borgia by Raphael in the Borghese Palace were really by the great hand. I replied that my impression was that both names were false.[3]

I am ashamed not to have sooner acknowledged your kind letter of the 9th – & now I must break off for callers have come in & I have no one to bear the brunt, being alone. So I promise to send a sequel to this. Kindest love to Enid

Ever your's truly

Eliz: Eastlake

1. Wilhelm von Bode (1845–1929), art historian and Director of the Painting Collection at the Gemäldegalerie in Dresden. His article 'The Berlin Renaissance Museum', *Fortnightly Review*, 50 (1891), pp. 506–15, caricatured Morelli's reputation for attribution based upon artists' renditions of ears, noses and fingers and cast him as a 'quack doctor'. Layard's 'castigation', as it was conceived rather than executed, appeared in his Introduction to Morelli's *Italian Painters* (London: John Murray, 1892), pp. 1–39.

2. Morelli had hoped that Elizabeth would undertake the translation herself. See letter from Morelli to Layard, Milan, 5 February 1890, BL, BM Add MS 38965 fols. 205–206.

3. Morelli attributes the portrait of a Cardinal to Jacopo Pontormo (*Italian Painters* [London: John Murray, 1892], p. 128 n. 9).

Letter to John Murray   *NLS Ms.42178*

7 FitzRoy Square

9 Novr 91

Dear Mr. Murray

I heard from Mr. Courtney, who wrote me a kind & courteous note, that he has resigned the Editorship of your Mag: He therefore returned me "Another letter from the Baltic" which I had just sent him. He added that he believed the Mag: would be "suspended". If this be true I shall be much grieved. If not actually certain I can only commend this last article to your tender mercies to give it a place in an early number.

It is probably the last attempt of my pen, & it is also one of the best. I have lately had my letters from Petersburg returned to me, not having seen them since I wrote them, almost 50 years ago, & they are so lively & full of interest that they have only wanted a little 'tossing up' to make an amusing article. It also gives a rather unique picture of high life at Petersburg. Should your Mag: not continue, then I shall encroach on

your kindness to tell me which, among the many present mags would
be likely to take an article of this kind.

I hope you are well, & keep your activity. Mine departs more &
more, which does not supprize me. I have every comfort this world can
give, but it cannot restore the "old familiar faces"!

I greatly admire your Archbishop Tait in this last Quarterly. Ever dear
Mr Murray yr's truly
Eliz Eastlake

Letter to A. H. Layard   *NLS Ms.42173*

7 FitzRoy Sqre
15. Novr 91
Dear Layard

I am late in fulfilling the <u>threat</u> of soon writing again. Meanwhile
I believe that the extracts you asked for are what you wanted. Your
introduction to Miss Joscelyn Ffoulkes' translation of dear Morelli's work
will interest me intensely. I have not yet seen that attack on him in
the Fortnightly – but I must & will get it. My little Editor friend Mr.
Vershoyle, has resigned his post, & also his FitzRoy Square lodgings,
& is gone to a small living in Suffolk. I leave Dr. Bode unreservedly
to your tender mercies, & shall enjoy the castigation you serve out to
him. I had some German connoisseur here the other day & who, after
looking through the little collection, asked me if I were any relation of
'Sir Charles Eastlake?' Germans are out of the pale of polite society.

I have been occupied lately with compiling "Another Letter from
the Baltic" which, to my surprize was returned to me by the Editor
of Murray's Mag:, with the regretful information that the Mag: was
about to be dropped, & that his office was over. I find it is too true.
Murray writes me "there are too many of us". Certainly the Mag: had
no great distinction – I fear therefore that they have lost by it. It is a
pity that one of Murray's own sons could not have edited it. Of course
my selfish thought is what to do with my article which is chiefly upon
the high Russian society of 50 years ago! – & rather interesting. Murray
recommends Blackwood, but I do not fancy their double columns,
or suggests making a little vol: with this article & the last, with the
addition of something more. It strikes me that something new to the
present generation might by made of 'Edinburgh Society' also 50 years
ago, & perhaps I may work this out.[1]

I have had a young German connoisseur here, German in name,

& American in education, whose enthusiasm for the old masters has interested me much. He brought a letter to me from that young Mr. Berenson whom you once kindly admitted into Ca' Capello. He tells me how prevelant an enthusiasm there exists among his young contemporaries.

I hope Miss Ffoulkes translation is good & compact. I remark that translations nowadays are very slip slop, & with questionable grammar.

I have not seen dear old Mr. Hawtrey of late, but hear that he is well.

My best love to Enid – I am quite well & hope that you both are Ever yr's truly
Eliz Eastlake

1. 'Reminiscences of St. Petersburg Society', *Longman's Magazine*, vol. 20 (June 1892), pp. 145–57 and 'Reminiscences of Edinburgh Society Nearly Fifty Years Ago', *Longman's Magazine*, vol. 21 (January 1893), pp. 250–64.

Letter to A. H. Layard   *NLS Ms.42173*

7 FitzRoy Sqre
29 Decr 91
My dear Layard

I shd like you to have a few words from me in time for the New Year, tho' I have little that is interestg to say. But your last kind letter – Novr 24 with the account of yr visit to our dear Empress Frederick preeminently deserves my best thanks. She is a shining light in her exalted sphere – much thrown away, I fear, among my little-loved Germans to whom she is truly caviar. I had hoped that she & her noble Husband were destined to be the rinascimento of Germany, but it did not deserve either of them. Trent is one of the few places where dear Sir Chas & I never were. I sympathize truly with you in a "republican antipathy to royalty." The history of royalty is, with a few exceptions, a sadly contemptible thing. People talk of their temptation to evil, they forget those temptations to good which their power & influence give them. The young Emperor with his arrogance & priggery suits his countrymen too well, & will probably leave them worse that he found them, & entail on them five (or six?) young Hohenzollern's into the bargain.

Not that I am in a humour to praise my own country, or rather our countrywomen, just now. The Russell & the Osbourne trials,[1] tho' not to be compared in depth of iniquity are a terrible revelation of female folly & wickedness. In point of fact all society was taken in. The wiseacres, including myself, had pitched on Major Hargreaves as the culprit – anybody indeed but the real criminal. The story quite haunts me. It is evident that the wretched woman did not possess one grain of conscience. The levity of the sin is its horrid part, its courage too astonishing. I can but hope that this fearful exposure may help to put fast women, with their slang & their cigars out of fashion. They are a stain on our country. Your sex come out with fly.g colours. Still, it must be remembered that my sex commit these disgraceful mistakes under the belief of pleasing yours!

I have thought every one fortunate who has been anywhere but in London in these last days. I have lived here 41 years but never remember a fog of such blackness & opaqueness. It cd be literally felt. It was terribly depressing – nobody moved who cd help it, & everything was delayed. We had five mortal days of it, hearing of Brighton being all sparkle & light. Of course I never go out in winter, but every body was as infirm as I. No end of family parties were prevented on Xmas Day. Two relations kindly made their way to me.

I am no longer thinking of publishing my 2nd letter from the Baltic. Murray took a fit of bearishness – not a rare thing in my experience – & the idea is given up. I have sent it to Blackwood's Maga – but hardly think it is in their line. It is time for me to give up scribbl.g now. Just now I had a note from dear old Hawtrey. He is quite well – but the fog prevented even his many friends.

I have seen Lady Charlotte's admission into the 'Fan Makers' Company. She well deserves the honor – I read the Master's address & her answers with interest.

You ask what I have been readg lately – really the number of notes & letters to answer at this time is so immense that I have no time to read. I have been sendg books to a number of little boys & of course have read them first. Now you & Enid will be soon in Rome. I rather envy you that.

Time to send you both my hearty good wishes with best love to Enid Ever yr's truly
Eliz Eastlake

1. Mrs Osbourne v. Major and Mrs Hargreaves for slander in charging her with stealing jewels. Mrs Osbourne was imprisoned for larceny and perjury when it was discovered that she had sold the jewels.

Letter to A. H. Layard   *NLS Ms.42173*

7 FitzRoy Sqre
7 Febry 92
Dear Layard

I am late in acknowledg.g your last kind letter – dated January 4th,
wh: has been my own loss, but Xmas & New Year bring even me so
much to do & to think of, that I take some time to recover! There are
so many to think of, & so many letters & notes to write, & so many
presents to send – to say nothing of five Norfolk turkeys – that I have
no time to please myself. In the first week of 92 I wrote above 50 notes
& letters, & read no end of little story-books. For I have three sets of
little boys to remember & quite enjoy to read first the books I send
them. I had quite an embarrass de richesses, tho' not without some silly
& stupid exceptions – for a good child's book should be a real work of
Art. However I did very well & had some juvenile underlined effusions
in return. Then we have had this terrible influenza period since, which
has interrupted every other thought. Happily it has not touched my
few remaining relatives but the loss of friends has been severe. Three
dear old gentlemen were carried off within 8 days – first an Admiral
(Dunlop) who had been married only 27 days! Then my next door
neighbour – Mr Dent – a most worthy & excellent man, a giver of
splendid roses in the depth of winter, & a dropper in when I was alone.
& then good General Wray, commander of the Turkish Contingent in
the Crimean War – a cousin of the Lewins, who used to come here
like a tame cat. I can't replace any of them. Then my other next door
neighbour at No.6 died the same day as Mr. Dent. So I was literally
encompassed. But the scourge has not entered these doors – thank God.
You will have seen also Ph: Hardwick's death, a great deliverance for
himself, for he suffered much. He has left an excellent little wife, &
two promising girls & two ditto boys – also a good deal of money.[1] I
will not speak of the young Prince – his death has elicited a deal of
dormant loyalty – the existence of which, in spite of the Pce of Wales'
peccadilloes, I never doubted. As for himself I am assured by a Lady
who aught to know, Lady Sarah Spencer, that he is taken from the evil
to come, for he <u>hated</u> his station, & felt himself utterly unequal to what
it expected & required from him.[2]

I am leading a quiet, vegetatg life – subsisting on what books I can
get. At last I got the Fortnightly with Dr. Bode's malevolent effusion,
& am thankful to have, with your help, defended dear Morelli to the
best of my power. He also offends me in another direction, in his total

neglect of dear old Waagen's name, who did the most for the Berlin gallery. But nothing surprizes me in a German – not even the cruelty, now published, in the German army, which I have long known with the resulting high percentage of suicide among the poor privates. But the lower Germans are so abject that they will never rise against their oppressors.

My thoughts are just now painfully occupied with the miscarriage of justice in Mrs Osbourne's case – which occasioned her discharge from the Guild Hall Court. If the whole rigour of the law cannot be carried out against her, it will do immense harm among our lower classes. I have already heard one lady declarg her not to be guilty, & could only answer "why then did she abscond!"

I know the kind of job you must have had with Miss Ffoulkes' translation, & am thankful it has passed through your revision – too many women write & translate nowadays with limited knowledge of grammar & construction. I have sometimes longed to write a short article with specimens & quotations. But I have scribbled my last now. As to readg I have followed your lead & am now immersed in the 'Duc de Nivernais' wh: I find most interestg. I am also readg Père Didon's "Jesus Christ" not so much in your line. I am also interested in an article on the Jews in Revue des deux Mondes by Leroy Deaulieu of last July. I was sorry to perceive the loss you had suffered in the death of yr old friend Mrs Burr under yr roof.[3]

I can but rejoice that you & Enid are not going to Rome, wh: is full.

1. Philip Charles Hardwick left £211,000 in his will.

2. The Prince of Wales' son, Prince Albert Victor, had died in January from the flu.

3. Margaretta Higford Burr died in Venice on 23 January 1892 but not under Layard's roof. See Enid Layard's Journals, vol. XII (BL Add MS 46164).

Letter to A. H. Layard   *NLS Ms.42173*

7 FitzRoy Sqre
22. Feb: 92
Dear Layard

Your proof sheets – so kindly sent – have been a <u>great</u> treat to me, & I laid them down with the comfortg conviction that dear Morelli had at length recd <u>thorough</u> justice – indeed you tell even those who thought they knew him well, as for instance myself. How true it is that a man is

known by his friends. His comprised a group of the choicest characters
– our Empress & you at the top. There is no accident in such a fact
– the noble & intelligent gravitate together. You will see I have had the
impertinence to suggest a few very immaterial hints in pencil – from
an inveterate habit of reading critically. Only when you miksquote me
– p.35 – & put 'quick' instead of 'genial', which puzzled me till I looked
up the article – have I used open; & I have no doubt you wd have
corrected that misprint.

I did not answer that portion of your letter of Feb: 9 in wh: you
speak of the removal of the Borghese Gallery into the country, &
also of the trouble entailed in the Doria Gallery by the disarrangemt
of the numbers. I have always felt that the abolition of the law of
primogeniture was a grave error in the Italian govt. I have lived too
much in countries – Gemany – where it does not exist, not to know
the evils wh: its absence entails – the pride & poverty of families,
& the class hatreds in the country itself. I look upon our unique
institution of <u>nobility</u>, as distinct from <u>noblesse</u>, as the real source
of English union, givg the title, honors, & wealth to only one at a
time, & bindg that one in closest union, through his younger childn,
with the great body of commoners. Socialism ought never to flourish
in England – though here & there introduced by the Germans with
whom it is <u>naturally</u> at home, its souce is malgovernments. The
accounts of the cruelty in the German army aught to open peoples'
eyes to the real rottenness of that govt. the suicides among the poor
privates is four times than in any other body of men. But as you well
know Germans are my favourite hatred.

You speak of Gregory, & heartily do I hope wish that he
may recover.[1] But he is in my very bad books now for his havg
recommended the Govt to return Burton as Director of our N. Gal:. He
is beyond the age of public service, he has <u>never</u> done his duty, & that
Gregory well knows, & it was an opportunity of relievg the Treasury
of a useless burden. I know no one to put in his place, & feel that for
a time the office might be suspended. No one knows perhaps so well
as I <u>how</u> the office ought to be filled. I have a great affection for Chas
Eastlake, but my opinion of Burton is formed independently [sic].

I do fear that John Murray is in his last illness. He does not mend
– is entirely in bed & gradually weaker. I am unspeakably sorry sorry
[sic] for his family, & even for his now almost unconscious wife, who
has a vague idea of him, & is angry if anyone sits in his chair. This I
know from his & my nephew Charles Eastlake Smith.

You speak of that <u>baggage</u> Mrs Osbourne. I can have no pity for her
as long as she is unrepentant. & I don't approve of her honest husband

sitting by her in court & holding her hand. That would not be allowed to the husband of a poor woman – less a culprit. Now give my best love to Enid. I like to hear of her reading to you.

Ever your's truly

Eliz Eastlake

I send the proof by this days post

1. Sir William Gregory died on 6 March 1892.

Letter to A. H. Layard   *NLS Ms.42173*

7 F. Sqre

7. April 1892

I am in your debt, dear Layard, for 2 letters now, & am late in acknowledge.g them. Increasg years & declining strength interfere somewhat with the writg table. For some time every body has ascribed every neglect of duty to the <u>weather</u>, but this won't serve now, for we have perpetual sunshine. It was most kind of you to explain to me the Trustees' motive for retaining Sir F.B.'s 'valuable services', & I bow entirely to them. I wish I could as heartily concur in your opinion of his merits. You ask me if I know Mr. Benson,[1] who married Halford's daughter. I do, up to a certain point, for he occasionally favours me with a visit, 'to talk a little about art'. I have photographs of some of his pictures. And he certainly has a genuine love for the Old Masters – tho' I should not say that his connoisseurship was at all profound, but perhaps quite sufficiently so to qualify him as a Trustee of N.G. & he is a gentlemanly nice young man.

Mrs Salis Schwabe takes her <u>congé</u> very philosophically – I gave her no hope from the first.[2] The picture, called 'Les Gemissements de la Terre' is I think permanently at 8 Clarges St, so you can see it (for yr own pleasure) when you come.

Now for another subject – dear John Murray's death! wh: I know affects you deeply & I need not say does the same with me. I have known him, I was going to say, before you were born. At all events for over 50 years & I question whether any unrelated person has known the family so intimately as I. It was about a month ago that he called here with his youngest daughter. I thought him greatly altered, & he said sorrowfully "infirmities! Infirmities!" On leaving this house he insisted on walking home, & arrived in A. Street so exhausted that he went to bed at once & never left it but for short periods. He was carried down once a day to sit next to his poor unconscious wife. I can conceive few incidents more <u>pathetic</u>! It is a great comfort to know that his death was entirely painless. Our mutual nephew, Chas Eastlake Smith, followed the coffin with the other members of the family. He writes me that St. James' church was crammed – & also the sad ceremony at Wimbledon equally crowded. He tells me that young Jack broke down, but that Hallam continued firm. I shall hear from my dear nephew what are the family arrangements. It is true that dear John Murray had taken a prejudice against me ever since I stood alone, & one wh: from reasons I cd not control it was was not in my power to remove. Peace to him! I look forward to the time when all misconceptions will be cleared up.

You will enjoy Florence, & the Uffizi – I hope it will do you both good. My best love to Enid, ever your's truly

Eliz Eastlake

1. Robert Benson (1850–1929), merchant banker and art collector, married Evelyn Holford. He was Trustee of the National Gallery from 1912.

2. Julie Salis Schwabe (1818–96), educationalist who helped to establish the Froebel Educational Institute. A letter from Elizabeth to Layard dated 9 March 1892 (NLS Ms.42173) reads: 'My attention has been lately called to a picture for which I shd like to bespeak your interest. Old Mrs Salis Schwabe whom everyone knows has been to me about the fine Ary Scheffer in her possession. She wants to convert it into a fund for establishing the 'Kinder Garten' system into some Italian school – & wd be thankful to dispose of it to the Nat: Gallery for £3.000 – but wd take £2.000 – & has been offered £4.000. From the specimens I have seen of Scheffer in his family home at Rotterdam I am inclined to rate a chef d'oeuvre by him very high – & so did Sir Chas. I have seen the picture in question – a <u>very</u> fine thing both in colour & expression – though I forget the subject.'

Letter to A. H. Layard   *NLS Ms.42173*

7 FitzRoy Sqre
28 April 92
Dear Layard

Though no longer in your debt I find myself bound to inflict another letter upon you. For I have meanwhile recd in your name a copy of Miss Ffoulkes' translation of Morelli's work. It makes a handsome vol: & I shall keep it for the present on my table & look into it from time to time. Meanwhile I have read your introduction again with renewed interest. Whether considered as a contribution to Art, or a defence of a friend, or a piece of writing I find it first rate, & enhancg in every way the value of the work. The young lady (I have no idea what she is like) is fortunate in havg had such able friends. I am very proud to possess the book.

Since your last letter – March 24th – you have gone thro' the pain of hearing of Murray's death. He is universally lamented, & I know from his & my mutual nephew what crowds attended both the funeral ceremonies at St James' & at Wimbledon. I know the general outline of his will, & of the removal of the poor unconscious lady to Wimbledon, which is to be her residence & that of her daughters. There is a pleasant society there who will not neglect them. Last Sunday week I had the unexpected pleasure of a visit from young John. I had seen him but once since he was a little boy, & that about 20 years ago, but I had always heard with pleasure of his intelligence & kindness. We did not meet without emotion. He had his little girl on his hand – a bright healthy-lookg child, but with the sad disfigurement of a hair lip [sic]. Those shd be confined to boys only! I hope I shall see him from time to time – but all power of hospitality is over on my part.

There seem to be no end of exhibitions going on now in London. Tomorrow I send friends & relatives to the Private View of the R. Academy – the Dinner as usual on the Saturday – & the opening on the first Monday of the month. I never have any fear of Leighton's not doing honor to the R.A. on these occasions. Meanwhile I have recd & read the Annual Report of the Nat: Gallery. I see the worthy Director adheres to his conception of the names of painters best fitted for the edification of the public – tho' such as 'Dou' & "Sir A. Mov' will hardly reach their comprehension.

I have not been reading anything new of late – I was caught by the title of a book which promised some gratification of my anti German sentiments, "A Roman in Britain" by H.C. Coote. I particularly object to being credited with a Teutonic origin, & have always felt that the Romans must have left enough behind them in Britain to relieve us of that charge. A careful history quite confirms that belief. It appears that the Roman colonists looked on the Britons as their most intelligent & promising pupils. Also that Anglo Saxons who succeeded were the most hopeless of barbarians. I feel much more comfortable & proud of my country since reading this work. Nor does the Emperor William bid fair to mitigate my prejudices. Of course there are a few Germans I like & respect, as I always did dear old Waagen, but the greater portion are slaves & sycophants – too poor to be honest, far less liberal.

Of course I am reading this Quarterly attentively & have enjoyed the capitally written article on the Archbishop of York, whom we knew, but the next, 'Culture & Anarchy' seems to me far fetched & very tedious.[1] Altogether I fancy the Q.R. is too heavy, though I am sure the dear old Editor does his best. There is nothing to take its place, & I am not sure that anything now is wanted.

I have been having a few photographs of these drawing room walls taken, which I understand promise to be successful. Of course you shall have copies.

The other day I had a visit from Mary Kay & her sister – both well & Mrs. K: most agreeable. Now with my best love to Enid who I hope is well I am

Your's ever truly

Eliz Eastlake

1. Mowbray Morris, 'Culture and Anarchy', *Quarterly Review*, vol. 174 (April 1892), pp. 317–44 is a review of Thomas Hardy's *Tess of the D'Urbevilles*.

Letter to John Murray IV   *NLS Ms.42178*

7 FitzRoy Square

2 May 92

Dear Mr Murray[1]

I was touched to find that the Quarterly was sent to me for this month. I have enjoyed it for so many years – from your Grandfather's & from your lamented Father – that I am doubly bound to set the present young generation free from such an incubus.

I therefore beg you to consider me for the short remainder of my life as one of your <u>abonnés</u> & consider me as no less grateful.

In this present number the article on Archbishop Thompson (whom we knew) is most interesting, but the pearl of the number – as far as I have read – however sad the subject, is that on 'The French decadence'. I remember the sensation produced by an article on French novels before you were born, which horrified the English world. This seems to me as terrible in disclosure, & still more powerfully treated.

Believe me yrs very truly

Eliz Eastlake

1. John Murray IV (1851–1928) began working for the family business in the 1880s and inherited a share of it (with his brother Hallam).

Letter to A. H. Layard   *NLS Ms.42173*

7 FitzRoy Sqre
10 Novr. 1892
Dear Layard

I need not say how truly welcome was yr letter of the 28. Octr & how ashamed I feel to be so late in acknowledge.g it. But it is the old story of excuses which seem to evaporate in relating. I have fits of work – so called – & fits of very genuine idleness, & have had both lately. And now we are enveloped in Novr fogs which are an excuse for anthing.

Your account of yr visit to the son of the Duchesse de Berri interests me much. I had been readg about her in the Duchesse de Contaut's [sic][1] memoirs wh: seem to be the latest tribute to old French court manners which will surely never be seen again.

Meanwhile I have seen your friend Miss Ffoulkes, who was looking well, & of course did not blush to me as she does to you. And I cd conscientiously congratulate her on the completion of her task. She is on the whole a good translator. I might suggest a little contractg & tightening up here & there, but she has made it a very readable book. I have also read the article in the Edinburgh, which is fairly done. I have no idea by whom.

I had no idea that Morelli has once been over to Wimbledon & had inspected the two <u>Pedrini</u>'s which we had purchased for Murray in Milan(?) Such ages had elapsed since I had been at Wimbledon that I had really forgotten the transaction. But I had a kind visit from young John Murray last Sunday, who reminded me of them, & told me of Morelli's visit. He is certainly no beauty, but he has a most pleasant manner, & I grieve that my age & infirmities prevent my welcomg him & his wife as I wd otherwise gladly do. He brought his wife with him, who also struck me as a little chatterbox, but that is not unwelcome at the head of a table like that in Albemarle Street. He is left, as you perhaps know, guardian to Ph: Hardwick's childn, & she cannot say too much of his kindness. I hear him spoken of highly too for his business powers. And when he was here he spoke in the kindest & most generous [sic] of the work that Hallam had done whilst he (John) was in Scotland.[2]

I am writing with the consciousness that, if not already in Engld, you may cross this letter. There can be no difficulty in bearing witness to Lady Westminster's singular competence to make a will. Tho' I had not seen her for years, yet I saw much of her at one time as she was always kind to me. I am sure the charge against yr friend Rassam[3] must be equally unjust, but indeed the B. Museum never behaved well to you, or you wd have been appointed a Trustee to an Institution you have benefited so grandly. There ought to be a better bust of you & whenever yr friends combine to have one I am ready to contribute.

You mention a notice of Henri de Rohan wh: you are preparing. I have no idea who he was, but I shall be glad to know. I have not been idle, but as Murray's Mag: ceased I turned to Longman's Mag: & find a very civil editor in one of the Longman family. In their June No. is a paper "Reminiscences of Petersburg Society", & perhaps next month, or Janry there will be "Reminiscences of Edinr Society", wh: in my young time was very interesting. No time to speak of yr beloved Stella! I hope she will come to London one day.[4]

With kindest love to Enid, ever yrs truly
Eliz Eastlake

1. *Memoirs of the Duchess de Gontaut*, 2 vols. (London: Chatto & Windus, 1894).

2. Alexander Henry Hallam Murray (1854–1934), son of John Murray III, who inherited a share in the family business. Hallam was also an amateur painter. He married Enid Layard's niece, Alicia du Cane.

3. Hormudz Rassam (1826–1910), Assyrian scholar who had assisted Layard in his first excavations, and continued on archaeological expeditions throughout the Near East. After 1882 he lived in Brighton.

4. Stella Dyer is often mentioned in Enid Layard's journal as reading to Layard and playing the violin for him.

Letter to A. H. Layard   *NLS Ms.42173*

7. F. Sqre
22 Janry 93
Dear Layard

I have treated you abominably for some time, & you have turned the other cheek to me in the most magnanimous way. For you have written me two delightful long letters without a word from me, till I am quite ashamed. But Christmas & New Year have become occasions on which one slaves from morng to night without getting a step forwarder. The torrent of cards, notes, letters, & appeals is simply overpowering, & on the top of all these I have been trying to do my usual rough summary of my years accounts, till I have been well nigh worn out. However,

I have killed off cards, notes, & even years' accounts & some of the
appeals, & have now come to the letters, among the first to your's.

Knowg your delightful Ca' Capello as I do there is always enough
to excite my envy, which is filled to the brim by the report of the fine
weather you have had. Still I don't doubt you must have had a touch
of the misery of cold darkness we have suffered here, from which we
are now emerging. Bronchitis has killed many. It had nothing to do
I believe with the death of dear old Thomson Hankey whom I shall
miss. You will be glad to hear that his illness was short & his end
without suffering. Had he lived longer something in one leg, I believe
the threatening of anurism, wd have given great pain. I shall miss him
much. He had ceased to be able to climb my stairs, but I cd go to him
in his ground floor romm, & with the help of his dear old wife's wheel
chair. I conclude his property was large, but he had plenty of nephews
& nieces to divide it among. "Seven nephews" he once wrote to me. He
was a man of clear mind & of generous feelings, & he bore the trials of
old age with great cheerfulness.

I have been reading lately a M.S. of the Memoirs of Lady De
Ros, who died about a year ago at 94, compiled by her daughter
Mrs Swinton (named Blanche Arthur as Goddaughter of the D: of
Wellington.) it is much made up of letters from friends of her time. She
wished me to look thro' it before publication, & so young John Murray
brought it to me himself, & completed the conquest of my affections!
The memoir concludes with the article of the Brussells ball, tho' before
Waterloo, given by Mrs Swinton's grandmother the Dss of Richmond
which is perhaps the best part of it.[1]

You know the Baroness Burdett Coutts well, or I shd congratulate
you on knowing her better still. I have stood in that relation to her
as to judge of her very fine, thoroughbred qualities. As to the risk of
marrying a man so much younger than oneself I begin to think that it
is a sure guarantee for domestic felicity! I have known several instances
of its success & I have a niece married now above a year to a young
man – rich, good looking, & of excellent character, who is much more
her junior than I like to own, but no two people can be happier.

I have recd Frizzoni's vol: of dear Morelli's Berlin Gallery, & have
written him a German note to acknowledge it, & look forward to readg
it carefully with great zest. I have no one to read to me as you happily
possess in yr beloved Stella, whose interesting character I quite believe
in. I wonder you don't do as good 'Bob Lowe' used to do, who, instead
of sitting with idle hands, learned to knit socks for himself![2] By the
way I recd a note from Lady Sherbrook yesterday, asking me a question
regardg his life which is being compiled by a "Mr. A: Patchett Martin"

a name I never heard. I never saw her, but I know she made him a very good wife.

I consider my literary career as concluded now. I have taken refuge in Longmans 6d Magazine wh: is liberal & courteous. I shd hardly think that finds its way to Venice. Shd it do so you will find me in this month's number. I like Miss Ffoulkes very much & thro' her a former friend, Lady Florentia Hughes,[3] & I have renewed intercourse. Tell Enid I think much of her, & applaud her wisdom in encouraging yr liking for so good a little girl as Stella, who I am sure is grateful to both of you.

Ever yrs truly
Eliz Eastlake

1. J. R. Swinton, *A Sketch of the Life of Georgiana, Lady de Ros, with Some Reminiscences of her Family and Friends, Including the Duke of Wellington* (London: John Murray, 1893).

2. Robert Lowe, Viscount Sherbrooke (1811–92), former politician.

3. Lady Florentia Hughes (1828–1909).

Letter to A. H. Layard   NLS Ms.42173

7 FitzRoy Sqre
29. Janry. 93
Dear Layard

You have seen my handwriting so recently that you will wonder what can be the reason for this fresh infliction. It is the renewal of an old story, which you may almost guess. A rumour has reached me that yr friend Burton is about to resign the Directorship, doubtless much to your sorrow, so I am sorry for you – & of course sorry also for the public good, but if such be unfortunately the case I am anxious to urge the experience & merits of my nephew Chas Eastlake.

I have long felt that, for the present at least, the two offices of Director & Secretary are not needed & that the double salary might be avoided & saved to the nation. I believe you feel as warmly as I do how well he has filled his post & how thoroughly he knows the duties of both situations. A small addition to what he now receives wd be ample. I shd make him welcome to all his uncle's notes (I made Burton welcome also, but he never took advantage of them) & many a picture cd be still tracked & followed up which has remained unnoticed during this interval.

I hear a rumour that Poynter may be invited to be Director, whether a painter largely employed wd accept it I cannot say, but this wd frustrate the economy of public funds, & also he is not versed in the work. I believe your fellow trustees Lords Northborne, Carlisle, & Saville wd not be disinclined to recommend the junction of the two offices in Charles' person. I am sure a more honorable public servant cd not be found, he has also for years aimed to make himself something of a connoisseur. I now leave the matter to yr judgement well aware of yr good will towards him whatever the result.

I have no news for you except that I heard from yr godson, Alick Ross, the other day now tutor to Sir George Smith's son at Prestonpans, who had got his pupil thro' a first 'exam' & seems very happy.

Love to dear Enid

Ever yrs' truly

Eliz Eastlake

Letter to William Ewart Gladstone   *NLS Ms.10150 f.52*

7 FitzRoy Square

5 May 93

Dear Mr Gladstone

I ventured to give you trouble not long ago, on a mistaken plea which I much regretted. This time I feel safe in believing that the affairs of the National Gallery are included under your Department.[1]

I see by a paper called "Art News & Gossip" that Sir Fred: Burton contemplates retirement from the Directorship. This will entail the choice of a successor, & I am anxious to intrude on you one or two suggestions which perhaps could reach you from no one else. There is no first-rate Connoisseur now in England. Sir Fred: Burton has never been one; but it is easy to secure good pictures at inordinate prices. Such being the case I venture to suggest that the duties of the Director, & of the Keeper & Secretary might be merged together, at a saving to the nation & at no loss to the country. My nephew Mr. C. Lock Eastlake has for years filled the post of Keeper & Secretary, & I am not singular in saying that he has filled them admirably. All the Trustees of the Gallery wd attest this. He has inherited much of Sir Charles' conscientious accuracy in all he undertakes. He is also a very respectable connoisseur, & has studied foreign galleries carefully. Will you kindly believe that I am biased by no nepotism in suggesting him for the double position. I have all Sir Charles' notes on pictures in all parts of the continent – I mean all pictures eligible for purchase – carefully arranged, which are at his service. I placed them at Sir Fred: Burtons' but he has not availed himself of them.

Pray recall me to Mrs Gladstone's kind remembrance & believe me dear Mr Gladstone yr's very truly
Eliz Eastlake

1. This letter is in an album of over 200 letters on the subject of the Directorship of the National Gallery, many correspondents (Lionel Cust, P. G. Hamerton, Humphry Ward, W. B. Richmond, Sidney Colvin, G. F. Watts) debating the merits of a painter versus a connoisseur. The album also contains a letter from Charles Lock Eastlake to Gladstone dated 31 August 1893 (MS 10150 f. 58) offering his services as Director and also suggesting that the posts of Keeper and Director be merged. There are several other letters here about the job description of the new Director. Poynter had already offered his own services in f. 40 on 14 March 1893 and in a PS states that he has the approval of Henry Layard.

Letter to A. H. Layard   NLS Ms.42173

7 FitzRoy Sqre
23. May 93
Dear Layard
Your last kind letter told me of dear Enid's typhoid fever. I heard from another quarter that she was recoverg as well as cd be wished & also that you were expected as soon as she cd travel. I was therefore remiss as not to answer yr letter at once, & then feared I might not catch you. Now I have been to yr house to enquire, & find that your are really expected on Monday. I hope this may be just in time, if not it's no loss to you. I am glad to hear that the cause which was expected to bring you has been done away with. Your good Rassam still claims your help, & I trust that may right him. I never saw him but once but I cd never forget him.[1]

Meanwhile English thoughts have been divided between Home Rule & the drought. Everyone hopes that the one may terminate as surely as the other has done. But it is not so enjoyable as the persistent fine weather has been, which lasted for the Queen to open the Institute, & for the Whitsuntide holiday people.

My life has been as quiet as usual – not pleasingly diversified by the Australian Bank's suspensions, in one of which I, & my friends the Lewins are involved, in the 'London Chartered Bank of Australia', namely, the share of wh: our dear friends the Grotes rather largely held. At present there has been no meeting announced.

Fresh reports of Sir Frederick Burton's resignation have appeared – & by Chas Eastlake's wish I wrote to Mr. Gladstone & said all that I thought prudent as to the function of the two offices – & that in Charles' person – I could tell him what perhaps no one else would – that there is no first-rate connoisseur in England now. But I could also assure him that Chas is a very respectable one – & is willing to seek to take advice & would have the use of all Sir Chas' notes. Meanwhile Sir Fred gives no sign of resigning – & of course would be foolish to do so while he can neglect work & draw his salary. I may add that I offered <u>him</u> the use of Sir Charles' notes (carefully & alphabetically arranged) but he had never availed himself of them.[2]

Now dear Layard I won't trouble you to read further, trusting to see you so soon. My kindest love to Enid – & congratulations to <u>you</u> on her recovery.

Ever yr's truly
Eliz Eastlake
I had immediate & courteous answer from Mr. Gladstone – but he can't move till Burton resigns.

1. See letter to Layard, 10 November 1892, n. 3.

2. Sir Edward Poynter (1836–1919) became Director of the National Gallery in 1894 and President of the Royal Academy in 1896.

Letter to John Murray IV   *NLS Ms.42178*

7 FitzRoy Square
29 June 93
Dear Mr. Murray

This letter will be conveyed to you by Mr. Berenson, who, though bearing a foreign name, is thoroughly English in speech & mind – brought up I believe in America. He is an enthusiast in the study of the Old Masters – one of a young band, much educated by Morelli, of whom you have heard from Layard. Mr. Berenson has written a memoir of Lorenzo Lotto – a very original painter of Raphael's time with a careful list of his chief works – which he would like you to publish.

The matter of course interested Sir Charles & me deeply & there are specimens of him in the National Gallery. His most important works are at Bergamo. I have read the MS with admiration, for it is most

pleasingly done. I know well the pros & cons of such a proposal but
I know well too that as the knowledge of Old Masters advances (for
which we are chiefly indebted to Morelli's scholars) fresh chapters are
opened & must be made known to the public. We are far from knowing
all the Old Masters yet & I know no one in England who can help. Mr.
Berenson is confident that a small public would respond. At all events I
venture to introduce to you an agreeable young gentleman.
Hoping that you are all well – & rejoicing in the rain. I am yr's very
truly
Eliz Eastlake

Letter to Enid Layard   BL Add 58223 f.137

7 FitzRoy Square
14 July 1893
Dear Enid
    I don't know whether the weather will allow me to come to your
door today but at all events I must send you the little pamphlet of
which I spoke. I have turned down the leaf at the "medical evidence
against the practise" which I want you especially to read. It is no joke
for any tender hearted woman to enter into this horrid subject at all,
but it would be vile cowardice to shrink from knowing the truth on a
subject which concerns such dreadful sufferings of defenceless creatures.
Even if such sufferings on their part did us good, most hearts would
hesitate to accept much good at such cost, but the truth is the reverse.
These horrors mislead those who practise them, & of course unutterably
demoralize them. I know that Layard's defence of vivisection is chiefly
naughty chaff, but I am jealous that one so noble as he should even
appear to defend such atrocities.[1]
    The subject is becoming doubly serious – for the results of this
medical demoralization is that the hospitals have become places of
experiment & consequently of suspicion. The poor are shunning them
& the rich withdrawing their subscriptions form these hospitals which
include vivisectors on their staff. The question won't rest – it is getting
hold of the national conscience as the slave trade did only those believe
in Pasteur who are ignorant of the truth. He cures those who have not
hydrophobia, but kills the few who go to him with it, & a great many
beside. A regular register is kept of his murders, chapter & verse, they
amount to hundreds now, & are always increasing.
    Don't fear, dear Enid, that I am going to pester you with this horrid

subject. I shall never mention it again unless you wish. Meanwhile should you care to read further I have plenty more literature at your service! It is false logic to believe that those who torture innocent animals care a straw for the welfare of their fellow creatures.

Excuse my blots.

Ever yours affectionately

Eliz Eastlake

1. Frances Power Cobbe's lobby group, the Victoria Street Society for the Protection of Animals from Vivisection, argued that anaesthesia should be compulsory in animal experiments involving surgery and that the use of cats, dogs and horses for vivisection should be prohibited. See Richard D. French, *Antivivisection and Medical Science in Victorian Society* (Princeton and London: Princeton University Press, 1975). French shows (p. 239) that women represented 40–60 per cent of the membership and that Cobbe recruited many titled women as patrons.

Chronological Bibliography of Works by Elizabeth Eastlake

* denotes previously uncredited publications

'Letters to John Henry Merck, from Goethe, *Herder, Wieland &c*' *Foreign Quarterly Review*, vol. 17 (July 1836), pp. 391–417.* (see letter, 21 June 1836)

(trans.) J. D. Passavant, *Tour of a German Artist in England with Notices of Private Galleries, and Remarks upon the State of Art*, 2 vols. (London: Saunders & Otley, 1836).

A Residence on the Shores of the Baltic; Described in a Series of Letters, 2 vols. (London: John Murray, 1841).

A Residence on the Shores of the Baltic; Described in a Series of Letters, 2 vols. (London: John Murray, 2nd edn, 1842).

'Jesse, Kohl, and Sterling on Russia', *Quarterly Review*, vol. 69 (March 1842), pp. 380–418.

'Books for Children', *Quarterly Review*, vol. 71 (December 1842), pp. 54–83.

'"The Lady of the Manor" – Evangelical Novels', *Quarterly Review*, vol. 72 (May 1843), pp. 25–53.

'Biographies of German Ladies', *Quarterly Review*, vol. 73 (December 1843), pp. 142–87.

The Jewess: A Tale from the Shores of the Baltic (London: John Murray, 1844).

A Residence on the Shores of the Baltic; Described in a Series of Letters, 2 vols. (London: John Murray, 3rd edn, 1844).

'The Wolves of Esthonia', *Fraser's Magazine*, 31 (April 1844), pp. 392–400.

'Children's Books', *Quarterly Review*, vol. 74 (June 1844), pp. 1–26.

'Coronation of the King of Sweden', *The Times*, 15 October 1844.

'Lady Travellers', *Quarterly Review*, vol. 76 (June 1845), pp. 98–136.

Livonian Tales (London: John Murray, 1846).

'Modern German Painting', *Quarterly Review*, vol. 77 (March 1846), pp. 323–48.

'Cathedral of Cologne', *Quarterly Review*, vol. 78 (September 1846), pp. 425–63.

'Planche's *History of Costume*', *Quarterly Review*, vol. 79 (March 1847), pp. 372–99.

'Music', *Quarterly Review*, vol. 83 (September 1848), pp. 481–515.

'Views of Edinburgh', *Fraser's Magazine*, vol. 38 (November 1848), pp. 481–94.* (see letter, 6 October 1848)

'Modern Frankfort', *Fraser's Magazine*, vol. 38 (September 1848), pp. 334–44.

'*Vanity Fair* and *Jane Eyre*', *Quarterly Review*, vol. 84 (December 1848), pp. 153–85.

(trans.) Kugler's *Handbook of Painting in Italy, Part I: Italian Schools, Translated by a Lady. Edited with notes, by Sir Charles L. Eastlake … Second Edition, thoroughly revised with much additional material*, 2 vols. (London: John Murray, 1851).

'Physiognomy', *Quarterly Review*, vol. 90 (December 1851), pp. 62–91.

'Art and Nature Under an Italian Sky', *Quarterly Review*, vol. 91 (June 1852), pp. 1–11.

Music and the Art of Dress: Two Essays Reprinted from the Quarterly Review (London: John Murray, 1852).

(trans.) Gustav Waagen, *Treasures of Art in Great Britain*, 2 vols. (London: John Murray, 1854).

(attrib.) 'The History of Rome', *Gentleman's Magazine*, vol. 39 (1853), pp. 348–54.

'Treasures of Art in Great Britain', *Quarterly Review*, vol. 94 (March 1854), pp. 467–508.

(with Dean Milman) 'The Late John Lockhart', *The Times*, 9 December 1854* (authenticated in Lang, *Life and Letters of John Gibson Lockhart*, vol. II, p. 400).

'Modern Painters [by Ruskin]', *Quarterly Review*, vol. 98 (March 1856), pp. 384–433.

(trans.) Gustav Waagen, *Galleries and Cabinets of Art in Great Britain* (London: John Murray, 1857).

'Photography', *Quarterly Review*, vol. 101 (April 1857), pp. 442–68.

'Michel Angelo', *Quarterly Review*, vol. 103 (April 1858), pp. 436–83.

'Late Prince Consort', *Quarterly Review*, vol. 111 (January 1862), pp.176–200.

(with Harriet Grote) 'Christian Art', *Quarterly Review*, vol. 116 (July 1864), pp. 143–76.

The History of Our Lord, commenced by the late Mrs. Jameson, continued and completed by Lady Eastlake (London: Longman, Green, Longman, Roberts & Green, 1864).

'Galleries of the Louvre', *Quarterly Review*, vol. 117 (April 1865), pp. 287–323.

Recueil de meubles et d'ornement intérieurs, composés et dessinés dans les differents styles depuis l'epoque Louis XIII, jusqu'a nos jours par E. Eastlake, vol. 1 (Brussels: C. Muquardt; London: Williams & Norgate; The Hague: Martinus Nijhoff, 1866).

(with Harriet Grote) 'British Museum', *Quarterly Review*, vol. 124 (January 1868), pp. 147–79.

Fellowship: Letters Addressed to My Sister Mourners (London: Macmillan & Co., 1868).

Recueil de meubles et d'ornement intérieurs, composés et dessinés dans les differents styles depuis l'epoque Louis XIII, jusqu'a nos jours par E. Eastlake, vol. 2 (Brussels: Goupil and Muquardt; London: Williams & Norgate; Paris: Rapilly, 1869).

Preface to Charles Eastlake's *Materials for a History of Oil Painting*, vol. II (London: Longmans, Green & Co., 1869).

Contributions to the Literature of the Fine Arts by Sir C. L. Eastlake: with a memoir by Lady Eastlake (London: John Murray, 1869).

'Exhibition of the Society of Female Artists', *Art Journal*, 1 March 1869.

'Otto Mündler', *The Times*, 21 April 1870.

(ed.) *Life of John Gibson, R.A., Sculptor* (London: Longmans, 1870).

'Crowe and Cavalcaselle on the History of Painting', *Edinburgh Review*, vol. 135 (January 1872), pp. 122–49.

(ed.) *Kugler's Handbook of Painting. The Italian Schools … Edited, with notes, by Sir Charles L. Eastlake … New Edition. Fourth Edition. Revised and Remodelled from the latest researches, by Lady Eastlake*, 2 parts (London: John Murray, 1874).

'Leonardo da Vinci', *Edinburgh Review*, vol. 141 (January 1875), pp. 89–126.

'Life and Works of Thorvaldsen', *Edinburgh Review*, vol. 142 (July 1875), pp. 1–29.

'Drink: Vice and the Disease', *Quarterly Review*, vol. 139 (October 1875), pp. 396–434.

Frescoes by Raphael on the Ceiling of the Stanza dell'Eliodoro in the Vatican, Drawn by N. Consoni and Engraved by L. Gruner with Descriptions by Lady Eastlake (London: Published for Louis Grave by Virtue & Co. Ltd, 1875).

'The Two Ampères', *Edinburgh Review*, vol. 143 (January 1876), pp. 74–101.

'The Letters and Works of Michel Angelo', *Edinburgh Review*, vol. 144 (July 1876), pp. 104–47.

'London Alms, and London Pauperism', *Quarterly Review*, vol. 142 (October 1876), pp. 373–402.

'Venice Defended', *Edinburgh Review*, vol. 146 (July 1877), pp. 165–98.

'Titian', *Edinburgh Review*, vol. 147 (January 1878), pp. 105–44.

'The Englishwoman at School', *Quarterly Review*, vol. 146 (July 1878), pp. 40–69.

'Bastiat, Apostle of Free Trade', *Edinburgh Review*, vol. 149 (April 1879), pp. 377–89.

'Albert Dürer', *Quarterly Review*, vol. 148 (October 1879), pp. 376–407.

(ed.) *Dr. Rigby's Letters from France in 1789* (London: Longmans, 1880).

Mrs. Grote, A Sketch by Lady Eastlake (London: John Murray, 1880).

'Germany, Past and Present', *Edinburgh Review*, vol. 152 (October 1880), pp. 503–40.

'Mrs Jameson', *The Encyclopaedia Britannica*, vol. 13 (Edinburgh: Adam & Charles Black, 1880), pp. 562–63.

'Madame de Stael: Life and Times', *Quarterly Review*, vol. 152 (July 1881), pp. 1–49.

'The Jacobin Conquest', *Quarterly Review*, vol. 153 (January 1882), pp. 132–78.

'John Gibson Lockhart', *The Encyclopaedia Britannica*, vol. 14 (Edinburgh: Adam & Charles Black, 1882), pp. 762–64.

'The Life and Works of Raphael', *Edinburgh Review*, vol. 157 (January 1883), pp. 168–204.

Five Great Painters: Essays Reprinted from the Edinburgh and Quarterly Review, 2 vols. (London: Longmans, Green & Co., 1883).

'The Late Mr. Rawdon Brown', *The Times*, 8 September 1883, p. 6, col. C.

'Madonna del Ansidei', *The Times*, 14 October 1884, p. 2, col. E.

'The Female School of Art', *Englishwoman's Review*, n.s. 155 (15 March 1886), pp. 102–104.★ (see letter, 13 March 1886).

(trans.) Professor Brandl's *Samuel Taylor Coleridge and the English Romantic School* (London: John Murray, 1887).

'Samuel Coleridge and the Romantic School', *Quarterly Review*, vol. 165 (July 1887), pp. 60–96.

'Thomas Webster, R.A.', *Murray's Magazine*, vol. 2 (July–December 1887), pp. 222–31.

'Kaspar Hauser', *Quarterly Review*, vol. 166 (April 1888), pp. 469–95.

'Reminiscences of Samuel Rogers', *Quarterly Review*, vol. 167 (October 1888), pp. 504–13.

'Venice: Institutions and Private Life', *Quarterly Review*, vol. 168 (January 1889), pp. 71–102.

'Alexander I of Russia and the Poles', *Quarterly Review*, vol. 170 (January 1890), pp. 80–111.

'An Old Letter from the Baltic', *Murray's Magazine*, vol. 8 (1890), pp. 487–503.

'Russia: People and Government', *Quarterly Review*, vol. 172 (January 1891), pp. 113–42.

'Giovanni Morelli: Patriot and Critic', *Quarterly Review*, vol. 143 (July 1891), pp. 235–52.

'Temper', *Murray's Magazine*, vol. 10 (September 1891), pp. 384–93.

'Reminiscences of St. Petersburg Society', *Longman's Magazine*, vol. 20 (June 1892), pp. 145–57.

'Reminiscences of Edinburgh Society Nearly Fifty Years Ago', *Longman's Magazine*, vol. 21 (January 1893), pp. 250–64.

Select Bibliography

Avery-Quash, Susanna, 'The Travel Notebooks of Charles Eastlake, 1830–65', *The Walpole Society*, vol. 74 (forthcoming, 2012).

Barlow, Paul and Colin Trodd (eds.), *Governing Cultures: Art Institutions in Victorian England* (London: Ashgate, 2000).

Borenius, Tancred, 'Eastlake's Travelling Agent', *Burlington Magazine*, vol. 83 (September 1943), p. 215.

Brake, Laurel, *Subjugated Knowledges: Journalism, Gender and Literature in the Nineteenth Century* (London: Macmillan, 1994).

Bruce, W. N. (ed.), *A. Henry Layard, Autobiography and Letters*, 2 vols. (London: John Murray, 1903).

Bullen, J.B., *The Myth of the Renaissance in Nineteenth-Century Writing* (Oxford: Clarendon, 1994).

Cardoso, Rafael and Colin Trodd (eds.), *Art and the Academy in the Nineteenth Century* (Manchester: Manchester University Press, 2000).

Catalogue of the Collection of Pictures, Chiefly by the Old Masters, formed by Sir C.L. Eastlake ... and sold by order of the Executors of Lady Eastlake ... which will be sold by auction by Messrs. Christie, Manson & Woods ... June 2, 1894 (London: William Clowes & Sons, 1894).

Catalogue of ... Drawings and Engravings, the property of Lady Eastlake, deceased, late of 7 Fitzroy Square, which will be sold by Auction by Messrs. Christie, Manson & Woods ... Tuesday, June 19, 1894 (London: William Clowes & Sons, 1894).

Catalogue of a small Collection of Objects of Art, the Property of Lady Eastlake, deceased ... Which will be sold by Auction by Messrs. Christie, Manson & Woods ... July 5, 1894 (London: William Clowes & Sons, 1894).

'Charles Eastlake', *Encyclopaedia Britannica* (Edinburgh: Adam & Charles Black, 9th edn, 1877), vol. 7, pp. 615–16.

Clarke, Meaghan, *Critical Voices: Women and Art Criticism in Britain 1800–1905* (Aldershot: Ashgate, 2005).

Conlin, Jonathan, *The Nation's Mantlepiece: A History of the National Gallery* (London: Pallas Athene, 2006).

Cooper, Robyn, 'The Popularization of Renaissance Art in Victorian England: The Arundel Society', *Art History*, vol. 1, no.3 (September 1978), pp. 263–92.

Denvir, Bernard, 'The Eastlakes', *Quarterly Review*, vol. 295 (January 1957), pp. 85–97.

— 'Dictator of Taste', *Guardian*, 23 December 1965, p. 4.

Dowd, Carol Togneri, 'The Travel Diary of Otto Mündler', *The Walpole Society*, vol. 51 (1985), pp. 69–254.

Easley, Alexis, *First Person Anonymous: Women Writers and Victorian Print Media, 1830–70* (Aldershot: Ashgate, 2004).

'Eastlake and Gibson', *Edinburgh Review*, vol. 131 (1870), pp. 392–417.

Eastlake Smith, Charles (ed.), *Journals and Correspondence of Lady Eastlake*, 2 vols. (London: John Murray, 1895).

Egerton, Judy, *National Gallery Catalogues: The British School* (London: National Gallery Publications, 1998).

Ernstrom, Adele M., '"Equally Lenders and Borrowers in Turn": The Working and Married Lives of the Eastlakes', *Art History*, 15.4 (December 1992), pp. 470–85.

— 'Why Should We Be Always Looking Back? "Christian Art" in Nineteenth-Century Historiography in Britain', *Art History*, 22.3 (1997), pp. 421–35.

Fales, Frederick Mario, and Bernard J. Hickey (eds.), *Austen Henry Layard: Tra l'Oriente e Venezia* (Rome: L'Erma di Bretschneider, 1987).

Fraser, Hilary, *The Victorians and Renaissance Italy* (Oxford: Blackwell, 1992).

Fraser, Hilary, Stephanie Green and Judith Johnston (eds.), *Gender and the Victorian Periodical* (Cambridge Studies in Nineteenth-Century Literature and Culture) (Cambridge: Cambridge University Press, 2003).

Frawley, Maria H., *A Wider Range: Travel Writing By Women in Victorian England* (London & Toronto: Associated University Presses, 1994).

Fyvie, John, *Some Famous Women of Wit and Beauty: A Georgian Galaxy* (London: Archibald Constable & Co., 1905).

Gage, J., 'Turner's Academic Friendships: C. L. Eastlake', *Burlington Magazine*, vol. 110 (December 1968), pp. 676–83.

Garver, Joseph, 'Lady Eastlake's "Livonian" Fiction', *Studia Neophilogica*, 51.1 (1979), pp. 17–29.

Gaunt, William, 'Charles Eastlake, a Victorian with a Flair for Pictures', *The Times*, 21 December 1965, p. 11, col. C.

Goodman, Nigel (ed.), *Dawson Turner, A Norfolk Antiquary and his Remarkable Family* (Phillimore, 2007).

Gould, Cecil, 'Eastlake and Molteni: The Ethics of Restoration', *Burlington Magazine*, 116 (1974), pp. 530–34.

— 'The Eastlakes', *Apollo*, 101 (May 1975), pp. 350–53.

Green, G. M., *Catalogue of the Eastlake Library in the National Gallery* (London: Eyre & Spottiswoode, for HMSO, 1872).

Griffiths, Ralph A., and John E. Law (eds.), *Rawdon Brown and the Anglo-Venetian Relationship* (Stroud: Nonsuch, 2005).

'Lady Eastlake', *The Lady's Own Paper*, no.16, Saturday 9 March 1867, p. 1.

Haskell, Francis, *Past and Present in Art and Taste: Selected Essays* (New Haven and London: Yale University Press, 1987).

— *Rediscoveries in Art* (Oxford: Phaidon, 1980).

Herrmann, Frank, 'Dr. Waagen's Works of Art and Artists in England', *Connoisseur*, 161 (March 1966), pp. 173–77.

— *The English as Collectors: A Documentary Chrestomathy* (London: John Murray, 1999 [Chatto & Windus, 1972]).

Hilton, Tim, *John Ruskin: The Early Years* (New Haven and London: Yale University Press, 1985).

Holmes, Sir Charles, and C. H. Collins Baker, *The Making of the National Gallery, 1824–1924* (London: The National Gallery, 1924).

Houghton, Walter E. (ed.), *The Wellesley Index to Victorian Periodicals 1824–1900*, 5 vols. (London: Routledge & Kegan Paul, 1966–89).

James, William, *The Order of Release: The Story of John Ruskin, Effie Gray and John Everett Millais, Told for the First Time in their Unpublished Letters* (London: John Murray, 1947).

Johnson, Wendell Stacy, 'The Bride of Literature: Ruskin, the Eastlakes and Mid Victorian Themes of Art', *Victorian Newsletter*, no. 26 (Fall1964), pp. 23–28.

Klonk, Charlotte, 'Mounting Vision: Charles Eastlake and the National Gallery of London', *Art Bulletin*, 85.2 (June 2000), pp. 331–47.

Korman, Sally, 'A *Saint Francis* by Botticelli in the National Gallery', *Apollo*, vol. 158.497 (July 2003), pp. 42–49.

Lang, Andrew, *The Life and Letters of John Gibson Lockhart*, 2 vols. (London: John C. Nimmo, 1897).

Law, John E., and Lene Østermark-Johansen (eds.), *Victorian and Edwardian Responses to the Italian Renaissance* (Aldershot: Ashgate, 2005).

Levey, Michael, 'A Little Known Director: Sir William Boxall', *Apollo*, 101 (May 1975), pp. 354–67.

— 'Botticelli and Nineteenth-Century England', *Journal of the Warburg and Courtauld Institutes*, 23 (1960), pp. 291–306.

Lochhead, Marion, *Elizabeth Rigby, Lady Eastlake* (London: John Murray, 1961).

— *John Gibson Lockhart* (London: John Murray, 1954).

Lutyens, Mary, *Millais and the Ruskins* (London: John Murray, 1967).

Macgregor, Neil, 'Passavant and Lady Eastlake: Art History, Friendship and Romance', in Hildegard Bauereisen and Martin Sonnabend (eds.), *Correspondances: Festschrift für Margret Stuffmann zum 24 Nov. 1996* (Mainz: H. Schmidt, 1996), pp. 166–74.

Mündler, Otto, 'Charles Lock Eastlake', *Zeitschrift für bildenden Kunst*, vol. 4 (1869), pp. 99ff.

Nichols, C. M. [Catherine Maud], 'Personal Reminiscences of Lady Eastlake' (1893), in *Norwich Scrapbooks, Collection Made by Edward A. Tillett* (Norwich, c. 1906), p. 339.

Onslow, Barbara, *Women of the Press in Nineteenth-Century Britain* (London: Palgrave, 2000).

Orr, Clarissa Campbell (ed.), *Women in the Victorian Art World* (Manchester and New York: Manchester University Press, 1995).

Østermark-Johansen, Lene, *Sweetness and Strength: The Reception of Michelangelo in Late Victorian England* (London: Ashgate Scholar Press, 1998).

Palgrave, Gwenllian F., *Francis Turner Palgrave: His Journals and Memories of his Life* (London: Longman & Co., 1899).

Palmer, C. J., and Stephen Tucker (eds.), *Palgrave Family Memorials* (privately printed, 1878).

Paston, George, *At John Murray's: Records of a Literary Circle 1843–92* (London: John Murray, 1932).

Pemble, John, *The Mediterranean Passion* (Oxford: Clarendon Press, 1987).

— *Venice Rediscovered* (Oxford: Oxford University Press, 1995).

Penny, Nicholas, 'Un'Introduzione ai taccuini di Sir Charles Eastlake', in Anna Chiara Tommasi (ed.), *Giovanni Battista Cavalcaselle Conoscitore e Conservatore*, alle origini della storia dell'arte Convegno internazionale di studi a cura di Donata Levi e Paola Marini Legnago, 28 novembre 1997–Verona, 29 novembre 1997 (Venice: Marsilio, 1998), pp. 277–89.

Poovey, Mary, *Uneven Developments: The Ideological Work of Gender in Mid-Victorian England* (London: Virago Press, 1989).

Reitlinger, Gerald, *The Economics of Taste*, 3 vols. (London: Barrie & Rockliff, 1961).

Robertson, David, *Sir Charles Eastlake and the Victorian Art World* (Princeton, NJ: Princeton University Press, 1978).

— 'The Lady Who Reviewed Jane Eyre', *Gazette of the Grolier Club*, 12 (February 1970), pp. 2–10.

Robinson, Ainslie, 'The History of Our Lord as Exemplified in Works of Art: Anna Jameson's coup de grâce', Women's Writing, 10.1 (2003), pp. 187–200.

Santori, Flaminia Gennari, '"They Will Form Such an Ornament for our Gallery": La National Gallery e la pittura di Carlo Crivelli', in Anna Chiara Tommasi (ed.) Giovanni Battista Cavalcaselle Conoscitore e Conservatore, alle origini della storia dell'arte Convegno internazionale di studi a cura di Donata Levi e Paola Marini Legnago, 28 novembre 1997–Verona, 29 novembre 1997 (Venice: Marsilio, 1998), pp. 291–312.

Schuster, Eugene I., Sir Charles Eastlake P.R.A. 1793–1865 [commemorative exhibition catalogue] (Plymouth: Plymouth City Art Gallery, 1965).

Secombe, Thomas, 'Elizabeth Eastlake', Dictionary of National Biography, vol. xxii, supplement (1909).

Shattock, Joanne, Politics and Reviewers: The 'Edinburgh' and the 'Quarterly' in the Early Victorian Age (Leicester: Leicester University Press, 1989).

Sherman, Claire Richter, with Adele M. Holcomb (eds.), Women as Interpreters of the Visual Arts, 1820–1979 (Westport, CT and London: Greenwood Press, 1981).

Simmons, Dorothy Anne, 'Austen Henry Layard and the Victorian Art World 1850–1870', unpublished PhD thesis, Oxford Brookes University, 2000.

'Sir Charles Eastlake', Fine Arts Quarterly Review, n.s. vol. 1 (July–October 1866).

Smiles, Samuel, A Publisher and his Friends: Memoir and Correspondence of John Murray, 2 vols. (London: John Murray, 1891).

Springall, Stephen, That Indomitable Old Lady: A Romance of Fitzroy Square (London: Henry J. Drane Ltd, 1908).

Stark, Susanne, 'Behind Inverted Commas': Translation and Anglo-German Cultural Relations in the Nineteenth Century (Clevedon: Multilingual Matters Ltd, 1999).

Steegman, John, 'Sir Charles Eastlake: 1793–1865', Architectural Review, vol. 138 (November 1965), p. 364.

— 'The Eastlakes and Lord Lindsay', The Listener, 14 July 1949, pp. 61–62.

— Victorian Taste: A Study of the Arts and Architecture, 1830–1870 (London: Century in Association with the National Trust, 1970 [1950]).

Stevenson, Sara, David Octavius Hill and Robert Adamson: Catalogue of their Calotypes taken between 1843 and 1847 in the Collection of the Scottish National Portrait Gallery (Edinburgh: National Galleries of Scotland, 1981).

Stonge, Carmen, 'Making Private Collections Public: Gustav Friedrich Waagen and the Royal Museum in Berlin', Journal of the History of Collections, 10.1 (1998), pp. 61–74.

Sutton, Denys, 'Aspects of British Collecting Part IV', Apollo, 123 (1985), pp. 84–129.

Thomas, Clara Love and Work Enough: The Life of Anna Jameson (London: Macdonald, 1967).

Thornton, Dora, and Jeremy Warren, 'The British Museum's Michelangelo Acquisitions and the Casa Buonarroti', Journal of the History of Collections, 10.1 (1998), pp. 9–29.

Waterfield, Giles, Layard of Nineveh (London: John Murray, 1963).

— with Florian Illies, 'Waagen in England: German Influence on 19th Century English Art, Museums and Collections', Jahrbuch der Berliner Museen, 37 (1995), pp. 47–59.

Waterfield, Gordon, 'Henry Layard, Nineteenth Century Aesthete', Apollo, 83 (1966), pp. 166–73.

Weinberg, D., 'Ruskin, Pater and the Rediscovery of Botticelli', Burlington Magazine, 129.1006 (1987), pp. 25–27.

Whitehead, Christopher, The Public Art Museum in Nineteenth Century Britain: The Development of the National Gallery (London: Ashgate, 2005).

Wilson, James, The Dark Clue (New York: Atlantic Monthly Press, 2001).

Wolk, L., 'Calotype Portraits of Elizabeth Rigby by David Octavius Hill and Robert Adamson', History of Photography, 7 (July–September 1983), pp. 167–81.

Index of Names

Page numbers with n refer to footnotes